J
REFERENCE
P9-AFA-773
Lake Oswego Public Library
WITHDRAWN
Lake Oswego, Oregon 97034

2002

5.00

2.+.20

McGraw-Hill Mathematics

McGraw-Hill School Division
New York Farmington

Senior Consulting Authors

Gunnar Carlsson, Ph.D.
Professor of Mathematics
Stanford University
Stanford, California

Ralph L. Cohen, Ph.D.
Professor of Mathematics
Stanford University
Stanford, California

Program Authors

Douglas H. Clements, Ph.D.
Professor of Mathematics Education
State University of New York at Buffalo
Buffalo, New York

Carol E. Malloy, Ph.D.
Assistant Professor of Mathematics Education
University of North Carolina at Chapel Hill
Chapel Hill, North Carolina

Lois Gordon Moseley, M.S.
Mathematics Consultant
Houston, Texas

Robyn R. Silbey, M.S.
Montgomery County Public Schools
Rockville, Maryland

McGraw-Hill School Division
A Division of The McGraw-Hill Companies

McGraw-Hill School Division
Two Penn Plaza
New York, New York 10121-2298

Printed in the United States of America
ISBN 0-02-100127-8
11 12 13 071/043 08 07

Contributing Authors

Mary Behr Altieri, M.S.
Mathematics Teacher
1993 Presidential Awardee
Lakeland Central School District
Shrub Oak, New York

Nadine Bezuk, Ph.D.
Professor of Mathematics Education
San Diego State University
San Diego, California

Pam B. Cole, Ph.D.
Associate Professor of
Middle Grades English Education
Kennesaw State University
Kennesaw, Georgia

Barbara W. Ferguson, Ph.D.
Assistant Professor of Mathematics
and Mathematics Education
Kennesaw State University
Kennesaw, Georgia

Carol P. Harrell, Ph.D.
Professor of English and English Education
Kennesaw State University
Kennesaw, Georgia

Donna Harrell Lubcker, M.S.
Assistant Professor of Education
and Early Childhood
East Texas Baptist University
Marshall, Texas

Chung-Hsing OuYang, Ph.D.
Assistant Professor of Mathematics
California State University, Hayward
Hayward, California

Contents

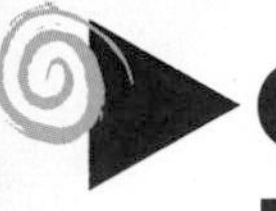

Chapter 1: Place Value and Money

Theme: Wild Wild Kingdom

Chapter 2: Addition and Subtraction

Theme: Fun Zone

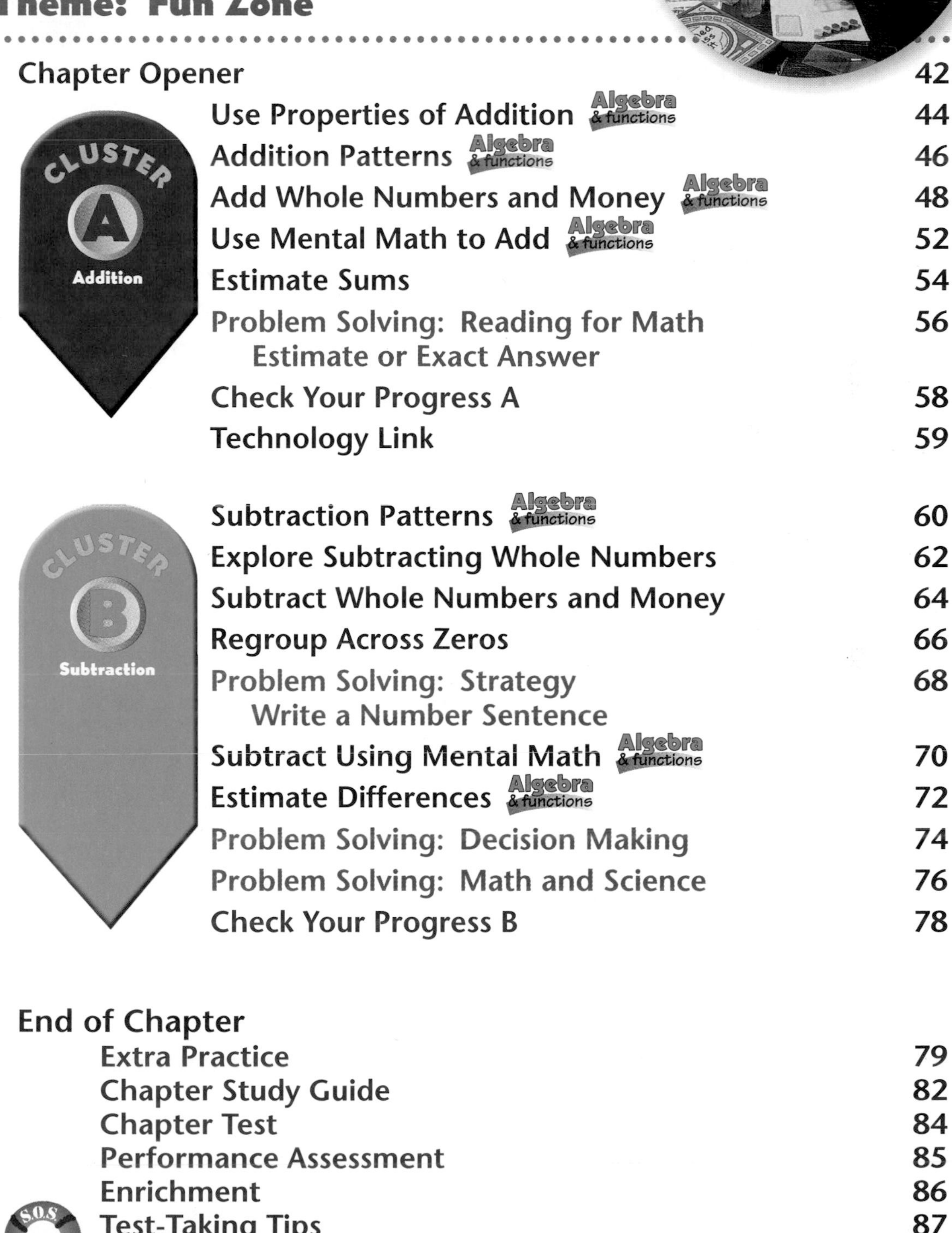

Chapter 3: Data, Statistics, and Graphing

Theme: Going Places

Chapter 4: Multiplication and Division Facts

Theme: Collectible Treasures

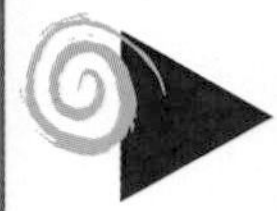

Chapter 5: Multiply by 1-Digit Numbers

Theme: Cool Forests and Hot Deserts

Chapter 6: Multiply by 2-Digit Numbers

Theme: Water, Water Everywhere

Chapter 7: Divide by 1-Digit Numbers

Theme: After School Activities

Chapter 8: Divide by 2-Digit Numbers

Theme: Fitness Counts

Chapter 9: Measurement

Theme: That's Entertainment!

Chapter 10: Geometry

Theme: Shaping the World

Chapter 11: Fractions and Probability

Theme: Amusement Parks

Chapter 12: Fraction Operations

Theme: Food for Thought

Chapter 13: Relate Fractions and Decimals

Theme: Bright Lights, Big Cities

Chapter 14: Decimal Operations

Theme: Planes, Trains, and Automobiles

CHAPTER 1 Place Value and Money

Theme: Wild Wild Kingdom

Use the Data

World Population of Endangered Species

African wild dogs	4,000
California condors	120
Porcupine caribou	150,000
Cheetahs	200
Pandas	1,000

Source: World Wildlife Fund

- The table above names some endangered species. Which species has the least number of animals? How can you use place value to order these animals from greatest to least? Tell how you did it.

What You Will Learn

In this chapter you will learn how to

- read and write whole numbers in the millions.
- compare, order, and round whole numbers and money.
- count money and make change.
- use and compare negative numbers.
- use strategies to solve problems.

Objective: Explore the concept of a million.

1-1 Explore: How Big Is a Million?

Learn

You can use what you know about place value models to explore how to build a model of 1,000,000.

Work Together

You Will Need
- **10-by-10 grids**
- **scissors**
- **tape**

▶ You know there are 10 ones in 1 ten, and there are 10 tens in 1 hundred. If you stack 10 hundreds, they make a thousand cube. You can use 10-by-10 grids to make a model of a thousand cube.

- Cut out six 10-by-10 grids.

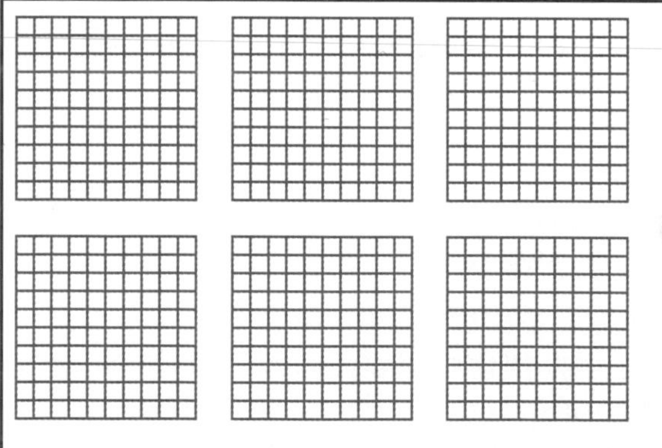

- Tape the grids together so that they form a cube.

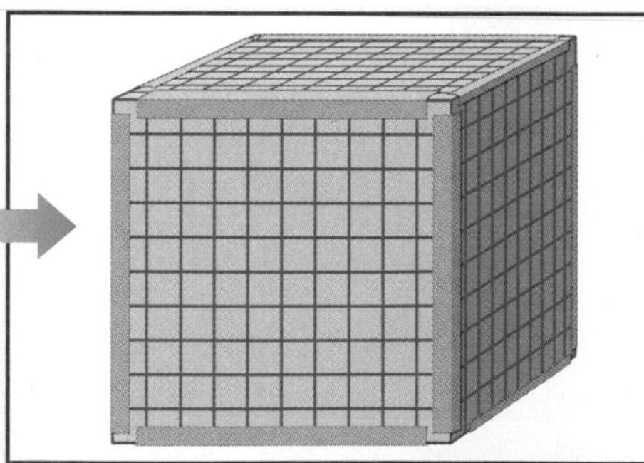

▶ There are 10 thousands in 10,000. Work with others to build a model of 10,000 using thousand cubes.

▶ There are 10 ten thousands in 100,000. How many thousand cubes would you need to build a model of 100,000? Draw a picture of this model.

▶ There are 10 hundred thousands in 1,000,000. How many thousand cubes would you need to build a model of 1,000,000?

Make Connections

You can use models and patterns to think about models for 1,000,000.

Using Models	Using Paper and Pencil
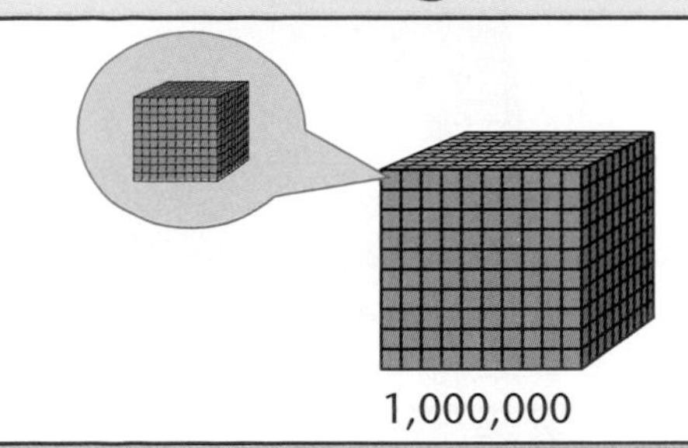 1,000,000	10 hundreds = 1,000 10 thousands = 10,000 10 ten thousands = 100,000 10 hundred thousands = 1,000,000

Try It **Find the answer.**

1. How many tens are in 1,000?
2. How many hundreds are in 100,000?
3. How many thousands are in 1,000,000?

Explain why 1,000 thousand cubes can be used to build a model of 1,000,000.

Practice **Find the answer.**

4. What number do these thousand models show?

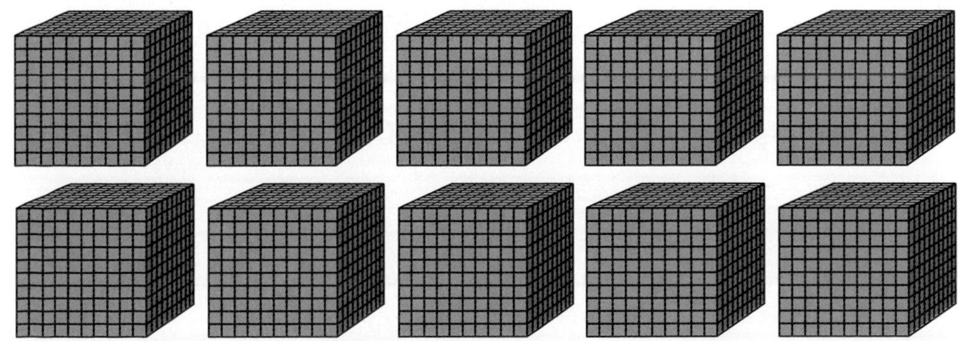

5. **Number Sense:** How long do you think it would take to count to 1,000,000? Explain how you found your answer.
6. **Language Arts:** How many pages do you need to have a million letters? Explain.

Objective: Count, read, and write whole numbers through 999,999,999.

1-2 Place Value Through Millions

Learn

Frank studies crocodiles and alligators in the Big Cypress National Preserve. The 729,000-acre preserve is home to many native animals and plants of Florida. What is the word name and expanded form for 729,000?

Frank Mazotti, wildlife biologist

Math Words

place value the value given to a digit by its place in a number

digit any of the symbols used to write numbers (0, 1, 2, 3, 4, 5, 6, 7, 8, 9)

period each group of three digits in a place value chart

standard form a way to write a number that shows only its digits

expanded form a way of writing a number as the sum of the values of its digits

Example 1

Use a **place value** chart to show the value of the **digit** in a number.

Thousands			Ones		
Hundreds	Tens	Ones	Hundreds	Tens	Ones
7	2	9	0	0	0

You can read or write 729,000 in different ways.

Use commas to separate **periods**.

Standard form: 729,000

Word name: seven hundred twenty-nine thousand

Short word name: 729 thousand

Expanded form: 700,000 + 20,000 + 9,000

Another Example

Standard form: 879,642,135

Word name: eight hundred seventy-nine million, six hundred forty-two thousand, one hundred thirty-five

Short word name: 879 million, 642 thousand, 135

Expanded form: 800,000,000 + 70,000,000 + 9,000,000 + 600,000 + 40,000 + 2,000 + 100 + 30 + 5

When Dinosaurs Lived on Earth

200,000,000 Years Ago
Crocodiles

140,000,000 Years Ago
Diplodocus

120,000,000 Years Ago
Iguanadon

80,000,000 Years Ago
Protoceratops

Crocodiles first appeared during the time of dinosaurs, about 200 million years ago. How many years ago did diplodocus live? Write the word name and the expanded form for the number.

Example 2

You can expand a place value chart to include millions.

Millions			Thousands			Ones		
Hundreds	Tens	Ones	Hundreds	Tens	Ones	Hundreds	Tens	Ones
1	4	0	0	0	0	0	0	0

Here are the different ways to write 140,000,000.

Standard form: 140,000,000

Word name: one hundred forty million

Short word name: 140 million

Expanded form: 100,000,000 + 40,000,000

Try It **Write the word name and expanded form for each number.**

1. 7,824
2. 86,012
3. 355,813
4. 18,434,904

Write the number in standard form.

5. fifty-one thousand, one hundred thirty-seven
6. 3 hundred 42 million, 5 hundred 2
7. 9 million, 47 thousand, 3 hundred 87
8. 2,000 + 600 + 8
9. 10,000 + 900 + 60 + 2
10. 3,000,000 + 70,000 + 2
11. 40,000,000 + 6,000 + 40 + 8

Look at the place value chart above. What patterns do you see?

Practice

Write the word name and the expanded form for each number.

12. 1,050 **13.** 80,788 **14.** 709,582 **15.** 7,961,888

16. 2,200,009 **17.** 100,329,089 **18.** 500,003,300 **19.** 136,055,766

Write the value of each underlined digit.

20. $\underline{3}$45,092 **21.** 256,4$\underline{5}$7 **22.** $\underline{7}$,609,004 **23.** $\underline{4}$0,075,411

24. $\underline{2}$37,999,228 **25.** 37,92$\underline{9}$,342 **26.** 373,285,$\underline{2}$75 **27.** 732,1$\underline{4}$0,842

Write each number in standard form.

28. five thousand, four hundred six

29. one hundred thousand, ninety-one

30. 60,000 + 600+ 90

31. 3,000 + 400 + 3

32. 2,000,000 + 90,000 + 3

33. thirty-two million, five hundred thirty-seven thousand, two hundred fifty-eight

34. five million, two hundred nine thousand, four hundred one

★35. one hundred less than four hundred thirty-five million, eight hundred sixty-seven thousand, four hundred nine

★36. one thousand more than three hundred thirty-two million, three hundred fifty thousand, five hundred ninety-seven

Algebra & functions **Find the missing number.**

37. 2,865 = 2,000 + ■ + 60 + 5

38. 68,768 = 60,000 + 8,000 + 700 + ■ + 8

39. 759,323 = 700,000 + 50,000 + 9,000 + 300 + 20 + ■

40. 680,912 = 600,000 + 80,000 + ■ + 10 + 2

41. 4,222,111 = 4,000,000 + ■ + 20,000 + 2,000 + 100 + 10 + 1

42.

Here's how Kevin wrote a number in standard form when given the expanded form. Tell what mistake he made. Explain how to correct it.

Problem Solving

43. Science: The Jurassic Period in Earth's history was from 205,000,000 to 138,000,000 years ago. Brachiosaurus were walking on Earth about 143,000,000 years ago. Write each of these numbers as short word names.

44. Literature: *How Much Is a Million?* is a children's book written by David Schwartz and illustrated by Steven Kellogg. In it, the author and illustrator show readers different ways to think of one million. Write your own explanation of how much one million is. Draw pictures to help.

45. Generalize: Explain how a zero in the ones place of a place value chart is like a zero in the millions place. How is it different?

46. Create a problem using place value through millions. Solve it. Ask others to solve it.

Use data from the chart for problems 47–50.

47. What is the word name for the amount of money the museum budgets for equipment?

48. What is $20,000 more than the budget for maintenance? What number is in the ten-thousands place of this number?

49. What is the total budget for the Natural History Museum?

★50. What is $5,000 less than the amount budgeted for new exhibits? Show this number in standard form, expanded form, and word name.

Natural History Museum Budget

Employee salaries	$5,100,000
Maintenance	$2,300,000
New exhibits	$7,100,000
Equipment	$3,900,000

Spiral Review and Test Prep

51. 4 × 3 **52.** 332 − 130 **53.** 820 + 134 **54.** 9 ÷ 3

55. 10 × 10 **56.** 911 − 160 **57.** 22 + 221 **58.** 64 ÷ 8

Choose the correct answer.

59. Which number shows 9 hundreds?

A. 493 **C.** 9,439
B. 34,913 **D.** 90,000

60. In $\underline{7}$62,803, what is the value of the underlined digit?

F. 700 **H.** 70,000
G. 7,000 **J.** 700,000

Extra Practice, page 31

1-3 Compare and Order Numbers and Money

Algebra & functions

Learn

Math Words

is less than (<)

is greater than (>)

Some birds move to other climates—or migrate—each year. Which migrates farthest?

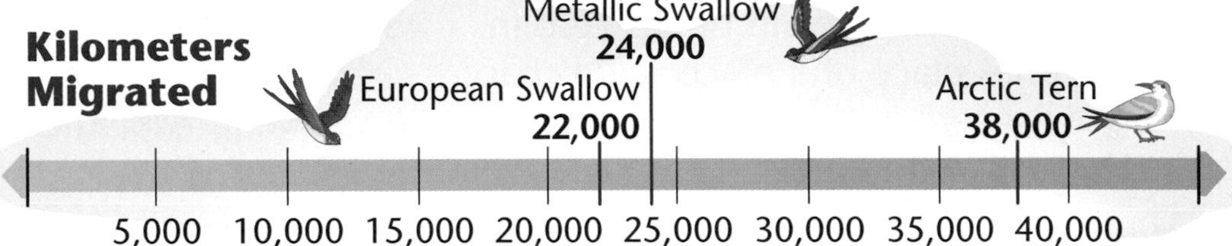

Example 1

You can use a number line to compare and order the distances.

Think: 22,000 comes before 24,000

22,000 **is less than** 24,000

$22{,}000 < 24{,}000$

Think: 38,000 comes after 24,000

38,000 **is greater than** 24,000

$38{,}000 > 24{,}000$

If 22,000 is less than 24,000, and 24,000 is less than 38,000, then 22,000 is less than 38,000.

The Arctic tern migrates farthest.

Scientists count 12,617 ovenbirds, 14,976 grosbeaks, and 9,401 yellow warblers. Order the number of birds from least to greatest.

Example 2

You can compare and order numbers using place value.

1

Line up the ones place. Then look at the greatest place. Compare the digits.

12,617
14,976
9,401

9,401 is the least number.

2

Compare the digits in the next place.

12,617
14,976

$4 > 2$, so 14,976 is the greatest number.

3

Write the numbers in order from least to greatest:

9,401
12,617
14,976

The correct order is yellow warblers, ovenbirds, and grosbeaks.

Kyle found a CD of bird songs listed for $7.13 in one store, $6.95 in another store, and $6.89 in a third. Which is the least expensive? the most expensive?

Example 3

You can compare and order money amounts the same way you did with whole numbers.

1 Compare the three amounts.

$7.13
$6.95
$6.89

7 > **6**, so $7.13 is the greatest number.

2 Compare the remaining two amounts.

$6.95
$6.89

8 < **9**, so $6.89 is less than $6.95.

3 Write the numbers in order from least to greatest.

$6.89
$6.95
$7.13

The least expensive is $6.89. The most expensive is $7.13.

Try It **Compare. Write >, <, or =.**

1. 4,908 ● 4,718
2. 16,547 ● 62,050
3. $23.45 ● $20.98
4. 8,342 ● 8,342
5. $426.10 ● $416.19
6. 295,931 ● 294,899

Order from greatest to least.

7. 3,566; 2,499; 3,422
8. 56,011; 52,993; 63,129
9. $647.34; $667.49; $657.99
10. $5.49; $5.42; $5.29
11. 9,100; 9,003; 9,010
12. 23,412; 23,510; 23,500

Order from least to greatest.

13. $57.99; $57.64; $56.34
14. 15,875; 13,655; 13,695
15. 249,009; 248,999; 248,090
16. 39,631; 39,511; 39,500
17. 873,239; 871,132; 871,735
18. $26.99; $27.34; $27.30

Explain why any 4-digit whole number is greater than any 3-digit whole number.

Practice

Compare. Write >, <, or =.

19. 9,965 ● 9,569

20. 28,050 ● 28,005

21. $125.47 ● $260.50

22. 72,816 ● 673,557

23. $9.07 ● $0.99

24. 123,152 ● 20,556

25. 143,524 ● 143,242

26. 643,342 ● 633,342

27. $525.43 ● $525.43

Order from greatest to least.

28. 540, 598, 567

29. $32.89; $28.12; $39.28; $42.75

30. 346,812; 327,905; 349,888

31. 182,976; 157,198; 157,340; 182,893

32. 222, 220, 212

33. $99.19; $98.99; $96.91

Order from least to greatest.

34. 4,448; 4,424; 4,406

35. $693.93; $622.39; $639.22; $693.23

36. 38,981; 37,982; 38,891

37. 659,341; 659,214; 659,218; 659,314

38. 711,002; 71,002; 710,002

39. 1001, 1011, 1101

40.

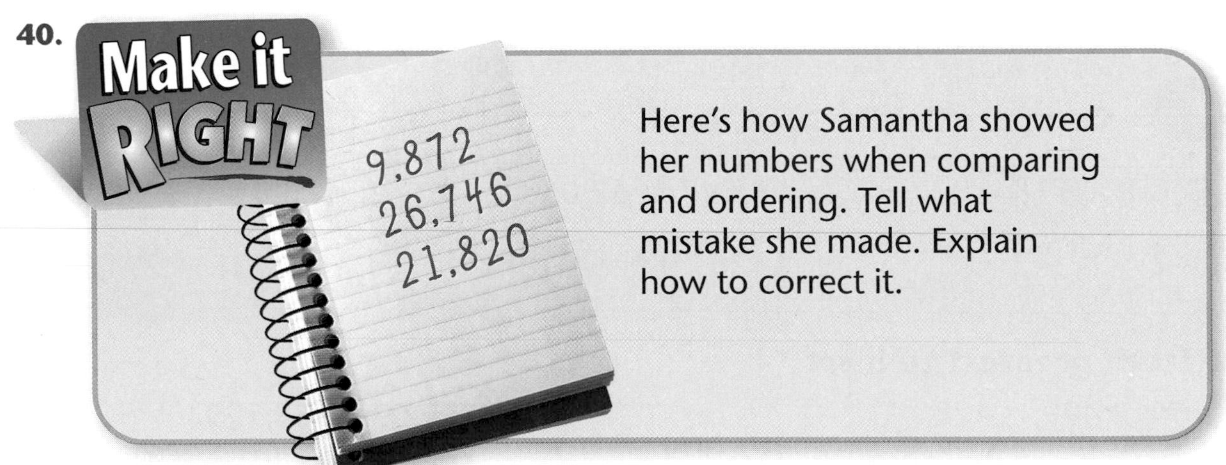

Here's how Samantha showed her numbers when comparing and ordering. Tell what mistake she made. Explain how to correct it.

Problem Solving

41. Sean is writing a folktale. In it, birds migrate different distances. The bird that migrates the farthest will find gold coins. The Canada goose migrates 13,200 miles. The falcon migrates 9,500 miles. The swallow migrates 19,342 miles. Which bird will find gold coins? Explain.

42. Each bird in Sean's folktale flies at a different height. The bird that flies the lowest will fall back to Earth. The Canada goose flies at 12,000 feet. The falcon flies at 21,700 feet. The swallow flies at 15,300 feet. Which bird will fall back to Earth? Use a number line to solve.

43. **Art:** John Audubon is famous for his drawings of birds. His book, *Birds of America,* contains 435 different pictures of birds. A certain bookstore has a collection of his books that is worth $72,432. How would you show this amount of money in word form? expanded form?

44. **Generalize:** List other times when you might place a group of items in order. Explain how you would put them in order.

★45. If you use each digit once, what is the greatest whole number you can make using 1, 4, 5, 6, and 9? the least?

★46. The symbol $\geq$ means greater than or equal to. The symbol $\leq$ means less than or equal to. Which number line shows numbers greater than 45? Which number line shows numbers greater than or equal to 45?

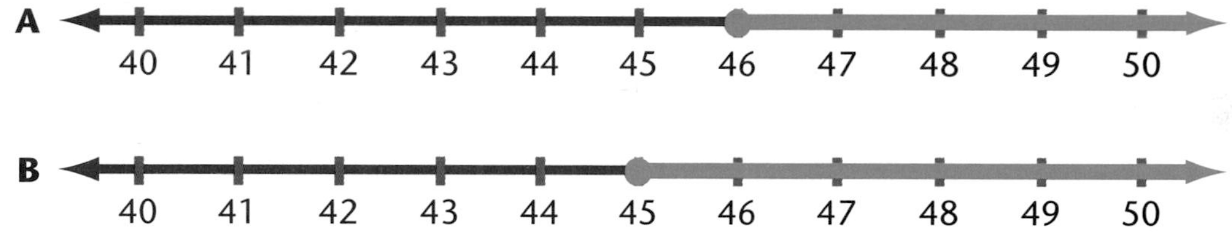

Spiral Review and Test Prep

47. What is one hundred less than four thousand, one hundred?

48. What is another name for ten 100s?

49. What is the value of the 7 in 73,458?

50. How many thousands are in one million?

Choose the correct answer.

51. Which is true?
    - **A.** 489 > 498
    - **B.** 560 < 543
    - **C.** 347 > 598
    - **D.** 346 < 598

52. Which is true?
    - **F.** 5,693 < 5,683
    - **G.** 5,692 < 5,683
    - **H.** 6,256 > 6,264
    - **J.** 6,256 > 6,234

53. What is the standard form for sixteen thousand, four hundred, thirty-two?
    - **A.** 6,432
    - **B.** 1,624
    - **C.** 16,432
    - **D.** 14,632

54. Which is ordered from least to greatest?
    - **F.** 34,445; 34,434, 43,534
    - **G.** 34,434; 34,445; 43,534
    - **H.** 43,534; 34,445; 34,434
    - **J.** Not Here

Objective: Identify the four steps in a problem-solving process.

1•4 Problem Solving: Reading for Math

Using the Four-Step Process

Cheetahs Move Faster Than Cars!

Read Look at how fast these animals can run! List these three animals from fastest to slowest.

Speeds of Animals

Name	Speed (miles in one hour)
Rabbit	45
African elephant	25
Cheetah	70

READING SKILL ▶

Steps in a Process

A process is a series of steps you do to complete a task.

- **What do you know?** The speed of each animal
- **What do you need to find?** The order of the animals from fastest to slowest.

MATH SKILL ▶

- Read the problem. Identify the important information.
- Make a plan for solving the problem.
- Follow your plan. Solve the problem.
- Look back to see if your answer makes sense.

Plan Compare two animals at a time. Order from fastest to slowest.

Solve Compare the speeds.

Rabbit and African elephant: $45 > 25$ **The rabbit is faster.**
Cheetah and rabbit: $70 > 45$ **The cheetah is faster.**

The correct order is cheetah, rabbit, and African elephant.

Look Back
- Is your answer reasonable? Explain.

Explain how the four-step process is useful.

Practice **Solve. Use the four-step process.**

1. A dolphin can move at a speed of about 25 miles each hour. A whale moves at a speed of 20 miles each hour. A barracuda moves at a speed of 30 miles each hour. Order these water animals from slowest to fastest.

2. A bat flies at a speed of only 15 miles each hour. An eagle can fly 105 miles farther in an hour. How far does an eagle fly in one hour?

Use data from Animal Facts for problems 3–8.

3. What is the order of the black bear, gorilla, and lion from greatest to least weight?

4. What is the order of the giraffe, hippopotamus, and elephant from least to greatest weight?

5. Which animal has the least weight?

6. Which animal has the greatest weight?

7. How much less does a giraffe weigh than a hippopotamus?

8. How much greater is the weight of a lion than a black bear?

Animal Facts
Weight of Male Animals

Animal	Weight (in pounds)
Black bear	275
Elephant	5,300
Giraffe	2,000
Gorilla	450
Hippopotamus	2,600
Lion	375

Spiral Review and Test Prep

Choose the correct answer.

A male kangaroo weighs 112 pounds. A male alligator weighs 498 pounds. Which one weighs more?

9. Which of the following statements is true?
   A. A male alligator weighs less than a male kangaroo.
   B. The weight of a male kangaroo is 211 pounds.
   C. The weight of a male alligator is 498 pounds.

10. Which plan can you use to solve the problem?
   F. Add 498 and 112.
   G. Compare 498 to 112.
   H. Subtract 112 from 498.

Extra Practice, page 32

Objective: Round whole numbers and money amounts through millions.

1-5 Round Numbers and Money

Learn

Math Word

round to find the nearest value of a number based on a given place value

Before trees near San Juan Capistrano Mission were cut down, a flock of as many as 2,342,675 swallows returned to the mission each year. To the nearest million, how many swallows returned?

There's More Than One Way!

Round 2,342,675 to the nearest million.

A

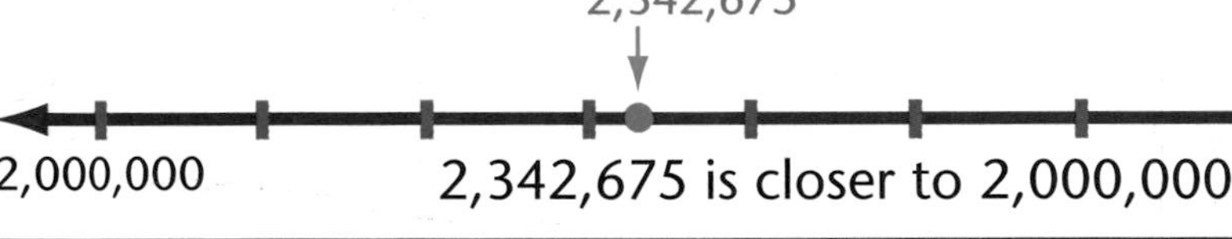

2,342,675 is closer to 2,000,000.

B

1 Find the digit in the millions place.

2,342,675

2 Look at the place to the right of the millions place.

2,**3**42,675

3 If the digit is less than 5, round down. If the digit is 5 or greater, round up.

$3 < 5$, so 2,342,675 rounds down to 2,000,000.

To the nearest million, 2,000,000 swallows returned each year.

More Examples

A

Round 698 to the nearest hundred.
698 rounds up to 700

Think: The digit in the tens place is 9, and $9 > 5$.

B

Round 5,234 to the nearest thousand.
5,234 rounds down to 5,000

Think: The digit in the hundreds place is 2, and $2 < 5$.

C

Round 683,682 to the nearest hundred thousand. 683,682 rounds up to 700,000

Think: The digit in the ten thousands place is 8, and $8 > 5$.

Kyle tells his friends that posters of the swallows cost about $7.00 each. Is this reasonable?

Prices for Swallow Posters

Store	Price
Cappy's Posters	$7.13
Swallow Center	$6.89
On the Wing	$6.95

Example

Round each price to the nearest dollar. To round money, you round the same way as with whole numbers.

1 Find the digit in the dollars place.

$7.13
$6.89
$6.95

2 Look at the place to the right of the dollars place.

$7.13
$6.89
$6.95

3 If the digit is less than 5, round down. If the digit is 5 or greater, round up.

$7.13 → $7.00
$6.89 → $7.00
$6.95 → $7.00

The price of each poster rounded to the nearest dollar is $7.00. Kyle's statement is reasonable.

More Examples

D Round $4.79 to the nearest ten cents.

$4.79 rounds up to $4.80

Think: The digit in the pennies place is 9. $9 > 5$

E Round $0.52 to the nearest ten cents.

$0.52 rounds down to $0.50

Think: The digit in the pennies place is 2. $2 < 5$

Try It **Round to the given place.**

1. 674 to the nearest ten
2. $0.86 to the nearest ten cents
3. 4,580 to the nearest hundred
4. 32,113 to the nearest thousand
5. $34.32 to the nearest dollar
6. 13,242,750 to the nearest million

Explain how to round to the nearest thousand.

Practice Round to the given place.

7. 826 to the nearest ten
8. $0.72 to the nearest ten cents
9. 3,870 to the nearest hundred
10. 32,113 to the nearest thousand
11. $45.76 to the nearest dollar
12. 372,632 to the nearest hundred thousand
13. $7.82 to the nearest ten cents
14. 14,556 to the nearest ten thousand
15. 4,762 to the nearest hundred
16. 4,591,218 to the nearest million
17. $18.32 to the nearest dollar
18. 67,822 to the nearest hundred thousand
19. 47,874 to the nearest thousand
20. 7,292,658 to the nearest million
21. $137.89 to the nearest dollar

Find the rule. Complete the table.

22.

Rule: ■					
Input	1,764,345	7,435,285	12,845,376	25,569,345	34,395,792
Output	2,000,000	■	■	■	■

23.

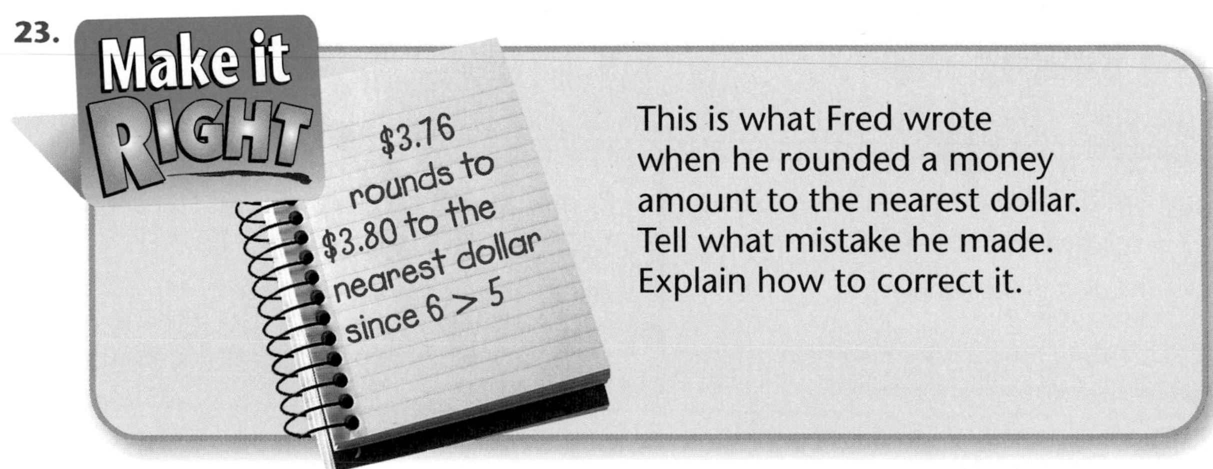

This is what Fred wrote when he rounded a money amount to the nearest dollar. Tell what mistake he made. Explain how to correct it.

Problem Solving

24. A bird-watching group reports that there are 2,753 songbirds in their area. To the nearest thousand, how many songbirds are there?

25. **Summarize:** How would you round $12.98 to the nearest ten dollars?

Use data from *Did You Know?* for problems 26–27.

26. About how many feathers does a Bewick swan have, rounded to the nearest hundred? nearest thousand? nearest ten thousand?

27. **Science:** The whistling swan has about 24,216 feathers. Which has more feathers, the whistling swan or the Bewick swan? Explain your answer.

28. **Collect data** about animals. Decide to which place you will round the numbers. Then show the numbers on a number line.

29. Zane raises $2,876 for a bird sanctuary. To the nearest thousand dollars, how much money has he raised?

30. The bird sanctuary records show that 24,753 people visited last year. A newspaper story states that about 25,000 people visited the sanctuary. Is this statement reasonable? Why?

★31. Olivia has $40.00. The price of a radio rounds down to $40.00. Can she buy it? Explain.

Spiral Review and Test Prep

32. $300 - 100$

33. $800 + 156$

34. 9×3

35. $25 \div 5$

36. $1{,}000 - 900$

37. 7×6

38. $\begin{array}{r} 70 \\ -20 \\ \hline \end{array}$

39. $\begin{array}{r} 400 \\ +200 \\ \hline \end{array}$

40. $\begin{array}{r} 3 \\ \times 8 \\ \hline \end{array}$

41. $\begin{array}{r} 5 \\ \times 8 \\ \hline \end{array}$

Choose the correct answer.

42. Which number has a 4 in the tens place?
   A. 5,604
   B. 5,400
   C. 5,040
   D. 4,000

43. Which number names $700 + 50 + 6$?
   F. 700,506
   G. 7,056
   H. 756
   J. Not Here

Check Your Progress A

Write the word name and expanded form for each number. **(pages 2–7)**

1. 15,030
2. 3,678,992
3. 208,573,800

Write each number in standard form. **(pages 2–7)**

4. 30,000 + 2,000 + 300 + 8
5. 5 million, 133 thousand, 3 hundred, 10

Compare. Write >, <, or =. **(pages 8–11)**

6. 4,908 ● 4,718
7. 16,547 ● 62,050
8. $16.16 ● $16.70
9. $6.18 ● $6.81
10. 1,111 ● 1,111.00
11. $22.00 ● $22.22

Order from greatest to least. **(pages 8–11)**

12. 6,556; 6,599; 6,499
13. $185.67; $183.21; $190.01
14. 287; 2,289; 21
15. 14.01; 141.01; 1.4

Order from least to greatest. **(pages 8–11)**

16. $34.09; $34.90; $33.09
17. 541,618,524; 541,218,524; 541,618,323

Round to the given place. **(pages 14–17)**

18. 43,976 to the nearest thousand
19. 136,036 to the nearest ten
20. 72,092 to the nearest hundred
21. $73.52 to the nearest dollar
22. 8,477,086 to the nearest ten thousand
23. $3.67 to the nearest ten cents

Solve. **(pages 2–17)**

24. Megan compares the prices of sweatshirts. The gray sweatshirt costs $32.95. The white sweatshirt costs $30.99. The blue sweatshirt costs $34.99. Which is the least expensive sweatshirt?

Journal

25. **Compare:** How is comparing, ordering, and rounding money amounts similar to doing the same with whole numbers?

Additional activities at www.mhschool.com/math

Use Place-Value Models to Compare Numbers

Rita has 4,235 pennies. Trevor has 4,223 pennies. Who has more pennies?

You can build models of the number of pennies each person has using place-value or base-ten models.

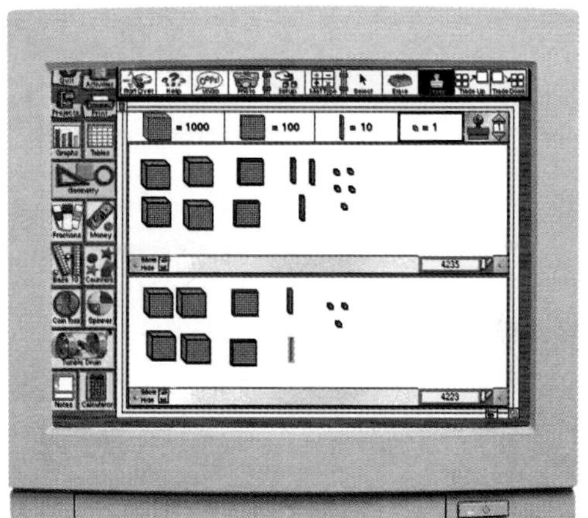

- Use a mat with two sections open.
- In the top section, start with the thousands and stamp out 4,235.
- In the bottom section, start with the thousands and stamp out 4,223.

The number boxes keep count as you stamp.

Who has the most pennies?

Use the computer to model each number. Then name the greater number.

1. 2,024 and 2,036
2. 3,612 and 3,710
3. 5,901 and 5,091
4. 6,521 and 6,512

Solve.

5. Misty has a collection of 1,235 postcards. Inez has a collection of 1,215 postcards. Who has more postcards?
6. Ms. Croson's class worked 2,705 minutes on a school project. Ms. Yen's class worked 2,714 minutes on the same project. Which class worked longer?
7. **Analyze:** How does using the model help you decide which number is greater?

For more practice use Math Traveler.™

Objective: Make a table to organize data and solve a problem.

Problem Solving: Strategy
Make a Table

Read

Mr. Singh's class voted on the type of fish they would buy to go into the new aquarium. They will buy the fish chosen by the greatest number of students.

Melissa-clownfish
Matthew-angelfish
Aaron-clownfish
Lee-puffer
Mei-clownfish
Kibbe-angelfish
Kim-puffer
Carlos-angelfish

Jake-angelfish
Brian-puffer
Crystal-clownfish
Abbey-clownfish
Demetrios-puffer
Nina-clownfish
Missy-angelfish
Sabrina-angelfish

Yuneng-puffer
Edwina-clownfish
Ryan-clownfish
Shani-angelfish
Lita-clownfish
Kelsey-clownfish
Kerstin-angelfish
Danny-clownfish

- **What do you need to know?** Students' choice of fish
- **What do you need to find?** Which type of fish is most popular

Plan

Collect and organize data to find out which fish will go into the aquarium.

Solve

Find which type of fish received the most votes. Organize the votes in a table.

Type of Fish	Tally	Number
angelfish	𝍸 |||	8
clownfish	𝍸 𝍸 |	11
puffer	𝍸	5

Mr. Singh's class will choose the clownfish for the aquarium.

Look Back

Does the answer make sense? How can you tell?

How does using a table help you solve a problem?

Practice

Use data from the list for problems 1–4.

Different Varieties of tetras, goldfish, and angelfish		
tetras-black neon tetra	goldfish-black moor	angelfish-gold angel
tetras-lemon tetra	goldfish-fan tail goldfish	angelfish-marble angel
tetras-white skirt	goldfish-lionhead	angelfish-silver angel
tetras-silver dollar		

1. How many varieties of angelfish are there?
2. Which type of fish has the greatest number of varieties?
3. **Science:** Unlike many other common aquarium fish, goldfish do not require a heated tank. How many varieties of goldfish are there?
4. How many varieties of fish are there altogether?
5. Alice, Jose, and Miko each like a different type of fish, either x-ray fish, paradise fish, or rainbow fish. Alice likes x-ray fish. Miko does not like rainbow fish. Who likes rainbow fish?

Problem Solving

Mixed Strategy Review

6. **Collect data** from other students about the type of fish they prefer. Make a table to organize your data. Write a problem that uses the data in your table. Solve it. Ask others to solve it.
7. Last month Aqua Inc. sold 28,324 freshwater fish and 9,892 saltwater fish. Which type of fish did they sell more of?
8. Aquarium World has 573,356 fish in stock. Round the number of fish to the nearest ten thousand.

CHOOSE A STRATEGY
- Logical Reasoning
- Draw a Picture
- Make a Graph
- Act It Out
- Make a Table or List
- Find a Pattern
- Guess and Check
- Write a Number Sentence
- Work Backward
- Solve a Simpler Problem

9. Akemi, Dakota, and Lucas are each writing a research report on one of these animals: hedgehogs, lemurs, and sea lions. Akemi is not writing about sea lions or hedgehogs. Lucas is writing about sea lions. What animal is Dakota writing about? Make a table to solve the problem.

★10. If you earn $10,000 a year, how long would it take you to earn $1,000,000? Explain your answer.

Extra Practice, page 33

Objective: Count coins and bills to find money amounts and make change.

1•7 Count Money and Make Change

Learn

Mario buys parakeet food for $7.67 in Gail's store. He gives Gail $10.00. How much change should Mario get?

Example

Gail can count up to find the change. Mario can check his change by counting the coins and bills.

1 *Start at $7.67. Count up to $10.00.*

Think: $7.68 → $7.69 → $7.70 → $7.75 → $8.00 → $9.00 → $10.00

2 *Count the bills and coins from greatest to least value.*

Think: $1.00 → $2.00 → $2.25 → $2.30 → $2.31 → $2.32 → $2.33

Gail should give Mario $2.33 as change.

Try It

Tell which coins and bills make the amount.

1. $0.78 **2.** $2.11 **3.** $5.28 **4.** $10.32

Find the amount of change.

5. Price: $0.56 Amount given: $1.00

6. Price: $2.35 Amount given: $5.00

7. Price: $7.28 Amount given: $10.00

How can you be sure to give change using the least number of coins and bills?

Practice Write the amount of money shown.

8. 

9. 

10. 

Tell which coins and bills make the amount.

11. \$0.89
12. \$3.39
13. \$7.87
14. \$10.06

Find the amount of change.

15. Price: \$0.79
Amount given: \$1.00
16. Price: \$2.07
Amount given: \$5.00
17. Price: \$4.19
Amount given: \$10.00

Algebra & functions **Find each missing number.**

18. \$3.45; \$3.55; ■; \$3.75
19. \$10.10; ■; \$10.30; \$10.40

Problem Solving

Use data from *Did You Know?* for problems 20–21.

20. At the San Diego Zoo, is there a greater number of birds or mammals? Explain.
21. Order the number of animals from greatest to least.
22. **What if** you have no quarters? Given \$10.00, make change for a tie that costs \$8.02.
23. **Analyze:** Explain how a clerk could skip-count to give \$2.45 in change. Which coins could the clerk use?

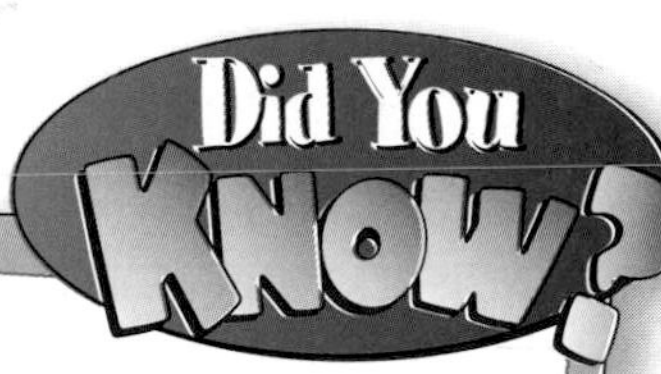

The San Diego Zoo is a 100-acre park. This zoo has the largest population of birds, reptiles, and mammals. There are 1,762 birds, 869 reptiles and amphibians, and 1,607 mammals.

Spiral Review and Test Prep

24. \$16 + \$4
25. \$82 − \$31
26. \$6 × 5
27. \$10 ÷ 2

Choose the correct answer.

28. Which is true?
    - A. 59 > 79
    - B. 37 < 37
    - C. 85 < 98
    - D. 54 < 44

29. Which shows 4,356,344 rounded to the nearest million?
    - F. 4,300,000
    - G. 4,000,000
    - H. 43,500,000
    - J. 5,000,000

Extra Practice, page 33

Objective: Use negative numbers to represent situations; compare negative numbers.

Negative Numbers

Learn

When you make a pledge, you owe money. How can you represent how much Anna owes? How can you represent the amount Nelson paid?

Math Words

negative number a number less than zero

positive number a number greater than zero

Save the Animals Fund
PLEDGE SHEET

Student	Pledge	Paid
Anna	$8	
Li	$4	
Nelson		$3

Example 1

You can represent the amount Anna owes as a **negative number**.	**Write:** $^{-}8$ **Read:** negative eight
The amount Nelson paid can be represented as a **positive number**.	**Write:** $^{+}3$ or 3 **Read:** positive three You do not have to write + to show that a number is positive.

You can use a number line to compare positive and negative numbers.

Example 2

Think: the numbers to the left are less than the numbers to the right.

Negative numbers are to the left of 0. Positive numbers are to the right of 0.

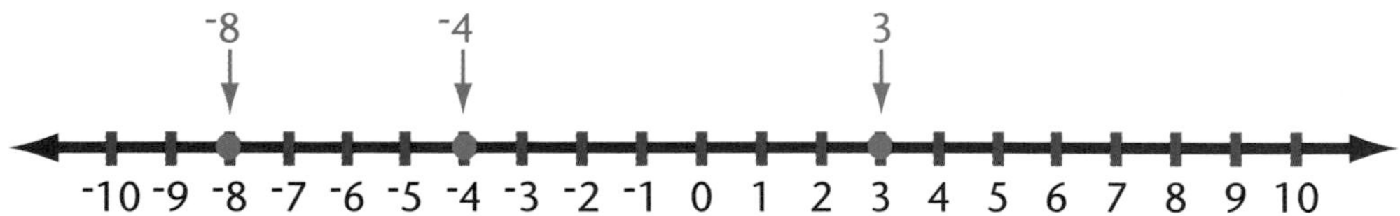

$^{-}8$ is to the left of $^{-}4$ on the number line, so $^{-}8 < {}^{-}4$.

$^{-}4$ is to the left of $^{+}3$ on the number line, so $^{-}8 < {}^{+}3$ and $^{-}4 < {}^{+}3$.

Try It

Write a positive or negative number to represent each situation.

1. You owe $14.
2. 12°F below zero
3. gain of 2 pounds

Explain how you can represent a loss of $5.00.

Practice **Write a positive or negative number to represent each situation.**

4. You earn $35.
5. 23°F above zero
6. You lose 3 pounds.
7. 18°F below zero
8. You owe $7.
9. 43 feet below sea level

Compare. Write $>$ or $<$. You may use a number line to help.

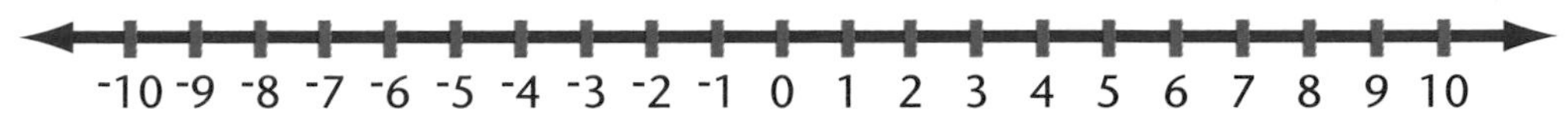

10. 2 ● $^-9$
11. $^-1$ ● 8
12. 3 ● $^-3$
13. $^-3$ ● $^-7$
14. $^-6$ ● 0
15. $^-7$ ● 7
16. 1 ● $^-6$
17. $^-1$ ● $^-9$
18. $^-5$ ● 0
19. 2 ● $^-1$

Describe a situation that can be represented by the integer.

20. $^-12$
21. $^+7$
22. $^-15$
23. $^-25$
24. $^-10$

Algebra & functions **Find the missing numbers in the counting pattern.**

25. $^-10$, ■, $^-8$, $^-7$, ■, ■, $^-4$, $^-3$, ■, $^-1$, ■

Problem Solving

26. **Science:** Some whales dive as deep as 460 meters below sea level looking for food. Write this depth as a negative number.

27. **Create a problem** for which you would compare negative numbers. Solve it. Ask others to solve it.

28. **Explain** why a negative number such as $^-1{,}934$ is less than a positive number like $^+1$.

★29. Use the number 3,203. Find the number with 1 less thousand, 4 more hundreds, 4 more tens, and 1 less one.

Spiral Review and Test Prep

30. $50 + 50$
31. $4{,}554 - 554$
32. 200×6
33. $12 \div 6$
34. $55 \div 5$
35. $100 + 1{,}000$

Choose the correct answer.

36. Which number is the greatest?
   - A. 5,687
   - B. 6,621
   - C. 21,341
   - D. 9,873

37. Which measures about 1 foot?
   - F. A house
   - G. A bedroom carpet
   - H. A bed
   - J. A computer screen

Extra Practice, page 33

Objective: Analyze data and make decisions.

Problem Solving: Application
Decision Making

Which store should Stacia go to? Why?

Stacia wants to buy 20 pounds of dog food for her Great Dane. There are several stores she can go to. Each store has a different cost for dog food. Each store is also a different distance from Stacia's house.

Cost of Gas to Drive to Store	
Name of Store	Cost of Gas
Pet Supply	$2.40
Animal World	$1.80
Pet's Place	$2.10
Discount Pet Food	$2.70

Read for Understanding

1. How much is 20 pounds of Nutripet at Discount Pet Food?
2. How much is 20 pounds of Nutripet at Pet Supply?
3. At which store is 20 pounds of dog food more expensive, Pet's Place or Animal World? How much more?
4. How much more is 20 pounds of dog food at Pet Supply than at Pet's Place?
5. Order the stores from the least expensive to the most expensive for 20 pounds of dog food.
6. Order the stores from the least to most expensive gas prices.

Make Decisions

7. For 20 pounds of Nutripet, which store is least expensive?
8. For which store is the cost of gas the most? the least?
9. What is the total cost to drive to Pet Supply and buy 20 pounds of dog food?
10. What is the total cost to drive to Animal World and buy 20 pounds of dog food?
11. What is the total cost to drive to Pet's Place and buy 20 pounds of dog food?
12. What is the total cost to drive to Discount Pet Food and buy 20 pounds of dog food?
13. Compare the total cost for Pet Supply and Animal World. What do you find?
14. Compare the total cost for Pet's Place and Discount Pet Food. What do you find?
15. Which store is the most expensive? least expensive?
16. What other things do you have to think about?

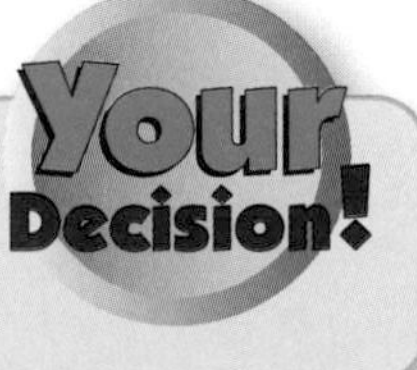

What is your recommendation for Stacia? Explain.

Problem Solving

Objective: Apply place value to investigate science concepts.

Problem Solving: Math and Science

How do you compare with your partner?

You Will Need
- ruler

Have you ever looked closely at a carton of eggs? It looks as if every egg is exactly the same, but each egg is really a little different.

Even though people have a lot in common, everyone is different. Let's see how you compare with another person in your class.

Hypothesize

If you compare yourself with your partner in 10 ways, how many times will you be the same (or almost the same)?

Procedure

1. Work with a partner and fill in the chart together.
2. Use what you know, or complete a quick activity, to answer each question.
3. Count how many times you and your partner have the same answer (or almost the same answer).

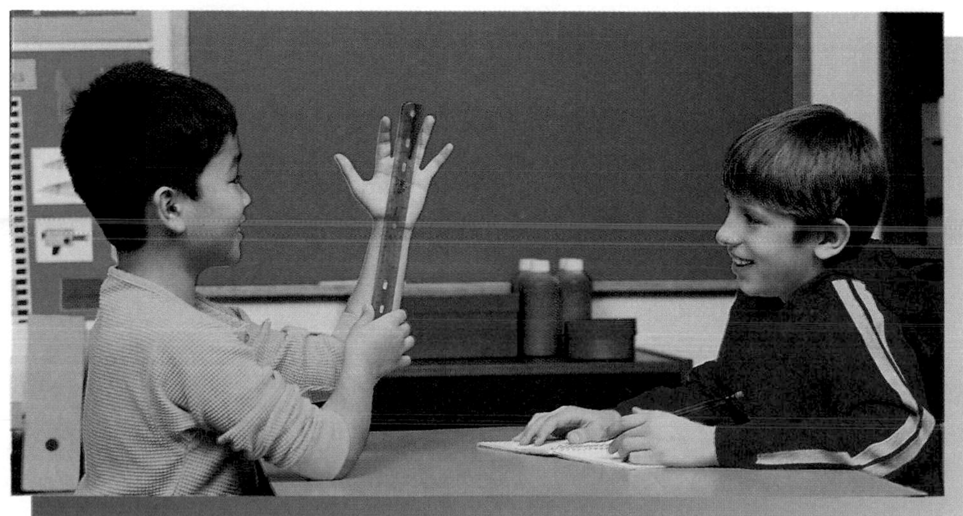

Data

Record your data. Copy and complete the chart. Decide whether you and your partner are the same.

	Same?	Student 1	Student 2
1.	Your favorite number		
2.	Number of hours you sleep each night		
3.	Number of push-ups you can do in 30 seconds		
4.	Number of objects in your desk right now		
5.	Number of cups of water you drank yesterday		
6.	Number of dogs and cats you know		
7.	Length of your arm from shoulder to wrist		
8.	How long you can stand on one foot		
9.	Number of times you breathe in one minute		
10.	Age		

Conclude and Apply

- How many times were you and your partner the same? different?
- Explain how you decided whether you and your partner were the same. Did the numbers have to be exactly alike? Why or why not?
- Why is it good to have variation in nature? What might happen if everyone were exactly the same?

Variation means that things are different from each other. Every living thing—each dog, ant, person, bacterium, and fish—varies (is different).

Going Further

1. Compare your chart with those of the whole class. Are there any questions to which almost everyone has the same answer? different answers?
2. Compare your chart to people who are older or younger than you. How do you compare?

Check Your Progress B

Write the money amount shown. (pages 22–23)

1.  

2.  

Tell which coins and bills make the amount. (pages 22–23)

3. \$1.35 4. \$4.53 5. \$5.85 6. \$7.31 7. \$9.67

Find the amount of change. (pages 22–23)

8. Price: \$3.47
   Amount given: \$5.00
9. Price: \$2.65
   Amount given: \$5.00
10. Price: \$6.23
    Amount given: \$10.00

Write a positive or negative number to represent each situation. (pages 24–25)

11. You owe \$47.
12. 52°F above zero
13. You grow 3 inches.
14. 5°C below zero
15. You lose \$32.
16. 25 feet below sea level

Compare. Write > or <. (pages 24–25)

17. $3 \bullet {}^{-}8$ 18. ${}^{-}4 \bullet 6$ 19. $7 \bullet {}^{-}7$ 20. ${}^{-}2 \bullet {}^{-}9$ 21. ${}^{-}8 \bullet 0$

Solve. (pages 20–25)

22. Angela, Bryan, Choon, and Derek like beetles, butterflies, ladybugs, and grasshoppers. Each likes a different insect. Angela likes beetles. Bryan does not like butterflies or grasshoppers. Derek picks butterflies. Who picks grasshoppers?

23. The low temperature on Monday was ${}^{-}5$°C. On Tuesday the low temperature was ${}^{-}10$°C. On which day was the temperature higher?

24. Tim's ticket costs \$8.75. He pays \$10.00 and receives \$2.25 change. Is this correct? Explain.

25. **Generalize:** Give examples of when you use negative numbers.

Extra Practice

Place Value Through Millions (pages 4–7)

Write the word name and the expanded form for each number.

1. 6,064
2. 8,372
3. 73,619
4. 42,001
5. 645,827
6. 215,253
7. 56,022,030
8. 357,002,030
9. 832,555,040
10. 566,349,123
11. 888,333,761
12. 526,230,007

Write the standard form for each number.

13. one hundred ten thousand, four hundred twenty-six
14. six hundred fifty-three thousand, four
15. 41 million, 439 thousand, 4 hundred, 49
16. 5,000,000 + 20,000 + 3,000 + 40 + 6
17. 80,000 + 5,000 + 400 + 60 + 2
18. 300,000 + 60,000 + 7,000 + 200 + 1
19. 6 million, 208 thousand, 5 hundred 60
20. 2 million, 312 thousand

Write the value of each underlined digit.

21. $\underline{3}$,456
22. $\underline{5}$4,289
23. $\underline{9}$24,532
24. 1,5$\underline{6}$9,867
25. 365,$\underline{3}$67,596
26. 1$\underline{6}$,743,218

Compare and Order Numbers and Money (pages 8–11)

Compare. Write >, <, or =.

1. 7,872 ● 7,782
2. \$36.14 ● \$36.41
3. 74,589 ● 75,499
4. 685,982 ● 684,892
5. 635,386 ● 635,386
6. \$98.38 ● \$98.57

Order the numbers from greatest to least.

7. \$4.60; \$4.78; \$4.87
8. 132,764; 132,467; 132,674

Order the numbers from least to greatest.

9. \$42.87; \$48.72; \$45.82
10. 254,452; 254,542; 254,425

Extra Practice

Problem Solving: Reading for Math Using the Four-Step Process (pages 12–13)

Solve. Use the four-step process.

1. The deepest a person has dived using compressed air is 510 feet. A sperm whale regularly dives to 3,720 feet. Some seals can dive to 1,968 feet. Which dive is the deepest?

2. The Komodo dragon grows to 10 feet. The saltwater crocodile grows to 20 feet. The Pacific leatherback turtle grows to 7 feet. Which reptile is shortest?

3. Linda has $14.75 to spend on lunch. Daphne has $12.75 and Lon has $9.89. Who has the most money for lunch?

4. Adult admission to the animal park is $4.98. Children pay $2.50 to get in. The admission price for seniors is $1.75. Who pays the most?

Round Numbers and Money (pages 14–17)

Round to the given place.

1. 323 to the nearest ten
2. $0.98 to the nearest ten cents
3. 2,380 to the nearest hundred
4. 45,710 to the nearest thousand
5. $57.29 to the nearest dollar
6. 282,315 to the nearest hundred thousand
7. $8.78 to the nearest ten cents
8. 16,759 to the nearest ten thousand
9. 2,567 to the nearest hundred
10. 7,481,328 to the nearest million
11. $17.72 to the nearest dollar
12. 89,322 to the nearest hundred thousand
13. 93,774 to the nearest thousand
14. 3,284,728 to the nearest million
15. $947.29 to the nearest dollar
16. 578,971 to the nearest ten thousand
17. 42,985 to the nearest thousand
18. 1,382,353 to the nearest million

Use 4,484,389 to round to the nearest

19. thousand.
20. ten thousand.
21. hundred thousand.
22. million.

Extra Practice

Problem Solving: Strategy Make a Table (pages 20–21)

Use the table to solve.

1. How many green catfish did Sam see?
2. How many catfish did Sam see altogether?
3. How many types of barbs did Sam see?
4. How many fish did Sam see altogether?

	How Many Seen
glass catfish	2
tiger barb	4
green catfish	5
tinfoil barb	3

Count Money and Make Change (pages 22–23)

Write the amount of money shown.

1.  

2.   

Tell what coins and bills make the amount.

3. \$1.71
4. \$6.63
5. \$7.26
6. \$9.19

Find the amount of change.

7. Price: \$6.35
   Amount given: \$10.00
8. Price: \$3.98
   Amount given: \$5.00
9. Price: \$1.19
   Amount given: \$2.00

Negative Numbers (pages 24–25)

Write a positive or negative number to represent each situation.

1. You owe \$64.
2. 35°F above zero
3. A cord shrinks 4 inches.
4. 67°C below zero
5. You earn \$17.
6. 78 feet below sea level
7. You lose \$12.
8. You cut 2 inches.
9. A plant grows 1 inch.

Compare. Write $>$ or $<$.

10. $1 \bullet {}^{-}8$
11. ${}^{-}2 \bullet 6$
12. $5 \bullet {}^{-}5$
13. ${}^{-}5 \bullet {}^{-}9$
14. ${}^{-}2 \bullet 0$
15. ${}^{-}7 \bullet 2$
16. $4 \bullet {}^{-}6$
17. ${}^{-}8 \bullet 0$
18. ${}^{-}4 \bullet {}^{-}2$
19. $0 \bullet {}^{-}3$

Chapter Study Guide

Language and Math

Math Words
is less than
is greater than
expanded form
place value
digit
negative number

Complete. Use a word from the list.

1. The number 98,552 is written as 90,000 + 8,000 + 500 + 50 + 2 in ____.
2. 47,798 ____ 47,987.
3. You can write 34 feet below sea level as a ____.
4. A symbol used to write a number is a ____.
5. You can compare numbers by looking at the ____ of their digits.

Skills and Applications

Place value through millions. (pages 2–7)

Example
Write 5,080,105 in word name and expanded form.

Solution
Word name: five million, eighty thousand, one hundred five
Expanded form: 5,000,000 + 80,000 + 100 + 5

Write each number in word name and expanded form.

6. 5,936
7. 34,907
8. 214,657
9. 4,987,109
10. 97,605,442
11. 905,001,590

Compare, order, and round numbers and money. (pages 8–11, 14–17)

Example
Order from greatest to least.
59,617; 45,671; 46,714

Solution
Start with the greatest place.
Compare the digits in each place.

59,617	5 > 4, so 59,617 is the
45,671	greatest number.
46,714	6 > 5, so 46,714 > 45,671

The numbers from greatest to least:
59,617; 46,714; 45,671

Order from greatest to least.

12. 33,998; 33,899; 33,999
13. $450.22; $450.44; $450.34

Compare. Write >, <, or =.

14. 8,273 ● 7,418
15. 1,670 ● 1,670
16. $65.79 ● $6.94
17. $5.63 ● $3.52

Round to the given place.

18. 8,909 (ten)
19. 65,823,551 (hundred thousand)

Count money and make change. (pages 22–23)

Example

What is the amount of change Sarah will get if she pays for a \$4.74 clip with \$5.00.

Solution

Start at \$4.74   \$4.75   \$5.00

The amount of change is \$0.26.

Find the amount of change.

20. Price: \$3.85
Amount given: \$5.00

21. Price: \$1.33
Amount given: \$5.00

22. Len bought a box of dog biscuits for \$3.22. He handed the clerk a five-dollar bill. What is the amount of change Len will get?

Use and compare negative numbers. (pages 24–25)

Example

Which is higher, 8°F below zero or 2°F below zero?

Solution

Use a number line. Compare.

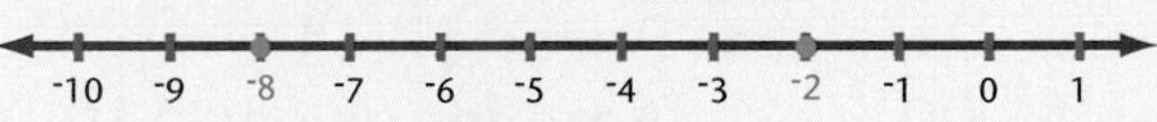

$^{-}8$ is to the left of $^{-}2$, so $^{-}2 > {}^{-}8$.

Write a positive or negative number for each situation.

23. You owe \$59. **24.** 16°F above zero

Compare. Write > or <.

25. 3 ● $^{-}4$ **26.** $^{-}1$ ● 3

27. 2 ● $^{-}2$ **28.** $^{-}5$ ● $^{-}7$

29. $^{-}9$ ● 0 **30.** $^{-}6$ ● $^{-}1$

Use strategies to solve problems. (pages 12–13, 20–21)

Example

Select the most popular fish.

pufferfish	pufferfish	triggers
triggers	gobies	gobies
gobies	gobies	triggers

Solution

Make a table to organize the data.

Type of Fish	Tally	Number
Pufferfish	||	2
Triggers	|||	3
Gobies	||||	4

Gobies are the most popular fish.

Make a table to solve.

31. Mr. Gonzales has these fish in his tank. Which type of fish does he have more of than any other?

red eye tetra	shark catfish
glass catfish	gold angelfish
marble angelfish	red eye tetra
shark catfish	shark catfish

32. Does Mr. Gonzales have more catfish or tetras?

33. How many shark catfish does he have?

Study Guide

Chapter Test

Write each number in standard form.

1. six hundred thirty-three thousand, sixty-eight
2. 300,000,000 + 4,000,000 + 500,000 + 90,000 + 6,000 + 2

Compare. Write >, <, or =.

3. 1,647,954 ● 1,357,859
4. $18.75 ● $18.90
5. $127.87 ● $127.87

Order the numbers from least to greatest.

6. $665.28; $664.82; $666.22
7. 2,595,282; 2,959,822; 2,594,282

Round to the given place.

8. 6,238 to the nearest hundred
9. 5,657,259 to the nearest hundred thousand
10. $16.55 to the nearest dollar
11. $2.56 to the nearest ten cents

Find the amount of change.

12. Price: $2.64
    Amount given: $5.00
13. Price: $0.96
    Amount given: $5.00
14. Price: $7.14
    Amount given: $10.00

Compare. Write > or <.

15. 9 ● $^{-}9$
16. $^{-}4$ ● 6
17. $^{-}4$ ● $^{-}6$

Solve.

18. The Bengal tiger weighs about 500 pounds, the Asian elephant about 11,000 pounds, the African lion about 400 pounds, and the blue whale about 320,000 pounds. Order the animals from heaviest to lightest.
19. Sal pledges to donate $45 to public television. How can you write this as a negative number?
20. For a math project, a group asks its members which pet they would like to have. Here are the results of the survey. Make a table to find which pet is most popular.

Harold	cat	Lexi	rabbit	Monica	cat
Simon	fish	Evon	dog	Jerome	cat
Andy	cat	Amber	fish	Kimi	rabbit
Carrie	dog	Peter	turtle	Trish	dog

Performance Assessment

Play this game with a partner.

For each turn, either you or your partner rolls the number cube to see how many digits the number can have for both players. Then each player draws cards in turn. Use the numbers on the cards to form the greatest possible number using each digit only once. Once the cards are down in place, they cannot be moved. Alternate who goes first for each round.

Compare numbers. The player with the greater number gets 1 point. The player with the greatest number of points after 5 turns is the winner.

You Will Need
- **a 1–6 number cube**
- **2 sets of cards labeled 0–9, one digit on each card**

Keep track of the game on a chart like the one below.

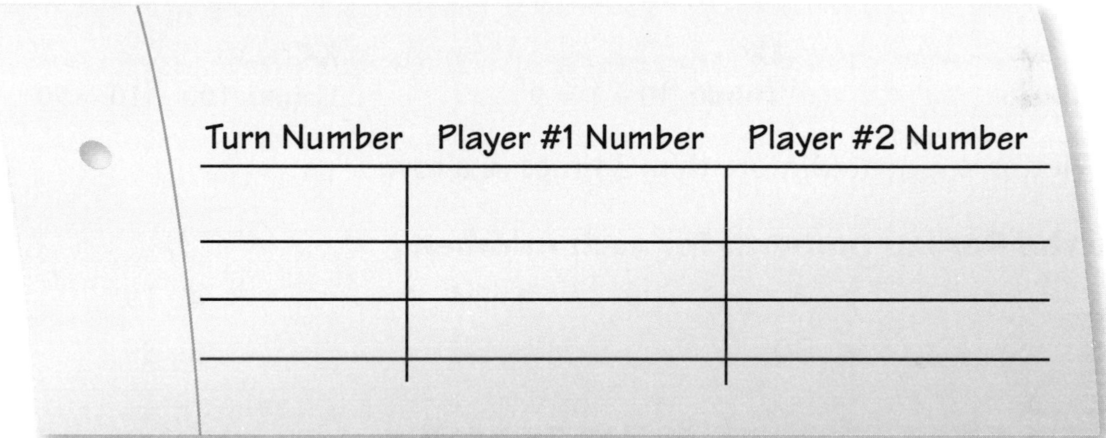

Turn Number	Player #1 Number	Player #2 Number

- Write how you compared the numbers.
- Write your strategy for placing the digits where you did.

A Good Answer
- shows the numbers compared for each turn.
- explains how they were compared.
- describes a strategy for placing the digits to form the greatest possible number.

You may wish to save this work for your portfolio.

Enrichment

Roman Numerals

A very long time ago, the Romans developed a system of numbers called **Roman numerals.** They used letters to symbolize numbers as shown in the table.

I	V	X	L	C
1	5	10	50	100

Numbers were made by putting the symbols together. You will use addition and subtraction when rewriting Roman numerals as numbers.

VII
Think: 5 + 1 + 1 = 7

LXII
Think: 50 + 10 +1 + 1 = 62

CLXI
Think: 100 + 50 + 10 + 1 = 161

IV
Think: 5 − 1 = 4

IX
Think: 10 − 1 = 9

XC
Think: 100 − 10 = 90

No letter is repeated more than 3 times in a row.

Write the Roman numeral for each number.

1. 2 **2.** 7 **3.** 14 **4.** 19

5. 24 **6.** 30 **7.** 36 **8.** 39

Write the number for each Roman numeral.

9. LVII **10.** LIX **11.** LXI **12.** LXIII

13. LXVII **14.** LXX **15.** LXXIV **16.** LXXVII

Solve.

17. Kara had LXIII dollars in her wallet. She spent VIII dollars on a book. How much does Kara have left?

18. **Generalize:** Why do you think Roman numerals are not used very often today?

19. **Generalize:** How are the numbers we use similar to Roman numerals? How are they different?

Test-Taking Tips

Using the **process of elimination** can help you choose the correct answer when you are taking a multiple-choice test.

Which number is 10,000 more than 465,832?

A. 10,832 **C.** 475,832
B. 455,832 **D.** 565,832

Use place value to think about the correct choice.

Choice A has too few places. Choice D has too many hundred thousands. You can eliminate choices D and A. Now you can choose between B and C. If the number is 10,000 greater than 465,832, the digit in the ten thousands should increase to 7. C is the correct choice.

Check for Success

Before turning in a test, go back one last time to check.

- ☑ I understood and answered the questions asked.
- ☑ I checked my work for errors.
- ☑ My answers make sense.

Read each problem. Eliminate answers you know are wrong. Choose the correct answer.

1. Which number is 1,000 less than 7,649?

A. 8,649 **C.** 7,549
B. 7,642 **D.** 6,649

2. Which number is greater than 12,498?

F. 12,398 **H.** 12,496
G. 12,489 **J.** 12,500

3. Which names the same number as 80,000 + 200 + 90?

A. 829 **C.** 82,900
B. 80,290 **D.** 800,290

4. What is the value of the 3 in 1,032?

F. Thirty **H.** Three
G. Three hundred **J.** Thirty thousand

5. Jill has 3 quarters more than Pat. Pat has $0.75. How much does Jill have?

A. $1.75 **C.** $1.25
B. $1.50 **D.** $1.00

6. Richard has $1.79. Which two coins are hidden by the squares?

F. 1 dime, 1 penny **H.** 1 dime, 1 nickel
G. 2 dimes **J.** 2 quarters

Test Prep

Spiral Review and Test Prep

Chapter 1

Choose the correct answer.

Number Sense

1. Which is the standard form for three hundred twenty-one million, four hundred ninety-five thousand, six hundred eighty-seven?

   A. 321,495,687 **C.** 321,687
   B. 321,459,687 **D.** 321,459

2. Which is 6,951,532 rounded to the nearest hundred?

   F. 6,950,000 **H.** 6,951,500
   G. 6,951,000 **J.** 6,951,600

3. Susan buys a stuffed animal for $3.45. She pays with a five-dollar bill. How much change should she get?

   A. $3.45 **C.** $1.55
   B. $2.55 **D.** $0.55

4. Which is correct?

   F. $6.96 > $6.99
   G. $23.39 > $24.39
   H. $43.29 < $44.29
   J. $87.89 < $86.99

Measurement and Geometry

5. What is the perimeter of this animal cage at the zoo?

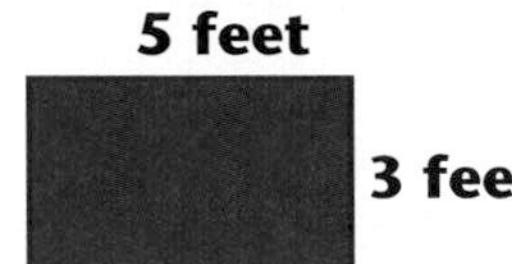

   A. 13 feet **C.** 16 feet
   B. 15 feet **D.** 8 feet

6. A bird has a wing span of $10\frac{1}{2}$ inches. How do you show this measurement to the nearest inch?

   F. 11 inches **H.** $10\frac{1}{2}$ inches
   G. 1 feet **J.** 10 inches

7. During the dry season in Australia, a water-holding frog burrows about 50 centimeters below the top of the soil. Which measurement is greater than 50 centimeters?

   A. 5 centimeters
   B. 10 centimeters
   C. 50 centimeters
   D. 50 meters

8. Which is the name of the figure shown?

   F. Trapezoid **H.** Square
   G. Rectangle **J.** Triangle

Statistics, Data Analysis, and Probability

Use the chart for problems 9–12.

Animal Lengths	
African giant earthworm	22 ft
Finback whale	85 ft
Giant squid	57 ft
Japanese spider crab	11 ft
Oarfish	46 ft
Saltwater crocodile	18 ft

Source: *The Random House Children's Encyclopedia*

9. Which two animals have a combined length of 107 feet?
   - A. Giant squid and oarfish
   - B. Finback whale and Japanese spider crab
   - C. Giant squid and saltwater crocodile
   - D. Finback whale and African giant earthworm

10. How much longer is a giant squid than an oarfish?
   - F. 103 feet
   - H. 39 feet
   - G. 11 feet
   - J. 46 feet

11. Which animal is exactly twice as long as the Japanese spider crab?
   - A. African giant earthworm
   - B. Saltwater crocodile
   - C. Oarfish
   - D. Chinese giant salamander

12. Which are the closest in length?
   - F. Oarfish and giant squid
   - G. Japanese spider crab and saltwater crocodile
   - H. Giant squid and finback whale
   - J. Oarfish and Japanese spider crab

Mathematical Reasoning

13. A giraffe is about 3 times as tall as a man. If a man is 6-foot tall, what is the height of a giraffe?
   - A. 12 feet
   - C. 24 feet
   - B. 18 feet
   - D. Not Here

14. A group of bikers rode for 4 miles the first day, 8 miles the second day, and 12 miles the third day. If the number of miles they ride continues to increase in the same way, how far will they ride on the sixth day?
   - F. 16 miles
   - H. 24 miles
   - G. 20 miles
   - J. 32 miles

15. Victor says the 4 in 890,040,317 represents the ten thousands place. Alex says it represents forty thousand. With whom do you agree?
   - A. Victor
   - C. Both Victor and Alex
   - B. Alex
   - D. Neither Victor nor Alex

16. Hal has read the first 68 pages of a 268-page book. How many pages does Hal have to read in order to finish the book?

    Write a number sentence you could use to solve the problem. Explain how you decided which type of number sentence to write.

SOS

CHAPTER 2

Addition and Subtraction

Theme: Fun Zone

Real Data

Number of Tickets	Prize
20 tickets	Small stuffed animal
60 tickets	Large stuffed animal
280 tickets	CD
450 tickets	Movie video
3,500 tickets	Game station

- One day at a carnival, you won 215 tickets. On the next day, you won 184 tickets. How can you use addition and subtraction to find how many points you still need to win the game station?

What You Will Learn

In this chapter you will learn how to

- add and subtract, using mental math.
- find sums and differences.
- estimate and find sums and differences.
- use strategies to solve problems.

Objective: Use addition properties.

2·1 Use Properties of Addition

Algebra & functions

Learn

Maria places 4 new baseball cards in a large album. Now she has 12 cards in all. How many cards had been in the album?

Math Words

Commutative Property Order of the numbers does not affect the sum.

variable a symbol used to represent a number or group of numbers.

Identity Property When 0 is added to a number, the sum is the number.

Example 1

You can use the **Commutative Property** and related facts to help you remember facts and solve the problem.

Find n if $4 + n = 12$.

Note: n is called a **variable**. Here it stands for the unknown number of cards.

If you know $8 + 4 = 12$, then you know $4 + 8 = 12$.

You can also use related subtraction facts.

If $n = 8$, then you know $12 - 8 = 4$ and $12 - 4 = 8$.

There had been 8 cards in the album.

You can use the Commutative Property, the **Identity Property**, and the related sentences when working with greater numbers.

Example 2

Find n if $27 - n = 27$.

If you know $27 + 0 = 27$, then you know $27 - 0 = 27$.

Try It **Write the related number sentences for each.**

1. 5, 7, 12 **2.** 6, 11, 17 **3.** 6, 27, 21

Tell how you can use a related number sentence to check the answer to $18 - 5 = n$.

Practice Complete each set of related number sentences.

4. $8 + 12 = t$
$v + 8 = 20$
$20 - 8 = v$
$20 - 12 = s$

5. $5 + 14 = n$
$14 + i = 19$
$19 - 14 = i$
$19 - i = 14$

6. $6 + 7 = h$
$7 + w = 13$
$13 - 6 = s$
$h - 7 = 6$

7. $8 + 16 = e$
$16 + t = 24$
$e - 8 = 16$
$24 - g = 8$

Find the sum or difference. Write the related number sentences.

8. $9 + 8$
9. $16 - 8$
10. $25 - 5$
11. $32 + 4$
12. $46 + 0$
13. $19 + 6$
14. $54 - 7$
15. $24 - 4$

Write the related number sentences for each set of numbers.

16. 6, 9, 15
17. 9, 9, 18
18. 2, 35, 37
19. 0, 39, 39
20. 12, 33, 45
21. 15, 25, 40
22. 32, 64
23. 20, 33, 53

Look at each set of numbers. Can you write a set of related number sentences? Why or why not?

★24. 3, 3, 3
★25. 6, 8, 14
★26. 4, 20, 24
★27. 10, 20, 40

Problem Solving

Use data from the chart for problems 28–29.

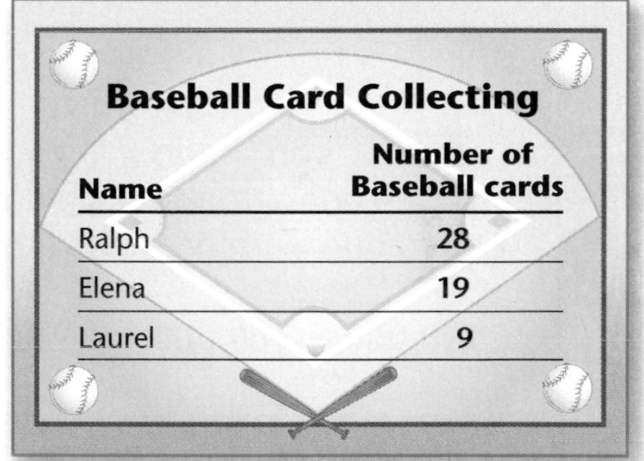

Baseball Card Collecting

Name	Number of Baseball cards
Ralph	28
Elena	19
Laurel	9

28. How many more cards does Ralph have than Elena?

29. **Analyze:** How are the numbers in the chart related? Give examples.

30. Five of 14 baseball cards are National League cards. How many cards are not National League?

Spiral Review and Test Prep

31. $4 + 5$
32. $12 - 3$
33. $8 + 3$
34. $17 - 9$

Choose the correct answer.

35. Chantal has 4 green model cars and 7 yellow model cars. How many cars does she have altogether?
A. 3
B. 11
C. 47
D. Not Here

36. Kimi has 12 marbles. She gives 4 to her brother. How many does she have left?
F. 8
G. 16
H. 52
J. 124

Extra Practice, page 79

Objective: Review adding multiples of 10, 100, and 1,000.

2•2 Addition Patterns

Algebra & functions

Learn

Math Words

pattern a series of numbers or figures that follow a rule

sum the answer for an addition problem

The ABC Toy Factory is making model car sets. The number of wheels needed is shown on the clipboard. How many wheels do they need?

Example

You can use a **pattern** to find a **sum** mentally.

Find: 500,000 + 700,000

Think: You can use basic facts and place value to help.

5 + 7 = 12	5 ones + 7 ones = 12 ones
50 + 70 = 120	5 tens + 7 tens = 12 tens
500 + 700 = 1,200	5 hundreds + 7 hundreds = 12 hundreds
5,000 + 7,000 = 12,000	5 thousands + 7 thousands = 12 thousands
50,000 + 70,000 = 120,000	5 ten thousands + 7 ten thousands = 12 ten thousands
500,000 + 700,000 = 1,200,000	5 hundred thousands + 7 hundred thousands = 12 hundred thousands

The ABC Toy Factory needs 1,200,000 wheels in all.

Try It

Write the number that makes each sentence true.

1.
$4 + 9 = n$
$40 + 90 = m$
$400 + 900 = r$
$4{,}000 + 9{,}000 = s$
$40{,}000 + 90{,}000 = t$

2.
$8 + 3 = d$
$800 + 300 = h$
$80{,}000 + 30{,}000 = b$
$800{,}000 + w = 1{,}100{,}000$

Sum it Up! Look at the addition patterns above. Explain how you used the pattern to add mentally.

Practice Write the number that makes each sentence true.

3. $7 + 8 = n$
   $70 + 80 = a$
   $700 + 800 = x$
   $7{,}000 + 8{,}000 = t$
   $70{,}000 + 80{,}000 = z$
   $700{,}000 + 800{,}000 = c$

4. $5 + 5 = j$
   $w + 50 = 100$
   $500 + u = 1{,}000$
   $5{,}000 + 5{,}000 = k$
   $q + 50{,}000 = 100{,}000$
   $500{,}000 + m = 1{,}000{,}000$

Add mentally.

5. 500 + 300
6. 4,000 + 9,000
7. 20,000 + 80,000
8. 600 + 900
9. 100,000 + 700,000
10. 800,000 + 400,000
11. 300,000 + 600,000

★12. 30 + 400 + 5,000 + 60,000 + 700,000

Problem Solving

13. The ABC Toy Factory made 50,000 paint sets its first year. This year, they have made 60,000 paint sets so far. How many paint sets have they made in all?

14. In May the Rocket Toy Company made $30,000 selling puzzles. In June they made $70,000. How much money did they make in the two months?

15. **Money:** Mark has 1 ten-dollar bill and 4 one-dollar bills. He buys a puzzle for $12.75. What change should he get?

16. **Explain** how you would add 400 + 700 + 300 + 800 + 100.

Spiral Review and Test Prep

Round to the nearest thousand.

17. 2,425
18. 7,632
19. 33,511
20. 74,299

Choose the correct answer.

21. Marco has 17 stamps in a stamp collection. He gives 9 stamps to a friend. Which number sentence shows how many stamps Marco has now?

    A. 17 + 9 = 26
    C. 9 + 17 = 26
    B. 17 − 8 = 9
    D. 17 − 9 = 8

22. Kayla has 15 yellow and red beads to make a necklace. She has 7 yellow beads. Which number sentence shows how many beads are red?

    F. 15 + 7 = 23
    H. 8 + 7 = 15
    G. 15 − 7 = 8
    J. 15 − 9 = 7

Objective: Review adding two or more whole numbers and money amounts.

2•3 Add Whole Numbers and Money

Learn

Have you ever played Skee Ball at an amusement park? Mark and Julie play at a boardwalk arcade. If they combine their scores, how many points will they have toward a prize?

> **Math Word**
>
> **Associative Property** when adding, the grouping of numbers does not affect the result

Example 1

Find: 239 + 185

1 Add the ones. Regroup if necessary.

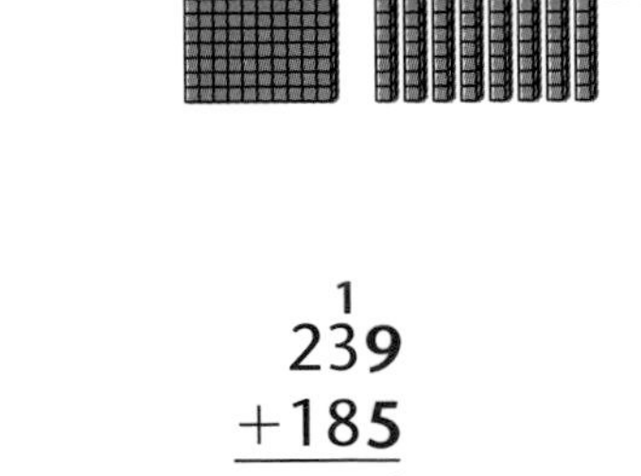

$$\begin{array}{r} {}^{1} \\ 239 \\ +185 \\ \hline 4 \end{array}$$

Think: 14 ones = 1 ten and 4 ones

2 Add the tens. Regroup if necessary.

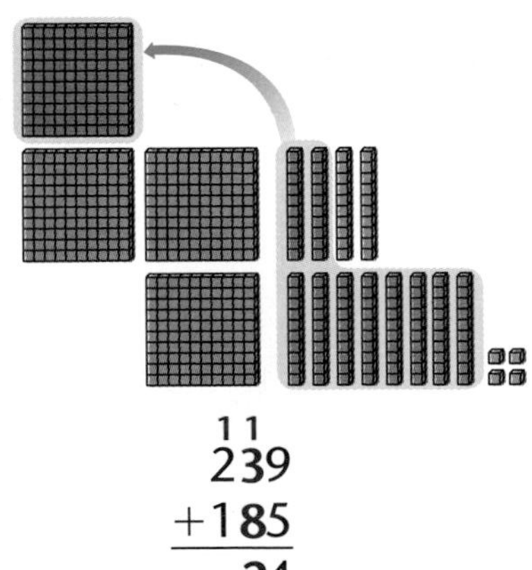

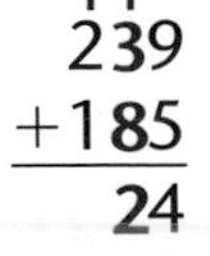

$$\begin{array}{r} {}^{1\,1} \\ 239 \\ +185 \\ \hline 24 \end{array}$$

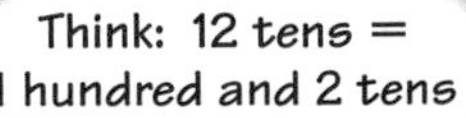

3 Add the hundreds. Regroup if necessary.

$$\begin{array}{r} {}^{1\,1} \\ 239 \\ +185 \\ \hline 424 \end{array}$$

Mark and Julie have 424 points.

Next, Mark and Julie play a video game. Mark scores points in three games. How many points does Mark score?

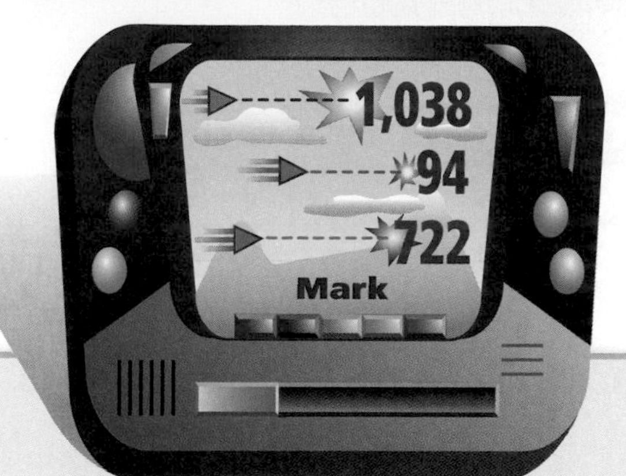

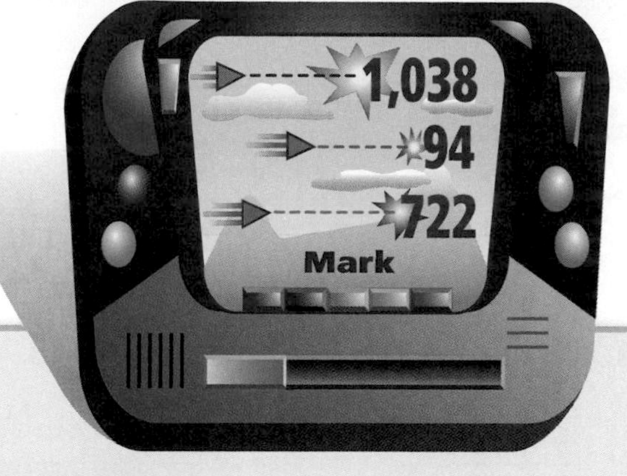

Example 2

Find: 1,038 + 94 + 722

You can use the Commutative Property and **Associative Property** to help you add. Use the properties to make tens.

1 Add the ones. Regroup if necessary.

```
     1
 1,038
    94
+  722
     4
```

Think:
8 + 2 = 10
10 + 4 = 14

2 Add the tens. Regroup if necessary.

```
    11
 1,038
    94
+  722
    54
```

Think:
1 + 9 = 10
10 + 3 + 2 = 15

3 Add the hundreds. Regroup if necessary.

```
   11
 1,038
    94
+  722
   854
```

4 Add the thousands.

```
   11
 1,038
    94
+  722
 1,854
```

Mark scored 1,854 points in all.

More Examples

A

```
  12 11
 534,857
     729
+  6,953
 542,539
```

B

```
  1  1 1
 $4,281.98
+    25.69
 $4,307.67
```

You can add money as you would whole numbers. Line up the decimal points. Add each place. Regroup if necessary.

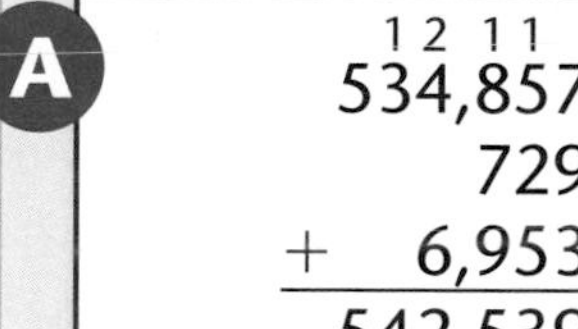

Find each sum.

1. 232 + 591
2. \$9.06 + 3.91
3. 3,067 + 2,693
4. \$142.09 + 7.23
5. 23,384 + 452

You are adding a 3-digit number, a 5-digit number, and a 2-digit number. Why is it important to line up the digits when adding?

Practice Find each sum.

6. 577 + 309

7. \$7.54 + 4.43

8. 4,112 + 3,855

9. \$23,806 + 684

10. \$0.98 + 0.47

11. 6,337 + 5,119 + 408

12. 54,890 + 527 + 5,034

13. \$546.09 + 3.27 + 25.03

14. 617,909 + 43,055 + 101,507

15. 311,997 + 3,984 + 103

16. 489 + 643
17. \$6.06 + \$0.97
18. 8,345 + 2,192
19. \$2,745 + \$866
20. 331,997 + 103
21. 123,905 + 87,345
22. \$1,564.01 + \$287.89
23. \$75.03 + \$6.73 + \$28.15
24. \$410.96 + \$0.97 + \$8.09 + \$27.38

Algebra & functions Find each sum. Use properties to help you.

25. 324 + 421 + 356
26. 811 + 429 + 300
27. 5,360 + 320 + 240
28. 8,451 + 3,840 + 349
29. 8,495 + 7,683 + 55

Write two addends for each sum. Each addend must be greater than 500.

★30. 1,560 ★31. 3,800 ★32. 8,462 ★33. 15,365 ★34. 654,359

35.

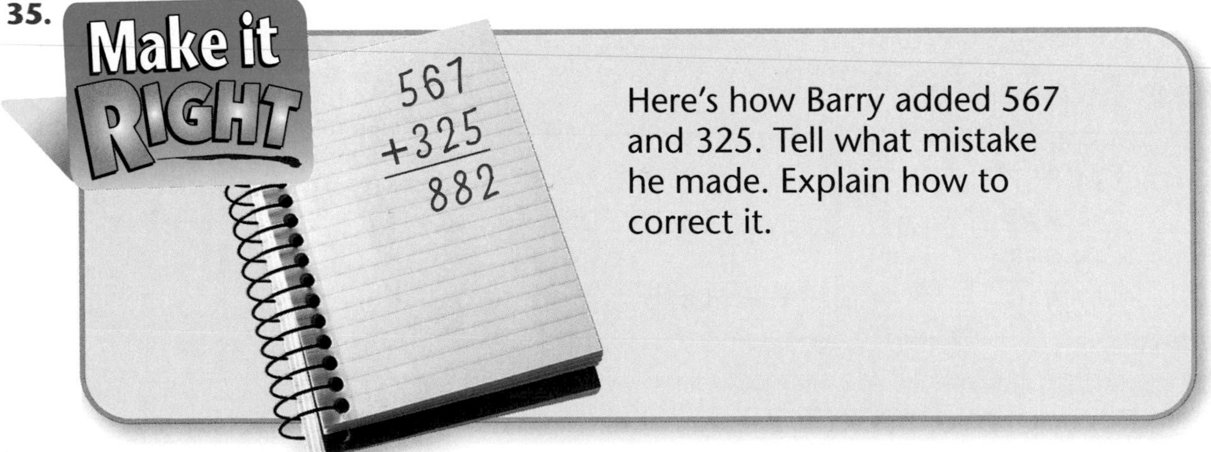

Here's how Barry added 567 and 325. Tell what mistake he made. Explain how to correct it.

Problem Solving

36. Jessie scores 289 points in a bowling game. He scores 176 points in the second game, and 134 points in the third game. What was his total for the three games?

37. **Generalize:** How do you use the Commutative Property and the Associative Property to add columns of numbers?

Use data from *Did You Know?* for problems 38–39.

38. How many pieces are in the puzzle with the most pieces ever?

39. **Measurement:** How can the puzzle with the most pieces be smaller than the largest?

40. Billy is thinking of a number that is less than 100. When you add 80 to this number, you get 150. What is the number?

41. **Analyze:** If you add two 4-digit numbers, what is the greatest number of digits that can be in the sum? the least number?

Did You Know?

The world's largest jigsaw puzzle was made up of 43,924 pieces. There were 160,560 more pieces in the puzzle that had the most pieces ever.

Use data from the table for problems 42–46.

42. Paula scores 8,078 points playing pinball. Between which two players would she rank?

43. Suki scores 5,316 points. Which players have fewer points?

44. Corey scores 1,000 points in his next game. How many points does he have now?

45. Holly scores 14,389 points on her next game. How many points does she score in all?

46. Erin scores 2,142 points fewer than Holly. How many points does Erin score?

TOP SCORES FOR JET PILOT

Player	Score
Holly	23,977
Roger	14,825
Anita	7,965
Chin	5,245
Corey	935

Spiral Review and Test Prep

Compare. Write >, <, or =.

47. 387 ● 378
48. 4,276 ● 3,853
49. 45,531 ● 54,387
50. 345,876 ● 347,441
51. 453,990 ● 453,990
52. 673,424 ● 774,392

Choose the correct answer.

53. Round $345.78 to the nearest ten dollars.
   A. $300
   B. $340
   C. $350
   D. $345

54. Find the number missing from the counting pattern:
   18, 28, 38, ■, 58, 68
   F. 39
   G. 48
   H. 47
   J. Not Here

Objective: Use mental math strategies to add.

2·4 Use Mental Math to Add

Learn

Math Words

compensation When adding, add a number to one addend and subtract the same number from the other addend to find the sum.

addend a number to be added

Have you ever used building blocks to construct something? Frank has a basic kit and a deluxe kit of Build It! How many pieces of Build It! does he have?

There's more than one way!

You can add mentally to solve.

Method A

When the numbers are close to a ten or hundred you can use **compensation**.

Add: $198 + 375$

$+2 \downarrow \qquad \downarrow -2$

$200 + 373 = 573$

Think: Add a number to one **addend** to make a hundred. Subtract the same number from the other addend. The sum remains the same.

Method B

You can also use the zig-zag method to add mentally.

Add: 198
+375

Think: $198 + \mathbf{300} = 498$

$498 + \mathbf{70} = 568$

$568 + \mathbf{5} = 573$

Frank has a total of 573 construction pieces.

Try It

Add mentally. Explain which method you used.

1. $183 + 517$ **2.** $298 + 476$ **3.** $595 + 231$ **4.** \$163 + \$597

When is it easier to use compensation than the zig-zag method? Why?

Practice Add mentally.

5. 52 + 87
6. 73 + 44
7. 65 + 21
8. \$83 + \$12
9. 45 + 32
10. 55 + 24
11. 98 + 32
12. \$129 + \$160
13. 187 + 602
14. 346 + 531
15. 598 + 421
16. \$649 + \$230
17. 620 + 303
18. 298 + 201
19. 432 + 266
20. \$548 + \$450
21. 277 + 331
22. 554 + 315
23. 3,101 + 2,297
24. 2,686 + 1,213

Algebra & functions **Write the letter of each missing number.**

25. $357 + n = 657$
26. $h + 412 = 912$
27. $150 + t = 850$

Choose from these numbers: 37, 43, 46, 56, 74, 99, 114, and 301. Find two numbers that have

★28. a sum of 99.
★29. a sum of 80.
★30. a sum of 400.

Problem Solving

31. Tanya has 2 metal building sets. One set has 457 pieces. The other set has 313 pieces. How many pieces does she have in all?

32. **Generalize:** Why does the sum not change when you add a number to one addend and subtract it from the other?

33. The Spensor family bought a robot building kit for \$239 and a model car building kit for \$112. How much did they spend in all?

34. **Create a problem** that could be solved using compensation. Solve it. Ask others to solve it.

Spiral Review and Test Prep

Find the amount of change.

35. Cost: \$0.35
Amount given: \$1.00

36. Cost: \$1.69
Amount given: \$5.00

37. Cost \$5.90
Amount given: \$10.00

Choose the correct answer.

38. What number is equal to 3 ten thousands + 5 hundreds + 4 tens + 7 ones?
A. 3,547
C. 300,547
B. 30,547
D. 3,457

39. Tamla's address has a 4 in the hundreds place. Which could be her address?
F. 8548
H. 4321
G. 9734
J. 2435

Estimate Sums

Learn

Math Word

estimate an answer that is close to the exact answer

Children at the Kiawa Day Camp sign up for craft activities. About how many children are signed up for wood carving and weaving?

Example

Estimate: 173 + 112

Round each number to find the sum mentally.

173 + 112
↓ ↓
200 + 100 = 300

Think: Round to the nearest hundred.

There are about 300 children signed up for craft activities.

More Examples

A Estimate: 4,372 + 381

Think: Round to the nearest hundred.
4,400 + 400 = 4,800

B Estimate: 25,377 + 5,065

Think: Round to the nearest thousand.
25,000 + 5,000 = 30,000

C Estimate: \$0.57 + \$0.32

Think: Round to the nearest ten cents.
\$0.60 + \$0.30 = \$0.90

D Estimate: \$4.25 + \$3.57

Think: Round to the nearest dollar.
\$4.00 + \$4.00 = \$8.00

Try It

Estimate. Tell how you rounded.

1. 167 + 872 **2.** \$0.42 + \$0.81 **3.** \$2.38 + \$7.89 **4.** 1,272 + 689

Sum it Up! Tell how you could round the numbers in problem 4 so that the estimate is closer to the exact sum.

Practice **Estimate each sum.**

5. 578 + 607 6. 321 + 408 7. \$4.67 + \$2.99 8. \$9.25 + \$7.56

9. 3,990 + 605 10. 507,900 + 458,033 11. 319,998 + 505,883

Add. Estimate to check that each answer is reasonable.

12. 4,706 + 2,990 13. \$51.65 + \$6.64 14. 40,119 + 3,974 15. 23,567 + 11,999

Compare. Write > or < to make a true sentence.

16. 186 + 238 ● 300 17. 352 + 132 ● 600 18. 8,321 + 8,200 ● 17,000

★19. 197 + 364 ● 213 + 312 ★20. 7,214 + 5,125 ● 6,302 + 5,415

Problem Solving

21. There are a total of 568 children at the Kiawa Day Camp. The Blackfoot Day Camp has 713 children. About how many children are at the two camps?

22. **Social Studies:** Campers visit a museum. They learn how the Iroquois made wampum from shells. One wampum belt has 256 shells in it. Another belt has 327 shells. About how many shells are in both belts?

23. The camp children made 4 beaded necklaces. They used a total of 1,587 beads. What is 1,587 rounded to the nearest thousand?

★24. **Analyze:** How will an estimated sum compare to the exact sum if you round each number up? down?

Spiral Review and Test Prep

How much money is shown?

25.

26.

Choose the correct answer.

27. Which is not part of the fact family?
 A. 2 + 8 = 10 C. 10 − 2 = 8
 B. 10 + 0 = 10 D. 8 + 2 = 10

28. Which is the expanded form of 1,702?
 F. 1,000 + 70 + 2 H. 170 + 2
 G. 1,000 + 700 + 2 J. 100 + 70

Objective: Form conclusions about whether to estimate or find an exact answer.

2·6

Problem Solving: Reading for Math

Estimate or Exact Answer

Boy Collects Over 900 Cards!

Read Chet has 428 football cards. He has 504 baseball cards. Is the headline reasonable?

READING SKILL ▶ **Form a Conclusion**

You form a conclusion when you make a decision based on past experience and the information given.

- **What do you know?** **The number of football cards and baseball cards**
- **What do you need to find?** **How the total compares to the headline**

MATH SKILL ▶ **Estimate or Exact Answer**

If you need an exact answer, you must use the numbers given.

If you do not need an exact answer, estimate.

Plan You must decide if you need an estimate or an exact answer.

Solve The headline says "over 900." This is not an exact sum. You can estimate to see if the headline is reasonable.
428 rounds to 400. 504 rounds to 500.

Find: $400 + 500 = 900$

The headline is reasonable.

Think: Both numbers were rounded down. The exact sum is greater than the estimate.

Look Back Is your answer reasonable? Explain.

Rewrite the problem so an exact answer is needed. Explain why it is needed.

Practice

Solve. Explain why you gave an estimate or exact answer.

1. Nora and Miko are collecting commemorative quarters. Nora has $12.50 worth of quarters. Miko has $18.75 worth of quarters. What is the total value of the girls' quarter collections?

2. Kevin, Luis, and Eli collect stamps. Kevin has 526 stamps in his collection. Luis has 772 stamps, and Eli has 698 stamps. Do the boys have more than 1,800 stamps altogether?

Use data from the Card Collectors Club for problems 3–8.

3. About how many cards do Kuri and Sean have altogether?

4. Dixie, Leon, and Tamala put their cards together to make one big collection. How many cards are in this collection?

5. If Ana, Dixie, and Sean put their cards together, will they have more than 2,000 cards?

6. What is the total number of cards owned by Tamala, Kuri, and Leon?

7. **What if** Sean got 237 more cards? Would he have the most cards?

8. About how many cards are owned by all of the club members?

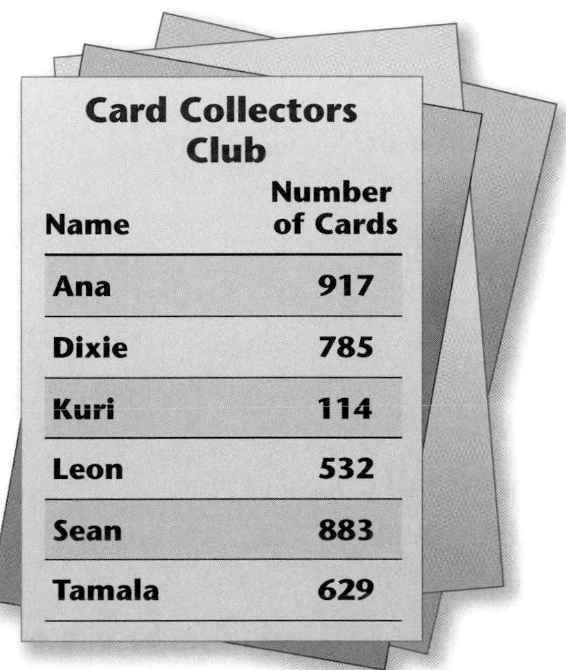

Card Collectors Club

Name	Number of Cards
Ana	917
Dixie	785
Kuri	114
Leon	532
Sean	883
Tamala	629

Spiral Review and Test Prep

Choose the correct answer.

The largest card collection at the Collectors Show has 3,741 cards. The next largest collection has 3,019 cards. Are there more than 6,000 cards in these two collections altogether?

9. Which of following statements is true?
   - A. The largest collection had 7,000 cards.
   - B. One collection at the show contained 3,019 cards.
   - C. The largest collection at the show had 3,714 cards.

10. Which number sentence will help you solve this problem?
    - F. $3{,}741 - 3{,}019 < 1{,}000$
    - G. $3{,}741 + 3{,}019 > 6{,}000$
    - H. $6{,}000 - 3{,}019 < 3{,}000$

Extra Practice, page 80

Check Your Progress A

Complete each set of related number sentences. (pages 44–45)

1. $2 + n = 6$
   $n + 2 = 6$
   $6 - 2 = n$
   $6 - n = 2$

2. $5 + 9 = t$
   $r + 5 = 14$
   $14 - 9 = p$
   $14 - p = 9$

3. $6 + 15 = b$
   $15 + c = 21$
   $21 - 6 = w$
   $21 - w = 6$

4. $5 + 26 = h$
   $26 + s = 31$
   $31 - 5 = m$
   $h - 26 = 5$

5. $9 + d = 11$
   $2 + 9 = f$
   $f - 2 = 9$
   $11 - g = 2$

6. $k + 17 = 34$
   $34 - 17 = k$

Find each sum. (pages 48–51)

7. $\begin{array}{r} 129 \\ +687 \\ \hline \end{array}$

8. $\begin{array}{r} \$5.08 \\ +\ 3.17 \\ \hline \end{array}$

9. $\begin{array}{r} 55{,}871 \\ +42{,}963 \\ \hline \end{array}$

10. $\begin{array}{r} 4{,}509 \\ +\ 358 \\ \hline \end{array}$

11. $\begin{array}{r} 567{,}909 \\ +\ 90{,}873 \\ \hline \end{array}$

12. $\begin{array}{r} \$389{,}052 \\ 67{,}801 \\ +\ 674 \\ \hline \end{array}$

Add mentally. (pages 52–53)

13. 800 + 600
14. 562 + 830
15. 4,697 + 466
16. 775 + 824

Estimate each sum. (pages 54–55)

17. 357 + 498
18. 530 + 4,217
19. 3,607 + 4,459
20. 6,123 + 2,598
21. 4,678 + 23,997
22. 25,990 + 65,003

Solve. (pages 44–55)

23. The gym has 767 female members and 624 male members. How many people belong to the gym?

24. A hobby stores sells picture frames for $39.95 each. The glass to go with the frame costs $19.25. Samantha has $60.00 to spend. Does she have enough money to buy one picture frame and glass? Use estimation to solve.

25. **Compare:** When is it easy to use the zig-zag method to add mentally?

Additional activities at www.mhschool.com/math

Use the Internet

Rico is gathering data on the land and water area of different countries of the world. He needs to find data for three different countries. He will use the data he collects to complete the table below. How can he use the Internet to gather the data?

Country	Land Area	Water Area	Sum	Difference

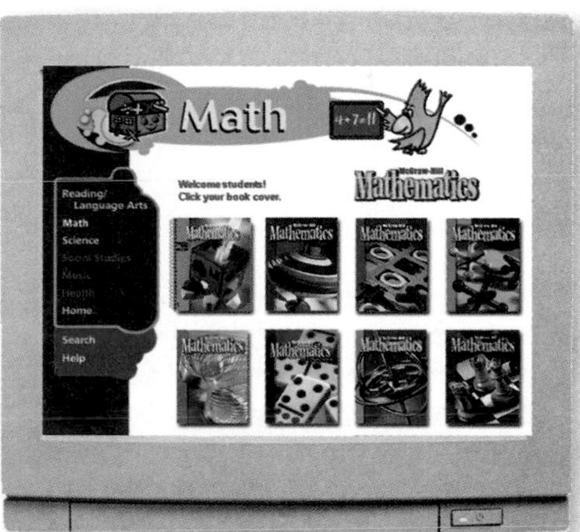

- Go to www.mhschool.com/math.
- Find the list of sites that provide world data.
- Click on a link.
- Find the data on land area of countries. Choose four countries for which data is given.
- Copy the table. Write the names of the countries you chose in your table.
- Record the land and water area for each country in the table.
- Find the sum of and the difference between the areas. Record the sum and difference in the table.

1. Which country has the greatest land and water area? the least?

2. Which country has the greatest difference between the areas? the least?

3. **Analyze:** Why does using the Internet make more sense than using another reference source to find the data needed to complete your table?

For more practice, use Math Traveler™.

Objective: Review subtracting multiples of 10, 100, and 1,000.

2·7 Subtraction Patterns

Algebra & functions

Learn

Math Word

difference an answer to a subtraction problem

Look at all the colors! Rachel and her mother buy two boxes of beads at a craft store. How many more mixed-color beads than pink beads do they buy?

Example

Find: 1,200,000 − 500,000

Think: You can use place value to help.

You can use patterns to find **differences** mentally.

12 − 5 = 7	12 ones − 5 ones = 7 ones
120 − 50 = 70	12 tens − 5 tens = 7 tens
1,200 − 500 = 700	12 hundreds − 5 hundreds = 7 hundreds
12,000 − 5,000 = 7,000	12 thousands − 5 thousands = 7 thousands
120,000 − 50,000 = 70,000	12 ten thousands − 5 ten thousands = 7 ten thousands
1,200,000 − 500,000 = 700,000	1,200 thousands − 500 thousands = 700 thousands

There are 700,000 more mixed-color beads than pink beads.

Try It

Subtract mentally.

1. 2,000 − 700

2. 9,000 − 4,000

3. 12,000 − 8,000

4. 50,000 − 5,000

Look at the subtraction patterns above. Explain how you use the pattern to subtract mentally.

Practice Write the number that makes each sentence true.

5.
$11 - 2 = c$
$110 - 20 = k$
$1{,}100 - 200 = j$
$11{,}000 - 2{,}000 = u$
$110{,}000 - 20{,}000 = p$
$1{,}100{,}000 - 200{,}000 = v$

6.
$9 - 4 = t$
$90 - w = 50$
$q - 400 = 500$
$9{,}000 - 4{,}000 = b$
$m - 40{,}000 = 50{,}000$
$900{,}000 - 400{,}000 = g$

Subtract mentally.

7. 1,300 − 500
8. 7,000 − 3,000
9. 8,000 − 7,000
10. 60,000 − 30,000
11. 140,000 − 90,000
★12. 2,500 − 500
★13. 23,000 − 3,000

Problem Solving

14. Rachel ordered boxes of straight pins. One box has 1,700,000 long pins. Another box has 800,000 short pins. How many more long pins are there than short pins?

15. **Art:** Batik is a textile art that involves dying waxed cloth. Rachel's Sewing Store had 11 bolts of fabric for batik and 4 bolts are left. How many were sold?

16. Last year, Rachel sold fabric for a total of $100,000. This year, she will sell enough fabric to make $60,000 more than last year. How much money will the store make this year?

17. **Explain** how you can use place value to help you subtract mentally.

Spiral Review and Test Prep

Add mentally.

18. 600 + 600
19. 9,000 + 1,000
20. 5,000 + 3,000
21. 60,000 + 30,000
22. 40,000 + 80,000
23. 700,000 + 700,000

Choose the correct answer.

24. Which is the expanded form for 609,467?
   A. 16 + 0 + 9 + 4 + 6 + 7
   B. 600,000 + 9,000 + 400 + 60 + 7
   C. 60,000 + 90,000 + 400 + 60 + 7
   D. 600,000 + 90,000 + 4,000 + 60 + 7

25. What number should replace *n* to make the number sentence true?
   $7{,}654 + n = 7{,}654$
   F. 7,654
   G. 1
   H. 0
   J. Not Here

Objective: Review subtracting whole numbers of up to 6-digit numbers.

2•8

Explore Subtracting Whole Numbers

Learn

You can use place-value models to explore subtracting whole numbers.

What is 423 − 255?

Work Together

▶ Use the place-value models to find 423 − 255.

- Show 423 using the hundred blocks.
- You will need to regroup to subtract.
- Regroup 1 hundred as 10 tens.
- Regroup 1 ten as 10 ones.

You Will Need
- **place-value models**

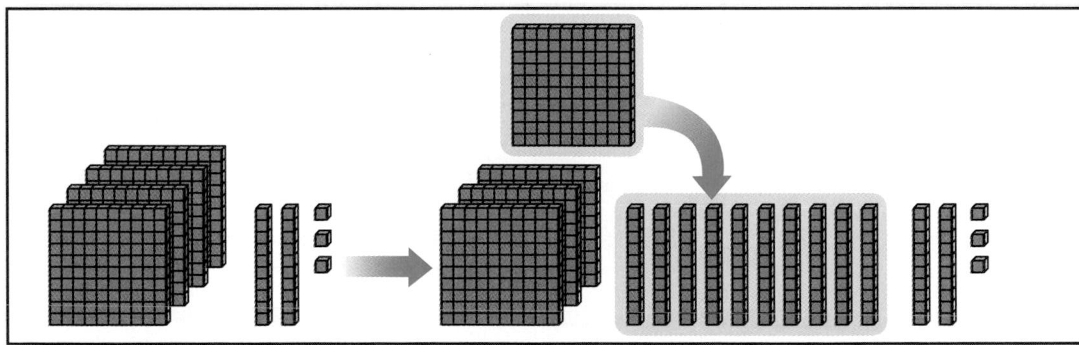

- Use the place-value models to subtract 255.
  Record your work and answer the question at the top of the page.

▶ Use the place value models to subtract. Record your work.

354 − 148   234 − 52   500 − 317   228 − 154   314 − 176

Make Connections

Here is how you can record subtraction.

Find: 361 − 185

Using Models | **Using Paper and Pencil**

1 Subtract the ones. Regroup if necessary.

Think: 6 tens 1 one = 5 tens 11 ones

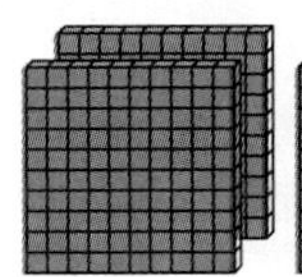

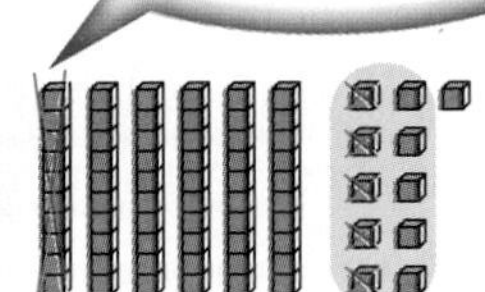

```
  5 11
 3 6 1
−1 8 5
     6
```

2 Subtract the tens. Regroup if necessary.

Think: 3 hundreds 5 tens = 2 hundreds 15 tens

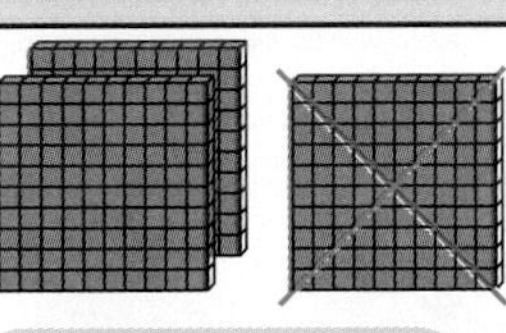

```
   15
 2 5 11
 3 6 1
−1 8 5
   7 6
```

3 Subtract the hundreds. Regroup if necessary.

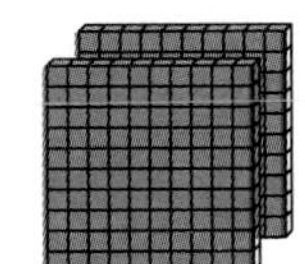
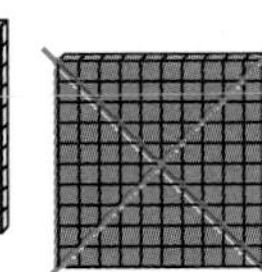
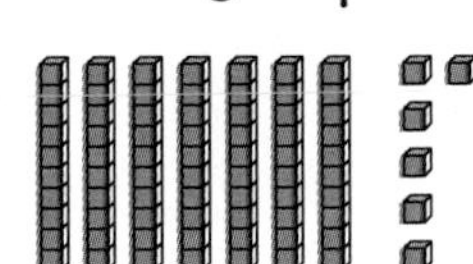

```
   15
 2 5 11
 3 6 1
−1 8 5
 1 7 6
```

Try It **Subtract. You may wish to use models.**

1. 567 − 299 **2.** 815 − 418 **3.** 736 − 628 **4.** 848 − 175 **5.** 425 − 136

6. 684 − 395 **7.** 468 − 289 **8.** 377 − 199

Sum it Up Show 736 − 87 using place value models.

Practice **Subtract.**

9. 927 − 683 **10.** 700 − 365 **11.** 557 − 98 **12.** 467 − 129 **13.** 864 − 375

14. 846 − 377 **15.** 754 − 385 **16.** 547 − 369

★**17. Analyze:** Look at problem 10. How many times do you need to regroup in the tens place? Explain why.

Objective: Review subtracting whole numbers and money.

2·9 Subtract Whole Numbers and Money

Learn

Matt and Kimi are playing a board game. How much more money does Matt have than Kimi?

Example

Find: $418 – $298

1 Regroup if necessary. Subtract the ones.

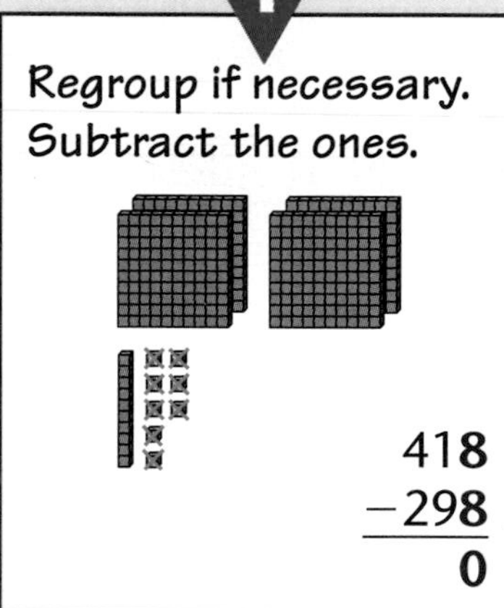

```
  418
- 298
    0
```

2 Regroup if necessary. Subtract the tens.

```
 3 11
 4̸ 1̸ 8
- 2 9 8
    2 0
```

3 Regroup if necessary. Subtract the hundreds.

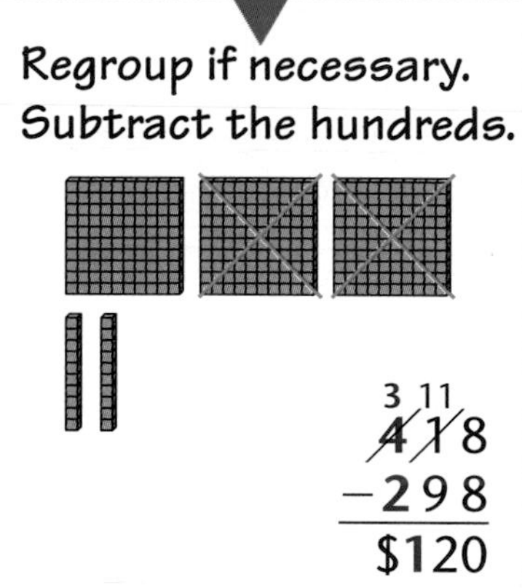

```
 3 11
 4̸ 1̸ 8
- 2 9 8
  $120
```

You can use addition to check subtraction: 120 + 298 = 418
Matt has $120 more than Kimi.

Another Example

```
          12
        6 2̸ 14
  $3,56 7̸,3̸ 4̸
 –  2,115.9 8
  $1,451.36
```

Think: Subtract money as you would whole numbers. Line up the decimal points. Subtract each place. Regroup if necessary.

Try It

Subtract. Check by adding.

1. 831 – 415 **2.** 7,673 – 3,459 **3.** $235.63 – 14.90

Why is it important to line up the digits when subtracting?

Practice

Subtract. Check by adding.

4. $688 - 309$
5. $\$8.57 - 1.59$
6. $5{,}677 - 458$
7. $\$23{,}766 - 909$
8. $\$4431 - 774$
9. $\$82.45 - 76.43$
10. $4{,}387 - 1{,}539$
11. $55{,}432 - 7{,}642$
12. $411{,}917 - 788$
13. $56{,}892 - 43{,}075$
14. $\$4{,}647.90 - 399.99$
15. $873{,}155 - 125{,}009$
16. $6{,}337 - 408$
17. $54{,}890 - 5{,}034$
18. $546{,}599 - 25{,}603$
19. $678{,}647 - 89{,}718$

20. 611,229 − 101,507
21. \$359.08 − \$47.85
22. 165,477 − 16,359

★23. (409,302 + 78,155) − 9,788
★24. (35,254 + 3,265) − 8,973

★25. (45,633 + 3,456) − 7,845
26. (73,287 − 28,742) + 9,000

Problem Solving

27. Francis scored 34,234 points in a board game. Leroy scored 5,678 fewer points than Francis. How many points did Leroy score?

28. Ted scored 7,912 points. Janet scored 1,213 points more than Ted. How many points did Janet score?

29. **Social Studies:** Chess is thought to have been invented in India in the fifth century. By the eleventh century, it had reached Europe. About how many years did it take to reach Europe?

30. **Analyze:** If you subtract a 3-digit whole number from a 4-digit whole number, what is the least number of digits the answer could have? Give an example.

Spiral Review and Test Prep

31. 592 + 327
32. 817 + 445
33. 3,567 + 2,702
34. 5,472 + 433

Choose the correct answer.

35. Which number shows 6 ten thousands?
   A. 456,455
   B. 659,645
   C. 1,266,500
   D. 6,636,460

36. Which is an example of the Commutative Property?
   F. $6 + 0 = 6$
   G. $6 + n = 6$
   H. $6 + 3 = 3 + 6$
   J. $(6 + 3) + 2 = 6 + (3 + 2)$

Extra Practice, page 80

Objective: Review subtracting up to 6-digit numbers across zeros.

2·10 Regroup Across Zeros

Valerie Darling and Arielle Ring

Learn

Valerie Darling and Arielle Ring started their own candle-making business to raise money for Romanian orphans. The girls raised $500, but spent $125 in supplies. How much money did the girls make for the children?

Example

Subtract: $500 – $125

1

Regroup the hundreds.

$$\begin{array}{r} \overset{4}{\cancel{5}}\overset{10}{\cancel{0}}0 \\ -125 \\ \hline \end{array}$$

Think: 5 hundreds = 4 hundreds, 10 tens

2

Regroup the tens.

$$\begin{array}{r} \overset{4}{\cancel{5}}\overset{\overset{9}{\cancel{10}}}{\cancel{0}}\overset{10}{\cancel{0}} \\ -125 \\ \hline \end{array}$$

3

Subtract.

$$\begin{array}{r} \overset{4}{\cancel{5}}\overset{\overset{9}{\cancel{10}}}{\cancel{0}}\overset{10}{\cancel{0}} \\ -125 \\ \hline 375 \end{array}$$

Think: 10 tens = 9 tens, 10 ones

Check: 375 + 125 = 500

The girls had $375 to give to the children.

Try It

Subtract. Check by adding.

1. 800 – 438 **2.** 7,000 – 5,902 **3.** $20,000 – 1,631

Look at problem 1. How many times was it necessary to regroup in the tens place? Explain.

Practice Subtract. Check by adding.

4. 908 − 319
5. \$5.00 − 1.59
6. 7,000 − 997
7. 40,000 − 788
8. \$40.00 − 9.56
9. 8,000 − 1,458
10. \$60,000 − 2,805
11. 30,000 − 7,053
12. \$4,000.00 − 29.08
13. 50,101 − 30,155
14. \$200,450 − \$69,999
15. \$870,800 − \$225,009
16. 60,005 − 31,188
17. \$544.00 − \$294.11
18. 900,099 − 203,854
19. 310,808 − 101,507

Problem Solving

20. Within a year, Arielle and Valerie gave \$4,500 to charities in Romania. Another group gave \$1,675. How much money was given altogether?

21. **Social Studies:** A group of college students sews capes for charities. The first sewing machine was invented in 1790. How old was the sewing machine in the year 2000?

22. A total of 3,000 candles were made to sell for a charity. Senior citizens made 875 of them. How many candles came from other groups?

Journal

23. **Explain:** Write a letter to a younger student, telling the student how to regroup in subtraction with 4-digit numbers.

★ 24. Another charity group raised \$35,725 selling blankets they knitted. They spent \$1,650 on supplies. How much are they able to donate?

25. Use the digits 5, 7, and 9 to write subtraction problems to show how to obtain the greatest difference and the least difference. You need to use all of the digits once.

Spiral Review and Test Prep

26. 4,357 + 1,689
27. 8,943 + 589
28. 46,254 + 3,643
29. 39,506 + 3,586

Choose the correct answer.

30. Skip-count to find which number comes next in the pattern.
3, 6, 9, 12, ■
A. 11 C. 15
B. 13 D. 16

31. Which number should replace *n* to make the number sentence true?
$(7 + 4) + 12 = 7 + (n + 12)$
F. 0 H. 11
G. 4 J. 32

Extra Practice, page 81

Objective: Write a number sentence to solve a problem.

Problem Solving: Strategy
Write a Number Sentence

Read

Read the problem carefully.

Nelson has a certain amount of money. He spends $41 to buy a stained-glass kit. He now has $10 left. How much money did Nelson have before he bought the kit?

- **What do you know?** Nelson spends $41; he has $10 left.
- **What do you need to find?** How much money he had

Plan

You can write a number sentence to find the missing number.

Solve

Amount he had	minus	cost of kit	equals	amount left.
↓	↓	↓	↓	↓
m	−	$41	=	$10

Think: Use a related sentence $41 + $10 = $51.

He had $51 before he bought the kit.

Look Back

Does your answer make sense? Check your answer.

How can you decide what kind of number sentence to write?

Practice Write a number sentence to solve.

1. Maya puts $8 in her savings account. She already had $32 in the account. How much money does Maya have in the account now?

2. Ms. Green had 29 buttons to sew on dolls. She has 14 buttons left. How many buttons has she already sewn on?

3. Jeanette has saved $18. How much more money does she need to buy a model airplane kit for $22?

4. The school choir has raised $1,428. They receive a donation. Now they have $3,250. How much was the donation?

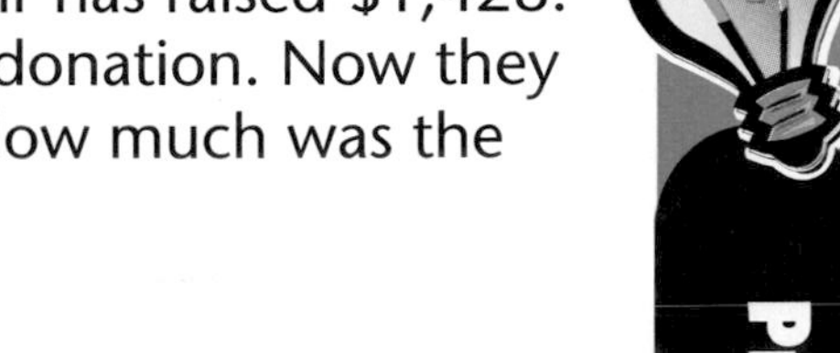

Mixed Strategy Review

CHOOSE A STRATEGY

- Find a Pattern
- Work Backward
- Use Logical Reasoning
- Write a Number Sentence
- Make a Table or List
- Guess and Check
- Make a Graph
- Solve a Simpler Problem

5. Haley earns $4.35 each week for delivering newspapers. How many weeks does she need to work to buy modeling clay for $9.95?

★6. On day 1, Cassie puts a nickel in a bank. Each day she doubles the amount she puts in the bank. At the end of 7 days, how much money will she have?

Use data from the table for problems 8–11.

7. Lisa has 4 one-dollar bills, 6 quarters, 7 dimes, 8 nickels, and 12 pennies. Find the total value of bills and coins.

Stained Glass Kit Price List

Red Glass	$39 each box
Blue Glass	$25 each box
Green Glass	$18 each box
Copper Molding	$2 each sheet

8. How much would it cost to buy a box of each color glass and 5 sheets of copper molding?

9. Mr. Tomba buys 2 boxes of blue glass, 3 boxes of green glass, and 1 box of red glass. He pays for them with 2 hundred-dollar bills. How much change does he get?

10. Becky bought a box of green glass and some copper molding. She spent $36. How many sheets of copper molding did she buy?

11. **Create a problem** using the data in the table. Write a number sentence to solve it. Ask others to solve it.

Extra Practice, page 81

Objective: Use mental math strategies to subtract.

2·12 Subtract Using Mental Math

Learn

Math Word

compensation
When subtracting two numbers, add or subtract the same number to find the difference.

Susan wants to order an explorer kit. She finds a kit for \$93 in a catalog. What is the sale price of the kit?

There's more than one way!

Find: \$93 − \$18

You can subtract mentally to solve. When the numbers are close to a ten or a hundred, you can use **compensation**.

Think: Add or subtract the same number. The difference remains the same. Make a ten or a hundred.

Method A

\$93 − \$18
+2 ↓ ↓ +2
\$95 − \$20 = \$75

Method B

\$93 − \$18
−3 ↓ ↓ −3
\$90 − \$15 = \$75

The sale price of the kit is \$75.

Example

Find: \$93 − \$22
You can also use the zig-zag method to subtract mentally.

$$\begin{array}{r} \$93 \\ -\ 22 \\ \hline \end{array}$$

Think: \$93 − \$20 = \$73
\$73 − \$2 = \$71

So \$93 − \$22 = \$71.

Try It

Subtract mentally. Explain your method.

1. \$1.85 − \$1.52
2. 276 − 199
3. 5,865 − 3,435

When is it easier to use compensation than the zig-zag method? Why?

Practice Subtract mentally.

4. 36 − 8
5. 93 − 28
6. 89 − 19
7. \$22 − \$17
8. 84 − 28
9. 96 − 35
10. 71 − 46
11. \$153 − \$48
12. 293 − 102
13. 777 − 200
14. 645 − 405
15. \$804 − \$680
16. 592 − 103
17. 712 − 408
18. 264 − 99
19. \$835 − \$197
20. 617 − 413
21. 909 − 614
22. \$345 − \$105
23. 4,975 − 1,225

Algebra & functions **Write the number that makes each sentence true.**

24. $847 - n = 247$
25. $m - 313 = 487$
26. $750 - p = 100$

Write each number as the difference of two numbers.

★27. 500
★28. 755
★29. 1,800
★30. 7,455
★31. 75,690

Problem Solving

Use data from the catalog page for problems 32–33.

32. Ronnie has \$46. Can he buy the Bird Feeder Kit and two Tangram Puzzles? Explain.

33. Marcy has 2 twenty-dollar bills, 3 one-dollar bills, and 2 half-dollars. Does she have enough money to buy the Radio Kit? Explain.

34. **Compare:** How is compensation different for addition and subtraction?

35. **Collect data** from a catalog of your choice. Write a money problem using only the dollar amounts given in the catalog.

Spiral Review and Test Prep

Add mentally.

36. 83 + 47
37. 48 + 95
38. 239 + 401
39. 698 + 257

Choose the correct answer.

40. Find n if $17 - n = 9$
  A. 26
  B. 12
  C. 8
  D. Not Here

41. Which is true?
  F. 1,435 > 1,453
  G. 1,345 < 1,435
  H. 1,434 > 1,443
  J. 1,434 = 1,443

Objective: Estimate differences of up to 6-digit numbers.

2•13 Estimate Differences

Learn

Kelsey and Kareem collect comic books. About how many more comic books does Kelsey have than Kareem?

Example

Estimate: 324 − 178

Round each number to find the difference mentally.

324 − 178
↓ ↓
300 − 200 = 100

Think: Round up or down to the nearest hundred.

Kelsey has about 100 more comic books.

More Examples

A Estimate: 3,690 − 469 — Round to the nearest hundred.
3,700 − 500 = 3,200

B Estimate: 13,442 − 6,187 — Round to the nearest thousand.
13,000 − 6,000 = 7,000

C Estimate: \$0.87 − \$0.41 — Round to the nearest ten cents.
\$0.90 − \$0.40 = \$0.50

D Estimate: \$6.79 − \$2.45 — Round to the nearest dollar.
\$7.00 − \$2.00 = \$5.00

Try It

Estimate each difference. Tell how you rounded.

1. 678 − 432 **2.** 4,578 − 1,890 **3.** \$4.69 − \$3.31

Tell how you can round the numbers in problem 2 another way to estimate. Is this estimate closer to the exact difference? How can you tell?

Practice Estimate each difference.

4. 384 − 98
5. $0.68 − $0.25
6. $0.98 − $0.31
7. 4,228 − 377
8. 5,622 − 2,641
9. 9,706 − 1,890
10. $71.89 − $21.65
11. 45,089 − 4,672
12. 43,870 − 12,677
13. $5,167.20 − $3,380.15
14. 436,966 − 178,056
15. 647,988 − 59,000
16. 670,067 − 340,899
17. 809,776 − 414,887
18. 687,005 − 119,694

Algebra & functions **Compare. Write > or < to make the sentence true.**

19. 324 − 212 ● 300
20. 6,832 − 3,720 ● 1,000

★21. 4,620 − 3,464 ● 3,921 − 1,121
★22. 8,521 − 3,252 ● 7,523 − 1,213

Problem Solving

Use data from *Did You Know?* for problems 23–24.

23. About how many years has Gasoline Alley been published in United States newspapers?
24. The main character, Skeezix, was introduced 3 years after the strip started. In what year was he introduced?

★25. **Analyze:** How will an estimated difference compare to the exact difference if you round each number up? down?

26. **Summarize:** Explain how you can use estimation to determine if an answer is reasonable.

The longest running comic strip in the United States is Gasoline Alley. This comic strip was first published in 1918.

Spiral Review and Test Prep

Order from least to greatest.

27. 2,572; 2,537; 2,687
28. 56,709; 60,532; 59,110
29. 127,062; 126,072; 126,702

Choose the correct answer.

30. Which number sentence is not part of the fact family?
    A. 14 − 8 = 6
    C. 14 − 6 = 8
    B. 8 + 6 = 14
    D. 6 + 14 = 20

31. Which number should replace n to make the number sentence true?
    $(8 + 6) + 9 = 8 + (n + 9)$
    F. 6
    H. 9
    G. 8
    J. Not Here

Extra Practice, page 81

Problem Solving: Application
Decision Making

The Outdoor Club at Woodcliff Elementary is planning a trip to the town carnival. There are 35 members in the club. The carnival has games, activities, and rides. The club members will be at the carnival from 10:00 A.M. until 3:00 P.M. For lunch, should they get take-out fast food, eat at the diner across the street, or buy food at the carnival?

You Decide!

Where should the club members eat lunch?

Option 1

BURGERS-TO-GO!

Only 5 miles from the carnival!

▶Jumbo Burger	$2.35
▶Chicken Sandwich	$1.49
▶French Fries	$0.69
▶Juice	$1.19
▶Milk	$0.45

Special of the day:
$5.00 off an order of 10 Jumbo Burgers!

Option 2

RUBY'S HEALTHY DINER MENU

Tuna Sandwich	$1.75
Cheese Sandwich	$1.25
Turkey Burger	$2.75
Garden Salad	$1.95
Fruit Salad	$1.50
Milk	$0.60

Option 3

Carnival Lunch Menu

• Tuna Sandwich	$2.25
• Turkey Sandwich	$2.50
• Burger	$3.25
• Garden Salad	$1.59
• Hot Dog	$2.25
• Juice	$1.75
• Milk	$0.75

Read for Understanding

1. What are the three different prices for milk?
2. How much would a tuna sandwich and a milk cost at the carnival?
3. At what place would you get the best price for a single burger?
4. You order a cheese sandwich and garden salad at Ruby's. How much is your lunch?
5. How much would a chicken sandwich, french fries, and juice cost at Burgers-to-Go?
6. How much more would a garden salad cost at Ruby's Healthy Diner than at the carnival?

Problem Solving

Make Decisions

7. If it usually takes a half hour to wait and order at Burgers-to-Go, then another 45 minutes to eat lunch, how much time will club members have left at the carnival?
8. Compare the price of juice at Burgers-to-Go and the carnival. Which is the better buy? How much money would you save?
9. Three club members have $12.50 altogether to spend for lunch at the carnival. What can they get so that each has the same lunch? Will they have any money left?
10. Ruby's Healthy Diner has 9 counter seats and 24 seats at tables. Can all of the club members eat there at the same time? Explain.
11. Ten club members want burgers. Which is the best place to get burgers? Explain.
12. What are the advantages and disadvantages of eating lunch at the carnival?
13. Which place for lunch is the least expensive? most expensive?
14. What are the advantages of going to Ruby's Healthy Diner?
15. If some of the club members prefer fruits and vegetables for lunch, where should they eat? Explain.
16. The club wants to go to a place with the most variety. Which place offers the most choices?
17. If most of the club members wanted to have a tuna sandwich and juice, where should they have lunch? Why?
18. Compare the price of milk at all three places. Which place has the least expensive price for milk? most expensive?

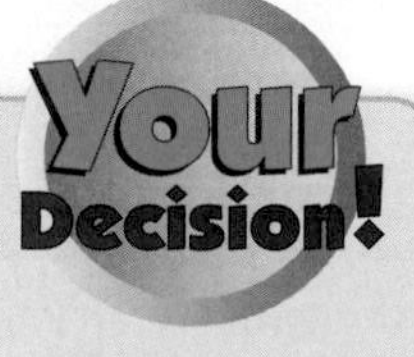

Which is the best place for the club members to eat lunch?

Objective: Apply addition and subtraction to investigate science concepts.

2·14 B

Problem Solving: Math and Science
Which materials block a magnet?

Your refrigerator may be covered with magnets holding papers and photos. Magnets work because they stick to the door without being blocked by the papers.

You Will Need
- **small magnet**
- **paper clips**
- **sheet of paper**
- **piece of aluminum foil**
- **tape**

Some things can block a magnet, making it difficult for objects to stick to it. In this activity, you will investigate which objects can block a magnet.

Hypothesize

Which objects will block a magnet—paper, aluminum foil, or tape?

Procedure

Wrap the magnet very well. Use a whole sheet of paper or foil, and wrap it several times.

1. Work with a partner.
2. Place the magnet in a pile of paper clips.
3. Count how many paper clips can hang from the magnet. Remove the clips.
4. Wrap the magnet completely in a sheet of paper. Repeat steps 2 and 3.
5. Wrap the magnet completely in a sheet of aluminum foil. Repeat steps 2 and 3.
6. Wrap the magnet completely with tape. Repeat steps 2 and 3.

Data

Copy and complete the chart to record the number of paper clips the magnet can hold.

Material	Paper Clips
Magnet only	
Magnet with paper	
Magnet with foil	
Magnet with tape	

Did You Know?

A material is shielding a magnet when it blocks the magnet from attracting other things.

Conclude and Apply

Find the difference in the number of paper clips used for each material.

Materials	Difference
Paper and foil	
Paper and tape	
Foil and tape	

- Which material blocks the magnet best? How do you know?
- Put the three materials in order from best blocker to worst.
- Explain the results of your activity in terms of shielding.

Going Further

1. Repeat the activity with three materials of your choice. Did you find a better blocker?
2. Design and complete an activity that demonstrates at what distance a magnet can still attract a paper clip.

Check Your Progress B

Write the number that makes each sentence true. **(pages 60–61)**

1.
$7 - 2 = b$
$70 - 20 = c$
$700 - 200 = d$
$7{,}000 - 2{,}000 = e$
$70{,}000 - 20{,}000 = f$
$700{,}000 - 200{,}000 = g$

2.
$11 - 6 = m$
$110 - n = 50$
$1{,}100 - 600 = o$
$p - 6{,}000 = 5{,}000$
$110{,}000 - 60{,}000 = q$
$1{,}100{,}000 - r = 500{,}000$

Find each difference. Check each answer. **(pages 62–67)**

3. $\begin{array}{r} 893 \\ -236 \\ \hline \end{array}$ **4.** $\begin{array}{r} 5{,}893 \\ -1{,}278 \\ \hline \end{array}$ **5.** $\begin{array}{r} 75{,}002 \\ -\ 8{,}764 \\ \hline \end{array}$ **6.** $\begin{array}{r} 65{,}903 \\ -40{,}076 \\ \hline \end{array}$

7. 4,509 − 358 **8.** 836,400 − 60,786 **9.** \$376,003 − \$123,411

Subtract mentally. **(pages 70–71)**

10. 26 − 12 **11.** 592 − 103 **12.** 545 − 405
13. 74 − 28 **14.** 888 − 200 **15.** 4,500 − 300

Estimate each difference. **(pages 72–73)**

16. 475 − 398 **17.** 679 − 128 **18.** 5,934 − 1,348
19. 8,133 − 3,672 **20.** 36,864 − 2,893 **21.** 78,320 − 61,035

Solve. **(pages 60–73)**

22. A camping club had 546 campers at a jamboree. A total of 1,200 people were invited. How many could not come to the jamboree? Write a number sentence.

23. There are 1,246 members in the camping club. There are 689 girls. How many are boys?

24. A craft store sells jumbo crafts kits for \$34.99. The regular kits cost \$18.25. How much more money is the jumbo kit?

25. **Compare:** What kind of numbers are easy to add or subtract mentally? Why?

Extra Practice

Use Properties of Addition (pages 44–45)

Complete the set of related number sentences.

1. $5 + c = 12$
   $c + 5 = 12$
   $12 - 7 = e$
   $12 - e = 7$

2. $7 + 8 = f$
   $h + 7 = 15$
   $15 - 8 = g$
   $15 - g = 8$

3. $6 + 15 = a$
   $15 + b = 21$
   $21 - 6 = z$
   $21 - z = 6$

Write the related number sentences for the set of numbers.

4. 5, 4, 9
5. 8 , 8, 16
6. 12, 2, 14
7. 0, 64, 64
8. 17, 5, 22

Addition Patterns (pages 46–47)

Write the number that makes each sentence true.

1. $5 + 8 = d$
   $50 + 80 = n$
   $5{,}000 + 8{,}000 = m$
   $50{,}000 + 80{,}000 = v$
   $500{,}000 + 800{,}000 = g$

2. $9 + 8 = t$
   $90 + 80 = s$
   $900 + y = 1{,}700$
   $9{,}000 + 8{,}000 = z$
   $k + 80{,}000 = 170{,}000$

Add mentally.

3. 400 + 300
4. 5,000 + 5,000
5. 10,000 + 60,000

Add Whole Numbers and Money (pages 48–51)

Find each sum.

1. 655 + 739
2. \$4.67 + 3.65
3. \$53.02 + 68.42
4. \$14,932 + 369
5. \$32.86 + \$40.64 + \$65.09
6. 55,871 + 3,654 + 32,864

Use Mental Math to Add (pages 52–53)

Add mentally.

1. 54 + 32
2. 83 + 23
3. 73 + 31
4. \$85 + \$25
5. 144 + 355
6. 468 + 321
7. 823 + 121
8. \$358 + \$120

Estimate Sums (pages 54–55)

Estimate each sum.

1. 473 + 313
2. 121 + 579
3. \$8.75 + \$3.98
4. 8,321 + 4,780
5. \$0.15 + \$0.88
6. 4,698 + 5,016

Extra Practice

Problem Solving: Estimate or Exact Answer (pages 56–57)

Solve. Explain why you gave an estimate or exact answer.

1. Ann and Jack collect stamps. Ann has 385 stamps. Jack has 193 stamps. About how many stamps do they have altogether?
2. Rico has 182 baseball cards. His brother Tim has 236 cards. How many cards do they have altogether?
3. Karl has saved \$3.83. Miko has saved \$8.29. Have they saved enough money to buy a CD for \$11.00?
4. Katie and Jack have a collection of 263 small and large marbles. If 127 marbles are small, how many are large?

Subtraction Patterns (pages 60–61)

Write the number that makes each sentence true.

1.
$13 - 6 = g$
$130 - 60 = f$
$1{,}300 - 600 = h$
$13{,}000 - 6{,}000 = b$
$130{,}000 - 60{,}000 = k$
$1{,}300{,}000 - 600{,}000 = x$

2.
$11 - 4 = p$
$j - 40 = 70$
$1{,}100 - 400 = b$
$11{,}000 - a = 7{,}000$
$110{,}000 - 40{,}000 = s$
$r - 400{,}000 = 700{,}000$

Subtract mentally.

3. 900 − 300
4. 15,000 − 7,000
5. 90,000 − 70,000
6. 1,400 − 700
7. 500,000 − 200,000
8. 120,000 − 60,000

Subtract Whole Numbers and Money (pages 64–65)

Subtract. Check by adding.

1. $\begin{array}{r} 478 \\ -115 \\ \hline \end{array}$
2. $\begin{array}{r} 6{,}392 \\ -\ 284 \\ \hline \end{array}$
3. $\begin{array}{r} 14{,}652 \\ -\ 363 \\ \hline \end{array}$
4. $\begin{array}{r} \$43.47 \\ -\ 24.39 \\ \hline \end{array}$

5. \$60.37 − \$3.68
6. 93,328 − 43,449
7. 238,906 − 45,835
8. \$454,148 − \$125,009
9. The jigsaw puzzle that James just completed has 350 pieces. He wants to work on a 1,275-piece puzzle next. How many more pieces are in the next puzzle?

Extra Practice

Subtract Across Zeros (pages 66–67)

Find each difference. Check by adding.

1. $\begin{array}{r} \$4.07 \\ -\ 2.78 \\ \hline \end{array}$
2. $\begin{array}{r} 6,302 \\ -\ 235 \\ \hline \end{array}$
3. $\begin{array}{r} \$34.00 \\ -\ 18.97 \\ \hline \end{array}$
4. $\begin{array}{r} \$40,200 \\ -\ 5,784 \\ \hline \end{array}$
5. $\begin{array}{r} 10,045 \\ -\ 994 \\ \hline \end{array}$
6. $\begin{array}{r} 30,002 \\ -11,378 \\ \hline \end{array}$
7. $\begin{array}{r} \$63,100 \\ -\ 28,843 \\ \hline \end{array}$
8. $\begin{array}{r} 700,034 \\ -306,654 \\ \hline \end{array}$
9. $\begin{array}{r} 120,701 \\ -105,803 \\ \hline \end{array}$
10. $\begin{array}{r} 450,063 \\ -\ 45,234 \\ \hline \end{array}$
11. $\begin{array}{r} 709,021 \\ -345,245 \\ \hline \end{array}$

Problem Solving Strategy: Write a Number Sentence (pages 68–69)

Write a number sentence.

1. On Monday Javier ran 15 miles. He ran 6 miles on Tuesday and 13 miles on Saturday. How many miles did he run that week?
2. Anya wants to do 50 sit-ups. She has already done 28. How many more will she have to do?

Subtract Using Mental Math (pages 70–71)

Subtract mentally.

1. 64 − 18
2. 85 − 34
3. 45 − 19
4. \$263 − \$59
5. 499 − 82
6. 545 − 297
7. 636 − 211
8. \$505 − \$149

Estimate Differences (pages 72–73)

Estimate each difference.

1. 565 − 218
2. 723 − 176
3. \$6.48 − \$2.29
4. \$14.75 − \$3.39
5. \$0.95 − \$0.36
6. \$3.79 − \$2.12
7. 7,167 − 489
8. 7,245 − 3,345

Chapter Study Guide

Language and Math

Math Words
addends
estimate
sum
difference

Complete. Use a word from the list.

1. Another word for total is ____.
2. When you ____, you find a number that is close to a another number.
3. The numbers that are added together are ____.

Skills and Applications

Addition of whole numbers and money. (pages 48–51)

Example
Find: 673 + 428

Solution
Add each place.
Regroup if necessary.

$$\begin{array}{r} {\scriptstyle 1\,1} \\ 673 \\ +428 \\ \hline 1{,}101 \end{array}$$

Add.

4. $\begin{array}{r} \$8.19 \\ +\ 2.77 \\ \hline \end{array}$

5. $\begin{array}{r} \$23.87 \\ +\ 16.32 \\ \hline \end{array}$

6. $\begin{array}{r} 67{,}139 \\ +\ 7{,}892 \\ \hline \end{array}$

7. $\begin{array}{r} 245{,}823 \\ +431{,}874 \\ \hline \end{array}$

8. $6,018.32 + $5,613.67

9. A store sold computer games last year for a total of $357,988. This year, computer games were sold for a total of $45,908. How much has the store made so far?

Subtraction of whole numbers and money. (pages 64–67)

Example
Find: 945 − 658

Solution
Subtract each place.
Regroup if necessary.

$$\begin{array}{r} {\scriptstyle 8\ 13\ 15} \\ \not{9}\,\not{4}\,\not{5} \\ -\ 6\ 5\ 8 \\ \hline 2\ 8\ 7 \end{array}$$

Subtract.

10. $\begin{array}{r} 731 \\ -167 \\ \hline \end{array}$

11. $\begin{array}{r} \$50.00 \\ -\ 24.78 \\ \hline \end{array}$

12. $\begin{array}{r} 67{,}042 \\ -\ 7{,}988 \\ \hline \end{array}$

13. $\begin{array}{r} 507{,}436 \\ -211{,}935 \\ \hline \end{array}$

14. $1,780.14 − $745.15

15. A hobby store received a shipment of video games for $60,000. It received another shipment of games for $5,618. How much more did the first shipment cost?

Add and subtract using mental math. (pages 52–53, 70–71)

Example
Subtract 98 − 48 mentally.

Solution
Add 2 to each number.

$$\begin{array}{c} 98 - 48 \\ {}_{+2}\downarrow \quad \downarrow_{+2} \\ 100 - 50 = 50 \end{array}$$

Add or subtract mentally.

16. 64 + 39
17. 73 + 37
18. 208 + 288
19. 675 − 314

Estimate sums and differences. (pages 54–55, 72–73)

Example
Estimate: 457 + 129

Solution
Round to nearest hundred.

$$\begin{array}{rcr} 457 & \rightarrow & 500 \\ \underline{+129} & \rightarrow & \underline{+100} \\ & & 600 \end{array}$$

Estimate each sum or difference.

20. 627 + 465
21. 2,499 + 4,181
22. 6,743 − 936
23. 50,455 + 2,945

Solve problems. (pages 56–57, 68–69)

Example
Ben buys a skateboard and pays for it with a hundred-dollar bill. He gets back $32.25 in change. How much is the skateboard?

Solution
Write a number sentence.
$100.00 − $32.25 = $67.75

Solve.

24. Andrea has $100.00. She buys a tennis racket for $67.59. How much change does she get?
25. Carmen has $20. He wants to buy an energy bar for $1.89, a water bottle for $7.29, and a lock for $11.98. Estimate to decide if he has enough money.

Study Guide

Chapter Test

Add or subtract. Check each answer.

1. $\begin{array}{r} 911 \\ -567 \\ \hline \end{array}$

2. $\begin{array}{r} 4,077 \\ +3,574 \\ \hline \end{array}$

3. $\begin{array}{r} \$6,000 \\ -\ \ 3,096 \\ \hline \end{array}$

4. $\begin{array}{r} 448,392 \\ +171,655 \\ \hline \end{array}$

5. $\begin{array}{r} 339 \\ +784 \\ \hline \end{array}$

6. $\begin{array}{r} \$78,436 \\ +\ \ 38,215 \\ \hline \end{array}$

7. $\begin{array}{r} \$76,115 \\ -\ \ 48,325 \\ \hline \end{array}$

8. $\begin{array}{r} 856,034 \\ -241,855 \\ \hline \end{array}$

9. $678.99 + $45.53

10. 619,332 − 428,445

11. $784.90 − $25.79

12. 730,117 + 53,907

Add or subtract mentally.

13. 47 + 52
14. 303 + 176
15. 900 − 600
16. 838 − 317

Estimate.

17. 827 + 378
18. 4,644 + 3,822
19. 916 − 449
20. 5,611 − 3,488

Solve.

21. Renee scored 167, 98, and 156 in three games of bowling. About how many points has she scored?

22. Yoshi collects baseball cards. He has 1,006. He put 389 cards into a baseball album. How many cards are not in the album? Write a number sentence.

23. Megan bought a paint set for $13.95, paintbrushes for $7.29, and an easel for $11.69. She paid for them with 2 twenty-dollar bills. What was her change?

24. Three students played a video game at an arcade. One student scored 4,671 points. Another student scored 3,057 points. Another scored 1,178 points. They need 10,000 points to win a prize. How many more points do they need?

25. A basic train set costs $115.98. Each additional car costs $18.59. Mr. Green wants to get a basic train set and 3 additional cars. He has $200.00 in his budget for hobbies. How much money will he have left over?

Performance Assessment

Your class is buying items to donate to the homeless shelter. You are in charge of selecting the grocery items to buy. You have $56.75 to spend.

You need to

- decide which items to buy.
- decide how many of each item to buy.
- keep track of your purchases so you do not go over the total amount you have to spend.
- show your work.

A Good Answer

- shows how many items were purchased.
- shows the amount of each item selected.
- does not go over the total allowed.
- shows how you added and subtracted to solve the problem.

You may wish to save this work for your portfolio.

Enrichment

Front-End Estimation

Another way of estimating is to use front-end estimation. In front-end estimation, you use the values of the "front" digits and then adjust the estimate by grouping the remaining digits.

Estimate $2.85 + $3.19 + $8.09.

$$\begin{array}{r} \$2.85 \\ 3.19 \\ +\ 8.09 \\ \hline \end{array} \quad \leftarrow \quad \begin{array}{l} \text{Add the front digits.} \\ 2 + 3 + 8 = 13 \end{array}$$

$$\left.\begin{array}{r} \$2.85 \\ 3.19 \\ +\ 8.09 \\ \hline \end{array}\right\} \text{about } \$1 \quad \begin{array}{l} \text{Look for combinations that make } \$1. \\ \text{Then adjust the estimate.} \\ 13 + 1 = 14 \end{array}$$

The front-end estimate is $14.

Now estimate 746 − 449.

$$\begin{array}{r} 746 \\ -\ 449 \\ \hline 300 \end{array} \quad \leftarrow \quad \begin{array}{l} \text{Subtract the front digits.} \\ 7 \text{ hundreds} - 4 \text{ hundreds} = 3 \text{ hundreds} \end{array}$$

$$\begin{array}{r} 746 \\ -\ 449 \\ \hline > 300 \end{array} \quad \leftarrow \quad \begin{array}{l} \text{Compare the remaining digits. See if you can regroup.} \\ \text{Then adjust the estimate.} \\ \text{The difference is less than 300.} \end{array}$$

Estimate. Use front-end estimation.

1. $\begin{array}{r} \$1.79 \\ 2.49 \\ +\ 3.56 \\ \hline \end{array}$ **2.** $\begin{array}{r} 2{,}671 \\ -1{,}743 \\ \hline \end{array}$ **3.** $\begin{array}{r} 277 \\ 419 \\ +687 \\ \hline \end{array}$ **4.** $\begin{array}{r} \$7.82 \\ -\ 4.26 \\ \hline \end{array}$ **5.** $\begin{array}{r} \$3.99 \\ 5.14 \\ +\ 2.09 \\ \hline \end{array}$

6. $\begin{array}{r} 789 \\ -\ 597 \\ \hline \end{array}$ **7.** $\begin{array}{r} 333 \\ 802 \\ +156 \\ \hline \end{array}$ **8.** $\begin{array}{r} 912 \\ -304 \\ \hline \end{array}$ **9.** $\begin{array}{r} \$8.86 \\ 2.01 \\ +\ 7.15 \\ \hline \end{array}$ **10.** $\begin{array}{r} \$12.87 \\ -\ \ 9.93 \\ \hline \end{array}$

11. **Generalize:** Explain why adjusting the estimate you make with the front-end digits helps you get a better estimate of a sum.

12. **Generalize:** When does it make sense to use a front-end estimate? When doesn't it? Give examples.

Test-Taking Tips

When you are taking a test, you will do better if you remember to **read the problem carefully.** It helps to read each item more than once.

A train ticket costs \$3.50. The senior-citizen price is \$2.00. How much would it cost for 2 tickets if one of the passengers is a senior citizen?

A. \$4.00 **C.** \$7.00
B. \$5.50 **D.** \$7.50

When you read the problem at first, you may decide that choice C, \$7.00, is correct since that is the cost of 2 tickets. But when you go back and read carefully, you may notice that one of the tickets purchased is for a senior citizen.

$\$3.50 + \$2.00 = \$5.50$
The total cost of the tickets is \$5.50.

B is the correct choice.

Read each problem carefully. Think about how you would answer it. Then read the problem again.

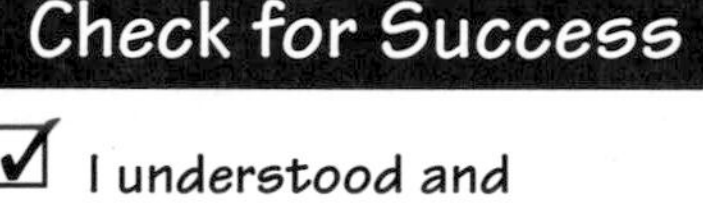

- ☑ I understood and answered the questions asked.
- ☑ I checked my work for errors.
- ☑ My answers make sense.

Choose the correct answer.

1. Theresa had 40 marbles in her collection. She gave away 12 and bought 8 more. How many marbles does she have now?
   A. 36 **C.** 52
   B. 48 **D.** 60

2. A ride on the Ferris wheel costs \$2.50. If you have a discount ticket, the ride costs \$1.75. How much would 3 rides cost, if one rider has a discount ticket?
   F. \$7.00 **H.** \$6.75
   G. \$5.25 **J.** \$3.75

3. Which number does not round to 2,000?
   A. 2,479 **C.** 1,876
   B. 2,013 **D.** 1,448

4. Gary did five loads of wash at \$0.75 a load. Which amount is not less than the money Gary spent to do his laundry?
   F. \$3.00 **H.** \$3.70
   G. \$3.10 **J.** \$3.90

Spiral Review and Test Prep

Chapters 1–2

Choose the correct answer.

Number Sense

1. What is 34,510 + 783?
   A. 112,810 C. 35,293
   B. 42,340 D. 35,000

2. What is \$5.00 − \$2.89?
   F. \$3.11 H. \$2.10
   G. \$2.11 J. \$2.01

3. What is 4,058 − 2,681?
   A. 2,637 C. 2,368
   B. 1,368 D. 1,377

4. What is \$8.59 rounded to the nearest dollar?
   F. \$10.00 H. \$8.00
   G. \$8.59 J. Not Here

Algebra and Functions

5. Which number sentence is true?
   A. $578 > 758$ C. $7,432 < 7,423$
   B. $2,377 = 2,733$ D. $9,554 > 9,514$

6. Which shows the order from greatest to least?
   F. \$7.52, \$7.25, \$7.15
   G. \$2.10, \$2.01, \$2.11
   H. \$5.95, \$5.99, \$5.59
   J. \$1.83, \$1.73, \$1.93

7. What is the sum of the next numbers in the pattern?
   4 + 8 = 12
   40 + 80 = 120
   400 + 800 = 1,200
   A. 4,000 C. 12,000
   B. 8,000 D. 120,000

8. Find the missing number.
   325 + 245 = ■ + 325
   Explain how you found your answer.

Statistics, Data Analysis, and Probability

Use data from the chart for problems 9–12.

Junior Varsity Basketball	
Name	Field Goal Points Scored
Luis	589
Saul	398
Marty	364
Abdul	611
Cleon	415
Mike	519

9. How many more points did Abdul score than Marty?

A. 247 **C.** 347
B. 257 **D.** 357

10. Cleon and Saul both play as guards. What are their total points?

F. 17 **H.** 803
G. 713 **J.** 813

11. Which two players scored more points than Mike?

A. Abdul and Saul **C.** Marty and Saul
B. Abdul and Luis **D.** Luis and Cleon

12. What is the total number of team points scored?

F. 1,896 **H.** 2,896
G. 2,796 **J.** 2,996

Measurement and Geometry

13. Which is the best estimate for the width of your math book?

A. 2 cm **C.** 20 cm
B. 2 m **D.** 20 mm

14. What is the area of the shaded figure?

F. 10 square units
G. 14 square units
H. 20 square units
J. Not Here

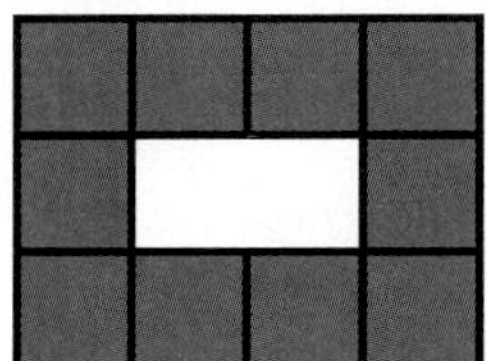

15. How many flat faces are in a cube?

A. 0 **C.** 4
B. 2 **D.** 6

16. How many angles are in a pentagon?

F. 6 **H.** 4
G. 5 **J.** 3

CHAPTER 3 Data, Statistics, and Graphing

Theme: Going Places

Use the Data

Favorite United States Cities to Visit

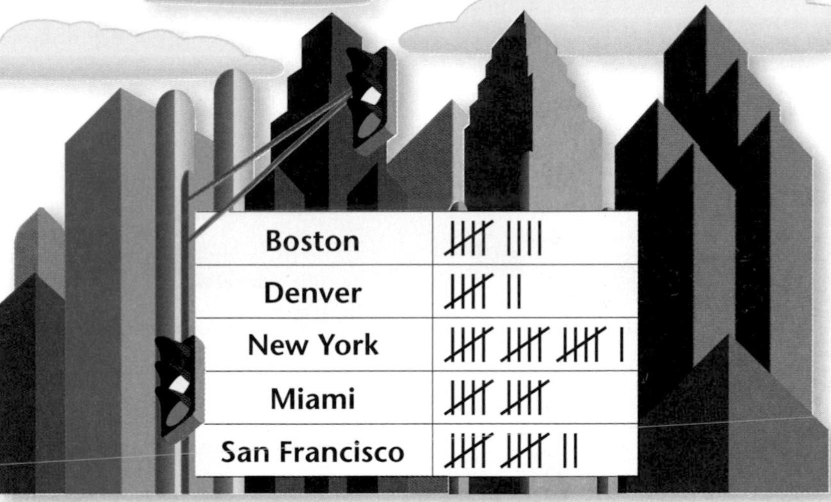

City	Tally
Boston	𝍸 ||||
Denver	𝍸 ||
New York	𝍸 𝍸 𝍸 |
Miami	𝍸 𝍸
San Francisco	𝍸 𝍸 ||

- How can you use tally marks to find the total number for each city?
- What conclusion can you make based on the data?

What You Will Learn

In this chapter you will learn how to
- tell time and find elapsed time.
- find range, median, and mode .
- collect and organize data in tables and graphs.
- use strategies to solve problems.

Objective: Tell time to the nearest minute.

3·1 Tell Time

Learn

Have you ever taken a trip to see a relative? Nina is going to visit her aunt. She will take the bus from Carlyle to Willistown. What time is it now? What time does Nina's bus leave Carlyle? What time does the bus arrive in Willistown?

Math Words

A.M. a name for time between 12:00 midnight and 12:00 noon

P.M. a name for time between 12:00 noon and 12:00 midnight

Town	Departure Time	Town	Arrival Time
Carlyle	9:30 A.M.	Long Beach	10:30 A.M.
Long Beach	10:45 A.M.	Willistown	1:45 P.M.
Willistown	2:00 P.M.	Brockport	4:00 P.M.

Example 1

Time Now	Bus Leaves	Arrives at Willistown

Write: 9:15 **A.M.**	**Write:** 9:30 A.M.	**Write:** 1:45 **P.M.**
Read: nine-fifteen, or a quarter after nine, or fifteen minutes after nine	**Read:** nine-thirty, or half-past nine, or thirty minutes after nine	**Read:** one forty-five, or a quarter to two, or fifteen minutes before two

More Examples

A

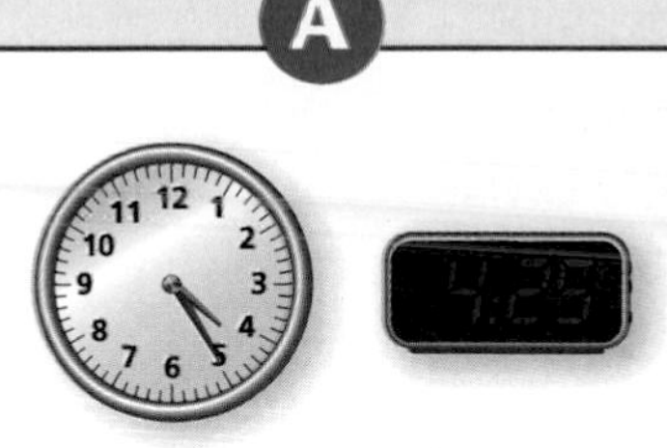

4:25

four twenty-five

B

6:42

six forty-two

C

10:17

ten-seventeen

Another bus makes 4 stops, one each quarter hour. How much time is that?

Example 2

15 minutes (min) = 1 quarter hour ($\frac{1}{4}$ h)

30 minutes (min) = $\frac{1}{2}$ hour ($\frac{1}{2}$ h) or 2 quarter hours

60 minutes (min) = 1 hour (1 h) or 4 quarter hours

The time it takes for the 4 bus stops is 1 hour.

Another bus makes 2 stops, one each half hour.

Example 3

Think: 30 minutes = $\frac{1}{2}$ hour

2 half hours = 1 hour

60 minutes = 1 hour

Time Facts

60 seconds = 1 minute

30 minutes = $\frac{1}{2}$ hour

60 minutes = 1 hour

90 minutes = $1\frac{1}{2}$ hours

180 minutes = 3 hours

Try It **Write each time using A.M. or P.M. Then write the time two ways in word form.**

1.

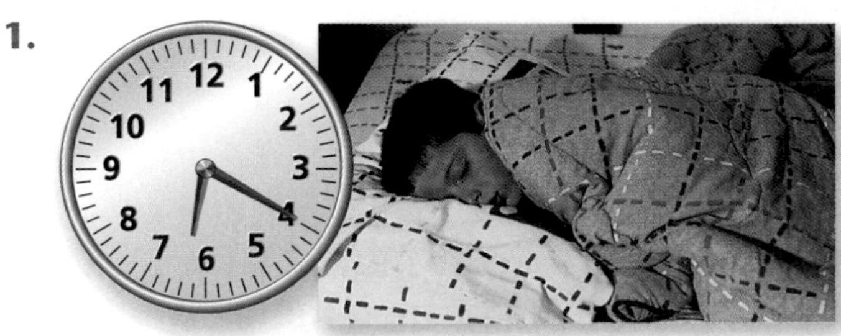

2.

Tell how much time.

3. 1 and 1 half hours = ▮ minutes

4. 180 minutes = ▮ hours

How do you use fractions to tell time?

Practice

Write the time in two ways using A.M. or P.M.

5.

6.

Name two activities that you enjoy doing that may take this amount of time.

7. about one minute
8. about one hour
9. about 10 hours

Tell how much time.

10. 15 minutes = ■ hour
11. ■ minutes = $\frac{1}{2}$ hour

★12. 1 hour 35 minutes = ■ minutes

★13. 145 minutes = ■ hour ■ minutes

Algebra & functions **Describe and complete the conversion patterns.**

14.

Hours	1	2	3	4	5
Minutes	60	120	180	■	■

15.

Seconds	30	■	90	120	150
Minutes	$\frac{1}{2}$	1	$1\frac{1}{2}$	■	$2\frac{1}{2}$

16.

The train Kerry wants to catch gets to the station at 10:30. Kerry looks at the clock at the station and tells the clerk, "It's 10:30. My train should be here and it is not." What is Kerry's error?

Problem Solving

17. **Analyze:** Claudia went to catch a bus at 7:30 A.M. Paulie went to catch a bus at half past seven in the evening. Could they be on the same bus? How do you know?

18. **Create a problem** that you can solve by changing minutes to hours. Solve it. Ask others to solve it.

Did You Know?

The continental United States is divided into four time zones. In 1883 these time zones were officially adopted based on research by Cleveland Abbe, an American meteorologist.

Use data from the map for problems 19 – 23.

19. What is the time difference in hours between New York and Portland?

20. What is the time difference in hours between Mountain Time and Central Time?

21. If it is 11:00 P.M. in Sacramento, what time is it in St. Louis?

22. If it is 6:00 P.M. in New York, what time is it in Denver?

★ **23.** Glenda flies from New York to Sacramento. She leaves New York at 1:00 P.M. Her flight takes 5 hours. What time is it when she arrives in Sacramento?

24. **Health:** Harley works out five days a week for 25 minutes a day to improve his heart rate. In hours and minutes, how much time does he spend working out each week?

Spiral Review and Test Prep

25. 95 + 36

26. \$7.64 + \$9.72

27. 906 − 147

28. \$8.78 − \$2.59

29. 600 − 547

Choose the correct answer.

30. Erin pays the exact bus fare with 2 quarters, a dime, and a nickel. How much is her bus fare?

A. 70 cents
B. 65 cents
C. 60 cents
D. 55 cents

31. Max wants to travel to England. The plane ticket costs \$350.75. So far Max has saved \$190.95. How much more must he save to buy the ticket?

F. \$240.20
G. \$240.80
H. \$159.80
J. \$159.20

Objective: Find and use elapsed time.

Elapsed Time

Learn

Math Word

elapsed time
the amount of time that passes from the start to the end of an activity

The Lloyd family is traveling from Miami, Florida, to Washington, D.C., on Flight 108. It left at 11:30 A.M. How long is the flight?

Destination	Flight	Arrival Time
Los Angeles	56	2:45 P.M.
Washington, D.C.	108	2:07 P.M.
Minneapolis	116	1:35 P.M.
Jackson	24	3:00 P.M.

Example 1

Count on to find the **elapsed time** between take-off and landing.

1

First, count on the hours.

11:30 A.M. ⟶ 12:30 P.M. ⟶ 1:30 P.M.

1 hour + 1 hour = 2 hours

2

Then, count on the minutes from where you left off.

1:30 P.M. ⟶ 2:00 P.M. ⟶ 2:07 P.M.

30 minutes + 7 minutes = 37 minutes

The flight took 2 hours and 37 minutes.

What time is 3 hours and 12 minutes after 10:00 P.M.?

Example 2

Think: Start at 10:00. Count on 3 hours: 10:00→11:00→12:00→1:00
Add on 12 minutes: 1:12 (Note: At 12:00 midnight and after write A.M.)

The time is 1:12 A.M.

How much time has passed?

1. Begin: 8:20 P.M.
   End: 10:55 P.M.
2. Begin: 9:30 A.M.
   End: 3:49 P.M.
3. Begin: 7:35 P.M.
   End: 12:53 A.M.

Tell how you find the elapsed time from 5:25 P.M. to 11:47 A.M.?

Practice How much time has passed?

4. Begin: 6:15 A.M.
   End: 10 A.M.

5. Begin: 10:25 A.M.
   End: 2:56 P.M.

6. Begin: 8:55 A.M.
   End: 3:23 P.M.

What time will it be in 30 minutes?

7. 

8.

9.

Write the missing numbers.

10. 3:22 P.M. is ■ minutes after 3:00 P.M.

11. 6:12 P.M. is ■ hours and ■ minutes after 4:00 P.M.

12. 7:45 A.M. is ■ hours and ■ minutes after 6:15 A.M.

★13. 9:00 A.M. is ■ hours and ■ minutes after 7:49 P.M.

Problem Solving

14. A car trip from Boston to New York took 4 hours and 21 minutes. The Kims left at 8:05 A.M. What time did they arrive in New York?

15. **Social Studies:** One of the oldest modern clocks was made in Rouen, France, in the year 1379. How many years ago was that?

16. **Analyze:** Becky goes to art school in the next town. Class begins at 10:20 A.M. The bus ride takes 1 hour and 19 minutes. Tell how you find what time Becky needs to leave to get to class on time.

17. Alex saved $300.00 for vacation. He takes a train trip from St. Louis to Phoenix. After buying his round-trip ticket, Alex has $175.50 to spend in Phoenix. How much was the round-trip train ticket?

Spiral Review and Test Prep

What is the value of the digit 6 in each number?

18. 56,134

19. 609,233

20. 2,361

Choose the correct answer.

21. $45.15 + $34.85
    A. $80.00
    B. $60.00
    C. $47.00
    D. $20.00

22. $215.89 − $75.89
    F. $260.00
    G. $140.00
    H. $250.00
    J. $150.00

Objective: Use a calendar and ordinal numbers.

3-3 Calendar

Learn

"My brother, Bob, returns from college on the Wednesday before Memorial Day!" said Gene. After a 12-day break, Bob will start his summer job. On what day will Bob start working?

Math Word

ordinal number a number used to tell order or position

May

Sunday	Monday	Tuesday	Wednesday	Thursday	Friday	Saturday
						1
2	3	4	5	6	7	8
9	10	11	12	13	14	15
16	17	18	19	20	21	22
23	24	25	26 Bob Comes Home	27	28	29
30	31 Memorial Day					

June

Sunday	Monday	Tuesday	Wednesday	Thursday	Friday	Saturday
		1	2	3	4	5
6	7	8	9	10	11	12
13	14	15	16	17	18	19
20	21	22	23	24	25	26
27	28	29	30			

Example

You can use a calendar to solve the problem.

1 Use the calendar. Find the Wednesday before Memorial Day.

Use **ordinal numbers** when you talk about dates.

The Wednesday before Memorial Day is May 26th.

2 Use May 26 as the first day and count on 12 days.

Gene's brother will start work on Monday, June 7.

Try It

Use the calendars for May and June for problems 1–5.

1. What is the date of the second Wednesday in June?
2. On what day of the week is Memorial Day?
3. You start vacation on June 1. You come back 2 weeks later. On what day and date do you return from vacation?

How much time has passed?

4. Start date: May 9
   Elapsed time: 22 days
   End date: ▮
5. Start date: May 15
   Elapsed time: ▮ days
   End date: June 16

How can you use a calendar to find the number of days from May 15 to Memorial Day?

Practice

Use the calendars for problems 6–9.

July						
Sunday	Monday	Tuesday	Wednesday	Thursday	Friday	Saturday
				1	2	3
4 Independence Day	5	6	7	8	9	10
11	12	13	14	15	16	17
18	19	20	21	22	23	24
25	26	27	28	29	30	31

August						
Sunday	Monday	Tuesday	Wednesday	Thursday	Friday	Saturday
1	2	3	4	5	6	7
8	9	10	11	12	13	14
15	16	17	18	19	20	21
22	23	24	25	26	27	28
29	30	31				

6. What is the date of the third Tuesday in August?

7. On what day of the week is Independence Day?

8. If your vacation begins on Independence Day to the following Saturday, how many days long is your vacation?

★**9.** You return from a 16-day vacation on Monday, August 2. On what day did you leave for vacation? How do you know?

Problem Solving

> A millennium is 1,000 years.
> A century is 100 years.
> A decade is 10 years.

10. The year 2001 begins a new millennium.
How many centuries are in a millennium?
How many decades are in a century?

11. How many days have passed since the start of the school year? How many days are left?

Use data from the table for problems 12–13.

12. How many decades after the first satellite did the first woman travel in space?

13. How many decades before the first shuttle flight was the first satellite launched?

History of United States Space Travel	
First satellite	1950s
First space flight	1960s
First shuttle flight	1970s
First woman in space	1980s

14. A plane will be the 142nd flight to take off this week. How many planes have taken off so far this week?

Spiral Review and Test Prep

15. 3,787 + 958 **16.** 1,003 − 684 **17.** 8,011 − 973 **18.** 1,576 + 96 + 98

Choose the correct answer.

19. Last year 10,502 tourists visited the aquarium. What is this number rounded to the nearest thousand?

A. 10,000 **C.** 11,000
B. 10,500 **D.** 1,500

20. There are 12 empty seats on a tour bus and 42 passengers. How many seats are on the bus in all?

F. 30 **H.** 54
G. 48 **J.** 58

Line Plots

Learn

Math Words

survey a collection of data that answers a question or questions

data information

line plot a vertical graph that uses Xs above a number line to show data

tally table a chart that keeps track of data by making a mark for each thing counted

Fourth-grade students in Springfield were asked how many miles from the center of town they live. The results of the **survey** are shown in the **data** to the right. Do more fourth-grade students live 4 miles or 6 miles away from town?

Example 1

You can solve this problem by using a **line plot** or **tally table**.

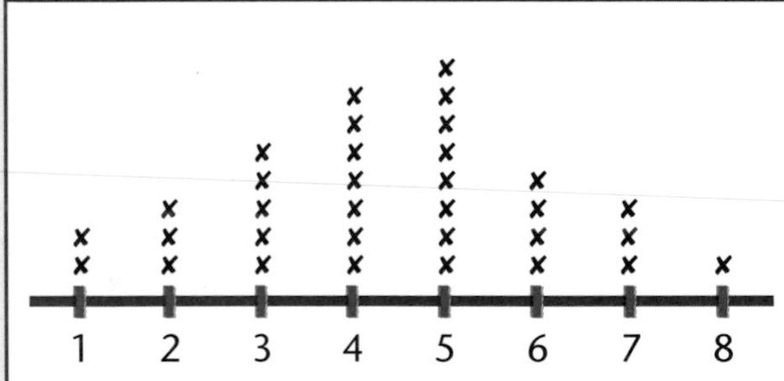

Miles from Town	Tally	Number
1	||	2
2	|||	3
3	𝍸	5
4	𝍸 ||	7
5	𝍸 |||	8
6	||||	4
7	|||	3
8	|	1

From the line plot and tally table you can see that there are more fourth-grade students that live 4 miles away than 6.

Try It

1. Make a tally table and line plot for the number of students on buses: 22, 23, 20, 25, 19, 21, 20, 22, 22
2. How many buses are included in the data?
3. How many more buses have 22 students than school buses with 19 students?

How are the tally table and the line plot similar?

Practice Solve.

4. Make a tally table and line plot for the number of minutes it takes students to travel from school to home: 12, 11, 10, 12, 15, 13, 14

5. What question do you think the survey asked?

6. What is the longest time it takes the students who were surveyed to get home from school?

7. How many students took part in this survey?

8. **Collect data** for a survey. Decide on a survey question for your class. Make a tally table and line plot for your data. Draw a conclusion based on your results.

★9. You collect data on how many students have traveled to states outside of the state in which they live. How would you set up a line plot?

Problem Solving

Use data from the tally table for problems 10 – 11.

10. The fourth graders read 3 books during the summer. The chart shows how many hours they read each week. Make a line plot for the data.

11. A new student reads for 12 hours each week. Redo the tally table to show this. How does the tally table help you compare the two sets of data to the original set?

Time Spent on Summer Reading List

Number of Hours per Week	Tally	Students
1	||	2
2	~~||||~~ |||	8
3	~~||||~~ ||	7
4	|||	3
5 or more	||	2

12. **Create a problem** using the results of your survey and the line plot you made in problem 9. Solve it. Ask others to solve it.

13. **Analyze:** Look at the line plot on the previous page. Are there any large batches of numbers in the data? What does this tell you?

Spiral Review and Test Prep

Round each number to the nearest thousand.

14. 34,578
15. 7,092
16. 690,573
17. 381,399

Choose the correct answer.

18. Which answer makes the number sentence true? 15 − ▮ = 9

A. 4 **B.** 5 **C.** 6 **D.** 7

19. Which makes the number sentence true? $4{,}465 - n = 0$

F. 4,465 **G.** 1 **H.** 0 **J.** 5

Objective: Find the range, median, and mode of a set of data.

3•5 Range, Median, and Mode

Mishelle Michaels, Meteorologist, Boston, MA.

Learn

You too can be a weather watcher. Many meteorologists rely on local schools to measure temperatures. The table below shows the temperatures recorded at 15 schools. You can describe the data in different ways.

Math Words

median the middle number in a group of numbers arranged in numerical order

mode the number or numbers that occur most often in a collection of data

range the difference between the greatest and the least numbers in a group of numbers

Temperature (°F)

Millroad	74	Center	75	Murphy	72	Carlton	71	Crestwood	71
Shore	71	Fallton	71	Riverdale	77	Paulie	70	Valley	74
Quenton	75	Elm	71	Hightop	65	Thomas	73	Hilltop	76

Example

Find the **median**.

Arrange the numbers in order from least to greatest. Find the middle number.

65 70 71 71 71 71 71 **72** 73 74 74 75 75 76 77

The median is 72.

Find the **mode**.

The number that occurs most often in the data is the number 71.

The mode is 71.

Find the **range**.

Subtract the least number from the greatest: $77 - 65 = 12$

The range is 12.

Most temperatures are clustered in the low- to mid-70s.

Try It

1. Find the range, median, and mode of this data.

T-shirts Sold Each Week	
Week 1:	10, 10, 12, 15, 18, 11, 10
Week 2:	12, 13, 13, 13, 15, 16, 16
Week 3:	15, 14, 14, 17, 17, 13, 13

Sum it Up! What do the range, median, and mode tell you about this data? What conclusion can you draw?

Practice

Use data from the line plot for problems 2–4.

2. Find the range, median, and mode from the line plot on the right.

3. What does the mode tell you about the data?

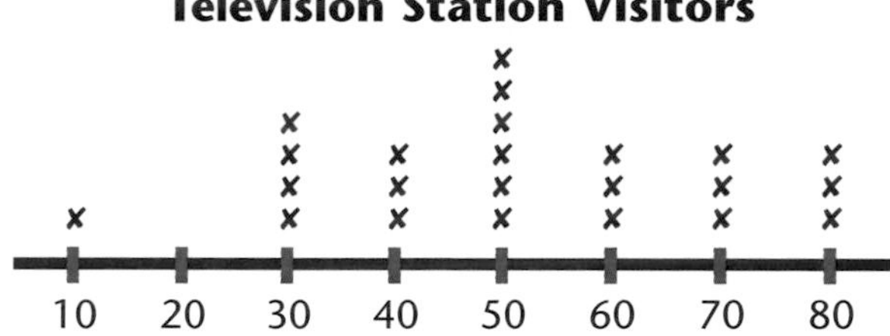

4. What does the median tell you about this data?

★5. Outliers are numbers that are separated from most of the data. Explain if there are any outliers in this data.

★6. **Analyze:** Can you find a middle number in the given data? How can you find the median?

Number of posters sold each day:
12, 12, 14, 16, 18, 18, 18,
20, 20, 20, 21, 21, 22, 22

Problem Solving

Use data from the table for problems 7–9.

7. Find the median, mode, and range for this set of data. Which day do you think had the best shows? Why?

8. Which had the greatest number of visitors, the News at Noon Show or the Talk It Over Show?

Number of Vistors Last Week

Days	1	2	3	4	5
News at Noon Show	20	25	20	50	15
Talk It Over Show	20	15	30	30	35

9. **Create a problem** about the data that can be answered using the median, mode, or range. Solve it. Ask others to solve it.

10. **Time:** A visitor watches the start of a show being taped at 12:15 P.M. It takes 50 minutes to tape the show. At what time is the show over?

Spiral Review and Test Prep

Use mental math to add or subtract.

11. 67 − 23
12. 62 − 45
13. 14 + 89
14. 35 + 41

Choose the correct answer.

15. $63.78 + $113.45
A. $177.23
B. $167.13
C. $177.13
D. Not Here

16. $3,091 − $698
F. $3,607
G. $3,393
H. $2,407
J. Not Here

Extra Practice, page 126

Objective: Identify information in problems as important, unimportant, missing, or extra.

3•6

Problem Solving: Reading for Math

Identify Extra and Missing Information

New Schedules Make Travel Easier

Read Bryan is going to Boston on May 10. He will take a train from New York City. The train leaves New York City at 6:58 A.M. and arrives in Boston at 12:20 P.M. On what day of the week will Bryan leave for Boston?

READING SKILL ▶ **Important and Unimportant Information**

Important facts help you solve the problem. Unimportant facts do not help you solve the problem.

- **What do you know?** Bryan leaves on May 10, at 6:58 A.M.; the train arrives at 12:20 P.M.
- **What do you need to find?** Day of the week Bryan leaves

MATH SKILL ▶ **Find Missing and Extra Information**

Identify and try to find any important information that is missing from the problem. If you cannot find it, then you cannot answer the problem.

Plan Find the day of the week for May 10. You can look for information in a calendar.

Solve You need to find the day of the week for May 10. You need a calendar or you need to know the day of the week that another date falls on. This important information is missing from the problem. It cannot be solved with the given information.

Look Back Is your answer reasonable?

How does identifying information as important or unimportant help you solve a problem?

Solve. Identify extra or missing information in problems 1–8.

1. Billie Sue visits her aunt in Baltimore each summer. She rides a train from Philadelphia to Baltimore. At 6:51 A.M., the train leaves Philadelphia. What time does it arrive in Baltimore?

2. Matt is taking a train from his home to college. The train leaves Chicago at 5:55 P.M. on August 20. It arrives in Dallas at 2:36 A.M. on August 21. How long is Matt's trip?

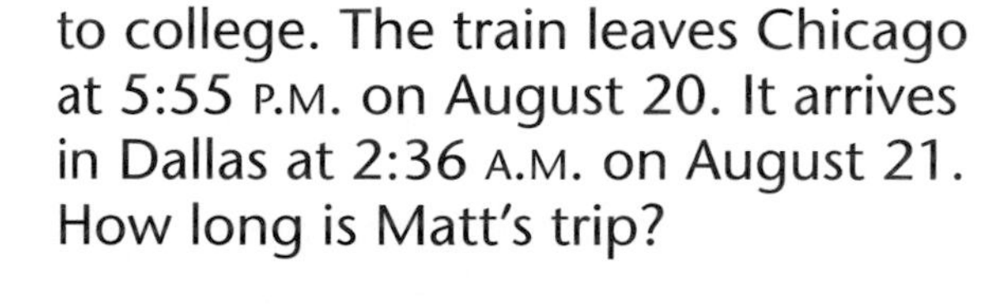

Use data from the flight schedule for problems 3–8.

3. How long is the flight from St. Louis to Omaha?

4. How much does one first-class ticket cost for Flight 755?

5. On Tuesday, August 5, Pete bought a ticket for Flight 321. His ticket is for the flight on August 21. On what day of the week will Pete fly from Phoenix to Salt Lake City?

Best Airways Flight Schedule

Flight	From	To	Departure Time	Arrival Time
107	Chicago	St. Louis	11:05 A.M.	12:15 P.M.
321	Phoenix	Salt Lake City	12:05 P.M.	2:37 P.M.
525	St. Louis	Omaha	8:50 A.M.	10:10 A.M.
755	Philadelphia	Atlanta	1:35 P.M.	3:41 P.M.

6. Is Flight 107 or Flight 525 shorter? How much shorter?

7. How fast does Flight 107 fly?

8. What is the order of flights from longest to shortest?

Spiral Review and Test Prep

Choose the correct answer.

A bus leaves Central Street at 12:45 P.M. It arrives at the first stop at 1:17 P.M. When will it arrive at the second stop?

9. Which of the following statements is true?
   - **A.** The ride to the first stop took about $\frac{1}{2}$ hour.
   - **B.** The bus left before noon.
   - **C.** It arrived at the first stop before 1:00 P.M.

10. What important information is missing?
    - **F.** When the bus leaves Central Street
    - **G.** The length of the trip between the first and second stop
    - **H.** When the bus arrives at the first stop

Check Your Progress A

Write the time in two ways using A.M. or P.M. **(pages 92–95)**

1.

2.

Tell how much time. **(pages 92–95)**

4. 60 min = ■ h
5. 30 min = ■ h
6. ■ min = 2 h
7. 180 min = ■ h
8. ■ min = $1\frac{1}{2}$ h
9. ■ min = $\frac{1}{2}$ h

How much time has passed? **(pages 96–97)**

10. Begin: 9:45 P.M.
End: 4:23 A.M.

11. Begin: 2:22 P.M.
End: 6:15 P.M.

12. Begin: 6:17 A.M.
End: 5:00 P.M.

13. Begin: 4:15 P.M.
End: 4:23 A.M.

14. Begin: 2:22 P.M.
End: 2:22 A.M.

15. Begin: 8:42 A.M.
End: 3:50 P.M.

Use the calendar for June for exercise 16. **(pages 98–99)**

June

Sunday	Monday	Tuesday	Wednesday	Thursday	Friday	Saturday
			1	2	3	4
5	6	7	8	9	10	11

16. Jess goes to camp on the 2nd of June. She stays for 5 days. What date does she leave?

Solve. **(pages 92–105)**

17. Billy spends a quarter of an hour doing homework for 5 nights. How much total time is this?

18. Make a line plot for the data in the table.

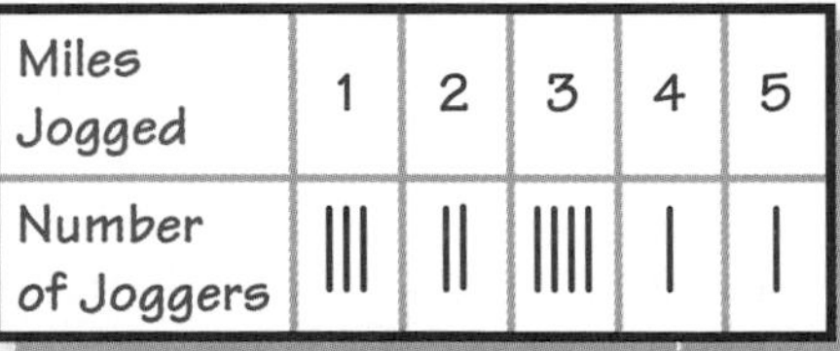
<table>
<tr><td>Miles Jogged</td><td>1</td><td>2</td><td>3</td><td>4</td><td>5</td></tr>
<tr><td>Number of Joggers</td><td>|||</td><td>||</td><td>||||</td><td>|</td><td>|</td></tr>
</table>

19. What is the range, median, and mode for the data in problem 18?

20. **Generalize:** Explain how you decide if a problem is missing information.

Use Graphs

On Monday, Mr. Brook's class gathered temperature data for a science experiment. They measured the temperature each hour one afternoon. They recorded a temperature of 64°F at 1 P.M., 59°F at 2 P.M., 46°F at 3 P.M., and 39°F at 4 P.M. During which hour did the temperature change the most?

You can use a computer program to graph the data to help find the greatest change.

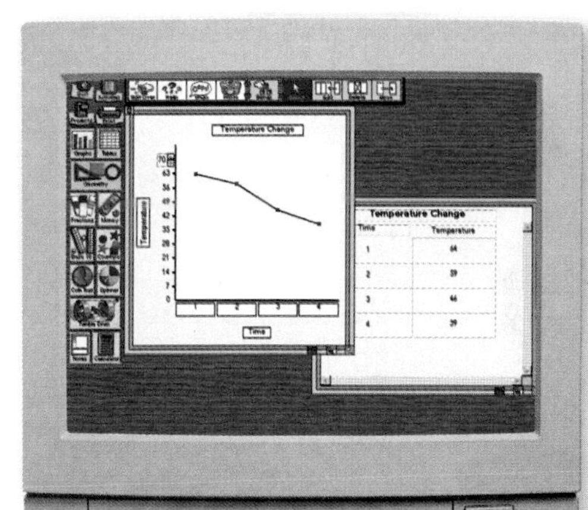

- Choose Line Graph.
- Enter the graph title and the labels for the axes.
- Change the scale on the vertical axis so the greatest number is 70.
- Click on the link at the bottom of the graph.
- Choose Table. Enter the data for the temperature in the second column.
- The line graph is drawn as you enter the data.

During which hour did the temperature change the most?

Use the computer to graph each set of data. Then tell during which hour the temperature changed the most.

1. On Tuesday, Ms. Harmon's class recorded a temperature of 36°F at 1 P.M., 39°F at 2 P.M., 37°F at 3 P.M., and 25°F at 4 P.M.
2. On Wednesday, Mr. Ricardo's class recorded a temperature of 22°F at 1 P.M., 35°F at 2 P.M., 32°F at 3 P.M., and 39°F at 4 P.M.
3. **Analyze:** How does using the computer help you redraw a line graph when the data changes?

For more practice, use Math Traveler™.

Objective: Work backward to solve a problem.

Problem Solving: Strategy
Work Backward

Read **Read the problem carefully.**

Bus Route P.M. Schedule			
Bus Stop	Time	Time	Time
Harris Street	3:00	6:30	7:00
Mini Mall	3:10	6:40	7:10
Athletic Club	3:32	7:02	7:32

Samuel and his father are going to the Athletic Club to play in a basketball tournament. The game starts at 7:30 P.M. It takes them about 35 minutes to walk to the Harris Street bus stop. Which bus should they take? When should they leave home?

- **What do you know?** **The game starts at 7:30 P.M.; it takes about 35 minutes to walk to the bus stop.**
- **What do you need to find?** **The bus they should take; the time they should leave**

Plan You can work backward to solve this problem. Use the bus schedule.

Solve Start by finding the last bus that can arrive at the Athletic Club before 7:30 P.M.

Think: **A bus arrives at the Athletic Club at 7:02 P.M. It leaves Harris Street at 6:30 P.M.**

Then find the time Samuel and his father need to leave home.

Think: **End time: 6:30 P.M.**
Elapsed time: 35 minutes ← Time to walk to bus stop
Start time: 5:55 P.M.

They should take the 6:30 P.M. bus and leave home by 5:55 P.M.

Look Back How can you work forward to check your answer?

What if they want to get to the club by 4:00 P.M.? How can you work backward to the latest time they should leave?

Practice **Work backward to solve.**

1. Mindy wants to eat before the 7:40 P.M. show. She needs about 45 minutes to order and eat her dinner. What is the latest time she can order?

2. Juan has $2.36 left. He used 7 quarters to buy a program for the show. Then he bought a bottle of water for $0.89. How much money did he start with?

3. Two tickets to the show cost $37.50. Michelle bought two tickets, and two programs for $2.79 each. She has $27.84 left in her wallet. How much money did she have to start with?

4. Sunny rides her bike for 15 minutes to the pond, 25 minutes to her friend's house, then 10 minutes back to her house. It is now 4:30 P.M. What time did Sunny start her bike ride?

Mixed Strategy Review

5. Michael works at the Arts Center. He drives 23 miles one way from his house to the center. He drives to and from the center 3 days a week. How far does he drive each week to the Arts Center?

★6. Since the new Arts Center opened, they have had 3 times the number of shows that played at the old theater. Next week, Guys and Dolls will be the nineteenth show in the new Arts Center. How many different shows were played at the old theater?

CHOOSE A STRATEGY
- Logical Reasoning
- Draw a Picture
- Make a Graph
- Act It Out
- Make a Table or List
- Find a Pattern
- Guess and Check
- Write a Number Sentence
- Work Backward
- Solve a Simpler Problem

Use data from the table for problems 7–9.

7. What is the range for the number of performances listed?

8. Which show had more than four thousand performances, but less than four thousand five hundred performances?

The Longest-Running Musicals on Broadway *as of March 31, 1998*

Show	Performances
Cats	6,463
A Chorus Line	6,137
Les Misérables	4,545
Phantom of the Opera	4,263
42nd Street	3,468

9. **Collect Data:** Use another resource to find out the current number of performances for each musical listed. Organize the data in a chart or graph. Use the data to create a problem. Solve it. Ask others to solve it.

Problem Solving

Extra Practice, page 126

Objective: Read and make pictographs.

3·8 Explore Pictographs

Learn

What do you like best about traveling to a new place? What kind of chart could show what other people like about traveling?

> **Math Words**
>
> **pictograph** a graph that shows data by using symbols
>
> **key** a list that tells how many items each symbol represents

Work Together

> **You Will Need**
> - graph paper

► *Choose a topic for a survey.*

Survey and collect data from members of your class.

Organize the data in a chart.

Favorite Places to Travel

Place	Votes
Mountains	12
Beach	21
Zoo	9

Make a **pictograph** to show the data in your chart.

Favorite Places

Mountains	☺ ☺
Beach	☺ ☺ ☺ ◐
Zoo	☺ ◐

Key: Each ☺ stands for 6 votes.

What symbols did you use in your pictograph?

What does each symbol represent in your **key**?

► *Make another pictograph with the same data from your survey. Change the symbols and the key.*

How is this pictograph like the first one?
How is it different?

Make Connections

Here is how to make a pictograph to show data about favorite places to travel.

Steps

- List the places.
- Choose a symbol to represent the results.
- Use a key to tell the number each symbol represents.
- Draw symbols to show the results.
- Write a title.

Favorite Places to Travel

Places	Votes
Mountains	🚗 half-🚗
Beach	🚗 🚗 🚗
Zoo	🚗 🚗 half-🚗
Theme Park	🚗 🚗

Key: Each 🚗 stands for 8 votes.
Each half-🚗 stands for 4 votes.

Try It Use data from the table for problems 1–4.

1. Make a pictograph to show the data.
2. What does each symbol in your pictograph represent?
3. How many people answered this survey?
4. Which ride received the most votes? How can you tell from the table? How can you tell from the pictograph?

Favorite Rides at Waterworld	
Ride	Number of Persons
Loop-de-Loop	24
Amazon Rapids	32
Niagara Falls	16
The Big Plunge	24

How did you decide on what symbols to use to make your key? How do you decide on its value?

Practice Use data from the table for problems 5–10.

5. Copy and complete the pictograph.
6. Which way to travel is the least favorite?
7. How many more people said they would rather travel by airplane than by car? How do you know?
8. **Analyze:** What if you use 1 💼 to represent 2 people? How will this change the pictograph?

Favorite Ways to Travel

Type	Votes	
Airplane	75	💼💼💼💼💼💼💼 half-💼
Train	30	💼💼💼
Car	50	
Bus	45	

KEY: Each 💼 represents 10 votes.
Each half-💼 represents 5 votes.

Extra Practice, page 127

Objective: Read and make bar graphs.

3·9 Bar Graphs

Learn

> **Math Words**
>
> **bar graph** a graph that displays data using bars of different heights
>
> **scale** equally spaced marks along a graph

What is your favorite zoo animal? Some Zoo Atlanta visitors named the animals they liked best. How can the data in the tally table be used to complete a graph?

Favorite Wild Animals

Panda	||||
Flamingo	||
Monkey	𝍸 𝍸 ||
Hornbill	𝍸 |
Tiger	𝍸 |||
Meerkat	𝍸

Example 1

The tally table shows the results of the fourth-grade survey. The results are shown in the **bar graph**.

The bars show the number of people who chose each animal. To complete the graph, follow these steps:

- *List the animals along the bottom of the graph.*
- *Write a* **scale** *with numbers along the left side of the graph, starting with zero.*
- *Draw bars to match the numbers of the data in the tally table.*
- *Write the title.*

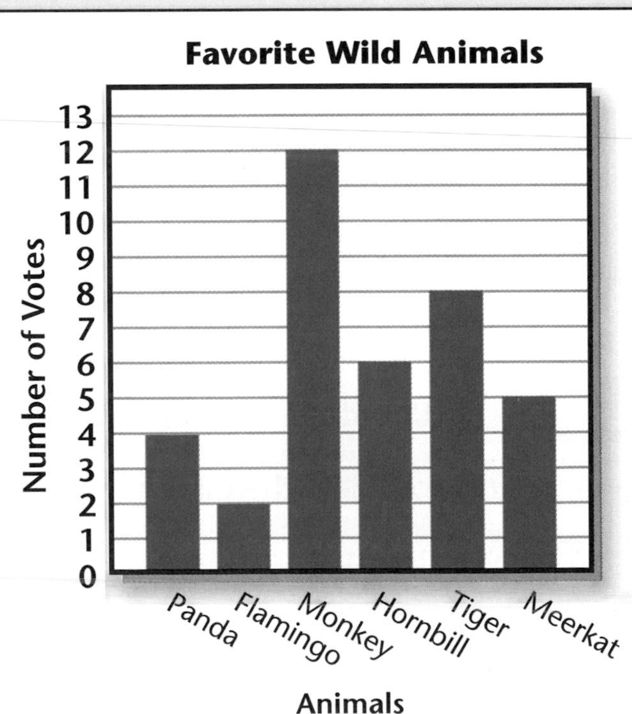

What if you wanted to know how many boys and girls liked each kind of animal?

Example 2

You can use a double bar graph to show the data. Each animal has two bars above it; one for girls and one for boys.

Favorite Animals		
Animal	Boys	Girls
Tiger	|||	|
Elephant	|	|
Panda	||||	卌 |||
Whale	||||	||
Gorilla	卌	|||
Wolf	|||	

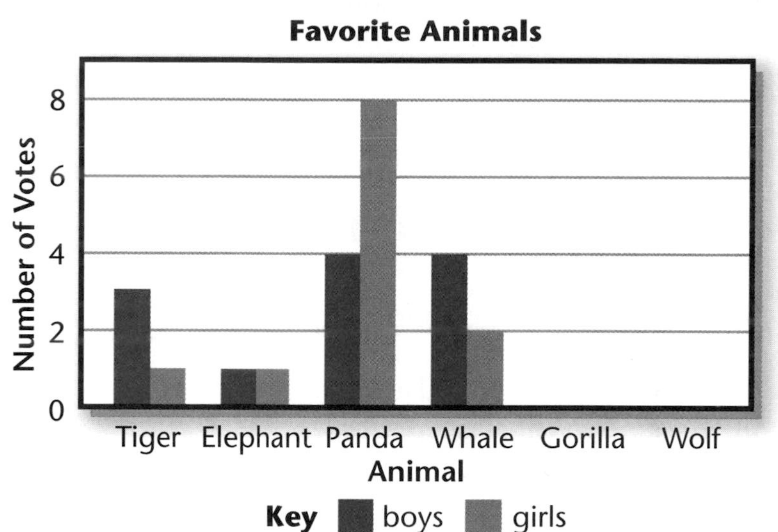

The double bars show the favorite animals of boys and of girls. To complete the graph, you would

- *complete the scale and the items along the bottom of the graph.*
- *draw double bars to match the numbers of the boys and the girls in the tally table.*

Try It **Copy and complete the graph for Example 2. Then answer the questions about the graph.**

1. Which animal is most popular? least popular?
2. If students only chose one favorite animal, then how many students were surveyed?
3. Which animal do the same number of boys and girls like? How many votes did this animal get?

In Example 1, how do you decide what the heights of the bars for the monkey, hornbill, tiger, and meerkat should be?

Practice

Use data from the bar graph for problems 4–7.

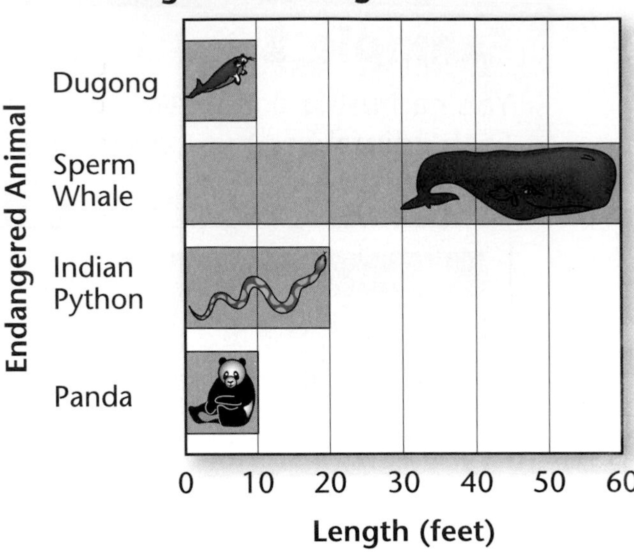

4. How much shorter is the python than the whale? Explain how you know.

5. Which animal is between 15 feet and 30 feet in length?

★6. **Analyze:** Why do you think the scale numbers increase by 10 rather than by 1?

7. Is the whale twice as long as the python and the dugong? How can you tell?

Use data from the bar graph for problems 8–11.

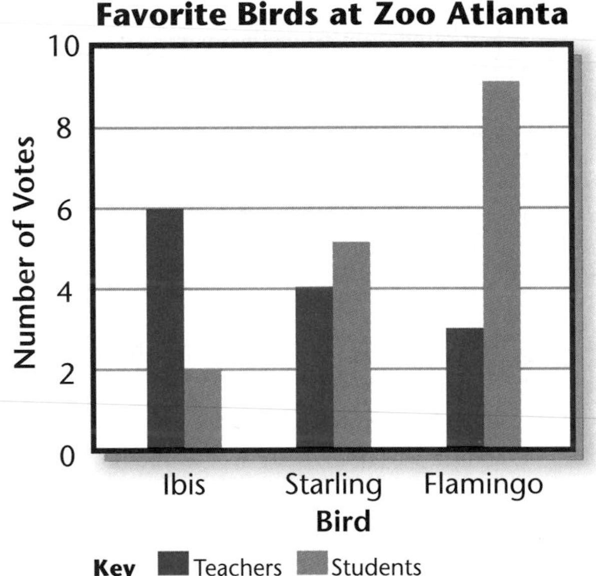

8. Why do you need 2 bars in this graph?

9. **Compare:** How do the scale numbers in this graph increase? What other scale numbers could you have used in this graph? Explain.

Another student makes the following statements about the graph. Do you agree with her? Why or why not?

10. More teachers than students like the starling.

11. More students than teachers like the flamingo.

12.

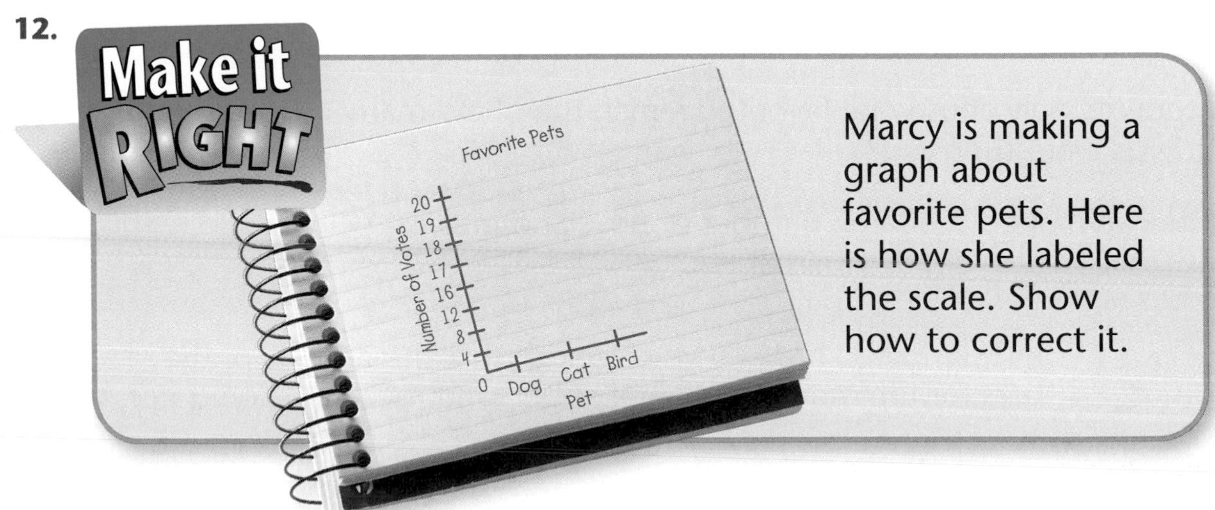

Marcy is making a graph about favorite pets. Here is how she labeled the scale. Show how to correct it.

Problem Solving

Use data from the chart for problems 13–17.

13. If you wanted to make a bar graph using the data in the table for length, what is a good scale to use? Why?

14. **Language Arts:** Choose two animals from the chart. Write a paragraph comparing and contrasting the animals. Use data from the chart in your paragraph.

15. What is the range in weight of the animals listed in the chart?

16. **What if** you want to make a graph of the data in the table for weight? What is a good scale to use? Why?

Heaviest Land Animals

Animal	Length (in Feet)	Weight (in Pounds)
African Elephant	24	14,432
White Rhinoceros	14	7,937
Hippopotamus	13	5,512
Giraffe	19	2,257
American Bison	13	2,202

Source: The Top 10 of Everything

17. **Science:** A carnivore is an animal that eats meat. The largest carnivore is the southern elephant seal, weighing 7,716 pounds. How much more does the heaviest land animal weigh?

18. **Generalize:** When is a bar graph more useful than data in a chart? than data in a pictograph? Explain your reasoning.

19. The Jordans live 756 miles from Zoo Atlanta. On Monday they drove 340 miles to visit the zoo. On Tuesday they drove 256 miles. How many miles will they drive on Wednesday to arrive at the zoo?

20. Kyle has $57.30 in his savings account at the end of the month. During the month he took out $25.00 and put in $14.98. How much money did he have at the beginning of the month?

Spiral Review and Test Prep

21. $\begin{array}{r} \$3.79 \\ 1.23 \\ +\ 0.38 \\ \hline \end{array}$

22. $\begin{array}{r} \$4.54 \\ 1.29 \\ +\ 0.34 \\ \hline \end{array}$

23. $\begin{array}{r} \$6.09 \\ -\ 4.66 \\ \hline \end{array}$

24. $\begin{array}{r} \$7.00 \\ -\ 4.18 \\ \hline \end{array}$

25. $\begin{array}{r} \$10.01 \\ -\ 3.38 \\ \hline \end{array}$

Choose the correct answer.

26. Which number sentence does not belong in the fact family?
    - **A.** $4 + 5 = 9$
    - **B.** $9 - 5 = 4$
    - **C.** $5 + 4 = 9$
    - **D.** $9 + 4 = 13$

27. It is 4:40 P.M. Marla will leave for the office in a quarter hour. What time will she leave?
    - **F.** 4:45 P.M.
    - **G.** 4:50 P.M.
    - **H.** 4:55 P.M.
    - **J.** 5:00 P.M.

Objective: Read and make coordinate graphs.

3·10 Coordinate Graphing

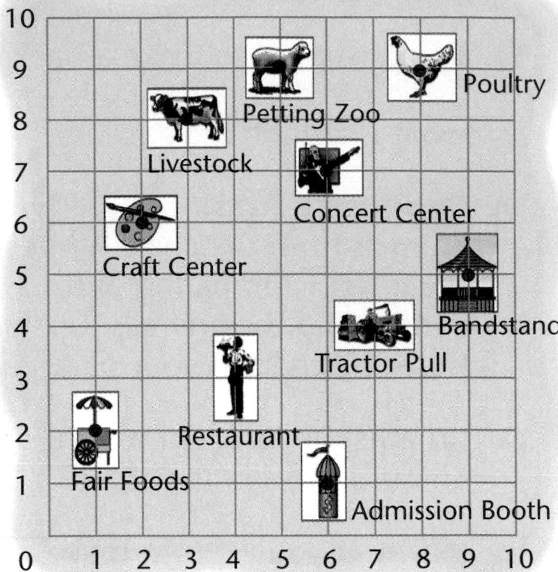

Algebra & functions **Learn**

Math Word

ordered pair
a pair of numbers that gives the location of a point on a graph, map, or grid

"Let's go to the Craft Center!" Mrs. Lopez suggested. How can the Lopez family use the map to find its location?

Example

You can use ordered pairs to name locations on the grid.

To tell where the Crafts Center is follow these steps:

1

- *Start at zero.*
- *Count two blocks to the right.*

First coordinate shows how far to go right.

(**2**, 6)

2

- *Then go 6 blocks up.*

Second coordinate shows how far to go up.

(2, **6**)

The 2 and 6 are an **ordered pair**. They are written as (2, 6).
The Craft Center is located at (2, 6).

Try It **Give the ordered pairs for each place on the grid.**

1. Petting Zoo
2. Admission Booth
3. Tractor Pull

Name the place at each location.

4. (6, 7)
5. (8, 9)
6. (9, 5)

Why is the order of numbers important in an ordered pair?

Practice Give the ordered pairs for each place on the grid.

7. Craft Center
8. Frog Jump
9. Petting Zoo
10. Kiddie Rides
11. Business Exhibit
12. Admission Booth

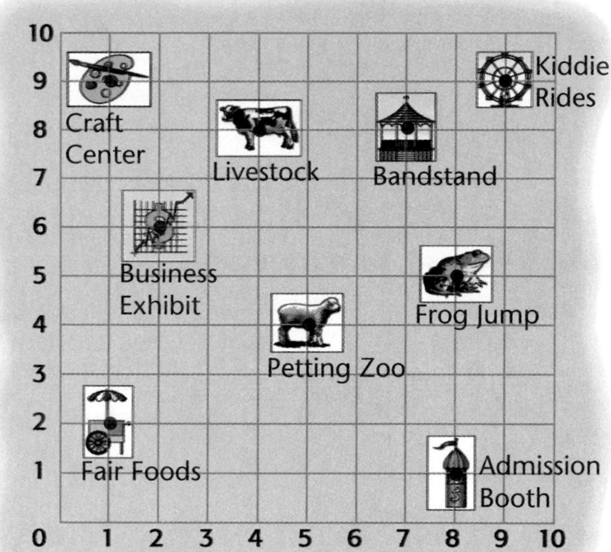

Name the place at each location.

13. (5, 4) 14. (7, 8) 15. (4, 8)

16. (1, 2) 17. (8, 5) 18. (1, 9)

Algebra & functions **Copy and complete the table.**

19.

Number of Ferris Wheel Carts	1	2	3	4	5
Number of Seats	4	8	■	■	■

★20. Use each pair of numbers in the table above as an ordered pair. Graph the numbers on graph paper. What do you notice?

Problem Solving

★21. If each grid line stands for 10 feet, how far is it from the Kiddie Rides to the Craft Center? from the Frog Jump to the Admission Booth?

22. **Generalize:** What can you say about the locations of any group of ordered pairs that have the same first number? the same second number?

Spiral Review and Test Prep

Tell how much time has passed.

23. Begin: 4:15 A.M.
End: 11 A.M.

24. Begin: 10:30 A.M.
End: 3:52 P.M.

25. Begin: 4:55 P.M.
End: 1:20 A.M.

Choose the correct answer.

26. What is $23.67 rounded to the nearest dollar?
A. $20.00 C. $24.00
B. $23.00 D. Not Here

27. What is the difference?
$11.16 − $7.67
F. $3.49 H. $4.51
G. $3.51 J. Not Here

Extra Practice, page 127

Objective: Explore reading and making line graphs.

3·11 Explore Line Graphs

Learn

Line graphs can be used to study how things change over time. For example, you can analyze data about the number of passenger planes that flew during the last 10 years.

Math Word

line graph a graph that uses a line to show the relationship between two sets of data

Work Together

You Will Need
- graph paper

► *Choose a topic to research.*
Collect the data.

- Organize the data in a chart.

Airline Flights	
Year	Number of Flights
1990	6,900
1991	6,800
1992	7,000
1993	7,200
1994	7,500
1995	8,000
1996	8,200
1997	8,200
1998	8,300
1999	8,400
2000	8,500

- Make a **line graph** to show the data in your chart.

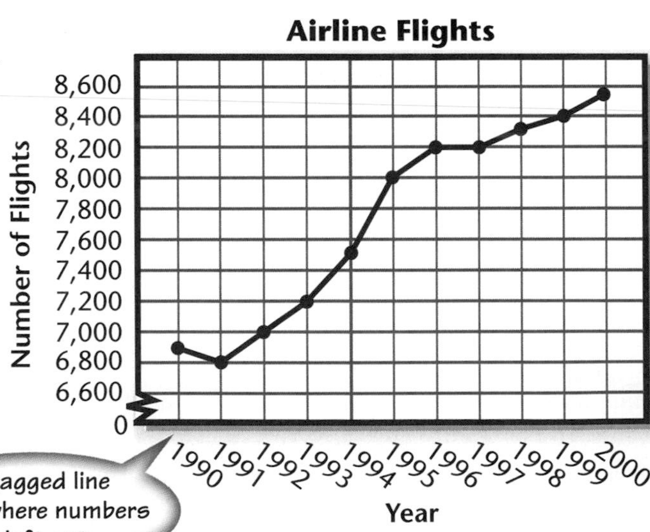

► *Make another line graph using the same data. Change the vertical scale so the numbers increase by a different number.*

How is this line graph like the first one? different?

How does changing the scale affect the line graph?

Make Connections

Here is how to make a line graph to show data about changing membership in a travel club.

Steps

- Choose the scale for the numbers that show the time and data.
- Label the graph.
- Plot the points that show the data.
- Connect the points with lines.
- Write a title.

Try It

Use data from the table for problems 1–4.

1. Make a line graph to show the data from the table.
2. What scale did you use to show the data?
3. How many members traveled by airplane in 2000?
4. What conclusion can you make from the data in your graph?

Airplane Travel by Travel Club

Year	Number of Members
1997	135
1998	140
1999	144
2000	150

Sum it Up What does the line graph tell you about this data?

Train Travel by Travel Club

Year	Number of Members
1940	186
1950	150
1960	87
1970	62
1980	51
1990	43
2000	36

Practice

Use data from the table for problems 5–7.

5. Copy and complete the line graph.
6. During which year listed was travel by train most popular? Why might that be?
7. **Analyze:** Based on the data, how many members do you predict will ride on trains in the year 2010? Explain your reasoning.

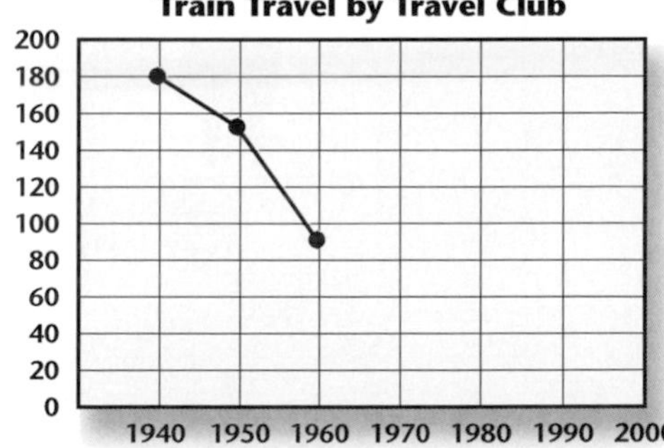

Extra Practice, page 127

Objective: Analyze data and make decisions.

3·12 A

Problem Solving: Application
Decision Making

You Decide!

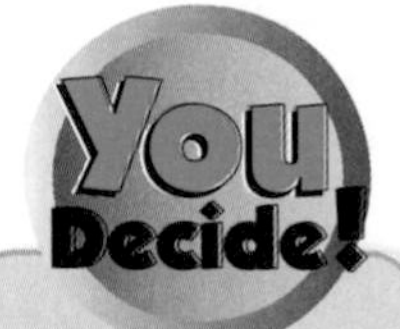

What should the schedule for the Nature Club members be?

What can the Sequoia Nature Club do today? They have from 8:00 A.M. to 5:00 P.M. and must stay together. Every member chose 3 activities and took a separate vote on what type of lunch to have. The tallies show the results.

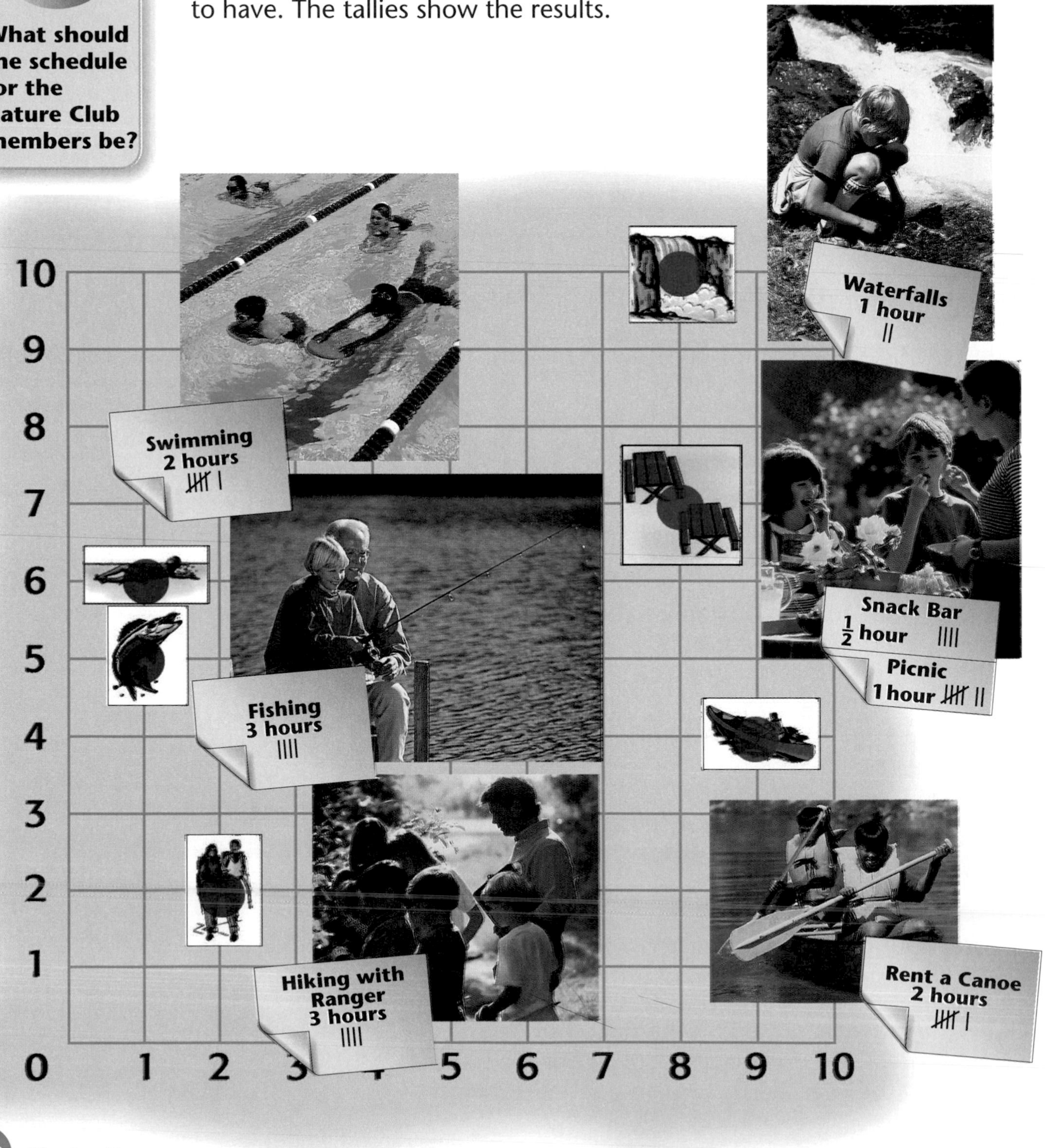

Waterfalls
1 hour
||
Swimming
2 hours
𝍸 |
Snack Bar
$\frac{1}{2}$ hour ||||
Picnic
1 hour 𝍸 ||
Fishing
3 hours
||||
Hiking with
Ranger
3 hours
||||
Rent a Canoe
2 hours
𝍸 |
0 1 2 3 4 5 6 7 8 9 10
1 2 3 4 5 6 7 8 9 10

Read for Understanding

1. Besides lunch, which activity is most popular? least popular?
2. How many members are in the Nature Club? How can you tell?
3. Where do you meet the ranger to go hiking?
4. Which activities will take the longest time to complete? How long?
5. Besides lunch, which activity takes the least amount of time?
6. Which type of lunch is more popular?
7. How much longer does hiking take than swimming?
8. It is a 5-minute walk for each block on the grid map. How many minutes will it take to get from the waterfalls to the picnic area?

Problem Solving

Make Decisions

9. How many hours of the day do you need to plan in your schedule? How can you tell?
10. **What if** you decide to start the day by going on a hike? What time will it be at the end of the hike?
11. If you wanted the hike to be the last activity, when would it have to begin?
12. Why might you choose the less popular choice for lunch for your schedule?
13. You decide to rent a canoe and swim after you see the waterfall. Which should you do first? Why?
14. Could you include all of the activities in the schedule if you decide you want to do them all? Why or why not?
15. Make a list of the things you must think about in order to decide on the day's schedule.
16. Which is more important in deciding on activities, the length of time or the number of votes? Why?
17. Can you rearrange the order of the activities in your schedule without having to change any of your choices?
18. Use the grid on the map to describe the route you should take to follow your schedule.

Your Decision!

What activities should the Nature Club do and when will each activity begin and end? Make a schedule.

Objective: Apply time and data to investigate science concepts.

Problem Solving: Math and Science

Does practice make perfect?

You Will Need
- **puzzle pieces**
- **scissors**
- **timer or clock**

In order to learn something new, you have to practice a lot. Some things you might practice include reciting math facts, playing the violin, and shooting baskets. The more you practice, the better your brain learns a skill.

In this activity, you will explore how your brain learns. You will solve a puzzle several times and see if practice improves how fast you can solve it.

Hypothesize

How many times will you need to repeat a puzzle to master it? How will you know when you have mastered the puzzle?

Procedure

1. Work with a partner. Take turns.
2. Cut out the puzzle pieces.
3. Time how long it takes to finish the first puzzle.
4. Record your data and repeat nine more times.

Data

Copy and complete the chart to record your data.

Attempt	Time to Complete the Puzzle
1	
2	
3	
4	
5	
6	
7	
8	
9	
10	

Your brain has two kinds of memory. Short-term memory helps you remember a new phone number long enough to dial it. Long-term memory helps you remember the words to a song you learned years ago.

Problem Solving

Conclude and Apply

- Describe what happened to the time as you repeated the puzzle over and over.
- How many times did you have to work the puzzle until you mastered it?
- What happened to your time after you mastered the puzzle?
- Make a line graph, comparing attempt number and time. What happened to the line on the graph after you mastered the puzzle?
- Explain how you used your short- and long-term memory to learn the puzzle.

Going Further

1. Repeat the activity, but shoot baskets instead. How many tries does it take until you make a shot? Is it harder to learn a puzzle or shoot a basket? How do you know?
2. Try the puzzle again a week later. Did you remember how to put together the puzzle?

Extra Practice, page 318

Check Your Progress B

Use data from the graphs for problems 1–6. **(pages 110–119)**

1. How many more students visited Grand Canyon than Mesa Verde?
2. What if 24 students visited Glacier Park? How would you show the data on the graph?
3. Which activity do students like the most? the least?
4. How many students like boating the best?
5. What is the range of temperatures?
6. What happened to the average temperature between July and August?

Parks Visited

Yellowstone	▲ ▲ ▲ ▲
Grand Canyon	▲ ▲ ▲ ▲ ▲ ▲
Mesa Verde	▲ ◭

KEY: Each ▲ represents 4 students.

Favorite Vacation Activities

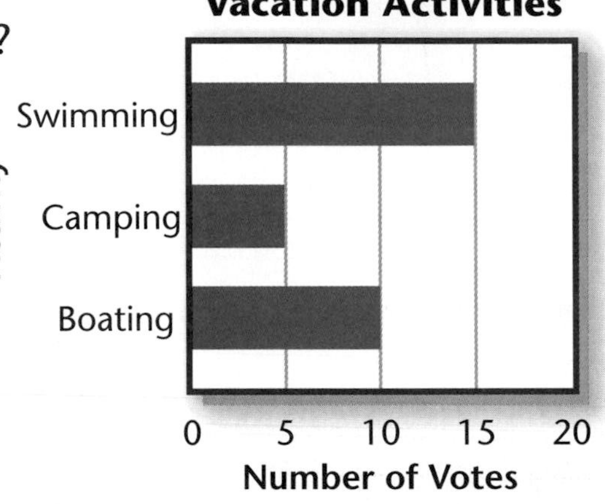

Average Daily Temperature

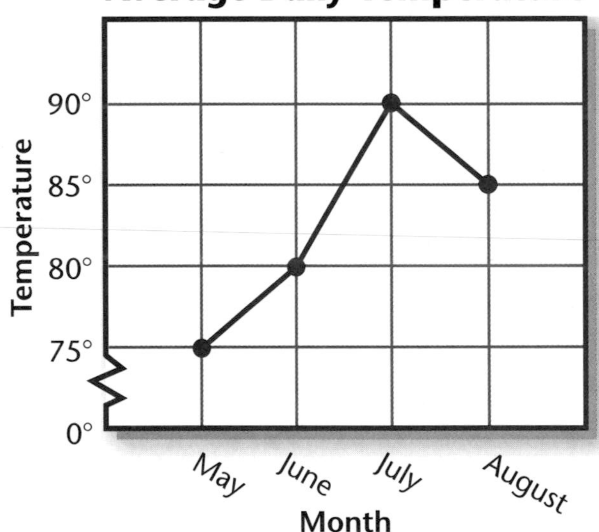

Solve. **(pages 108–119)**

7. Earl needs 40 minutes to wash his car. He then needs 10 minutes to get gas and 15 minutes to drive to his friend's house. Earl must meet his friend at 10:00 A.M. How late can he start to wash his car?
8. The coordinates on a map show the school is at (2, 3). The mall is 2 blocks to the right and 1 block up from the school. What are the coordinates of the mall's location?
9. School starts at 8:15 A.M. Dee wakes up and takes 20 minutes to shower and brush her teeth, 10 minutes to get dressed, 15 minutes to eat breakfast, and 15 minutes to walk to school. How late can Dee get up and still get to school on time?

Journal

10. **Generalize:** Explain how you identify the location of a point on a map using ordered pairs.

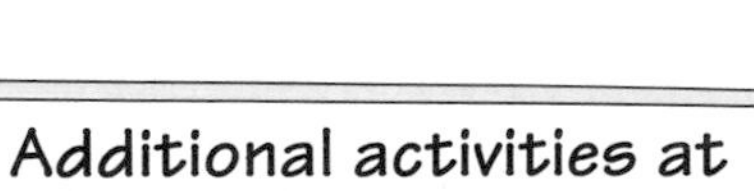

Extra Practice

Tell Time (pages 92–95)

Write the time two ways using A.M. or P.M.

1.

2. 

Tell how much time.

3. 135 minutes = ▮ hours ▮ minutes

4. 45 minutes = ▮ hour

Elapsed Time (pages 96–97)

How much time has passed?

1. Begin: 7:10 A.M.
   End: 8:15 A.M.

2. Begin: 10:30 P.M.
   End: 12:16 A.M.

3. Begin: 12:05 P.M.
   End: 3:49 P.M.

What time will it be in 30 minutes?

4.

5.

6. 

Calendar (pages 98–99)

Use the calendar for September for problems 1 – 3.

1. On what day and date is Labor Day?

2. On what day of the week is September 15?

3. Solve the following problem and identify the missing or extra information: On September 9, Marina went to visit her grandfather in Decatur, Georgia. She traveled on the train for $2\frac{1}{2}$ hours. She will visit her grandfather for 10 days. On what day will she leave Decatur?

September						
Sunday	Monday	Tuesday	Wednesday	Thursday	Friday	Saturday
			1	2	3	4
5	6 Labor Day	7	8	9	10	11
12	13	14	15	16	17	18
19	20	21	22	23	24	25
26	27	28	29	30		

Extra Practice

Line Plots (pages 100–101)

Use data from the line plot for problems 1–3.

Travelers' Survey Results
Number of Miles Driven in 1 Day

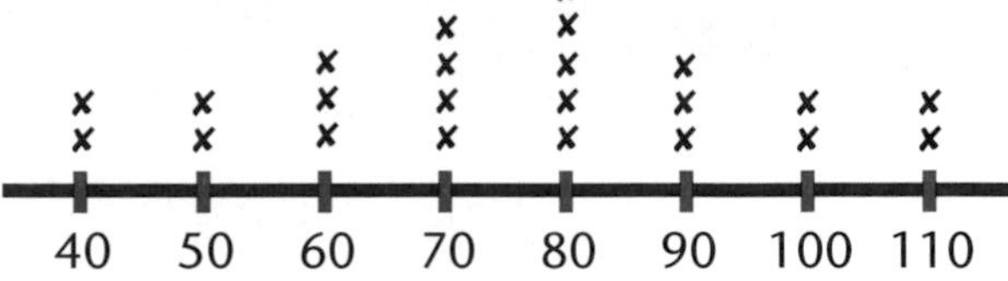

1. How many travelers drove 70 miles in one day?
2. What if you added 1 more traveler for each of 40, 60, and 80 miles in 1 day? How would that change the data?
3. How many travelers drove 80 or more miles in a day?

Range, Median, and Mode (pages 102–103)

Use data from the line plot for problems 1–3.

1. What is the range of the miles driven? How do you know?
2. What is the median of the miles driven? How do you know?
3. What is the mode of the miles driven? How do you know?

Problem Solving: Reading for Math Identify Extra and Missing Information (pages 104–105)

Solve. Identify extra or missing information in each problem.

1. June is taking a late train from her home to visit her cousins. The train leaves Savannah at 11:05 P.M. It arrives in Charleston at 1:36 A.M. on July 13. How long is June's trip?
2. James takes a plane to Sacramento to visit his uncle. He arrives at 7:45 A.M. When did James's plane leave?

Problem Solving: Strategy Work Backward (pages 108–109)

Solve.

1. Ellen takes a bus trip to visit her aunt. The bus leaves at 12:45 P.M. It takes Ellen 45 minutes to get to the station, 10 minutes to buy a ticket, and 15 minutes to shop for some items. What time does Ellen need to leave to catch the 12:45 P.M. bus?
2. Ellen buys a bus ticket for $4.50, a magazine for $3.95, and a can of juice for $0.95. She has $4.25 left. How much money did she start with?

Extra Practice

Explore Pictographs (pages 110–111)

Use data from the pictograph for problems 1–2.

1. How many votes did Sacramento Zoo receive?
2. Which zoo received the least amount of votes?

Favorite California Zoos

Los Angeles Zoo	🐼 🐼 🐼
The Oakland Zoo	🐼 🐼 🐼 🐼 🐼 🐼
Sacramento Zoo	🐼 🐼 🐼 🐼

KEY: Each 🐼 represents 5 votes.

Bar Graphs (pages 112–114)

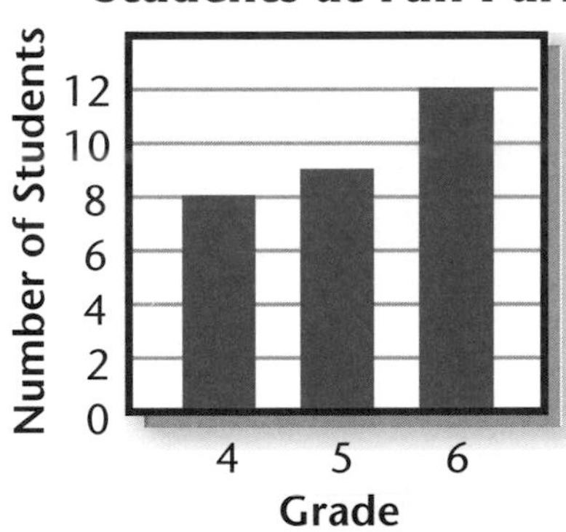

Use data from the bar graph for problems 1–2.

1. How many more children in Grade 6 went to Fun Park than in Grade 5?
2. How many children went to Fun Park in all?

Coordinate Graphing (pages 116–117)

Give the ordered pairs for each place on the grid.

1. Big Chute
2. Roller Coaster
3. Whirl-Around

Name the place at each location.

4. (3, 2)
5. (1, 5)
6. (8, 1)
7. (3, 7)

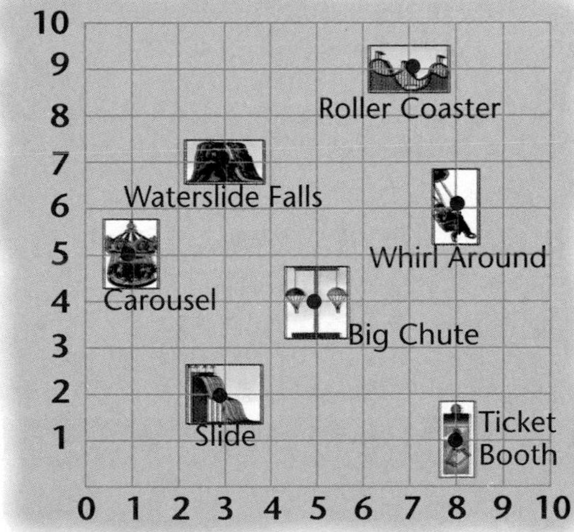

Line Graph (pages 118–119)

Use data from the line graph for problems 1–2.

1. How many inches did the plant grow from Week 1 to Week 2?
2. Between which two weeks did the plant grow the most?

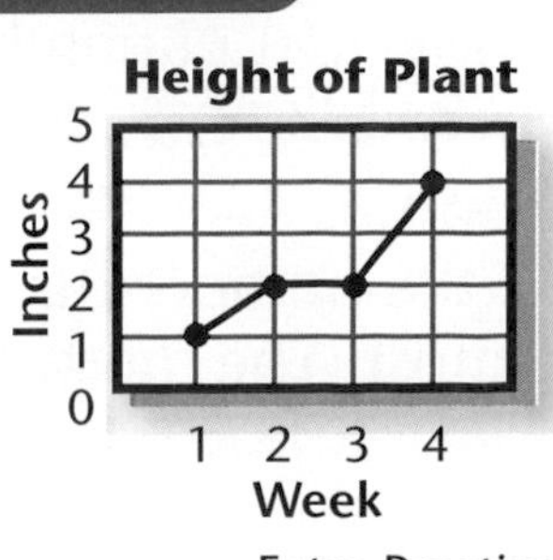

Chapter Study Guide

Language and Math

Math Words

key
pictograph
line graph
mode
range
elapsed time

Complete. Use a word from the list.

1. A graph that uses pictures to show data is called a ____.
2. Part of a graph that tells how many numbers a symbol represents is called a ____.
3. The difference between the greatest and least numbers in a group of numbers is called the ____.
4. ____ is the amount of time that passes from the start of an activity to the end.

Skills and Applications

Tell time and find elapsed time. (pages 92–99)

Example

Find how much time has passed from 10:25 A.M. to 3:15 P.M.

Solution

Count on the hours.
10:25 → 2:25 = 4 h
Count on the minutes.
2:25 → 3:15 = 50 min
Total time: 4 h 50 min

5. Begin time: 9:15 P.M.
   End time: 11:35 A.M.
   Elapsed time:
6. Begin time: 11:45 A.M.
   End time: ■
   Elapsed time: 4 h 25 min

Find range, median, and mode. (pages 102–103)

Example

What is the mode of the following set of numbers:
1, 1, 2, 3, 3, 3, 3, 4, 4, 4, 6

Solution

Find the number that appears the most. The mode is 3.

7. What is the range?
8. What is the median?
9. What would the median be if 6 fives were added to the set?

Collect and organize data in tables and graphs. (pages 100–101, 110–119)

Example

Use the line graph to solve the problem.

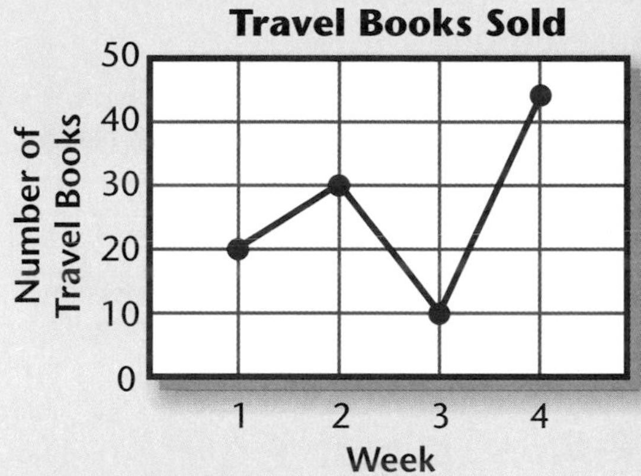

How many books were sold during Week 4?

Solution

Find the dot above Week 4. Look at the number in the scale. It is between 40 and 50. This means 45 books were sold.

10. Use the line graph. How many books were sold during Week 1?

Use data from the table for problems 11–13.

Book Store Survey	
Favorite Type of Book	Votes
Travel	35
Mystery	45
Cookbook	20
Humor	25

11. Make a bar graph to show the results of the survey.

12. **What if** you made this bar graph into a pictograph with a key of 1 📖 = 7 votes? How many 📖 would you use for travel?

13. Draw a coordinate grid with 0–5 scale. How would you show the point (3, 4)?

Use strategies to solve problems. (pages 104–105, 108–109)

Example

Jason gets to work at 9:15 A.M. He left his house and walked 25 minutes to work. What time did he leave his house?

Solution

Think: End time: 9:15 A.M.
Elapsed time: 25 minutes ← Time to walk to work
Start time: 8:50 A.M.
He left his house at 8:50 A.M.

14. Zach wants to go to a 7:15 P.M. movie. It takes him 25 minutes to walk to the theater and 10 minutes to buy a ticket and get popcorn. What time does he need to leave to make the movie on time?

15. Millie made some beaded necklaces. She put 38 beads on each necklace. When she was finished, she had 15 beads left. What missing information do you need to find out how many beads she started with?

Chapter Test

1. Write the time in two ways.

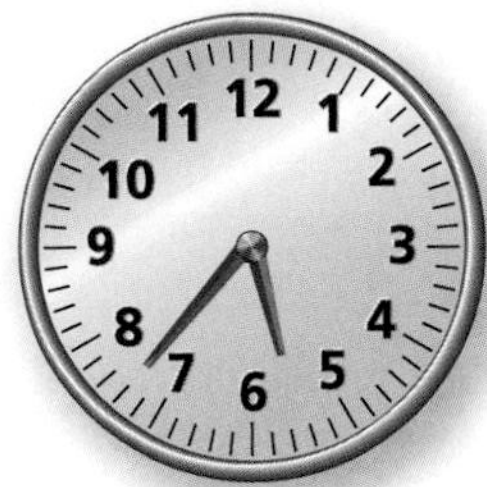

2. How much time has passed?
   Start time: 6:25 P.M.
   End time: 12:05 A.M.
   Elapsed time:

Number of Letters in First Name

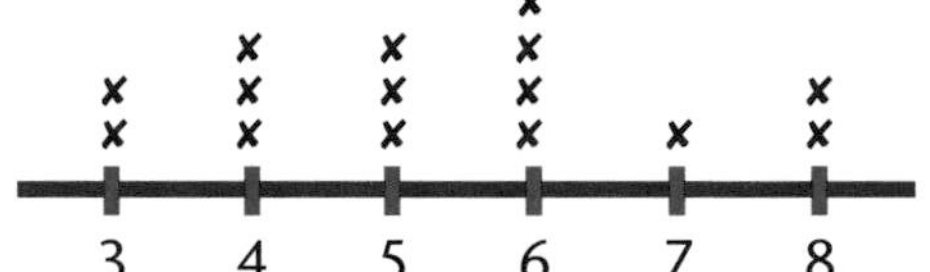

Use data from the line plot for problem 3.

3. Find the median, mode, and range.

Use data from the bar graph for problems 4–5.

4. Which day had the most visitors? the least?

5. How many more visitors were there on Saturday than on Friday?

Visitors at Sea World

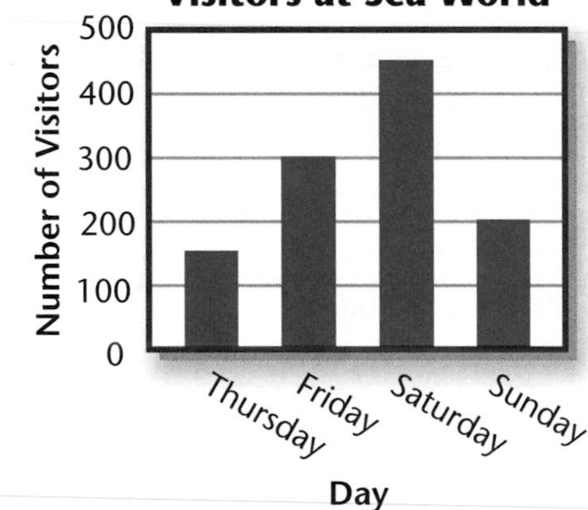

Give the ordered pair for the place on the grid.

6. Lions' Den

Name the place at the location.

7. (1, 5)

Solve.

8. Suppose you were making a pictograph with the following key: 1 🯅 is equal to 2 persons. How many 🯅 would you need to draw to show 7 persons?

9. Nina wants to go to a show at 2:30 P.M. It will take her 1 hour and 15 minutes on the bus to get to the theater and another 10 minutes to buy her ticket. What time does she have to leave to make the show on time?

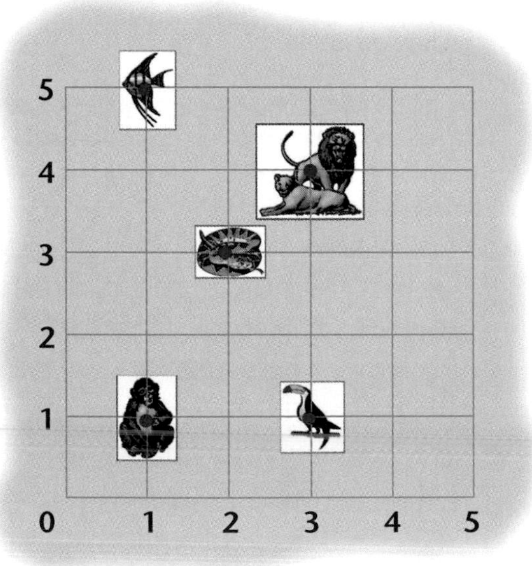

10. Can you solve the following problem? If not, what missing information do you need to solve it? Benjamin bought two tickets to a show. He spent $2.95 on a program. He had $5.15 left. How much money did he have to start with?

Performance Assessment

What are some of the places you travel to? Some might be far away in another part of the country. Others might be in your own town or city.

Make a table like the one shown below that shows 5 places that you have traveled to or hope to travel to. These do not have to be vacation places. You can include travel to a relative's house or perhaps a shopping mall that you like. Include the amount of time it takes to travel to these places.

Place I Travel To	Time It Takes to Get There
Amusement Park	30 minutes

After you make your table, use the data to make a bar graph. Draw a conclusion based on the data in the graph.

A Good Answer

- shows a completed table with a time given for each destination.
- shows a correctly drawn bar graph with the data from the table displayed.
- has a reasonable conclusion based on the data in the graph.

You may want to save your work in your portfolio.

Assessment

Enrichment

Stem-and-Leaf Plots

15	35	60
9	59	33
33	67	39
63	5	13
	13	

A stem-and-leaf plot is another way of showing data.

The chart at the right shows the ages of all the people in Jay's extended family.

You can use a stem-and-leaf plot to organize the data. Use the numbers in the chart.

First, you draw lines for the "stem" and the "leaf."

The "stems" are the tens digits. List each different tens digits once.

Stem	Leaf
0	
1	
3	
5	
6	

The "leaves" are the ones digits. List each ones digit. List them in order.

Stem	Leaf
0	5 9
1	3 3 5
3	3 3 5 9
5	9
6	0 3 7

Compare the chart and the stem-and-leaf plot. Can you see how the stem-and-leaf plot organizes the data?

1. How is the stem-and-leaf plot easier to read than the chart?

Make a stem-and-leaf plot for each set of data.

2. Test Scores: 72, 75, 78, 82, 85, 89, 90, 90, 91, 93, 95, 99

3. Temperatures: 56, 58, 59, 59, 62, 65, 66, 66, 66, 70, 73, 79, 82, 87

4. Heights: 42, 44, 44, 46, 48, 51, 53, 53, 55, 56, 60, 61

5. Number of Students: 19, 20, 23, 24, 25, 25, 26, 27, 30, 30, 31, 32

Test-Taking Tips

On some tests you will need to use given information to make a graph and solve problems.

Erin's parents have made a line graph showing her height on her birthday.

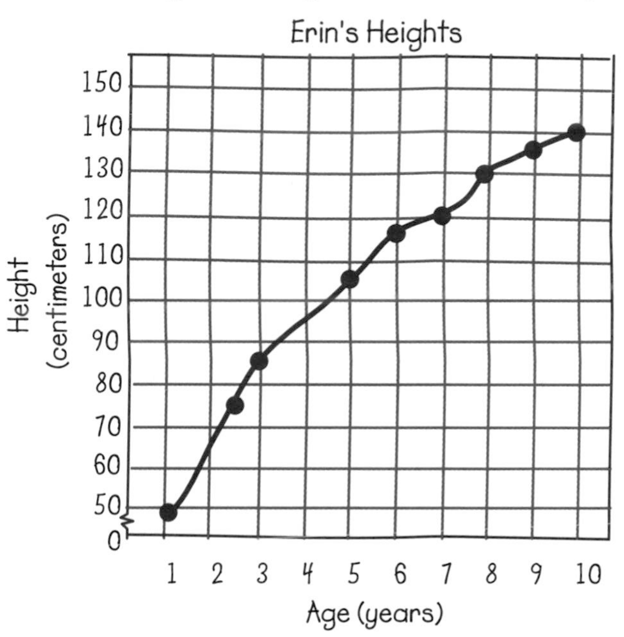

Check for Success

Before turning in a test, go back one last time to check.

- ☑ I understood and answered the questions asked.
- ☑ I checked my work for errors.
- ☑ My answers make sense.

Use data from the table for problems 1–3.

1. Make a line graph. Label your graph.

Money Raised	$125	$130	$150	$135	$160	$160	$180
Years	1995	1996	1997	1998	1999	2000	2001

2. In which two years did they raise the same amount of money?

3. Write a statement describing the data in the graph.

Use data from the table for problems 4–6.

4. Make a line graph. Label your graph.

Temperature	40°	45°	45°	50°	55°	60°	60°
Time	7 A.M.	8 A.M.	9 A.M.	10 A.M.	11 A.M.	12 noon	1 A.M.

5. When was the lowest temperature recorded?

6. Draw a conclusion based on the graph.

Test Prep

Spiral Review and Test Prep

Chapters 1–3

Choose the correct answer.

Number Sense

1. What is 25,843 rounded to the nearest thousand?
   - A. 24,000
   - B. 24,500
   - C. 25,000
   - D. 26,000

2. Marion has a twenty-dollar bill. She buys a train ticket for $8.35 and a magazine for $3.79. How much change does she get?
   - F. $16.21
   - G. $11.65
   - H. $8.86
   - J. $7.86

3. What is the best estimate for 6,789 + 1,437?
   - A. 8,000
   - B. 7,000
   - C. 6,000
   - D. 1,000

4. Which is the same as 90 minutes?
   - F. 1 hour, 15 minutes
   - G. 2 hours
   - H. 3 half hours
   - J. 4 quarter hours

Measurement and Geometry

5. About how much water would you need to fill a bathtub?
   - A. 50 gallons
   - B. 50 quarts
   - C. 50 pints
   - D. 50 cups

6. About how much would a math book weigh?
   - F. About 2 ounces
   - G. About 5 ounces
   - H. About 2 pounds
   - J. About 20 pounds

7. First-class airfare from Chicago to Los Angeles costs $948.79. Coach fare is $515.25. About how much do you save if you fly coach?
   - A. About $50.00
   - B. About $400.00
   - C. About $500.00
   - D. About $600.00

8. What is the shape on the side of a cube?
   - F. Square
   - G. Circle
   - H. Pentagon
   - J. Triangle

Statistics, Data Analysis, and Probability

Use data in the pictograph for problems 9–12.

Favorite Vacation States

California	☺ ☺ ☺ ☺ ☺ ☺ ☺ ◐
New York	☺ ☺ ☺ ☺ ☺ ☺
Texas	☺ ☺ ☺ ☺ ☺
Florida	☺ ☺ ☺ ☺ ☺ ◐

KEY: One ☺ represents 2 persons, half ◐ represents 1 person.

9. How many people chose Florida as their favorite vacation state?

A. 5 **C.** 10
B. $5\frac{1}{2}$ **D.** 11

10. Which state got 15 votes?

F. Florida **H.** New York
G. Texas **J.** California

11. How many more people like California than New York?

A. $1\frac{1}{2}$ **C.** 6
B. 3 **D.** Not Here

12. If three more people voted for Texas, how many more ☺ would you add to the graph?

F. $1\frac{1}{2}$ **H.** 6
G. 3 **J.** 4

Mathematical Reasoning

13. There are 8 rows of seats in a minibus. Each row has 4 seats. Which number sentence shows how to find how many seats in all?

A. $8 - 4 = 4$ **C.** $8 \times 4 = 32$
B. $8 + 4 = 13$ **D.** $8 \div 4 = 2$

14. The sum of two numbers is 500. One addend is 50 more than the other addend. What are the two numbers?

F. 250 and 250 **H.** 225 and 275
G. 225 and 300 **J.** 200 and 300

15. Jeff works out for 10 minutes on Monday, 20 minutes on Tuesday, and 40 minutes on Wednesday. If he continues the pattern, how many minutes will he work out on Thursday?

A. 50 minutes **C.** 75 minutes
B. 60 minutes **D.** 80 minutes

16. Beth paints 4 rows of squares in a design. There are 4 squares in each row. Each square has 2 circles. How many circles are in the design? Explain how you found your answer.

CHAPTER 4

Multiplication and Division Facts

Theme: Collectible Treasures

Use the Data

Dolls from Around the World

Type of Doll	Number of Tallies
Kachina Dolls	𝍸 ||||
Peruvian Dancer Dolls	𝍸 |||
Noh Dolls	||||
Zulu Dolls	𝍸
Russian Nesting Dolls	||||

- If you have 5 shelves on which to place these dolls, how could you arrange them so there is an equal number on each shelf? How can you use multiplication or division to solve the problem?

What You Will Learn

In this chapter you will learn how to
- multiply facts through 12.
- divide facts through 12.
- use the properties of multiplication.
- use inverse operations.
- use strategies to solve problems.

Objective: Review the meaning of multiplication.

4•1 The Meaning of Multiplication

Algebra & functions **Learn**

The Science Club gathers rock samples and displays them in a box. How many rocks are there?

Math Words

array objects or symbols displayed in rows and columns

factors numbers that are multiplied to give a product

product the answer in multiplication

Example

You can use multiplication to solve this problem.

Make an **array** *to model the problem.*

Write what the array shows:
4 rows of 3 counters.

Write a multiplication sentence.

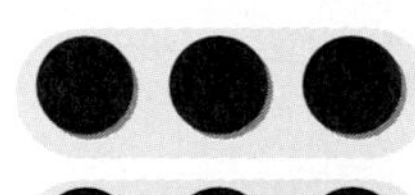

$4 \times 3 = 12$ (4 ↑ **factor**, 3 ↑ factor, 12 ↑ **product**) or

$$\begin{array}{r} 4 \\ \times 3 \\ \hline 12 \end{array}$$

4 ← factor
×3 ← factor
12 ← product

They gathered 12 rocks in all.

Try It **Find each product and write a multiplication sentence.**

1. 4 × 4 **2.** 2 × 8 **3.** 5 × 3 **4.** 1 × 9 **5.** 7 × 3

Explain how to model 6 groups of 3. Show how you find the total and record your work.

Practice **Find each product.**

6. $\begin{array}{r} 4 \\ \times 5 \\ \hline \end{array}$ 7. $\begin{array}{r} 5 \\ \times 9 \\ \hline \end{array}$ 8. $\begin{array}{r} 6 \\ \times 2 \\ \hline \end{array}$ 9. $\begin{array}{r} 8 \\ \times 3 \\ \hline \end{array}$ 10. $\begin{array}{r} 7 \\ \times 1 \\ \hline \end{array}$ 11. $\begin{array}{r} 6 \\ \times 4 \\ \hline \end{array}$

12. 2×4 13. 3×8 14. 5×6 15. 4×9 16. 7×4

17. 5×7 18. 8×5 19. 6×3 20. 4×8 21. 2×3

Algebra & functions **Write the number that makes each sentence true.**

22. $2 \times (k \times 4) = 24$ 23. $(m \times 7) \times 5 = 35$ 24. $4 \times (2 \times h) = 40$

Problem Solving

25. Lisa arranged her books on 3 shelves with 9 books on each shelf. How many books does Lisa have?

26. Lil and Will each have a rock collection. Lil has 36 rocks. Will has 42 rocks. Who has more rocks? how many more?

27. **Analyze:** Hunter finds the product of 5×7 by adding $7 + 7 + 7 + 7 + 7$. Will he get the correct product? Explain.

28. In Karina's club, there are 5 tables with 5 people at each table. How many people are in Karina's club?

Spiral Review and Test Prep

Give the value of each underlined digit.

29. 30,<u>9</u>87 30. 7<u>8</u>8,994 31. 1,043,2<u>2</u>7 32. 20,<u>0</u>32,648

Choose the correct answer.

33. What is the difference when 30,000 is subtracted from 150,000?
  - A. 1,200
  - B. 12,000
  - C. 120,000
  - D. 1,200,000

34. What is the range for this set of test grades?
83, 70, 81, 94, 70, 85, 79
  - F. 24
  - G. 70
  - H. 80.2
  - J. 81

Extra Practice, page 179

4·2 Properties of Multiplication

Algebra & functions

Learn

Math Words
- Commutative Property of Multiplication
- Identity Property of Multiplication
- Zero Property of Multiplication

Beads can be used as decorations, jewelry, and money. What if you put these beads into 5 groups of 3? Would the total number of beads stay the same? What if there is only 1 row of 5? What if there are 0 rows of 5?

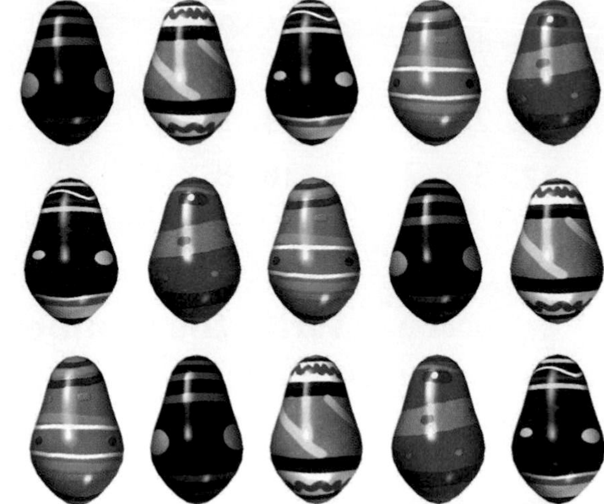

Example

You can use these properties of multiplication to answer the questions.

Commutative Property

The order of the numbers does not affect the product.

3 groups of 5 beads = 15 beads $3 \times 5 = 15$

5 groups of 3 beads = 15 beads $5 \times 3 = 15$

The number of beads stays the same.

Identity Property

The product of 1 and a number is the number.

1 row of 5 beads = 5 beads

$1 \times 5 = 5$

Zero Property

The product of 0 and a number is zero.

0 rows of 5 beads = 0 beads

$0 \times 5 = 0$

Try It **Multiply. Then use the Commutative Property to write a different multiplication sentence.**

1. 5×4 **2.** 8×1 **3.** 7×4 **4.** 0×3 **5.** 6×6

Sum it Up! How can the properties of multiplication help you remember facts? Give an example.

Practice **Multiply. Then use the Commutative Property to write a different multiplication sentence.**

6. 7×3 **7.** 9×5 **8.** 7×1 **9.** 0×0 **10.** 1×6

11. 1×4 **12.** 3×8 **13.** 6×5 **14.** 7×0 **15.** 7×6

16. 2×5 **17.** 6×3 **18.** 1×1 **19.** 5×4 **20.** 0×9

Write + or × to make each sentence true.

21. 4 ● 4 = 8 **22.** 8 ● 2 = 16 **23.** 5 ● 1 = 6 **24.** 5 ● 5 = 25

★**25.** 4 ● 2 = 2 ● 6 ★**26.** 3 ● 1 = 1 ● 4 ★**27.** 4 ● 3 = 6 ● 2 ★**28.** 3 ● 0 = 3 ● 1

Problem Solving

29. **Social Studies:** The Chinese abacus uses beads to do calculations. Write two multiplication sentences to show how many beads are in the top part of the abacus.

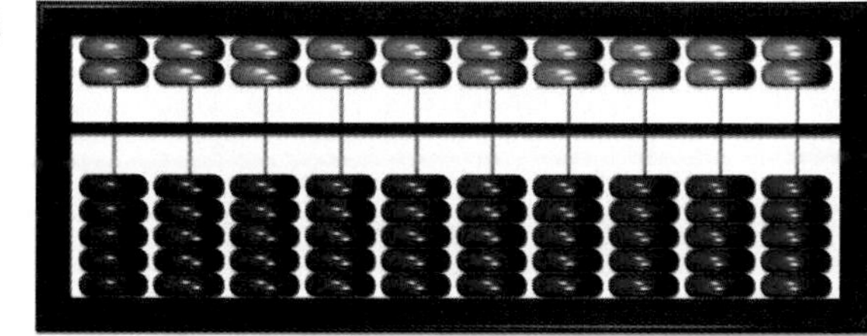

30. Lani uses 538 beads to make a belt. She has 1,487 beads left in the box. How many beads did she have to start with?

31. **Art:** Temari balls are used as decoration in Japan. Yoshi is putting beads on his Temari ball. He puts on 3 rows of beads with 7 beads in each row. What other way can he put the beads in equal groups and still have 21 beads?

32. **Compare:** How are the Identity Properties of Addition and Multiplication alike? How are they different?

33. Kayla is using beads to make 4 bracelets. She puts 8 beads on each bracelet. How many beads does she use?

Spiral Review and Test Prep

Round each to the nearest hundred thousand.

34. 476,900 **35.** 309,725 **36.** 115,987 **37.** 750,750

Choose the correct answer.

38. Ronnie buys lunch for $6.79. He pays for it with a ten-dollar bill. What is his change?

A. $4.31 **C.** $4.21
B. $3.21 **D.** Not Here

39. Anita has 6 quarters, 3 dimes, 4 nickels, and 2 pennies. How much money does she have?

F. $1.98 **H.** $2.00
G. $1.80 **J.** $2.02

Extra Practice, page 179

Objective: Review multiplying by 2, 3, 4, and 6.

4-3 Multiply by 2, 3, 4, and 6

Learn

Math Words

skip-count to count by twos, fives, tens, and so on

multiple the product of any two whole numbers

David collects stamps from foreign countries. He displays the stamps in 2 groups of 5 stamps each. How many stamps does he have in all?

Example 1

Find: 2×5

To help you recall this fact quickly, you can **skip-count**.
Skip-count by 5s two times to find the total number of stamps.

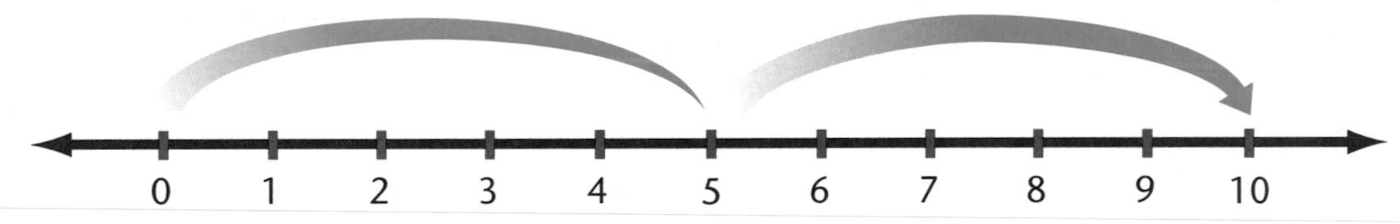

The numbers 5 and 10 are **multiples** of 5.

There are 10 stamps in all.

What if David has 4 album pages with 3 stamps on each page? How many stamps are there in all?

Example 2

Find: 4×3

To help recall these facts quickly, you can double a known fact to find a new fact.

$$4 \times 3 = 2 \times 3 + 2 \times 3$$
$$6 + 6 = 12$$

So $4 \times 3 = 12$.

There are 12 stamps in all.

David has 3 pages of an album and puts 5 postcards on each page. How many postcards are there in all?

What if David has 6 pages with 4 postcards on each page? How many postcards are in his album?

Example 3

Find: 3×5

You can use a known fact.

3 groups of 5 = 2 groups of 5 plus 5

$3 \times 5 = 2 \times 5 + 5$

$= 10 + 5 = 15$

There are 15 cards in the album.

Example 4

Find: 6×4

You can double a known fact.

$6 \times 4 = (3 \times 4) + (3 \times 4)$

$12 + 12 = 24$

There are 24 cards.

Try It **Write a multiplication sentence to solve.**

1.

2.

3.

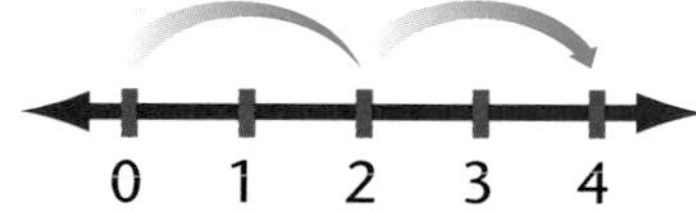

Multiply. Show your methods.

4. 3×8
5. 6×3
6. 7×3
7. 6×2
8. 2×8
9. 3×9
10. 5×1
11. 5×5
12. 3×2
13. 6×6
14. 7×8
15. 6×1
16. 5×1
17. 6×2
18. 4×7
19. 5×8
20. 4×2
15. 2×7

Show how you can double a known fact to find 4×6.

Practice Write a multiplication sentence to solve.

22.

23.

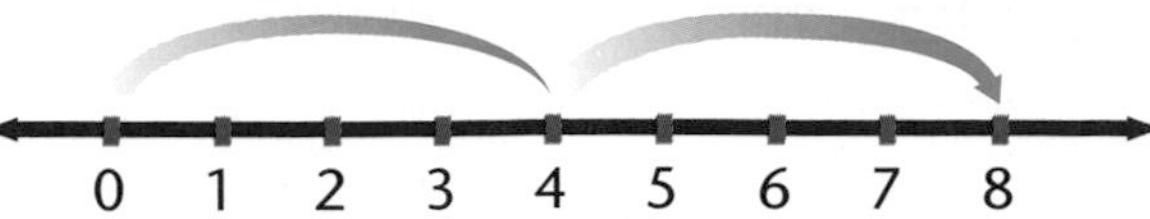

Multiply.

24. 3×4 **25.** 2×9 **26.** 6×6 **27.** 3×2 **28.** 2×8

29. 4×7 **30.** 4×5 **31.** 2×9 **32.** 4×9 **33.** 6×4

34. $\begin{array}{r} 3 \\ \times 6 \\ \hline \end{array}$ **35.** $\begin{array}{r} 4 \\ \times 8 \\ \hline \end{array}$ **36.** $\begin{array}{r} 4 \\ \times 0 \\ \hline \end{array}$ **37.** $\begin{array}{r} 2 \\ \times 2 \\ \hline \end{array}$ **38.** $\begin{array}{r} 7 \\ \times 4 \\ \hline \end{array}$

39. $\begin{array}{r} 5 \\ \times 2 \\ \hline \end{array}$ **40.** $\begin{array}{r} 7 \\ \times 6 \\ \hline \end{array}$ **41.** $\begin{array}{r} 4 \\ \times 3 \\ \hline \end{array}$ **42.** $\begin{array}{r} 8 \\ \times 4 \\ \hline \end{array}$ **43.** $\begin{array}{r} 9 \\ \times 6 \\ \hline \end{array}$ **44.** $\begin{array}{r} 6 \\ \times 8 \\ \hline \end{array}$

45. $\begin{array}{r} 3 \\ \times 3 \\ \hline \end{array}$ **46.** $\begin{array}{r} 9 \\ \times 4 \\ \hline \end{array}$ **47.** $\begin{array}{r} 7 \\ \times 6 \\ \hline \end{array}$ **48.** $\begin{array}{r} 2 \\ \times 6 \\ \hline \end{array}$ **49.** $\begin{array}{r} 8 \\ \times 2 \\ \hline \end{array}$ **50.** $\begin{array}{r} 4 \\ \times 6 \\ \hline \end{array}$

★**51.** $(2 + 2) \times 9$ ★**52.** $(8 - 2) \times 3$ ★**53.** $6 \times (3 + 2)$

Algebra & functions

54. If  = 6, then how many is   ?

55. If = 4, then how many is ?

56.

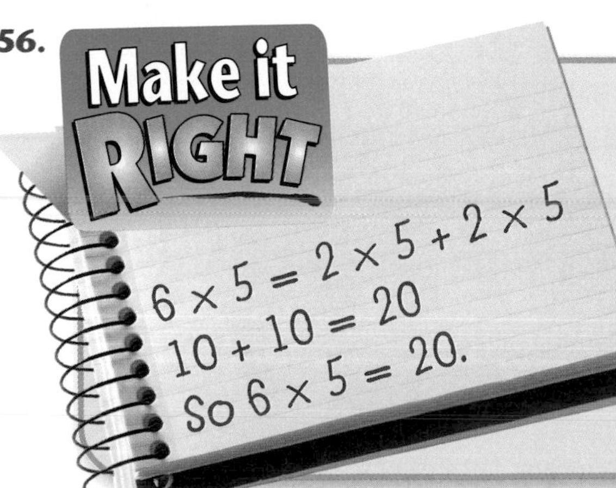

Peter finds 6×5. Here is how he doubled a known fact to find the product. What mistake did he make? Show how to correct it.

Problem Solving

Use data from the sign for problems 57–58.

57. Postcards come in packages of 9. If Harley buys 6 packages, how many postcards does he have? How much change will he get from $20.00?

58. Samuel buys 6 packs of postcards and Nathan buys 4 packs. How much does each pay?

59. A box of postcards has 8 cards in it. How many cards are in 6 boxes?

60. Aunt Holly has been collecting postcards for 20 years. She has 3,569 cards in her collection. How many more cards does she need to collect to have 10,000 cards?

61. Sally spent $0.86 on postcards. She has $2.89 left. How much money did she start with?

62. **Explain** how you can find 9×9 using known facts for 3.

63. **Analyze:** Jorge uses subtraction to find other facts. To find 4×8, he thinks, "$5 \times 8 = 40$, and $40 - 8 = 32$, so $4 \times 8 = 32$." Explain why this works.

Spiral Review and Test Prep

64. $\begin{array}{r} 382 \\ +486 \\ \hline \end{array}$ **65.** $\begin{array}{r} 713 \\ -276 \\ \hline \end{array}$ **66.** $\begin{array}{r} 15{,}782 \\ -\ 9{,}467 \\ \hline \end{array}$ **67.** $\begin{array}{r} \$38.96 \\ +\ \ 9.78 \\ \hline \end{array}$ **68.** $\begin{array}{r} 3{,}007 \\ -\ \ 849 \\ \hline \end{array}$

Choose the correct answer.

69. Shawna organized her doll collection. She started at 11:15 A.M. and finished at 1:20 P.M. How much time did she spend on this task?

A. 2 hours 15 minutes
B. 1 hour 5 minutes
C. 5 minutes
D. Not Here

70. What is the median for this set of numbers?

$8, $10, $8, $10, $5, $5, $8

F. $5
G. $8
H. $10
J. Not Here

Extra Practice, page 179

Objective: Review multiplying by 5 and 10.

4·4 Multiply by 5 and 10

Learn

Quilts are made from a collection of squares of fabric that are sewn together. When the quilt is finished, it will have 5 rows of 5 squares each. How many squares of fabric are in the quilt?

Example 1

Multiply 5×5 to find the number of fabric squares.

To recall this fact quickly, you can skip-count by fives.

The numbers 5, 10, 15, 20, and 25 are multiples of 5.

There are 25 squares of fabric in the quilt.

What if there are 4 rows of 10 squares each? How many squares are in the quilt?

Example 2

Find 10×4 to solve.

You can use mental math to find the number of squares.
Think: 4 tens = 40

There are 40 squares of fabric in the quilt.

Try It

Multiply. Show your methods.

1. 5×9
2. 3×10
3. 7×5
4. 10×6

How does skip-counting help you multiply?

Practice **Multiply.**

5. 10×1 6. 4×8 7. 4×9 8. 2×10 9. 5×8

10. 3×10 11. 7×3 12. 9×5 13. 5×3 14. 5×2

15. 10×10 16. 6×8 17. 10×7 18. 6×10 19. 5×5

20. $\begin{array}{r} 5 \\ \times 3 \\ \hline \end{array}$ 21. $\begin{array}{r} 6 \\ \times 5 \\ \hline \end{array}$ 22. $\begin{array}{r} 10 \\ \times 6 \\ \hline \end{array}$ 23. $\begin{array}{r} 5 \\ \times 7 \\ \hline \end{array}$ 24. $\begin{array}{r} 8 \\ \times 5 \\ \hline \end{array}$ ★25. $\begin{array}{r} 15 \\ \times 10 \\ \hline \end{array}$ ★26. $\begin{array}{r} 70 \\ \times 5 \\ \hline \end{array}$

Tell whether the number is a multiple of 2, 5, or 10.

27. 8 28. 12 29. 15 30. 25 31. 20

Problem Solving

Use data from *Did You Know?* for problems 32–33.

32. Suppose that 25,968 of the individual quilts came from the United States. About how many quilts would be from other countries?

33. **Create a problem** using the information in *Did You Know?* Solve it. Then give it to another student to solve.

34. If all squares are the same, which is larger—a quilt that has 6 rows of 5 squares, or a quilt that has 9 rows of 3 squares? Explain.

35. **Analyze:** What happens when you multiply an even number by 5? an odd number? What patterns do you notice?

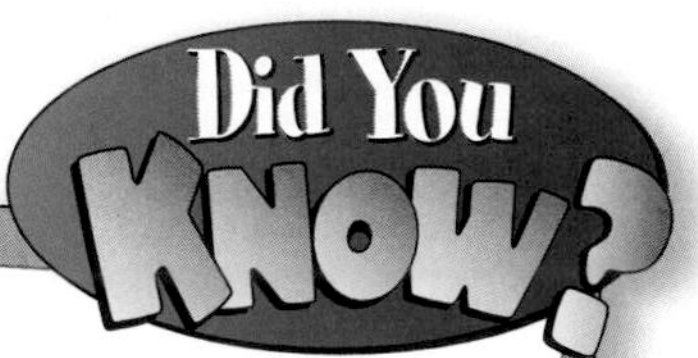

The largest collection of quilts in the world is made up of over 42,000 individual quilts from different countries. Altogether the quilts take up 16 football fields and weigh over 53 tons.

Spiral Review and Test Prep

36. $937 - 414$ 37. $787 - 354$ 38. $5,499 - 459$ 39. $3,976 - 545$

Choose the correct answer.

40. In a pictograph, ▣ stands for 5 quilts. How many quilts does  stand for?

A. 5 C. 25

B. 40 D. 50

41. Using the information in problem 40, which shows 25 quilts?

F. ▣▣▣▣

G. 

H. ▣▣▣

J. Not Here

Objective: Review multiplying by 7, 8, and 9.

4•5 Multiply by 7, 8, and 9

Learn

Raoul's shell collection is displayed in a showcase. He has 7 showcases. He puts the number of shells shown in each showcase. How many seashells does Raoul have in all?

Example 1

Find: 7×5

To help you recall a fact, you can add to a known fact.

$6 \times 5 = 30$

Think: 6 groups of 5 + 5

$30 + 5 = 35$

So $7 \times 5 = 35$.

Raoul has 35 seashells.

Example 2

Find: 8×6

You can double a fact with a factor of 4 to find a product with a factor of 8.

Think: $8 \times 6 = (4 \times 6) + (4 \times 6) = 24 + 24 = 48$

So $8 \times 6 = 48$.

Example 3

Find: 9×5

You can use a fact with a factor of 10 to find a product with a factor of 9.

Think: 10 groups of 5 − 5

$10 \times 5 = 50$

$50 - 5 = 45$

So $9 \times 5 = 45$.

Try It

Multiply. Show your methods.

1. 7×8 **2.** 9×7 **3.** 8×8 **4.** 9×10

What strategy would you use to multiply 9×9?

Practice Multiply.

5. 7×6	**6.** 8×6	**7.** 7×4	**8.** 8×9	**9.** 9×9
10. 7×7	**11.** 7×5	**12.** 9×5	**13.** 8×4	**14.** 8×3
15. 8×8	**16.** 7×8	**17.** 9×7	**18.** 8×10	**19.** 5×5
20. 0×9	**21.** 6×8	**22.** 6×9	**23.** 0×7	**24.** 7×9
25. 6×6	**26.** 10×2	**27.** 6×7	**28.** 8×0	**29.** 9×4

Algebra & functions **Find the rule. Then complete the table.**

30.

Rule: ■						
0	1	2	3	4	5	6
0	7	14	21	■	■	■

31.

Rule: ■						
0	1	2	3	4	5	6
0	8	16	24	■	■	■

Problem Solving

Use data from the chart for problem 32.

32. Science: Invertebrates are animals without backbones. Most shells once belonged to one of the invertebrates listed in the table. About how many species of shelled invertebrates are there in all?

33. Raoul has 8 starfish in his collection. Each starfish has 5 "arms." How many arms are there on all his starfish?

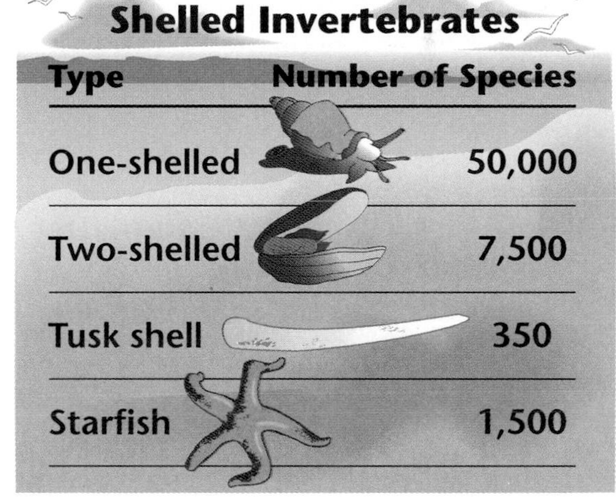

Shelled Invertebrates

Type	Number of Species
One-shelled	50,000
Two-shelled	7,500
Tusk shell	350
Starfish	1,500

34. Analyze: Lisa doubled a product twice to find the product 8×5. What product did she double? Explain.

Spiral Review and Test Prep

Round each to the nearest ten.

35. 838 **36.** 5,641 **37.** 6,995 **38.** $156.50

Choose the correct answer.

39. Which time is the same as 4:15?

- **A.** Fifteen minutes to five
- **B.** A quarter after four
- **C.** Four-thirty
- **D.** Fifteen minutes to four

40. Which is 35,018 in expanded form?

- **F.** $30,000 + 5,000 + 100 + 8$
- **G.** $3,000 + 500 + 10 + 8$
- **H.** $30,000 + 500 + 10 + 8$
- **J.** Not Here

Extra Practice, page 180

Objective: Make a judgment to decide the best operation to use.

4·6 Problem Solving: Reading for Math

Choose an Operation

Ella Sticks with Gift

Read Ella collects stickers. She received 6 packs of stickers as a gift. Each pack contains 8 stickers. How many stickers did Ella receive altogether?

READING SKILL ▶

Make a Judgment

When you make a judgment, you decide something using what you know and the information given in the problem.

- **What do you know?** How many packs she received; How many stickers are in each pack
- **What do you need to find?** Total number of stickers
- **What judgment is called for?** Which operation to use

MATH SKILL ▶

Choose the Operation

Understanding what the problem is asking you to find can help you decide which operation to use.

Plan To find the total you can add repeatedly, or you can multiply once. So multiplication is the best operation.

Solve Ella has 6 packs of stickers. There are 8 stickers in each pack.

$6 \times 8 = 48$ Ella received a total of 48 stickers.

Look Back

- How can you check your answer?

How do you choose which operation to use when solving a problem?

Practice **Solve. Tell how you chose the operation.**

1. Ella has 318 stickers in her collection. Her friend, Myra, has 279 stickers in her collection. What is the total number of stickers in the girls' collections?

2. Rory bought 5 packs of sports stickers. Each pack contains 8 stickers. How many stickers did Rory buy?

Use data from the table for problems 3–7.

3. How many rainbow stickers does the Sticker Shack have?

4. Max bought all the sports car stickers at the Sticker Shack. How many stickers did he buy?

5. How many packs of frog and kitten stickers are at the Sticker Shack altogether?

6. Sara bought 1 pack each of butterfly, frog, and rainbow stickers. How many stickers did Sara buy?

7. Which two types of stickers does the Sticker Shack have an equal number of?

Sticker Inventory

Sticker Type	Number of Packs	Stickers in Each Pack
Butterflies	9	4
Frogs	7	8
Kittens	8	7
Rainbows	10	6
Sports cars	9	9

8. Choose reasonable numbers to complete the problem. Solve it.

Jill buys ▮ rolls of star stickers. There are ▮ stickers in each roll. How many stickers did Jill buy?

Spiral Review and Test Prep

Choose the correct answer.

Al has 6 albums full of stickers. Each album has 10 pages. How many pages are there altogether?

9. Which is true?
   - A. There are 6 pages in each album.
   - B. Al has 60 albums full of stickers.
   - C. The albums have 60 pages altogether.

10. Which number sentence can you use to solve the problem?
    - F. $10 - 6 = 4$
    - G. $10 + 6 = 16$
    - H. $10 \times 6 = 60$

Extra Practice, page 180

Objective: Review patterns in the multiplication table.

4·7 Multiplication Table and Patterns

Algebra & functions

Learn

Math Words

square number the product of a number multiplied by itself

prime number a whole number greater than 1 with only itself and 1 as factors

"This postcard completes the 7th page of my scrapbook!" said Victoria. If each page has 8 postcards, how many postcards does Victoria have in the scrapbook?

×	0	1	2	3	4	5	6	7	8	9	10	11	12
0	0	0	0	0	0	0	0	0	0	0	0	0	0
1	0	1	2	3	4	5	6	7	8	9	10	11	12
2	0	2	4	6	8	10	12	14	16	18	20	22	24
3	0	3	6	9	12	15	18	21	24	27	30	33	36
4	0	4	8	12	16	20	24	28	32	36	40	44	48
5	0	5	10	15	20	25	30	35	40	45	50	55	60
6	0	6	12	18	24	30	36	42	48	54	60	66	72
7	0	7	14	21	28	35	42	49	56	63	70	77	84
8	0	8	16	24	32	40	48	56	64	72	80	88	96
9	0	9	18	27	36	45	54	63	72	81	90	99	108
10	0	10	20	30	40	50	60	70	80	90	100	110	120
11	0	11	22	33	44	55	66	77	88	99	110	121	132
12	0	12	24	36	48	60	72	84	96	108	120	132	144

Example 1

Find: 7×8

Look at where the 7s row and the 8s column meet in the table.

$7 \times 8 = 56$

Victoria has 56 postcards.

In the table, the pattern of **square numbers** is shown in red. The pattern of **prime numbers** is shown in blue.

Try It **Copy and complete the table.**

1. 5×5 **2.** 6×4 **3.** 7×5 **4.** 9×3 **5.** 8×4

Sum it Up What pattern do you see wherever you find the row and column or the column and row for any two factors? What property does this illustrate?

Practice **Multiply.**

6. 6 × 9　　7. 11 × 4　　8. 8 × 5　　9. 9 × 10　　10. 8 × 7

11. 6 × 6　　12. 5 × 12　　13. 9 × 3　　14. 7 × 7　　15. 10 × 11

16. $\begin{array}{r}10\\ \times\ 0\\ \hline\end{array}$　　17. $\begin{array}{r}9\\ \times 1\\ \hline\end{array}$　　18. $\begin{array}{r}11\\ \times\ 3\\ \hline\end{array}$　　19. $\begin{array}{r}12\\ \times\ 6\\ \hline\end{array}$　　20. $\begin{array}{r}8\\ \times 8\\ \hline\end{array}$　　21. $\begin{array}{r}12\\ \times 12\\ \hline\end{array}$

Use the table to solve.

22. Which columns have only even numbers?

23. Which rows have only even numbers?

24. What pattern do you see in the 2, 4, and 8 columns?

25. What pattern do you see in the 5 and 10 columns?

Compare. Write >, <, or =.

26. 8 + 1 ● 4 × 2　　27. 16 − 9 ● 3 × 6　　28. 12 × 10 ● 8 + 4

29. 5 × 6 ● 20 + 10　　30. 11 − 6 ● 5 × 2　　31. 6 × 8 ● 12 × 4

Problem Solving

32. **Analyze:** What pattern do you see in Row 1? in Column 1?

34. Triangular numbers can be shown as triangles. List the triangular numbers in the table. What pattern do you notice?

1 | 3 | 6 | 10 | 15

33. Square numbers can be shown as squares. Where are these numbers in the table? What do you notice about their factors? What other square numbers can you name?

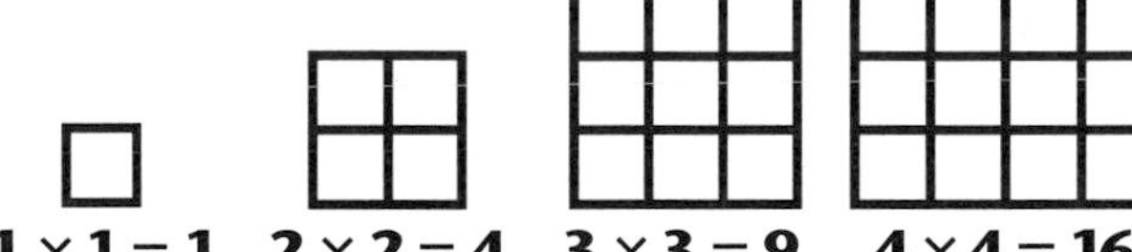

Spiral Review and Test Prep

Write in order from greatest to least.

35. 1,234; 1,378; 980; 1,700

36. 16,142; 9,043; 16,875; 10,202

Choose the correct answer.

37. Which is 3,000 + 400 + 5 in standard form?

A. 3,405　　**C.** 3,045

B. 3,450　　**D.** 345

38. Which is $28.55 rounded to the nearest dollar?

F. $28　　**H.** $29

G. $28.50　　**J.** Not Here

Extra Practice, page 180

Facts Practice: Multiplication

Multiply.

1. 3×4	**2.** 5×2	**3.** 4×6	**4.** 9×3	**5.** 6×3
6. 6×5	**7.** 10×4	**8.** 5×3	**9.** 3×3	**10.** 5×5
11. 4×4	**12.** 4×2	**13.** 9×7	**14.** 8×4	**15.** 9×5
16. 8×5	**17.** 7×4	**18.** 9×0	**19.** 8×8	**20.** 2×9
21. 3×7	**22.** 5×4	**23.** 7×5	**24.** 8×6	**25.** 7×8
26. 9×9	**27.** 6×9	**28.** 7×6	**29.** 2×7	**30.** 1×8
31. 0×10	**32.** 6×6	**33.** 7×7	**34.** 1×1	**35.** 8×2
36. $\begin{array}{r} 5 \\ \times 8 \\ \hline \end{array}$	**37.** $\begin{array}{r} 6 \\ \times 4 \\ \hline \end{array}$	**38.** $\begin{array}{r} 4 \\ \times 9 \\ \hline \end{array}$	**39.** $\begin{array}{r} 7 \\ \times 8 \\ \hline \end{array}$	**40.** $\begin{array}{r} 8 \\ \times 4 \\ \hline \end{array}$
41. $\begin{array}{r} 10 \\ \times\ 8 \\ \hline \end{array}$	**42.** $\begin{array}{r} 5 \\ \times 3 \\ \hline \end{array}$	**43.** $\begin{array}{r} 6 \\ \times 7 \\ \hline \end{array}$	**44.** $\begin{array}{r} 11 \\ \times\ 6 \\ \hline \end{array}$	**45.** $\begin{array}{r} 12 \\ \times\ 1 \\ \hline \end{array}$
46. $\begin{array}{r} 8 \\ \times 9 \\ \hline \end{array}$	**47.** $\begin{array}{r} 6 \\ \times 9 \\ \hline \end{array}$	**48.** $\begin{array}{r} 5 \\ \times 10 \\ \hline \end{array}$	**49.** $\begin{array}{r} 12 \\ \times\ 4 \\ \hline \end{array}$	**50.** $\begin{array}{r} 8 \\ \times 6 \\ \hline \end{array}$
51. $\begin{array}{r} 11 \\ \times\ 4 \\ \hline \end{array}$	**52.** $\begin{array}{r} 12 \\ \times\ 7 \\ \hline \end{array}$	**53.** $\begin{array}{r} 9 \\ \times 8 \\ \hline \end{array}$	**54.** $\begin{array}{r} 12 \\ \times\ 3 \\ \hline \end{array}$	**55.** $\begin{array}{r} 11 \\ \times\ 1 \\ \hline \end{array}$
56. $\begin{array}{r} 12 \\ \times\ 2 \\ \hline \end{array}$	**57.** $\begin{array}{r} 8 \\ \times 7 \\ \hline \end{array}$	**58.** $\begin{array}{r} 12 \\ \times\ 5 \\ \hline \end{array}$	**59.** $\begin{array}{r} 7 \\ \times 9 \\ \hline \end{array}$	**60.** $\begin{array}{r} 12 \\ \times 9 \\ \hline \end{array}$
61. $\begin{array}{r} 8 \\ \times 5 \\ \hline \end{array}$	**62.** $\begin{array}{r} 6 \\ \times 8 \\ \hline \end{array}$	**63.** $\begin{array}{r} 3 \\ \times 9 \\ \hline \end{array}$	**64.** $\begin{array}{r} 11 \\ \times\ 9 \\ \hline \end{array}$	**65.** $\begin{array}{r} 12 \\ \times 12 \\ \hline \end{array}$

Add, subtract, or multiply.

1. $3 + 7$
2. $6 - 3$
3. $7 + 6$
4. 7×7
5. $5 - 2$
6. $8 - 3$
7. $9 + 4$
8. 1×7
9. $15 - 6$
10. $9 + 5$
11. 5×10
12. $8 + 7$
13. 9×9
14. $13 - 7$
15. $6 + 7$
16. $5 + 3$
17. $18 - 9$
18. $15 - 7$
19. $8 + 3$
20. 7×8
21. $14 - 5$
22. $4 + 5$
23. $7 + 2$
24. 3×9
25. $10 - 9$
26. 5×3
27. $9 + 3$
28. 4×6
29. $6 + 9$
30. $6 + 5$
31. $14 - 7$
32. 0×6
33. $11 - 2$
34. 6×8
35. $13 - 4$
36. $5 + 2$
37. 6×5
38. $12 - 6$
39. $11 - 3$
40. 10×7
41. 8×7
42. $16 - 8$
43. 6×3
44. 8×2
45. $9 + 9$
46. $\begin{array}{r} 5 \\ \times 7 \\ \hline \end{array}$
47. $\begin{array}{r} 8 \\ +8 \\ \hline \end{array}$
48. $\begin{array}{r} 5 \\ +8 \\ \hline \end{array}$
49. $\begin{array}{r} 16 \\ -\ 7 \\ \hline \end{array}$
50. $\begin{array}{r} 3 \\ \times 4 \\ \hline \end{array}$
51. $\begin{array}{r} 17 \\ -\ 8 \\ \hline \end{array}$
52. $\begin{array}{r} 6 \\ +6 \\ \hline \end{array}$
53. $\begin{array}{r} 8 \\ \times 8 \\ \hline \end{array}$
54. $\begin{array}{r} 4 \\ +3 \\ \hline \end{array}$
55. $\begin{array}{r} 9 \\ -0 \\ \hline \end{array}$
56. $\begin{array}{r} 4 \\ \times 9 \\ \hline \end{array}$
57. $\begin{array}{r} 5 \\ +3 \\ \hline \end{array}$
58. $\begin{array}{r} 7 \\ \times 9 \\ \hline \end{array}$
59. $\begin{array}{r} 18 \\ -\ 9 \\ \hline \end{array}$
60. $\begin{array}{r} 8 \\ \times 9 \\ \hline \end{array}$
61. $\begin{array}{r} 8 \\ +2 \\ \hline \end{array}$
62. $\begin{array}{r} 9 \\ +8 \\ \hline \end{array}$
63. $\begin{array}{r} 8 \\ +0 \\ \hline \end{array}$
64. $\begin{array}{r} 7 \\ \times 7 \\ \hline \end{array}$
65. $\begin{array}{r} 14 \\ -\ 9 \\ \hline \end{array}$
66. $\begin{array}{r} 4 \\ +8 \\ \hline \end{array}$
67. $\begin{array}{r} 11 \\ \times\ 7 \\ \hline \end{array}$
68. $\begin{array}{r} 12 \\ -\ 6 \\ \hline \end{array}$
69. $\begin{array}{r} 11 \\ -\ 7 \\ \hline \end{array}$
70. $\begin{array}{r} 10 \\ \times\ 4 \\ \hline \end{array}$
71. $\begin{array}{r} 9 \\ +3 \\ \hline \end{array}$
72. $\begin{array}{r} 15 \\ -\ 7 \\ \hline \end{array}$
73. $\begin{array}{r} 9 \\ -3 \\ \hline \end{array}$
74. $\begin{array}{r} 11 \\ -\ 8 \\ \hline \end{array}$
75. $\begin{array}{r} 2 \\ \times 8 \\ \hline \end{array}$
76. $\begin{array}{r} 7 \\ \times 4 \\ \hline \end{array}$
77. $\begin{array}{r} 10 \\ -\ 5 \\ \hline \end{array}$
78. $\begin{array}{r} 8 \\ +6 \\ \hline \end{array}$
79. $\begin{array}{r} 12 \\ \times\ 2 \\ \hline \end{array}$
80. $\begin{array}{r} 4 \\ +9 \\ \hline \end{array}$
81. $\begin{array}{r} 13 \\ -\ 5 \\ \hline \end{array}$
82. $\begin{array}{r} 11 \\ \times\ 4 \\ \hline \end{array}$
83. $\begin{array}{r} 18 \\ -\ 9 \\ \hline \end{array}$
84. $\begin{array}{r} 7 \\ \times 3 \\ \hline \end{array}$
85. $\begin{array}{r} 7 \\ +8 \\ \hline \end{array}$

For additional practice, use Fact Dash.

Objective: Review finding the product of three factors.

4•8 Multiply Three Numbers

Algebra & functions

Learn

Math Word

Associative Property of Multiplication

Can you use a yo-yo? Timothy Crump is a yo-yo expert! Suppose he buys yo-yos from 2 companies. He buys 6 different styles from each company and gets each style in 4 different colors. How many yo-yos does he buy in all?

Timothy Crump Herndon, Virginia

Example

Find $2 \times 6 \times 4$ to solve. You can use the **Associative Property** to multiply three factors. The grouping of the numbers does not affect the answer.

1 Use parentheses to show grouping.

$2 \times 6 \times 4 = (2 \times 6) \times 4$

2 Look for a known fact to multiply.

2×4 is a known fact.

3 Use the Commutative Property to change the order, if necessary.

$$\begin{aligned}(2 \times 6) \times 4 &= (6 \times 2) \times 4 \\ &= 6 \times (2 \times 4) \\ &= 6 \times 8 \\ &= 48\end{aligned}$$

Multiply inside the parentheses first.

He buys 48 yo-yos in all.

More Examples

A $3 \times (2 \times 7) = (3 \times 2) \times 7 = 6 \times 7 = 42$

B $(8 \times 2) \times 5 = 8 \times (2 \times 5) = 8 \times 10 = 80$

Try It

Multiply. Use mental math to solve.

1. $(3 \times 6) \times 2$ **2.** $3 \times (5 \times 3)$ **3.** $(8 \times 4) \times 2$ **4.** $5 \times (9 \times 2)$

Sum it Up Show how to use properties to multiply $(9 \times 2) \times 5$.

Practice Multiply.

5. $(5 \times 2) \times 2$
6. $(9 \times 3) \times 2$
7. $8 \times (7 \times 1)$
8. $(6 \times 3) \times 3$
9. $(2 \times 6) \times 4$
10. $2 \times (5 \times 4)$
11. $(3 \times 5) \times 2$
12. $(2 \times 9) \times 3$
13. $3 \times (4 \times 3)$
14. $(8 \times 3) \times 2$
15. $9 \times (0 \times 8)$
16. $(7 \times 1) \times 7$

Complete the multiplication sentence.

17. $(7 \times 4) \times 1 = ■$
18. $6 \times (5 \times 0) = ■$
19. $8 \times 2 = ■ \times 8$

★20. $6 \times 9 = 6 \times (■ \times 3)$

★21. $(2 \times 3) \times 4 = (2 \times 3) \times (2 \times ■)$

Problem Solving

22. **Collect Data:** Survey 5 other students to see how many CDs and cassette tapes they have. Show your data in a pictograph. Write a problem about the data in your graph.

Use data from the chart for problems 23–24.

23. How many more yo-yos does Eric have than Betty? than Michelle?

24. Which two collectors have about as many yo-yos as Eric has?

★25. Mateo bought yo-yos at a convention to add to his collection. He bought 12 yo-yos at the first table. Then he bought 4 yo-yos at each of the 6 other tables. How many yo-yos did he get in all?

★26. **Logical Reasoning:** Find as many ways as you can to show the number 90, using three numbers and at least two operations.

Yo-Yo Collectors

Name	Total Number of Yo-Yos
Eric	80
Betty	59
Maria	57
Bob	50
Michelle	37

Spiral Review and Test Prep

27. $\$6.32 - \$4.14$
28. $\$9.45 + \$0.75$
29. $\$84.38 - \$57.49$

Choose the correct answer.

30. Tala listened to CDs from 7:20 P.M. to 8:05 P.M. How long is this?
    - A. 1 hour 15 minutes
    - B. 25 minutes
    - C. 45 minutes
    - D. 35 minutes

31. What is the range for this set of data?
    10, 15, 10, 18, 2
    - F. 10
    - G. 12
    - H. 11
    - J. 16

Extra Practice, page 180

Check Your Progress A

Write a multiplication sentence to solve. (pages 138–139)

1. 

2. 

Multiply. Then use the Commutative Property to write a different multiplication sentence. (pages 140–141)

3. 8×2
4. 7×6
5. 3×1
6. 0×5

Multiply. (pages 142–149, 152–157)

7. 6×5
8. 10×6
9. 6×3
10. 2×3
11. 4×0
12. 9×2
13. 9×7
14. 1×8
15. $2 \times 7 \times 5$
16. $1 \times 6 \times 8$
17. $11 \times 4 \times 0$
18. $5 \times 4 \times 2$
19. $\begin{array}{r} 11 \\ \times\ 8 \\ \hline \end{array}$
20. $\begin{array}{r} 7 \\ \times 8 \\ \hline \end{array}$
21. $\begin{array}{r} 9 \\ \times 6 \\ \hline \end{array}$
22. $\begin{array}{r} 12 \\ \times\ 5 \\ \hline \end{array}$

Solve. (pages 138–157)

23. Daniel puts 9 books on each of 8 shelves. How many books does he have in all? Which operation did you use to solve the problem?

24. Lee buys 8 packs of baseball cards for his collection. There are 5 cards in each pack. How many cards does Lee buy? If he buys 2 more packs, how many cards will he have?

25. **Explain** how the properties of multiplication can help you with basic multiplication facts.

Additional activities at
www.mhschool.com/math

Use Tables to Multiply

Tamara is on a committee that is planning a banquet. They are going to rent 9 tables for the banquet. They must decide if they need to rent tables to seat 6, 8, 10, or 12 people. How many people can be seated if they rent tables that seat 6 people? that seat 8 people? that seat 10 people? that seat 12 people?

You can use a spreadsheet table to multiply.

- Click on the table key.
- Label the columns *People per Table, Number of Tables,* and *Total Number of People.*
- In *People per Table,* enter the number of people that can be seated.
- In *Number of Tables,* enter 9.
- In *Total Number of People,* enter a formula to multiply *People per Table* by *Number of Tables.*
- How many people can be seated if they rent tables that seat 6 people? 8 people? 10 people? 12 people?

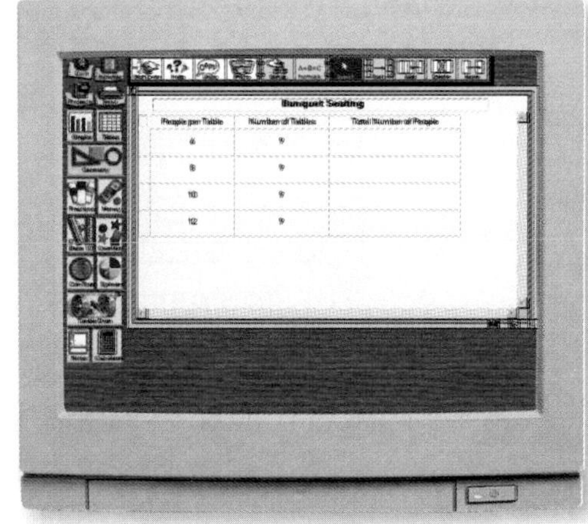

Use the computer to create a table to find each set of products. Then use your table to complete each number sentence.

1. $4 \times 5 = n$
$5 \times 5 = b$
$6 \times 5 = m$
$7 \times 5 = p$

2. $6 \times 8 = t$
$8 \times 8 = s$
$10 \times 8 = e$
$12 \times 8 = j$

3. $4 \times 4 = w$
$6 \times 4 = f$
$8 \times 4 = h$
$10 \times 4 = u$

4. $3 \times 12 = y$
$4 \times 12 = k$
$5 \times 12 = v$
$6 \times 12 = z$

5. Analyze: How does using the table help when you have to multiply several times?

For more practice, use Math Traveler™.

Objective: Relate multiplication and division facts.

4·9 Relate Multiplication and Division Facts

Algebra & functions

Learn

Math Words

quotient the result of division

dividend a number to be divided

divisor the number by which the dividend is divided

Beverly is arranging her collection of toy cars. If she puts 8 cars on each shelf, how many shelves does she need for 32 cars?

Example

Find: 32 ÷ 8

You can use a related multiplication fact to help you quickly recall the **quotient**.

Think:
■ x 8 = 32
4 x 8 = 32

32 ÷ 8 = 4 or $8\overline{)32}$ with quotient 4

32 = **dividend**, 8 = **divisor**, 4 = quotient; in $8\overline{)32}$: 4 ← quotient, 32 ← dividend, 8 = divisor

She needs 4 shelves.

Try It

Divide.

1. 12 ÷ 4
2. 16 ÷ 4
3. 9 ÷ 3
4. 18 ÷ 3
5. 20 ÷ 4
6. 6 ÷ 2
7. 24 ÷ 8
8. 32 ÷ 4
9. 28 ÷ 7
10. 21 ÷ 3

Sum it Up! What related multiplication fact can you use to find 56 ÷ 8?

Practice Divide.

11. $45 \div 9$ **12.** $21 \div 3$ **13.** $28 \div 7$ **14.** $16 \div 8$ **15.** $25 \div 5$

16. $10 \div 1$ **17.** $18 \div 6$ **18.** $40 \div 5$ **19.** $60 \div 5$ **20.** $48 \div 4$

21. $6\overline{)36}$ **22.** $5\overline{)30}$ **23.** $5\overline{)15}$ **24.** $3\overline{)27}$ **25.** $6\overline{)42}$

Problem Solving

26. Robert has 72 toy cars. He wants to put an equal number of cars on 8 shelves. How many cars go on each shelf?

27. Jessica also has 72 toy cars, but she has only 6 shelves. How many cars can go on each shelf?

Use data from *Did You Know?* for problems 28–30.

28. Write the number of labels in Teiichi's collection in expanded form.

29. How many more labels does Teiichi have than Robert?

30. If Teiichi and Robert combined their collections, how many labels would they have altogether?

31. How many toy cars can be bought with \$36.00 if each car costs \$4.00?

32. Generalize: How are multiplication and division related? Use examples to explain.

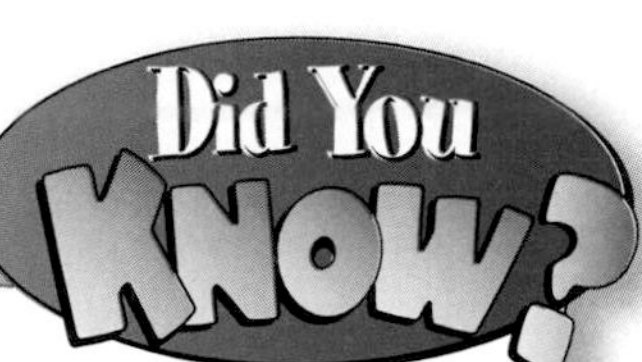

Teiichi Yoshizawa of Japan has a collection of 743,512 different matchbox labels from 130 countries. Robert Jones of Indiana has 280,000 matchbox labels in his collection.

Spiral Review and Test Prep

33. $\$10.00 \times 3$ **34.** $\$3.00 + \$10.00$ **35.** $\$10.00 - \$7.00$ **36.** $\$10 - \$0.30$

37. $3 \times 2 \times 5$ **38.** $1 + 8 + 10$ **39.** 11×0 **40.** $11 + 0$

Choose the correct answer.

41. Theo left town on March 29. He returned on April 2. How many days was Theo gone?

A. 3 **C.** 4
B. 5 **D.** 6

42. On a pictograph, each ● stands for 4 balls. How many balls does ●●●●●●●●● stand for?

F. 32 **H.** 36
G. 34 **J.** 38

Extra Practice, page 180

Objective: Solve a problem by acting it out with models.

Problem Solving: Strategy
Act It Out

Read

Read the problem carefully.

The Marble Collectors' Club luncheon is today! The club president wants to seat 24 members so that every table is filled. Each round table seats 5 people. Each rectangular table seats 6. Which shape tables should she use? How many tables will she need?

- **What do you know?** **There are 24 members; the round tables seat 5; the rectangular tables seat 6**
- **What do you need to find?** **Which shape tables she should use; how many tables she will need**

Plan

One way to solve the problem is to act it out using models.

Solve

Model using round tables.

Four tables are filled and 4 people are left over.

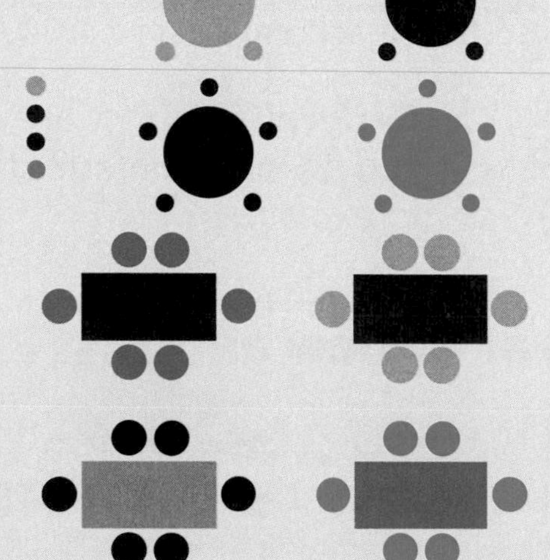

Model using rectangular tables.

The president of the club should use the rectangular tables. She will need 4 tables. Zero people will be left over.

Look Back

Does your answer make sense? What other methods could you use to solve the same problem?

How did acting out the problem help you solve it?

Practice **Solve.**

1. **What if** 45 members of the club are going to attend the luncheon? Which tables should the president use? How many tables will she need?

2. For placemats, Meg is going to cut 2-foot by 1-foot rectangles from a piece of fabric with a starry background. The fabric is 4 feet wide and 3 feet long. How many placemats can she cut from one piece of fabric?

3. Elroy is delivering 63 sandwiches to the luncheon. He has a large box that will fit 9 sandwiches. He has a smaller box that will fit 8 sandwiches. Which box should he use if he wants to put an equal number of sandwiches in each box? How many boxes will he need?

4. Courtney wants to create a display of 28 UFO photos. She has a large poster that will fit 10 photos. She also has 3 smaller posters. How can she arrange the photos on the posters so that she has an equal number on the 3 smaller posters?

Problem Solving

Mixed Strategy Review

CHOOSE A STRATEGY

- Logical Reasoning
- Draw a Picture
- Make a Graph
- Act It Out
- Make a Table or List
- Find a Pattern
- Guess and Check
- Write a Number Sentence
- Work Backward
- Solve a Simpler Problem

5. Pedro is bringing two science fiction books to the luncheon. Together the books have 242 pages. One book has 119 pages. How many pages is the other book?

★ 6. Walter has been saving money to buy a model robot. He puts $6.00 in his bank account for 6 weeks in a row. He already had $17.82 in the account. The model costs $35.59. How much money will he have left in his account after he buys the model?

Use data from the table for problems 7–9.

7. Which country has almost twice as many collectors as France?

8. How many more collectors are there in the country with the greatest number of collectors than in the country with the least number of collectors?

9. **Create a problem** using the data in the table. Solve it. Have others solve it.

Science Fiction Collectors Around the World

Country	Collectors
England	14,509
France	13,955
Japan	25,394
Australia	17,642

Extra Practice, page 181

Objective: Review using related multiplication facts to find division facts for 2 through 12.

Divide by 2 through 12

Learn

Mrs. Pavlik has a collection of 54 Ukrainian eggs. She gives each of her 6 grandchildren the same number of eggs. How many eggs will Mrs. Pavlik give each grandchild?

There's more than one way!

Find 54 ÷ 6 to solve.

Method A

You can count backward in groups of 6 on a number line.

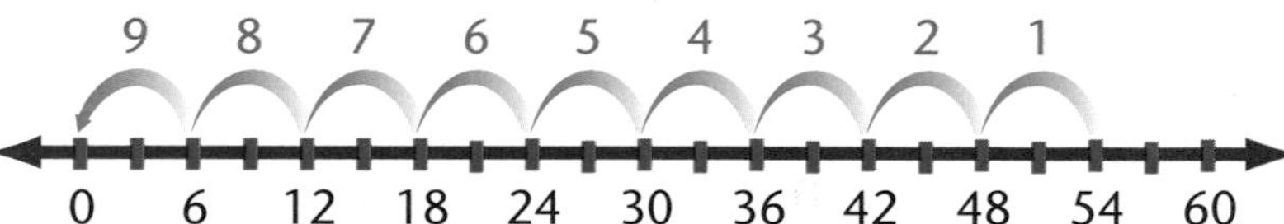

Think: 54, 48, 42, 36, 30, 24, 18, 12, 6, 0

There are 9 jumps from 54 to 0.

So $54 \div 6 = 9$.

Each grandchild gets 9 eggs.

Method B

You can use a related multiplication sentence to find the quotient.

Think: What number times 6 is 54?

$\blacksquare \times 6 = 54$

$9 \times 6 = 54$

So $54 \div 6 = 9$.

Each grandchild gets 9 eggs.

Akemi collects Temari balls. She has 21 balls. She puts 7 balls on a shelf. How many shelves will she need?

Example 1

Find: $21 \div 7$

You can use a related multiplication sentence.

Think: What number times 7 is 21?

$\blacksquare \times 7 = 21$

$3 \times 7 = 21$

So $21 \div 7 = 3$.

She needs 3 shelves.

What if Akemi has 40 Temari balls and puts 10 on each shelf? How many shelves does she need?

Example 2

Find: $40 \div 10$

Think: $40 = \blacksquare$ groups of 10

40 = 4 groups of 10

So $40 \div 10 = 4$.

She needs 4 shelves.

Try It **Divide.**

1. $8 \div 2$
2. $10 \div 5$
3. $42 \div 6$
4. $48 \div 12$
5. $63 \div 9$
6. $11\overline{)55}$
7. $7\overline{)84}$
8. $4\overline{)28}$
9. $3\overline{)33}$
10. $8\overline{)72}$

What method would you use to find $45 \div 9$?

Practice **Divide.**

11. 25 ÷ 5 12. 18 ÷ 2 13. 12 ÷ 12 14. 16 ÷ 2 15. 30 ÷ 10

16. 36 ÷ 6 17. 33 ÷ 11 18. 14 ÷ 2 19. 27 ÷ 3 20. 35 ÷ 5

21. 40 ÷ 5 22. 8 ÷ 4 23. 15 ÷ 3 24. 45 ÷ 5 25. 10 ÷ 2

26. $7\overline{)35}$ 27. $6\overline{)30}$ 28. $11\overline{)88}$ 29. $9\overline{)18}$ 30. $8\overline{)16}$

31. $8\overline{)40}$ 32. $5\overline{)25}$ 33. $7\overline{)14}$ 34. $5\overline{)50}$ 35. $12\overline{)144}$

Algebra & functions **Find the rule. Then complete the table.**

36.

Rule ■						
0	11	22	33	■	■	■
0	1	2	3	4	5	6

37.

Rule ■						
0	12	24	36	■	■	■
0	1	2	3	4	5	6

How much does each can weigh?

★38.

★39.

40.

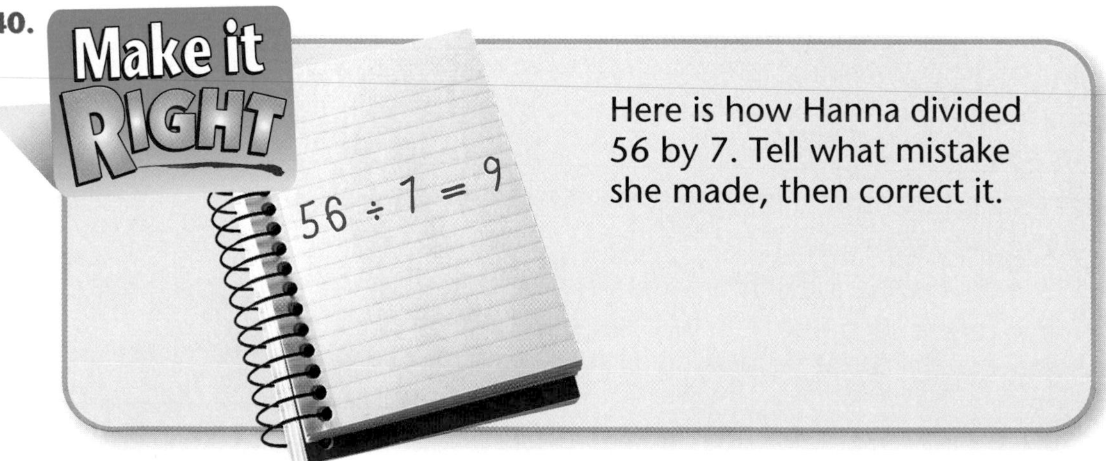

Here is how Hanna divided 56 by 7. Tell what mistake she made, then correct it.

Problem Solving

41. **What if** Mrs. Pavlik had 5 grandchildren and a collection of 40 eggs? How many eggs would each grandchild get if they all got the same number of eggs?

42. **Art:** The Imperial Winter Egg made with 3,000 diamonds was sold for \$5,587,308.00. The second most valuable decorative egg was sold for \$2,141,563.00. For how much more money did the Imperial Winter egg sell?

Use data from the line plot for problems 43–45.

The Craft Club polled students aged 5 to 10 to see how many dolls they owned. The line plot shows the results.

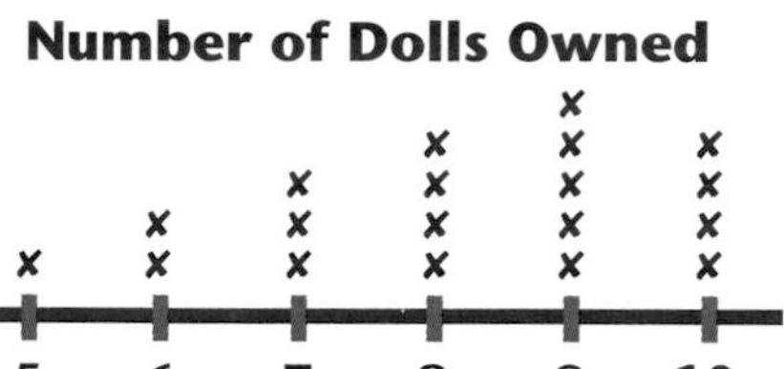

43. What is the median?

44. What is the mode?

45. What is the range?

Problem Solving

46. There are 144 decorative eggs at a museum. The museum curator places them in display cases. She places 12 eggs in each case. How many cases does she need?

47. Mrs. Pavlik sends a box of Ukrainian eggs to one of her grandchildren. She spends $45.99 on the eggs and $12.45 to mail them. How much does she spend in all?

★48. The collectors' fair at school was held from 3:30 P.M. to 5:45 P.M. Mike and Brian came 25 minutes early to help set up and did not leave until 30 minutes after the fair closed. How long were they at the fair?

★49. George evenly divided his collection of 12 eggs into 3 storage boxes. Jeff evenly divided 15 eggs into 5 boxes. Who has more eggs in each box? How many more does he have?

50. Martine plans to display part of her Temari ball collection at a craft show. She wants to put 8 balls in each of 5 cases. She has 65 balls in her collection. How many balls does she plan to leave home?

51. **Generalize:** Addition and subtraction are called inverse operations because one operation undoes the other. Are multiplication and division inverse operations? Give an example.

Spiral Review and Test Prep

52. 319 + 1,329

53. 7,468 − 5,430

54. 9,257 + 6,159

Choose the correct answer.

55. Which item tells how to find (3, 2) on a grid starting at (0, 0)?
   A. right 3, up 2
   B. right 5
   C. right 2, up 3
   D. up 5

56. A painter takes 1 day to prepare the house and 4 days to paint it. The house must be done by March 13. What is the latest starting date?
   F. March 6
   G. March 9
   H. May 9
   J. March 10

Extra Practice, page 181

4•12

Objective: Review using inverse operations to find missing factors.

Fact Families

Algebra & functions

Learn

Nicole has 30 foreign coins in her collection. She wants to arrange them with 6 coins in each row. How many rows of coins can she make?

Example 1

Find: 30 ÷ 6

You can use a fact family to find the number of groups.

6 × 5 = 30
5 × 6 = 30
30 ÷ 5 = 6
30 ÷ 6 = 5

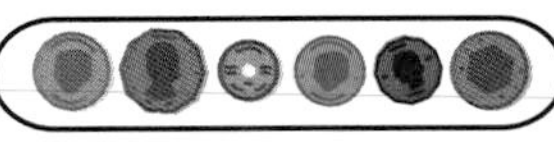
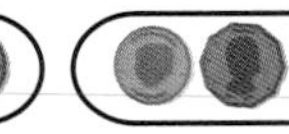

She can make 5 rows of coins.

More Examples

A

2 × 4 = 8
4 × 2 = 8
8 ÷ 4 = 2
8 ÷ 2 = 4

B

9 × 1 = 9
1 × 9 = 9
9 ÷ 1 = 9
9 ÷ 9 = 1

C

3 × 3 = 9
9 ÷ 3 = 3

Nicole also has a collection of 48 silver dollars that she keeps in a coin collector's book. She places 8 silver dollars in the slots on each page. How many pages are in her coin book?

Example 2

Find: $48 \div 8$

You can find the missing factors.

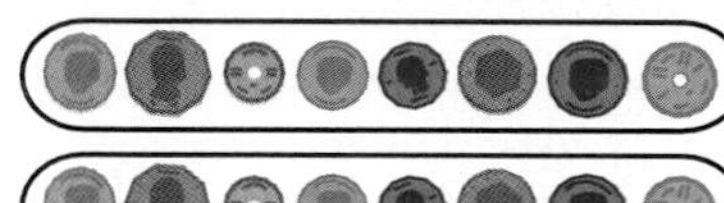

Think: There are 8 silver dollars on each page for a total of 48 coins.

$8 \times \blacksquare = 48$

$8 \times 6 = 48$

So $48 \div 8 = 6$.

There are 6 pages in the book.

Try It

Complete each fact family.

1. $3 \times 9 = t$
$9 \times h = 27$
$27 \div 3 = p$
$r \div 9 = 3$

2. $5 \times 7 = a$
$m \times 5 = 35$
$35 \div 7 = w$
$n \div 5 = 7$

3. $6 \times 6 = v$
$36 \div u = u$

4. $9 \times 5 = m$
$5 \times n = 45$
$45 \div 9 = p$
$r \div 5 = 9$

5. $7 \times 9 = a$
$b \times 7 = 63$
$c \div 9 = 7$
$63 \div d = 9$

6. $5 \times 10 = f$
$10 \times g = 50$
$50 \div h = 10$
$50 \div k = 5$

Find each missing factor.

7. $5 \times n = 40$
$40 \div 8 = y$

8. $8 \times d = 24$
$24 \div 3 = s$

9. $7 \times k = 56$
$56 \div 8 = j$

How are addition and subtraction fact families like multiplication and division fact families?

Practice **Complete each fact family.**

10. $6 \times 7 = p$
$7 \times b = 42$
$42 \div 6 = g$
$z \div 7 = 6$

11. $7 \times 7 = c$
$49 \div r = r$

12. $12 \times 5 = l$
$t \times 12 = 60$
$60 \div 5 = f$
$q \div 12 = 5$

13. $11 \times 8 = s$
$t \times 11 = 88$
$88 \div 11 = u$
$88 \div v = 11$

14. $4 \times 8 = w$
$y \times 4 = 32$
$32 \div 8 = z$
$a \div 4 = 8$

15. $12 \times 12 = j$
$144 \div k = 12$

Find each missing factor.

16. $4 \times n = 16$
$16 \div 4 = m$

17. $9 \times d = 63$
$63 \div 7 = e$

18. $8 \times y = 8$
$8 \div 1 = x$

19. $7 \times t = 56$
$56 \div 8 = p$

20. $11 \times r = 88$
$88 \div 8 = b$

21. $3 \times h = 27$
$27 \div 9 = k$

Write a multiplication and division fact family for each group of numbers.

22. 3, 5, 15 **23.** 8, 8, 64 **24.** 7, 10, 70 **25.** 6, 8, 48

26. 6, 11, 66 **27.** 4, 8, 32 **28.** 12, 7, 84 **29.** 4, 9, 36

Divide. What patterns do you see?

30. $0 \div 3$ $0 \div 4$ $0 \div 6$ $0 \div 9$

31. $3 \div 3$ $7 \div 7$ $5 \div 5$ $1 \div 1$

32. $4 \div 1$ $5 \div 1$ $7 \div 1$ $9 \div 1$

33.

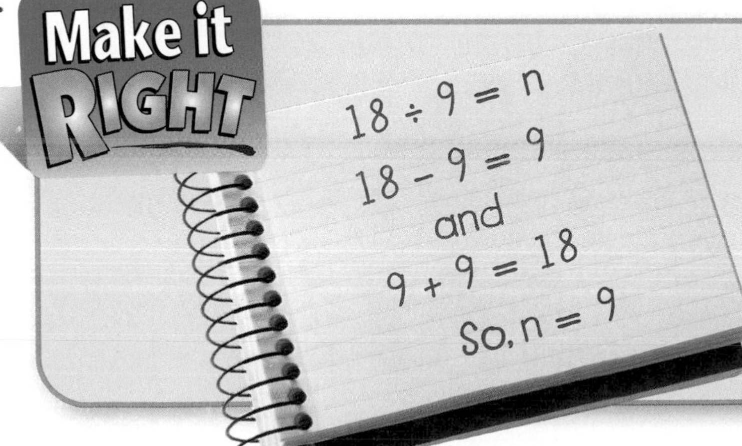

Here is the related fact Kenny used to divide $18 \div 9$. Tell what mistake he made. Explain how to correct it.

Problem Solving

34. Bill has a collection of 64 books that he wants to donate to the library. He wants to put an equal number of books in each box. Write a number sentence to show how he could divide the books into equal groups.

★35. A high speed coin press can make about 40,000 coins each hour. How many coins can be made in 2 hours? in 3 hours? Explain how you could use patterns to find how many coins could be made in 10 hours.

36. **Spatial Reasoning:** Which shape does not belong? Why?

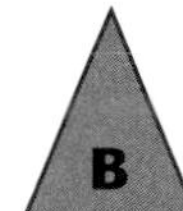

Use data from the chart for problems 37–39.

37. What is the difference between the coin worth the greatest value and the coin worth the least?

38. How much more money is the Lincoln head penny worth than the Liberty half dollar?

★39. Suppose a coin collector had all of the coins listed in a collection. What would his collection be worth? How much would he profit if he sold the collection at an auction for $850?

Values of Some Rare Coins

1939 Lincoln Head penny	$175
1933-D Buffalo nickel	$85
1935 Mercury head dime	$275
1930 Liberty quarter	$145
1938 Liberty half dollar	$115

40. **Analyze:** For which of these can you find an answer: 0×4 or $4 \div 0$? Explain.

Spiral Review and Test Prep

Write each number in standard form.

41. $6{,}000 + 200 + 70 + 7$

42. $700 + 90 + 8$

43. $10{,}000 + 500 + 9$

Choose the correct answer.

44. Rena goes to a movie that starts at 6:20 P.M. The movie is 2 hours and 10 minutes long. What time does it end?

A. 8:30 A.M.
B. 7:20 A.M.
C. 8:30 P.M.
D. 7:20 P.M.

45. Barry buys 2 packs of stickers for $3.00 each and a sticker album for $6.00 Which number sentence shows how much he spent altogether?

F. $(2 \times 3) \times 6$
G. $(2 + 3) + 6$
H. $(2 + 3) \times 6$
J. $(2 \times 3) + 6$

Extra Practice, page 181

Facts Practice: Division

Divide.

1. $6 \div 2$ **2.** $10 \div 5$ **3.** $24 \div 3$ **4.** $4 \div 2$ **5.** $9 \div 3$

6. $3 \div 3$ **7.** $44 \div 11$ **8.** $12 \div 2$ **9.** $42 \div 7$ **10.** $40 \div 8$

11. $36 \div 4$ **12.** $24 \div 4$ **13.** $16 \div 8$ **14.** $27 \div 9$ **15.** $32 \div 4$

16. $18 \div 3$ **17.** $8 \div 4$ **18.** $54 \div 6$ **19.** $56 \div 7$ **20.** $63 \div 9$

21. $8 \div 2$ **22.** $28 \div 7$ **23.** $81 \div 9$ **24.** $49 \div 7$ **25.** $15 \div 5$

26. $54 \div 9$ **27.** $18 \div 2$ **28.** $36 \div 12$ **29.** $16 \div 2$ **30.** $72 \div 8$

31. $36 \div 6$ **32.** $30 \div 5$ **33.** $14 \div 2$ **34.** $96 \div 8$ **35.** $21 \div 3$

36. $44 \div 4$ **37.** $64 \div 8$ **38.** $15 \div 3$ **39.** $45 \div 5$ **40.** $20 \div 4$

41. $16 \div 4$ **42.** $30 \div 6$ **43.** $56 \div 8$ **44.** $27 \div 3$ **45.** $25 \div 5$

46. $40 \div 5$ **47.** $28 \div 4$ **48.** $72 \div 9$ **49.** $36 \div 9$ **50.** $45 \div 9$

51. $8\overline{)72}$ **52.** $6\overline{)30}$ **53.** $5\overline{)5}$ **54.** $9\overline{)18}$ **55.** $8\overline{)16}$

56. $8\overline{)40}$ **57.** $7\overline{)63}$ **58.** $7\overline{)14}$ **59.** $4\overline{)48}$ **60.** $11\overline{)77}$

61. $12\overline{)12}$ **62.** $7\overline{)35}$ **63.** $6\overline{)54}$ **64.** $8\overline{)64}$ **65.** $5\overline{)40}$

66. $5\overline{)20}$ **67.** $3\overline{)6}$ **68.** $4\overline{)16}$ **69.** $5\overline{)55}$ **70.** $2\overline{)24}$

71. $1\overline{)8}$ **72.** $11\overline{)121}$ **73.** $10\overline{)120}$ **74.** $3\overline{)27}$ **75.** $8\overline{)96}$

"Go Fish" for Facts

You Will Need
- **index cards**

What to Do Number of players: 3

1. Write the number sentences for 12 fact families on index cards. Put one fact on each card.
2. Mix up the cards. Deal 8 cards to each player. Put the rest in a pile facedown.
3. The dealer asks the player on the left for a fact that the dealer needs in order to complete a fact family for one of the cards he or she has. If the second player has that card, it goes to the dealer.
4. The dealer asks for another fact until the second player does not have the fact asked for. Then the second player says, "Go fish." The dealer picks a card from the top of the pile. Then the second player asks the third player for cards, and so on.
5. When a fact family is completed, the player puts those cards faceup in his or her pile.
6. The game ends when there are no more cards in the stack or to be asked for. The player with the most fact families wins.

For more practice, use Fact Dash.

Objective: Analyze data and make decisions.

Problem Solving: Application

Decision Making

How should she arrange her trophies and ribbons in the showcase?

Lily has been competing in bowling tournaments for many years. She has a collection of trophies and ribbons she has won in the tournaments. Lily wants to make a showcase for her trophies and ribbons. The showcase will have shelves for the trophies and display frames for the ribbons.

Number of Trophies	Number of Ribbons
First Place: 10	First Place: 21
Second Place: 14	Second Place: 15
Third Place: 4	Third Place: 8

Mel's Hardware Shelf Sale!

Thursday through Saturday
3-shelf sets: $39.95
4-shelf sets: $49.95
5-shelf sets: $59.95
Each shelf holds 4 trophies!

Creative Crafts Display Frames

Small display frames (holds 4 ribbons) $5.00 each
Medium display frames (holds 6 ribbons) $7.00 each
Large display frames (holds 8 ribbons) $9.00 each

Read for Understanding

1. How many trophies does Lily have in all? how many ribbons?

2. If she wants to divide all her trophies into equal groups, what are some possible equal groups she could use?

3. If she wants to divide all her ribbons into equal groups, what are some possible equal groups she could use?

4. Which kinds of trophies or ribbons can be divided into 3 equal groups? how many in each group?

5. Which kinds of trophies can be divided into 4 equal groups? how many in each group?

6. Which kinds of ribbons can be divided into 4 equal groups? how many in each group?

7. Which kinds of trophies can be divided into 5 equal groups? how many in each group?

8. Which kinds of ribbons can be divided into 5 equal groups? how many in each group?

9. How many small frames does she need for the third-place ribbons?

10. How many 3-shelf sets does she need to display all her second-place trophies?

Problem Solving

Make Decisions

11. How many trophies can she display on the 3-shelf set? the 4-shelf set? the 5-shelf set?

12. **What if** Lily decides to put all of her trophies on shelves with an equal number on each shelf? How many shelves does she need? Which shelf sets could she buy? Explain. How much would it cost?

13. **What if** she wants to put only her first- and second-place trophies on shelves with an equal number on each shelf? How many shelves does she need? Which shelf sets could she buy? How much would it cost?

14. How many small frames would Lily need to display all of her ribbons with an equal number in each frame? How much would it cost?

15. Can Lily use the frames to show an equal number of her first-place ribbons? Explain.

16. What are two ways she could display her third-place ribbons in frames with an equal number in each frame?

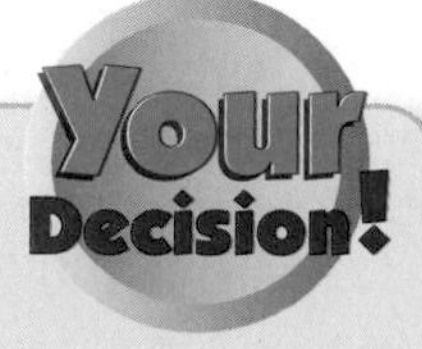

What is your recommendation for Lily? Explain.

Objective: Apply multiplication and division facts to investigate science concepts.

Problem Solving: Math and Science

Ramp races: How does height affect distance?

You Will Need
- **6 math textbooks**
- **crayon**
- **ruler or meterstick**

You and a friend coast down a hill without pedaling. Next, you coast down a steeper hill as far as you can go. Which ride takes you farther from the base of the hill?

In this activity, you will see how far a crayon rolls past a ramp when the ramp gets steeper.

Hypothesize

What will happen to the distance a crayon rolls past a ramp as the ramp gets steeper?

Procedure

1. Work with a partner. Place a book flat on the floor.
2. Lean another book against it to make a ramp.
3. Place a crayon at the top of the tilted book and let it go.
4. Measure how far the crayon traveled past the bottom of the ramp (to the nearest centimeter).
5. Repeat two times and record the longest distance.
6. Put another book on the stack. Repeat steps 3 to 5.
7. Add a third book to the stack. Repeat steps 3 to 5.
8. Add a fourth book to the stack. Repeat steps 3 to 5.
9. Add a fifth book to the stack. Repeat steps 3 to 5.

Data

For each ramp, copy and complete a chart to record the greatest distance that the crayon traveled.

Ramp height	Distance traveled
1 book	
2 books	
3 books	
4 books	
5 books	

Did You Know?

The taller the ramp, the faster the crayon is moving when it reaches the bottom. The speed of an object is how fast it moves.

Conclude and Apply

- Which crayon traveled the farthest? Which crayon traveled the shortest distance?
- Use division to calculate how many times farther the crayon traveled for the 2-, 3-, 4-, and 5-book ramps than it did for the 1-book ramp. Round to the nearest whole number.

	2 Book	3 Book	4 Book	5 Book
Number of Times				
Farther than 1-Book Ramp				

- Do you see a pattern? Describe it.
- If the pattern continues, how far will a crayon travel if released from a 10-book ramp? a 20-book ramp?
- Explain the ramp activity in terms of speed.

Going Further

1. Design and complete an activity to check your prediction for the 10-book ramp.

2. Design and complete an activity to compare how different objects (pens, pencils, chalk, balls, etc.) roll off the ramp.

Check Your Progress B

Find each missing factor. **(pages 160–161)**

1. $4 \times n = 48$
$48 \div 12 = m$

2. $9 \times x = 99$
$99 \div 9 = s$

3. $u \times 10 = 60$
$60 \div 6 = w$

Divide. **(pages 164–167)**

4. $56 \div 7$ **5.** $48 \div 8$ **6.** $16 \div 4$ **7.** $24 \div 6$ **8.** $81 \div 9$

9. $40 \div 4$ **10.** $36 \div 12$ **11.** $33 \div 11$ **12.** $27 \div 9$ **13.** $72 \div 8$

14. $40 \div 5$ **15.** $49 \div 7$ **16.** $25 \div 5$ **17.** $64 \div 8$ **18.** $63 \div 9$

Write a multiplication and division fact family for each group of numbers. **(pages 168–171)**

19. 9, 8, 72 **20.** 3, 12, 36 **21.** 5, 5, 25

Solve. **(pages 160–177)**

22. Jacob has 54 baseball cards. He puts them in an album with 6 cards on each page. How many pages does he fill?

23. There are 42 members of the Shell Collectors' Club. There are 7 tables at the Shell Convention luncheon. An equal number of members sit at each table. How many members sit at one table?

24. A small display box holds 4 rocks and a large display box holds 6 rocks. Tammy has 64 rocks in her collection. She wants to put an equal number of rocks in each box. Which boxes should she use to display them? How many boxes will she need?

25. **Generalize:** What happens when you multiply an odd number by an odd number, an odd number by an even number, and an even number by an even number? Show your work.

Extra Practice

The Meaning of Multiplication (pages 138–139)

Find each product and write a multiplication sentence.

1. 4×5 2. 3×3 3. 2×6 4. 1×7 5. 9×5

Properties of Multiplication (pages 140–141)

Find the product. Then use the Commutative Property to write a different multiplication sentence.

1. 2×4 2. 6×1 3. 7×3 4. 0×4 5. 5×6

Multiply by 2, 3, 4 and 6 (pages 142–145)

Multiply.

1. 5×4 2. 2×6 3. 7×4 4. 0×4 5. 2×4

6. 6×2 7. 6×4 8. 7×2 9. 5×2 10. 4×5

11. 4×4 12. 4×3 13. 2×8 14. 8×4 15. 4×9

16. 3×9 17. 6×5 18. 7×3 19. 3×8 20. 6×0

21. $\begin{array}{r} 1 \\ \times 3 \\ \hline \end{array}$ 22. $\begin{array}{r} 3 \\ \times 3 \\ \hline \end{array}$ 23. $\begin{array}{r} 4 \\ \times 6 \\ \hline \end{array}$ 24. $\begin{array}{r} 7 \\ \times 6 \\ \hline \end{array}$ 25. $\begin{array}{r} 6 \\ \times 9 \\ \hline \end{array}$ 26. $\begin{array}{r} 6 \\ \times 6 \\ \hline \end{array}$

Solve.

27. In a collection there are 9 crowns each in 4 cases. How many crowns are there in all?

28. In a photo album there are 9 pages. If 3 photos fit on a page, how many photos are there in all?

Multiply by 5 and 10 (pages 146–147)

Multiply.

1. 5×5 2. 9×10 3. 5×0 4. 5×8 5. 5×4

6. $\begin{array}{r} 10 \\ \times\ 5 \\ \hline \end{array}$ 7. $\begin{array}{r} 5 \\ \times 7 \\ \hline \end{array}$ 8. $\begin{array}{r} 8 \\ \times 10 \\ \hline \end{array}$ 9. $\begin{array}{r} 5 \\ \times 6 \\ \hline \end{array}$ 10. $\begin{array}{r} 5 \\ \times 9 \\ \hline \end{array}$ 11. $\begin{array}{r} 12 \\ \times\ 5 \\ \hline \end{array}$

Solve.

12. Julia has 5 boxes of comic books. Each box has 10 books in it. How many comic books does she have in all the boxes?

Extra Practice

Multiply by 7, 8, and 9 (pages 148–149)

Multiply.

1. 7×6
2. 9×6
3. 8×8
4. 3×9
5. 9×4
6. 7×9
7. 6×9
8. 10×8

Problem Solving: Reading for Math Choose an Operation (pages 150–151)

Solve. Tell how you chose the operation.

1. Tracy bought 3 packs of baseball cards. Each pack contains 7 cards. How many cards did Tracy buy?
2. Cassie has 138 marbles in her collection. Her brother Jacob has 219 marbles. How many do they have in all?

Multiplication Table and Patterns (pages 152–153)

Copy and complete the table.

×	0	1	2	3	4	5	6	7	8	9	10	11	12
11	0	11	22	33	44	55							
12	0	12	24	36	48	60							

Multiply Three Numbers (pages 156–157)

Multiply.

1. $(3 \times 5) \times 2$
2. $2 \times (5 \times 4)$
3. $(7 \times 3) \times 2$
4. $2 \times (6 \times 4)$

Solve.

5. Lacey has 5 holders for her CDs. There are 2 rows for each holder. She puts 6 CDs in each row. How many CDs does she have?

Relate Multiplication and Division Facts (pages 160–161)

Divide. Use a related multiplication fact.

1. $72 \div 8$
2. $49 \div 7$
3. $0 \div 10$
4. $55 \div 5$
5. $60 \div 12$

Solve.

6. Ray has 48 leaves in his scrapbook. He put 6 leaves on each page. How many pages are in his scrapbook?

Extra Practice

Problem Solving: Strategy Act It Out (pages 162–163)

Solve.

1. Luisa has 18 book covers from her favorite science fiction books. She wants to hang them on her wall in equal rows. She has room for 2 to 6 rows. How can she arrange the book covers? List all the ways.

2. Roger's dog won 24 blue ribbons. Roger wants to put an equal number of ribbons in some frames. He has frames that will hold 4 ribbons and 5 ribbons. Which frames should he use? How many frames will he need?

Divide by 2 Through 12 (pages 165–167)

Divide.

1. 8 ÷ 4	**2.** 10 ÷ 5	**3.** 14 ÷ 2	**4.** 15 ÷ 3	**5.** 36 ÷ 6
6. 25 ÷ 5	**7.** 18 ÷ 2	**8.** 20 ÷ 4	**9.** 24 ÷ 6	**10.** 21 ÷ 3
11. 72 ÷ 8	**12.** 40 ÷ 8	**13.** 9 ÷ 9	**14.** 63 ÷ 7	**15.** 21 ÷ 7
16. 48 ÷ 12	**17.** 66 ÷ 11	**18.** 48 ÷ 8	**19.** 32 ÷ 8	**20.** 28 ÷ 7
21. 56 ÷ 7	**22.** 18 ÷ 9	**23.** 16 ÷ 8	**24.** 72 ÷ 9	**25.** 27 ÷ 9
26. 36 ÷ 4	**27.** 35 ÷ 5	**28.** 32 ÷ 4	**29.** 16 ÷ 2	**30.** 27 ÷ 3

Solve.

31. Maria has 88 model cars to put into display cases. If a display case can hold 8 cars, how many cases does she need?

Fact Families (pages 168–171)

Write a multiplication and division fact family for each group of numbers.

1. 7, 5, 35 **2.** 11, 11, 121 **3.** 6, 7, 42 **4.** 12, 9, 108

Solve.

5. Becky has 45 marbles. She wants to put an equal number of marbles into 5 bags. How many marbles will go in each bag?

6. Claude arranges 4 rows of marbles. Each row has 9 marbles in it. How many marbles does Claude have?

Chapter Study Guide

Language and Math

Complete. Use a word from the list.

1. In the division sentence $72 \div 8 = 9$ the ____ is 9.
2. The multiplication sentences $3 \times 4 = 12$ and $4 \times 3 = 12$ show the ____ Property.
3. In $4 \times 8 = 32$, the 32 is a (an) ____.
4. A ____ is formed by multiplying a number by itself.
5. The multiplication sentence $3 \times (2 \times 1) = (3 \times 2) \times 1$ is an example of the ____ Property.

Math Words

- Associative Property
- Commutative Property
- divisor
- factor
- product
- quotient
- square number

Skills and Applications

Multiply facts through 12. (pages 142–149)

Example

Find: 6×12

Solution

Double a known fact.

$(3 \times 12) + (3 \times 12) =$

$36 + 36 = 72$

Multiply.

6. 5×2
7. 5×5
8. 8×4
9. 2×7
10. 12×4
11. 7×11
12. 8×8
13. 9×9
14. 7×3
15. 6×7

Use properties of multiplication. (pages 140–141)

Example

These properties can help you multiply.

Commutative Property

$5 \times 4 = 20$ $4 \times 5 = 20$

Identity Property

$3 \times 1 = 3$ $1 \times 4 = 4$

Zero Property

$4 \times 0 = 0$ $0 \times 8 = 0$

Associative Property

$7 \times (2 \times 5) = 7 \times 10 = 70$

Find each product. Then use the Commutative Property to write a different multiplication sentence.

16. 4×3
17. 2×1
18. 4×7
19. 3×0

Multiply.

20. $8 \times (0 \times 7)$
21. $5 \times (2 \times 8)$
22. $(9 \times 4) \times 1$
23. $(6 \times 2) \times 5$

Divide facts through 12. (pages 164–167)

Example

Divide: $15 \div 5$

Solution

Use a related multiplication fact.

$5 \times \blacksquare = 15$

$5 \times 3 = 15$

$15 \div 5 = 3$

Divide.

24. $42 \div 7$
25. $14 \div 7$
26. $64 \div 8$
27. $27 \div 9$
28. $7\overline{)35}$
29. $3\overline{)21}$
30. $8\overline{)56}$
31. $9\overline{)72}$

Identify fact families and missing factors. (pages 160–161, 168–171)

Example

Write a fact family for 7, 8, and 56.

Solution

$7 \times 8 = 56$

$8 \times 7 = 56$

$56 \div 8 = 7$

$56 \div 7 = 8$

Write a multiplication and division fact family for each group of numbers.

32. 9, 9, 81
33. 7, 9, 63

Find each missing number.

34. $3 \times n = 21$
35. $12 \div n = 6$
36. $n \div 7 = 4$

Use strategies to solve problems. (pages 150–151, 162–163)

Example

Belle wants to put 16 rocks from her collection into each of 4 square-shaped display boxes. Can she put an equal number in each box? How?

Solution

Act out the problem using models.

 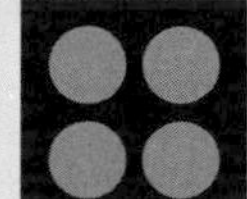 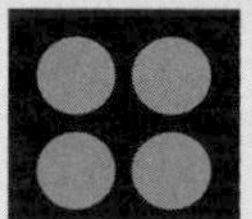 

She can put 4 rocks in each box.

Solve.

37. Wendi has invited 26 of her postcard-collecting friends to dinner. She wants an equal number of people at each table, including herself. Should she seat 8 or 9 guests at each table? How many tables does she need?

38. Wendi buys one tablecloth for each table at her dinner party for $5.00 each. How much does she spend if she buys 4 tablecloths? Which operation did you use? Why?

Study Guide

Chapter Test

Multiply.

1. 6×7 2. 10×6 3. 7×3 4. 5×6 5. 7×7

6. $\begin{array}{r} 7 \\ \times 4 \\ \hline \end{array}$ 7. $\begin{array}{r} 6 \\ \times 4 \\ \hline \end{array}$ 8. $\begin{array}{r} 4 \\ \times 8 \\ \hline \end{array}$ 9. $\begin{array}{r} 6 \\ \times 0 \\ \hline \end{array}$ 10. $\begin{array}{r} 4 \\ \times 9 \\ \hline \end{array}$ 11. $\begin{array}{r} 6 \\ \times 8 \\ \hline \end{array}$

12. $2 \times 4 \times 5$ 13. $5 \times 1 \times 3$

Divide.

14. $54 \div 9$ 15. $45 \div 5$ 16. $15 \div 3$ 17. $28 \div 7$ 18. $81 \div 9$

19. $5\overline{)40}$ 20. $7\overline{)49}$ 21. $5\overline{)25}$ 22. $8\overline{)64}$ 23. $9\overline{)63}$

Write a multiplication and division fact family for each group of numbers.

24. 5, 5, 25 25. 9, 11, 99 26. 4, 12, 48

Find the missing factors.

27. $4 \times n = 32$
$32 \div 8 = m$
28. $9 \times d = 36$
$36 \div 4 = e$
29. $8 \times y = 96$
$96 \div 12 = x$

Solve.

30. Mario puts 5 books about baseball on each of 5 shelves. How many books about baseball does he have?

31. Keesha has 35 baseball cards. She wants to divide them equally among 7 friends. How many cards will each friend get?

32. There are 48 people who attend game night. Mario wants to put an equal number of people at each table. Should he use tables that seat 4 or 5 people? Explain.

33. Lee buys a package of baseball cards for \$2.00, a package of baseballs for \$6.00, and a baseball magazine for \$3.00. How much does he spend in all? What operation did you use? Why?

Performance Assessment

For their school open house week, some fourth graders brought in their collections. The chart at the right shows the types of collections and the number of items in each collection.

Collection	Number
Pins	48
Bean Bag Toys	36
Dolls	50
Model Cars	66
Seashells	42
Books	54

The items in each collection can be packed up in boxes of 4, 5, 6, 8, 9, 10, or 12.

Make a chart like the one below to show how the items can be packed to use the fewest number of boxes without having any left over.

Collection	Total Number of Items	Number per Box	Number of Boxes

A Good Answer

- shows a completed chart.
- shows that the items have been divided into groups of 4, 5, 6, 8, 9, 10, or 12.
- shows the mathematics you used to find the fewest number of boxes.

You may wish to save this work for your portfolio.

Enrichment

Sieve of Eratosthenes

A number that has exactly two factors, itself and 1, is a **prime number.** A **composite number** is one that has more than two factors: itself, 1, and at least one other factor.

Many years ago a Greek mathematician named Eratosthenes discovered a way to identify prime numbers. This is called the **Sieve of Eratosthenes.**

1	2	3	4	5	6	7	8	9	10
11	12	13	14	15	16	17	18	19	20
21	22	23	24	25	26	27	28	29	30
31	32	33	34	35	36	37	38	39	40
41	42	43	44	45	46	47	48	49	50
51	52	53	54	55	56	57	58	59	60
61	62	63	64	65	66	67	68	69	70
71	72	73	74	75	76	77	78	79	80
81	82	83	84	85	86	87	88	89	90
91	92	93	94	95	96	97	98	99	100

Start with a hundreds chart.

- Cross out 1 because it does not have exactly two factors.
- Circle 2. There are exactly two factors of 2: 1 and itself. Two is a prime number.
- Now cross out all the multiples of 2.
- Circle 3. It is a prime number. Cross out all the multiples of 3. Why have some already been crossed out?
- 4 has already been crossed out as a multiple of 2.
- Circle 5. It is a prime number. Why? Cross out all multiples of 5.

1. Complete the rest of the chart. Continue to circle the prime numbers and cross out their multiples.

Write prime or composite.

2. 2   3. 11   4. 39   5. 17   6. 47

7. 27   8. 33   9. 41   10. 93   11. 81

12. When you reached 10, you should have found that all the multiples had already been crossed out. Explain why.

Test-Taking Tips

Some multiple-choice tests include **"Not Here"** as one of the choices. Sometimes the correct answer is not given.

Angela needs 48 party invitations. The invitations come in packages of 8. How many packages does she need to buy?

A. 5 **C.** 40
B. 8 **D.** Not Here

Solve the problem, then check the answer choices.

You need to find out how many groups of 8 are in 48. Divide 48 by 8.

She needs 6 packages.

Check the answer choices. Six is not one of the choices. Check your work: $6 \times 8 = 48$. So the correct answer is choice D, Not Here.

Check for Success

Before turning in a test, go back one last time to check.

- ☑ I understood and answered the question asked.
- ☑ I checked my work for errors.
- ☑ My answers make sense.

Choose the correct answer. Check your work before you choose.

1. Which is a related fact for $72 \div 8 = 9$?

A. $8 \times 8 = 64$ **C.** $9 \times 9 = 81$
B. $8 \times 9 = 72$ **D.** Not Here

2. Which number is missing?
1, 2, 4, 7, 11, 16, ____, 29

F. 21 **H.** 26
G. 22 **J.** Not Here

3. There are cans of juice arranged in 10 rows of 9. You remove 3 cans from each of 4 rows. How many cans are left?

A. 78 **C.** 88
B. 87 **D.** Not Here

4. Which of the following is true?

F. $63 \div 9 = 48 \div 8$
G. $6 \times 2 = 84 \div 7$
H. $35 \div 5 = 3 \times 3$
J. Not Here

5. Which number belongs in the ■?
$3 \times 2 \times ■ = 24$

A. 2 **C.** 4
B. 3 **D.** Not Here

6. Joe saved $18.75 one week, twice that the second week, and $12.90 the third week. How much did Joe save in 3 weeks?

F. $37.50 **H.** $60.40
G. $49.79 **J.** Not Here

Spiral Review and Test Prep

Chapters 1–4

Choose the correct answer.

Number Sense

1. Linda paid $15.25 for a cap and scarf. The scarf cost $6.79. How much did she pay for the cap?
   A. $22.04 **C.** $8.56
   B. $9.46 **D.** $8.46

2. Which is 9 hundred 6 thousand fourteen in standard form?
   F. 960,014 **H.** 90,614
   G. 906,014 **J.** 9,614

3. Which number sentence solves the problem? Alison has a photo album with 8 pages. She has 4 photos on each page. How many photos are in the album?
   A. $8 + 4 = 12$ **C.** $8 - 4 = 4$
   B. $8 \times 4 = 32$ **D.** $8 \div 4 = 2$

4. Steven has a total of 56 stamps. He puts 8 stamps on each page of an album. How many pages does he have?
   F. 7 pages **H.** 5 pages
   G. 6 pages **J.** 4 pages

Algebra and Functions

5. What is the product of the next fact in the pattern?
   $3 \times 2 = 6$
   $3 \times 4 = 12$
   $3 \times 6 = 18$
   $3 \times 8 = 24$
   A. 3×9 **C.** 30
   B. 27 **D.** Not Here

6. Which multiplication fact could you use to solve $63 \div 9$?
   F. 9×5 **H.** 9×7
   G. 9×6 **J.** 9×8

7. What is the missing number?
   $7 \times (■ \times 2) = 42$
   A. 3 **C.** 9
   B. 8 **D.** 33

8. Which makes the number sentence true?
   3×5 ● $64 \div 8$
   F. $=$ **H.** $<$
   G. $+$ **J.** $>$

Statistics, Data Analysis, and Probability

Use data from the bar graph for problems 9–11.

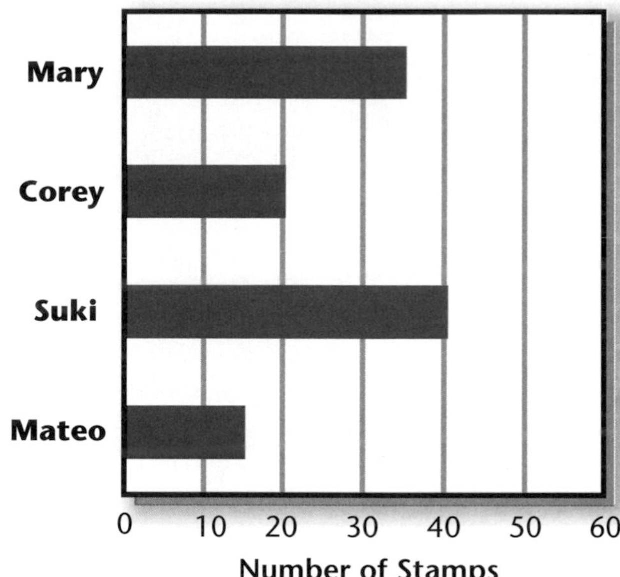

9. How many stamps did Mary collect?
   - A. 30
   - B. 35
   - C. 40
   - D. Not Here

10. How many more stamps did Suki collect than Mateo?
    - F. 15
    - G. 25
    - H. 30
    - J. 40

11. How many stamps did the children collect in all?
    - A. 110
    - B. 100
    - C. 90
    - D. 85

12. Lucy scored 80, 85, 90, 80, 85, and 80 on six math tests. She got an 85 on her seventh test. What is her median test score?
    - F. 80
    - G. 85
    - H. 88
    - J. 90

Mathematical Reasoning

13. Matt is building a rectangular fence. Each corner needs 1 post. He needs to put 8 posts on each side corner and 2 extra posts for a gate. How many posts does he need?
    - A. 32
    - B. 34
    - C. 38
    - D. 40

14. Ben scored 6 three-point field goals and 4 two-point field goals in a basketball game. Which number sentence shows how to find his total?
    - F. $(6 \times 3) + (4 \times 2)$
    - G. $6 + 3 + 4 + 2$
    - H. $(6 - 3) + (4 - 2)$
    - J. $(6 \div 3) + (4 \div 2)$

15. The sum of two numbers is equal to 483. The difference between the larger and smaller is 1. Which are the numbers?
    - A. 240, 243
    - B. 241, 242
    - C. 400, 83
    - D. 482, 1

16. School starts at 8:30 A.M. It takes Jessica 15 minutes to walk to school. What is the latest time she can leave for school and not be late? Explain.

CHAPTER 5

Multiply by 1-Digit Numbers

Theme: Cool Forests and Hot Deserts

Use the Data

Trees

Name	Amount of Growth Each Year (in feet)
Joshua tree	2
Poplar	10
Red alder	9
Willow	8

Source: Encarta 98

- How tall is each tree after 6 years?
- How can you use multiplication to solve the problem?

What You Will Learn

In this chapter you will learn how to
- multiply multiples of 10, 100, and 1,000.
- multiply multi-digit numbers.
- estimate products, including money.
- use a function and/or an equation.
- use strategies to solve problems.

Objective: Review using patterns to multiply mentally.

5•1 Patterns of Multiplication

Algebra & functions

Learn

Math Words

factors numbers that are multiplied to give a product

product the answer in multiplication

Rob plans group hiking trips. The beginner hiking trip costs $2,000. The advanced trip costs $5,000. What is the cost of 4 beginner trips? 3 advanced trips?

Hiking Trips
Monument Valley, Utah

Beginner	$2,000
Advanced	$5,000

Example

You can use patterns of **factors** and **products** to multiply mentally.

$4 \times 2 = 8$	$3 \times 5 = 15$
$4 \times 20 = 80$	$3 \times 50 = 150$
$4 \times 200 = 800$	$3 \times 500 = 1{,}500$
$4 \times 2{,}000 = 8{,}000$	$3 \times 5{,}000 = 15{,}000$

Four beginner trips cost $8,000 and the 3 advanced trips cost $15,000.

More Examples

A

$6 \times 5 = 30$
$6 \times 50 = 300$
$6 \times 500 = 3{,}000$
$6 \times 5{,}000 = 30{,}000$

B

$7 \times 8 = 56$
$7 \times 80 = 560$
$7 \times 800 = 5{,}600$
$7 \times 8{,}000 = 56{,}000$

Try It

Multiply. Use mental math.

1. 90×4
2. 6×80
3. 6×500
4. 3×600
5. 200×3
6. 8×200
7. $1{,}000 \times 4$
8. 500×5

What happens to a product when a zero is added to one of the factors?

Practice Copy and complete.

9. $2 \times 9 = \blacksquare$
$2 \times \blacksquare = 180$
$\blacksquare \times 900 = 1{,}800$
$2 \times 9{,}000 = \blacksquare$

10. $7 \times 3 = \blacksquare$
$7 \times \blacksquare = 210$
$\blacksquare \times 300 = 2{,}100$
$7 \times 3{,}000 = \blacksquare$

11. $6 \times 8 = \blacksquare$
$6 \times \blacksquare = 480$
$\blacksquare \times 800 = 4{,}800$
$6 \times 8{,}000 = \blacksquare$

Multiply. Use mental math.

12. $\begin{array}{r} 40 \\ \times\ 9 \\ \hline \end{array}$ **13.** $\begin{array}{r} 20 \\ \times\ 6 \\ \hline \end{array}$ **14.** $\begin{array}{r} 300 \\ \times\ \ 8 \\ \hline \end{array}$ **15.** $\begin{array}{r} 7{,}000 \\ \times\ \ \ 4 \\ \hline \end{array}$ **16.** $\begin{array}{r} 60{,}000 \\ \times\ \ \ \ 6 \\ \hline \end{array}$

17. 40×2 **18.** 4×60 **19.** 8×800 **20.** 400×4

21. $3 \times 80{,}000$ **22.** $4 \times 40{,}000$ ★**23.** $3 \times 120{,}000$ ★**24.** $5 \times 300{,}000$

Find each missing number.

★**25.** $a \times 3 = 90$ ★**26.** $2 \times b = 100$ ★**27.** $8 \times c = 400$ ★**28.** $d \times 4 = 320$

★**29.** $6 \times t = 2{,}400$ ★**30.** $7 \times w = 2{,}100$ ★**31.** $y \times 7 = 3{,}500$ ★**32.** $z \times 1 = 6{,}000$

Problem Solving

33. A group of tourists will travel 3,500 miles by airplane one way. How many miles will the tourists travel round trip?

34. Social Studies: Rob arranged for a group to visit the Arabian Desert in Egypt. It covers 70,000 square miles. The Great Sandy Desert in Australia covers 150,000 square miles. How much larger is the Great Sandy Desert?

35. Analyze: Why does the product of 5 and 800 have one more zero than the product of 3 and 400?

Spiral Review and Test Prep

★**36.** 4×6 **37.** $867 + 948$ **38.** $54 \div 9$ **39.** $521{,}209 - 8{,}985$

Choose the correct answer.

40. How many minutes is $\frac{1}{4}$ hour?

A. 45 minutes **C.** 25 minutes
B. 30 minutes **D.** 15 minutes

41. Round $546.32 to the nearest dollar.

F. $564.00 **H.** $546.00
G. $547.00 **J.** Not Here

Objective: Review using models to multiply 2-digit numbers by 1-digit numbers.

Explore Multiplying by 1-Digit Numbers

Learn

You can use graph paper to explore multiplying by 1-digit numbers. What is 6 × 29?

Work Together

You Will Need
- centimeter graph paper

Find 6 × 29 using graph paper.

- Draw a rectangle that is 6 squares high and 29 squares wide.
- How many squares are inside the rectangle? How did you find the number of squares?

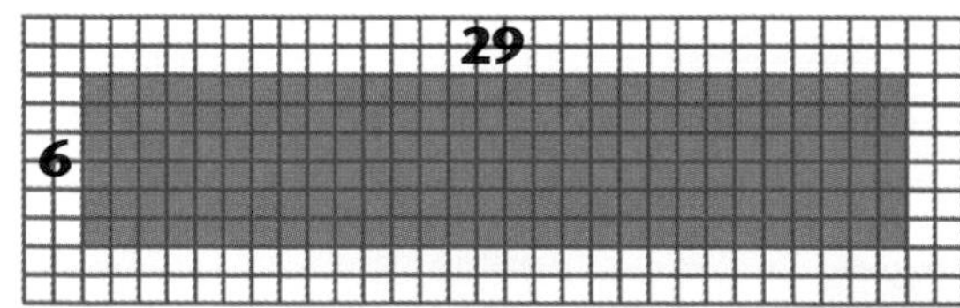

- Use graph paper to multiply. Record your work.

4 × 17	5 × 32	8 × 27
3 × 43	6 × 37	7 × 23
2 × 18	5 × 21	3 × 13
4 × 17	9 × 12	1 × 16

Make Connections

Here is how you can find the product.

Find: 6×29

Using Models

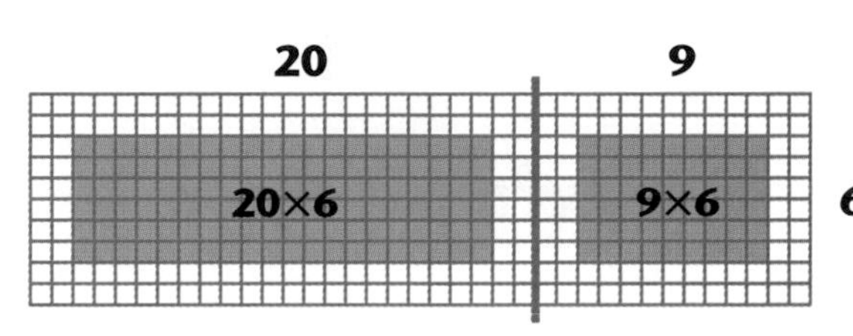

Using Paper and Pencil

$$\begin{array}{r} 29 \\ \times\ 6 \\ \hline 54 \\ +120 \\ \hline 174 \end{array}$$

54 ← Multiply the ones. 6×9

+120 ← Multiply the tens. 6×20

174 ← Add.

Try It **Find each product. You may use graph paper.**

1. 38×3
2. 19×4
3. 43×5
4. 27×8
5. 56×9
6. 45×6
7. 6×33
8. 9×14
9. 8×19
10. 4×58
11. 7×47

Explain how to multiply a 2-digit number by a 1-digit number.

Practice **Find each product.**

12. 38×5
13. 22×6
14. 18×7
15. 26×8
16. 37×9
17. 23×9
18. 82×3
19. 18×4
20. 26×5
21. 41×6
22. 47×7
23. 56×5
24. 4×65
25. 3×28
26. 7×34
27. 2×73
28. 4×39
29. **Analyze:** How can you use tens and ones models to find 4×37? Use pictures to explain your reasoning.

Objective: Review multiplying 2-digit numbers by 1-digit numbers.

5•3 Multiply by 1-Digit Numbers

Learn

Cactus plants can grow in deserts or in sunny windows. If there are 14 cactus plants on each of the 3 shelves, how many cactus plants are there altogether?

There's more than one way!

Find: 3×14

Method A

You can use graph paper.
Divide the rectangle into two smaller rectangles.
Add the two products to find 3 × 14.

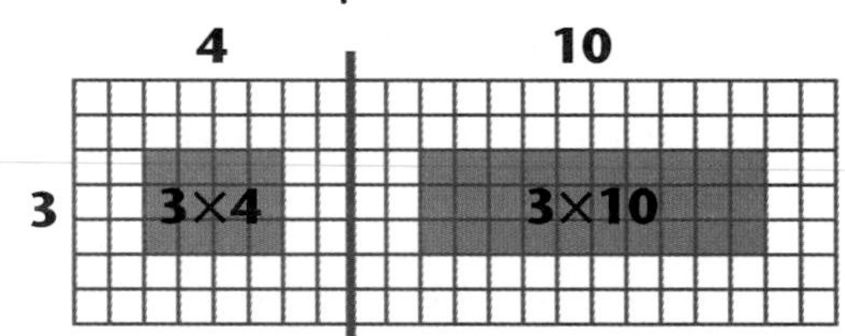

$$\begin{array}{rl} 14 & \\ \times\ 3 & \\ \hline 12 & \leftarrow 3 \times 4 \\ +30 & \leftarrow 3 \times 10 \\ \hline 42 & \end{array}$$

Method B You can use place-value models to show regrouping.

1

Multiply the ones.
Regroup if necessary.

Think: 3 × 4 ones = 12 ones
12 ones = 1 ten 2 ones

2

Multiply the tens.
Add the tens.

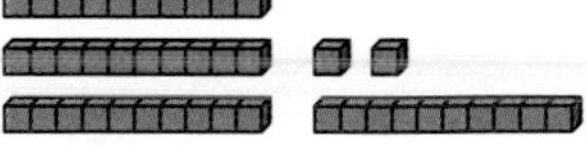

Think: 3 × 1 ten = 3 tens
3 tens + 1 ten 2 ones =
4 tens 2 ones

There are 42 cactus plants.

There are 27 cactus plants on each of the 5 shelves.
How many cactus plants are there?

Example

Find: 5×27

Multiply the ones.
Regroup if necessary.

$$\begin{array}{r} \scriptstyle 3 \\ 27 \\ \times\ 5 \\ \hline 5 \end{array}$$

5×7 ones $= 35$ ones
35 ones $=$ 3 tens 5 ones

2

Multiply the tens.
Add all the tens.
Regroup if necessary.

$$\begin{array}{r} \scriptstyle 3 \\ 27 \\ \times\ 5 \\ \hline 135 \end{array}$$

5×2 tens $= 10$ tens
10 tens $+$ 3 tens $=$ 13 tens
$5 \times 27 = 135$

There are 135 cactus plants.

More Examples

$$\begin{array}{r} \scriptstyle 4 \\ 67 \\ \times\ 6 \\ \hline 402 \end{array}$$

B

$$\begin{array}{r} \scriptstyle 2 \\ \$0.36 \\ \times\quad 4 \\ \hline \$1.44 \end{array}$$

Multiply as with whole numbers. Write a dollar sign and decimal point in the product.

Try It

Copy and complete.

1.
$$\begin{array}{r} 88 \\ \times\ 2 \\ \hline 16 \\ +160 \\ \hline ■■■ \end{array}$$

2.
$$\begin{array}{r} 67 \\ \times\ 4 \\ \hline ■■ \\ +240 \\ \hline 268 \end{array}$$

3.
$$\begin{array}{r} 28 \\ \times\ 6 \\ \hline 48 \\ +■■■ \\ \hline 168 \end{array}$$

4.
$$\begin{array}{r} 46 \\ \times\ ■ \\ \hline 18 \\ +120 \\ \hline 138 \end{array}$$

Multiply.

5. 4×20 **6.** $6 \times \$0.19$ **7.** 3×29 **8.** 4×26 **9.** 4×53

Show how you would multiply 6×57.

Practice Multiply.

10. $\begin{array}{r} 17 \\ \times\ 3 \\ \hline \end{array}$ 11. $\begin{array}{r} 21 \\ \times\ 4 \\ \hline \end{array}$ 12. $\begin{array}{r} \$0.33 \\ \times\quad 5 \\ \hline \end{array}$ 13. $\begin{array}{r} 72 \\ \times\ 3 \\ \hline \end{array}$ 14. $\begin{array}{r} \$0.42 \\ \times\quad 8 \\ \hline \end{array}$ 15. $\begin{array}{r} 57 \\ \times\ 9 \\ \hline \end{array}$

16. 13×6 17. 7×26 18. 3×31 19. $6 \times \$0.54$ 20. 5×68

21. 44×7 22. 2×27 23. $6 \times \$0.50$ 24. 7×19 25. 63×3

26. 42×6 27. 28×3 28. 5×77 29. 4×16 30. $8 \times \$0.73$

31. Multiply 34 by 7.

32. Multiply 61 by 4.

33. Multiply 5 by 32.

34. Multiply 8 by 53.

Use the numbers from Lists A and B for problems 35–36.

List A: 6, 7, 8 List B: 67, 76, 86

★35. Choose one number from each list to find a product between 530 and 540.

★36. Choose one number from each list to find a product between 510 and 520.

37.

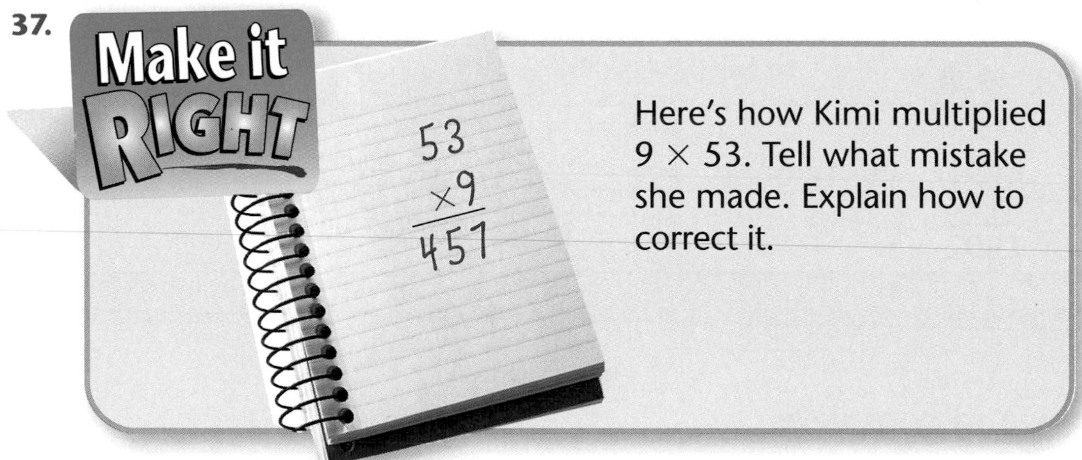

Here's how Kimi multiplied 9×53. Tell what mistake she made. Explain how to correct it.

Problem Solving

38. There are 29 members in a gardening club. Each donates 3 plants to the community gardens. How many plants do they donate altogether?

39. Marco wants to take photos of the desert landscape. He buys a roll of film for \$4.29 and some batteries for \$6.99. He pays with \$20. How much change does he get?

40. The cactus in Ann's window is 3 inches tall. A cactus she sees in the Painted Desert is 27 times as tall. How tall is the cactus in the desert?

41. **Create a problem** multiplying a 2-digit number by a 1-digit number. Solve it. Ask others to solve it.

Use data from the table for problems 42–45.

Items at The Wildlife Company		
Name	Number of Boxes	Number in Each Box
Wildlife videos	5	14
Rain forest T-shirts	6	26
Desert T-shirts	4	37
Animals of the Rain Forest books	8	43

42. How many *Animals of the Rain Forest* books are there altogether?

43. Are there more rain forest T-shirts or desert T-shirts? how many more?

44. Are there more T-shirts than books?

★**45.** How many items are there in all?

46. **Social Studies:** In 1942 General Patton started training troops for World War II in the California desert. The soldiers slept in tents at night. In one area there were 19 tents with 4 soldiers in each tent. How many soldiers were in that area?

★**47.** **Spatial Reasoning:** There are 8 clay pots in each box. How many clay pots are there altogether in the boxes?

Spiral Review and Test Prep

48. 12,900 + 3,000

49. \$263,824 + \$422,376

50. 140,000 − 60,000

51. 320 − 110

52. \$18.11 + \$2.00

53. 11,111 − 2,222

54. \$76.23 − \$3.24

55. 23,000 + 5,000

56. 452,000 + 81,000

Choose the correct answer.

57. Which is the same as 36 ÷ 4?

A. 4 ÷ 36 **C.** $36\overline{)4}$

B. 4 × 36 **D.** $4\overline{)36}$

58. Which multiplication fact is related to 18 ÷ 2?

F. 2 × 18 **H.** 1 × 18

G. 2 × 9 **J.** 8 × 1

Objective: Review estimating products.

5•4 Estimate Products

Learn

Math Words

estimate to find an answer that is close to the exact answer

round to find the nearest 10; 100; 1,000 and so on

Ruth sells postcards of ferns, berries, and mushrooms that grow in Olympic National Park in Washington. On a typical day she sells about 34 postcards. About how many postcards can she sell in 4 days?

34 postcards

Example

You can **estimate** to solve the problem.

Estimate: 4×34

Round the greater factor.

Think: 4×34 Round to the nearest ten.

$\downarrow \quad \downarrow$

$4 \times 30 = 120$

Ruth can sell about 120 postcards in 4 days.

More Examples

A

Estimate: 5×175

Round to the nearest hundred.

Think:
$5 \times 200 = 1,000$

B

Estimate: $8 \times 2,631$

Round to the nearest thousand.

Think:
$8 \times 3,000 = 24,000$

C

Estimate: $7 \times \$9.25$

Round to the nearest dollar.

Think:
$7 \times \$9.00 = \$63.00$

Try It **Estimate each product. Tell how you rounded.**

1. $6 \times \$52$
2. 3×189
3. $7 \times \$3.41$
4. $4 \times 5,286$

Why do you round the greater factor to estimate?

Practice Estimate each product.

5. 7×35
6. $3 \times \$94$
7. 17×8
8. 26×5
9. $4 \times \$68$
10. 457×7
11. 227×8
12. 198×6
13. 2×736
14. $8 \times \$5.45$
15. 626×4
16. $\$2.39 \times 7$
17. 912×6
18. 564×5
19. 291×7
20. $4 \times 6{,}784$
21. $6 \times 2{,}364$
22. $5 \times \$76.45$
23. $7 \times 3{,}561$
24. $3 \times 6{,}468$

Algebra & functions Compare. Write $>$ or $<$.

25. 7×37 ● 8×28
26. 6×123 ● 4×298
27. 5×378 ● 9×345

★28. $(325 + 16) \times 4$ ● $1{,}200$

★29. $(428 + 89) \times 5$ ● $2{,}500$

Problem Solving

30. A customer buys 4 postcards from Ruth for $0.55 each. Estimate how much the customer pays.

31. **Compare:** How does estimating using only the first digit in the greatest place compare with rounding to the greatest place?

32. Chim has $20.00. He wants to buy 3 of Ruth's small paintings like the one shown. Each costs the same amount. Does he have enough money? How do you know?

33. **Health:** During the winter, Ruth lives in Arizona and paints sunsets. People who live in hot, desert-like climates often suffer from heat stroke. This can be a problem if the temperature reaches a high of 114°F. What is this temperature rounded to the nearest ten?

Spiral Review and Test Prep

34. $12 - 5$
35. $18 \div 3$
36. $4 \times 3 \times 7$
37. $369 + 705 + 423$

Choose the correct answer.

38. $34{,}452$ ● $34{,}542$
    - A. $<$
    - B. $>$
    - C. $=$
    - D. Not Here

39. How many minutes are in 4 hours?
    - F. 120 minutes
    - G. 140 minutes
    - H. 180 minutes
    - J. 240 minutes

Extra Practice, page 221

Objective: Form conclusions about using an overestimate or underestimate to solve a problem.

Problem Solving: Reading for Math

Use an Overestimate or Underestimate

Getting Back to Nature

Read

A total of 196 people are taking a trip. Four buses have been ordered. Each bus holds 52 people. Should a fifth bus be ordered for the trip?

READING SKILL ▶

Form a Conclusion

You form a conclusion when you make a decision. This decision is based on facts you know.

- **What do you know?** **196 people on the trip; 4 buses ordered; each bus holds 52 people**
- **What do you need to find out?** **If another bus is needed**

MATH SKILL ▶

Overestimating and Underestimating

To overestimate, round factors up. The estimate is greater than the exact product. To underestimate, round factors down. The estimate is less than the exact product.

Plan

To find if another bus is necessary estimate the product.

Underestimate to make sure that everyone gets a seat on a bus.

Solve

Estimate: 52×4 **Round 52 down.**

$50 \times 4 = 200$ **Compare the product with the number**

$200 > 196$ **of people.**

Four buses will hold all the people going on the trip.

Look Back

Is your answer reasonable?

When would you underestimate a product? overestimate?

Solve. Tell why you used an overestimate or underestimate.

1. A ticket for the trip costs $18. The 5-member Rico family has $100 set aside for special outings. Do the Ricos have enough money to buy the tickets?

2. Each of the 196 people on the trip will receive a pamphlet. The pamphlets come in packs of 24. Trip organizers were given 6 packs of pamphlets. Are there enough pamphlets for each person?

Use data from the pamphlet for problems 3–7.

3. On Monday, a group of 117 students will visit the forest. What is the least number of nature walks that must be held so that each student goes on a walk?

4. Each person who attends a plant naming show receives a packet of plant seeds. The rangers have 200 packets. Is that enough for the shows that day?

5. Last Wednesday, a total of 273 people visited the forest. Could every visitor have seen the Park history film? Explain.

6. A group of 90 campers wants to take a nature walk. How many walks will have to be given for all the campers to go on a nature walk?

7. The rangers have 6 boxes of plant seeds. Each box holds 24 packs. How many full shows at the outdoor arena will this supply?

Trail National Forest

Activity	Schedule	Number of People
Nature walk	Every hour	32
Park history film	6 shows daily	36
Plant naming show	4 shows daily	48

Spiral Review and Test Prep

Choose the correct answer.

Five students want to buy their teacher a book for $17.75. The students give $4 each. Is this enough money?

8. Which statement is true?
   - A. The book cost $4.
   - B. The students will have a total of $20.
   - C. The book costs $20.

9. To be sure they have enough money, the students
   - F. overestimate the book's cost.
   - G. underestimate the book's cost.
   - H. overestimate the money given.

Problem Solving

Check Your Progress A

Multiply. Use mental math. (pages 192–193)

1. 3×80 **2.** 6×300 **3.** 4×700 **4.** $8 \times 4{,}000$ **5.** $3 \times 80{,}000$

Multiply. (pages 196–199)

6. 8×23 **7.** 9×34 **8.** $7 \times \$54$ **9.** 5×68 **10.** $7 \times \$0.82$

11. 3×74 **12.** 6×48 **13.** 2×68 **14.** 4×36 **15.** $6 \times \$0.52$

Estimate each product. (pages 200–201)

16. 4×28 **17.** 5×884 **18.** 6×338 **19.** $7 \times \$4.29$ **20.** $8 \times 3{,}674$

Solve. (pages 192–203)

21. A group of hikers allows 19 cups of water each day for each hiker. They estimate that each hiker will drink 120 cups in 6 days. Did they overestimate or underestimate? Explain why an estimate is necessary.

22. **Art:** Watercolor paint is made with ground pigments and gum arabic. Each container of gum needs to be mixed with 14 containers of water. If an artist has 3 containers of gum and 14 containers of water, how many containers of paint can be made?

23. Frank wants to buy 6 black-and-white photographs of Death Valley. Each photograph costs $45. How much does he pay for all 6 of them?

24. Carolyn buys 8 postcards at each stop on her bus tour. She makes 16 stops. How many postcards does she buy?

25. **Summarize:** Write a letter to a younger neighbor. Explain in your letter how to multiply a 2-digit number by a 1-digit number.

Additional activities at
www.mhschool.com/math

Use Place-Value Models to Multiply

The fourth and fifth graders at Northside Elementary School are going on a field trip. There are 28 students, teachers, and parents going from each of 8 classes. How many people are going on the trip?

You build a model of 8 groups of 28 people using place-value or base-ten models.

- Choose multiplication as the type of mat.
- Stamp out 2 tens and 8 ones in each of the 8 sections at the top of the mat.

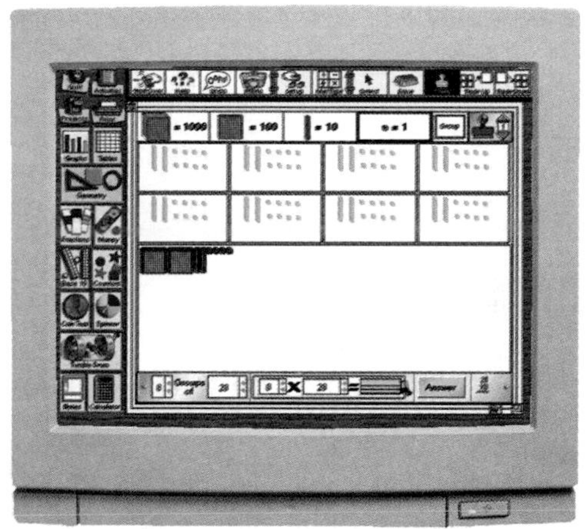

The number boxes keep count as you stamp.

How many are going on the trip?

Use the computer to model each multiplication. Then write the product.

1. 5×52 **2.** 9×76 **3.** 7×123 **4.** 8×109

Solve.

5. Rachael stores her CDs in cases. Each case holds 8 CDs and she has 14 full cases. How many CDs does she have in the cases?

6. Mica collects baseball cards. He has 9 boxes of cards and each box contains 120 cards. How many baseball cards does he have?

7. **Analyze:** How does modeling the problem help you multiply?

For more practice, use Math Traveler™.

Objective: Review multiplying greater numbers by 1-digit numbers.

5•6 Multiply Greater Numbers

Learn

Foresters sometimes take photographs of different campgrounds to design another campground. Roy has 2 boxes with 164 photos in each box. How many photos does he have?

Foresters like Roy Renkin manage public forests and parks.

Example 1

Find: 2×164

1 Multiply the ones. Regroup if necessary.

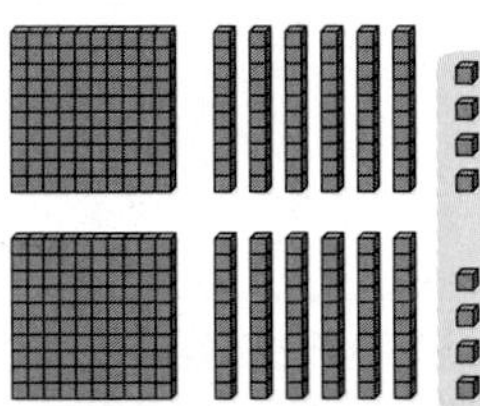

$$\begin{array}{r} 164 \\ \times \quad 2 \\ \hline 8 \end{array}$$

Think: 2×4 ones $= 8$ ones

2 Multiply the tens. Add all the tens. Regroup if necessary.

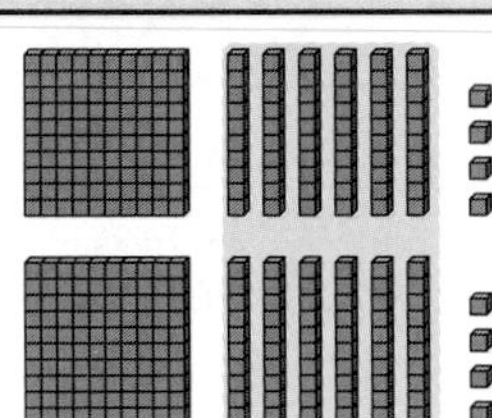

$$\begin{array}{r} \overset{1}{1}64 \\ \times \quad 2 \\ \hline 28 \end{array}$$

Think: 2×6 tens $= 12$ tens
12 tens = 1 hundred 2 tens

3 Multiply the hundreds. Add all the hundreds. Regroup if necessary.

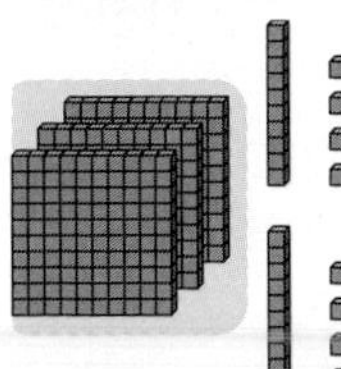

$$\begin{array}{r} \overset{1}{1}64 \\ \times \quad 2 \\ \hline 328 \end{array}$$

Think: 2×1 hundred $= 2$ hundreds
2 hundreds + 1 hundred = 3 hundreds

Check: You can estimate to check the reasonableness of the answer. Estimate: $2 \times 200 = 400$

Roy has 328 photos.

328 is reasonably close to 400.

Roy puts another 1,225 photos into each of 6 boxes.
How many photos does he organize?

Example 2

Find: $6 \times 1{,}225$

1 Multiply the ones.
Regroup if necessary.

$$\begin{array}{r} \overset{3}{} \\ 1{,}225 \\ \times \quad 6 \\ \hline 0 \end{array}$$

Think: 6×5 ones $= 30$ ones
30 ones $=$ 3 tens 0 ones

2 Multiply the tens.
Add all the tens.
Regroup if necessary.

$$\begin{array}{r} 1\,3 \\ 1{,}225 \\ \times \quad 6 \\ \hline 50 \end{array}$$

Think: 6×2 tens $= 12$ tens
12 tens $+$ 3 tens $=$ 15 tens
15 tens $=$ 1 hundred 5 tens

3 Multiply the hundreds.
Add all the hundreds.
Regroup if necessary.

$$\begin{array}{r} 1\,1\,3 \\ 1{,}225 \\ \times \quad 6 \\ \hline 350 \end{array}$$

Think: 6×2 hundreds $= 12$ hundreds
12 hundreds $+$ 1 hundred $=$ 13 hundreds
13 hundreds $=$ 1 thousand 3 hundreds

4 Multiply the thousands.
Add all the thousands.
Regroup if necessary.

$$\begin{array}{r} 1\,1\,3 \\ 1{,}225 \\ \times \quad 6 \\ \hline 7{,}350 \end{array}$$

Think: 6×1 thousand $= 6$ thousands
6 thousands $+$ 1 thousand $=$ 7 thousands

Check for reasonableness: Estimate: $6 \times 1{,}200 = 7{,}200$

Roy has organized 7,350 photos.

7,350 is reasonably close to 7,200.

Try It **Multiply. Check for reasonableness.**

1. $\begin{array}{r} 209 \\ \times \quad 4 \\ \hline \end{array}$
2. $\begin{array}{r} \$3.17 \\ \times \quad 3 \\ \hline \end{array}$
3. $\begin{array}{r} 458 \\ \times \quad 6 \\ \hline \end{array}$
4. $\begin{array}{r} 6{,}723 \\ \times \quad 5 \\ \hline \end{array}$
5. $\begin{array}{r} 88{,}613 \\ \times \quad 2 \\ \hline \end{array}$
6. 5×344
7. $7 \times \$6.09$
8. $8 \times 4{,}007$
9. $9 \times 61{,}480$
10. $7 \times 21{,}826$
11. $5 \times 48{,}753$
12. $8 \times \$138.73$
13. $37{,}937 \times 8$

Explain how multiplying 3-digit numbers is like multiplying 2-digit numbers. How is it different?

Practice Multiply. Check for reasonableness.

14. 609×6 **15.** $\$465 \times 7$ **16.** 719×4 **17.** $\$2.28 \times 5$ **18.** 164×9

19. $4,539 \times 7$ **20.** $\$5,098 \times 4$ **21.** $3,036 \times 4$ **22.** $\$68.30 \times 9$ **23.** $4,509 \times 3$

24. 6 × 29,558 **★25.** 4 × $2,139.82 **★26.** 5 × 360,309

27. Multiply 3 by 9,898. **28.** Multiply 7 by 2,334.

29. Multiply 6 by 4,502. **30.** Multiply $17.39 by 8.

Find only the products between 1,200 and 60,000.

★31. 3 × 5,188 **★32.** 8 × 8,829 **★33.** 9 × 257

★34. 2 × 504 **★35.** 7 × 6,741 **★36.** 9 × 35,768

Copy and complete.

37.

Rule: Multiply by 3			
Input	367	1,237	31,286
Output	▮	▮	▮

38.

Rule: Multiply by 4,869				
Input	2	4	6	8
Output	▮	▮	▮	▮

39.

Here is how Carlos multiplied 7 × 6,509. Tell what mistake he made. Explain how to correct it.

Problem Solving

40. Jan is going to take a camping trip to Death Valley National Monument in the California desert. The fee is $29 for each night. How much will it cost to stay for 9 nights?

41. Analyze: If you multiply a 1-digit number by a 4-digit number, what is the greatest number of digits the product could have? Explain.

Use data from *Did You Know?* for problems 42–45.

42. How many years ago was the tree reported?

43. Wood from the Australian eucalyptus is valued at $9 a foot. How much would this tree be worth?

44. A forester had a tree cut down that was 85 feet less than this Australian eucalyptus. The tree was cut into 10-foot logs. How many logs were there?

45. **What if** 75 years later, 180 eucalyptus seedlings were planted in each of 7 areas of a national forest? When were they planted? How many were planted?

46. **Create a problem** multiplying greater numbers. Solve it. Ask others to solve it.

47. **Science:** Balsam fir trees grow about 50 feet tall. Redwood trees grow more than 5 times as tall. How tall do the redwoods grow?

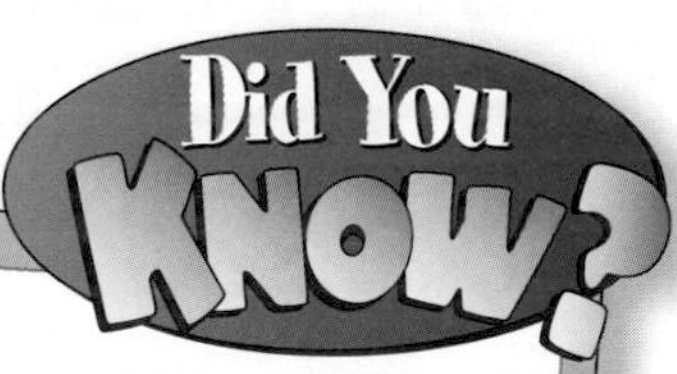

The tallest tree ever measured was an Australian eucalyptus. It measured 435 feet tall and was reported by forester William Ferguson in 1872.

Source: *The Guinness Book of Records*

Spiral Review and Test Prep

48. $\begin{array}{r} 3,974 \\ 39 \\ +\ 627 \\ \hline \end{array}$

49. $\begin{array}{r} 8,432 \\ -\ 265 \\ \hline \end{array}$

50. $\begin{array}{r} 9 \\ \times 8 \\ \hline \end{array}$

51. $\begin{array}{r} 4 \\ \times 6 \\ \hline \end{array}$

52. $5\overline{)40}$

53. $\begin{array}{r} 12 \\ \times 13 \\ \hline \end{array}$

54. $6\overline{)72}$

55. $\begin{array}{r} 620 \\ -\ 92 \\ \hline \end{array}$

56. $\begin{array}{r} 211 \\ 18 \\ +123 \\ \hline \end{array}$

57. $\begin{array}{r} 17 \\ \times\ 3 \\ \hline \end{array}$

Choose the correct answer.

58. What is 507,809 written in expanded form?
   - **A.** 500,000 + 70,000 + 8,000 + 90
   - **B.** 500,000 + 70,000 + 8,000 + 9
   - **C.** 500,000 +7,000 +800 + 9
   - **D.** 500,000 +7,000 +8,000 + 9

59. What is the range of this set of data: 34 22 28 35 21 34 20?
   - **F.** 34
   - **G.** 28
   - **H.** 15
   - **J.** 14

Objective: Find a pattern to solve a problem.

Problem Solving: Strategy
Find a Pattern

Read **Read the problem carefully.**

Tamara arranged pine cones into different groups. She started with one pine cone in the first group. In the next group she put 2 pine cones. She put 4 pine cones in the third group, 8 pine cones in the fourth, and so on. If the number in each row continues to increase in the same way, how many pine cones does she put in the eighth group?

- **What do you know?** **The number in the first four rows**
- **What do you need to find?** **The number to put in the eighth group**

Plan One way to solve the problem is to find a pattern. Look at how the number of pine cones in each group changes.

Solve The number of pine cones doubles each time.

$1 \xrightarrow{\times 2} 2 \xrightarrow{\times 2} 4 \xrightarrow{\times 2}$

Continue the pattern to find how many pine cones will be in the eighth group.

$1 \xrightarrow{\times 2} 2 \xrightarrow{\times 2} 4 \xrightarrow{\times 2} 8 \xrightarrow{\times 2} 16 \xrightarrow{\times 2} 32 \xrightarrow{\times 2} 64 \xrightarrow{\times 2} 128$

Tamara puts 128 pine cones in the eighth group.

Look Back Is there another way to describe the pattern above?

What other strategies could you use to solve this problem?

Practice **Find a pattern to solve. Describe the pattern.**

1. As a plant cell grows, one cell divides into two cells. Two cells divide into four cells, four into eight, and so on. How many cells will there be after seven divisions?

2. Ben gathers acorns. On the first day he gathered 11 acorns. On the second day he gathered 22 acorns, the third day 33 acorns, and on the fourth day 44 acorns. How many will he gather on the eleventh day?

3. Tamara planned to use wood for a group of outdoor sculptures. The first sculpture weighed 6 pounds. The second one weighed 18 pounds. The third one weighed 54 pounds. What comes next according to your pattern? How many pounds will the wood weigh in the fifth sculpture?

4. On a bike trip in the Petrified Forest, two bikers take turns carrying the heavier pack. The first biker starts off with the heavier pack. They change after every 12 miles. They have biked 110 miles so far. How many times have they changed? Who is now carrying the heavier pack?

Problem Solving

Mixed Strategy Review

5. Wood ducks are nesting under the pine trees. One year 3 pairs of wood ducks built nests. The next year 7 pairs built nests. The third year 11 pairs built nests. Describe the pattern. How many nests should there be in the fifth year?

6. **Create a problem** that can be solved by finding a pattern. Solve it. Ask others to solve it.

CHOOSE A STRATEGY

- Logical Reasoning
- Draw a Picture
- Make a Graph
- Act It Out
- Make a Table or List
- Find a Pattern
- Guess and Check
- Write a Number Sentence
- Work Backward
- Solve a Simpler Problem

Use data from the chart for problems 7–9.

7. Which two trees are twice the height of the big leaf maple?

8. The sawmill cut up a tree that reached its maximum height. It sold half the length of the tree to a builder. A carpenter bought half that length. There is 45 feet of wood left from the tree. What kind of tree was it?

9. Find the maximum height of these trees: lodgepole pine, red alder, black cottonwood. What tree(s) could be next to make a pattern? Explain the pattern.

Trees in Oregon

Name	Maximum Height (in Feet)
Big leaf maple	100
Black cottonwood	200
Douglas fir	250
Grand fir	250
Lodgepole pine	100
Ponderosa pine	180
Red alder	150
Western red cedar	200

Extra Practice, page 222

Objective: Use a table to explore functions and graph them.

5•8 Functions and Graphs

Algebra & functions

Learn

Math Words

function a relationship in which one quantity depends upon another quantity

equation a mathematical statement with an equal sign

coordinates the numbers in an ordered pair

ordered pair a pair of numbers that gives the location of a point on a graph

It sometimes rains hard in the Redwood National Park. If it rained this hard for 2 hours, how much rainfall would there be? in 3 hours? in 4 hours?

Rainfall 8 millimeters each hour

There's more than one way!

Method A

One way to solve this problem is to make a **function** table. The amount of rain that falls depends upon the time period you are considering.

Time (hours)	Amount (mm)
1	8
2	16
3	24
4	32

Think: Each number in the **Time** row is multiplied by 8 to find the amount of rainfall.

Method B

Another way to solve this problem is by writing an **equation**. You multiply the time by the amount of rain that falls in 1 hour.

Let r be the total amount of rainfall.

Let t be the time period.

So r equals 8 times t.

$r = 8t$

Now you can substitute different values for t to find the value of r.

2 hours	3 hours	4 hours
$r = 8 \times 2$	$r = 8 \times 3$	$r = 8 \times 4$
$r = 16$	$r = 24$	$r = 32$

In 2 hours the amount of rainfall would be 16 millimeters; in 3 hours, 24 millimeters; and in 4 hours, 32 millimeters.

An environmental club plans a tree-planting campaign. They live close to a forest where trees are being cut down to make paper. How many seedlings will they plant if 2 trees are cut down? 12 trees?

SAVE TREES! PLANT SEEDLINGS!

Help us reach our goal of planting 2 seedlings for every tree cut down in the Shawnee Woods.

The Shawnee Tree Campaign

Example

You can write and graph an equation to solve the problem.

1

Let y be the number of seedlings to plant.

Let x be the number of trees cut down.

If 2 seedlings will be planted for every tree cut, write the equation:

$y = 2x$

2

Make a table of values for the equation. Show the **coordinates** of the **ordered pairs**.

X	0	1	2	3	4
Y	0	2	4	6	8

Think: $y = 2x$

$y = 2 \times 3$ Substitute for x to find y.

$y = 6$

3

Plot the ordered pairs. Connect the points with a line.

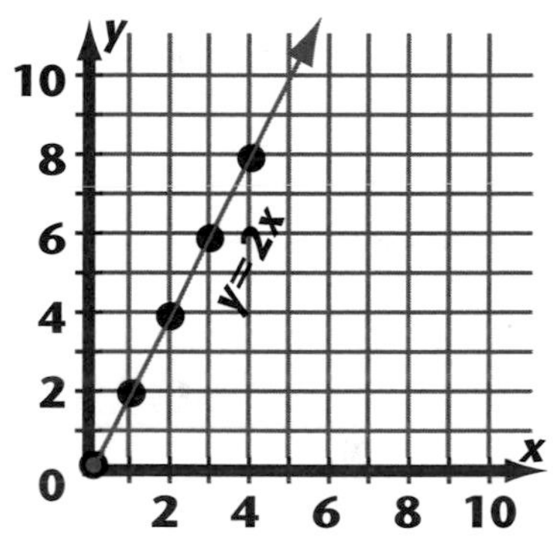

The club will plant 4 seedlings if 2 trees are cut down and 24 seedlings if 12 trees are cut down.

Try It **Copy and complete each table. Then graph the function.**

1. $y = 2x + 1$

X	0	1	2	3
Y	1	3	■	■

2. One kind of seedling grows 4 times faster than another kind. $y = 4x$

X	0	1	2	3
Y	0	4	■	■

Explain how you can use a graph to find values.

Practice

Copy and complete each table. Then write an equation.

3. One plant grows 5 centimeters more each month than another plant.

p	1	2	3	4	5
g	6	7	■	■	■

4. One tree grows 3 times as fast as another.

m	1	2	3	4	5
j	3	6	■	■	■

★5. One number is 2 more than 3 times another number.

k	1	2	3	4	5
p	5	8	■	■	■

★6. One number is 1 less than 2 times another number.

c	1	2	3	4	5
d	1	3	■	■	■

Copy and complete each table. Then graph the function.

7. Each member of the Junior Rangers Club plants 3 pine saplings. Then they each choose one other sapling to plant.

$b = 3a + 1$

a	0	1	2	3
b	1	4	■	■

8. The lumber company has agreed to plant 5 trees for every tree a Junior Ranger plants.

$s = 5r$

r	0	1	2	3
s	0	5	■	■

9. $d = 3c - 1$

c	1	2	3	4
d	2	5	■	■

10. $l = 2k + 1$

k	0	1	2	3
l	1	3	■	■

11.

Here's how Annie wrote an equation from the following table. Tell what mistake she made. Explain how to correct it.

a	0	2	4	6
b	1	5	9	13

Problem Solving

12. The Tree-Savers give out 5 small trees to every new member. How many trees do they give out to 5 new members? 10 new members? Write and solve an equation.

13. It costs $5 for each person to go to a red wood photography exhibit. How much would it cost for 6 people to go? Write and solve an equation.

Use data from *Did You Know?* for problems 14–16.

14. **Time:** About how many trees would be cut down from 8:00 A.M. to 10:00 P.M.?

15. Over the next 3 years, what would be the least number of species we could lose? the greatest number?

16. **Collect data** on the number of animals in the rain forest. Order the data from greatest to least.

★ 17. **Create a problem** solved by making a graph. Solve it. Ask others to solve it.

18. A camp charges $8 each night. A fire permit costs an extra $9 for the entire visit. How much would it cost for 5 nights along with a fire permit? Write and solve an equation.

19. **Explain** how the function $y = 2x + 3$ is a way of finding a second number when a first number is given.

★20. **What if** one kind of tree grows 3 inches each year and another kind grows 5 inches each year. Show a graph for each tree. Tell how the lines are different.

Did You Know?

The rain forest is home to as many as 30 million species. Some 500,000 trees are cut down every hour in tropical rain forests. When the trees are cut down, the plants and animals lose their homes and can become extinct. We lose 20,000 to 100,000 species every year when the rain forests are destroyed.

Spiral Review and Test Prep

21. 100,000 − 386
22. $3 \times 2 \times 5$
23. 65,908 + 392
24. $12 \div 4$
25. $311.10 − $45.98
26. 9 + 6
27. $21 \div 3$

Choose the correct answer.

28. How many minutes are in $1\frac{1}{2}$ hours?
    - A. 30
    - B. 60
    - C. 90
    - D. 120

29. What is the value of 4 in 641,298,537?
    - F. 4
    - G. 4,000
    - H. 4,000,000
    - J. 40,000,000

Objective: Analyze data and make decisions.

Problem Solving: Application
Decision Making

Eight members of a photography club plan to go on a camping trip to the Painted Desert in Arizona. They have asked you to help them choose their food.

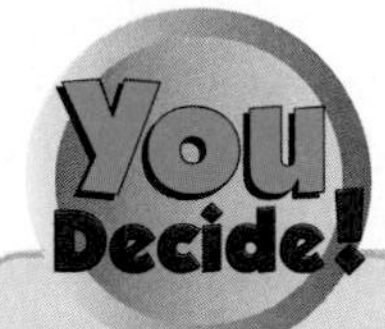

Choose 1 breakfast, 1 lunch, 1 dinner, and snacks for the trip.

breakfast

Cereal	$2.79 a box	2 boxes
Milk	$2.49 a gallon	1 gallon
Bagels	$1.49 a package	2 packages

lunch

Mayonnaise	$1.79 a jar	1 jar
Bread	$1.39 a loaf	2 loaves
Cheese	$2.89 a package	2 packages
Tuna	$0.89 a can	4 cans

dinner

Rice	$2.19 a box	1 box
Chicken wings	$2.45 a package	2 packages
Baked beans	$1.29 a can	3 cans
Hot dogs	$3.19 a package	2 packages
Buns	$1.49 a package	2 packages
Vegetables	$1.19 a can	3 cans
Juice	$3.49 a bottle	1 bottle

snacks

Granola bars	$2.39 a box	2 boxes
Grapes	$1.29 a pound	2 pounds
Oatmeal cookies	$1.99 a box	2 boxes
Bananas	$0.69 a pound	3 pounds

Read for Understanding

1. How much would it cost to buy the bananas?
2. How much would you spend on bread?
3. How much would you spend on cereal?
4. How much would you spend on chicken wings?
5. What is the price for 2 packages of hot dogs?
6. How much would you spend on grapes?
7. How much would it cost to buy the two packages of bagels?
8. What is the cost of buying 2 packages of cheese?
9. How much would you spend on 3 cans of beans?
10. How much would it cost to buy the 4 cans of tuna fish?

Problem Solving

Make Decisions

11. What foods would you choose for breakfast?
12. What foods would you plan for lunch?
13. What would you buy for dinner?
14. One member of the club is vegetarian. What would you plan for dinner?
15. One member of the club is allergic to milk and cheese. What would you plan for breakfast? for lunch?
16. Many club members will want a snack between lunch and dinner. Choose a snack that would boost their energy.
17. Which costs more, breakfast or snacks? Explain.
18. Compare the cost of lunch with the cost of dinner. Which is less?
19. Compare the cost of lunch with the cost of breakfast. Which is more?
20. Make a list of other things you should think about before making your decision.

Your Decision!

What is your recommendation for the menus? How much would you spend on food?

Objective: Apply multiplication to investigate science concepts.

Problem Solving: Math and Science

How much water do you use each day?

You Will Need
- **measuring cups (optional)**

Whoosh! You let the water run before you fill your glass to take a drink. Do you have any idea how much water you just used?

Because clean water is an important resource, everyone should be aware of how much they use. And you probably use a lot more than you think!

Hypothesize

Estimate how much water you use each day.

Procedure

1. Work with a partner or small group.
2. Make a list of all the places you use water.
3. Record the number of times you use that source of water. (For example, how many times do you drink a glass of water?)
4. Estimate, measure, or research how much water is involved in each activity. (For example, a drinking glass holds about 1 cup.)
5. Multiply to find the amount of water you use for each activity.
6. Find the total amount of water used.

Data

Copy and complete the chart to record your data.

Activity	Number of Times a Day	Amount of Water for Each Use	Amount of Water Each Day

Problem Solving

Conclude and Apply

- How much water do you use each day?
- **What if** a cup of water costs $0.10, how much money do you spend on water each day?
- Is clean water a renewable or nonrenewable resource? Explain.

Natural resources include things like water, trees, oil, coal, and soil. A renewable resource can be replaced, while a nonrenewable one cannot.

Going Further

1. Find the water use of the entire class. Use the data to find the water use of the whole school for one day. Estimate the water use of the school for one year.
2. Make a list of at least five ways to use less water.

Check Your Progress B

Multiply. Check for reasonableness. **(pages 206–209)**

1. $3,428 \times 5$
2. $65,183 \times 3$
3. $\$1.38 \times 7$
4. $1,293 \times 8$
5. $6,732 \times 6$
6. $\$9.35 \times 8$
7. $23,116 \times 7$
8. $22,308 \times 9$
9. $\$25.76 \times 5$
10. $39,532 \times 4$
11. $4,743 \times 6$
12. $\$53.25 \times 6$

Copy and complete each table. Then write an equation. **(pages 212–215)**

13. One desert animal can run 3 times as fast as another animal.

a	1	2	3	4	5
b	3	6	■	■	■

14. One number is 3 less than another number.

t	5	10	15	20	25
d	2	7	■	■	■

Copy and complete each table. Then graph the function. **(pages 212–215)**

15. There are 7 people in each minivan on the tour of the Painted Desert.

$d = 7t$				
t	1	2	3	4
d	7	14	■	■

16. You can rent a canoe for \$2 an hour and buy juice for the trip for \$3.

$c = 2d + 3$				
d	0	1	2	3
c	3	5	■	■

Solve. **(pages 206–215)**

17. A forest covers an area of 2,322 acres. Ten years ago it was 4 times as large. What was the area ten years ago?

18. A tour of the desert costs \$23.75 per person. How much would a tour cost for a family of 5?

19. Admission to a museum is \$8.50 a person. Visitors can also buy a videotape for \$12.95. How much does it cost for a family of 6 to go to the museum and purchase a videotape? Write and solve an equation.

20. **Explain** what the equation $y = x + 4$ means and show how it can be represented in different ways.

Additional activities at
www.mhschool.com/math

Extra Practice

Patterns of Multiplication (pages 192–193)

Multiply. Use mental math.

1. 30×8 2. 50×5 3. 200×6 4. $6{,}000 \times 7$ 5. $40{,}000 \times 8$

6. 9×900 7. $8 \times 3{,}000$ 8. $5{,}000 \times 6$ 9. $3 \times 70{,}000$ 10. $4 \times 60{,}000$

Solve.

11. Mr. Estefan led a tour to the desert. Members of the tour sketched 6 unusual desert plants. There were 20 members on the tour. Write a multiplication sentence that shows how many sketches they made in all.

Multiply 2-Digit Numbers by 1-Digit Numbers (pages 196–199)

Multiply.

1. 44×8 2. 89×4 3. 38×9 4. 55×7 5. 68×5

6. 6×56 7. 3×87 8. 49×6 9. 2×97 10. 58×5

Solve.

11. As part of a library project, 18 fourth-grade students read aloud books about desert animals to young children. Each student reads 6 books. How many books do they read altogether?

Estimate Products (pages 200–201)

Estimate each product.

1. 45×6 2. 258×3 3. 646×4 4. $\$32.97 \times 5$ 5. $5{,}428 \times 2$

6. 8×46 7. 832×6 8. $3 \times \$9.74$ 9. $7{,}408 \times 5$ 10. $7 \times 6{,}824$

Extra Practice

Problem Solving: Reading for Math Use an Overestimate or Underestimate (pages 202–203)

1. A total of 98 students are going camping. Each tent holds 5 people. The school has 21 tents. Should they get another one?

2. There are 27 fourth graders plus 2 adults going on a hike. Each hiker needs 6 cups of water. Is 180 cups enough?

Multiply Greater Numbers (pages 206–209)

Multiply. Check for reasonableness.

1. $\begin{array}{r} 801 \\ \times \quad 8 \\ \hline \end{array}$ 2. $\begin{array}{r} 288 \\ \times \quad 6 \\ \hline \end{array}$ 3. $\begin{array}{r} 6{,}709 \\ \times \quad 3 \\ \hline \end{array}$ 4. $\begin{array}{r} 4{,}792 \\ \times \quad 5 \\ \hline \end{array}$ 5. $\begin{array}{r} 25{,}861 \\ \times \quad 9 \\ \hline \end{array}$

6. $\begin{array}{r} \$0.64 \\ \times \quad 7 \\ \hline \end{array}$ 7. $\begin{array}{r} \$3.96 \\ \times \quad 8 \\ \hline \end{array}$ 8. $\begin{array}{r} \$5.16 \\ \times \quad 4 \\ \hline \end{array}$ 9. $\begin{array}{r} \$34.27 \\ \times \quad 6 \\ \hline \end{array}$ 10. $\begin{array}{r} \$92.11 \\ \times \quad 9 \\ \hline \end{array}$

11. 4 × 306 12. 7 × 382 13. 2,887 × 3 14. 6,504 × 5 15. 50,561 × 8

16. $4.30 × 8 17. 7 × $3.98 18. 615 × 9 19. 542 × 2 20. 8 × $29.76

Solve.

21. **Science: What if** a piece of leaf is magnified 150 times under a microscope? If the actual size of the leaf piece is 6 millimeters, what is the magnified size?

22. Pine seedlings are on sale for $4.99 each. How much do 6 seedlings cost?

Problem Solving: Strategy Find a Pattern (pages 210–211)

Solve.

1. In an architect's drawing, there are 81 cacti in the ninth row, 72 in the eighth row, 63 in the seventh row. Describe the pattern. If the number keeps decreasing by the same amount how many cacti are in the third row?

2. The following amounts of rainfall were recorded for 3 months: 7 inches, 14 inches, 21 inches. Describe a pattern. If the pattern continues, how much rain will fall in the next month?

Extra Practice

Functions and Graphs (pages 212–215)

Copy and complete each table. Then write an equation.

1. One number is 2 more than another number.

w	1	2	3	4	5
r	3	4	■	■	■

2. One seedling needs 3 times more water than another seedling.

f	1	2	3	4	5
h	3	6	■	■	■

3. One number is 1 less than another number.

l	2	4	6	8	10
w	1	3	■	■	■

4. One forest gets twice as much rain as another forest.

a	2	3	4	5	6
b	4	6	■	■	■

Copy and complete each table. Then graph the function.

5.

$d = 3c + 2$				
c	0	1	2	3
d	2	5	■	■

6. One wildflower has 4 times as many petals as another one.

$q = 4p$				
p	0	1	2	3
q	0	4	■	■

7.

$d = 3c - 2$				
c	1	2	3	4
d	1	4	■	■

8.

$y = 2v - 1$				
v	1	2	3	4
y	1	3	■	■

Chapter Study Guide

Language and Math

Math Words
- ordered pairs
- factors
- function
- product
- estimate

Complete. Use a word from the list.

1. In 78×4, the ____ are 78 and 4.
2. An example of a ____ is $y = 3x$.
3. You use ____ to plot points to graph a function.

Skills and Applications

Multiply multiples of 10; 100; and 1,000. (pages 192–193)

Example
Find: $3 \times 6{,}000$

Solution
Use multiplication patterns.

$3 \times 60 = 180$
$3 \times 600 = 1{,}800$
$3 \times 6{,}000 = 18{,}000$

Find each product.

4. 30×5
5. 6×80
6. 600×7
7. $6{,}000 \times 5$
8. $4 \times 40{,}000$

Multiply multidigit numbers (pages 194–199, 206–209)

Example
Find: 3×152

Solution
Multiply each place.

Regroup.
$$\begin{array}{r} ^{1}\\ 152 \\ \times \quad 3 \\ \hline 456 \end{array}$$

Think:
$3 \times 2 = 6$
$3 \times 50 = 150$
$3 \times 100 = 300$
$300 + 150 + 6 = 456$

Find each product.

9. $\begin{array}{r} 36 \\ \times\ 7 \\ \hline \end{array}$
10. $\begin{array}{r} 334 \\ \times\ \ 5 \\ \hline \end{array}$
11. $4 \times 7{,}570$
12. $9 \times \$0.28$
13. $5 \times \$31.76$
14. $4 \times \$77.68$
15. $6 \times 18{,}765$
16. $8 \times 6{,}709$

Estimate products, including money. (pages 200–201)

Example
Estimate: 4×37

Solution
Round the greater factor. $37 \rightarrow 40$.
Multiply $4 \times 40 = 160$

Estimate each product.

17. $4 \times \$56$
18. 5×322
19. $\$728 \times 3$
20. 6×107
21. Each of 4 boys picks 29 pears. About how many pears are there altogether?

Use a function or an equation. (pages 212–215)

Example

Copy and complete each table. Then graph the function.

Admission to an exhibit costs $3 for each person. How much will it cost for 5 people to enter the exhibit?

Solution

1	2	3	4	5
$3	$6	$9	$12	$15

$y = 3x$ $y = 3 \times 5 = \$15$

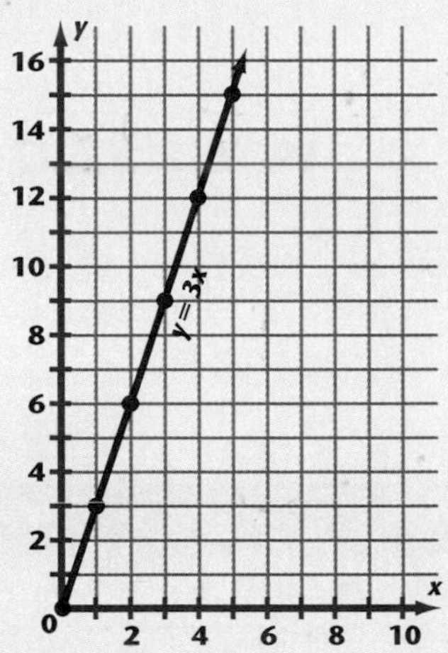

It will cost $15.

Copy and complete each table. Then graph the function.

22. There are 6 times as many pine trees as oaks in the forest.

r	1	2	3	4	5
s	6	12	▮	▮	▮

23. One number is 4 more than another number.

p	1	2	3	4	5
q	5	6	▮	▮	▮

Study Guide

Use strategies to solve problems. (pages 202–203, 210–211)

Example

There is a stack of books on forestry. There are 3 books in the first row, 6 in the second row, and 9 in the third row. If the number of books continues to increase in the same way how many would be in the sixth row?

Solution

Find a pattern to solve a problem.

3 →(+3) 6 →(+3) 9 →(+3) 12 →(+3) 15 →(+3) 18

There would be 18 books in the sixth row.

Solve.

24. Miko and her parents want to go on a trip to a rain forest. Roundtrip airline tickets cost $385 each. They have saved $12,000. Have they saved enough money to pay for 3 tickets? Explain.

25. Carlos is making a flower display. He puts 6 flowers in the first row, 12 flowers in the second row, 24 in the third row, and 48 in the fourth row. If the number of flowers in each row keeps increasing in the same way, how many would he put in the sixth row?

Chapter Test

Multiply.

1. $\begin{array}{r} 487 \\ \times \quad 3 \\ \hline \end{array}$
2. $\begin{array}{r} 700 \\ \times \quad 8 \\ \hline \end{array}$
3. $\begin{array}{r} \$2.17 \\ \times \quad 8 \\ \hline \end{array}$
4. $\begin{array}{r} 6,688 \\ \times \quad 4 \\ \hline \end{array}$
5. $8.56 × 5
6. 6 × 539
7. 20,000 × 2
8. 7 × 4,628
9. 7 × 39,628
10. 5 × $86.29
11. 4,296 × 9
12. 4 × $53.82
13. 7,000 × 6
14. 4 × 34,269
15. 3 × 8,974

Estimate each product.

16. 3 × 762
17. 6 × 5,709
18. 4,362 × 9
19. 8 × 8,697

Solve.

20. On their summer vacation, the Hayes family drove 150 miles each day for 6 days. How many miles did they drive?

21. There are 5 times as many hikers as campers in the forest. Copy and complete the table. Then graph the function.

$t = 5p$				
p	0	1	2	3
t	0	5	■	■

22. Six years ago, 2,584 deer were counted in a nature survey. This year, 6 times as many deer are counted. How many deer are counted this year?

23. A subscription to a wildlife magazine is $37.50 each year. Mrs. Hollings is buying one subscription for each of her 9 grandchildren. How much do the subscriptions cost?

24. Byron plans a weekend camping trip for 113 hikers. His 2 buses for the trip can each hold 49 people. Does he need to get a third bus? Should he overestimate or underestimate?

25. An article in the newspaper said that the estimated number of backpackers in the forests had increased over the past several months. The data given was April: 125, May: 175, June: 225, July: 275. What would be the estimated number of backpackers for September if the numbers continued to increase in this pattern?

Performance Assessment

For your social studies project you are building a model of a forest. You want to include four different kinds of miniature trees in your model.

Kind of Tree	Cost of Tree
Elm	$0.08 each
Maple	$0.05 each
Oak	$0.07 each
Pine	$0.09 each

You need to include between 25 and 59 of each kind of tree. There should be a different number of each type of tree.

Include a plan for the number of trees you will need to buy. Then find the cost.

Record your work in a chart like the one below.

Type of Tree	Number	Total Cost
	Total Cost	

A Good Answer

- shows a plan for the number of trees to buy.
- shows a completed chart.
- shows the mathematics you used to find the total cost.

You may want to save this work in your portfolio.

Enrichment

Napier's Rods

Years ago, a famous Scottish mathematician named John Napier invented a way to make using a Hindu method of multiplying easier. He used a set of rods.

Make a rod like the one below. It will serve as a guide when you are multiplying.

X
1
2
3
4
5
6
7
8
9

Make rods for each number from 1 to 9 like the rods for 2, 6, and 8 shown below.

2	6	8
0/2	0/6	0/8
0/4	1/2	1/6
0/6	1/8	2/4
0/8	2/4	3/2
1/0	3/0	4/0
1/2	3/6	4/8
1/4	4/2	5/6
1/6	4/8	6/4
1/8	5/4	7/2

Use the rods to multiply 4 × 348.

You will need the 3, 4, and 8 rods.

- Line up the guide rod and the rods for 3, 4, and 8. Use the numbers in the fourth row, since you are multiplying by 4.
- Begin with the right hand rod, the 8 rod. Add as shown by the direction of the arrows. Regroup when necessary.

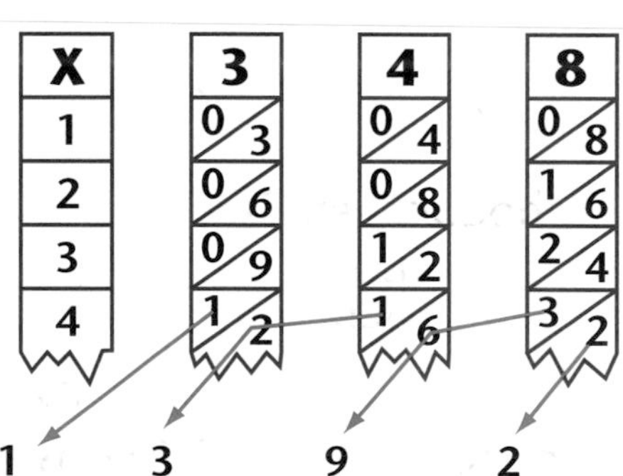

Use the Napier's rods that you have made to multiply.

1. 3 × 239
2. 6 × 519
3. 4 × 537
4. 7 × 627
5. 5 × 481
6. 8 × 351
7. Describe the numbers that are on each of Napier's rods.

Test-Taking Tips

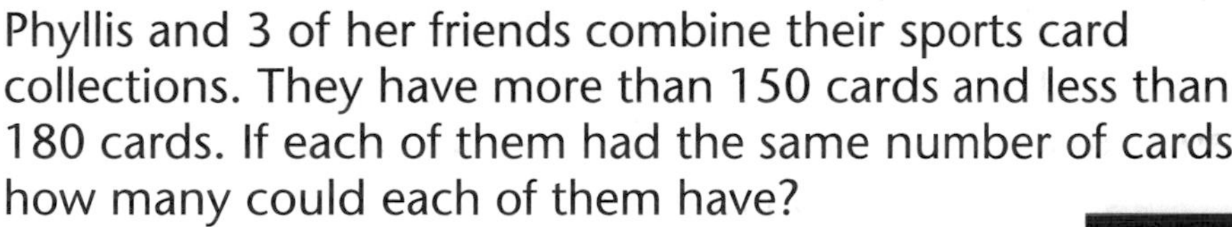

S.O.S.

When you are taking a test, you may come upon problems for which you can use mental math to find the correct choice.

Phyllis and 3 of her friends combine their sports card collections. They have more than 150 cards and less than 180 cards. If each of them had the same number of cards how many could each of them have?

A. 10 **C.** 40
B. 20 **D.** 50

Look at each answer choice and use mental math. There were 4 friends in all.

Think: $4 \times 10 = 40$ less than 150
$4 \times 20 = 80$ less than 150
$4 \times 40 = 160$ greater than 150 and less than 180

So choice C, 40, is the correct answer.

Check for Success

Before turning in a test, go back one last time to check.

- ☑ I understood and answered the questions asked.
- ☑ I checked my work for errors.
- ☑ My answers make sense.

Choose the correct answer. Use mental math if possible.

1. Clyde raised \$80 for his club. Zack raised 3 times as much. How much money did Zack raise?
   A. \$83 **C.** \$240
   B. \$180 **D.** \$243

2. Sean bought ten 8-packs of cups. He used 4 cups. How many cups did he have left?
   F. 42 cups **H.** 80 cups
   G. 76 cups **J.** 84 cups

3. A school hires 4 buses for a school trip. Each bus holds 42 students. What is the total number of students that can fit on the buses?
   A. 48 **C.** 164
   B. 84 **D.** 168

4. Kim has \$80. The bike costs \$250. How much more does she need to buy the bike?
   F. \$120 **H.** \$160
   G. \$150 **J.** \$170

5. There were a total of 420 people who paid \$5 each to see a play. How much did the box office collect?
   A. \$420 **C.** \$4,200
   B. \$2,100 **D.** \$20,100

6. One book has 200 pages. A second book has twice as many pages. A third book has 150 more pages than the first and second books together. How many pages does the third book have?
   F. 400 **H.** 750
   G. 650 **J.** 1,200

Spiral Review and Test Prep

Chapters 1–5

Choose the correct answer.

Number Sense

1. 547×8
   A. 4,026 C. 4,376
   B. 4,375 D. 4,426

2. Which is the same as 6×7?
   F. 49 H. $6 + 7$
   G. 7×6 J. $7 + 6$

3. It takes Will 180 minutes to row down the river. How many hours is this?
   A. 5 hours C. 3 hours
   B. 4 hours D. 2 hours

4. Outdoor Stores, Inc. has $20,000 to remodel the store. The carpenter charges $9,523. The electrician charges $2,709. A plumber will charge the store $3,648. The rest will be used for a new roof. How much money is there for a new roof?
   F. $4,120 H. $601
   G. $7,768 J. $35,880

Algebra and Functions

5. Which shows that one number is 3 more than another number?
   A. $y = x + 3$ C. $1 + 3 = x$
   B. $y = 3$ D. $3x$

6. 42,304 ● $42,304 \times 1$
   F. > H. =
   G. < J. Not Here

7. These prices are in order from greatest to least. Which could be the missing price?

   $62.21, $53.88, ■, $35.76

   A. $24.87 C. $42.87
   B. $34.98 D. $53.98

8. Which number sentence has the same answer as 6×3?
   F. $9 + 2$ H. $38 + 2$
   G. 4×4 J. 9×2

Statistics, Data Analysis, and Probability

Use data from the table for problems 9–12.

Daily Sign-Up at Town Forest	
Hiking	卌 |||
Nature trails	卌 卌
Biking	|||
Fishing and boating	卌 ||||
Camping	卌 卌 ||
Wildlife viewing	卌 |
Scenic drives	卌 卌 卌 |||

9. What is the range of this data?

A. 15 **C.** 13
B. 14 **D.** 16

10. Each person who signed up for camping will bring 4 friends. How many campers are there?

F. 65 **H.** 50
G. 70 **J.** 60

11. Those who are biking will rent equipment for one day. Each bike costs $24 each day. Helmets cost $4 each day. How much will the bikers pay altogether for equipment?

A. $72 **C.** $84
B. $80 **D.** $21

12. Which activity has 3 times as many people as wildlife viewing?

F. Camping **H.** Nature trails
G. Scenic drives **J.** Hiking

Mathematical Reasoning

13. A classroom library has 8 shelves of 7 books each. They receive a book donation that gives them 10 times the original number. How many equal number of books will fit on the 8 shelves?

A. 7 **C.** 70
B. 8 **D.** 80

14. To change hours to minutes, which of these do you need to know?

F. How many seconds are in a minute
G. How many minutes are in an hour
H. How many hours are in a day
J. How may days are in a week

15. A forest ranger drove 132 miles during one week. The next week, the ranger drove 306 miles. Which operation would you use to find out how many more miles the ranger drove during the second week than the first week?

A. Addition **C.** Multiplication
B. Subtraction **D.** Division

16. Create a word problem that involves multiplication. The answer must be 120 trees. Explain how you solved it.

CHAPTER 6 Multiply by 2-Digit Numbers

Theme: *Water, Water Everywhere*

Use the Data

Deepest Freshwater Lakes in North America

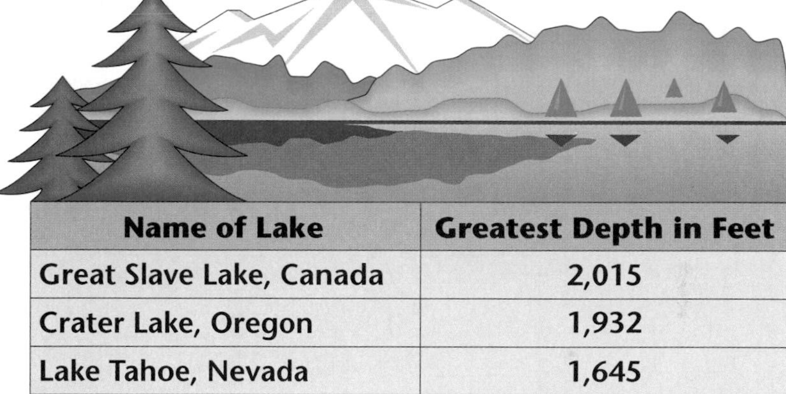

Name of Lake	Greatest Depth in Feet
Great Slave Lake, Canada	2,015
Crater Lake, Oregon	1,932
Lake Tahoe, Nevada	1,645

Source: *The Top Ten of Everything*

- What if a diver goes down to the bottom of the deepest part of Crater Lake and comes back up? How can you use multiplication to find out the total distance the diver swam? What is the total distance?

What You Will Learn

In this chapter you will learn how to
- multiply multiples of 10; 100; and 1,000.
- multiply a multidigit number by a 2-digit number.
- estimate products, including money amounts.
- use strategies to solve problems.

Objective: Use multiplication patterns to multiply by 2-digit numbers.

6•1 Patterns of Multiplication

Algebra & functions

Learn

Volunteers care for our beaches by cleaning up the litter. Suppose the bags they fill each hold 20 gallons of trash. How many gallons of trash do they pick up in 1 day? in 4 days?

Volunteers fill 1,000 bags with litter each day.

Example

You can use multiplication patterns to find products mentally.

$2 \times 1 = 2$	$2 \times 4 = 8$
$20 \times 1 = 20$	$20 \times 4 = 80$
$20 \times 10 = 200$	$20 \times 40 = 800$
$20 \times 100 = 2{,}000$	$20 \times 400 = 8{,}000$
$20 \times 1{,}000 = 20{,}000$	$20 \times 4{,}000 = 80{,}000$

They pick up 20,000 gallons of trash in 1 day; 80,000 gallons in 4 days.

More Examples

A	B
$4 \times 5 = 20$	$2 \times 9 = 18$
$40 \times 5 = 200$	$20 \times 9 = 180$
$40 \times 50 = 2{,}000$	$20 \times 90 = 1{,}800$
$40 \times 500 = 20{,}000$	$200 \times 90 = 18{,}000$
$40 \times 5{,}000 = 200{,}000$	$2{,}000 \times 90 = 180{,}000$

Try It

Multiply. Use mental math.

1. 60×10 **2.** $80 \times 1{,}000$ **3.** 50×30 **4.** 100×40

How can you use patterns and basic facts to help you multiply using mental math?

Practice Find each missing number.

5. $4 \times 8 = k$
$40 \times r = 320$
$40 \times 80 = y$
$40 \times 800 = l$

6. $c \times 8 = 64$
$80 \times 8 = s$
$h \times 80 = 6{,}400$
$80 \times 800 = v$

7. $4 \times 5 = q$
$z \times 5 = 200$
$40 \times b = 2{,}000$
$400 \times 50 = u$

Multiply. Use mental math.

8. 20×100	9. 70×50	10. 60×300	11. $1{,}000 \times 90$
12. 80×60	13. 600×40	14. $50 \times 5{,}000$	15. $80 \times 4{,}000$
16. 900×30	17. $2{,}000 \times 40$	18. 70×600	19. $5{,}000 \times 40$
20. $8{,}000 \times 30$	21. $60 \times 1{,}000$	22. 800×50	23. 90×90
24. 70×70	25. $2{,}000 \times 90$	26. 70×800	27. $5{,}000 \times 60$

Algebra & functions **Find each missing number.**

28. $40 \times n = 1{,}200$
29. $80 \times l = 80{,}000$
30. $z \times 200 = 8{,}000$
★31. $300 \times y = 3{,}000{,}000$
★32. $f \times 5{,}000 = 2{,}500{,}000$

Problem Solving

33. Every week each beach lifeguard collects 30 pounds of trash from the beach. How much trash would 70 lifeguards collect?

34. **Logical Reasoning:** The product of two numbers is 2,400. One number is 20 more than the other. What are the two numbers?

Spiral Review and Test Prep

Complete. Write $>$, $<$, or $=$.

35. 1,243 ● 1,423
36. 12,121 ● 12,112
37. 342,003 ● 342,003

Choose the correct answer.

38. Pablo bought a beach ball for $2.95 and a sand pail set for $5.59. He paid for it with a ten-dollar bill. What was his change?
A. $8.54
B. $2.56
C. $2.46
D. $1.46

39. Winnie spent $5.69 for sunscreen and $13.25 for a beach towel. She had $4.48 left. How much money did she start with?
F. $23.42
G. $23.32
H. $18.94
J. Not Here

Objective: Use models to multiply 2-digit numbers by 2-digit numbers.

6•2

Explore Multiplying by 2-Digit Numbers

Learn

You can use centimeter graph paper to explore multiplying 2-digit numbers.

What is 15×23?

Work Together

You Will Need
- **centimeter graph paper**

Use the graph paper to multiply 15 × 23.

- ▶ Draw a rectangle to show the factors.
- ▶ Use the first factor as the length and the second factor as the width of the rectangle.
- ▶ Find the products of the two factors without counting all the squares in the grid.
- ▶ Record your results in a table like the one shown below.
- ▶ Answer the question above.

15

23

First Factor	Second Factor	Product
15	23	

- ▶ Choose two new 2-digit factors. Use the graph paper to multiply. Record your results in the table. Repeat four times.

Make Connections

You can use the Distributive Property to break apart the factors to find a product.

Using Models | **Using Paper and Pencil**

Draw arrays for tens and ones in each of the factors.

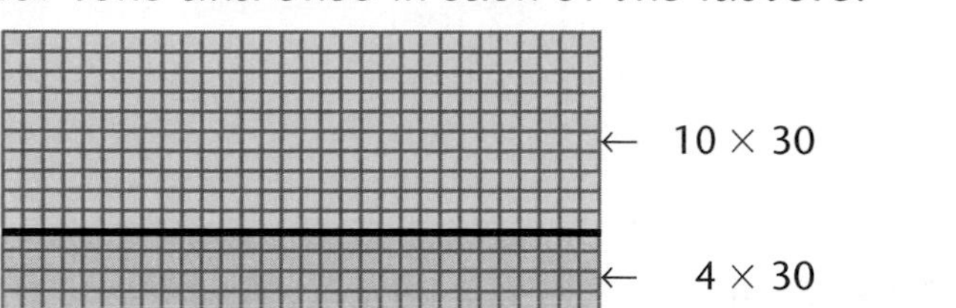

$$\begin{array}{r} 30 \\ \times 14 \\ \hline 300 \\ +120 \\ \hline 420 \end{array}$$

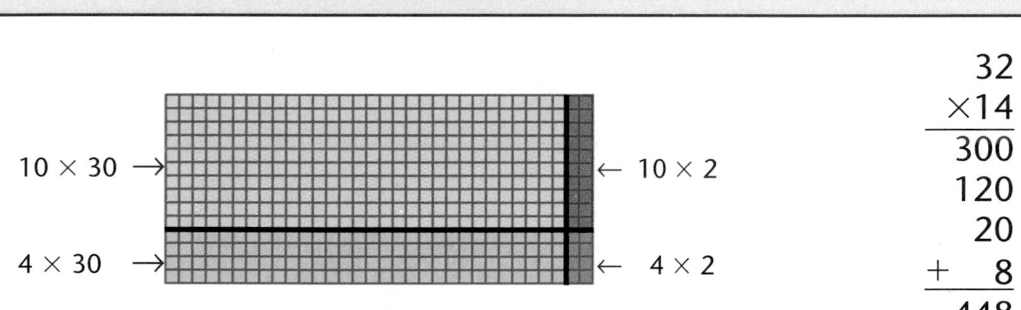

$$\begin{array}{r} 32 \\ \times 14 \\ \hline 300 \\ 120 \\ 20 \\ + \quad 8 \\ \hline 448 \end{array}$$

Try It **Multiply. You may need to tape grids together.**

1. 25 × 30	**2.** 31 × 12	**3.** 50 × 18	**4.** 42 × 20	**5.** 16 × 42
6. 28 × 15	**7.** 33 × 22	**8.** 15 × 19	**9.** 17 × 24	**10.** 34 × 14

Sum it Up Show how you could find 25 × 47.

Practice **Multiply.**

11. 15 × 40	**12.** 27 × 14	**13.** 30 × 27	**14.** 33 × 25	**15.** 23 × 44
16. 18 × 16	**17.** 38 × 27	**18.** 12 × 29	**19.** 13 × 44	**20.** 37 × 29
21. 20 × 15	**22.** 12 × 17	**23.** 32 × 11	**24.** 41 × 21	**25.** 80 × 15

26. Analyze: You can find 12 × 40 by solving: 12 × 4 tens = 48 tens = 480. How is this like breaking apart factors to find the product? How is it different?

Objective: Multiply multidigit numbers by multiples of 10.

6•3 Multiply by Multiples of 10

Learn

A diver wearing a JIM suit, a deep-sea diving outfit, can descend 32 feet into the ocean in 1 minute. After 30 minutes, how deep is the diver?

There's more than one way!

Multiply: 30×32

You can use graph paper to multiply.

Method A

Break apart the factors.
Then add the parts.

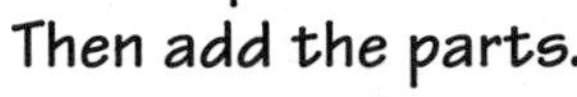

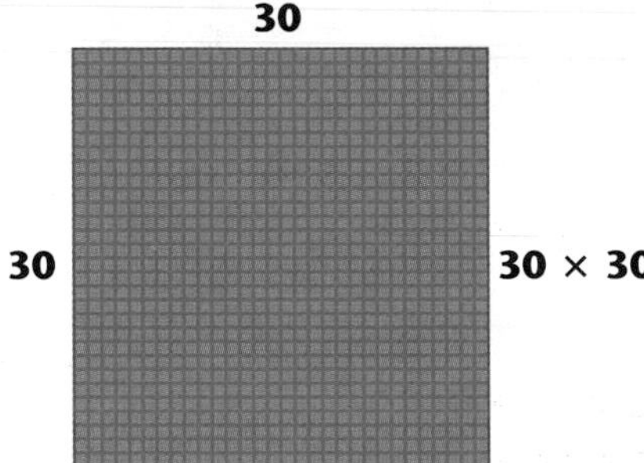

Think: 32 is 30 + 2.
Multiply each part by 30.

$$\begin{array}{r} 30 \\ \times 30 \\ \hline 900 \end{array} \qquad \begin{array}{r} 2 \\ \times 30 \\ \hline 60 \end{array}$$

$$900 + 60 = 960$$

You can use paper and pencil to multiply.

Method B

1 Multiply by the ones.

$$\begin{array}{r} 32 \\ \times 30 \\ \hline 0 \end{array}$$

Think: 0 ones × 32

2 Multiply by the tens.

$$\begin{array}{r} 32 \\ \times 30 \\ \hline 960 \end{array}$$

Think: 3 tens × 32

The diver is 960 feet deep after 30 minutes.

Try It

Multiply.

1. 20×36 **2.** 19×60 **3.** 40×212 **4.** $50 \times 3{,}109$

What is the same about all of the products in problems 1 through 4? Explain.

Practice **Multiply.**

5. $\begin{array}{r} 37 \\ \times 20 \\ \hline \end{array}$ 6. $\begin{array}{r} 42 \\ \times 30 \\ \hline \end{array}$ 7. $\begin{array}{r} 165 \\ \times\ 20 \\ \hline \end{array}$ 8. $\begin{array}{r} 376 \\ \times 10 \\ \hline \end{array}$ 9. $\begin{array}{r} 1,427 \\ \times\ \ 30 \\ \hline \end{array}$

10. 50 × 53 11. 40 × 349 12. 98 × 90 13. 60 × 5,832

14. 487 × 50 15. 60 × 321 16. 80 × 4,227 17. 20 × 2,116

18. 6,084 × 70 19. 24,567 × 80 ★20. 535,102 × 30 ★21. 646,794 × 80

Algebra & functions **Find each missing number.**

22. $34 \times n = 680$ 23. $250 \times d = 7,500$

24. $1,505 \times h = 60,200$ 25. $t \times 3 = 192$

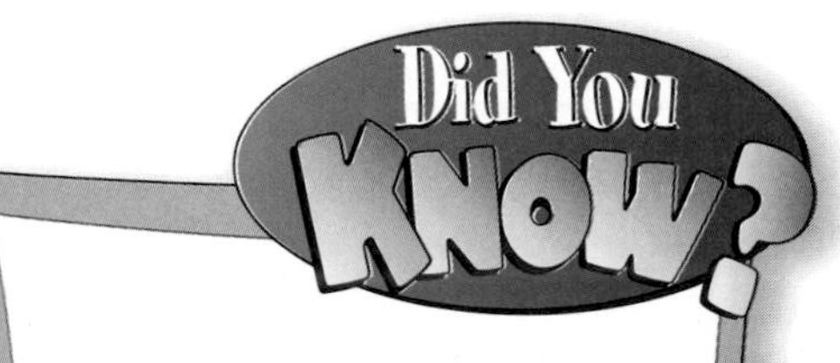

A nautical mile is about 6,076 feet. It is used to measure distances at sea. A league is a distance that measures depth and is about 3 nautical miles.

Problem Solving

Use data from *Did You Know?* for problems 26–28.

26. **Science:** How many feet are in a league?

27. **Science:** How many feet are in 30 nautical miles?

28. What is the difference in length between a nautical mile and a land mile of 5,280 feet?

29. **Generalize:** What rule can you write for multiplying a number by a multiple of 10?

Spiral Review and Test Prep

Use data from the line graph for 30–31.

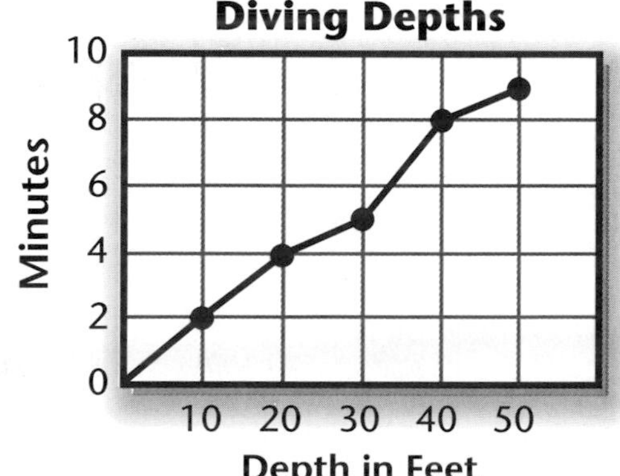

30. How long does it take the diver to reach a depth of 50 feet?

31. How deep is the diver after 4 minutes?

Choose the correct answer.

32. \$315.65 + \$1,265.42
   - A. \$4,310.07
   - B. \$2,681.07
   - C. \$1,581.07
   - D. \$1,481.07

33. \$500.25 − \$1.99
   - F. \$498.26
   - G. \$480.01
   - H. \$301.25
   - J. Not Here

Objective: Make inferences to solve multistep problems.

6•4

Problem Solving: Reading for Math

Solve Multistep Problems

Sail Beautiful Sunrise Lake

Read The Sunrise Lake marina offers 4 sailing classes daily. Each class holds 24 people. Classes are held every day of the 90-day season. How many people can take sailing classes in a season?

READING SKILL ▶ **Make Inferences**

An inference is a conclusion arrived at by reasoning.

- **What do you know?** — **4 classes a day; each class holds 24 people; 90 days in a season**
- **What can you infer?** — **You need to find the total number of people taking classes each day.**
- **What do you need to find?** — **Number of people who can take classes in a season**

MATH SKILL ▶ **Solve Multistep Problems**

Some problems take more than one step to solve. You must decide how to solve each step and in what order.

Plan Multiply to find the total. Then, multiply again to find the total number for a season.

Solve

$4 \times 24 = 96$ So 96 people can take classes each day.

$90 \times 96 = 8,640$ So 8,640 people can take sailing classes in one season.

Look Back Can you solve these steps in a different order?

How did making an inference help you solve this problem?

Practice **Solve. Tell what inference you made.**

1. During one hour, Ted caught 6 fish. Emil caught twice as many fish as Ted. Estimate the number of fish the boys will catch if they fish for 2 hours.

2. Sara and Tim rented a canoe from 9:30 A.M. until 12:30 P.M. After lunch, they rented another canoe from 1:30 P.M. to 3:00 P.M. For how many minutes did they rent the canoe?

Use data from the Rental Chart for problems 3–8.

Sunrise Lake Resort Rentals

Item	Fee
Canoe	\$8 each $\frac{1}{2}$hour
Fishing Pole	\$4 each $\frac{1}{2}$hour
Paddle Boat	\$28 each $\frac{1}{2}$hour
Rowboat	\$15 each $\frac{1}{2}$hour

3. A group of vacationers rented a paddle boat for 5 hours. How much did they pay for the rental?

4. Mr. Wallace rented fishing poles for himself and four family members. They fished from 11:15 A.M. to 2:15 P.M. How much did he pay for this rental?

5. During the first week of June, 4 rowboats were rented for a total of 18 hours each. Altogether, how much did these rentals cost?

6. Five canoes were rented for 90 minutes each. What was the total fee for this rental?

7. How much does it cost to rent a fishing pole and paddle boat for 3 hours?

8. Cara rented a fishing pole for 3 hours. Her brother rented a canoe for 30 minutes less. How much did they pay for their rentals?

Spiral Review and Test Prep

Choose the correct answer.

Tomas rented 2 life vests for \$2 an hour each. He rented a small sailboat for \$16 an hour. He sailed for 3 hours. How much did he pay in all?

9. Which statement is true?
   - **A.** Tomas paid \$6 for the life vests.
   - **B.** He paid \$48 to rent the sailboat.
   - **C.** Tomas sailed for 2 hours.

10. Which "hidden question" must you solve?
    - **F.** How many hours did he sail?
    - **G.** How much did he pay for the sailboat each hour?
    - **H.** How much did he pay to rent 2 life vests for 3 hours?

Extra Practice, page 263

Objective: Multiply 2-digit numbers by 2-digit numbers.

Multiply by 2-Digit Numbers

Learn

It's fun to take a boat tour on Lake Michigan. Each month the boat makes 45 tours. How many miles does the boat travel in one month?

Example 1

Find: 21×45

1 Multiply by the ones. Regroup if necessary.

$$\begin{array}{r} 45 \\ \times 21 \\ \hline 45 \end{array} \leftarrow 1 \times 45$$

2 Multiply by the tens. Regroup if necessary.

$$\begin{array}{r} \overset{1}{4}5 \\ \times 21 \\ \hline 45 \\ 900 \end{array} \leftarrow 20 \times 45$$

3 Add the products.

$$\begin{array}{r} \overset{1}{4}5 \\ \times 21 \\ \hline 45 \\ +900 \\ \hline 945 \end{array}$$

The boat travels 945 miles in one month.

More Examples

A

$$\begin{array}{r} \overset{1}{3}4 \\ \times 23 \\ \hline 102 \\ +680 \\ \hline 782 \end{array}$$

B

$$\begin{array}{r} \$\overset{1}{0}.\overset{2}{2}5 \\ \times \quad 41 \\ \hline 25 \\ +\ 1000 \\ \hline \$10.25 \end{array}$$

You can multiply money amounts the same way you multiply whole numbers.

Insert the dollar sign and decimal point.

An all-day boat tour with lunch costs $24 for each person. How much would the all-day tour cost for a group of 68 people?

Find: 68 × $24

1 Multiply by the ones. Regroup if necessary.

$$\begin{array}{r} {}^{3} \\ \$24 \\ \times\ 68 \\ \hline 192 \end{array} \leftarrow 8 \times 24$$

2 Multiply by the tens. Regroup if necessary.

$$\begin{array}{r} {}^{2} \\ {}^{\not 3} \\ \$24 \\ \times\ 68 \\ \hline 192 \\ 1440 \end{array} \leftarrow 6 \times 24$$

3 Add the products.

$$\begin{array}{r} {}^{2} \\ {}^{\not 3} \\ \$24 \\ \times\ 68 \\ \hline 192 \\ +1\,440 \\ \hline 1{,}632 \end{array}$$

It costs $1,632 for 68 people.

More Examples

C

$$\begin{array}{r} {}^{1} \\ {}^{\not 3} \\ 54 \\ \times 49 \\ \hline 486 \\ +2160 \\ \hline 2{,}646 \end{array}$$

D

$$\begin{array}{r} {}^{3} \\ {}^{\not 4} \\ \$0.76 \\ \times\ 58 \\ \hline 6\ 08 \\ +38\ 00 \\ \hline \$44.08 \end{array}$$

Try It **Find each product.**

1. $\begin{array}{r} 31 \\ \times 17 \\ \hline \end{array}$

2. $\begin{array}{r} \$26 \\ \times\ 14 \\ \hline \end{array}$

3. $\begin{array}{r} 19 \\ \times 37 \\ \hline \end{array}$

4. $\begin{array}{r} 43 \\ \times 58 \\ \hline \end{array}$

5. $\begin{array}{r} \$0.87 \\ \times\ 15 \\ \hline \end{array}$

6. 37 × $26
7. 84 × 31
8. 55 × $0.48
9. 43 × 61

If you multiply 11 × 36, will you need to regroup ones? Why or why not?

Practice Find each product.

10. $\begin{array}{r} 15 \\ \times 25 \\ \hline \end{array}$ 11. $\begin{array}{r} \$0.33 \\ \times \quad 18 \\ \hline \end{array}$ 12. $\begin{array}{r} 63 \\ \times 32 \\ \hline \end{array}$ 13. $\begin{array}{r} \$0.52 \\ \times \quad 17 \\ \hline \end{array}$ 14. $\begin{array}{r} 84 \\ \times 28 \\ \hline \end{array}$

15. $39 × 24 16. 42 × 36 17. $0.57 × 93 18. 78 × 81

19. 38 × 65 20. 18 × 97 21. $0.95 × 88 22. 86 × 79

★23. 24 × 76 × 2 ★24. 33 × 59 × 6 ★25. 48 × 51 × 9

Algebra & functions Find each product.

26. $(10 + 5) \times (10 + 2) = n$ 27. $(20 + 7) \times (30 + 3) = m$

28. $(30 + 6) \times (10 + 3) = r$ 29. $(40 + 9) \times (50 + 5) = p$

30. 

Here is how Rebecca found 26 × 58. Tell what mistake she made. Explain how to correct it.

Problem Solving

31. A boat makes 36 trips each month. Each trip is 67 miles long. How many miles does the boat travel in a month?

32. Each boat can hold up to 98 passengers. If the boat is full for 31 trips, how many passengers is that?

33. **Spatial Reasoning:** A picture frame is 60 inches long by 15 inches wide. How many pictures with a length of 30 inches and a width of 15 inches can fit inside the frame? Explain.

★34. A juice company delivers 45 cartons of juice to be sold on the boat. There are 3 layers of cans in each carton and 12 cans in each layer. How many cans are there in all?

Use data from the chart for problems 35–40.

35. How many more square miles is Lake Michigan than Lake Ontario?

36. Which of the Great Lakes is about 3 times the size of Lake Erie?

37. Which of the Great Lakes is almost exactly 3 times the size of Lake Ontario?

38. In what order are the lakes listed?

39. What is the total area for all of the Great Lakes?

40. **Create a problem** using the data in the table. Solve it. Ask others to solve it.

41. The snack bar on a tour boat charges $0.75 for a small bottle of juice. Each of the 54 people in a tour group buys a bottle. How much do they spend altogether?

42. **Geography:** Lake Superior is the highest of the Great Lakes at 600 feet above sea level. Its outlet is the Saint Marys River. This river falls 21 feet over a series of rapids and empties into Lake Huron. How high above sea level is Lake Huron?

The Great Lakes

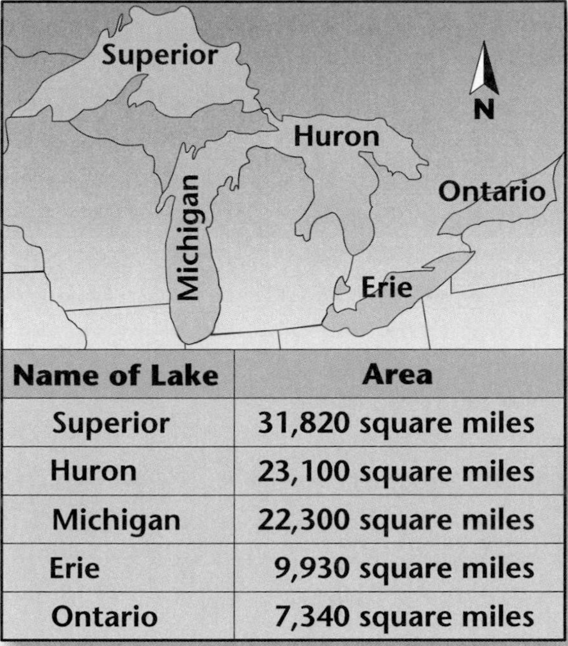

Name of Lake	Area
Superior	31,820 square miles
Huron	23,100 square miles
Michigan	22,300 square miles
Erie	9,930 square miles
Ontario	7,340 square miles

Spiral Review and Test Prep

43. $1,237 + 978$

44. $2,006 - 489$

45. 327×8

46. $8\overline{)40}$

47. $\$1.76 \times 5$

48. $45 \div 9$

49. 42×7

50. $89 + 96$

51. $120 - 84$

52. 16×8

53. $\$0.46 \times 5$

54. $56 \div 8$

55. $900 - 8$

56. 97×8

57. $84 \div 7$

Choose the correct answer.

58. What is 34,562 rounded to the nearest hundred?

A. 35,000
B. 34,500
C. 34,600
D. 34,000

59. What is the next product in the pattern?

$3 \times 2 \quad 3 \times 4 \quad 3 \times 6 \quad ■$

F. 3×7
G. 3×9
H. 18
J. 24

Objective: Estimate products.

6.6 Estimate Products

Learn

Mr. and Mrs. Lundberg are saving their money to take a cruise. They saved $42 a week for 52 weeks. Have they saved enough money?

Sea Maiden Cruise Ship

Couples Cruise for $1,895

Math Words

estimate to find an answer that is close to an exact answer

round to find the nearest value of a number based on a given place value

factor numbers that are multiplied to give a product

Example

Estimate to solve the problem.

Round each **factor** so you can multiply mentally.

Estimate: $42 × 52

Think: $42 × 52

↓ ↓

$40 × 50 = $2,000

$2,000 > $1,895

The Lundbergs have saved enough money to take the cruise.

More Examples

A

Estimate: 54 × 367

Think: 50 × 400 = 20,000

B

Estimate: 4,482 × 89

Think: 4,000 × 90 = 360,000

Try It

Estimate each product. Tell how you rounded.

1. 56 × 18 **2.** 84 × 371 **3.** 49 × $5,250 **4.** 91 × 645

5. 372 × 48 **6.** 754 × 34 **7.** $1,925 × 25 **8.** 5,289 × 78

Tell how estimating 48 × 1,214 by rounding 1,214 to the nearest hundred instead of to the nearest thousand affects the estimate.

Practice **Estimate each product.**

9. 72 × \$49
10. 55 × 630
11. 85 × \$29
12. 12 × 28
13. 91 × 432
14. 83 × 654
15. 35 × 950
16. 59 × \$419
17. 45 × \$1,925
18. 28 × 4,155
19. 74 × 2,915
20. 75 × \$3,545
21. 58 × 92
22. \$712 × 15
23. 854 × 244
24. 90 × \$4,672

Algebra & functions **Compare. Write > or <.**

25. 47 × 35 ● 2,000
26. 59 × 195 ● 1,000
27. 21 × 217 ● 4,000

★28. 47 × 13 ● 38 × 32

★29. 54 × 25 ● 15 × 31

Problem Solving

30. Cabins aboard a luxury cruise ship cost \$2,145 each trip. About how much money would a travel club of 27 people spend on cabins?

31. **Generalize:** How does an exact product compare to an estimate found by rounding up both factors? by rounding down both factors?

32. **Collect Data:** Take a survey to find out how many have been on a boat and what kind of boat they were on. Share the results with other students in the class.

★33. The Queen Elizabeth II was launched in 1967. Suppose the ship crosses the Atlantic Ocean 64 times each year. Estimate how many times the ship would have crossed the ocean since it was launched.

Spiral Review and Test Prep

Use the pictograph to answer each question.

34. How many more trips did the Ocean Storm make than the Sail-Away?

35. How many trips did the three ships make altogether?

Number of Trips

Sea Maiden	⛵ ⛵ ⛵ ⛵
Sail-Away	⛵ ⛵ ½⛵
Ocean Storm	⛵ ⛵ ⛵ ⛵ ⛵ ⛵

KEY: Each ⛵ is equal to 4 trips.

Choose the correct answer.

36. 7 × 356
    - A. 3,592
    - B. 2,596
    - C. 2,496
    - D. 2,492

37. 56 ÷ 8
    - F. 6
    - G. 7
    - H. 8
    - J. 9

Extra Practice, page 264

Check Your Progress A

Multiply. **(pages 234–235)**

1. 50×200
2. 300×40
3. $20 \times 9{,}000$
4. 60×300
5. 500×80
6. $70 \times 4{,}000$

Multiply. **(pages 236–239, 242–245)**

7. $\begin{array}{r} \$28 \\ \times\ 14 \\ \hline \end{array}$
8. $\begin{array}{r} 57 \\ \times\ 31 \\ \hline \end{array}$
9. $\begin{array}{r} \$0.66 \\ \times\quad 87 \\ \hline \end{array}$
10. $\begin{array}{r} 95 \\ \times\ 76 \\ \hline \end{array}$
11. $\begin{array}{r} \$0.84 \\ \times\quad 35 \\ \hline \end{array}$

12. $48 \times \$73$
13. $\$0.92 \times 27$
14. 83×54

Estimate the product. **(pages 246–247)**

15. 25×623
16. 34×54
17. 65×351
18. $17 \times \$899$
19. 42×68
20. $19 \times \$674$

Solve. **(pages 234–247)**

21. You can rent a canoe for $3.50 an hour from 9:00 A.M. to noon. After noon the price is $4.00 each hour. How much will you pay to rent a canoe from 11:00 A.M. to 2:00 P.M.?

22. There are 70 students on a class trip. They are taking a cruise around the harbor. Each ticket for the cruise costs $20. How much money do the students spend on the cruise tickets?

23. A ship makes 75 trips. Each trip is 97 miles. How many miles does the ship travel?

24. There is a $27 charge for baggage over 40 pounds. About how much money is collected for 265 overweight bags?

25. **Compare:** How is multiplying by a 2-digit number like multiplying by a 1-digit number? How is it different?

Use the Internet

Mr. Cooper owns a restaurant in St. Louis, Missouri. He is planning to open two new restaurants in other cities in the United States. He needs to find out how many miles it is to travel to these cities, both by road and by air. He will need to travel to each new restaurant he opens 12 times the first year. How can he use the Internet to find the mileage between the cities?

City	Mileage	Round Trip Mileage	Total Mileage for 12 Round Trips

- Go to www.mhschool.com/math.
- Find the list of sites that provide information about U.S. cities.
- Click on a link.
- Find the data for the mileage by road between cities. Choose two cities for which data is given.
- Copy the table. Record the mileage.
- Find the data for mileage by air between cities. Choose two cities for which data is given.
- Copy the table. Record the mileage.
- Find the round trip mileage for each city in each table.
- Find the total mileage for 12 round trips for each city in each table.

1. Suppose Mr. Cooper does not want to travel by plane and wants to drive as little as possible. Which city should he choose? Why?

2. **Analyze:** Why does using the Internet make more sense than using another reference source to find the mileage?

For more practice, use Math Traveler™.

Objective: Multiply greater numbers by 2-digit numbers.

6•7 Multiply Greater Numbers

Learn

The fourth-grade science class visits the *U.S.S. Nautilus.* During one mission the submarine traveled 346 miles each day for 36 days. How many miles did it travel in all?

The U.S.S. Nautilus could travel 346 miles in a day.

Example 1

Find: 36×346

1 Multiply by the ones. Regroup if necessary.

$$\begin{array}{r} {}^{2\,3} \\ 346 \\ \times 36 \\ \hline 2076 \end{array}$$

2 Multiply by the tens. Regroup if necessary.

$$\begin{array}{r} {}^{1\,1} \\ {}^{2\,\not{3}} \\ 346 \\ \times\ \ 36 \\ \hline 2076 \\ +10380 \\ \hline \end{array}$$

3 Add the products.

$$\begin{array}{r} {}^{1\,1} \\ {}^{\not{2}\,\not{3}} \\ 346 \\ \times\ \ 36 \\ \hline 2\,076 \\ +10\,380 \\ \hline 12{,}456 \end{array}$$

12,456 is reasonably close to 12,000.

Check for reasonableness: Estimate: $40 \times 300 = 12{,}000$
The submarine traveled 12,456 miles.

More Examples

A

$$\begin{array}{r} {}^{2} \\ {}^{\not{2}} \\ 504 \\ \times\ \ 67 \\ \hline 3\,528 \\ +30\,240 \\ \hline 33{,}768 \end{array}$$

B

$$\begin{array}{r} {}^{2} \\ {}^{\not{2}} \\ \$6.72 \\ \times\ \ \ \ 34 \\ \hline 26\,88 \\ +201\,60 \\ \hline \$228.48 \end{array}$$

Each month, around 12,498 visitors come to see the U.S.S. Nautilus. How many visitors would that be for 36 months?

Example 2

Find: 36 × 12,498

1 Multiply by the ones. Regroup if necessary.

```
 1 2 5 4
 12,498
×     36
  74 988
```

2 Multiply by the tens. Regroup if necessary.

```
  1 2 2
 1 2 5 4  (crossed out)
  12,498
×     36
  74 988
+374 940
```

3 Add the products.

```
  1 2 2
 1 2 5 4  (crossed out)
  12,498
×     36
  74 988
+374 940
 449,928
```

Check for reasonableness: Estimate: 40 × 12,000 = 480,000
In 36 months, 449,928 visitors would see the U.S.S. Nautilus.

449,928 is reasonably close to 480,000.

More Examples

A

```
 4 25
 2 13  (crossed out)
  5,739
×    64
 22 956
+344 340
 367,296
```

B

```
 2 4 3  2
 3 6 4  3  (crossed out)
  $348.65
×      57
  2 440 55
+17 432 50
$19,873.05
```

Try It **Multiply. Check that each answer is reasonable.**

1. 531 × 22

2. $1.58 × 67

3. 3,275 × 26

4. $252.31 × 38

5. 19,578 × 19

6. 519 × 44 **7.** $16.70 × 25 **8.** 32,884 × 27 **9.** 60,722 × 11

You multiply 42 × $5.15 and get $21.63. Is that a reasonable answer? Explain.

Practice Multiply. Check that each answer is reasonable.

10. 227×86
11. $\$5.15 \times 31$
12. 479×34
13. 562×18
14. $\$1.98 \times 19$
15. $1,209 \times 27$
16. $\$64.31 \times 18$
17. $7,588 \times 23$
18. $\$40.99 \times 53$
19. $\$234.11 \times 14$
20. $32,730 \times 28$
21. $63,121 \times 36$
22. $54,702 \times 36$
23. $\$119.53 \times 48$
24. $34,867 \times 63$
25. $71,295 \times 42$
26. 41×378
27. $32 \times \$11.25$
28. $51 \times 48,725$
29. $83 \times \$526.18$

Given each set of digits, make the greatest and least product by multiplying two 2-digit numbers. Use each digit once.

30. 8, 4, 6, 2
31. 4, 9, 7, 3
★32. 5, 3, 8, 1
★33. 7, 5, 3, 7

34.

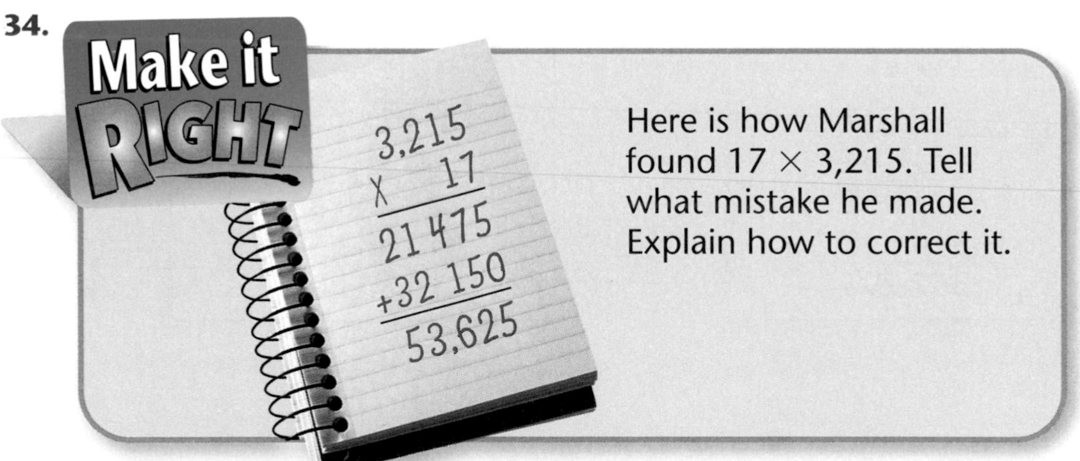

Here is how Marshall found $17 \times 3,215$. Tell what mistake he made. Explain how to correct it.

Problem Solving

35. In 1960 the U.S.S. *Triton* traveled underwater for an average of 938 kilometers each day for 84 days. How many kilometers did the *Triton* travel underwater in that trip?

36. **Health:** Deep-sea divers use special tanks of air to prevent illness at depths greater than 250 feet. A deep sea diver dives to 625 feet. For how many feet of this dive does the diver need to use the air in a special tank?

Use data from the sign for problems 37–38.

Deluxe Boat Rides

Adults	$12.95
Children under 12	$ 6.50
Senior Citizens	$ 7.75
Lunch	$ 3.25

37. Mrs. Hamilton, her two children, and her elderly grandmother went for a boat ride. They bought 4 lunches on the trip. How much did their trip cost?

38. A group of 38 senior citizens took the Deluxe Boat Ride. How much did their trip cost?

39. **Analyze:** What is the greatest number of digits a product could have if you multiply a 4-digit number by a 3-digit number?

40. **Time:** A submarine leaves port at 8:15 A.M. on Tuesday. It returns to port after 3 days, 5 hours, and 35 minutes. What time and day does the submarine return?

41. **Language Arts:** Ships at sea often used Morse Code to transmit messages. The codes for the numbers 1, 2, 3, and 4 are shown. If the pattern continues, what would be the Morse Code for the number 5?

1	• - - - -	**3**	• • • - -
2	• • - - -	**4**	• • • • -

42. **Collect Data:** Survey another class to find out if they prefer to swim in a lake, an ocean, or a swimming pool. Organize the results in a graph. Share the results with your class.

Spiral Review and Test Prep

43. 27×8

44. $1,006 - 589$

45. $\$32,947 + 5,649$

46. 52×8

47. $15,912 - 10,456$

Choose the correct answer.

48. Find the missing number.
$n \times 6 \times 2 = (5 \times 8) + 8$
   - A. 6
   - B. 5
   - C. 4
   - D. 2

49. Tanya found 541 − 79 to get 462. How can she check her answer?
   - F. 541 + 79
   - G. 462 + 79
   - H. 462 − 79
   - J. Not Here

Objective: Make a graph to solve problems.

Problem Solving: Strategy
Make a Graph

Aquatic Beach Sandcastle Competition.

Read

Read the problem carefully.

Each year, San Francisco, California, hosts the Aquatic Beach Sandcastle Competition. How could a newspaper display this data to show the age group that had the most people in the contest?

- **What do you know?** How many people participated in each age group
- **What do you need to find?** In which age group the most people participated

Age Group (Years)	Number of People
7 and under	425
8 to 11	450
12 to 15	375
16 and up	475

Plan

You want a display that allows you to compare the data quickly. You can make a pictograph.

Solve

Make the pictograph. Then compare the number of symbols for each age group.

The age group 16 and up has the most symbols.

So more participants were 16 years and older than any other age group.

Number of Sandcastle Builders

7 and under	
8 to 11	
12 to 15	
16 and up	

KEY: Each [symbol] is equal to 50 participants, each [half symbol] is equal to 25 particpants .

Look Back

Can you compare the data another way?

Why is it easier to compare the data by looking at a graph than a table?

Practice **Use data in the table to solve problems 1–6.**

1. Make a graph to show the data in the chart.
2. Which contest had the most people? the least?
3. How many more people participated in the contest in Seal Beach than in Malibu?
4. **What if** there were 1,175 people in a contest held in Miami Beach? How would the graph change?
5. What is the range in the number of people in the contests?
6. What is the total number of people who participated in the sandcastle-building contests?

Sandcastle-Building Contests

Location	Number of People
Port Aransas, TX	1,250
Wenatchee, WA	1,675
Seal Beach, CA	1,775
Atlantic City, NJ	1,525
Malibu, CA	1,375

Problem Solving

Mixed Strategy Review

7. **Time:** A boat returns from a deep-sea fishing trip at 3:40 P.M. The boat was out on the ocean for 11 hours and 25 minutes. Before docking at the marina, the boat stopped to get gas for 15 minutes. What time did the boat leave for the trip?
8. The fee for entering the fishing contest is $15. If 34 people enter the contest, how much do they pay in fees in all?

★9. Cassette tapes come in lengths of 30 minutes, 60 minutes, and 90 minutes. A local radio station wants to play music during $4\frac{1}{2}$ hours of a beach contest. What combination of tapes could they use to have continuous music for the whole contest?

10. **Collect Data:** Survey students to find how many have participated in a beach contest. Organize the results in a graph. Create a problem based on the graph. Solve it. Ask others to solve it.

CHOOSE A STRATEGY
- Logical Reasoning
- Draw a Picture
- Make a Graph
- Act It Out
- Make a Table or List
- Find a Pattern
- Guess and Check
- Write a Number Sentence
- Work Backward
- Solve a Simpler Problem

Extra Practice, page 265

Objective: Use strategies to multiply.

6•9 Multiply Using Mental Math

Learn

Math Word

compensation multiplying a factor by a number and dividing the other factor by the same number for mental math

Tiger sharks swim in the ocean. How far can a tiger shark swim in 12 hours?

The tiger shark can swim 15 miles per hour.

There's more than one way!

You can multiply using mental math.

Method A

You can use **compensation**.

Think:

$15 \times 12 \rightarrow (15 \times 2) \times (12 \div 2) \rightarrow 30 \times 6 = 180$

You can also multiply mentally using compatible numbers.

Method B

Use the Distributive Property to break the factors into compatible numbers.

$15 \times 12 \rightarrow (10 \times 12) + (5 \times 12)$

$120 + 60$

180

Remember: Do the operations inside the parentheses first.

The shark can travel 180 miles.

Multiply. Use mental math. Explain which method you used.

1. 16×20
2. 24×12
3. 14×30
4. 42×7

How can you use the Distributive Property to multiply 25×45?

Practice Multiply. Use mental math.

5. 18 × 14
6. 20 × 44
7. 15 × 35
8. 45 × 40
9. 33 × 22
10. 21 × 55
11. 84 × 12
12. 77 × 11
13. 42 × 30
14. 50 × 25
15. 60 × 16
16. 48 × 18

★17. (3 × 4) × 300
★18. (5 × 3) × 200
★19. (5 × 5) × 400

Algebra & functions Complete each table.

20.

Rule: Multiply by 25					
Input	30	32	48	120	160
Output	■	■	■	■	■

21.

Rule: Multiply by 12					
Input	18	42	86	120	240
Output	■	■	■	■	■

Problem Solving

Use data from *Did You Know?* for problems 22–24.

22. **What if** a marlin could swim for 10 hours at its top speed? How many miles could it travel?

23. **What if** a blue fin tuna and a sailfish could swim for 12 hours at top speed? How many miles farther would the sailfish be?

24. A spine-tailed swift can fly at top speeds of 106 miles per hour. How much faster is the bird than the sailfish?

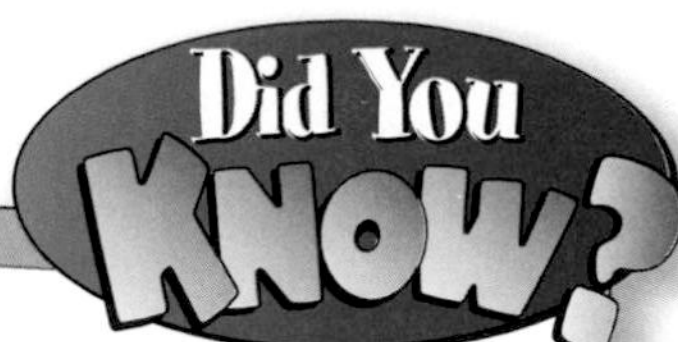

The sailfish is the fastest fish in the world, swimming at a top speed of 68 miles per hour. The marlin can go as fast as 50 miles per hour, and the blue fin tuna can travel at speeds up to 46 miles per hour.

Spiral Review and Test Prep

25. 321×7

26. $426 + 968$

27. $1,710 - 789$

28. 430×8

29. $5,155 + 397$

Use the numbers below to choose the correct answer.

5 3 4 4 8 6 2 4 3 9 6 4 7

30. What is the median of the data?
 A. 3
 B. 4
 C. 5
 D. 6

31. What is the range of the data?
 F. 5
 G. 6
 H. 7
 J. 9

Extra Practice, page 265

Objective: Analyze data and make decisions.

Problem Solving: Application

Decision Making

Which kind of boat or boats will they rent?

Learn

The 5 members of a family are on a day trip to Lake Lanier in Georgia. They want to go for a boat ride on the lake.

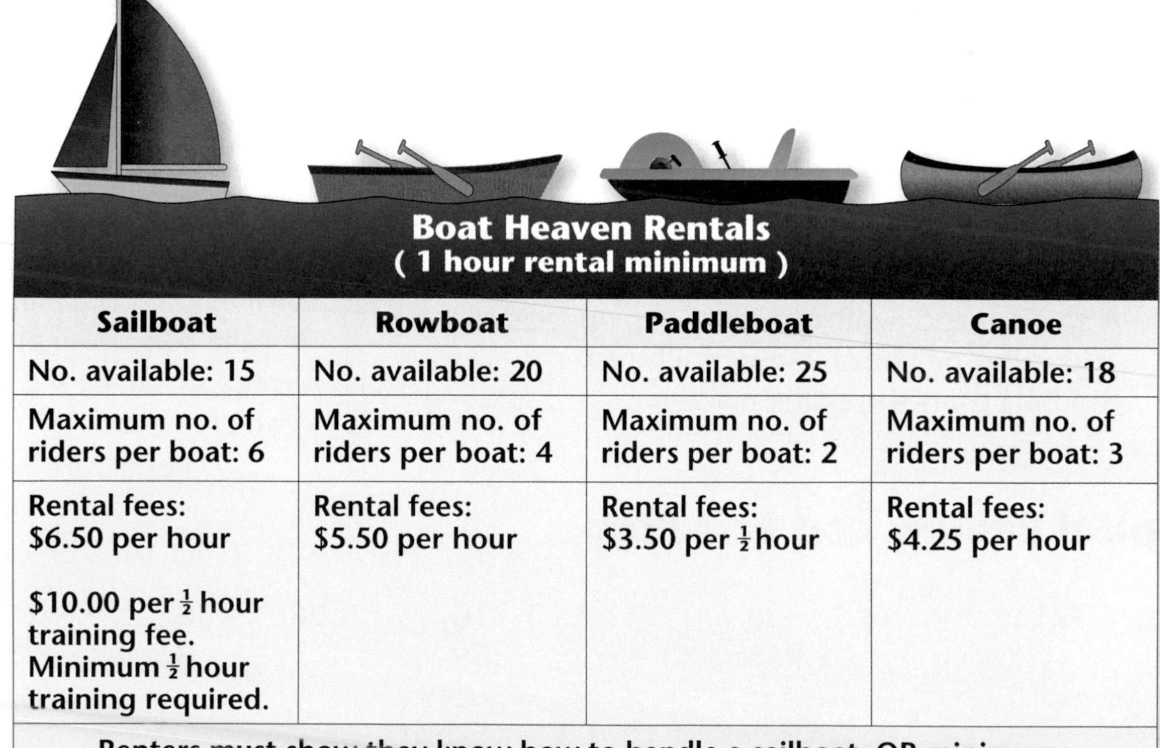

Boat Heaven Rentals
(1 hour rental minimum)

Sailboat	Rowboat	Paddleboat	Canoe
No. available: 15	No. available: 20	No. available: 25	No. available: 18
Maximum no. of riders per boat: 6	Maximum no. of riders per boat: 4	Maximum no. of riders per boat: 2	Maximum no. of riders per boat: 3
Rental fees: $6.50 per hour $10.00 per $\frac{1}{2}$ hour training fee. Minimum $\frac{1}{2}$ hour training required.	Rental fees: $5.50 per hour	Rental fees: $3.50 per $\frac{1}{2}$ hour	Rental fees: $4.25 per hour
Renters must show they know how to handle a sailboat, OR minimum half-hour training required at a fee of $10.00.			

Read for Understanding

1. What does "1 hour rental minimum" mean?
2. How much is the minimum training fee?
3. Which type of boat holds the most people?
4. For which type of boat is the greatest number available?
5. What is the cost of renting each type of boat for 1 hour?
6. Which kind of boat costs the most to rent for 1 hour?
7. What would the cost be for a full hour of training?
8. What kind of boat has the least number available?

Problem Solving

Make Decisions

9. How many of each type of boat do you need to rent if everyone in the family decides to go on the same type of boat?
10. How much will it cost to rent that number of each type of boat for 1 hour?
11. For which type of boat do you think it is most likely that people will need training? Why?
12. **What if** the family needs training to rent a sailboat? How much will it cost to rent one for 2 hours?
13. Which type of boat moves the fastest? How might this affect your decision?
14. **What if** the family needs training to rent each canoe they need? How much will it cost to rent them for 2 hours?
15. Make a list of other things you must think about before deciding which kind of boat to rent.
16. Suppose the family arrives at the lake at 10:30 A.M. They plan to meet friends for lunch at 1:00 P.M. How much time do they have at the lake?
17. **What if** the three members of the family need a half-hour training each, while the other members of the family want to use a paddleboat in the meantime. What would the cost be?
18. Suppose three members of the family want to canoe for three hours while the other members want to use a paddleboat for two hours. What would the cost be?

Your Decision!

Which boat or boats will the family rent? How long will they ride? Explain why you made this decision.

Objective: Apply multiplying 1-digit numbers to investigate science concepts.

Problem Solving: Math and Science

How many times does your heart beat each day?

Your heart works hard. Even when you sit or sleep, your heart beats all the time.

You Will Need
- **timer or clock**

How many times do you think your heart beats in a minute? an hour? a day? In this activity, you will calculate how many times your heart beats each day.

Hypothesize

Estimate how many times your heart beats each day.

Procedure

1. Measure your heart rate for 1 minute.
2. Calculate the number of beats in one hour. (Hint: Multiply your heart rate for each minute times 60 since 1 hour = 60 minutes.)
3. Calculate the number of beats in one day. (Hint: 1 day = 24 hours.)

★4. Calculate the number of beats for a year.

Where can you feel your heart beat? Place two fingers (not the thumb) on the side of your neck. Place your hand over your heart. Place two fingers on the inside of your wrist.

Data

Copy and complete the chart to record your observations.

Time	Estimate Number of Heartbeats
Each minute	
Each hour	
Each day	
★ Each year	

Conclude and Apply

- Why would it be difficult to count the number of heartbeats in a day? Explain how math made your job easier.
- Round the number of beats for a day to the nearest 10,000. Collect the data for the whole class. What was the range of heartbeats? Which number was most common? Make a bar graph to display the data from the class.
- Marty's heart beats 70 times each minute. Tamara's heart beats 60 times each minute. How many more times does Marty's heart beat each day?
- Explain how exercise can reduce the number of times your heart beats each day.

Did You Know?

Your heart is a type of muscle. Just like the muscles in your arms or legs, it will get stronger with exercise. A strong heart pumps blood better and can beat less often.

Problem Solving

Going Further

1. Collect heartbeat data from people younger and older than you. Does the number of heartbeats increase or decrease with age? Why do you think so?

2. Design and do an activity to measure how many times you will breathe today.

Check Your Progress B

Multiply. **(pages 250–253)**

1. $\begin{array}{r} 415 \\ \times\ 21 \\ \hline \end{array}$
2. $\begin{array}{r} 327 \\ \times\ 13 \\ \hline \end{array}$
3. $\begin{array}{r} 4,217 \\ \times\ 53 \\ \hline \end{array}$
4. $\begin{array}{r} 5,904 \\ \times\ 42 \\ \hline \end{array}$
5. $\begin{array}{r} 32,457 \\ \times\ 27 \\ \hline \end{array}$
6. $\begin{array}{r} \$6.14 \\ \times\ 17 \\ \hline \end{array}$
7. $\begin{array}{r} \$0.89 \\ \times\ 85 \\ \hline \end{array}$
8. $\begin{array}{r} \$13.42 \\ \times\ 33 \\ \hline \end{array}$
9. $\begin{array}{r} \$57.07 \\ \times\ 25 \\ \hline \end{array}$
10. $\begin{array}{r} \$48.98 \\ \times\ 51 \\ \hline \end{array}$
11. 45 × 3,405
12. 7 × 11,278
13. 72 × 32,064

Multiply. Use mental math. **(pages 256–257)**

14. 14 × 24
15. 25 × 12
16. 18 × 40
17. 12 × 39
18. 17 × 28
19. 46 × 5
20. 15 × 14
21. 19 × 21

Use data from the table for problems 22–23. **(pages 250–257)**

22. Make a graph to compare the data.
23. How many more people were in the 8 to 11 group than were in the 12 to 15 group?
24. A fishing license costs $35.50. How much will it cost the 12 members of the fishing club to buy licenses?
25. **Analyze:** How can you find the product of 79 × 245 if you know that the product of 80 and 245 is 19,600?

Water Sports Contests

Age Group (Years)	Number of People
7 and under	108
8 to 11	156
12 to 15	132
16 and up	144

Extra Practice

Patterns of Multiplication (pages 234–235)

Multiply mentally.

1. 30×100
2. 40×80
3. 20×400
4. $2,000 \times 80$
5. 90×60
6. 500×70
7. $50 \times 4,000$
8. $60 \times 8,000$

Multiply by Multiples of 10 (pages 238–239)

Multiply.

1. 48×20
2. 18×30
3. 24×40
4. 37×50
5. 219×60
6. 165×80
7. 449×50
8. 118×60
9. $1,357 \times 60$
10. $6,042 \times 70$
11. 529×80
12. 413×50
13. $9,127 \times 30$
14. 60×74
15. 689×30
16. $80 \times 4,876$
17. There are 5,256 square feet of surface to paint on a ship. A painting crew paints 20 ships with this same surface. How many square feet does the crew paint?
18. A cruise ship takes 678 passengers to and from Bermuda each week. How many passengers go on the cruise in 50 weeks?

Problem Solving: Reading For Math Multistep Problems (pages 240–241)

Solve. Tell what inference you made.

1. Tickets to the waterpark cost $24 for adults and $16 for children. How much will it cost for 10 adults and 20 children to go to the waterpark?
2. The waterpark is open for 8 hours each day. The boats for the water effect ride leave 30 times each hour. Each boat holds 20 people. How many people can go on the ride each day?

Extra Practice

Multiply by 2-Digit Numbers (pages 242–245)

Multiply.

1. 41×23
2. 14×26
3. $\$0.16 \times 16$
4. 36×29
5. 11×85
6. $\$37 \times 28$
7. 42×38
8. $\$0.47 \times 91$
9. 68×54
10. 97×21
11. 48×56
12. $88 \times \$0.33$
13. 53×26
14. $73 \times \$0.65$
15. A tour boat made 37 trips. Each time the boat had a sold-out crowd of 87 passengers. How many passengers did the boat carry in all?

Estimate Products (pages 246–247)

Estimate the product.

1. 75×28
2. 572×88
3. 314×64
4. $\$2,509 \times 64$
5. $8,689 \times 73$
6. 54×29
7. 8×52
8. 3×753
9. 19×812
10. 65×19
11. 97×243
12. $39 \times \$589$
13. 89×375

Multiply Greater Numbers (pages 250–253)

Multiply. Check that each answer is reasonable.

1. 197×24
2. $\$2.67 \times 55$
3. 529×28
4. $\$50.27 \times 23$
5. $3,679 \times 23$
6. $\$20.08 \times 44$
7. $8,745 \times 27$
8. $\$995.04 \times 15$

Solve.

9. A sailor works out 25 minutes every day. How many minutes does the sailor work out in one regular year?
10. Steamboat A takes 1,349 passengers on a river tour every day. Steamboat B takes 1,423 passengers on the same tour each day. After 21 days how many more passengers has Steamboat B taken on tour than Steamboat A?

Extra Practice

Problem Solving: Strategy Make a Graph (pages 254–255)

Use data from the table for problems 1–3.

1. Make a graph to display the data.
2. How many more people chose Clear Lake than chose Mono Lake?
3. Draw a conclusion based on the information in your graph?

Favorite Lake	
Lake	Number of People
Mono	240
Shasta	220
Clear	260
Honey	180

Multiply Using Mental Math (pages 256–257)

Multiply. Use mental math.

1. 14×30
2. 34×12
3. 15×40
4. 40×35
5. 16×14
6. 20×55
7. 24×40
8. 50×45
9. 16×42
10. 21×44
11. 18×24
12. 33×33
13. 41×30
14. 51×25
15. 70×17
16. 48×14
17. 60×35
18. 25×40
19. 44×22
20. 55×10
21. 80×20
22. 19×31
23. 18×30
24. 17×20
25. A dolphin can swim 37 miles in an hour at top speed. If it could maintain this speed for 12 hours, how far would it travel?
26. A cruise ship travels 25 miles in one hour. If it maintains that speed, how far will it travel in 48 hours?
27. Suppose a canoe can be rented for $16 an hour. How much would it cost to rent it for 15 hours?
28. A speed boat travels at 45 miles an hour. If it maintains this speed, how many miles will it travel over 18 hours?

Chapter Study Guide

Language and Math

Complete. Use a word from the list.

1. To estimate 34 × 198, you ____ the factors to 30 × 200.
2. When you multiply 56 × 145, you need to ____ the ones.
3. When you multiply 25 × 18, you can use the ____ to find the product mentally.
4. In 30 × 20 = 600, the 600 is the ____.

Math Words
Distributive Property
estimate
factor
product
regroup
round

Multiply multiples of 10; 100; and 1,000. (pages 234–235)

Example
Multiply: 40 × 2,000

Solution
Use patterns.

$$4 \times 2 = 8$$
$$40 \times 2 = 80$$
$$40 \times 20 = 800$$
$$40 \times 200 = 8{,}000$$
$$40 \times 2{,}000 = 80{,}000$$

Multiply.

5. 30 × 100
6. 50 × 80
7. 70 × 400
8. 4,000 × 60
9. 60 × 60
10. 200 × 90
11. 40 × 50
12. 600 × 40
13. A lifeboat holds 23 people. There are 57 lifeboats aboard a ship. How many people can fit aboard the lifeboats?

Multiply a multidigit number by a 2-digit number.
(pages 238–239, 242–245, 250–253, 256–257)

Example
Multiply: 26 × 43

Solution
Multiply each place.
Regroup if necessary.
Add the products.

$$\begin{array}{r} {}^{1}\\ 43 \\ \times 26 \\ \hline 258 \\ +860 \\ \hline 1{,}118 \end{array}$$

Multiply.

14. $\begin{array}{r} 31 \\ \times\ 47 \\ \hline \end{array}$
15. $\begin{array}{r} \$0.26 \\ \times\ \quad 62 \\ \hline \end{array}$
16. $\begin{array}{r} 461 \\ \times\ 27 \\ \hline \end{array}$
17. $\begin{array}{r} \$23.11 \\ \times\ \quad 55 \\ \hline \end{array}$
18. $\begin{array}{r} \$1{,}461 \\ \times\ \quad 27 \\ \hline \end{array}$
19. $\begin{array}{r} 52{,}073 \\ \times\ \quad 39 \\ \hline \end{array}$
20. 85 × $45.11
21. 67 × 60,912
22. A cruise ship receives 2,055 packages of paper cups. Each package contains 75 paper cups. How many cups is that in all?

Estimate products. (pages 246–247)

Example

Estimate: 27×63

Solution

Round the factors so you can multiply mentally.

27×63

$\downarrow \quad \downarrow$

$30 \times 60 = 1{,}800$

Estimate the product.

23. 54×37
24. 28×471
25. 67×18
26. 269×23
27. 167×92
28. 578×78
29. $\begin{array}{r} 425 \\ \times\ 36 \\ \hline \end{array}$
30. $\begin{array}{r} 967 \\ \times\ 68 \\ \hline \end{array}$
31. Jeff worked for 21 days last month. He cleaned 212 fish each day. About how many fish did Jeff clean?

Use strategies to solve problems. (pages 240–241, 254–255)

Example

Which type of museum had the most visitors?

Type of Museum	Number of Visitors
Whaling	35,525
Air and Space	35,750
Submarine	35,675
Riverboat	35,175

Solution

You can make a graph to help you compare the data.

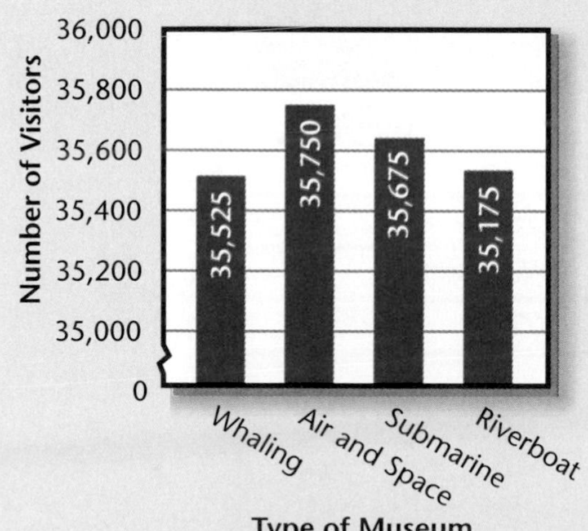

The Air and Space Museum had the most visitors.

Solve.

32. How many more people went to the Air and Space Museum than went to the Riverboat Museum?
33. A group of students take an 11:45 A.M. bus to go to the Whaling Museum. The bus trip is 50 minutes long. The students spend $2\frac{1}{2}$ hours at the museum then take the bus home. What time do they get home?

Chapter Test

Multiply.

1. $\begin{array}{r} 30 \\ \times\ 50 \\ \hline \end{array}$
2. $\begin{array}{r} 51 \\ \times\ 18 \\ \hline \end{array}$
3. $\begin{array}{r} 21 \\ \times\ 45 \\ \hline \end{array}$
4. $\begin{array}{r} 80 \\ \times\ 36 \\ \hline \end{array}$
5. $\begin{array}{r} 300 \\ \times\ 68 \\ \hline \end{array}$
6. $\begin{array}{r} 315 \\ \times\ 48 \\ \hline \end{array}$
7. $\begin{array}{r} 5,000 \\ \times\ 20 \\ \hline \end{array}$
8. $\begin{array}{r} \$4.45 \\ \times\ 89 \\ \hline \end{array}$
9. $\begin{array}{r} \$30.13 \\ \times\ 58 \\ \hline \end{array}$
10. $\begin{array}{r} 6,000 \\ \times\ 97 \\ \hline \end{array}$

11. 40 × 72
12. 13 × $78.05
13. 38 × 7,000
14. 59,132 × 48
15. 83 × 73,552
16. 50 × 80
17. 25 × $0.95

Estimate.

18. 24 × 13
19. 87 × 215
20. 68 × $569
21. 83 × 925

Solve.

22. A dock worker earns $28.79 an hour. Suppose the dock worker works 8 hours a day, 5 days a week for 46 weeks. How much does the dock worker earn?

23. Ted is following a boat race. Use the data from the chart to make a graph to show which part of the race is the longest.

Boat Race	
Part	Distance (Miles)
1	1,525
2	1,750
3	975
4	1,775

24. A cargo ship delivers 58 cartons of bananas. Each carton sells for $135.95. How much do the cartons sell for in all?

25. A ship weighs 78,956 tons. At each of 3 stops it picks up 1,678 tons of cargo. At the fourth stop it delivers 2,984 tons of cargo. What is the total weight of the ship now?

Performance Assessment

You are the manager of a company that gives whale-watching tours.

Each of your boats goes out 24 times a week. Find the total number of passengers possible for each boat during the course of a week.

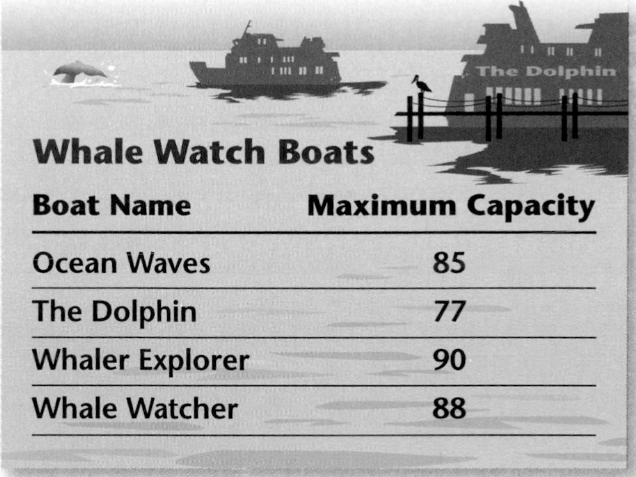

Whale Watch Boats

Boat Name	Maximum Capacity
Ocean Waves	85
The Dolphin	77
Whaler Explorer	90
Whale Watcher	88

Record your work on a chart like the one below.

Name of Boat	Number of Passengers	Number of Times Boat Goes Out	Total Number of Passengers
		24	
		24	

A Good Answer
- shows a completed chart.
- shows the mathematics you used to find the total number of passengers possible for each boat.

You may want to save this work in your portfolio.

Enrichment

Lattice Multiplication

Long ago, Hindu mathematicians in India used the **lattice method of multiplication** to multiply greater numbers. You can use graph paper to try this way of multiplying.

Find: 137×42

- Set-up a 3-by-2 grid since you are working with 3- and 2-digit numbers. Draw a line through each of the squares. This forms lattices.

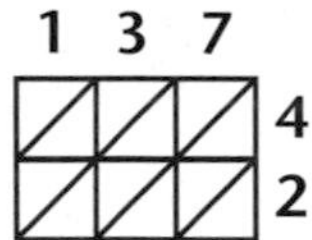

- Record the digits of the 3-digit factor across the top, one above each square. Do the same for the 2-digit factor along the right side.
- Multiply each top digit by each side digit. Write the products in the lattices. Start with 7×4. Then multiply 7 and 2.

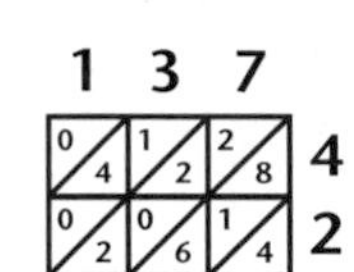

- Continue to multiply the digits until the grid is complete. If you do not need both lattices in a square, write a zero.

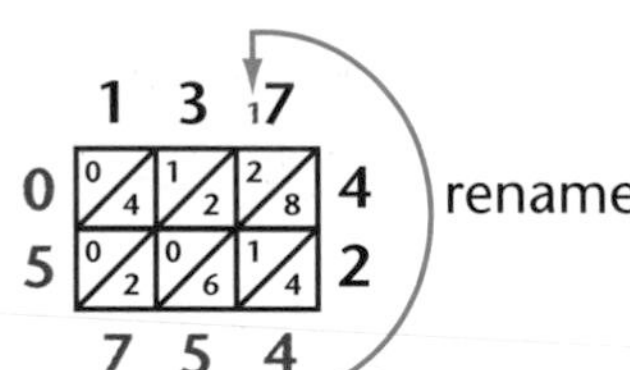

- Look at the strips formed by the lattices. Start with the lower right lattice. Add the digits in each diagonal. Rename to the next diagonal when you need to.
- Write the product by looking at the digits around the outside of the grid. Start at the top left corner.

05754 Therefore $137 \times 42 = 5{,}754$

Use lattice multiplication to find the product. Show your work.

1. 125×24
2. 219×43
3. 523×18
4. 629×13
5. What place value does the sum of the digits in the first strip on the right represent?

Test-Taking Tips

When taking a test, there are times when you might want to **estimate to eliminate incorrect answer choices.**

Mason bought shoes for $27.95, a jacket for $84, and a pair of jeans for $42.50. How much did he spend?

A. $126.50 **C.** $164.75
B. $154.75 **D.** $224.75

Estimate how much Mason spent.
30 + 80 + 40 = 150
He spent about $150.

Look at the answer choices.
Choice A and D are not close to the estimate.
Choice B is very close to the estimate.
Choice C is also reasonable.
Calculate the answer
$27.95 + $84 + $42.50 = $154.75.

B is the correct choice.

Check for Success

Before turning in a test, go back one last time to check.

- ☑ I understood and answered the questions asked.
- ☑ I checked my work for errors.
- ☑ My answers make sense.

Choose the correct answer.
Estimate to help you choose.

1. There were 23,677 people at the baseball game. There were still 15,078 empty seats. How many people could have gone to the game altogether?

A. 8,599 **C.** 38,755
B. 9,599 **D.** 48,755

2. Janice practices the piano a total of 12 hours each week. How many hours does she practice in a year? (Hint: there are 52 weeks in a year.)

F. 480 **H.** 752
G. 800 **J.** 624

3. Gene read one book that was 119 pages, a play that was 47 pages, and a poem that was 9 pages. How many pages did he read total?

F. 140 **H.** 250
G. 175 **J.** 380

4. Rob mows lawns to earn money. He charges $12 for each lawn. He mowed two lawns on Saturday and three on Sunday. How much did Rob earn altogether?

F. $30 **H.** $45
G. $40 **J.** $60

Spiral Review and Test Prep

Chapters 1–6

Choose the correct answer.

Number Sense

1. $25 \times 14 = n$
   - **A.** $5 \times 5 \times 7$
   - **B.** 50×7
   - **C.** 350×5
   - **D.** $(20 \times 14) + 14$

2. $\$2,507 - \$398 = t$
   - **F.** \$2,391
   - **G.** \$2,309
   - **H.** \$2,291
   - **J.** \$2,109

3. Which number is in the thousands place in 1,234,657?
   - **A.** 1
   - **B.** 2
   - **C.** 3
   - **D.** 4

4. Will bought 2 notepads and a pen. He spent \$3.55. Each notepad sells for \$1.35. How much did the pen cost?
   - **F.** \$2.70
   - **G.** \$2.20
   - **H.** \$1.85
   - **J.** \$0.85

Measurement and Geometry

5. A tablecloth is 68 inches long and 45 inches wide. Rosa wants to put a ribbon around the edges of the tablecloth. How much ribbon will she need?
   - **A.** 90 inches
   - **B.** 113 inches
   - **C.** 226 inches
   - **D.** 3,060 inches

6. What is the length of the object to the nearest centimeter?

   - **F.** 1 cm
   - **G.** 5 cm
   - **H.** 20 cm
   - **J.** 80 cm

7. Which item weighs about 2 pounds?
   - **A.** Television
   - **B.** Kitten
   - **C.** Chair
   - **D.** Orange

8. How many faces and edges does this shape have?

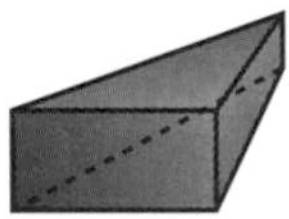

   - **F.** 2 faces, 5 edges
   - **G.** 4 faces, 5 edges
   - **H.** 5 faces, 9 edges
   - **J.** 4 faces, 8 edges

Statistics, Data Analysis, and Probability

Use data from the chart for problems 9–12.

Fred's Pizzeria	
Large pizza	$13.75
Small pizza	$9.35
1-foot hero	$7.79
3-foot hero	$22.50
Large soda	$2.15
Small soda	$1.49

9. Elm Street School is having a party for its fourth graders. The principal orders 12 small pizzas and a 3-foot hero. How much does he spend?
   A. $31.85 C. $134.70
   B. $112.20 D. $187.50

10. How much do you save by ordering a 3-foot hero instead of three 1-foot heroes?
   F. $0.97 H. $14.71
   G. $0.87 J. $23.37

11. The Carters order a large pizza and 4 small sodas. How much more does the pizza cost than the sodas?
   A. $7.79 C. $12.26
   B. $8.79 D. $19.71

12. Ben buys a 1-foot hero and a large soda. He pays with a twenty-dollar bill. What is his change? Explain how you found your answer.

Algebra and Functions

13. What is the next product in the pattern?
   $5 \times 2 = 10$
   $50 \times 2 = 100$
   $50 \times 20 = 1,000$
   A. 2,000 C. 10,000
   B. 5,000 D. 100,000

14. Which is an example of Commutative Property?
   F. $4 \times 3 = 4 \times 3$
   G. $5 \times 1 = 5$
   H. $(3 \times 2) \times 4 = 3 \times (2 \times 4)$
   J. $7 + 0 = 7$

15. If prices continue to increase in the same way, how much do 5 tickets cost?
   1 ticket = $4
   2 tickets = $8
   3 tickets = $12
   A. $13 C. $20
   B. $16 D. $24

16. What is the location of the school?

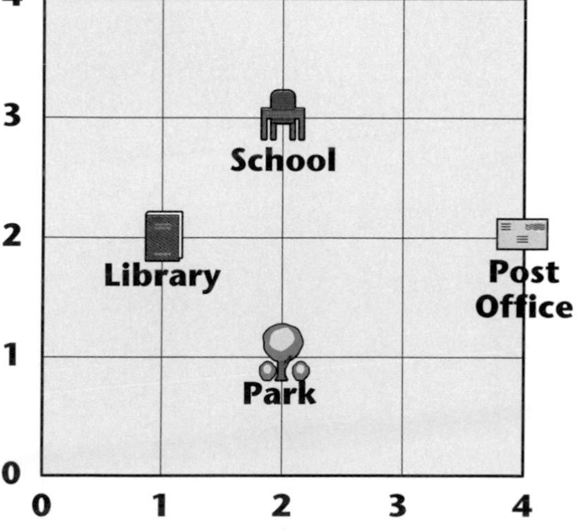

   F. (3, 2) H. (2, 3)
   G. (2, 1) J. (4, 2)

CHAPTER 7 Divide by 1-Digit Numbers

Theme: After-School Activities

Use the Data

After-School Activities	9–14 Year Olds
Do Homework	☺☺☺☺☺☺☺☺☺
Play Video Games	
Read Books	☺☺☺☺
Watch TV	☺☺☺☺☺☺☺☺

Key: ☺ stands for 5 students.

- **What if** 25 people responded that they play video games after school? How many ☺ do you need to show this on the graph? How can you use division to solve this problem?

What You Will Learn

In this chapter you will learn how to
- divide multiples of 10.
- divide multidigit numbers by 1-digit numbers.
- estimate quotients.
- find means (averages).
- use strategies to solve problems.

Objective: Review using mental math strategies to divide multiples of 10, 100, and 1,000.

7·1

Division Patterns

Algebra & functions

Learn

Math Words

quotient the result of division

dividend a number to be divided

divisor the number by which the dividend is divided

Sean races mountain bikes on the weekends. He finishes a 5,600-meter race. How many meters is each lap?

There's more than one way!

Find: 5,600 ÷ 7

Method A

You can find division patterns by using ones, tens, and hundreds.

56 ones ÷ 7 = 8 ones ⟷ 56 ÷ 7 = 8
56 tens ÷ 7 = 8 tens ⟷ 560 ÷ 7 = 80
56 hundreds ÷ 7 = 8 hundreds ⟷ 5,600 ÷ 7 = 800

Method B

You can find division patterns by using related multiplication patterns.

8 × 7 = 56	So	56 ÷ 7 = 8
80 × 7 = 560	So	560 ÷ 7 = 80
800 × 7 = 5,600	So	5,600 ÷ 7 = 800

Each lap is 800 meters.

Try It

Write the number that makes each sentence true.

1. $9 \div 3 = n$
$90 \div 3 = x$
$900 \div 3 = a$

2. $48 \div 6 = y$
$d \div 6 = 80$
$4{,}800 \div 6 = c$

3. $40 \div b = 5$
$e \div 8 = 50$
$4{,}000 \div 8 = g$

Look at the division patterns above. What happens to the **quotient** when the number of zeros in the **dividend** increases and the **divisor** remains the same?

Practice Divide.

4. $2\overline{)80}$ 5. $6\overline{)540}$ 6. $7\overline{)\$420}$ 7. $4\overline{)1{,}200}$ 8. $5\overline{)\$4{,}000}$

9. $320 \div 8$ 10. $\$180 \div 2$ 11. $490 \div 7$ 12. $140 \div 2$ 13. $350 \div 7$

14. $630 \div 9$ 15. $6{,}400 \div 8$ 16. $3{,}600 \div 4$ 17. $30{,}000 \div 5$ 18. $48{,}000 \div 6$

19. How many \$5 are in \$650?

★20. How many nickels are in \$3.50?

Algebra & functions Find the missing number.

21. $100 \div 2 = n$ 22. $240 \div 6 = z$ 23. $210 \div 7 = b$ 24. $270 \div 9 = a$

25. $280 \div d = 7$ 26. $240 \div x = 30$ 27. $y \div 7 = 60$ 28. $k \div 2 = 700$

Problem Solving

29. It takes Joe 9 minutes to run one lap. The whole race takes 180 minutes. How many laps does he run?

30. **Analyze:** If $5{,}600 \div 7 = 800$, what does $56{,}000 \div 7$ equal? How do you know?

Use data from the sign for problems 31–33.

31. Sheena buys a bike and 2 extra tires. How much do they cost in all?

32. Ralph wants to save to buy a bike, a bike lock, an 1 extra tire. He plans to save 5 equal amounts. How much should he save each time?

33. Each case holds 24 bike locks. The store has 12 cases. How much money can the store sell all of the bike locks for?

Spiral Review and Test Prep

34. $549 + 375$ 35. $\$241 - \$32$ 36. $312 + 49$ 37. 358×6 38. 32×45

Choose the correct answer.

39. Tina takes piano lessons every Monday. The lesson begins at 4:15 P.M. and ends at 5:00 P.M. How long is Tina's piano lesson?
   A. 15 minutes C. 75 minutes
   B. 45 minutes D. 85 minutes

40. What is the median for this group of numbers?
   40, 45, 45, 55, 50, 40, 60
   F. 20 H. 45
   G. 40 J. 49

Objective: Use models to divide.

7·2 Explore Division

Learn

Math Word

remainder the number less than the divisor that remains after the division is completed

You can use place-value models to explore division.

What is 125 divided by 4?

Work Together

You Will Need
- **place-value models**

- ► Use the place-value models to find 125 ÷ 4. Show 125 as 1 hundred and 2 tens and 5 ones. Put the models into 4 equal groups. Regroup as needed.
- ► Record your work. What is 125 ÷ 4?

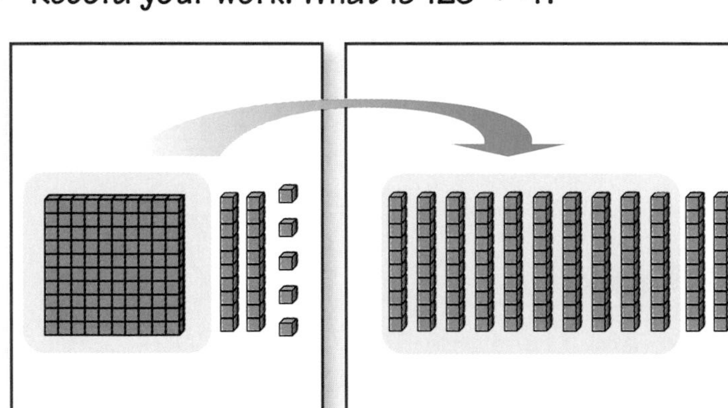

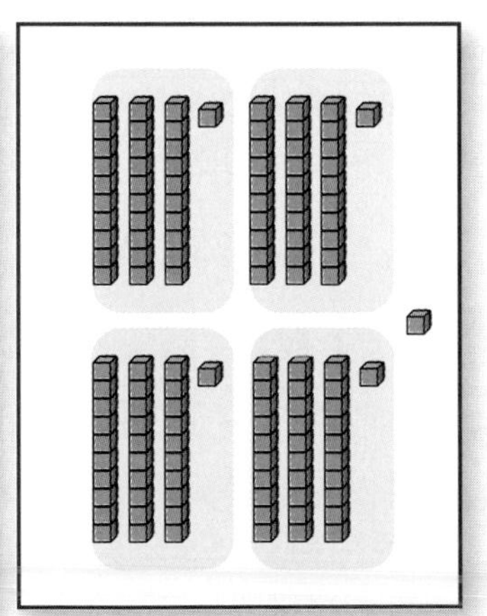

- ► Try some more.

68 ÷ 3   478 ÷ 2   193 ÷ 6   184 ÷ 5   54 ÷ 3

Make Connections

Here is how to record how to find a quotient with a **remainder**.

Find: 131 ÷ 3

Using Models | **Using Paper and Pencil**

1 Regroup 1 hundred and 3 tens as 13 tens. Place 4 tens in each group.

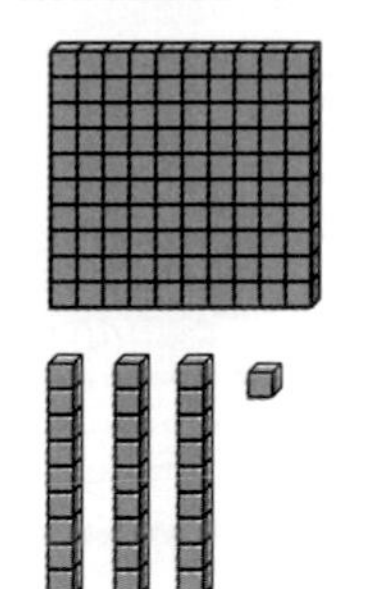

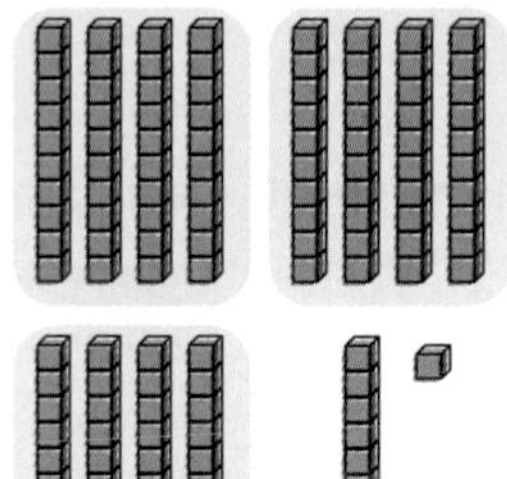

$$\begin{array}{r} 4 \\ 3\overline{)131} \\ -12 \\ \hline 1 \end{array}$$

← **4** tens in each group
← **12** tens used
← **1** ten left

2 Regroup the remaining ten into ones.

$$\begin{array}{r} 4 \\ 3\overline{)131} \\ -12\downarrow \\ \hline 11 \end{array}$$

Bring down 1 one
← **11** ones in all

3 Then place 3 ones in each group.

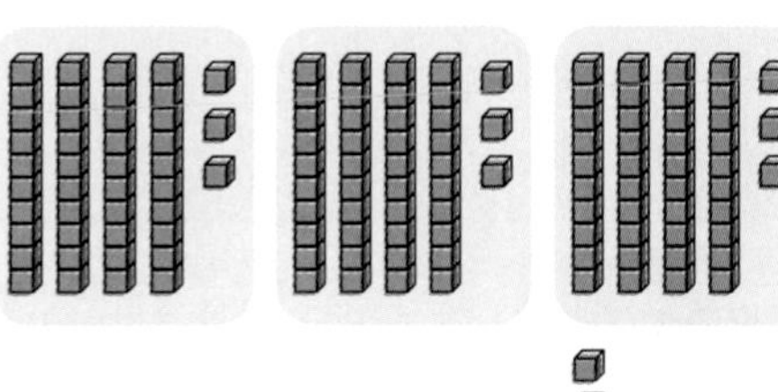

$$\begin{array}{r} 43 \\ 3\overline{)131} \\ -12\downarrow \\ \hline 11 \\ -\ 9 \\ \hline 2 \end{array}$$

← **3** ones in each group
← **9** ones used
← The **2** left is the **remainder**.

131 ÷ 3 = 43 R2

Try It **Divide. You may use place-value models.**

1. $4\overline{)44}$
2. $2\overline{)26}$
3. $5\overline{)178}$
4. 292 ÷ 7
5. 294 ÷ 9
6. 358 ÷ 3

Sum it Up Explain how to use place-value models to find 173 ÷ 3 and show how you record your work.

Practice **Divide.**

7. $3\overline{)51}$
8. $2\overline{)26}$
9. $8\overline{)173}$
10. $7\overline{)289}$
11. $6\overline{)346}$
12. $2\overline{)446}$
13. 57 ÷ 5
14. 159 ÷ 7
15. 497 ÷ 6
16. 582 ÷ 5
17. 637 ÷ 7
18. 434 ÷ 8
19. **Analyze:** Tara solved a division problem. The divisor is 6. The quotient is 28. The remainder is 2. What is the dividend?

Objective: Review dividing 3-digit numbers by 1-digit numbers.

7·3 Divide 3-Digit Numbers

Learn

Math in ACTION

Glenn talked local flower shops into giving flowers to a senior citizen hospital. Suppose Glenn has 216 flowers. He places 6 flowers in each vase. How many vases can he fill?

Glenn Suravech from Montebello, CA

Example 1

Find: 216 ÷ 6

1 Model 216. Decide where to place the first digit in the quotient.

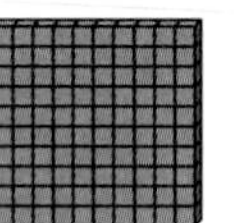
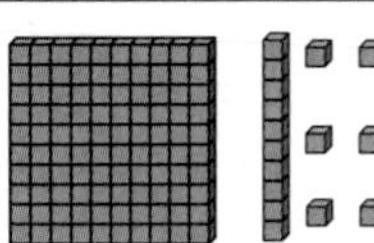

$6\overline{)216}$ **Think:** $6\overline{)2}$ Not enough hundreds.

$\begin{array}{r} x \\ 6\overline{)216} \end{array}$ **Think:** $6\overline{)21}$ Enough tens. The first digit is in the tens place.

2 Regroup the hundreds. How many tens can be put in each of 6 groups?

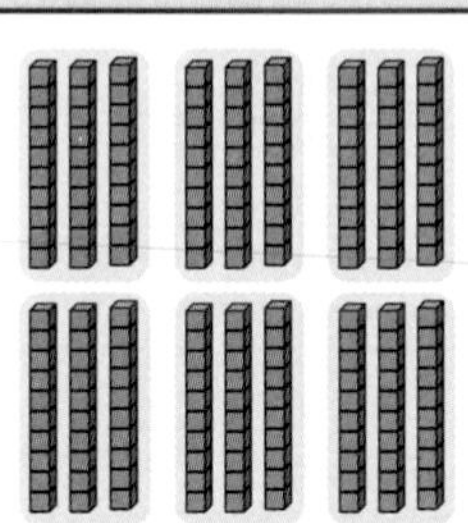

$$\begin{array}{r} 3 \\ 6\overline{)216} \\ -18 \\ \hline 3 \end{array}$$

← Multiply: $3 \times 6 = \mathbf{18}$

← Subtract: $21 - 18 = \mathbf{3}$; Compare: $3 < 6$

3 Regroup the tens. How many ones can be put in each of 6 groups? How many are left?

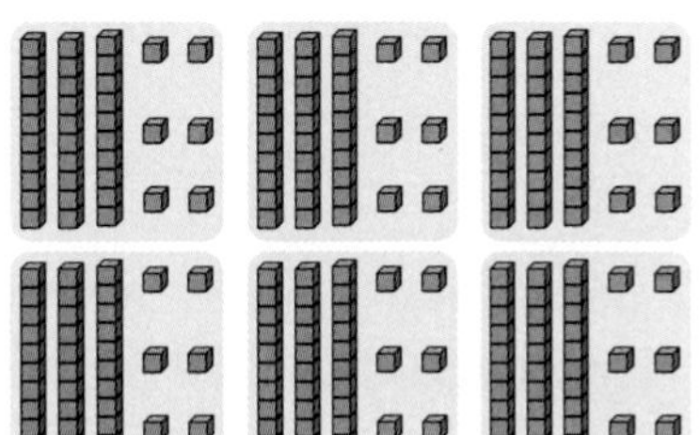

$$\begin{array}{r} 36 \\ 6\overline{)216} \\ -18{\downarrow} \\ \hline 36 \\ -36 \\ \hline 0 \end{array}$$

← Multiply: $6 \times 6 = \mathbf{36}$

← Subtract: $36 - 36 = \mathbf{0}$; Compare: $0 < 6$

4 Check. Use the inverse relationship between division and multiplication.

divisor → $\begin{array}{r} 36 \\ 6\overline{)216} \end{array}$ 36 ← quotient, 216 ← dividend

So $\begin{array}{r} 36 \\ \times\ 6 \\ \hline 216 \end{array}$ 36 ← quotient, 6 ← divisor, 216 ← dividend

Glenn can fill 36 vases.

Another store donates 258 vases. The vases are packed 4 to a box. How many full boxes are there? How many vases are in the unfilled box?

Example 2

Find: $258 \div 4$

1 Place the first digit of the quotient.

```
   x
4)258
```

Think:
4)25
The first digit is in the tens place.

2 Divide the tens.

```
   6
4)258
 -24  ← Multiply: 6 × 4
   1  ← Subtract: 25 − 24
        Compare: 1 < 4
```

Think:
Find the closest fact not greater than 25.
$7 \times 4 = 28$ Too big!
$6 \times 4 = 24$ OK

3 Bring down the ones. Divide the ones.

```
  64R2
4)258
 -24↓
   18
  -16  ← Multiply: 4 × 4
    2  ← Subtract: 18 − 16
         Compare: 2 < 4
```

Think:
Find the closest fact not greater than 18.
$4 \times 4 = 16$

Check the answer. Multiply. Add if there is a remainder.

$64 \times 4 + 2 = 258$ ✓ (64: quotient; 4: divisor; 2: remainder; 258: dividend)

There are 64 full boxes and 2 vases in the unfilled box.

Try It **Divide. Check your answer.**

```
1.    16■ R■        2.    1■■ R7       3.    1■8 R■       4.    ■54 R2
    5)829               8)935              7)971              3)464
     -5                  -8                 -■                 -3
      32                  1■                 27                 16
     -30                 - 8                -21                -15
       29                  55                 61                 ■■
      -■■                 -48                -■■                -12
        4                   ■                  5                  ■
```

Without dividing, how do you know that the quotient of $547 \div 3$ is a 3-digit number?

Practice **Divide. Check your answer.**

5. $4\overline{)56}$
6. $5\overline{)65}$
7. $8\overline{)954}$
8. $9\overline{)942}$
9. $2\overline{)\$426}$
10. $3\overline{)335}$
11. $7\overline{)342}$
12. $8\overline{)295}$
13. $5\overline{)468}$
14. $2\overline{)120}$
15. $84 ÷ 4
16. 93 ÷ 4
17. 749 ÷ 6
18. 842 ÷ 7
19. $908 ÷ 6
20. 438 ÷ 8
21. 484 ÷ 6
22. 675 ÷ 7
23. 383 ÷ 4
24. 248 ÷ 3
25. Divide 573 by 4.
26. Divide 884 by 7.
27. Divide 156 by 3.

Use each digit in the box once. Write a division sentence with a 1-digit divisor and the greatest possible quotient.

★28. 3 4 5 9

★29. 2 6 7 8

★30. 1 4 5 6

Algebra & functions **Find each missing number.**

31. $875 \div n = 125$
32. $c \div 6 = 172$
33. $320 \div m = 160$

★34. $(150 + 10) \div s = 20$

★35. $(242 + t) \div 5 = 50$

★36. $844 \div (2 + k) = 211$

37.

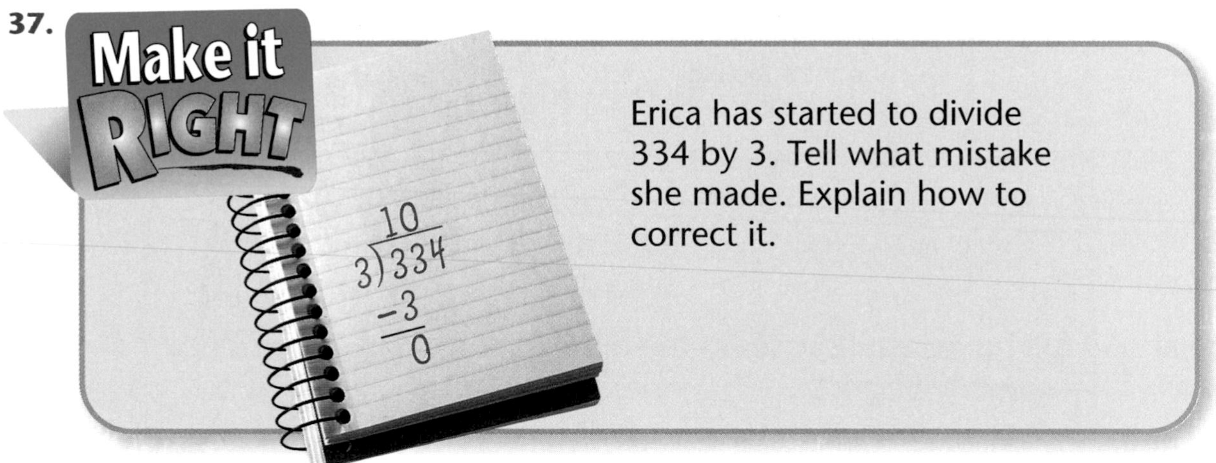

Erica has started to divide 334 by 3. Tell what mistake she made. Explain how to correct it.

Problem Solving

38. Florists donate 213 flowers on Monday, 179 on Tuesday, and 225 on Wednesday. How many flowers were donated in three days?

39. **Health:** Petting an animal can be good for a senior citizen's health. One day Jane and her assistants bring 24 animals from her pet store to each of 5 floors at a retirement center. How many animals does Jane bring?

40. **Explain** the steps you would take to find 794 ÷ 3. Show how to check your answer.

41. Florist donates 576 flowers. A youth group puts 3 flowers in each vase. How many vases can they fill?

Use data from *Did You Know?* for problems 42–45.

42. **Social Studies:** The food banks are grouped into 6 regions. If there are about the same number of food banks in each region, how many food banks are there in each region?

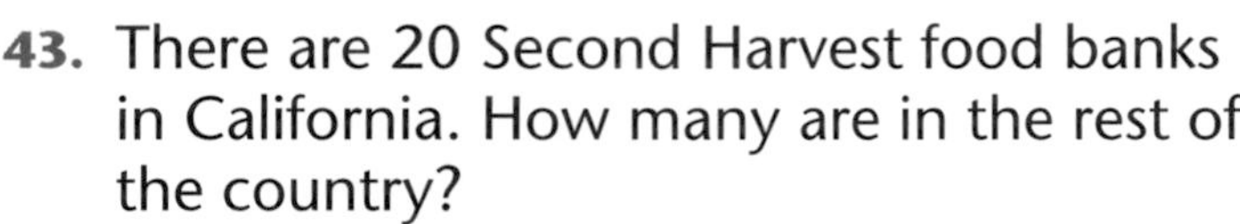

43. There are 20 Second Harvest food banks in California. How many are in the rest of the country?

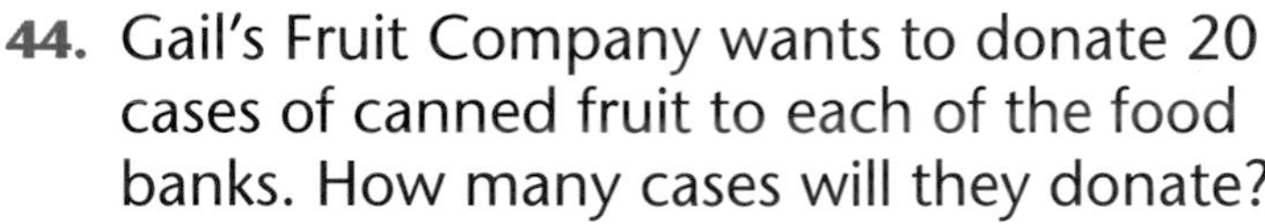

44. Gail's Fruit Company wants to donate 20 cases of canned fruit to each of the food banks. How many cases will they donate?

★ 45. About how many people other than children and seniors are helped by Second Harvest each year?

Second Harvest is the largest charitable hunger relief organization in the United States. Its 188 food banks help more than 26 million Americans each year. This includes 8 million children and 4 million seniors.

Spiral Review and Test Prep

46. $\begin{array}{r} 237 \\ +583 \\ \hline \end{array}$

47. $\begin{array}{r} \$10.05 \\ -\quad 5.83 \\ \hline \end{array}$

48. $\begin{array}{r} 72 \\ \times\ 8 \\ \hline \end{array}$

49. $\begin{array}{r} 87 \\ \times 64 \\ \hline \end{array}$

50. $\begin{array}{r} 437 \\ 65 \\ +609 \\ \hline \end{array}$

51. $\begin{array}{r} 1{,}502 \\ -\quad 647 \\ \hline \end{array}$

52. $\begin{array}{r} 1{,}783 \\ +2{,}376 \\ \hline \end{array}$

53. $\begin{array}{r} \$1.74 \\ \times\quad 3 \\ \hline \end{array}$

54. $\begin{array}{r} 78 \\ \times 28 \\ \hline \end{array}$

55. $9\overline{)108}$

56. \$2.37 − \$0.97

57. 156×5

58. $324 + 7 + 86$

59. 27×42

Choose the correct answer.

60. Eli's family left their house at 2:15 P.M. They arrived at the camp 2 hours and 20 minutes later. What time did they arrive at the camp?

    A. 4:35 P.M.
    B. 5:35 P.M.
    C. 4:02 P.M.
    D. 4:35 A.M.

61. What is a rule for this function table?

2	3	4	5
8	12	16	20

F. Add 6.
G. Multiply by 3.
H. Multiply by 4.
J. Add 15.

Extra Practice, page 311

Objective: Divide 3-digit numbers by 1-digit numbers.

7·4 Quotients with Zeros

Learn

Each day after school Juan and Rita make friendship bracelets to sell at a flea market. They have a box of 316 beads to make 3 bracelets. Each bracelet has the same number of beads. How many beads are in each bracelet?

Example

Find: 316 ÷ 3

1 Place the first digit in the quotient.

```
   x
3)316
```

Think: 3)3 The first digit is in the hundreds place.

2 Divide the hundreds.

```
   1
3)316
 -3
  0
```

Multiply: 1 × 3 = 3
Subtract: 3 − 3 = 0
Compare: 0 < 3

Think: Use the closest fact not greater than 3. 1 × 3 = 3

3 Bring down the tens. Divide the tens.

```
   10
3)316
 -3↓
  01
 - 0
   1
```

Multiply: 0 × 3 = 0
Subtract: 1 − 0 = 1
Compare: 1 < 3

Think: Use the closest fact not greater than 1. 0 × 3 = 0

4 Bring down the ones. Divide the ones.

```
   105 R1
3)316
 -3↓
  01
 - 0↓
   16
  -15
    1
```

Multiply: **5 × 3 = 15**
Subtract: 16 − 15 = 1
Compare: 1 < 3

Think: Use the closest fact not greater than 16. 5 × 3 = 15

Check: 3 × 105 + 1 = 316.
They will use 105 beads for each bracelet.

Try It

Divide. Check your answer.

1. 4)417 **2.** 6)$612 **3.** 2)608 **4.** 708 ÷ 7 **5.** 918 ÷ 9

When do you get a zero in the tens place of a quotient?

Practice **Divide. Check your answer.**

6. $6\overline{)68}$
7. $7\overline{)145}$
8. $4\overline{)\$428}$
9. $5\overline{)567}$
10. $4\overline{)57}$
11. $4\overline{)\$120}$
12. $3\overline{)\$315}$
13. $9\overline{)683}$
14. $2\overline{)39}$
15. $3\overline{)341}$
16. $4\overline{)419}$
17. $8\overline{)138}$
18. $3\overline{)207}$
19. $7\overline{)702}$
20. $5\overline{)549}$
21. $122 ÷ 2
22. $424 ÷ 3
23. 725 ÷ 9
24. 61 ÷ 2
25. 541 ÷ 3
26. $735 ÷ 7
27. 639 ÷ 6
28. 925 ÷ 9
29. 241 ÷ 6
30. 323 ÷ 4

Find only those quotients that are greater than 800.

31. 4,345 ÷ 4
32. 1,123 ÷ 3
33. 1,605 ÷ 2
34. 7,236 ÷ 9

Problem Solving

35. Juan and Rita make a $102 profit selling their friendship bracelets. They share their profit equally. How much money does Rita get?

36. **Create a division** problem in which the quotient has a zero in the ones place. Solve it. Explain how you chose your problem.

Use data from the table for problems 37–38.

37. You buy 3 packs of craft sticks and 2 jars of glue and pay with a twenty-dollar bill. How much change will you receive?

38. **Art:** Juan bought 2 boxes of beads to make 6 bracelets. He will use the same number of beads for each bracelet. How many beads will he use for each bracelet?

Crafts Price List		
Item	Number	Cost
Plastic beads	Box of 305	$4
Craft string	1 6-foot roll	$2
Craft sticks	100 pack	$3
Craft glue	1 8-ounce jar	$1

Spiral Review and Test Prep

39. 135 + 65
40. 108 − 25
41. 36 × 4
42. 72 ÷ 6
43. 565 ÷ 5

Choose the correct answer.

44. Tanya and Amy have 68 cards altogether. Tanya has 2 cards more than Amy. How many cards does Amy have?
    A. 32
    B. 33
    C. 34
    D. 35

45. Which is equal to 6 × 32?
    F. 3 × 3 × 32
    G. 32 ÷ 6
    H. 6 × 8 × 4
    J. Not Here

Objective: Make an inference to interpret remainders and solve problems.

7•5

Problem Solving: Reading for Math

Interpret the Remainder

Soccer Club Celebrates

Read

The Hillside Soccer Club had a great year! A group of 156 people will celebrate at the soccer banquet. Each banquet table can seat 8 people. How many tables should be set up for the dinner?

READING ▶ SKILL

Make Inferences

You make an inference when you draw a conclusion from something known or hinted at.

- **What do you know?** 156 people; each table seats 8 people.
- **What can you infer?** Everyone needs a seat at a table.

MATH ▶ SKILL

Interpret the Remainder

- Sometimes you use only the quotient.
- Sometimes the remainder is part of the answer.
- Sometimes you add 1 to the quotient.

Plan

Separate the total number of people into equal groups. Divide.

Everyone will need a seat. Decide what you will do with the remainder if there is one.

Solve

$156 \div 8 = 19$ R4 ← **19 full tables with 4 people left**

To make sure that everyone has a seat at a table, add 1 to the quotient. So 20 tables should be set up for the dinner.

Look Back

- Is your answer reasonable?

How did you use an inference to help you decide how to interpret the remainder?

Solve. Tell what inference you made and how you interpreted the remainder.

1. A container with 150 ounces of juice will be on a table. If the juice is shared equally, how many 6-ounce cups will be poured?
2. The team collects $200 to give to their 6 coaches. Each coach gets the same amount. The rest of the money will go into the team fund. How much money goes into the team fund?
3. A total of 85 soccer balls will be given away. The balls are packed 6 to a box. How many balls will be left?
4. The 24 members of the school band are going to perform at the dinner. Each car holds 5 members. How many cars do they need?

Use data from the Soccer News for problems 5–8.

5. Awards will be given to 14 club members. These awards will cost the club $84. How many tickets need to be sold to pay for the awards?
6. Six club officials will speak at the dinner. Each speaker will talk for the same amount of time. How many minutes long will each speech be?
7. Sal pays $80 for tickets. How many tickets does he buy?
8. Nara has $48. How many tickets can she buy?

Spiral Review and Test Prep

Choose the correct answer.

Some team members and their families plan to rent vans to go to the dinner. There are 39 people in all. Each van holds 7 people. How many vans will they need to rent?

9. Which of the following statements is true?
   - A. The team has 39 members.
   - B. A van holds 7 people.
   - C. Everyone can fit in 1 van.
10. How do you interpret the remainder to solve this problem?
    - F. Use only the quotient.
    - G. Use only the remainder.
    - H. Add 1 to the quotient.

Objective: Estimate quotients by using compatible numbers.

7·6 Estimate Quotients

Learn

Math Words

compatible numbers numbers that are close to the numbers in a problem and easy to divide mentally

Evan's skates have a special meter that shows how far he has skated. Each turn of the wheel adds 6 inches to the meter. About how many times has the wheel turned?

There's more than one way!

Estimate: $213 \div 6$

To estimate the quotient, you can use **compatible numbers** that help you divide mentally.

Find a number close to 213 that you can divide by 6.

Method A

Think of the basic fact: $18 \div 6 = 3$

180 is close to 213

$180 \div 6 = 30$

So far, the wheel has turned about 30 times.

Method B

Think of the basic fact: $24 \div 6 = 4$

240 is close to 213

$240 \div 6 = 40$

So far, the wheel has turned about 40 times.

Try It

Estimate. Show the compatible numbers you use.

1. $5\overline{)642}$ **2.** $3\overline{)172}$ **3.** $9\overline{)348}$ **4.** $\$4{,}682 \div 8$ **5.** $50{,}153 \div 7$

Which estimate is for a distance greater than what Evan has skated?

Practice **Estimate. Use compatible numbers.**

6. $5\overline{)564}$ 7. $2\overline{)130}$ 8. $4\overline{)210}$ 9. $9\overline{)291}$ 10. $7\overline{)226}$

11. $5\overline{)3,784}$ 12. $3\overline{)2,507}$ 13. $6\overline{)2,578}$ 14. $8\overline{)3,712}$ 15. $2\overline{)4,737}$

16. 832 ÷ 9 17. 172 ÷ 4 18. \$6.87 ÷ 3 19. 508 ÷ 7 20. 537 ÷ 6

21. 4,127 ÷ 6 22. \$7,332 ÷ 9 23. \$6,604 ÷ 8 24. 43,548 ÷ 8

25. 3,684 ÷ 5 26. 4,374 ÷ 9 27. 5,721 ÷ 8 28. 31,248 ÷ 5

29. 2,326 ÷ 6 30. 43,129 ÷ 7 ★31. \$665,604 ÷ 8 ★32. 413,548 ÷ 5

Problem Solving

33. A skate park has \$4,750 to spend on 6 new ramps. About how much can they spend on each ramp? Explain.

34. Taylor buys a helmet and pads. He pays with 3 twenty-dollar bills. How much change does Taylor receive?

35. **Compare:** Which is an easier way to estimate 149 ÷ 7: use the compatible numbers 140 ÷ 7, or round the dividend 150 ÷ 7? Explain.

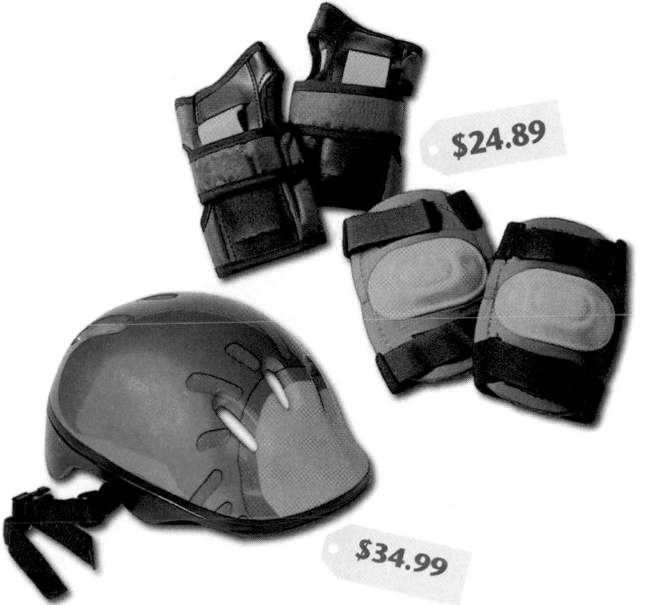

Spiral Review and Test Prep

36. $\begin{array}{r} 755 \\ +329 \\ \hline \end{array}$ 37. $\begin{array}{r} 2,003 \\ -\ \ 549 \\ \hline \end{array}$ 38. $\begin{array}{r} 54 \\ \times\ 6 \\ \hline \end{array}$ 39. $\begin{array}{r} 68 \\ \times 17 \\ \hline \end{array}$ 40. $7\overline{)35}$

41. \$649 + \$384 42. 68 × 23 43. 5,699 − 2,568 44. 723 × 7

45. \$13.95 + \$24.78 + \$36.75 46. (13 × 6) × (7 + 3)

Choose the correct answer.

47. Which number is 7 thousands 8 tens 9 ones in standard form?
   - A. 7,890
   - B. 7,089
   - C. 7,098
   - D. 789

48. Find the missing number.
   $n \times (4 + 5) = (3 \times 4) + (3 \times 5)$
   - F. 1
   - G. 3
   - H. 4
   - J. 5

Extra Practice, page 312

Objective: Divide 4-digit numbers by 1-digit numbers.

7•7 Divide 4-Digit Numbers

Learn

Piece by piece, Tamla and 4 friends are making mosaics using these tiles. Each mosaic uses the same number of tiles. How many tiles will each mosaic use?

Example 1

Find: 1,376 ÷ 5

1 Place the first digit in the quotient.

$$5\overline{)1{,}376}\quad \text{quotient digit: } x$$

Think: $5\overline{)13}$ The first digit is in the hundreds place.

2 Divide the hundreds.

$$\begin{array}{r} 2 \\ 5\overline{)1{,}376} \\ -1\,0 \\ \hline 3 \end{array}$$

Multiply: $2 \times 5 = 10$

Subtract: $13 - 10 = 3$

Compare: $3 < 5$

Think: Use the closest fact not greater than 13.

3 Bring down the tens. Divide the tens.

$$\begin{array}{r} 27 \\ 5\overline{)1{,}376} \\ -1\,0\downarrow \\ \hline 37 \\ -35 \\ \hline 2 \end{array}$$

Multiply: $7 \times 5 = 35$

Subtract: $37 - 35 = 2$

Compare: $2 < 5$

Think: Use the closest fact not greater than 37.

4 Bring down the ones. Divide the ones.

$$\begin{array}{r} 275 \text{ R1} \\ 5\overline{)1{,}376} \\ -1\,0\downarrow \\ \hline 37 \\ -35\downarrow \\ \hline 26 \\ -25 \\ \hline 1 \end{array}$$

Multiply: $5 \times 5 = 25$

Subtract: $26 - 25 = 1$

Compare: $1 < 5$

Think: Use the closest fact not greater than 26.

Check: You can check the reasonableness of your answer by estimating. Each mosaic will use 275 tiles.

Think: 1,500 ÷ 5 = 300 275 is reasonably close to 300.

Everyone loves Buddy, the school mascot. Luis has designed a mosaic of Buddy with 4 equal sections. He has 3,634 tiles. How many tiles will be in each section?

Example 2

Find: 3,634 ÷ 4

1 Place the first digit in the quotient.

```
     x
4)3,634
```

Think: $4\overline{)36}$ The first digit is in the hundreds place.

2 Divide the hundreds.

```
     9
4)3,634
 -3 6
    0
```

Multiply: $4 \times 9 = 36$

Subtract: $36 - 36 = 0$

Compare: $0 < 4$

Think: Use the closest fact whose product is not too great.

3 Bring down the tens. Divide the tens.

```
     90
4)3,634
 -3 6↓
    03
  -  0
     3
```

Compare: $3 < 4$

There are not enough tens.

Write 0 in the the quotient.

4 Bring down the ones. Divide the ones.

```
     908 R2
4)3,634
 -3 6↓ |
    03 |
  -  0↓
     34
    -32
      2
```

Multiply: $4 \times 8 = 32$

Subtract: $34 - 32 = 2$

Compare: $2 < 4$

Check for reasonableness. Estimate: 3,600 ÷ 4 = 900

There will be 908 tiles in each section.

Think: 908 is reasonably close to 900

Try It **Divide. Check your answer.**

1.
```
   1,2■4 R■
3)3,763
 -■
  07
 - 6
   16
  -15
   13
  -■■
    1
```

2.
```
   ■,3■7 R2
4)5,230
 -4
  12
 -12
   ■■
  -00
    30
   -28
     2
```

3.
```
     51■ R2
6)3,110
 -30
   11
  - ■
   50
  -■■
    2
```

4.
```
    $8■■ R3
5)$4,378
  -■■
    37
   -35
    28
   -■■
     3
```

How do you decide where to place the first digit in the quotient of 4,879 ÷ 8?

Practice Divide. Check your answer.

5. $6\overline{)6,744}$ **6.** $8\overline{)\$9,056}$ **7.** $3\overline{)8,395}$ **8.** $4\overline{)8,721}$ **9.** $3\overline{)9,056}$

10. $2\overline{)\$1,642}$ **11.** $5\overline{)4,657}$ **12.** $9\overline{)2,713}$ **13.** $8\overline{)\$5,638}$ **14.** $7\overline{)7,561}$

15. $6,888 ÷ 6 **16.** 9,726 ÷ 3 **17.** 7,803 ÷ 9 **18.** 2,227 ÷ 8 **19.** 8,147 ÷ 4

20. 4,859 ÷ 6 **21.** 4,906 ÷ 7 **22.** 8,202 ÷ 4 **23.** $5,768 ÷ 7 **24.** 3,947 ÷ 3

25. 5,450 ÷ 6 **26.** 9,182 ÷ 3 **27.** 6,749 ÷ 3 **28.** 4,678 ÷ 6 **29.** 3,516 ÷ 5

30. Divide 5,513 by 2. **31.** Divide 2,750 by 9. **32.** Divide 8,242 by 8.

33. Divide 6,524 by 4 **34.** Divide 4,573 by 6 **35.** Divide 7,049 by 7

Algebra & functions **Compare. Write > or <.**

36. 1,978 ÷ 3 ● 1,198 ÷ 2 **37.** 2,792 ÷ 7 ● 2,541 ÷ 6 **38.** 3,367 ÷ 4 ● 4,654 ÷ 5

39. 4,369 ÷ 2 ● 4,521 ÷ 3 **40.** 5,103 ÷ 4 ● 5,614 ÷ 3 **41.** 7,810 ÷ 5 ● 6,846 ÷ 7

★**42.** (3,452 + 1,376) ÷ 4 ● 4,269 ÷ 3

★**43.** (8,347 − 3,464) ÷ 5 ● (2,469 + 4,537) ÷ 6

44.

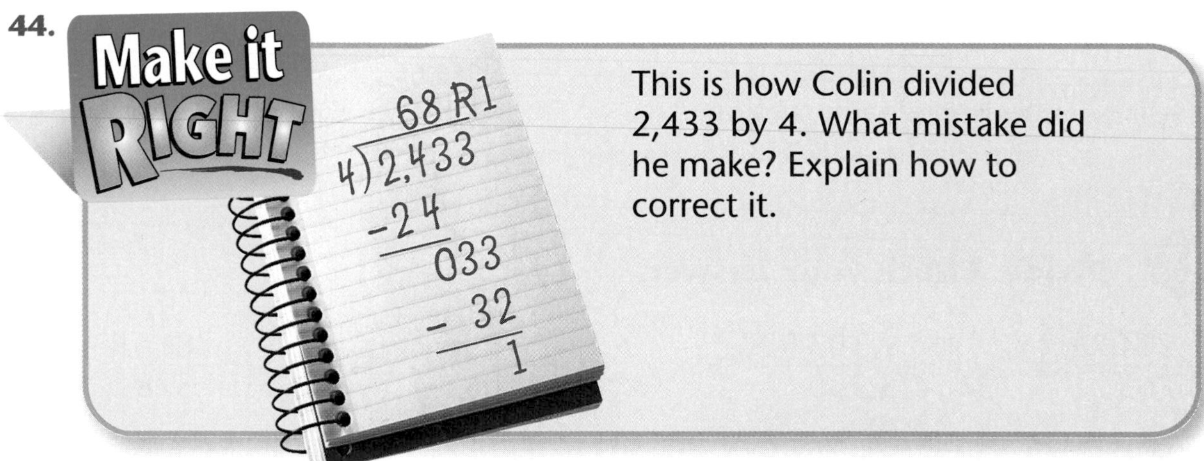

This is how Colin divided 2,433 by 4. What mistake did he make? Explain how to correct it.

Problem Solving

45. A large mosaic kit has 5,100 tiles separated equally into 4 bags. How many tiles are in each bag?

46. Lila makes 3 mosaic serving trays. Each tray uses 1,345 tiles. How many tiles does Lila use?

47. **Summarize:** How do you decide where to place the first digit in a quotient?

48. The art club has 2,525 tiles. They share the tiles equally among 4 projects. How many tiles are left?

Use data from the table for problems 49–51.

49. Niko can make 6 small mosaic trays from one kit. If each tray has the same number of tiles, how many tiles are in each tray?

50. Each suncatcher that Dylan makes uses 5 pieces of stained glass. How many kits does Dylan need to make 30 suncatchers?

51. **Create a problem** using data from the table. Solve it. Ask others to solve it.

ART SUPPLIES

MATERIAL	NUMBER IN KIT
Mosaic tiles	3,408 tiles
Stained glass	75 pieces

52. **Art:** Louis C. Tiffany (1848–1933) created a process for making a special type of colorful glass called favrile glass. For how many years did he live?

Spiral Review and Test Prep

53. 549 − 267 **54.** 72 × 21 **55.** \$899.72 + \$249.89 **56.** 8 × 396

Use data from the graph for problems 57–60.

57. In which month were the greatest number of awards given?

58. How many awards were given in all?

59. How many more awards were given in July than in September?

60. If the awards in August were shared equally by 6 people, how many awards did each get?

Choose the correct answer.

61. What number is equal to (6 × 1,000) + (4 × 100) + (7 × 10)?

A. 647 **C.** 6,470
B. 6,047 **D.** 6,000,470

62. Find the missing number.
4,764 × ■ = 4,764

F. 0 **H.** 4,764
G. 1 **J.** Not Here

Objective: Divide 5-digit numbers by 1-digit numbers.

7-8 Divide 5-Digit Numbers

Learn

"What a great break for us!" Paul exclaimed. He and his band have been invited to play in a concert at a local stadium. The stadium has 5 levels each with the same number of seats. How many seats are in each level?

Example

Find 12,350 ÷ 5 to solve the problem.

1 Place the first digit in the quotient.

```
    x
5)12,350
```

Think: 5)12
The first digit is in the thousands place.

2 Divide each place.

```
   2,470
5)12,350
 -10↓||
   23 ||
  -20↓|
    35|
   -35↓
     00
    - 0
      0
```

3 Multiply to check.

```
  2 3
  2,470
×     5
 12,350
```

There are 2,470 seats in each level.

Remember: For each place, multiply, subtract, compare, and bring down.

Try It

Divide. Check your answer.

1. 4)54,684 **2.** 3)70,962 **3.** 40,736 ÷ 6 **4.** 48,300 ÷ 8

Where will you place the first digit in each? Why? 4)82,342 4)17,476

Practice Divide. Check your answer.

5. $6\overline{)73{,}926}$
6. $3\overline{)94{,}446}$
7. $4\overline{)98{,}732}$
8. $2\overline{)\$73{,}504}$
9. $7\overline{)85{,}500}$
10. $8\overline{)29{,}969}$
11. $9\overline{)\$77{,}310}$
12. $2\overline{)42{,}115}$
13. $8\overline{)\$16{,}386}$
14. $6\overline{)58{,}503}$
15. $3\overline{)\$33{,}157}$
16. $5\overline{)15{,}125}$
17. $11{,}245 \div 9$
18. $\$376.26 \div 2$
19. $14{,}214 \div 7$
20. $38{,}924 \div 6$
21. $\$9{,}565 \div 5$
22. $18{,}028 \div 3$
23. $8{,}189 \div 9$
24. $88{,}888 \div 8$

Algebra & functions Find each missing number.

25. $45{,}345 \div n = 9{,}069$
26. $\$638.28 \div t = \$106.38$
27. $32{,}109 \div x = 4{,}587$

★28. $(7{,}124 + b) \div 5 = 3{,}145$

★29. $(c - 13{,}089) \div 2 = 25{,}356$

Problem Solving

30. Over 3 days, Paul's band played for 36,915 people. If there were the same number of people at each concert, how many people were at each concert?

31. **Analyze:** What is the least number of digits that there can be in the quotient when you divide a 5-digit number by a 1-digit number?

Spiral Review and Test Prep

Find the range, median, and mode.

32. 4, 6, 8, 2, 0, 5, 4
33. 245, 278, 212
34. 32, 35, 36, 31, 36

Choose the correct answer.

35. Tom divides 49 by 3. He gets 16 R1. How can he check his answer?
   - A. $(49 \times 3) + 1$
   - C. $(3 \times 16) + 1$
   - B. $(16 \times 1) + 3$
   - D. Not Here

36. Jake is 3 years older than Tina and 4 years younger than Neka. Tina is 18 years old. How old is Neka?
   - F. 25 years old
   - H. 19 years old
   - G. 21 years old
   - J. 17 years old

37. $59 \div 7$ means the same as
   - A. $7 \div 59$
   - C. $59\overline{)7}$
   - B. $7\overline{)59}$
   - D. 7×59

38. What number is missing from this addition pattern?
   5, 8, 11, 14, ____, 20
   - F. 15
   - H. 20
   - G. 17
   - J. 21

Extra Practice, page 312

Check Your Progress A

Write the number that makes each sentence true. **(pages 276–277)**

1. $54 \div n = 9$
$540 \div 6 = r$
$5{,}400 \div 6 = m$

2. $63 \div b = 9$
$630 \div w = 70$
$6{,}300 \div 9 = s$

3. $32 \div 8 = k$
$320 \div y = 40$
$g \div 8 = 400$

Divide. **(pages 280–285, 290–295)**

4. $2\overline{)91}$ **5.** $9\overline{)87}$ **6.** $8\overline{)52}$ **7.** $5\overline{)683}$

8. $7\overline{)724}$ **9.** $3\overline{)342}$ **10.** $4\overline{)\$752}$ **11.** $7\overline{)3{,}693}$

12. $3{,}864 \div 4$ **13.** $365 \div 5$ **14.** $\$5{,}648 \div 4$ **15.** $\$8{,}920 \div 7$

16. $12{,}546 \div 6$ **17.** $87 \div 2$ **18.** $2{,}345 \div 6$

Use data from the chart for problems 19–21. **(pages 288–289)**

These fruits are packed with about the same number in each box. Use compatible numbers to estimate the number in each box. Show the compatible numbers you use.

Fruit	Oranges	Apples	Pears	Peaches
Total	264	329	178	418

19. 8 boxes of apples **20.** 9 boxes of pears **21.** 6 boxes of oranges

Solve. **(pages 276–295)**

22. All 1,978 members of the drama club are going on the theater tour. Each van holds 9 members. How many vans will they need?

23. Pablo has gathered 268 rocks for his collection. He puts them in display cases. Each case holds 6 rocks. How many cases does he need?

24. **Explain:** Fred estimated $4{,}351 \div 6$. Will his estimate be greater or less than the exact quotient?

Journal

25. Misha has raised \$19,728. He wants to give the same amount to each of 4 charities. How much will each get?

Additional activities at www.mhschool.com/math

Use Place-Value Models to Divide

Three classes at West Elementary School bought 317 flowers to plant around their building. Each class will plant the same number of flowers. How many flowers will each class plant? Are any flowers left over?

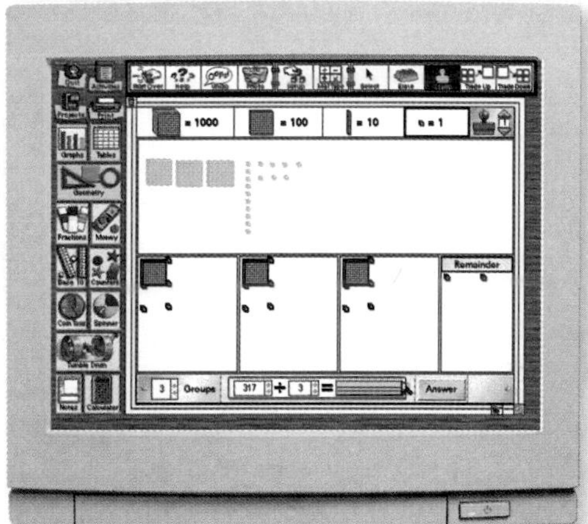

You can build a model of how the classes divide the flowers using place-value or base-ten models.

- Choose division as the type of mat.
- Stamp out the number of flowers.
- Group them into 3 equal groups.
- Regroup the models if necessary.

The number boxes keep count as you stamp and group.

- How many flowers will each class plant?
- Are any flowers left over?

Use the computer to model each division. Then write the quotient.

1. 420 ÷ 5 **2.** 614 ÷ 6 **3.** 962 ÷ 4 **4.** 1,574 ÷ 9

Solve.

5. Eric needs to buy 192 paper plates for a picnic. The paper plates come in packages of 8. How many packages does he need to buy?

6. There are 1,204 students attending an assembly in the school auditorium. Each row in the auditorium seats 9 students. How many rows in the auditorium are completely full? How many students are not sitting in a full row?

7. Analyze: How does modeling the problem help you divide?

For more practice, use Math Traveler™.

Objective: Compare unit costs to find the better buy.

Find the Better Buy

Learn

Math Word
per for each

Luis compares the unit prices of jars of glitter model paint to find the better buy. What is the unit price of the 8-ounce jar? Which jar is the better buy?

Example

Find $12.80 ÷ 8 to find the unit price of the 8-ounce jar.

1 Divide the way you divide whole numbers.

```
    1 60
8)$12.80
 -  8
   4 8
  -4 8
     00
   -  0
      0
```

2 Place the dollar sign and the decimal point where they belong in the quotient.

```
   $1.60
8)$12.80
 -  8
   4 8
  -4 8
     00
   -  0
      0
```

3 Compare the unit prices

$\$1.60 < \$1.75$

The unit price of the 8-ounce jar is $1.60 **per** ounce. It is the better buy.

Try It

Find each unit price. Find the better buy.

1. 2 ounces for $4.24
   4 ounces for $8.32
2. 3 pounds for $13.23
   5 pounds for $22.55
3. 6 feet for $19.86
   8 feet for $26.88

How is dividing money the same as dividing whole numbers? How is it different?

Practice

Find each unit price. Find the better buy.

4. 3 ounces for \$8.91
   4 ounces for \$11.40
5. 5 cups for \$37.70
   7 cups for \$53.34
6. 4 yards for \$105.44
   9 yards for \$248.22
7. 2 pounds for \$1.78
   6 pounds for \$4.92
8. 3 gallons for \$98.25
   8 gallons for \$265.20
9. 2 inches for \$19.70
   9 inches for \$87.75
10. 6 quarts for \$77.10
    8 quarts for \$94.00
11. 3 pints for \$65.55
    7 pints for \$155.05
12. 3 feet for \$2.85
    5 feet for \$4.40
13. 3 pounds for \$3.69
    4 pounds for \$4.12
14. 7 yards for \$67.45
    9 yards for \$97.44
15. 8 cups for \$124.89
    5 cups for \$79.15

Problem Solving

Use data from the flyer for problems 16–18.

16. Which jar is the best buy?
17. How much more does one ounce of the most expensive jar cost than one ounce of the best buy?
18. The unit cost of a 16-ounce jar is \$0.05 less than the unit cost of an 8-ounce jar. What is the total cost of the jar?
19. **Explain** how you can use division to determine the best buy.

Ari's Crafts
Special Today!
Glo-Paint!

2-ounce jar \$4.36
6-ounce jar \$12.72
8-ounce jar \$16.64

Spiral Review and Test Prep

20. $\begin{array}{r} 1{,}643 \\ +\ \ 498 \\ \hline \end{array}$

21. $\begin{array}{r} 4{,}065 \\ -\ \ 468 \\ \hline \end{array}$

22. $\begin{array}{r} 36 \\ \times\ 8 \\ \hline \end{array}$

23. $\begin{array}{r} 35 \\ \times 32 \\ \hline \end{array}$

24. $5\overline{)38}$

25. $560 + 31$
26. $2{,}500 - 200$
27. 40×60
28. $4{,}200 \div 7$

Choose the correct answer.

29. Mr. Morris will buy stock with \$551. The stock is \$8 for each share. How many shares will he buy?
    A. 4,416 **C.** 600
    B. 68 **D.** 120

30. Which is not a divisor if the remainder is 4?
    F. 3 **H.** 6
    G. 5 **J.** 8

Extra Practice, page 313

Objective: Solve problems by using the guess-and-check strategy.

Problem Solving: Strategy
Guess and Check

30 golf balls

Read — **Read the problem carefully.**

A worker at Seashore Minigolf has a basket of 30 golf balls for a minigolf party. There are more than 5 people in the party. The golf balls are passed equally to people in the party. After the golf balls are passed around, 6 are left.

How many people are in the party?
How many golf balls does each person get?

- **What do you know?** **30 golf balls altogether; more than 5 people in the party; 6 balls are leftover.**
- **What do you need to find?** **Number of people in the party; number of golf balls each person gets.**

Plan — One way to solve the problem is to make a guess, check it, and revise your guess until you find the correct answer.

Solve

Guess: 6 people in the party
Check: $30 \div 6 = 5$ → **There are no golf balls left. Try a different number.**

Guess: 7 people in the party
Check: $30 \div 7 = 4$ R2 → **There are 2 golf balls left. Try a different number.**

Guess: 8 people in the party
Check: $30 \div 8 = 3$ R6 → **One possible answer is that there are 8 people in the party. Each person gets 3 golf balls and 6 balls are left.**
6 golf balls are left.

Look Back — Is your answer reasonable? What operations do you use to check your answer?

How do you make your first guess? How do you revise it?

Practice Use guess and check to solve.

1. Malik puts 61 books in a bookcase. He has the same number of books on each shelf with 5 books left. There is one more shelf than the number of books on each shelf. How many shelves are filled? How many books does each shelf hold?

2. Jenny is making sand art. A bottle holds 8 inches of sand. Jenny wants to have 2 inches more of red sand than blue sand. How many inches of each color will she use?

3. There are 24 cars in the Sports Place parking lot. There are twice as many 4-door cars as 2-door cars. How many of each kind are there?

4. Austin buys small, medium, and large T-shirts for his family at $12, $15, and $20. The total cost is $59. How many of each size does he buy?

Mixed Strategy Review

CHOOSE A STRATEGY
- Logical Reasoning
- Draw a Picture
- Make a Graph
- Act It Out
- Make a Table or List
- Find a Pattern
- Guess and Check
- Write a Number Sentence
- Work Backward
- Solve a Simpler Problem

5. **Logical Reasoning:** When Carl divided a number by 5 and then subtracted 7 from the quotient, he got 4. What number was Carl thinking of?

6. **Science:** There are 332 dimples on a golf ball. They help the ball travel through the air easily. What is 332 rounded to the nearest hundred?

Use data from the table for problems 7–9.

7. Which player had the lowest score in the Masters Tournament?

8. In golf, the lowest score is the best score. Which players are tied for the third-best score in the Masters Tournament?

9. **Create a problem** using data from the table. Solve it. Ask others to solve it.

10. **Spatial Reasoning:** Four people can sit at a small square table. If 2 tables are pushed together, 6 people can sit at them. If 20 square tables are placed together in a row, how many people can sit at the long table that results?

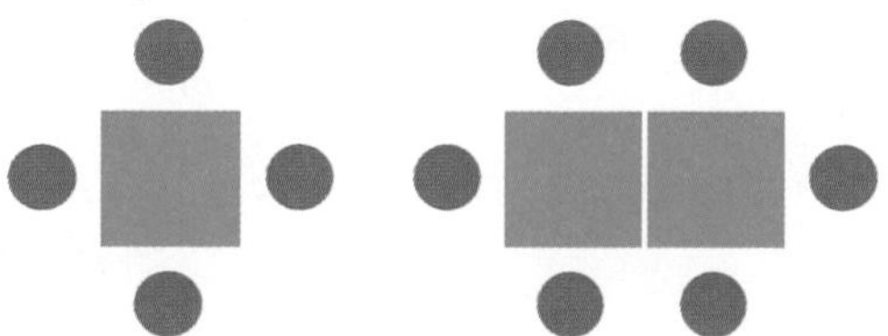

Best Winning Scores at Masters Tournament

Player	Score (over 4 rounds)
Tiger Woods	270
Jack Nicklaus	271
Raymond Floyd	271
Ben Hogan	274
Ben Crenshaw	274

Problem Solving

Extra Practice, page 313

Objective: Use models to find the mean of a set of numbers.

7·11 Explore Finding the Mean

Learn

Math Words

mean the quotient when the sum of two or more numbers is divided by the number of addends

average another word for mean

Tiffany plays on the school basketball team. In her last 3 games she scored 6 points, 9 points, and 3 points. What is the mean, or average, number of points Tiffany scored the last 3 games?

Work Together

You Will Need

- connecting cubes

► Use connecting cubes to show the points.

- Make stacks of cubes to show the number of points for each game.
- Rearrange the cubes so that the stacks are all the same height.
- Count the number of cubes in each stack. This is the **mean** number of points.
- Record your work in a table as shown.

Number of Stacks	Total Number of Cubes	Mean
3	$6 + 9 + 3 = 18$	$18 \div 3 = 6$

Tiffany's mean score is 6 points.

► Use connecting cubes to help you find the mean for each set of numbers. Record your work. Think about how you rearrange the cubes to make equal stacks.

15, 8, 17, 9, 6   7, 12, 3, 5, 13   2, 6, 10

Remember: Before you count, check to be sure that each stack has the same number of cubes.

Make Connections

In her next 4 basketball games Tiffany scores 8, 6, 3, and 7 points. What is her mean score for these 4 games?

Here are two ways you can find the mean or **average**.

	Using Models	Using Paper and Pencil
Make stacks of cubes to show each number.		Add all of the numbers. $8 + 6 + 3 + 7 = 24$
Rearrange the cubes into equal stacks.		Divide the sum by the number of addends. $24 \div 4 = 6$

Tiffany's mean score is 6 points.

Try It **Find the mean. You may use connecting cubes.**

1. 15, 10, 2
2. 10, 8, 12, 6, 4
3. 2, 4, 6, 12
4. 5, 9, 10

Suppose Tiffany scored only 4 points in the first game. How would this change her mean score?

Practice **Find the mean.**

5. 14, 8
6. 15, 15, 3
7. 20, 0, 7
8. 1, 3, 18, 2
9. 10, 0, 4, 2
10. 12, 8, 4, 3, 3
11. 4, 5, 6, 1
12. 10, 10, 3, 2, 5
13. 11, 9, 10, 12, 8, 10, 3
14. 5, 4, 6, 7, 5, 8, 3, 2
15. 2, 2, 2, 2, 4, 4, 4, 4
16. **Analyze:** Suppose you add a 0 to the set of numbers in problem 1 above. Does that change the mean? Why or why not?

Objective: Find the mean of a set of numbers.

7•12 Find the Mean

Learn

Fourth-grade members of the school band were asked how many hours they listen to music each week. This table shows the results of the survey. What is the mean number of hours these band members listen to music each week?

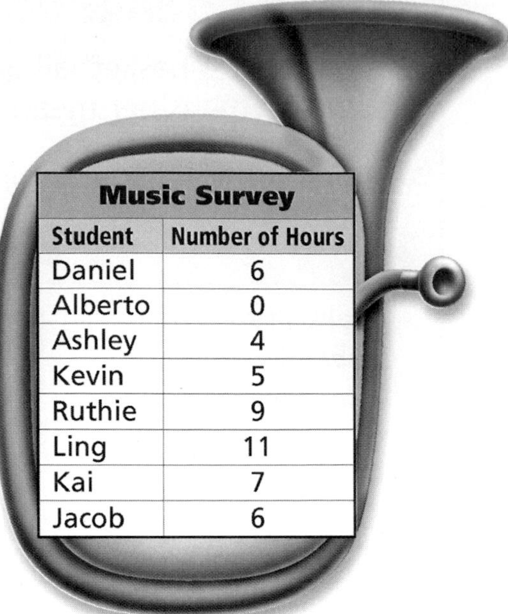

Music Survey

Student	Number of Hours
Daniel	6
Alberto	0
Ashley	4
Kevin	5
Ruthie	9
Ling	11
Kai	7
Jacob	6

Example

Find the mean for the set of numbers: 6, 0, 4, 5, 9, 11, 7, 6.

1. **Add the numbers.** $6 + 0 + 4 + 5 + 9 + 11 + 7 + 6 = 48$

2. **Count the number of addends.** $6 + 0 + 4 + 5 + 9 + 11 + 7 + 6 = 48$
   There are 8 addends.

3. **Divide the sum by the number of addends.** $48 \div 8 = 6$

The mean number of hours is 6.

Try It **Find the mean.**

1. Number of tickets sold
   11, 33, 55, 202, 101, 6
2. Number of meals served
   752, 864, 328
3. Daily attendance
   26, 25, 27, 26, 27, 25
4. Quiz scores
   20, 18, 19, 20, 17, 16, 16

Does the mean of a set of numbers have to be a number in the set? Why or why not?

Practice Find the mean.

5. 75, 32, 4
6. 32, 125, 64, 127
7. 64, 583, 650, 0, 443
8. 12, 12, 12, 12
9. 100, 1, 200, 2, 300, 3
10. 35, 46, 17, 119, 75, 14
11. 234, 630, 544, 17, 23, 154
12. 12, 25, 38, 14, 0, 42, 16
13. 11, 33, 55, 202, 101, 6
14. 752, 864, 328
15. 25, 19, 16, 24
16. 17, 7, 12, 3, 2, 13

Problem Solving

Use data from the graph for problems 17–20.

17. During which week did the band practice the most?

18. What is the mean number of hours the band practiced all 6 weeks?

19. **Compare:** Which is greater, the mean number of practice hours or the mode?

★20. How many hours would the band have to practice in week 7 for the mean number of hours to be 8?

21. Justin and Sonia spent $7.50 altogether at their band's fundraiser. Justin spent $3.00 more than Sonia. How much did each spend at the fundraiser?

Band Practice

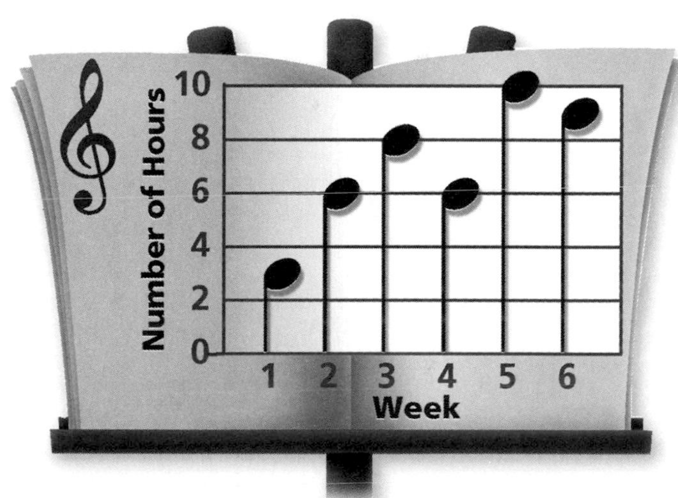

Spiral Review and Test Prep

22. $\begin{array}{r} 598 \\ +321 \\ \hline \end{array}$

23. $\begin{array}{r} 2,345 \\ -\ 876 \\ \hline \end{array}$

24. $\begin{array}{r} 423 \\ \times\ 4 \\ \hline \end{array}$

25. $6\overline{)77}$

26. $5\overline{)573}$

Choose the correct answer.

27. Rod did homework for 35 minutes on Monday, 1 hour on Tuesday, and 43 minutes on Wednesday. What is the range in the number of minutes he did homework for these 3 days?
 A. 25 minutes
 B. 36 minutes
 C. 46 minutes
 D. 52 minutes

28. Mr. Malson will set up exactly 8 chairs in each row in the all-purpose room. There are 265 students who need seats. What is the fewest number of rows Mr. Malson will set up?
 F. 33
 G. 34
 H. 35
 J. 36

Objective: Apply division to making decisions.

Problem Solving: Application

Decision Making

Should they take buses, a train, or cars to the aquarium?

The Science Club at Greenville Elementary School is planning an after-school class trip to the Oceanside aquarium. There will be 148 members on the trip. They will leave after school at 3:00 P.M. and return around 8:00 P.M.

Option 1 The Bus

Bus Charge: $100 for each bus round trip
Each bus can hold 44 children.
Bus Driver: $10 for each hour

Option 2 The Train

Train Ticket Prices
$8 one-way from
6:00 A.M.– 6:00 P.M.

$5 one-way from
6:01 P.M.– 11:00 P.M.

Greenville	Spring Hill	Midtown	Waterville	Oceanside
2:00 pm			2:35 pm	2:50 pm
3:15 pm		3:35 pm		5:05 pm
5:00 pm	5:10 pm	5:25 pm	5:40 pm	6:00 pm

Oceanside	Waterville	Midtown	Spring Hill	Greenville
6:10 pm	6:20 pm	6:35 pm	6:50 pm	7:10 pm
7:40 pm		8:00 pm		8:30 pm
9:00 pm				9:35 pm

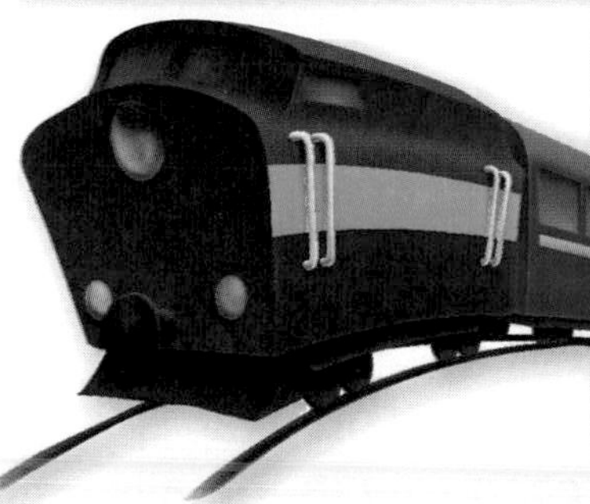

Option 3 The Car

4 students in each car
About $15 for gas for the round trip

Read for Understanding

1. What are the two different charges for a bus?
2. What time is the first train to Oceanside after school gets out?
3. If you take the 3:15 P.M. train from Greenville to Oceanside, what time do you arrive? How much does the ticket cost?
4. If you take the 7:40 P.M. train from Oceanside to Greenville, what time do you arrive? How much does the ticket cost?
5. If the club uses cars, about how many members will be in each car?
6. About how much is the gas for one car to make the trip?

Problem Solving

Make Decisions

7. Suppose the club decides to use cars. How many cars will they need?
8. Estimate the total price for gas if 37 cars are used.
9. What if five members decide not to go on the trip? How many cars are needed?
10. If the club uses cars that can hold 4 members each, what is the actual cost of the gas?
11. What are some advantages and disadvantages of using cars?
12. Are 3 buses enough to take the entire class? Why or why not?
13. How much are buses for the trip, not including the bus drivers?
14. Find the number of hours the trip will last. How much will it cost for one bus driver for the trip?
15. What is the total price for all bus drivers?
16. What are the advantages of chartering buses?
17. Suppose that the class takes the 3:15 P.M. train from Greenville to Oceanside and returns on the 7:40 P.M. train. How much would the round trip cost per student?
18. How much will it cost for all members to take the train?
19. If all 148 members go on the class trip, what is the cost to go by car? by bus? by train?
20. Which way is the least expensive?

What is your recommendation for the club? Explain.

Objective: Apply division to investigate science concepts.

Problem Solving: Math and Science

Do light or heavy objects fly farther?

You are playing catch with a friend. First you throw a small, light softball then a big, heavy basketball. Which ball do you think you can throw farther? Why?

You Will Need
- **paper clip**
- **big eraser**
- **connecting cubes**
- **ruler**
- **meterstick (optional)**

Hypothesize

Which object will travel farther? Why? Do an activity to check your answer.

Safety

Wear goggles to protect your eyes, and work away from other people.

Procedure

1. Lay the ruler across the cubes, like a seesaw.
2. Put a paper clip on one end of the seesaw.
3. "Chop" down on the other end with your hand.
4. Measure how far the paper clip traveled.
5. Record your data and repeat four more times.
6. Repeat the activity again five times with the eraser.

Data

Find the mean, or average, distances that the paper clip and the eraser traveled. Copy and complete the chart to record your work.

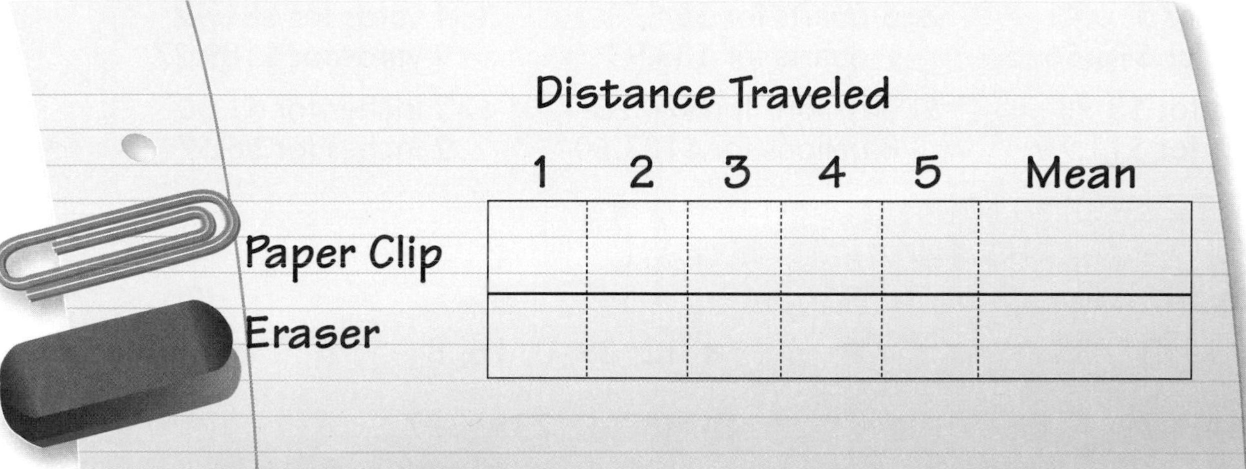

Distance Traveled

	1	2	3	4	5	Mean
Paper Clip						
Eraser						

Conclude and Apply

- Which object traveled farther? How do you know?
- Use division to decide how many times farther one object traveled than the other.
- Explain the results of the activity in terms of **gravity.**

Going Further

1. Repeat the activity with 5 different objects and rank them from best to worst.
2. Experiment with the size of the seesaw and describe its effect on your data.

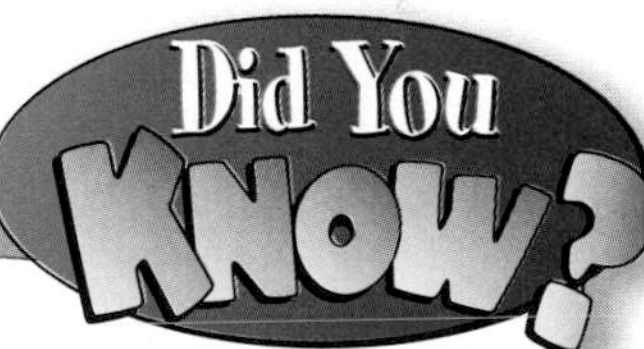

Gravity is the force that pulls objects together. The Earth's gravity is so strong that it attracts everything near it, including people, buildings, paper clips, and erasers.

Check Your Progress B

Find each unit price. Find the better buy. (pages 298–299)

1. 3 ounces for $10.41
4 ounces for $13.56

2. 5 quarts for $64.80
7 quarts for $83.93

3. 4 yards for $81.92
9 yards for $189.27

4. 2 pounds for $3.98
6 pounds for $11.70

5. 3 gallons for $74.25
8 gallons for $183.60

6. 2 inches for $1.30
9 inches for $6.57

Find the mean. (pages 302–305)

7. 34, 36, 35, 37, 33

8. 12, 29, 0, 16, 8

9. 345, 354, 339

10. 480, 0, 235, 377

11. 35, 46, 17, 120, 75, 13

12. 35, 39, 32, 44, 41, 37

13. Number of meals served for lunch: 76, 82, 77, 85, 75

14. Number of cousins each student has: 4, 6, 12, 8, 20, 10, 24

15. Points scored in the last 7 games: 12, 14, 16, 18, 12, 15, 18

16. Number of students in class: 25, 27, 28, 28, 27

Solve. (pages 298–305)

17. Ron keeps track of the weekly attendance for the rocketry club. Here are the numbers for last month: 13, 14, 11, and 10. What was the average attendance last month?

18. Of the 28 students in the class, 2 more students join the running club than join the art club. How many students join each club?

19. A 4-pack of AA batteries costs $3.88. An 8-pack of the batteries costs $7.12. Which is the better buy?

Journal

20. Analyze: Can the mean of a set of numbers be greater than the greatest number in the set? Why or why not?

Extra Practice

Division Patterns (pages 276–277)

Use mental math to divide.

1. $3\overline{)900}$	**2.** $3\overline{)240}$	**3.** $4\overline{)3{,}600}$	**4.** $7\overline{)350}$
5. 8,000 ÷ 4	**6.** 270 ÷ 9	**7.** 2,800 ÷ 7	**8.** \$480 ÷ 6
9. 2,400 ÷ 3	**10.** 2,100 ÷ 7	**11.** 480 ÷ 8	**12.** \$140 ÷ 2

Divide 3-Digit Numbers (pages 280–283)

Divide. Check your answer.

1. $4\overline{)613}$	**2.** $2\overline{)\$378}$	**3.** $7\overline{)603}$	**4.** $3\overline{)488}$
5. $6\overline{)152}$	**6.** $4\overline{)574}$	**7.** $5\overline{)654}$	**8.** $4\overline{)329}$
9. 663 ÷ 5	**10.** 347 ÷ 2	**11.** 785 ÷ 6	**12.** 649 ÷ 5
13. 175 ÷ 6	**14.** 275 ÷ 8	**15.** 824 ÷ 9	**16.** 573 ÷ 7

Quotients with Zeros (pages 284–285)

Divide. Check your answer.

1. $8\overline{)842}$	**2.** $4\overline{)415}$	**3.** $7\overline{)912}$	**4.** $2\overline{)\$202}$
5. 525 ÷ 5	**6.** 953 ÷ 9	**7.** \$637 ÷ 7	**8.** 634 ÷ 6

Problem Solving: Reading for Math Interpret the Remainder (pages 286–287)

Solve. Tell what you do with the remainder.

1. Andrew has 614 trading cards. He stores the cards in plastic sleeves. Each sleeve holds 9 cards. How many sleeves does he need?

2. Leona is making hair bows to sell at a crafts fair. She uses a 9-inch piece of ribbon for each bow. How many bows can she make with 22 feet of ribbon? How much ribbon will be left?

Extra Practice

Estimate Quotients (pages 288–289)

Estimate. Use compatible numbers.

1. 58 ÷ 3 **2.** 562 ÷ 8 **3.** 649 ÷ 9 **4.** 4,230 ÷ 7 **5.** 3,328 ÷ 4

6. 72 ÷ 7 **7.** 92 ÷ 9 **8.** 441 ÷ 9 **9.** 346 ÷ 7 **10.** 716 ÷ 5

11. 3,183 ÷ 5 **12.** 4,317 ÷ 6 **13.** 1,792 ÷ 3 **14.** 35,222 ÷ 4 **15.** 23,794 ÷ 8

Solve.

16. **Social Studies:** The 5 smallest towns in the country have a total population of 963 people. Each town has about the same population. About what is the population of each town?

Divide 4-Digit Numbers (pages 290–293)

Divide. Check your answer.

1. $7\overline{)7868}$ **2.** $4\overline{)\$9,544}$ **3.** $3\overline{)9,380}$ **4.** $5\overline{)7,831}$ **5.** $3\overline{)6,045}$

6. $2\overline{)\$1,864}$ **7.** $5\overline{)2,684}$ **8.** $9\overline{)3,620}$ **9.** $8\overline{)4,858}$ **10.** $7\overline{)7,355}$

11. 6,984 ÷ 6 **12.** 3,775 ÷ 5 **13.** 7,413 ÷ 9 **14.** 4,330 ÷ 8 **15.** $8,727 ÷ 3

Divide 5-Digit Numbers (pages 294–295)

Divide. Check your answer.

1. $8\overline{)\$16,488}$ **2.** $6\overline{)47,405}$ **3.** $3\overline{)63,435}$ **4.** $5\overline{)20,266}$

5. 12,345 ÷ 9 **6.** $46,736 ÷ 2 **7.** 16,244 ÷ 8 **8.** 41,800 ÷ 7

Solve.

9. A 5-level arena seats 34,535 people. If each level has the same number of seats, how many seats are on each level?

10. A box of 4 puzzles has 4,264 puzzle pieces in it. If each puzzle has the same number of pieces, how many pieces are in each puzzle?

Extra Practice

Find the Better Buy (pages 298–299)

Find each unit price. Find the better buy.

1. 6 ounces for $2.40
   3 ounces for $1.26
2. 2 cups for $5.24
   6 cups for $12.66
3. 4 yards for $82.00
   9 yards for $177.75
4. 3 pounds for $6.72
   8 pounds for $17.16
5. 3 gallons for $91.71
   7 gallons for $218.75
6. 2 inches for $17.52
   9 inches for $72.54

Problem Solving: Strategy Guess and Check (page 300–301)

Solve.

1. Sean spends $76 on a hockey stick and gloves. The stick costs $4 more than the gloves. How much does each cost?
2. There were a total of 12 goals scored in the game between the Mustangs and the Tigers. The Mustangs won by 2 goals. What was the score of the game?
3. Mike and Keisha have $0.95 altogether. Mike has $0.25 more than Keisha. How much does Keisha have?
4. Walter bought 2 shirts for $49. The red shirt cost $5 less than the white shirt. How much did the white shirt cost?

Find the Mean (pages 304–305)

Find the mean.

1. Number of minutes each student spends on homework:
   25, 40, 60, 30, 45
2. Number of students in fourth-grade classrooms:
   21, 24, 18
3. Test scores: 78, 92, 88, 90

Solve.

4. Meg wants to get at least a 94 test average in math. She has one more test to take. So far her test grades are 94, 100, 93, and 92. What is the lowest grade she can get on the last test and still get a 94 average?
5. Ms. Biasi gives her students problems each school day. Bryan scored 70 on Monday. His score increased 5 points each day for the rest of the week. What is Bryan's weekly average?

Chapter Study Guide

Language and Math

Complete. Use a word from the list.

1. When 40 is divided by 8, the ____ is 5.
2. Another word for average is ____.
3. When 15 is divided by 6, the ____ is 3.
4. In 8 ÷ 4, 8 is the ____.
5. In 6 ÷ 2, 2 is the ____.

Math Words

compatible number
dividend
divisor
mean
quotient
remainder

Skills and Applications

Divide multiples of 10 by 1-digit numbers. (pages 276–277)

Example

Find: 7,200 ÷ 6

Solution

Use patterns.

$$72 \div 6 = 12$$
$$720 \div 6 = 120$$
$$7{,}200 \div 6 = 1{,}200$$
$$72{,}000 \div 6 = 12{,}000$$

Divide.

6. 350 ÷ 7
7. 540 ÷ 6
8. $450 ÷ 5
9. 720 ÷ 9
10. 6,400 ÷ 8
11. 32,000 ÷ 4

Divide by 1-digit divisors. (pages 278–285, 290–295)

Example

Find: 1,216 ÷ 3

Solution

Decide where to place the first digit. Divide each place.

```
    405 R1
 3)1,216
  -1 2      ← Multiply 4 × 3
     01     ← Subtract. Compare. Bring down.
   -  0     ← Multiply 0 × 3
     16     ← Subtract. Compare. Bring down.
    -15     ← Multiply 5 × 3
      1     ← Subtract. Compare.
```

Divide.

12. 89 ÷ 7
13. 745 ÷ 6
14. $3.48 ÷ 2
15. 1,067 ÷ 5
16. 2,020 ÷ 3
17. 24,335 ÷ 4
18. How many teams of 9 players can be formed from a group of 1,323 people?
19. A 4-ounce jar of paste costs $2.56. An 8-ounce jar costs $4.96. Which jar is the better buy?

Estimate quotients. (pages 288–289)

Example

Estimate the quotient: 4,587 ÷ 5

Solution

Use compatible numbers:

4,587 ÷ 5
↓ ↓
4,500 ÷ 5

Since 4,500 ÷ 5 = 900, the quotient of 4,587 ÷ 5 is **about** 900.

Estimate the quotient. Show the compatible numbers you use.

20. 361 ÷ 6

21. 724 ÷ 9

22. 4,307 ÷ 7

23. 8,230 ÷ 9

24. Carol worked 4 days and earned $325. About how much did Carol earn each day?

25. The Computer Club wants to buy software for $345. If 8 members are sharing the cost equally, about how much will each member pay?

Find the mean. (pages 302–305)

Example

Find the average number of snowstorms each year.

Snowstorms	
Years	Number
1	3
2	6
3	7
4	4

Solution

Read the table to find the number for each year: 3, 6, 7, and 4.

Add: 3 + 6 + 7 + 4 = 20

Divide: 20 ÷ 4 = 5

The average number of storms is 5.

Find the mean of each set of numbers.

26. 8, 10, 9, 9, 8, 10

27. 23, 29, 44

28. 19, 0, 20, 9

29. 5, 56, 41, 369, 29

Solve.

30. Ty bowled four games. He scored 97, 108, 120, and 111. What is Ty's mean score?

31. Gail saved $348 in 3 months. What is the mean amount she saved each month?

Use strategies to solve problems. (pages 286–287, 300–301)

Example

There are twice as many boys as girls among the 54 members of a club. How many girls are there?

Solution

Guess: There are 36 boys.
Divide to find the number of girls.
36 ÷ 2 = 18
Check: 36 + 18 = 54
There are 18 girls in the club.

Solve.

32. Of the 48 balls sold, three times as many tennis balls were sold as soccer balls. How many soccer balls were sold?

33. Nadia's cheesecake recipe uses 5 eggs. If Nadia has 2 dozen eggs, how many cheesecakes can she make?

Chapter Test

Divide.

1. $58 \div 6$
2. $600 \div 3$
3. $47 \div 2$
4. $240 \div 6$
5. $286 \div 6$
6. $196 \div 9$
7. $320 \div 4$
8. $\$4,800 \div 8$
9. $8\overline{)5,816}$
10. $5\overline{)483}$
11. $3\overline{)\$8.25}$
12. $6\overline{)6,145}$
13. $7\overline{)49,000}$
14. $4\overline{)32,974}$
15. $9\overline{)9,027}$
16. $5\overline{)\$34.55}$

Estimate. Show the compatible numbers you use.

17. $352 \div 9$
18. $658 \div 8$
19. $685 \div 5$
20. $579 \div 7$

Solve.

21. There are 1,278 people signed up for the charity walk. They are separated into 9 groups. How many people are in each group?

22. Together Jane and Niko have 28 collectible dolls. Niko has 4 more dolls than Jane. How many dolls does each girl have?

23. Bert went to basketball camp. The table shows the number of points he scored in the practice games. What is the mean number of points he scored?

Monday	Tuesday	Wednesday	Thursday	Friday
6	9	8	2	5

24. A package of 4 rolls of film costs $8.60. A package of 3 rolls costs $6.15. Which is the better buy?

25. The 46 members of the Riverton Glee Club want to rent vans to go to a concert. Each van holds 7 people. How many vans will they need?

Performance Assessment

You are in charge of buying the juice boxes for your soccer team picnic.

Make a chart that shows each unit price. Use the chart to answer these questions. Show your work.

- Which pack is the best buy?
- What is the average or mean unit price for a juice box?

Number of Boxes in Pack	Price of Pack	Unit Price

A Good Answer

- has a complete chart with each unit price.
- clearly shows how you found the unit prices.
- shows the steps you used to find the average unit price.

You may want to save this work in your portfolio.

Assessment

Enrichment

Divisibility Rules

One number is **divisible** by another number if there is no remainder when you divide.

1. Copy and complete this multiplication table.

Factors	5	8	11	14	17	20
2						
5						
10						

Look at the ones digits in the products in the table.

2. What do you notice about the ones digits of all the products that have 2 as a factor? Are they odd or even?

3. What do you notice about the ones digits of all the products that have 5 as a factor?

4. What do you notice about the ones digits of all the products that have 10 as a factor?

5. **Generalize:** Write a statement about the divisibility of a number that has another number as a factor.

	A number is divisible by:	Examples:
2	if the ones digit is even (0, 2, 4, 6, 8).	56, 122, 314
5	if the ones digit is 0 or 5.	35, 120, 315
10	if the ones digit is 0.	80, 540, 880
3	if the sum of its digits is divisible by 3.	123 $(1 + 2 + 3 = 6; 6 \div 3 = 2)$
6	if it is divisible by both 2 and 3.	144 even and $(1 + 4 + 4 = 9; 9 \div 3 = 3)$
9	if the sum of its digits is divisible by 9.	198 $(1 + 9 + 8 = 18; 18 \div 9 = 2)$

Of 2, 3, 5, 6, 9, and 10, list which numbers each number is divisible by.

6. 335

7. 1,268

8. 261

9. 6,300

10. Use divisibility rules to solve mentally. You want to share some beads evenly among 6 people. Would you buy a package of 4,671; 48,372; or 54,793?

Test-Taking Tips

S.O.S.

The problems you find on tests sometimes contain extra information that you do not need to solve the problem.

It is important to read the problem carefully, decide on the facts you need, and **cross out any extra information** that may confuse you.

Robert waited for the train for 12 minutes. He got on the train at 9:10 A.M. and got off the train at 9:30 A.M. How long was Robert's train ride?

A. 20 minutes **C.** 40 minutes

B. 30 minutes **D.** 1 hour 30 minutes

To find how long Robert's train ride took, you need to know when it started and when it ended. You do not need to know how long Robert waited for the train.

Started: He got on the train at 9:10 A.M.

Ended: He got off the train at 9:30 A.M.

9:10 to 9:30 is 20 minutes.
The correct answer is A.

Check for Success

Before turning in a test, go back one last time to check.

- ☑ I understood and answered the questions asked.
- ☑ I checked my work for errors.
- ☑ My answers make sense.

Read the problem. Cross out the extra information. Then choose the correct answer.

1. Fredda has a collection of 27 dolls. The dolls are from 12 cities from Europe. How many dolls will be on each of 3 shelves, if there is the same number on each?

   A. 5 **C.** 9

   B. 8 **D.** 12

2. Four sailboats were in a race. If the boats had sailed 3 miles at the halfway point, how many miles long is the race?

   F. 4 **H.** 8

   G. 6 **J.** 12

3. The fourth grade has a 30-minute lunch period. They need 40 servings for their class lunch. How many cans do they need, if each can serves 8?

   A. 2 **C.** 48

   B. 5 **D.** 320

4. Suzanne shopped at the furniture store for 3 hours. She found 1 chair that costs $65. If 4 chairs are bought together, they cost $204. How much will 6 chairs cost?

   F. $125 **H.** $270

   G. $135 **J.** $334

Spiral Review and Test Prep

Chapters 1–7

Choose the correct answer.

Number Sense

1. 1,327 − 1,309 =
   - **A.** 3×6
   - **B.** $12 \div 3$
   - **C.** $6 + 6$
   - **D.** $12 - 3$

2. What is 4,587 rounded to the nearest hundred?
   - **F.** 4,000
   - **G.** 4,500
   - **H.** 4,600
   - **J.** 5,000

3. Liza bought a dress that cost $35.50 with tax. She paid the cashier and got back a five-dollar bill in change. How much money did Liza give the cashier?
   - **A.** $45
   - **B.** $40
   - **C.** $45.50
   - **D.** $40.50

4. Carly and Bailey paid $11.00 for movie tickets. Carly paid the adult price of $7.75 for her ticket. Bailey paid the child's price for his. How much is the child's price for a movie ticket? Explain how you solved this problem.

Measurement and Geometry

5. Mr. Park is making punch for the school picnic. He wants to make 6 gallons of punch with apple juice and grape juice. He has 11 quarts of apple juice. How much grape juice does he need?
   - **A.** 4 gallons
   - **B.** 13 quarts
   - **C.** 21 pints
   - **D.** Not Here

6. What is the perimeter of the figure?

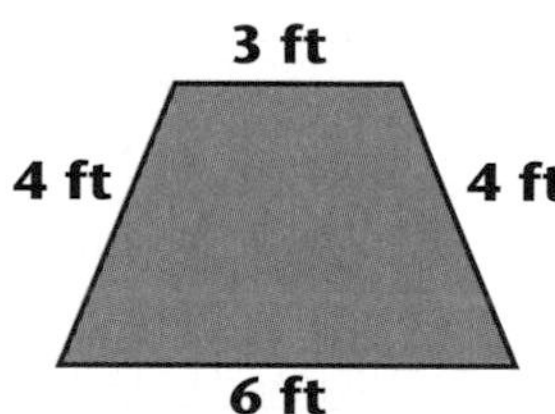

   - **F.** 16 feet
   - **G.** 17 feet
   - **H.** 18 feet
   - **J.** 24 feet

7. A bookcase is 3 meters tall. What is its height in centimeters?
   - **A.** 30 cm
   - **B.** 3,000 cm
   - **C.** 300 cm
   - **D.** Not Here

8. What is the name of the figure shown?

   - **F.** Pyramid
   - **G.** Cone
   - **H.** Cube
   - **J.** Cylinder

Statistics, Data Analysis, and Probability

Use data from the bar graph for problems 9–12.

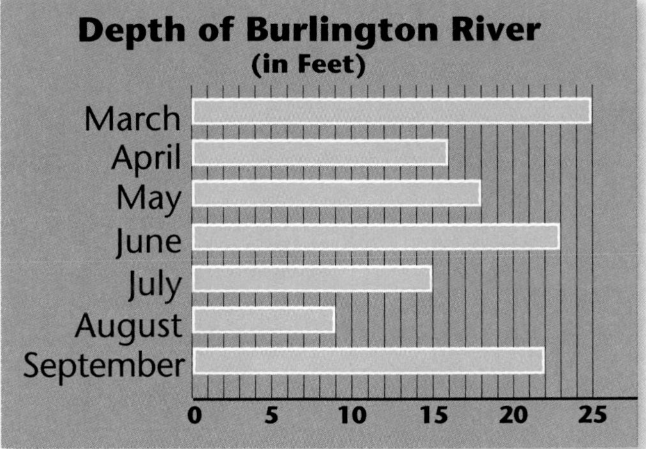

9. How much deeper was the Burlington River in June than in August?
   - A. 32 feet
   - B. 23 feet
   - C. 14 feet
   - D. 9 feet

10. When was the Burlington River about twice as deep as it was in August?
    - F. May
    - G. April
    - H. July
    - J. September

11. Roberto dropped a coin in the river. It fell to a depth of less than 5 yards. When might Roberto have dropped the coin?
    - A. Only during August
    - B. Only during July
    - C. During August or July
    - D. During May or July

12. Between which two months did the depth of the river change the most?
    - F. Between August and September
    - G. Between June and July
    - H. Between May and June
    - J. Between March and April

Mathematical Reasoning

13. Marilee scored 97, 95, and 84 on three of her last four math tests. Her average for the four tests was 90. Which is a reasonable estimate for her fourth test score?
    - A. 95
    - B. 100
    - C. 80
    - D. 65

14. Molly read for 30 minutes on Monday, 45 minutes on Tuesday, and 60 minutes on Wednesday. Which statement describes the pattern Molly is using?
    - F. Add 15 minutes each day.
    - G. Subtract 15 minutes each day.
    - H. Add 30 minutes each day.
    - J. Double the number of minutes.

15. A basketball player scored a total of 2,491 points. Of those points, the player scored 805 field goals worth 2 points each, and 111 field goals worth 3 points each. The rest were made on 1-point free throws. How many free throws did the player score?
    - A. 1,575
    - B. 548
    - C. 770
    - D. Not Here

16. Eric scored two touchdowns and a field goal in a football game. Touchdowns are worth 6 points and field goals are worth 3 points. Which shows how to find Eric's point total?
    - F. $6 + 2 \times 3$
    - G. $2 \times 3 + 6$
    - H. $6 \times 2 + 3$
    - J. Not Here

CHAPTER 8 Divide by 2-Digit Numbers

Theme: Fitness Counts

Use the Data

Number of calories used by a 100-pound person in 1 hour

Activity	Calories Used
Bicycling fast	480
In-Line skating	300
Aerobics	240
Swimming moderate	360

Source: American Dietary Association

- How many calories would you use each minute doing these activities? How can you use division to solve this problem?

What You Will Learn

In this chapter you will learn how to
- divide multiples of 10 by a 2-digit number.
- divide a multidigit number by a 2-digit number.
- estimate quotients.
- evaluate expressions.
- use strategies to solve problems.

Objective: Use mental math to divide by multiples of 10.

8·1 Division Patterns

Algebra & functions

Learn

The Oakdale Soccer Club is having a skills day. There are 1,600 students at the event. The coaches want to put the players into groups of 20. How many groups of 20 are there?

There's more than one way!

Find: $1{,}600 \div 20$

There is more than one way to find quotients mentally.

Method A

You can find division patterns by using related multiplication patterns.

$2 \times 8 = 16$	$16 \div 2 = 8$
$20 \times 8 = 160$	$160 \div 20 = 8$
$20 \times 80 = 1{,}600$	$1{,}600 \div 20 = 80$

Method B

You can use basic facts and division patterns to find quotients.

$16 \div 2 = 8$

$160 \div 20 = 8$

$1{,}600 \div 20 = 80$

The coaches can make 80 groups of 20.

Try It **Write the number that makes each sentence true.**

1. $64 \div 8 = n$
$640 \div 80 = n$
$6{,}400 \div 80 = p$

2. $36 \div 9 = f$
$360 \div 90 = f$
$3{,}600 \div 90 = y$

3. $30 \div k = 6$
$d \div 50 = 6$
$3{,}000 \div 50 = h$

Divide. Use mental math.

4. $600 \div 20$ **5.** $\$3{,}500 \div 70$ **6.** $36{,}000 \div 40$

How does knowing basic division facts help you find $32{,}000 \div 40$?

Practice

Write the number that makes each sentence true.

7. $63 \div 9 = n$
$630 \div 90 = n$
$6{,}300 \div 90 = s$

8. $48 \div 6 = f$
$480 \div 60 = f$
$4{,}800 \div 60 = y$

9. $9 \div t = 3$
$j \div 30 = 3$
$9{,}000 \div 30 = m$

Divide. Use mental math.

10. $60\overline{)240}$ **11.** $60\overline{)540}$ **12.** $60\overline{)18{,}000}$ **13.** $20\overline{)1{,}000}$

14. $4{,}800 \div 80$ **15.** $24{,}000 \div 30$ **16.** $\$2{,}500 \div 50$ **17.** $32{,}000 \div 40$

18. $2{,}700 \div 30$ **19.** $630{,}000 \div 70$ **20.** $42{,}000 \div 70$ **21.** $\$81{,}000 \div 90$

★**22.** How many $20 are in $1,800?

★**23.** How many dimes are in $26.00?

Find each missing number.

24. $12{,}000 \div a = 300$ **25.** $w \div 50 = 5$ **26.** $140{,}000 \div v = 2{,}000$

★**27.** $400{,}000 \div 40 = r$ ★**28.** $x \div 80 = 80{,}000$ ★**29.** $b \div 70 = 30{,}000$

Problem Solving

30. There are 800 intramural soccer players in Midville. The coaches put the players on teams of 10. How many teams are there?

31. **Analyze:** The dividend is 5,600. The divisor and the quotient have a difference of 10. Write the division sentence.

32. **Health:** Mia plays soccer for 60 minutes. She uses about 5 calories each minute. How many calories does she use in all?

33. A soccer stadium holds 27,000 people. Each section of the stadium has 90 seats. How many sections are there?

Spiral Review and Test Prep

34. $3{,}492 + 653$ **35.** $5{,}692 - 2{,}374$ **36.** $\$320 \times 4$

Choose the correct answer.

37. Casey and his brother share the cost of a soccer ball equally. If each boy spends $9.25, what is the cost of the soccer ball?

A. $9.50 **C.** $18.50
B. $18.25 **D.** $19.50

38. There are 58 members of a soccer club going to a professional game. They will take cars that hold 6 people. How many cars do they need?

F. 9 **H.** 11
G. 10 **J.** 348

Extra Practice, page 351

Objective: Use models to divide by 2-digit numbers.

8·2 Explore Dividing by 2-Digit Numbers

Learn

Math Word

remainder the number less than the divisor that remains after the divsion is completed

You can use place-value models to explore dividing by 2-digit numbers.

What is 115 ÷ 12?

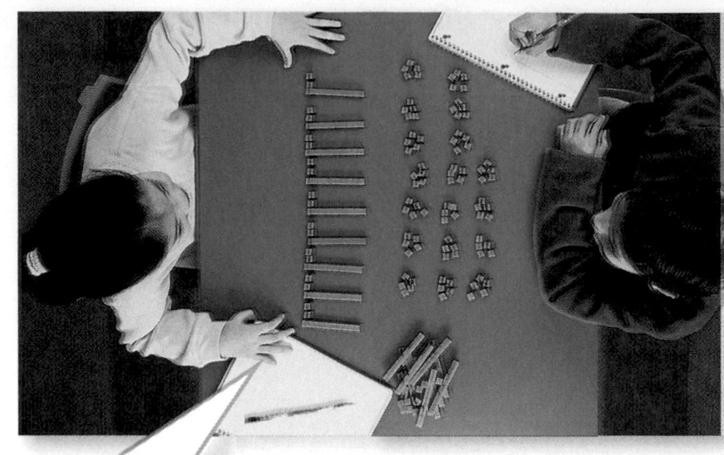

Work Together

► Use place-value models to find 115 ÷ 12.

You Will Need
- **place-value models**

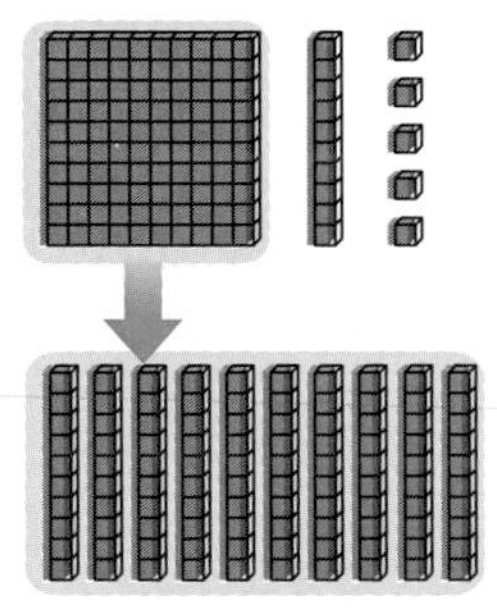

- Show 115 using place value models.
- Regroup the hundred as 10 groups of ten.

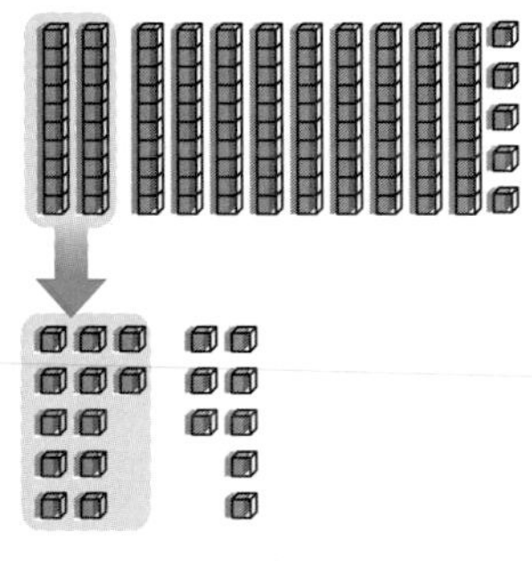

- Regroup the tens as needed.
- Divide the models into groups of 12.

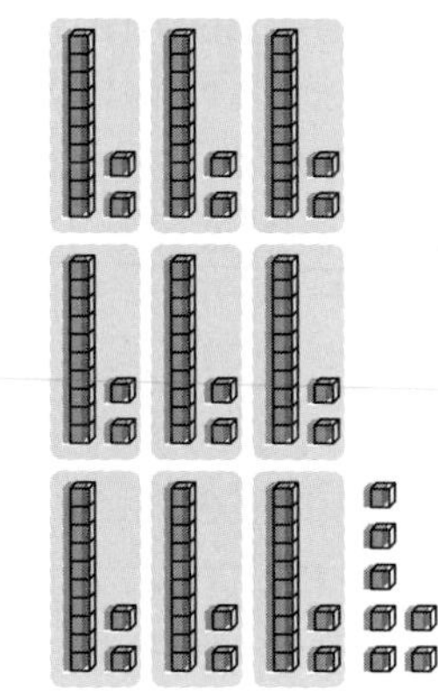

- Count the number of groups.
- Count the number of ones left over.
- Record your work and answer the question at the top of the page.

► Use place-value models to divide. You can find the number of groups. Record your work.

75 ÷ 15   86 ÷ 33   96 ÷ 18   132 ÷ 21   142 ÷ 33

Make Connections

You can show division in two ways.

Find: 184 ÷ 13

Using Models

Regroup the hundreds as tens.
Regroup the tens as ones.
Place the tens and ones in 13 groups.

Using Paper and Pencil

$$\begin{array}{r} 1 \\ 13\overline{)184} \\ -13 \\ \hline 5 \end{array}$$

1 ← no hundreds; 1 ten in each group; 13 tens used; 5 tens left

$$\begin{array}{r} 14 \\ 13\overline{)184} \\ -13\downarrow \\ \hline 54 \end{array}$$

Bring down 4 ones. 54 ← 54 ones in all

$$\begin{array}{r} 14\text{ R2} \\ 13\overline{)184} \\ -13\downarrow \\ \hline 54 \\ -52 \\ \hline 2 \end{array}$$

52 ← 52 ones used; 2 ← The 2 left is the **remainder**.

There are 13 groups with 14 in each group and 2 left.

184 ÷ 13 = 14 R2

Try It **Divide. You may use place-value models.**

1. 78 ÷ 13
2. 109 ÷ 22
3. 155 ÷ 31
4. 185 ÷ 16
5. 259 ÷ 35
6. $14\overline{)99}$
7. $18\overline{)121}$
8. $26\overline{)347}$
9. $42\overline{)481}$
10. $52\overline{)676}$

Explain how to use place value models to find 179 ÷ 14.

Practice **Divide. You may use place-value models.**

11. $22\overline{)92}$
12. $14\overline{)119}$
13. $17\overline{)135}$
14. $13\overline{)79}$
15. $12\overline{)133}$
16. 83 ÷ 15
17. 134 ÷ 24
18. 158 ÷ 11
19. 128 ÷ 16
20. 215 ÷ 14
21. **Analyze:** What is the greatest possible remainder when you divide a number by 15? How do you know?

Objective: Divide 2-digit numbers by multiples of 10.

8-3 Divide 2-Digit Numbers by Multiples of 10

Learn

All 64 members of the Little League are going to a Charleston River Dogs baseball game. The section that they will sit in has seats in rows of 30. How many rows will they fill? How many members will be in the unfilled row?

Example

Find: $64 \div 30$

1 Model 64. Decide where to place the first digit in the quotient.

$30\overline{)64}$

Think: $30 < 60$ So there are enough tens. The first digit is in the **tens** place.

2 How many groups of 30 can be made?

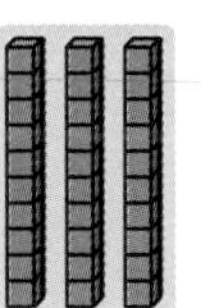

$$\begin{array}{r} 2 \\ 30\overline{)64} \\ -60 \\ \hline 4 \end{array}$$

← Multiply: $2 \times 30 = 60$

← Subtract: $64 - 60 = 4$

Compare: $4 < 30$

3 How many ones are left? Write the remainder.

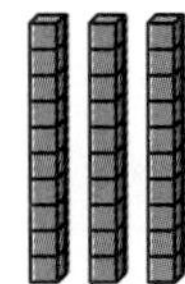

$$\begin{array}{r} 2\text{R}4 \\ 30\overline{)64} \\ -60 \\ \hline 4 \end{array}$$

They will fill 2 rows, with 4 people in the unfilled row.

Try It

Divide.

1. $10\overline{)47}$ **2.** $10\overline{)55}$ **3.** $52 \div 10$ **4.** $68 \div 30$ **5.** $81 \div 40$

Explain how you would find $67 \div 20$.

Practice **Divide.**

6. $20\overline{)62}$ 7. $30\overline{)93}$ 8. $20\overline{)44}$ 9. $10\overline{)71}$ 10. $10\overline{)99}$

11. $40\overline{)67}$ 12. $20\overline{)83}$ 13. $50\overline{)72}$ 14. $20\overline{)34}$ 15. $30\overline{)68}$

16. $38 \div 30$ 17. $29 \div 10$ 18. $65 \div 20$ 19. $94 \div 30$ 20. $76 \div 10$

Algebra & functions **Find each missing number.**

21. $36 \div n = 1$ R6 22. $58 \div y = 5$ R8 ★ 23. $(70 - 7) \div t = 3$ R3

Problem Solving

Use data from *Did You Know?* for problems 24–25.

24. **What if** during the game in 1979, the Phillies had scored about the same number of runs in each inning? About how many runs would this be?

25. **What if** at one game there are 2,300 fewer than the maximum crowd? How many fans are at the game?

26. **Social Studies:** Baseball games between college teams have been played since the Civil War (1861–1865). About how many years have college baseball teams been playing against each other?

27. **Create a problem** dividing a 2-digit number by a multiple of 10. Solve it. Ask others to solve it.

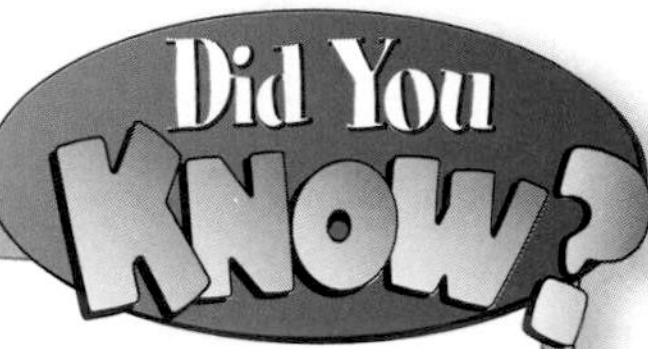

Wrigley Field is the home of the Chicago Cubs. It holds a maximum of 38,765 people. In 1979 the Philadelphia Phillies beat the Cubs 23–22 in 10 innings.

Spiral Review and Test Prep

28. $642 \div 6$ 29. 905×3 30. $8{,}975 - 4{,}689$ 31. $108 \div 12$

Choose the correct answer.

32. The Royals got 3 hits in each inning. How many hits did they have by the end of the ninth inning?
   A. 27
   B. 12
   C. 6
   D. 9

33. A player got 35, 41, and 32 home runs in the last 3 seasons. How many did the player average in these 3 years?
   F. 36
   G. 35
   H. 33
   J. Not Here

Objective: Divide by 2-digit divisors.

8-4 Divide by 2-Digit Divisors

Learn

Math Words

quotient the result of division

dividend a number to divide

divisor the number by which the dividend is divided

Joey's hockey team is selling ads in its journal to help raise money for a trip to the tournament. How many ads does the team need to sell to cover the cost of the trip?

Example 1

Find: $105 ÷ $35

1 Model 105. Decide where to place the first digit in the quotient.

$$\begin{array}{r} x \\ \$35\overline{)\$105} \end{array}$$

Think: 35 > 1 not enough hundreds
Think: 35 > 10 not enough tens
Think: 35 < 105 enough ones
The first place is in the ones place.

2 Regroup as needed. How many groups of 35 can be made?

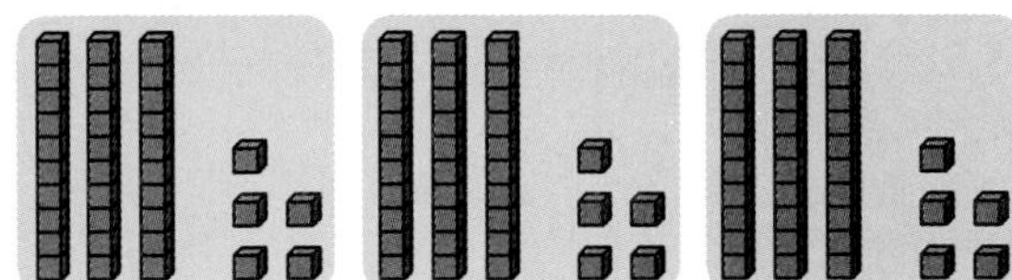

$$\begin{array}{r} 3 \\ \$35\overline{)\$105} \\ -105 \\ \hline 0 \end{array}$$

← Multiply: 3 × 35 = 105
← Subtract: 105 − 105 = 0
Compare: 0 < 35

3 Check. Use the inverse relationship between division and multiplication.

divisor → $\$35\overline{)\$105}$ ← **dividend**, with 3 ← **quotient**

$$\begin{array}{r} 3 \\ \times\ \$35 \\ \hline \$105 \end{array}$$

3 ← quotient
× $35 ← divisor
$105 ← dividend

Joey's team needs to sell 3 advertisements.

Over the last three seasons, Joey played a total of 42 games. He had 128 goals scored against him in these games. What was the average number of goals scored against Joey in each game?

Example 2

Find: 128 ÷ 42

1 Place the first digit.

x
42)128

Think:
42 > 1 42 > 12
Not enough hundreds or tens. Enough ones.

2 Divide the ones.

3 R2
42)128
−126 ← Multiply: 3 × 42 = 126
2 ← Subtract: 128 − 126 = 2
Compare: 2 < 42

3 Check the answer. Multiply. Add if there is a remainder.

42
× 3
126
+ 2
128

Joey had an average of 3 goals scored against him in each game.

More Examples

A

35 R1
23)806
−69
116
−115
1

B

$0.38
68)$25.84
−20 4
5 44
−5 44
0

Divide the way you divide whole numbers. Place the dollar sign and the decimal point where they belong in the quotient.

Try It **Divide. Check your answer.**

1. 37)683 **2.** 34)891 **3.** 52)$31.72 **4.** 37)2,450 **5.** 39)$32.76

6. $7.52 ÷ 47 **7.** 918 ÷ 21 **8.** $37.50 ÷ 15 **9.** 3,652 ÷ 56 **10.** 7,268 ÷ 62

Explain how you would divide 921 ÷ 23.

Practice **Divide. Check your answer.**

11. $21\overline{)86}$ **12.** $77\overline{)3{,}572}$ **13.** $13\overline{)\$85.02}$ **14.** $37\overline{)1{,}526}$ **15.** $42\overline{)\$60.90}$

16. 568 ÷ 62 **17.** \$9.80 ÷ 35 **18.** 325 ÷ 11 **19.** 4,629 ÷ 84 **20.** \$28.80 ÷ 48

21. 672 ÷ 28 **22.** 2,355 ÷ 33 **23.** \$91.12 ÷ 68 **24.** 4,761 ÷ 11 **25.** 8,168 ÷ 47

Algebra & functions **Solve.**

26. $(2{,}100 + 42) \div 49 = n$

27. $(1{,}000 + 120) \div 85 = t$

★**28.** $(600 + 48) \div (12 \times 3) = m$

★**29.** $(1{,}000 + 35) \div (9 \times 5) = (s - 2)$

30.

This is how Corey solved the division problem 690 ÷ 43. Tell what mistake he made. Explain how to correct it.

Problem Solving

31. A team wants to sell 240 books to raise money. If there are 15 players, what is the number of books each player must sell?

32. Britanny is reading a 105-page book on hockey. She plans to read 15 pages each day. How many days will it take Brittany to read the book?

33. Skate laces are available in boxes of 20 pairs for \$30.00 or boxes of 100 pairs for \$120.00. Which is the better buy? Why?

34. The girls' soccer team wants to buy new uniforms for \$770.00. If there are 22 girls on the team, how much does each uniform cost?

35. Fun Fitness Sportswear Company ordered 108 boxes of soccer jerseys. Each box contains 16 jerseys. If the company wants to send the same number of jerseys to 15 stores, how many jerseys will each store get? How many will be left?

Use data from the table for problems 36–40.

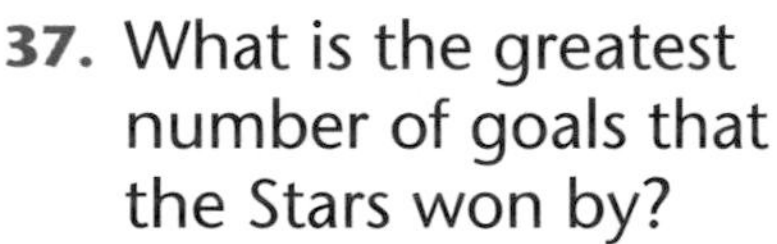

36. How many games did the Stars win? How many did they lose?

Scores of Hockey Games

Team	game A	game B	game C	game D	game E	game F
	Number of Goals					
Stars	5	8	3	4	1	3
Opponent	3	2	3	3	3	0

37. What is the greatest number of goals that the Stars won by?

38. What is the mean number of goals the Stars scored in these games?

★**39.** How many goals would the Stars have to score in the next game to have the mean number of goals be 5?

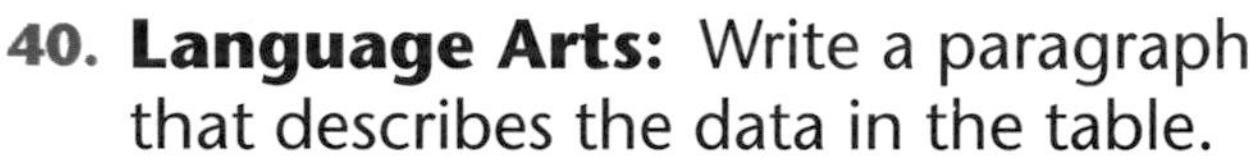

40. **Language Arts:** Write a paragraph that describes the data in the table.

41. A bicycle tour of California took 127 hours. How many days and hours did the tour take?

42. Carmine has a 192-foot rope. She needs to divide it into 12 equal sections for a game. How many sections will she have?

43. **Logical Reasoning:** Lois opens the book she is reading to chapter 2. The product of the two page numbers is 272. What are the page numbers?

44. A sports drink company has 1,968 containers of a sports drink mix. If the company ships the same number of containers to 72 schools, how many containers will each school get? How many will be left?

45. **Generalize:** What is the greatest number of digits you can have in a quotient if you divide a 3-digit dividend by a 2-digit divisor? Explain by giving an example.

Spiral Review and Test Prep

46. $89 \div 8$ **47.** 345×6 **48.** $76 \div 6$ **49.** 8×196 **50.** $38 \div 4$

Choose the correct answer.

51. A hockey game begins at 6:05 P.M. and ends at 7:25 P.M. How long is the game?

A. 20 minutes **C.** 80 minutes
B. 40 minutes **D.** 120 minutes

52. A player signs a contract that is worth between 2 million and 5 million dollars. Which could be an actual amount of the contract?

F. \$5,002,000 **H.** \$1,854,900
G. \$3,876,000 **J.** \$376,500

Extra Practice, page 351

Objective: Estimate quotients by using compatible numbers.

8•5 Estimate Quotients

Math in ACTION

Learn

Chris lives in Elk City, Oklahoma. What if he had to travel 512 miles to a tournament? He plans to ride 60 miles each day. How many days will the trip take?

Chris Coy won silver medals at the junior world racquetball championship. He plays with an artificial foot.

Math Words

estimate finding an answer that is close to an exact answer

compatible numbers numbers that are close to the numbers in a problem and easy to divide mentally

Example

To **estimate** the quotient for this problem, you can use **compatible numbers** that help you divide mentally.

512 is close to 540.

$540 \div 60 = 9$

Think of the basic fact: $54 \div 6 = 9$

The trip will take about 9 days.

More Examples

A Estimate: $\$584 \div 23$
Think: $\$600 \div 20 = \$30$

B $3,300 \div 38$
Think: $3,200 \div 40 = 80$

Try It

Estimate each quotient. Show the compatible numbers you use.

1. $23\overline{)788}$ **2.** $67\overline{)\$2,084}$ **3.** $394 \div 50$ **4.** $865 \div 11$

Which two pairs of compatible numbers can you use to estimate the quotient for the problem $366 \div 12$?

Practice Estimate the quotient. Choose compatible numbers.

5. $52\overline{)361}$
6. $11\overline{)6,893}$
7. $42\overline{)3,577}$
8. $73\overline{)2,922}$
9. $58\overline{)189}$
10. 924 ÷ 32
11. 236 ÷ 80
12. 927 ÷ 89
13. 491 ÷ 11
14. 3,476 ÷ 72
15. 997 ÷ 11
16. 6,325 ÷ 73
17. 1,458 ÷ 50
18. 5,365 ÷ 62
★19. 80,212 ÷ 92
★20. 48,560 ÷ 68

Algebra & functions **Compare. Write > or <.**

21. 356 ÷ 72 ■ 483 ÷ 12
22. 765 ÷ 15 ■ 832 ÷ 72
23. 1,348 ÷ 62 ■ 4,767 ÷ 40
24. 5,612 ÷ 80 ■ 7,300 ÷ 70

Problem Solving

25. Mateo is training for a 160-mile bike race. On one day of training Mateo rode 168 miles. He rode at a speed of 28 miles per hour. About how many hours did Mateo ride that day?

26. **Science:** Many people use bike riding as a serious form of exercise. If a bike club plans to cover 45 miles a day, how many days will it take to complete a trip of 278 miles? Explain.

27. Sheila rode her bike 22 miles each day for 7 days. Nathan rode 25 miles each day for 5 days and rested on the weekend. Which cyclist rode farther this week? how much farther?

28. **Analyze:** If you estimate 7,148 ÷ 12 using 7,200 ÷ 12, is the estimate greater or less than the actual quotient? How do you know?

Spiral Review and Test Prep

29. 185 × 32
30. $10\overline{)64,000}$
31. 247 × 56
32. $100\overline{)900}$
33. 84 ÷ 9
34. 325 × 24
35. 76 ÷ 5
36. 127 × 63

Choose the correct answer.

37. Kari buys a box with 4 tire tubes. The price of the box is $19.00. What is the price for 1 tube?
    - A. $4.50
    - B. $4.75
    - C. $15.00
    - D. $23.00

38. Reid buys some parts for his bike. The parts cost $6.19. How much change does he get from a ten-dollar bill?
    - F. $16.19
    - G. $4.81
    - H. $3.81
    - J. Not Here

Extra Practice, page 352

Objective: Change an estimate to adjust the quotient.

8·6 Adjust the Quotient

Learn

Look at this sign. How many sessions are needed for the members who signed up so far?

Example 1

Find: $337 \div 52$

1 Place the first digit.

$52\overline{)337}$ with x above the ones place

Think:

$52 > 3$ $52 > 33$
Not enough hundreds or tens. Enough ones.
Try 7 in the ones place.

Multiply: $7 \times 52 = 364$
Compare: $364 > 337$
Too high. Try 6.

2 Divide the ones.

$$\begin{array}{r} 6\text{R}25 \\ 52\overline{)337} \\ -312 \\ \hline 25 \end{array}$$

←Multiply: $6 \times 52 = 312$
←Subtract: $337 - 312 = 25$
Compare: $25 < 52$

3 Check the answer. Multiply. Add any remainders.

$$\begin{array}{r} 52 \\ \times\ 6 \\ \hline 312 \\ +\ 25 \\ \hline 337 \end{array}$$

You can also check the reasonableness by estimating.

Think: $350 \div 50 = 7$
6 is reasonably close to 7.

They need 7 sessions. There are 6 full sessions and one partially filled session of 25.

Try It

Divide. Check your answer.

1. $89\overline{)338}$
2. $98\overline{)504}$
3. $176 \div 43$
4. $355 \div 47$

How do you know when the first estimate of a quotient is too high? too low?

Practice Divide. Check your answers.

5. $64\overline{)430}$ 6. $49\overline{)\$392}$ 7. $36\overline{)329}$ 8. $55\overline{)428}$ 9. $43\overline{)189}$

10. $108 ÷ 27 11. 432 ÷ 55 12. 482 ÷ 83 13. 168 ÷ 35 14. 413 ÷ 45

15. 653 ÷ 82 ★16. 1,912 ÷ 45 ★17. 1,008 ÷ 26 ★18. $10.75 ÷ 25

Algebra & functions **Divide only those with quotients between $6.00 and $9.00.**

19. $69.85 ÷ 11 20. $95.26 ÷ 22 21. $53.82 ÷ 23 22. $97.80 ÷ 12

Problem Solving

23. Vince wants to do 350 sit-ups every week. If he does 60 each day, can Vince complete all 350 sit-ups in 5 days? Explain.

24. **Create a problem** that uses division by a 2-digit number. Solve it. Ask others to solve it.

Use data from the table for problems 25–27.

25. Tim swims for 30 minutes. Regina takes part in a 60-minute, low-impact aerobics class. Who uses more calories? how many more?

26. **Health:** How many calories do you use in one minute of swimming?

★27. **Explain:** How do you use division to find how many calories a person uses doing each activity for 45 minutes?

Number of Calories Used

Exercise	Calories Used in 60 Minutes
Aerobics, low impact	227
Swimming	360
Stair-treadmill	272
Rowing machine	318

Spiral Review and Test Prep

28. 212 ÷ 5 29. 366 ÷ 6 30. 146 ÷ 4 31. 362 × 14 32. 228 × 43

Choose the correct answer.

33. Colleen worked out for 45 minutes in the morning, then for 30 minutes in the afternoon. How long was her workout that day?
    - A. 15 minutes
    - B. $1\frac{1}{4}$ hours
    - C. $1\frac{1}{2}$ hours
    - D. $1\frac{3}{4}$ hours

34. Gym members can pay $8.00 to attend a class with a weight lifter. If 42 people sign up for the class, how much money will the members pay?
    - F. $34.00
    - G. $50.00
    - H. $326.00
    - J. $336.00

Objective: Form conclusions about using an overestimate or an underestimate to solve a problem.

8•7

Problem Solving: Reading for Math

Use an Overestimate or Underestimate

Let the Games Begin!

Read A total of 78 fourth-grade students will participate in Field Day. Each student will receive a visor. The visors come in boxes of 24. How many boxes are needed?

READING SKILL

Form a Conclusion

You form a conclusion when you make a decision based on the information given and what you know.

- **What do you know?** 78 students, 24 visors per box
- **What do you need to find?** Number of boxes needed

MATH SKILL

Overestimating and Underestimating

When dividing, you overestimate when you round down the divisor. You underestimate when you round up the divisor.

Plan Estimate the number of boxes needed. Since you want to make sure that each student gets a visor, overestimate.

Solve A box holds 24 visors. Round both numbers to a compatible pair.

Divide. $80 \div 20 = 4$

So 4 boxes of visors are needed.

Look Back How could you check your answer?

When would you underestimate a quotient? When would you overestimate a quotient?

Solve. Tell why you used an overestimate or an underestimate.

1. Each pack of blue ribbons costs $9. The Field Day Committee set aside $52 to pay for blue ribbons. How many packs can be purchased?

2. A box of gold medals holds 32 medals. The Field Day Committee needs 150 medals. How many boxes should be purchased?

Use data from the list for problems 3–6.

3. The committee bought a piece of rope that is 70 feet long. How many Field Day ropes can be made from this piece?

4. Sports stickers will be given to 28 students. Does the committee have enough stickers to give each of these students 3 stickers?

5. Flags will be shared by Field Day participants. How many students will share each flag?

Field Day Supply List	
Amount	Item
6	15-foot rope
75	sports stickers
39	flags
3	fruit drink containers

6. Each container of fruit drink mix makes 25 cups of liquid. A total of 34 students ordered fruit drink. Is there enough mix for each student who ordered the beverage to have 2 cups? Explain.

7. A pack of two whistles costs $9. The committee set aside $30 for 8 whistles. Is this enough to buy all the whistles needed? Explain.

Spiral Review and Test Prep

Choose the correct answer.

There are 40 adults working at Field Day. Each adult gets a special shirt. The shirts are sold in packs of 12. How many packs of shirts should they buy?

8. Which statement is true?
   - A. Shirts are sold in packs of 4.
   - B. Four shirts are needed.
   - C. Each pack holds a dozen shirts.

9. To be sure they buy enough shirts, they ____
   - F. underestimate the number of shirts in a pack.
   - G. overestimate the number of packs.
   - H. underestimate the number of adults.

Check Your Progress A

Divide. Use mental math. (pages 324–325)

1. $60\overline{)420}$ 2. $50\overline{)1{,}500}$ 3. $90\overline{)810}$ 4. $3{,}000 \div 50$ 5. $12{,}000 \div 40$

Divide. (pages 326–333; 336–337)

6. $30\overline{)68}$ 7. $40\overline{)89}$ 8. $20\overline{)47}$ 9. $10\overline{)51}$ 10. $60\overline{)66}$

11. $33\overline{)147}$ 12. $11\overline{)\$1.43}$ 13. $66\overline{)597}$ 14. $17\overline{)\$4.25}$ 15. $18\overline{)\$37.44}$

16. $892 \div 34$ 17. $\$82.96 \div 61$ 18. $345 \div 63$ 19. $\$48.30 \div 46$ 20. $106 \div 26$

Estimate. Use compatible numbers. (pages 334–335)

21. $12\overline{)579}$ 22. $92\overline{)622}$ 23. $34\overline{)6{,}135}$ 24. $70\overline{)\$5{,}530}$ 25. $78\overline{)3{,}889}$

26. $532 \div 88$ 27. $\$4{,}962 \div 68$ 28. $332 \div 42$ 29. $2{,}391 \div 75$

Solve. (pages 324–339)

30. A basketball player signs a contract for $12 million over 5 years. If he gets the same amount each month, how much does he get each month?

31. Franklin is the team's leader in 3-point field goals. In 40 games he scored 86 of these field goals. About how many 3-point field goals has he scored per game?

32. They are expecting 600 fans at a basketball game. Game programs come in packs of 36. About how many packs of programs are needed for the game?

33. **Compare:** How is dividing by a 2-digit number and dividing by a 1-digit number alike? How is it different?

Use the Internet

Tremain's school is having a career day. Each student is doing research to find out about careers they are interested in. Tremain wants to choose four careers and then gather data about the salaries of these careers. How can he use the Internet to gather the data?

Career	Yearly Salary	Monthly Salary

- Go to www.mhschool.com/math.
- Find the list of sites that provide career information.
- Click on a link.
- Find the careers. Choose four careers.
- Copy the table. Write the name of the careers in your table.
- Record the yearly salary for each career.
- Find the monthly salary for each career.

1. Which career has the greatest monthly salary? The least?

2. **Analyze:** Why does using the Internet make more sense than using another reference source to find the information about careers?

For more practice, use Math Traveler™.

Objective: Choose a strategy to solve the problem.

Problem Solving: Strategy
Choose a Strategy

Read

Read the problem carefully.

Camille is placing cones on her driveway to practice skating. She draws a starting line with chalk. Camille places the first cone 4 feet from the starting line. She wants to place the rest of the cones 4 feet apart for a total of 20 yards. How many cones does she need?

- **What do you know?** The first cone is 4 feet from the starting line; Cones will be every 4 feet for 20 yards
- **What are you asked to find?** The number of cones needed

Plan

Some problems can be solved in more than one way. To solve this problem you can draw a diagram or write a number sentence.

Think: Remember to look for hidden questions.

Solve

First, you have to know how many feet are in 20 yards.

$20 \times 3 = 60$ feet

Draw a diagram.

Count by 4s to 60. Then count the cones.

Remember: 1 yard = 3 feet.

Write a number sentence. $60 \div 4 = 15$

Camille will use 15 cones.

Look Back

Is there another way you can solve this problem?

Which strategy do you prefer to use to solve this type of problem? Why?

Practice **Solve. Tell which strategy you used.**

1. Camille wants to practice sharper turns. She uses the same 20-yard distance in the driveway and begins at the starting line. This time she places the cones 3 feet apart. How many cones will she use?

2. Camille has many extra wheels for her skates. She keeps the wheels in a box that is 1 foot wide and 1 foot long. Each wheel is about 3 inches wide. How many rows of wheels will fit in the box?

3. Camille's dad is helping her make a skating ramp. He has 6 sheets of 8-foot-long plywood. They need several 4-foot pieces of plywood for the ramp. How many 4-foot pieces can they cut?

4. **Art:** Camille uses a square piece of oak for a plaque that measures 2 feet on each side. She needs sections that are 4 inches wide and 6 inches long for pictures. How many pictures can she fit on the plaque?

Mixed Strategy Review

5. **Time:** A gymnastics exhibition began at 11:30 A.M. and finished at 2:10 P.M. How long was the exhibition?

6. For 4 weeks in July, Roberto swims every Monday, Wednesday, and Friday. During the next 4 weeks he swims these same days and also swims each Saturday. How many days did Roberto swim during this 8-week period?

7. A total of $2,750.00 in prize money is given out at a sports competition. The first-place finisher gets 4 times as much as the second-place finisher. Third place earns half as much as second place. How much do the first-, second-, and third-place finishers earn?

8. The town of Ashville is building a skate park that is 64 feet long and 40 feet wide. The park will be surrounded by a fence. Each section of fencing is 8 feet long. How many sections are needed for the park?

★9. A golf shop buys 45 golf hats for $675.00 The shop also buys 32 golf books. Each book is the same price as 1 hat. How much does the golf shop pay in all?

10. **Create a problem** that can be solved by drawing a diagram or writing a number sentence. Solve it. Ask others to solve it.

CHOOSE A STRATEGY

- Logical Reasoning
- Draw a Picture
- Make a Graph
- Act It Out
- Make a Table or List
- Find a Pattern
- Guess and Check
- Write a Number Sentence
- Work Backward
- Solve a Simpler Problem

Extra Practice, page 353

Objective: Use rules for the order of operations.

8·9 Order of Operations

Algebra & functions

Learn

In the last football game, the Jets scored 2 field goals, 3 touchdowns, and 2 running conversions. How many points did they score?

Touchdown – running or catching the ball in the end zone, worth 6 points
Conversion – after a touchdown, running or passing the ball into the end zone or kicking through the goal posts; running or passing conversion, 2 points, kicking conversion, 1 point
Field Goal - placekicking the ball between the goal post, worth 3 points
Safety - tackling a ball carrier in his own end zone, worth 2 points

Math Word

expression a group of numbers and symbols that shows a mathematical quantity

Use these rules for solving a problem having more than one operation.

Order of Operations	
1.	Do the operations in parentheses first.
2.	Multiply and divide from left to right.
3.	Add and subtract from left to right.

Example

1 Write an **expression** to solve the problem.

Number of field goals		Points for a field goal		Number of touchdowns		Points for a touchdown		Number of running conversions		Points for a running conversion
2	×	3	+	3	×	6	+	2	×	2

2 Simplify the expression using the order of operations.

$$2 \times 3 + 3 \times 6 + 2 \times 2$$
$$\downarrow \quad \downarrow \quad \downarrow$$
$$6 + 18 + 4$$

3 Add.
$6 + 18 + 4 = 28$

The Jets scored 28 points.

More Examples

A $(3 \times 4) + (8 \times 2)$
$12 + 16 = 28$

B $(8 + 12) \div (10 - 5)$
$20 \div 5 = 4$

Try It

Simplify. Use the proper order of operations.

1. $(8 - 6) \times 8$ **2.** $(24 - 10) \div 7$ **3.** $36 \div 9 \times 2$ **4.** $16 - (7 + 5)$

Sum it Up Tell how to simplify this expression: $16 \div (5 - 3)$.

Practice **Write which operation should be done first.**

5. $6 \times 5 - 10$
6. $(15 - 7) \div 4$
7. $(8 + 4) \times 3$
8. $22 - 12 + 4$
9. $2 + 6 \times 7$
10. $8 \times 3 \div 6$
11. $45 \div (6 + 3)$
12. $(7 + 3) \times 6$

Simplify. Use the proper order of operations.

13. $3 \times 5 + 6$
14. $12 \div 6 - 2$
15. $(5 + 9) \div 2$
16. $2 \times 6 - 7$
17. $48 \div (4 \times 3)$
18. $9 + 5 \times 2$
19. $5 \times 5 - 5$
20. $(3 + 8) \times 4$
21. $4 \times 7 + 3 \times 3$
22. $(21 \div 7) \times 9 + 2$
23. $(7 + 8) \times (8 - 5)$

★24. $2 + (22 - 16) \times 3 + 8 - 16$

★25. $[6 \times 3 + 8 \div 2] \times (3 + 3) + 3$

Problem Solving

Use data from *Did You Know?* for problem 26.

26. How many points were scored in all by the longest completed passes?

27. **Collect data** about football. Use your data to write a problem. Solve it. Ask other to solve it.

★28. The home team scored 4 touchdowns, 2 running conversions, and 2 field goals. The visitors scored 2 touchdowns and 2 kicking conversions. Write expressions and show the score of the game.

29. **Analyze:** John says the value of $3 + 6 \times 2$ is 18. Is he correct? Why or why not?

The longest pass completion ever in the NFL was 99 yards. It has happened 8 times. Each pass resulted in a touchdown.

Spiral Review and Test Prep

30. 6×113
31. 5×437
32. $9\overline{)365}$
33. $7\overline{)483}$
34. $6\overline{)549}$

Choose the correct answer.

Number of Touchdowns Scored Each Game									
3	4	2	5	2	2	3	3	5	1

35. What is the mean?
    - A. 2
    - B. 3
    - C. 4
    - D. 5

36. What is the range?
    - F. 0
    - G. 2
    - H. 4
    - J. 6

Objective: Analyze and make decisions.

Problem Solving: Application
Decision Making

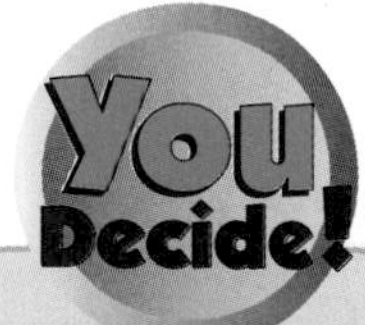

Should they make the hiker bars or buy boxes of them already made?

The Lakewood hiking club needs $110 for new equipment. To raise money, the members plan to sell nutritious hiker bars.

Hiker Bars

Ingredients for Hiker Bars (1 batch makes 48 bars)
Time: 1/2 hour to prepare; 45 minutes to bake

- 4 ounces chunky peanut butter
- 2 medium bananas (mashed)
- 4 ounces fruit juice
- 4 eggs
- 1 teaspoon baking powder
- 5 ounces dates (chopped)
- $\frac{1}{2}$ teaspoon salt
- 3 ounces butter
- 4 ounces molasses
- 7 ounces whole wheat flour
- 2 teaspoon vanilla
- 5 ounces oat or wheat cereal (crushed)
- 5 ounces of peanuts (chopped)

Option 1

Shopping List

48-ounce jar chunky peanut butter	$3.36
5-pound bag of whole wheat flour	$1.35
26-ounce box of salt	$0.59
1 pound baking powder	$2.29
1 dozen eggs	$1.92
16 ounces of peanuts	$1.28
2 ounces vanilla	$2.81
16 ounces butter	$2.24
32 ounces fruit juice	$3.84
16-ounce box of cereal	$2.88
16-ounce jar of molasses	$2.72
6 banana bunch	$1.28
16 ounces of dates	$2.24

Option 2

GRANOLA Hiker BARS
12 PACK FOR $9.36

Read for Understanding

1. How many hiker bars does the recipe make?
2. How many hiker bars come in a box? How much does the box cost?
3. What ingredients do they need to buy to make the hiker bars?
4. How long does it take to make 1 batch of hiker bars?
5. How many eggs do you need to make 1 batch of hiker bars?
6. How much money does the club need to raise?

Make Decisions

7. What will it cost to buy all of the ingredients needed to make 1 batch?
8. What is the unit cost of each hiker bar you make with the recipe?
9. How many batches of hiker bars can they make with the ingredients they bought? How many bars would that be?
10. How many boxes of bars would you need to buy to have that many hiker bars? How much does it cost to buy that many boxes?
11. How much money would they make on each bar from selling the homemade bars for a $1.00 each?
12. How much money would they make on each bar from selling the boxed bars for a $1.00 each?
13. How many homemade hiker bars do they need to sell to reach their goal?
14. How many boxed bars do they need to sell to reach their goal?
15. What are some advantages of making the hiker bars from the recipe? disadvantages?
16. What are some advantages of buying boxes of hiker bars? disadvantages?

What is your recommendation for the Hiking Club? Explain.

Problem Solving

Objective: Apply dividing by 2-digit numbers to investigate science concepts.

Problem Solving: Math and Science

Does eating improve performance?

Did you ever notice that when you feel hungry you sometimes also feel tired? In this activity you will explore how eating affects your ability to perform. You will see if eating lunch helps you do more sit-ups.

You Will Need
- **timer or clock**

Hypothesize

How many sit-ups do you think you can do right before lunch? after lunch?

Safety

Wait at least 30 minutes after eating before doing vigorous exercise.

Procedure

1. Work in a group. Take turns.
2. One student will be the timer.
3. Right before you eat lunch, count how many sit-ups you can do in 60 seconds.
4. Repeat at least 30 minutes after lunch.

Data

Copy and complete a chart to record your data.

Number of Sit-ups		
Student	Before Lunch	After Lunch

Problem Solving

Conclude and Apply

- Did you do more sit-ups before or after lunch?
- Use subtraction to find how many more sit-ups you did.
- Use division to find how many times more sit-ups you did. Round to the nearest whole number.
- Can you conclude that the food from lunch gave you more energy? Why or why not?
- Talk to your partner. In what ways could you improve this activity?
- Explain the activity in terms of energy conversion.

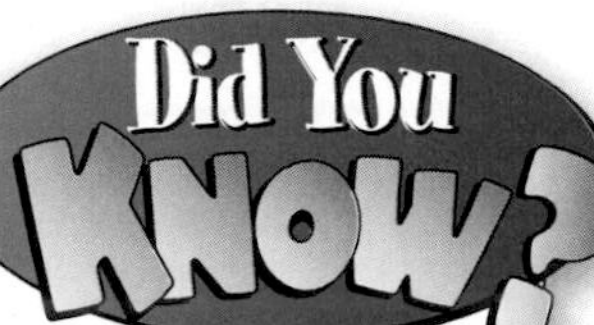

When you exercise, your body converts food and oxygen into energy. That energy helps power your muscles. It may also be released as heat. This whole process is called energy conversion.

Going Further

1. Design and complete an activity that determines whether or not food improves your ability to do mental tasks such as tests or puzzles.
2. Collect all of the data from the class and make a bar graph showing how many times more sit-ups each person could do after lunch.

Check Your Progress B

Simplify. Use the proper order of operations. **(pages 344–345)**

1. $3 + 2 \times 4$
2. $(4 + 5) \times 5$
3. $3 + (9 \div 3) - 2$
4. $2 \times 4 + 24 \div 3$
5. $9 - 8 \div 2$
6. $6 + (12 \div 4)$
7. $6 \times 4 + 1$
8. $1 + 9 \times 1$
9. $12 - 2 \times 3$
10. $8 \times 6 \div 12$
11. $9 + 8 \times 2$
12. $8 \div 2 - 1$
13. $(343 - 298) \div (3 \times 3)$
14. $(3 \times 12) - (8 + 24 \div 6)$
15. $(18 + 31) \div 7 \times 9$
16. $(443 - 387) \div (2 \times 2)$
17. $5 \times 11 - (6 + 57) \div 7$
18. $(51 - 3) \div 8 \times 3$
19. $3 \times (10 + 2) - (80 - 8) \div 9$
20. $(43 + 17) \div 6 \times (108 \div 9)$

Solve. **(pages 342–345)**

21. Jason buys a bag containing 15 baseballs at a total cost of \$18.75. What is the cost for 1 baseball?

22. A basketball player scores 8 two-point field goals and 2 three-point field goals in a game. How many points does she score in the game? Write an expression and find the number of points.

23. A box of 20 hockey pucks costs \$55.80. What is the cost for each puck?

24. Gail ordered 6 cases of tennis balls and 6 cases of handballs. Each case has 24 containers. Each container of tennis balls holds 3 balls. Each container of handballs holds 4 balls. How many balls did Gail order in all? Write an expression. Find the total number of balls.

25. **Explain** why the rules for order of operations are needed.

Extra Practice

Division Patterns (pages 324–325)

Divide. Use mental math.

1. 4,000 ÷ 40
2. 48,000 ÷ 80
3. 270 ÷ 30
4. 420,000 ÷ 60
5. $90\overline{)81{,}000}$
6. $70\overline{)5{,}600}$
7. $50\overline{)40{,}000}$
8. $20\overline{)1{,}800}$

Solve.

9. There are 48,000 seats in a stadium. There are 80 sections of seats in the stadium. How many seats are in each section?

Divide 2-Digit Numbers by Multiples of 10 (pages 328–329)

Divide.

1. 48 ÷ 40
2. 89 ÷ 40
3. 73 ÷ 10
4. 64 ÷ 30
5. 67 ÷ 20
6. 95 ÷ 30
7. 56 ÷ 10
8. 38 ÷ 30
9. 44 ÷ 20
10. 47 ÷ 10

Solve.

11. There are 82 players trying out for the all-star team. The coaches put the players into groups of 20. How many groups of 20 are there? How many are in the incomplete group?

Divide by 2-Digit Divisors (pages 330–333)

Divide.

1. $79\overline{)670}$
2. $28\overline{)\$6.72}$
3. $53\overline{)4{,}707}$
4. $41\overline{)\$71.75}$
5. $34\overline{)3{,}128}$
6. $48\overline{)3{,}711}$
7. $54\overline{)\$33.48}$
8. $75\overline{)\$78.75}$
9. 1,638 ÷ 39
10. 965 ÷ 56
11. $78.84 ÷ 36
12. 2,167 ÷ 34
13. $85.02 ÷ 78
14. 1,102 ÷ 84
15. 1,804 ÷ 44
16. 1,743 ÷ 33
17. 2,439 ÷ 26
18. $56.64 ÷ 24
19. 2,836 ÷ 37
20. $86.68 ÷ 44

Solve.

21. A swimmer finishes a 1,500-meter race in 25 minutes. How many meters does she swim each minute?

Extra Practice

Estimate Quotients (pages 334–335)

Estimate. Use compatible numbers.

1. $429 \div 58$
2. $256 \div 49$
3. $1{,}728 \div 42$
4. $1{,}836 \div 31$
5. $19\overline{)158}$
6. $63\overline{)558}$
7. $32\overline{)2{,}458}$
8. $82\overline{)4{,}913}$

Solve.

9. In the last 2 weeks, Franco rode his bike for a total of 232 miles. He rode the same distance each day. About how many miles did Franco ride each day? Show the compatible numbers you use.

Adjust the Quotient (pages 336–337)

Divide.

1. $54\overline{)325}$
2. $92\overline{)825}$
3. $66\overline{)465}$
4. $88\overline{)512}$
5. $29\overline{)118}$
6. $58\overline{)409}$
7. $73\overline{)440}$
8. $67\overline{)594}$
9. $78\overline{)286}$
10. $81\overline{)568}$
11. $52\overline{)301}$
12. $57\overline{)515}$

Problem Solving: Reading for Math Use an Overestimate or Underestimate (pages 338–339)

Solve.

1. A total of 354 students go to Field Day. Each student will be given a fruit snack. The snacks are sold in boxes of 12. The teachers bring 30 boxes. Is this reasonable? Explain.
2. Buses will take 446 students to a ball game. Each bus holds 42 students. Fred says to rent 8 buses. Is this reasonable? Explain.
3. A ticket to the game costs $19. The sports club has $600. Is this enough money to buy 28 tickets? Explain.
4. The soccer team wants to raise $315 for supplies. There are 32 members on the team. About how much money does each player need to raise for them to reach their goal?

Extra Practice

Problem Solving: Strategy Choose a Strategy (pages 342–343)

Use data from the price list for problems 1–3.

Dumbbells

All dumbbells sold in packages of 25 or individually. Package prices are listed.

Price List

1-pound weights	\$12.00
2-pound weights	\$24.00
5-pound weights	\$62.25
10-pound weights	\$99.50

1. Fitness World buys 50 five-pound weights. How much do they cost?
2. How much does 1 ten-pound weight cost?
3. In a store display, the dumbbells are arranged by weight from the least to the greatest and back to the least. What is the weight of the fourth dumbbell on display?
4. The weight room is 75 feet wide. Each weight machine is 6 feet wide. For safety there needs to be 3 feet on either side of each machine. How many machines can fit in a line across the width of the room?
5. It costs \$15 to buy equipment for a team at the Special Olympics. The entry fee is \$33 for each athlete. You want to raise money to support a team. How much do you need if there are 5 members?

Order of Operations (pages 344–345)

Write which operation should be done first.

1. $6 + 5 \times 10$
2. $(4 + 10) \div 2$
3. $(20 - 12) \times 4$
4. $15 - 10 + 3$
5. $30 - 9 \div 3$
6. $7 \times 6 \div 6$
7. $36 \div (6 + 3)$
8. $(8 + 8) \div 4$

Simplify. Use the proper order of operations.

9. $4 \times 6 + 3$
10. $24 \div 3 - 5$
11. $5 + (9 - 2)$
12. $2 \times (10 - 5)$
13. $64 \div (2 + 6)$
14. $9 - 5 + 2$
15. $16 \div 2 - 7$
16. $(15 - 7) \times 4$
17. $(23 \times 2) + (45 \div 15)$
18. $63 \div (6 \times 12 \div 8)$
19. $(325 \div 5) \times (350 \div 70)$
20. $7 \times 8 + 736 \div 32$

Chapter Study Guide

Language and Math

Math Words

compatible numbers
dividend
divisor
expression
order of operations
quotient

Complete. Use a word from the list.

1. You use the order of operations to find the value of a(n) ____.
2. In the division problem 320 ÷ 80, the ____ is 80.
3. When you divide, you can think of ____ to estimate the quotient.
4. The rule for solving a problem when there is more than one operation is called ____.

Divide multiples of 10 by a 2-digit number. (pages 324–325)

Example

Find: 2,800 ÷ 40

Solution

Use patterns.

28 ÷ 4 = 7
280 ÷ 40 = 7
2,800 ÷ 40 = 70

Divide.

5. 14,000 ÷ 20
6. 4,000 ÷ 50
7. 2,400 ÷ 30
8. 3,600 ÷ 60
9. 54,000 ÷ 60
10. 20,000 ÷ 40

Divide a multidigit number by a 2-digit number. (pages 326–333, 336–339)

Example

Find: 2,054 ÷ 33

Solution

Place the first digit in the quotient.

$$\begin{array}{r} 62 \text{ R8} \\ 33\overline{)2{,}054} \\ -1\,98 \\ \hline 74 \\ -66 \\ \hline 8 \end{array}$$

Divide the tens.
Multiply 6 × 33 = 198
Subtract 205 − 198 = 7
Bring down the ones.
Divide the ones.
Multiply: 2 × 33 = 66
Subtract: 74 − 66 = 8
Compare: 8 < 33

Divide.

11. 67 ÷ 20
12. \$85.44 ÷ 24
13. 2,275 ÷ 58
14. 414 ÷ 15
15. $18\overline{)\$50.22}$
16. $17\overline{)1{,}090}$
17. $42\overline{)\$52.92}$
18. $25\overline{)1{,}548}$

Estimate quotients. (pages 334–335)

Example

Estimate: $336 \div 42$

Think: $320 \div 40 = 8$

Solution

Use compatible numbers.

$336 \div 42$ is about 8.

Estimate. Use compatible numbers.

19. $\$358 \div 68$ **20.** $472 \div 57$

21. $652 \div 78$ **22.** $265 \div 32$

23. $72\overline{)\$2,164}$ **24.** $82\overline{)5714}$

25. $\$849 \div 12$

Use order of operations to evaluate expressions. (pages 344–345)

Example

Find: $(3 + 4) \times 8 \div 2$

Solution

Use the order of operations.

- Perform the operations inside the parentheses first.
- Multiply and divide from left to right.
- Add and subtract from left to right.

$(3 + 4) \times 8 \div 2$
$7 \times 8 \div 2$
$56 \div 2 = 28$

Write which operation should be done first.

26. $7 + 3 - 1$ **27.** $64 \div (12 - 4)$

Simplify. Use order of operations.

28. $(21 + 42) \div 7$ **29.** $4 \times 24 \div 2$

30. $6 \times (450 \div 90)$ **31.** $15 - 3 \times 4$

Use strategies to solve problems. (pages 338–339, 342–343)

Example

Starting 50 meters from the starting line, a runners club plans to put spotters every 50 meters along a race route. The race is 1,000 meters long. How many spotters do they need?

Solution

Write a number sentence or draw a diagram.

2 4 6 8 10 12 14 16 18 20
0 100 200 300 400 500 600 700 800 900 1000

Write a number sentence.

Divide: $1,000 \div 50 = 20$

They need 20 spotters.

Solve.

32. A store clerk wants to stack 55 cans of tennis balls in a triangular display. How many cans would be in the bottom row?

33. Each pack of awards costs \$25. The school has \$507 set aside for awards. Is this enough to buy the 20 packs of awards they need? Explain.

Study Guide

Chapter Test

Divide. Use mental math.

1. $240{,}000 \div 30$
2. $72{,}000 \div 80$
3. $2{,}100 \div 70$
4. $36{,}000 \div 90$

Divide.

5. $322 \div 39$
6. $453 \div 48$
7. $\$43.68 \div 12$
8. $601 \div 45$
9. $849 \div 26$
10. $861 \div 21$
11. $\$83.52 \div 36$
12. $1{,}429 \div 23$
13. $38\overline{)1{,}041}$
14. $36\overline{)\$63.36}$
15. $92\overline{)2{,}392}$
16. $84\overline{)3{,}205}$
17. $41\overline{)8{,}961}$
18. $55\overline{)9{,}845}$
19. $67\overline{)4{,}842}$
20. $72\overline{)5{,}748}$

Estimate each quotient. Use compatible numbers.

21. $822 \div 88$
22. $448 \div 52$
23. $7{,}284 \div 81$
24. $6{,}367 \div 78$

Simplify. Use the proper order of operations.

25. $81 \div (3 \times 3)$
26. $(37 + 53) \div 5$
27. $8 + 9 \times 16$
28. $3 \times 4 + 18 \div 6$
29. $(4 + 5) \div 3 \times 5$
30. $(8 - 4) + (180 \div 36) \div 5$

Solve.

31. The coach buys each player on her team the same snack. She has \$37.48 to spend on snacks for the 12 players. About how much can she spend on each snack?

32. There are 330 players at Soccer Day. Each team must have 15 players. How many teams are there?

33. Twice as many students as teachers were at Field Day. If there were 456 people at Field Day, how many were teachers?

Performance Assessment

Your school is preparing for field day. There are 267 students who will be taking part in the events.

Each student is entered in every event.

The chart shows some of the events and the number of students that can be in each session.

Field Day Notes	
Relay Races	25 per session
Three-Legged Race	40 per session
Rope Climb	15 per session
Obstacle Course	32 per session

Decide how many sessions are needed for each type of event. Make a chart like the one below to record your work.

Event Name	Total Number of Students	Number per Session	Number of Sessions

A Good Answer

- shows a completed chart.
- shows the mathematics you used to do your work.

You may want to save this work for your portfolio.

Enrichment

Factor Trees

Any composite number can be written as the product of prime number factors. A prime number is a number that has two factors — itself and 1. You can find the prime number factors by making a factor tree.

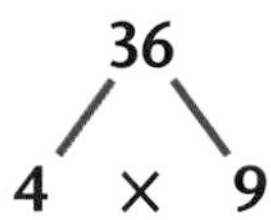

Write 36 as the product of 2 factors.

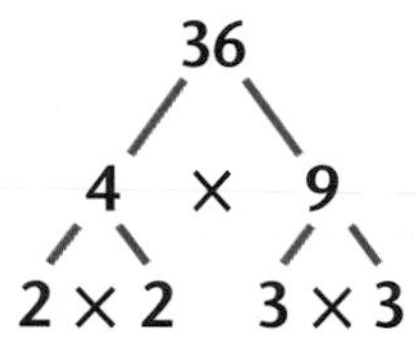

Write 4 and 9 as the product of two factors. The factors are all prime:
$2 \times 2 \times 3 \times 3 = 36$
This is the prime factorization of 36.

Sometimes you need to continue factoring one of the numbers.

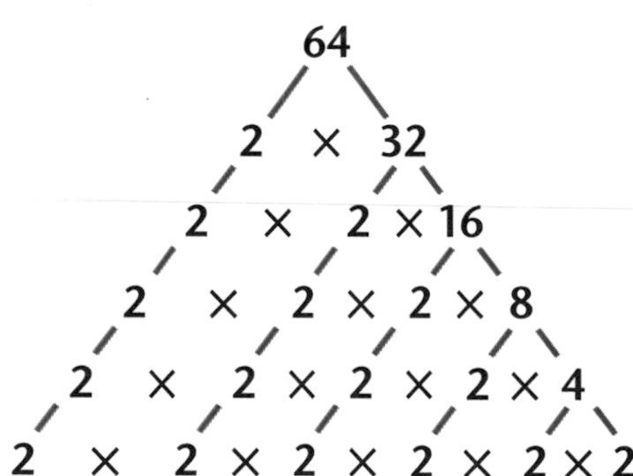

You cannot make a factor tree for a prime number.

43

It cannot split into factors other than 1 and itself.

Draw a factor tree for each number.

1. 24 **2.** 50 **3.** 96 **4.** 60 **5.** 48

6. **Generalize:** Will you end up with the same prime factors for a number no matter which 2 factors you start with? Explain.

Test-Taking Tips

S.O.S.

For some types of test questions, you will find that drawing a diagram can help you choose the correct answer.

There are six students in a row. Dave is between Dan and Ed. Emily is after Ed. Dan, Lou, and Kira are before Dave. Kira is not first. Which of the following shows the order of students from first to last?

A. Lou, Kira, Dan, Dave, Ed, Emily
B. Lou, Dan, Kira, Dave, Ed, Emily
C. Lou, Dan, Dave, Ed, Kira, Emily
D. Lou, Kira, Dave, Dan, Ed, Emily

Check for Success

Before turning in a test, go back one last time to check.

- ☑ I understood and answered the questions asked.
- ☑ I checked my work for errors.
- ☑ My answers make sense.

You need to find the order of the students. Draw a diagram to help you.

- Dave is between Dan and Ed.

X _______ X _______ X
Dan Dave Ed

- Emily is after Ed.

X _______ X _______ X _______ X
Dan Dave Ed Emily

- Dan, Lou, and Kira are before Dave. Kira is not first.

X ____ X ____ X ____ X ____ X ____ X
Lou Kira Dan Dave Ed Emily

Now look at your answer choices. The correct order is there. The correct answer choice is A.

Choose the correct answer. Draw a picture or diagram to help you.

1. Jane arranged 9 pictures in 3 rows. The second and third rows each have two more pictures than the row above them. How many pictures are in the second row?
   A. 1 **B.** 2 **C.** 3 **D.** 5

2. Louis, Becky, Carl, and Flo were the top four finishers in a race. Becky finished before Carl, but after Flo. Louis finished before Flo. Who won the race?
   F. Becky **G.** Carl **H.** Flo **J.** Louis

3. Four people can sit at a square table. How many people can sit at 5 square tables placed end-to-end to form a rectangle?
   A. 12 **B.** 14 **C.** 16 **D.** 20

4. Bo has 30 feet in which to set up a ball toss game. He sets buckets 4 feet apart. How many buckets can he set up?
   F. 6 **G.** 7 **H.** 8 **J.** 9

Spiral Review and Test Prep

Chapters 1–8

Choose the correct answer.

Number Sense

1. Which names the same number as $15 \times 82 = n$?
   A. $15 \times 80 + 2$
   B. $15 \times 40 + 42$
   C. $(15 \times 80) + (15 \times 2)$
   D. $(20 \times 14) + 14$

2. The Jets and the Falcons were tied at the end of the basketball game. In overtime the Jets scored 5 two-point field goals. The Falcons scored 1 three-point field goal. By how many points did the Jets win?
   F. 7 H. 9
   G. 4 J. 8

3. A store sells baseball cards. There are 6 cards in a package and 24 packages in a case. How many cards are in a case?
   A. 30 C. 124
   B. 144 D. Not Here

4. A stadium has 33,489 seats. Which number of fans would not fit in the stadium?
   F. 33,389 H. 33,849
   G. 33,479 J. 32,984

Measurement and Geometry

5. Tom Dempsey of the New Orleans Saints kicked a 63-yard field goal in 1970. How many feet is this?
   A. 21 feet C. 630 feet
   B. 126 feet D. 189 feet

6. A bat is 40 inches long. What is this length in feet and inches?
   F. 2 feet 4 inches H. 3 feet 4 inches
   G. 1 foot 4 inches J. 4 feet 4 inches

7. A baseball weighs about 5 ounces. Which item weighs less than a baseball?
   A. Puppy C. Paper clip
   B. Watermelon D. Bat

8. A baseball player hits a home run 360 feet long. How many yards is this?
   F. 100 yards H. 90 yards
   G. 120 yards J. 1,080 yards

Statistics, Data Analysis, and Probability

Use data from the table for problems 9–12.

Most Overall Tennis Titles

Player	Singles	Doubles	Mixed Doubles
King	6	10	4
Navratilova	9	7	3
Ryan	0	12	7
Lenglen	6	6	3
Brough	4	5	4

9. How many singles titles did these players win in all?
A. 25 **C.** 35
B. 15 **D.** Not Here

10. Including regular and mixed doubles, how many more doubles titles did King win than singles titles?
F. 4 **H.** 6
G. 8 **J.** 10

11. Which player won the most doubles and mixed doubles titles?
A. Lenglen **C.** King
B. Navratilova **D.** Ryan

12. How many titles in all did these players win?
F. 86 **H.** 96
G. 76 **J.** Not Here

Algebra and Functions

13. What is the next quotient in the pattern?

$27 \div 9 = 3$
$270 \div 9 = 30$
$2{,}700 \div 9 = 300$

A. 30 **C.** 300
B. 3 **D.** 3,000

14. Suppose that you burn 318 calories in 60 minutes doing high-impact aerobics. How many calories would you burn in 30 minutes?
F. 258 **H.** 159
G. 636 **J.** Not Here

15. Look at the pattern. What is the price for 1 ticket?
Group Event Ticket Prices
20 tickets = $440
25 tickets = $550
30 tickets = $660
A. $18 **C.** $20
B. $24 **D.** $22

16. A "pay-per-view" movie costs $3.00. Make a graph to show how much it would cost a family to view 8 movies.

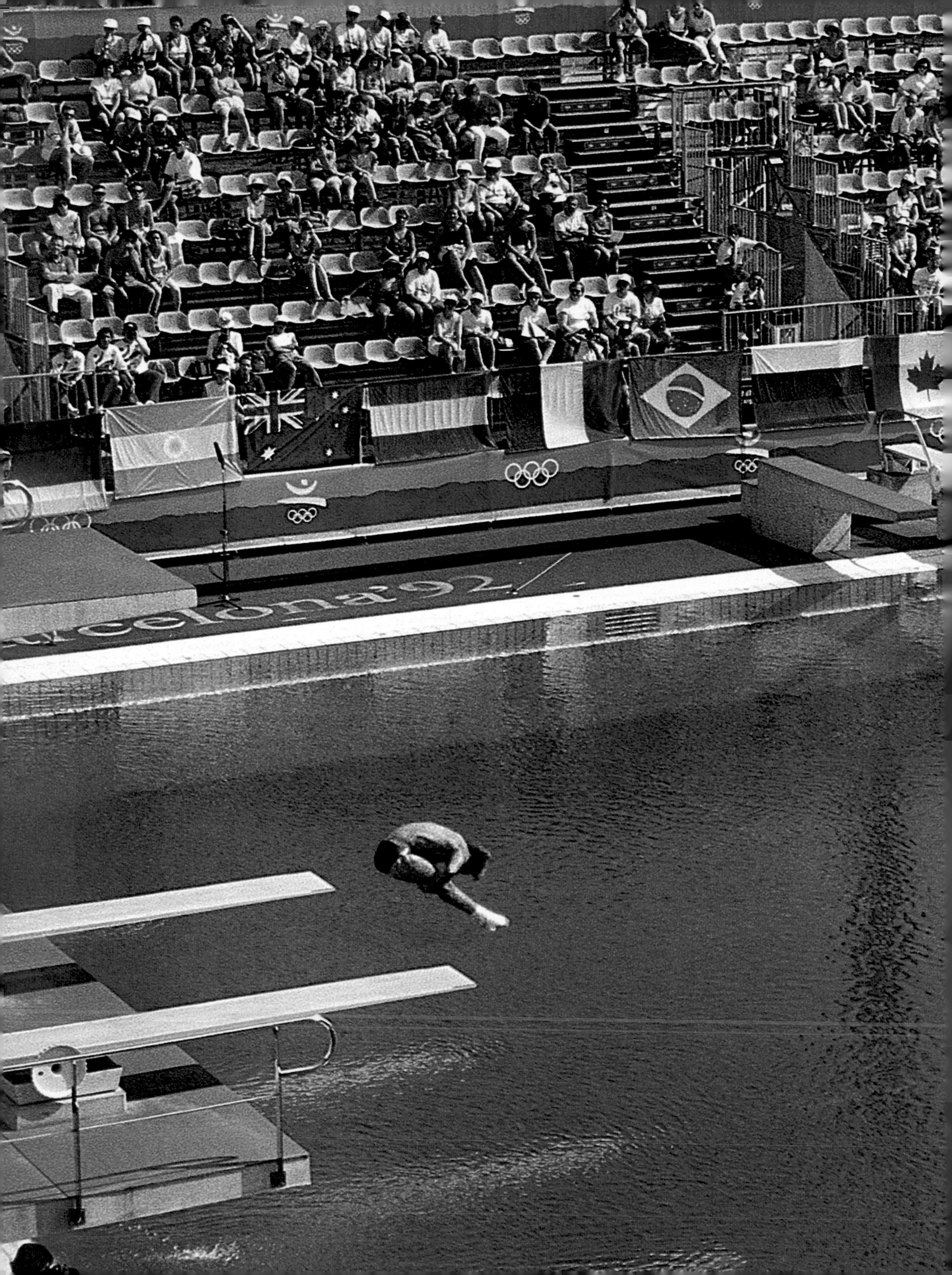
celona'92

Measurement

Theme: That's Entertainment!

Use the Data

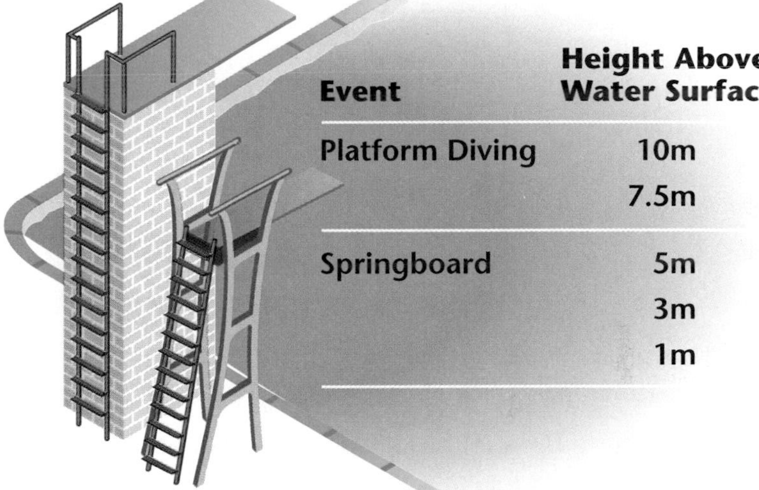

Event	Height Above Water Surface
Platform Diving	10m
	7.5m
Springboard	5m
	3m
	1m

- How far above the water is the diver in the highest springboard event?
- What is the height of the highest dive event?
- Which unit do you think is used to measure the amount of water in the pool?

What You Will Learn

In this chapter you will learn how to

- estimate and measure length.
- estimate and measure weight, mass, and capacity.
- estimate and measure temperature.
- convert units of measure.
- use strategies to solve problems.

Objective: Review estimating and measuring length in customary units.

Explore Customary Length

Learn

Math Word

length the measurement of distance between two endpoints

You can use an inch ruler, yardstick, or tape measure to explore measuring lengths in customary units.

Customary Units of Length
1 foot (ft) = 12 inches (in.)
1 yard (yd) = 3 feet (ft)
1 mile (mi) = 1,760 yards (yd)
1 mile (mi) = 5,280 feet (ft)

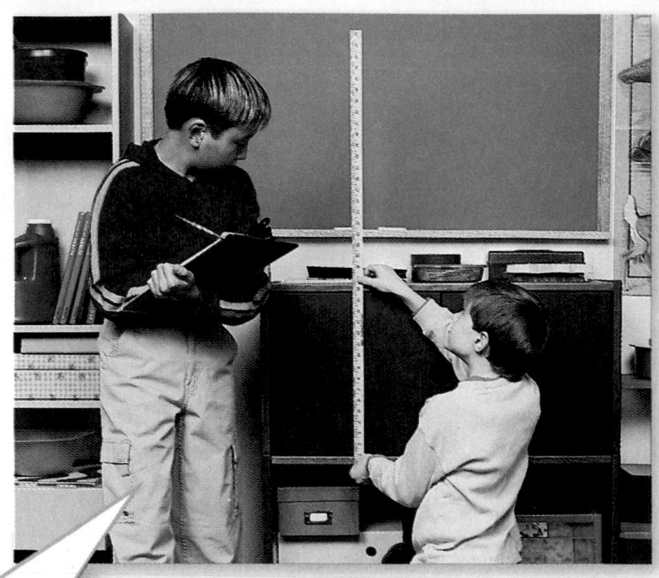

Work Together

You Will Need
- **inch ruler**
- **yardstick**
- **tape measure**

- Use a ruler to measure classroom objects: bulletin board, desk, eraser, marker, paper clip, chalkboard, and notebook. Remember that any measurement is an estimate.
  - Choose the appropriate unit of **length**.
  - Estimate the lengths.
  - Record your work in a table.

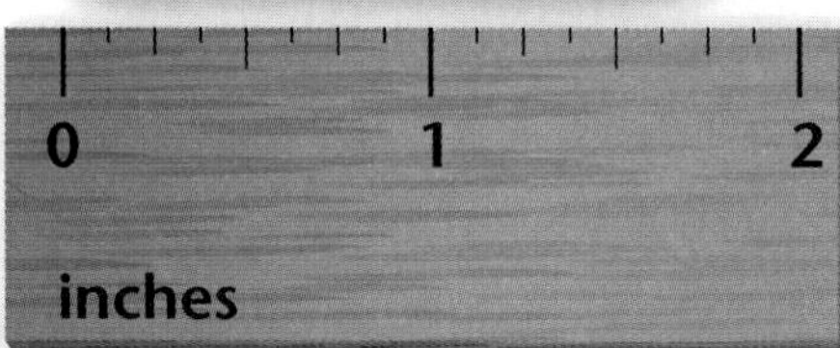

Object	Estimate	Actual Measurement

- To find a more exact measurement, measure to the nearest half inch, quarter inch, and eighth inch.
- Choose other objects in the classroom to measure. Choose which unit you will use to measure. Compare estimates and measurements with other students.

Make Connections

You can use inches, feet, yards, or miles to measure length.

Object	Measuring Tool and Unit
Tablecloth 	Use a ruler to measure the width to the nearest inch or fraction of an inch.
Banner 	Use a tape measure to measure the length to the nearest foot or yard.
Distance you drive to school. 	Use the odometer in a car to measure distance to the nearest mile.

Try It **Estimate and then measure. Tell what unit and tool you use.**

1. Your stride
2. Your height
3. Your arm span

How do you choose the appropriate unit of measure to use?

Practice **Estimate and then measure. Tell what unit and tool you use.**

4. The length of your foot
5. The height of a door
6. Your arm reach

Choose the best estimate.

7. The height of a room
   A. 3 yards C. 3 inches
   B. 3 feet D. 3 miles
8. The distance around a desktop
   F. 84 miles H. 84 feet
   G. 84 inches J. 84 yards
9. The width of the classroom
   A. 30 yards C. 30 feet
   B. 30 miles D. 30 inches
10. **Analyze:** When would you choose to measure to the nearest quarter inch or eighth inch?

Extra Practice, page 395

Objective: Review estimating and measuring capacity and weight in customary units.

9•2

Customary Capacity and Weight

Learn

Jorge is pouring juice to serve after the school play. How much juice is he pouring into the bowl?

Math Words

capacity a measure of dry or liquid volume of a container

weight a measurement that tells how heavy an object is

Customary Units of Capacity

8 fluid ounces (fl oz) = 1 cup (c)
2 cups (c) = 1 pint (pt)
2 pints (pt) = 1 quart (qt)
4 quarts (qt) = 1 gallon (gal)

Example 1

You can use different containers to measure **capacity**.

1 fluid ounce (fl oz) | 1 cup (c) | 1 pint (pt) | 1 quart (qt) | 1 gallon (gal)

Jorge pours 4 quarts, or 1 gallon, of punch into the bowl.

Jorge cuts 16 strawberries to put into the punch. What unit can be used to measure how much he uses?

Customary Units of Weight

16 ounces (oz) = 1 pound (lb)

2,000 pounds (lb) = 1 ton (T)

Example 2

You can use **weight** to find how heavy an object is.

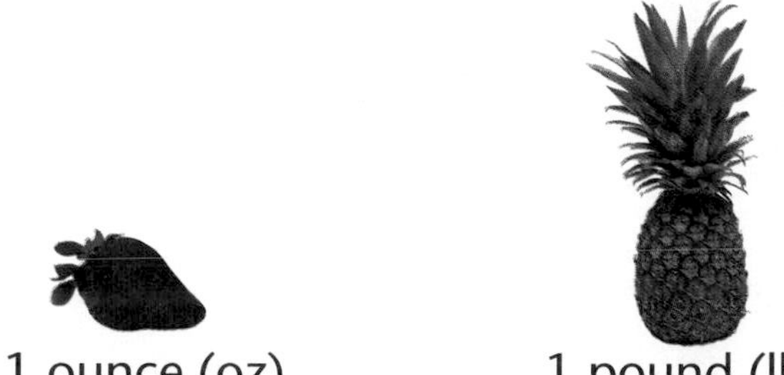

1 ounce (oz) 1 pound (lb)

1 ton (T)

Jorge put 16 ounces or 1 pound of strawberries into the punch.

Try It **Which object holds more? Estimate the capacity for each.**

1. A thermos or a bathtub
2. A soup spoon or a mug
3. A drinking glass or a waste basket
4. A swimming pool or a frying pan

Which object weighs more? Estimate the weight for each.

5. A math book or an eraser
6. An elephant or a horse
7. A paper napkin or a lunchbox
8. Eyeglasses or a shoe

Choose the correct estimate.

9. 

A. 8 c C. 8 pt
B. 8 qt D. 8 fl oz

10. 

F. 22 oz H. 22 T
G. 22 lb J. 2 lb

11. 

A. 3 gal C. 3 pt
B. 30 c D. 30 qt

Which is more reasonable for the weight of a bag of apples—1 pound or 1 ounce? How do you know?

Practice

Which object holds more? Estimate the capacity for each.

12. A bicycle drink bottle or a mop bucket

13. A laundry basket or a cereal bowl

Which object weighs more? Estimate the weight of each.

14. A backpack or a piece of chalk

15. An apple or a watermelon

Choose the best estimate.

16.

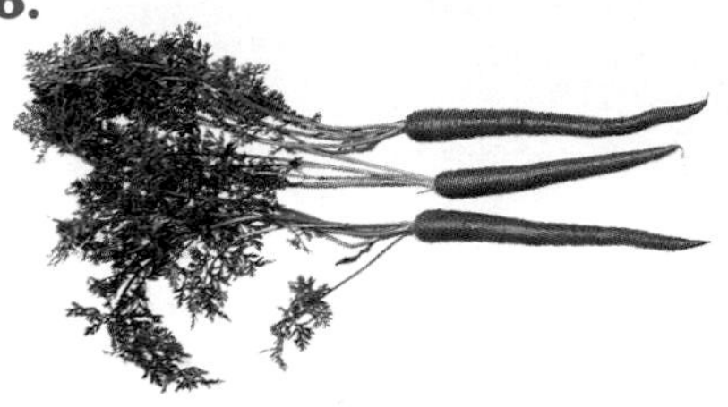

A. 4 oz C. 4 T
B. 4 lb D. 44 lb

17.

F. 1 gal H. 1 pt
G. 1 qt J. 1 c

18.

A. 40 oz C. 40 lb
B. 4 T D. 4 oz

19.

F. 12 oz H. 12 lb
G. 12 T J. 4 lb

20.

A. 800 gal C. 800 qt
B. 800 pt D. 800 c

21.

F. 10 pt H. 10 c
G. 10 qt J. 10 gal

22.

Fiona wrote this estimate in her notebook. Tell what mistake she made. Explain how to correct it.

Problem Solving

23. Jorge says that he needs only 8 ounces each of pineapple juice and orange juice to make punch for a large group. Do you think this is reasonable? Why or why not?

24. **Compare:** Do all quart containers have to have the same shape? Why or why not?

Use data from the chart for problems 25–27.

25. Jorge needs enough turkey to feed the guests at the party after the play. Does he buy a 9-pound turkey or a 9-ounce turkey?

26. All of the guests will be seated in equal groups at tables of 4 and 6. Draw a diagram to show how the guests will be seated.

27. Jorge wants to make enough punch so that everyone at the party can have at least 2 cups. How many cups is this altogether?

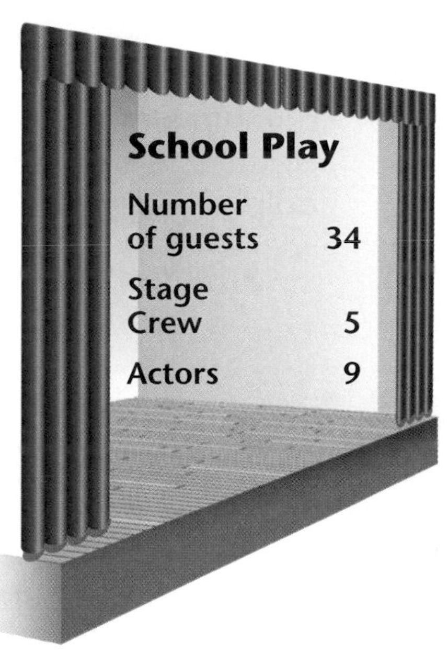

School Play

Number of guests	34
Stage Crew	5
Actors	9

28. **Collect Data:** Plan a party for your class. Find out what kinds of cold cuts the other students like. Use the data to make a shopping list, including the weight of each meat.

29. **Logical Reasoning:** It is about 4 inches high, weighs about 1 pound, and there are about 2 cups in it. People like to eat what is in it on cold days. What is it?

★**30.** How would you balance the second scale? (Hint: You can mix the containers.)

Spiral Review and Test Prep

31. 549 + 913 **32.** 6,047 − 2,972 **33.** 468 × 34 **34.** $75\overline{)303}$

Choose the correct answer.

35. Erica starts rehearsal at 11:20 A.M. and rehearses for 2 hours 25 minutes. What time does rehearsal end?

A. 12:20 P.M. **C.** 1:45 A.M.
B. 12:45 A.M. **D.** 1:45 P.M.

36. There are 128 ounces of punch and 16 guests. If each person gets the same amount, how much punch does each get?

F. 4 ounces **H.** 16 ounces
G. 8 ounces **J.** 112 ounces

Extra Practice, page 395

Objective: Explore simple conversions of length, capacity, and weight.

9·3 Convert Customary Units

Algebra & functions

Learn

Mrs. Tallchief and her grandchildren watch a dolphin jump into the air. How many inches does the dolphin jump?

Example 1

You can multiply when converting, or changing, larger units to smaller units. Convert 6 feet to inches.

Multiply to find how many inches the dolphin jumps.

6 feet = ▮ inches ⟶ $6 \times 12 = 72$ ⟶ 6 feet = 72 inches

Think: 12 inches = 1 foot. Since inches are smaller than feet, you need to multiply to get a greater number.

The dolphin jumps 72 inches.

How many feet is 48 inches?

Example 2

You can divide when converting smaller units to larger units.

Convert 48 inches to feet.

Divide to find how many feet.

48 inches = ▮ feet $48 \div 12 = 4$ 48 inches = 4 feet

Think: 1 foot = 12 inches. Since feet are larger than inches, you need to divide to get a lesser number.

The hoop is 4 feet wide.

Another Example

A killer whale is 4 yards long. How many feet is that?

Convert 4 yards to feet.

4 yards = ▮ feet $4 \times 3 = 12$ 4 yards = 12 feet

Think: 1 yard = 3 feet

How many pounds is 560 ounces?

Example 3

Convert 560 ounces to pounds.

Divide to find how many pounds.	560 ounces = ■ pounds 560 ÷ 16 = 35 560 ounces = 35 pounds	**Think:** 16 ounces = 1 pound

A baby dolphin weighs 35 pounds.

How many quarts is 10 gallons?

Example 4

Convert 10 gallons to quarts.

Multiply to find how many quarts.

10 gallons = ■ quarts ⟶ 10 × 4 = 40 ⟶ 10 gallons = 40 quarts

Think: 1 gallon = 4 quarts

There are 40 quarts in the tank.

More Examples

A baby blue whale can weigh up to 2 tons. How many pounds is this?

Convert 2 tons to pounds.

2 tons = ■ pounds

2 × 2,000 = 4,000

Think: 1 ton = 2,000 pounds

2 tons = 4,000 pounds

B

A fish bowl holds 64 fluid ounces. How many cups is this?

Convert 64 fluid ounces to cups.

64 fluid ounces = ■ cups

64 ÷ 8 = 8

Think: 8 fluid ounces = 1 cup

64 fluid ounces = 8 cups

Try It **Write the number that makes each sentence true.**

1. 4 ft = ■ in. **2.** 12 ft = ■ yd **3.** 4 mi = ■ yd **4.** 7 yd = ■ ft

How do you rename a larger unit of measure to a smaller unit of measure? a smaller unit to a larger unit?

Practice Write the number that makes each sentence true.

5. 2 gal = ■ qt
6. 4 pt = ■ qt
7. 4 lb = ■ oz
8. 80 oz = ■ lb
9. 12 yd = ■ ft
10. ■ pt = 8 qt
11. 9 ft = ■ in.
12. 96 in. = ■ ft
13. 1 gal = ■ pt
14. 300 ft = ■ yd
15. 4 qt = ■ pt
16. 3,520 yd = ■ mi
17. 4 pt = ■ c
18. ■ qt = 2 gal
19. 12 c = ■ qt
20. 120 in. = ■ ft
21. 15 ft = ■ yd
22. ■ qt = 8 pt
23. 160 oz = ■ lb
24. ■ pt = 16 c
25. 32 oz = ■ lb
26. 4 lb = ■ oz
27. 5 mi = ■ yd
28. 4 T = ■ lb

★29. 1 lb 3 oz = ■ oz
★30. 2 T 500 lb = ■ lb
★31. 4 qt 2 pt = ■ c
★32. 5 qt = ■ gal ■ qt
★33. 38 oz = ■ lb ■ oz
★34. 15 qt = ■ gal ■ qt

Copy and complete the table.

35.

Gallons	$\frac{1}{2}$	1	2	3
Quarts	2	4	■	■
Pints	■	■	16	24
Cups	8	■	■	■

36.

Ounces	32	■	■
Pounds	2	3	4

37. 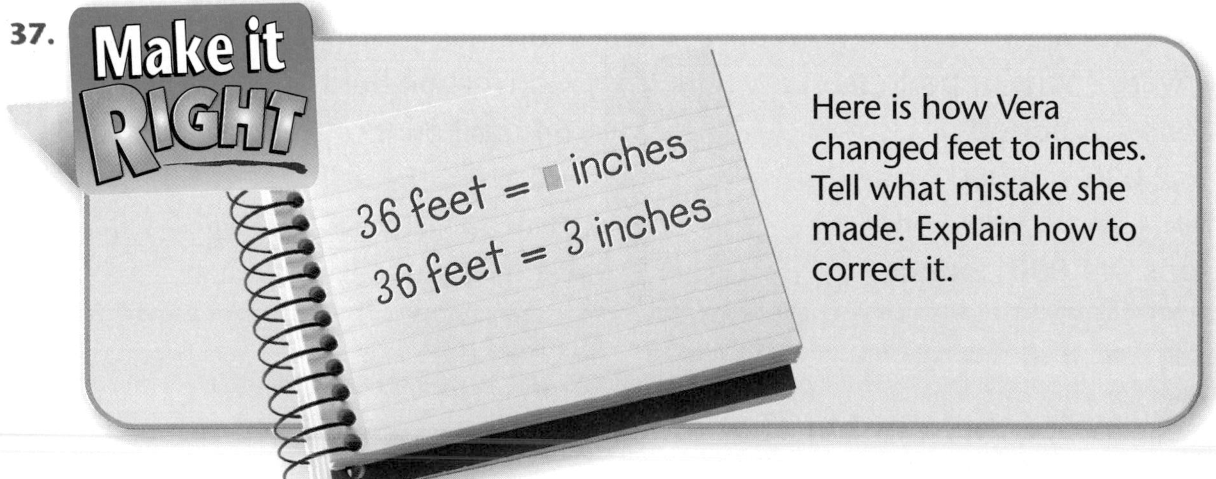

Here is how Vera changed feet to inches. Tell what mistake she made. Explain how to correct it.

Problem Solving

38. Each day a manatee eats 50 pounds of plants. How many ounces does the manatee eat?

39. The manatees live in a 100,000 gallon tank. How many quarts of water are in the tank?

40. There are enough seats for 2,204 people to see the show at an aquarium. Each row has 58 seats. How many rows are there?

41. A sea lion tank is 75 feet long. Suppose a sea lion swims back and forth in the tank 4 times. How many yards does the sea lion swim?

42. A dolphin trainer stands on a diving board that is 5 yards high. How many feet high is the diving board?

43. Two orcas about the same size weigh 12 tons altogether. About how many pounds does each orca weigh?

44. **Logical Reasoning:** A dolphin weighs more than a harbor seal but less than an elephant seal. An elephant seal does not weigh more than an orca. Write the animals in order from greatest to least by weight.

★45. Year-round passes for adults at an aquarium are \$74.95. Mrs. Tallchief pays \$194.85 for herself and her two grandchildren. How much is a ticket for one child?

46. An aquarium has 623 passes to distribute equally to 5 schools. How many passes are distributed to each school? How many are left?

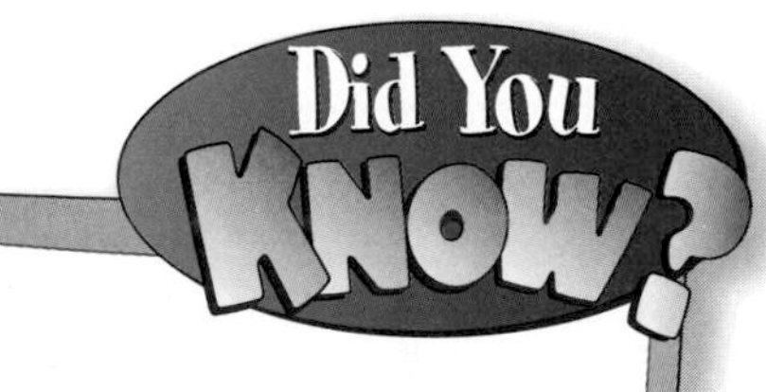

The largest animal that has ever lived is the blue whale. Lengths up to 100 feet have been recorded, with weights estimated at more than 100 tons. Some whales, such as the sperm whale, are capable of diving to depths of more than 3,300 feet.

Use data from *Did You Know?* for problems 47–50.

47. **Science:** About how many pounds might a blue whale weigh?

48. **Science:** About how many inches long is a blue whale?

49. **Science:** About how many yards might a sperm whale dive?

50. **Analyze:** Marcy says a blue whale can dive more than a mile deep. Is this reasonable?

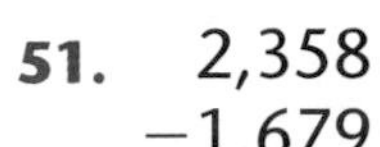

Spiral Review and Test Prep

51. $\begin{array}{r} 2{,}358 \\ -1{,}679 \\ \hline \end{array}$

52. $73\overline{)658}$

53. $\begin{array}{r} 509 \\ \times \quad 4 \\ \hline \end{array}$

54. $\begin{array}{r} 4{,}762 \\ \times \quad 7 \\ \hline \end{array}$

55. $\begin{array}{r} 42{,}538 \\ +65{,}987 \\ \hline \end{array}$

Choose the correct answer.

56. Find the average for this set of numbers.

47 15 83 58 67

A. 54   C. 265
B. 58   D. Not Here

57. The sea lion show begins at 2:20 and ends at 3:05. How long is the show?

F. 25 minutes   H. 45 minutes
G. 35 minutes   J. 65 minutes

Extra Practice, page 395

Objective: Compare and contrast information to check for reasonableness.

9•4

Problem Solving: Reading for Math

Check for Reasonableness

Sounds of Bolivia

Read Bolivian musicians like Randy play many different instruments. The quena, or flute, is 13 inches long. Is it reasonable to say that it is about 2 feet long?

Math in ACTION

Randy Ferrufino plays in a Bolivian musical group that celebrates his family's heritage.

READING SKILL ▶ **Compare and Contrast**

When you compare and contrast, you look at two or more items. You look for ways they are alike or different.

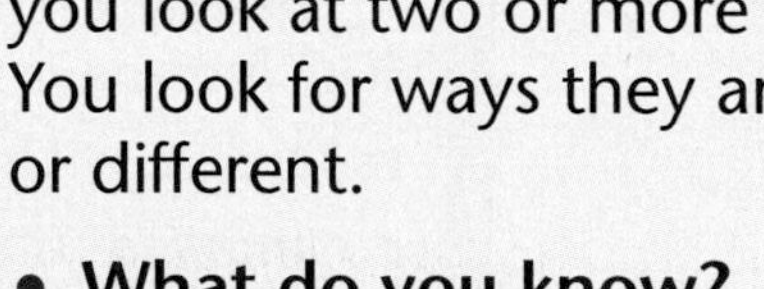

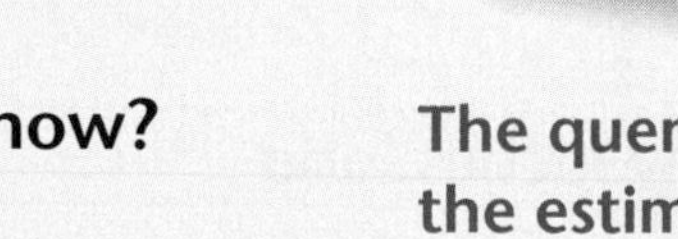

- **What do you know?** The quena is 13 inches long the estimation is about 2 feet
- **What do you need to find?** If the estimation is reasonable

MATH SKILL ▶ **Check for Reasonableness**

You can decide if an answer is reasonable by comparing it with the information given and with what you know.

Plan You need to check the estimate. You can use your knowledge of customary units of length.

Solve Compare the estimate with what you know.

The quena measures 13 inches. 12 inches = 1 foot

The estimate is not reasonable because 13 is closer to 12 than it is to 24.

Look Back Does your answer make sense?

Sum it Up! What would be a reasonable estimate of the length of the quena?

Practice Solve. Explain your answer.

1. Liz's drum is 60 inches long. She says that it is 5 feet. Is her statement reasonable?

2. The distance from Sal's home to the library is 2,640 feet. Sal calculates this distance as 7,920 yards. Is her calculation reasonable?

Use data from the list for problems 3–7.

3. Liz says the distance from the kitchen to the living room is 1 foot. Is her statement reasonable?

4. Liz says the distance from home to school is 5,280 yards. Is her statement reasonable?

5. Bob says Liz travels 14 feet from her house to the bus stop. Is his statement reasonable?

6. Liz calculates that the distance from her kitchen to her living room is 108 inches. Is her calculation reasonable?

7. Liz estimates she travels 10,000 feet going to and from school. Is this estimate reasonable?

8. Dixie's bedroom is 12 feet long. She says that her room is more than 200 inches long. Is her statement reasonable?

Spiral Review and Test Prep

Choose the correct answer.

Tami is 62 inches tall. She says that she is more than 5 feet tall.

9. Which statement is true?
   - **A.** Tami is 6 feet tall.
   - **B.** Tami's height is 2 yards.
   - **C.** Tami is 62 inches tall.

10. Her statement is reasonable because ____
    - **F.** 62 inches = 5 feet.
    - **G.** 62 inches < 5 feet.
    - **H.** 62 inches > 5 feet.

Extra Practice, page 396

Check Your Progress A

Choose the best estimate. **(pages 364–369)**

1. 

   F. 3 c   H. 3 gal
   G. 3 pt   J. 1 c

2. 

   A. 8 oz   C. 8 T
   B. 8 lb   D. 4 oz

3. 

   F. 1 c   H. 1 qt
   G. 1 pt   J. 1 gal

4. The length of a table
   A. 2 in.   C. 2 yd
   B. 2 ft   D. 2 mi

5. The distance across a lawn
   F. 50 in.   H. 5 mi
   G. 50 ft   J. 50 mi

6. The distance from one city to another
   A. 10 in.   C. 10 yd
   B. 10 ft   D. 10 mi

Write the number that makes each sentence true. **(page 370)**

7. 5 ft = ■ in.
8. 18 ft = ■ yd
9. 3 mi = ■ yd
10. 5 yd = ■ ft
11. 2 gal = ■ pt
12. 8 pt = ■ qt
13. 5 lb = ■ oz
14. 176 oz = ■ lb
15. 24 c = ■ pt
16. 5 gal = ■ qt

Solve. **(pages 364–375)**

17. Mrs. Johnson is making punch for a party. Does she use 4 quarts of juice or 4 fluid ounces of juice?

18. Mrs. Johnson hangs 24 feet of streamers across the room. How many inches is that?

19. Glenda is planning a party for 100 people. She decides to order 4 pounds of cold cuts. Is this reasonable? Explain why or why not.

20. **Explain** how you decide if the weight of an object should be given in ounces, pounds, or tons.

Additional activities at
www.mhschool.com/math

Use a Table to Convert Measurements

Derrick has three containers of milk. The containers hold 4 cups, 16 cups, and 20 cups of milk. How many quarts of milk does each container hold?

You can use a spreadsheet table to convert measurements.

Click on the table key.

Label the columns Cups and Quarts.

In the column labeled Cups, enter the capacities in cups of the three containers.

In the column labeled Quarts, enter a formula to convert cups to quarts.

How many quarts of milk does each container hold?

Use the computer to convert each measurement to quarts.

1. 12 cups
2. 24 cups
3. 32 cups
4. 8 cups

Solve.

5. Shauna has 8 yards of ribbon. How many inches of ribbon does she have?
6. A turkey weighs 12 pounds. How many ounces does the turkey weigh?
7. Kyle drinks 16 fluid ounces of water. How many cups does he drink?
8. A truck weighs 2 tons. How many pounds does the truck weigh?
9. **Analyze:** How does using the table help you convert cups to quarts?

For more practice, use Math Traveler™.

Objective: Review estimating and measuring length in metric units.

9·5 Explore Metric Length

Learn

You can use a centimeter ruler, meter stick, or tape measure to explore measuring lengths in metric units.

Metric Units of Length

10 millimeters (mm) = 1 centimeter (cm)

10 centimeters = 1 decimeter (dm)

100 centimeters = 1 meter (m)

1,000 meters = 1 kilometer (km)

Work Together

You Will Need
- centimeter ruler
- meter stick
- tape measure

▶ *Use a ruler to measure classroom objects.*
- Choose the appropriate unit.
- Estimate the lengths to the nearest unit.
- Record your work in a table.

Object	Estimate	Actual Measurement

▶ *To find a more exact measurement, measure those objects you measured in centimeters in millimeters. Record your work.*

▶ *Compare estimates and measures with other students.*

Make Connections

You can use millimeters, centimeters, meters, and kilometers to measure length.

Object		Measuring Tool and Unit
Stamp	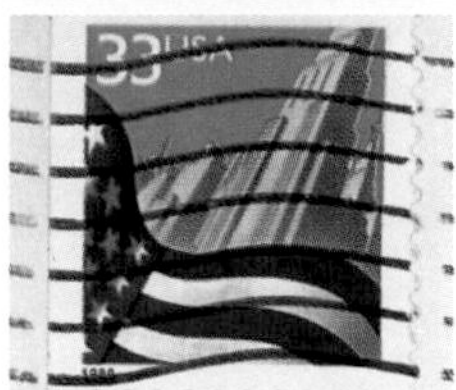	Use a ruler to measure the width to the nearest millimeter.
Invitation		Use a ruler to measure the length to the nearest decimeter.
Mailbox		Use a tape measure or meter stick to measure the height to the nearest meter.
Distance between cities		Use the odometer in the truck to measure the distance to the nearest kilometer.

Try It **Estimate and then measure. Tell what unit and tool you use.**

1. Your shoe
2. Your desk
3. The chalkboard

Sum it Up When you measure the length of an object, how do you decide which unit and measuring tool to use?

Practice **Choose the best estimate.**

4. The length of your classroom
   7 m or 7 dm
5. The width of a piece of construction paper
   8 m or 8 dm
6. The distance to the art supply store
   21 cm or 21 m
7. **Analyze:** Claire says her room is 3 dm wide. Is this reasonable? Why or why not?

Extra Practice, page 396

Objective: Review measuring capacity in metric units.

Metric Capacity and Mass

Learn

Margie and Linda both buy a sports drink during the movie. How much did they buy between the two of them?

Math Word

mass amount of matter an object has

Metric Units of Capacity

1,000 milliliters = 1 liter (L)

Example 1

Capacity is a measure of the dry or liquid volume of a container.

1 milliliter (mL)

1 liter (L)

20 liters (L)

1 liter (L) = 1,000 milliliters (mL)

Margie and Linda have 2 liters of liquid.

Another Example

An aquarium has 50 liters of water.

The snack bar clerk opens a bag of peanuts. The bag has a mass of 1 kilogram. How many grams is that?

Metric Units of Mass

1,000 grams (g) = 1 kilogram (kg)

Example 2

Mass measures the amount of matter that makes up an object.

1 gram (g)

1 kilogram (kg)

The bag has a mass of 1,000 grams.

Estimate and then measure the capacity of each object. Order the objects from least to greatest capacity.

1. A juice box
2. A spoon
3. A can of soda

Estimate and then measure the mass of each object. Order the objects from least to greatest mass.

4. A granola bar
5. A pair of sneakers
6. A sticker

Choose the correct estimate.

7. 

2 kg or 2 g

8. 

3 g or 3 kg

9. 

500 L or 500 mL

What would you measure using liters? using kilograms?

Estimate and then measure the capacity of each object. Order the objects from least to greatest capacity.

10. A thermos **11.** A sink **12.** A small paper cup

Estimate and then measure the mass of each object. Order the objects from least to greatest mass.

13. Your math book **14.** An apple **15.** A box of chalk

Choose the best estimate.

16. 

500 g or 500 kg

17. 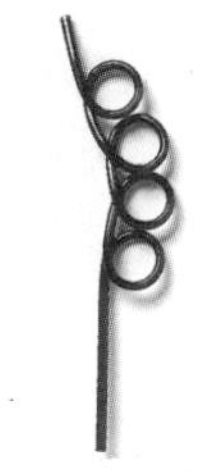

2 mL or 2 L

18. 

2 g or 2 kg

19. 

5 kg or 5 g

20. 

1 L or 1 mL

21. 

2 g or 2 kg

Algebra & functions **Copy and complete the tables.**

22.

Liter	1	2	■	4	■
Milliliter	1,000	■	3,000	■	■

23.

Kilogram	■	2	3	4	5
Gram	1,000	■	■	■	■

24. What pattern do you see in these tables for milliliters and grams?

25. 

A fourth-grade teacher tells the class to write their height and mass using metric measures. This is what Lisa wrote. Tell what mistake she made and show how to correct it.

Problem Solving

26. A shipment of boxes of raisins arrives at the theater. Does the shipment have a mass of 15 kilograms or 15 grams?

Cartoons are filmed in frames. A sound cartoon film is usually projected at a speed of 24 frames each second. The first full-length animated feature film lasted 82 minutes. It had about 447,000 photographed drawings.

Use data from *Did You Know?* for problems 27–30.

27. **Time:** About how many frames would a cartoon have in one minute of film?
28. About how many drawings appeared in each minute of this film?
29. Carly starts to watch a video of the first animated feature film at 2:00 P.M. What time does the movie end?

★30. **What if** a cartoon is 12 minutes long? How many frames would be in the film?

31. Robin works at the snack counter in the movie theater. She needs to fill a tank with juice. Does she order 20 liters of juice or 20 milliliters of juice?
32. A movie reel has 36 frames in each meter of film. How many frames would there be in one kilometer of film?
33. A movie theater serves about 200 liters of soda each hour. How many liters are served during a $2\frac{1}{2}$ hour film?
34. **Collect data** from different food packages. Record a variety of metric mass and capacity measurements. Convert these measures to other metric units.

Spiral Review and Test Prep

35. $45 + 56$

36. $156 - 29$

37. 78×7

38. $504 \div 6$

39. $264 + 9$

40. $457 + 919$

41. $13{,}765 - 367$

42. 415×36

43. $3{,}048 \div 24$

44. 519×56

Choose the correct answer.

45. Darren spends \$4.15 on a book and \$3.79 on pens. He has \$6.28 left. How much money did he start with?

    A. \$1.66 **C.** \$14.12
    B. \$7.94 **D.** \$14.22

46. Brandon spends \$13.16 for 4 videos. How much was each video?

    F. \$3.25 **H.** \$4.29
    G. \$3.29 **J.** Not Here

Extra Practice, page 396

Objective: Review simple metric conversions.

9·7 Convert Metric Units

Algebra & functions

Learn

Kevin and his sister Allie go to the circus. They see a high-wire act that is 20 meters above the ground. How many centimeters is that?

Example 1

Convert 20 meters to centimeters.

Multiply to find how many centimeters above the ground the act is.

20 meters = ▮ centimeters   20 × 100 = 2,000   20 m = 2,000 cm

Think:
1 m = 100 cm
Since meters are larger than centimeters, multiply to get a greater number.

The high-wire act is 2,000 centimeters above the ground.

A bag of elephant food weighs 5,000 grams. How many kilograms is that?

Example 2

Convert 5,000 grams to kilograms.

Divide to find how many kilograms.

5,000 grams = ▮ kilograms
5,000 ÷ 1,000 = 5
5,000 grams = 5 kilograms

Think:
1,000 g = 1 kg
Since kilograms are larger than grams, divide to get a lesser number.

The food weighs 5 kilograms.

An elephant drinks 3 liters of water. How many milliliters is that?

Example 3

Convert liters to milliliters.

Multiply to find how many milliliters.

3 liters = ▮ milliliters
3 × 1,000 = 3,000
3 liters = 3,000 milliliters

Think: 1 liter = 1,000 milliliters

Try It **Write the number that makes each sentence true.**

1. 30 mm = ▮ cm
2. 3,000 mL = ▮ L
3. 7 kg = ▮ g

Explain how to convert 20 millimeters to centimeters.

Practice

Write the number that makes each sentence true.

4. 8 m = ■ cm
5. 10 L = ■ mL
6. 4 km = ■ m
7. 9 kg = ■ g
8. 10 m = ■ dm
9. 8,000 mL = ■ L
10. 100 mm = ■ cm
11. 30,000 mL = ■ L
12. 12 dm = ■ cm
13. ■ mL = 40 L
14. 200 mm = ■ cm
15. 20 kg = ■ g
16. 15 m = ■ dm
17. 10,000 g = ■ kg
18. ■ m = 15,000 cm

Compare. Write >, <, or =.

19. 50 cm ■ 5 m
20. 200 cm ■ 2 m
21. 1,500 mL ■ 1 L
22. 4,000 g ■ 4 kg
23. 60 L ■ 600 mL
24. 40 cm ■ 4 dm

Problem Solving

25. The animal trainer feeds the circus lions 8 kilograms and 400 grams of food each day. How many grams of food do the lions eat?
26. **Science:** A tiger has a mass of 227 kilograms. A horse has a mass of 568 kilograms. Which has the greater mass? How much greater?
27. The circus tent holds 57 rows of seats. Each row contains 134 seats. How many people can the circus tent seat?
28. **Health:** A person should drink about 2,400 milliliters of water each day. About how many liters is that?
29. **Generalize:** How does the decimal point move when you convert from larger metric units to smaller metric units? from smaller metric units to larger metric units?

Spiral Review and Test Prep

30. $\begin{array}{r} 345 \\ +987 \\ \hline \end{array}$
31. $\begin{array}{r} 97 \\ -43 \\ \hline \end{array}$
32. $\begin{array}{r} 59 \\ \times\ 9 \\ \hline \end{array}$
33. 828 ÷ 9
34. $\begin{array}{r} 7{,}987 \\ +\ \ 498 \\ \hline \end{array}$

Choose the correct answer.

35. There are 35 cartons containing 325 bags of peanuts each. How many bags of peanuts is that?
    - A. 11,050
    - B. 11,375
    - C. 11,700
    - D. Not Here
36. A stadium seats 6,808 people. If each row contains 74 seats, how many rows are there?
    - F. 91
    - G. 92
    - H. 93
    - J. 94

Extra Practice, page 397

Objective: Use logical reasoning to solve problems.

Problem Solving: Strategy
Logical Reasoning

Read **Read the problem carefully.**

A carnival worker needs to fill an animal's drinking tank with 6 gallons of water. He has a 5-gallon pail and an 8-gallon pail. How can he use these pails to get exactly 6 gallons of water into the tank?

- **What do you know?** **6 gallons water needed, 5-gallon and 8-gallon pails available**
- **What do you need to find?** **How to get exactly 6 gallons of water into the tank.**

Plan Use the difference in the capacities of the two pails to find how to fill the tank. You can use a table to keep track.

Solve How much water in each:

- Fill 8-gallon pail.
- Pour water from 8-gallon pail to fill 5-gallon pail.
- Pour 3 gallons left in the 8-gallon pail into the tank.

8 gal	5 gal	Tank
8 gal	0	0
3 gal	5 gal	0
0	5 gal	3 gal

Now you can empty the water from the 5-gallon pail and repeat steps 1 through 3 to get 6 gallons in the tank.

Look Back Why is making a table helpful for solving this problem?

How do you use logical reasoning to solve the problem?

Practice Use logical reasoning to solve each problem.

1. Dan needs to put 6 cups of sea salt into the saltwater tank. He has a 7-cup container and a 5-cup container. How can he use the containers to measure 6 cups?

2. Beth went to visit the aquarium 2 days before Brittany. Mark went to the aquarium 4 days after Beth. The children went to the aquarium on Monday, Wednesday, and Friday. When did each person go to the aquarium?

3. The freshwater fish tank has 3 times as many fish as the saltwater fish tank. The saltwater tank has 2 more fish than the turtle tank has turtles, which has twice as many turtles as the frog tank. If the frog tank has 4 frogs, how many animals do the other tanks have?

4. The shark tank gets food 15 minutes before the amphibian tank. The amphibian tank gets food 5 minutes after the turtle tank. The turtle tank gets food 20 minutes before the penguins. The penguins get food at 10:30. What time do the other tanks get food?

Mixed Strategy Review

5. The giant ocean tank at the Monterey Bay Aquarium in California holds about 750,000 gallons of water. The tank at the New England Aquarium holds almost 190,000 gallons of water. Does the tank at the Monterey Bay Aquarium have about 2 times, 4 times, or 6 times the capacity of the tank at the New England Aquarium?

6. The tank at the New England aquarium is 23 feet deep. How many inches deep is that?

CHOOSE A STRATEGY

- Logical Reasoning
- Draw a Picture
- Make a Graph
- Act It Out
- Make a Table or List
- Find a Pattern
- Guess and Check
- Write a Number Sentence
- Work Backward
- Solve a Simpler Problem

7. **Create a problem** that can be solved using logical reasoning. Solve it. Ask others to solve it.

8. The aquarium has a collection of 156 tropical fish. They want to expand their collection to 500 fish. If the aquarium gets 8 new fish a week, how long will it be before they reach their goal?

★9. The Ryan family pays a total of $24.80 to see the exhibit at the aquarium. Two adult tickets cost $8.95 each. There are 3 children in the family. How much does one child's ticket cost?

★10. There are 64 fish in the tropical fish exhibit. There are twice as many red fish as there are blue fish. If 40 fish are colors other than red and blue, how many are red? How many are blue?

Problem Solving

Extra Practice, page 397

Objective: Measure temperature in degrees Fahrenheit and degrees Celsius.

Temperature

The temperature of the ice surface must be 32°F or colder for the ice to remain frozen.

Learn

Math Words

temperature a measurement that tells how hot or cold something is

degrees Fahrenheit a unit for measuring temperature

degrees Celsius a unit for measuring temperature

The temperature at the surface of the skating rink must be cold enough to keep the ice from melting. **Temperature** can be measured in **degrees Fahrenheit** (°F) and **degrees Celsius** (°C). What is the warmest possible surface temperature in degrees Celsius?

Example

Compare the scale on the two thermometers.

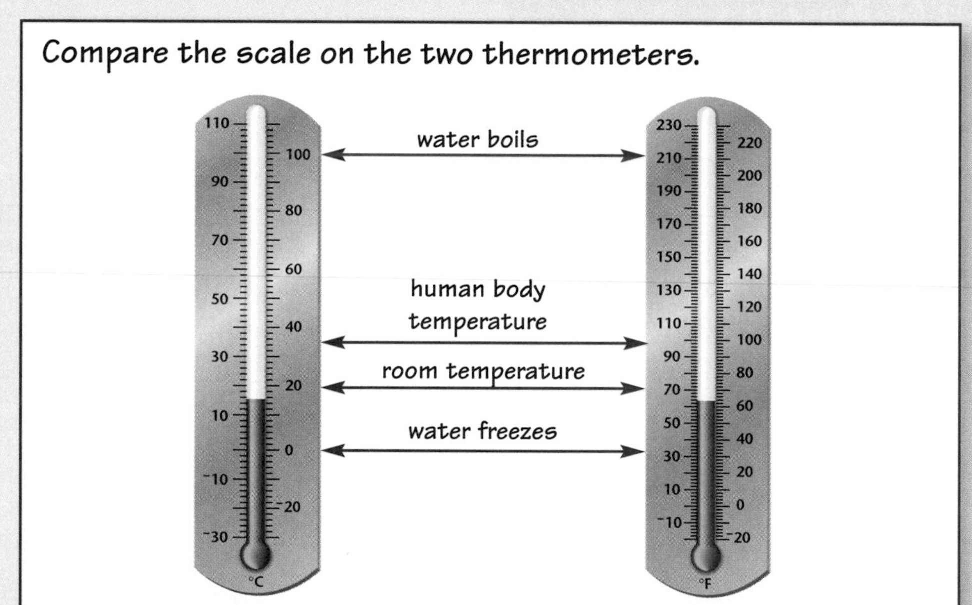

The temperature at the ice surface must be at most 0° C.

Try It

Give a reasonable temperature for each.

1. A glass of ice
2. The classroom temperature
3. The temperature in the sunlight

Which temperature is warmer, 32°F or 32°C? Explain how you know.

Practice **Give a reasonable temperature for each.**

4. A cup of soup
5. The temperature in a refrigerator
6. The temperature in the shade

Choose the best estimate.

7. To make a snowman
30°F or 30°C
8. To swim in the ocean
27°F or 27°C
9. To go hiking
68°F or 68°C
10. To wear heavy winter gear
⁻2°F or 20°C
11. To wear shorts and a t-shirt
87°F or 87°C
12. To wear a parka
20°F or 20°C

Problem Solving

13. Suppose it is 64°F during the daytime. It drops 12° degrees during the night. What temperature is it during the night?
14. Suppose it is 0°C during the day. It drops 5 degrees during the night. What temperature is it during the night?
★15. Suppose it is 6°C during the day. It drops 16 degrees during the night. What temperature is it during the night?

Use data from the line graph for problems 16–18.

Average Daily Temperature

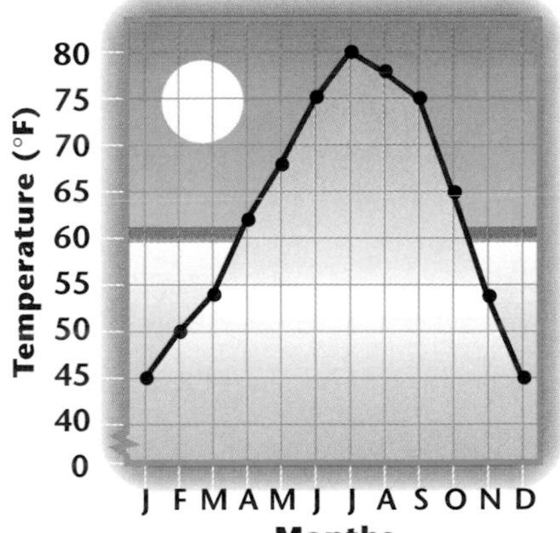

16. During which month is the average temperature the highest?
17. How much does the average temperature drop from September through December?
18. Marsha wants to go swimming in July. Is this reasonable? Why?

Spiral Review and Test Prep

Write the number that makes each sentence true.

19. 5 ft = ▮ in.
20. 21 ft = ▮ yd
21. 3 lb = ▮ oz
22. 96 oz = ▮ lb

Choose the correct answer.

23. Ron wants to measure the length of his room for new carpet. Which unit of measure should he use?
A. Inches
B. Yards
C. Miles
D. Not Here

24. Find the missing number.
$63 \div n = 9$
F. 54
G. 12
H. 8
J. 7

Extra Practice, page 397

Objective: Analyze data and make decisions.

Problem Solving: Application

Decision Making

Mr. Martin invites 11 of his son Jason's friends to a soccer party. The party will start at 12:30 P.M. and end at 4:30 P.M. Mr. Martin plans to serve drinks, sandwiches, and fruit snacks.

What should Mr. Martin buy for the party?

hero (turkey, salami, and cheese)	$12 a foot (minimum 1 yard)
turkey	$4.99 for each pound
salami	$3.99 for each pound
cheese	$2.29 for each pound
rolls	$0.35 each

Fran's Fruits and Vegetables

apples	$1.25 for each pound
grapes	$1.50 for each pound
pineapple	$2.75 each
cantaloupe	$1.50 each

Bob's Beverages

apple juice (pt)	$1.39
orange juice (qt)	$2.99
spring water (qt)	$1.85

Read for Understanding

1. How many children will be at the party?
2. How long is the party planned for?
3. What is the cost of a yard-long hero?
4. How much will it cost to buy a pound of apples?
5. How much will it cost to buy one roll for each child at the party?
6. What is the total cost for one bottle of each drink?

Make Decisions

7. If a yard-long hero is cut into pieces that are 3 inches long, how many pieces are in the hero?
8. If each child eats 2 pieces, how many feet of hero will Mr. Martin need to order? How much would this hero cost?
9. Mr. Martin thinks that 6 ounces of cold cuts is enough for one sandwich. If each child has 2 sandwiches, how many pounds of cold cuts will he need to buy?
10. If Mr. Martin buys an equal amount of cheese, turkey, and salami, how many pounds of each should he buy? How much would it cost altogether?
11. What is the total cost of making sandwiches?
12. Mr. Martin estimates that each child at the party will drink 3 cups of beverages. How many cups will he need for the party?
13. A punch recipe calls for 2 quarts of orange juice, 4 quarts of spring water, and 4 quarts of apple juice. How many cups of punch will the recipe make?
14. A punch bowl holds a gallon of punch. How many times will Mr. Martin be able to fill the bowl?
15. Mr. Martin thinks that one cantaloupe will be enough for 4 children. How many cantaloupes will he need? How much will he spend?
16. A fruit salad recipe calls for 24 ounces of grapes, $\frac{1}{2}$ pound of apples, and a pineapple. How much will it cost to make the fruit salad?
17. What else should you consider before deciding what to buy?

What is your recommendation for the soccer party? Explain.

Problem Solving

Objective: Apply measurement to investigate science concepts.

Problem Solving: Math and Science

Which color heats up most?

You Will Need
- **3 thermometers**
- **black paper**
- **white paper**
- **aluminum foil**
- **paper clips or rubber bands (optional)**

You and a friend are playing outside on a hot, sunny day. You are wearing white shorts and a white T-shirt, but your friend is wearing a black shirt and shorts. Which one of you will feel the heat the most?

Different colors react to heat differently. In this activity, you will decide which color heats up most.

Hypothesize

Rank white, black, and shiny silver in terms of which will heat the most, middle, and least.

Procedure

1. Record the starting temperature of each thermometer.
2. Fold the black and white papers and aluminum foil into a small pocket.
3. Insert the bulb of the thermometer into the pocket. You must be able to read the thermometer.
4. Use a paper clip or rubber band to secure the thermometer in the pocket.
5. Place all three thermometers in a sunny window or under a lamp. Wait 10 minutes. Without moving the thermometers, read the temperatures.

Data

Copy and complete the chart to record your observations.

	Start Temperature	Finish Temperature	Difference
Black			
White			
Foil			

White objects are white because they reflect all colors of light. Black objects are black because they absorb all colors of light.

Conclude and Apply

- Calculate the difference between each start and finish temperature.
- Which color heated up the most? the least?
- Use subtraction to find how many more degrees the hottest thermometer changed than the coolest. Is this a big difference?
- Why did you have to put the thermometers in a sunny window or under the lamp?
- If you were playing outside on a sunny day, which color clothing would you like to wear? Why?
- Explain the results of the activity in terms of the reflection or absorption of light.

Going Further

1. Repeat the activity to compare red, blue, and yellow paper.
2. Use paper or aluminum foil to design a hat that would keep you cool in the sun.
3. Describe an outfit you would wear to absorb the most heat. What kind of outfit would absorb the least amount of heat?
4. What color should you paint a container that you want to stay cool? warm?

Check Your Progress B

Choose the best estimate. **(pages 378–383)**

1. 

   A. 2 mL **C.** 2 L
   B. 20 mL **D.** 20 L

2. 

   F. 3 g **H.** 3 kg
   G. 30 g **J.** 30 kg

3. 

   A. 1 g **C.** 10 kg
   B. 100 g **D.** 1 kg

4. The length of carpet
   A. 3 mm **C.** 3 dm
   B. 3 cm **D.** 3 m

5. The distance across town
   F. 5 mm **H.** 5 m
   G. 5 cm **J.** 5 km

6. The capacity of a washing machine
   A. 6 mL **C.** 60 mL
   B. 6 L **D.** 60 L

Write the number that makes each sentence true. **(page 384)**

7. 3 m = ▮ mm
8. 4 m = ▮ dm
9. 30 kg = ▮ g
10. 6 km = ▮ m
11. 2,000 g = ▮ kg
12. 4,000 mL = ▮ L
13. 7 L = ▮ mL
14. 54,000 mm = ▮ m
15. 37 L = ▮ mL
16. 16 kg = ▮ g

Solve. **(pages 386–389)**

17. A fin whale can grow up to 80 feet long. Which is about the same length: a car, a school gym, or a highway?
18. Scotty measures a 2-meter distance around the frame of a picture. How many centimeters is that?
19. The temperature outside is 20°C. Should you wear a sweater or T-shirt?

20. **Explain** how you decide if the length of an object should be given in centimeters, meters, or kilometers.

Additional activities at
www.mhschool.com/math

Extra Practice

Explore Customary Length (pages 364–365)

Choose the best estimate.

1. The length of a fork
   A. 7 yd C. 7 ft
   B. 17 ft D. 7 in.
2. The height of a table
   F. 1 yd H. 3 in.
   G. 1 ft J. 1 in.
3. The height of a room
   A. 15 ft C. 5 mi
   B. 15 yd D. 15 mi

Customary Capacity and Weight (pages 366–369)

Choose the best estimate.

1. 
   A. 2 fl oz C. 2 pt
   B. 2 c D. 2 gal
2. 
   F. 5 fl oz H. 5 qt
   G. 5 pt J. 5 gal
3. 
   A. 20 gal C. 20 pt
   B. 20 qt D. 20 fl oz
4. 
   F. 8 oz H. 8 lb
   G. 80 oz J. 80 lb
5. 
   A. 6 oz C. 6 lb
   B. 60 oz D. 60 lb
6. 
   F. 2 oz H. 2 lb
   G. 200 oz J. 20 lb

Convert Customary Units (pages 370–373)

Write the number that makes each sentence true.

1. 24 yd = ■ ft
2. 132 in. = ■ ft
3. 600 ft = ■ yd
4. 5,280 ft = ■ mi
5. 6 pt = ■ c
6. ■ qt = 3 gal
7. 12 c = ■ qt
8. 10 qt = ■ pt
9. 2 gal = ■ pt
10. 4 qt = ■ c
11. ■ pt = 9 qt
12. ■ pt = 14 c
13. 48 oz = ■ lb
14. 10 lb = ■ oz
15. 176 oz = ■ lb
16. 5 T = ■ lb

Solve.

17. The length of a blue whale measures about 33 yards. The length of a finback whale measures about 84 feet. Which of these whales is longer? How much longer?

Extra Practice

Problem Solving: Reading for Math Check for Reasonableness (pages 374–375)

Tell if each situation is reasonable or unreasonable. Make changes to make it reasonable.

1. Shawna runs the 400-kilometer race for the track team.
2. Cecily's younger sister weighs 43 ounces.
3. Jason fills a 6-liter punch bowl for a party.

Explore Metric Length (pages 378–379)

Choose the best estimate.

1. The length of a whale
   A. 30 km C. 30 dm
   B. 30 m D. 30 mm
2. The depth of a pool
   F. 2 km H. 2 dm
   G. 2 m J. 2 mm
3. The length of a goldfish
   A. 8 mm C. 8 dm
   B. 8 cm D. 8 km

Solve.

4. A pitcher contains 1 liter of juice. John uses the pitcher to fill three 100-milliliter containers and two 250-milliliter containers. Can he fill another 250-milliliter container? Explain.
5. Kristy's thermos bottle holds 3 liters. How many milliliters can she put in the bottle if there are already 1,250 milliliters of water in the bottle?

Metric Capacity and Mass (pages 380–383)

Choose the best estimate.

1. 

   40 mL or 40 L
2. 

   100 cm or 100 mm
3. 

   25 g or 25 kg
4. The span of a hand
   A. 17 mm C. 17m
   B. 17 cm D. 17 km
5. The mass of a granola bar
   F. 150 mg H. 150 g
   G. 150 cg J. 150 kg
6. The capacity of a tea cup
   A. 250 mL C. 250 L
   B. 250 cL D. 250 kL

Extra Practice

Convert Metric Units (pages 384–385)

Write the number that makes each sentence true.

1. 11 m = ▮ cm
2. 15 L = ▮ mL
3. 6 kg = ▮ g
4. 3 kg = ▮ g
5. 9 m = ▮ dm
6. 12,000 mL = ▮ L
7. 400 mm = ▮ cm
8. 16,000 mL = ▮ L
9. 21 dm = ▮ cm
10. ▮ mL = 50 L
11. 350 mm = ▮ cm
12. 18 kg = ▮ g
13. 18 m = ▮ dm
14. 34,000 g = ▮ kg
15. ▮ m = 12,000 cm
16. 111,000 g = ▮ kg
17. ▮ mg = 14 kg
18. 3,000 L = ▮ kL

Problem Solving: Strategy Logical Reasoning (pages 386–387)

Use logical reasoning to solve.

1. What is the easiest way to fill a pitcher with 1-gallon of liquid using only a 3-gallon container and a 4-gallon container?
2. Juan needs to measure 6 quarts of water. He has a 5-quart jar and a 7-quart jar. How can he use them to measure 6 quarts?
3. Members of a fourth grade class are waiting in line to get into the aquarium. Raúl is behind Angelo and in front of Pete. Kate is in front of Angelo. Brianne is last in line. Raúl is in what place in the line?
4. Millie, Alan, and Kate are wearing souvenir T-shirts from their visit to the aquarium. One is blue, one is white, and one is red. Neither girl is wearing a blue shirt. Millie wishes she had a red shirt. What color is each child wearing?

Temperature: Fahrenheit and Celsius (pages 388–389)

Choose the most appropriate temperature.

1. To go for a sleigh ride
   25°F or 25°C
2. To go to the beach
   83°F or 83°C
3. To wear a sweater
   58°F or 58°C

Solve.

4. Caroline said, "If the temperature is 95 degrees tomorrow, we will swim in the lake." Did she mean 95°C or 95°F? Explain.

Chapter Study Guide

Language and Math

Math Words
capacity
degrees Celsius
degrees Fahrenheit
length
mass
weight
temperature

Complete. Use a word from the list.

1. Water freezes at zero ____.
2. A kilogram is a metric unit of ____.
3. You can use pounds to measure ____.
4. You can measure the ____ of a spoon in fluid ounces.
5. The ____ of a stamp can be measured in millimeters.

Estimate and measure length in customary or metric units. (pages 364–365, 378–379)

Example
Which is the best estimate?

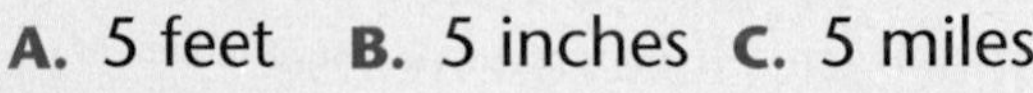

A. 5 feet **B.** 5 inches **C.** 5 miles

Solution
Five inches is too short. Five miles is too long. Five feet is the most reasonable estimate.

Choose the best estimate.

6. Pencil length
   A. 8 in.
   B. 8 ft
7. Hallway length
   F. 20 ft
   G. 20 in.
8. Movie screen height
   A. 12 m
   B. 12 dm
9. CD case width
   F. 140 cm
   G. 140 mm

Estimate and measure weight, mass, or capacity in customary or metric units. (pages 366–369, 380–383)

Example
Which is the best estimate?

A. 6 fl oz **B.** 6 c **C.** 6 pt

Solution
Six cups and 6 pints are too much. Six fluid ounces is reasonable.

Choose the best estimate.

10. Capacity of a soup bowl
    A. 25 mL
    B. 25 L
    C. 250 mL
11. Capacity of a sink
    F. 12 qt
    G. 12 pt
    H. 12 fl oz
12. Mass of a loaf of bread
    A. 500 g
    B. 50 g
    C. 5 kg
13. Weight of a bicycle
    F. 25 T
    G. 25 lb
    H. 25 oz

Estimate and measure temperature in degrees Fahrenheit or degrees Celsius. (pages 388–389)

Example
When would you wear only a shirt and jeans outside?
22°F or 22°C

Solution
22°C.
22°F is below freezing.

Choose the most appropriate temp.

14. When you wear shorts
    85°F or 85°C

15. When you go skiing
    6°C or 50°F

16. When you go to a picnic
    35°F or 35°C

17. When you go swimming
    27°C or 27°F

Convert units of measure. (pages 370–373, 384–385)

Example
A picnic table is 6 feet long. How many inches is that?

Solution
Multiply to change between feet and inches.
$6 \times 12 = 72$; **Think:** 1 foot = 12 inches
6 feet = 72 inches

Write the number that makes each sentence true.

18. 63 ft = ▮ yd
19. 60 cm = ▮ mm
20. 25 L = ▮ mL
21. 5 qt = ▮ c
22. 6,000 g = ▮ kg
23. 32 oz = ▮ lb

Use strategies to solve problems. (pages 374–375, 386–387)

Example
Cara performed her act 2 days after Brian. Marge did hers 4 days before Cara. The acts were performed on Monday, Wednesday, and Friday. When did each person perform?

Solution
You can use logical reasoning to solve the problem. Cara performed her act after both Brian and Marge. So, she must have performed on Friday. Since Cara performed 2 days after Brian, he must have performed on Wednesday. Marge performed on Monday.

Solve.

24. You have 3 glasses—2 fluid ounces, 5 fluid ounces, and 8 fluid ounces. What is the easiest way to fill a jar with 6 fluid ounces?

25. Renee said that the label on a box of crackers says that the mass is 453 kilograms. Is this reasonable? Explain.

Chapter Test

Choose the best estimate.

1. The length of a stage
   - A. 10 yd
   - B. 10 ft
   - C. 10 in.
   - D. 5 ft

2. The height of a television screen
   - F. 52 m
   - G. 52 dm
   - H. 52 cm
   - J. 52 km

3. The capacity of a bathtub
   - A. 40 qt
   - B. 40 gal
   - C. 40 pt
   - D. 40 c

4. The capacity of an eyedropper
   - F. 3 L
   - G. 3 mL
   - H. 30 mL
   - J. 30 L

5. The weight of a CD
   - A. 6 oz
   - B. 6 lb
   - C. 6 T
   - D. 16 lb

6. The mass of a bag of potatoes
   - F. 50 g
   - G. 50 kg
   - H. 5 kg
   - J. 5 g

Write the number that makes each sentence true.

7. 10 m = ▮ cm
8. 8 L = ▮ mL
9. 4 m = ▮ cm
10. 9 ft = ▮ in.
11. 45,000 mL = ▮ L
12. 9,000 g = ▮ kg
13. 550 mm = ▮ cm
14. 17,000 mL = ▮ L
15. 15 dm = ▮ mm
16. ▮ oz = 16 lb
17. 24 pt = ▮ gal
18. 40 kg = ▮ g
19. 3 yd = ▮ ft
20. 60,000 lb = ▮ T
21. ▮ lb = 80 oz

Solve.

22. Abdul says that the temperature outside is about 28°F and that he is going outside to swim. Is this reasonable? If not, how could you change the situation to make it reasonable?

23. Ethel wants enough cider to serve 3 cups each to 16 people. How many gallons should she buy?

24. When Carl went fishing, he threw back all of his fish that weighed less than 3 pounds. He caught fish weighing 54 ounces, 27 ounces, and 36 ounces. How many fish did he keep?

25. Jonah is 2 inches shorter than Hannah. Hannah is 3 inches taller than Joe. Chris is 4 inches taller than Joe. Who is tallest? shortest?

Performance Assessment

Your class wants to play a guessing game. Divide up into teams of three players each. The first player will describe an object in the classroom without naming it. Use as many attributes as possible to identify the size, weight, shape, and color of the object.

The other two players will be allowed two guesses apiece to name the object. Switch roles so everyone has a chance to describe an object.

Record each description and who guessed the object.

A Good Answer

- shows as many attributes as possible for an object.
- shows which player guessed correctly.

You may wish to save this work for your portfolio.

Enrichment

Relating Customary and Metric Measurement

The metric system is used in most countries of the world. The customary system is used mostly in the United States.

Comparing these systems can help you understand them better.

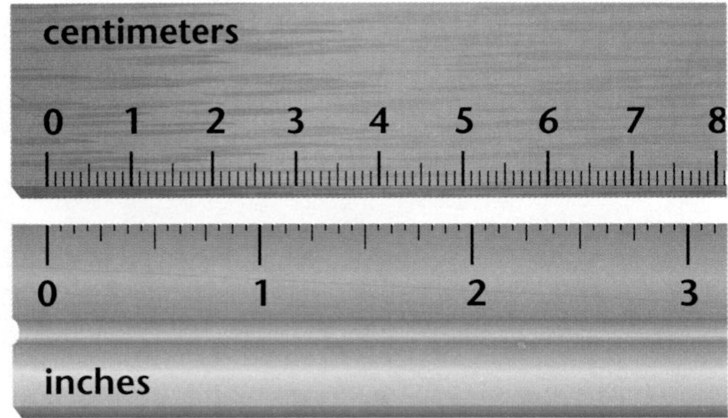

There are about 2.5 centimeters in one inch.

A liter is about one quart.

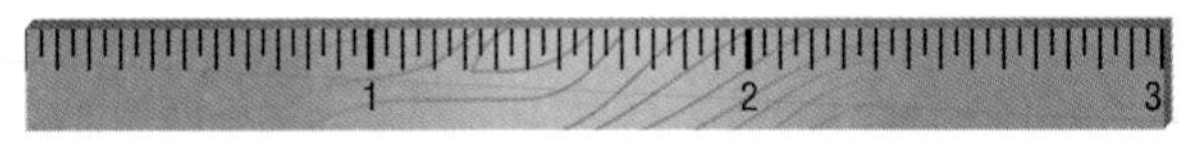

A meter is a little longer than a yard. It is about 39 inches long.

There are about 1.5 kilometers in a mile.
1 Kilogram is about 2 pounds.

Copy and complete.

1. A 2-liter bottle of juice is about ____ quarts.
2. A 4-inch pencil is about ____ centimeters.
3. A 2-meter leash is about ____ inches.
4. Candy weighing 3 kilograms is about ____ pounds.
5. A race of 3 kilometers is about ____ miles.

Test-Taking Tips

You can use the inch or centimeter side of your ruler to solve many problems. Make sure that you use the correct measurements.

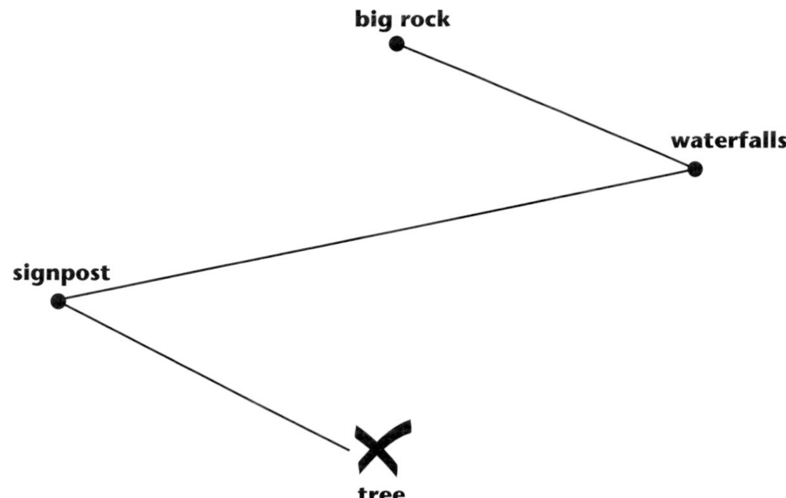

Roberta is on a treasure hunt. Use the map and measure to the nearest inch. How many inches is it from the big rock to the tree under which the treasure is buried? Use your inch ruler to answer the question.

A. 2 **C.** 6
B. 4 **D.** 8

First measure from the big rock to the waterfalls. It is 2 inches. Then measure from the waterfalls to the signpost. It is 4 inches. Next measure from the signpost to the tree. It is 2 inches. Add to find the total: $2 + 4 + 2 = 8$. The correct choice is D.

Check for Success

Before turning in a test, go back one last time to check.

- ☑ I understood and answered the questions asked.
- ☑ I checked my work for errors.
- ☑ My answers make sense.

Solve the problems. Use your centimeter ruler to choose the correct answer.

1. Janet made a bracelet out of beads. The bracelet is 6 centimeters long. Which of these could be the bracelet?

F.

G.

H.

J.

Test Prep

Spiral Review and Test Prep

Chapters 1–9

Choose the best answer.

Number Sense

1. What is 35,478 rounded to the nearest thousand?
   A. 35,000 **C.** 36,000
   B. 35,500 **D.** 40,000

2. A store has 3,028 CDs in stock. The store receives a case of CDs. The case has 14 rows of 16 CDs each. How many CDs does the store have now?
   F. 3,252 **H.** 3,058
   G. 3,232 **J.** 224

3. A family goes to dinner and to a baseball game. They spend more than $525 but less than $575. What could be the exact amount that they spend?
   A. $522.74 **C.** $578.25
   B. $568.75 **D.** $499.35

4. Gene estimated 613 ÷ 6 using the numbers 600 ÷ 6. Will his estimate be greater than or less than the exact quotient? Explain.

Measurement and Geometry

5. Ms. Jones is making dresses for a bridal party. She needs 9 yards of satin fabric. She has 5 feet of fabric. How many more feet of fabric does she need?
   A. 4 feet **C.** 23 feet
   B. 22 feet **D.** 48 feet

6. A tree is 9 meters tall. What is the height in centimeters?
   F. 90 centimeters
   G. 900 centimeters
   H. 9,000 centimeters
   J. 90,000 centimeters

7. A bottle-nosed dolphin weighs 200 kilograms. How many grams is that?
   A. 2,000 grams **C.** 200,000 grams
   B. 20,000 grams **D.** Not Here

8. Byron is making punch. He uses 5 quarts of orange juice and 6 cups of pineapple juice. How many cups of punch will there be?
   F. 11 cups **H.** 20 cups
   G. 16 cups **J.** 26 cups

Statistics, Data Analysis, and Probability

Use data from the bar graph for problems 9–12.

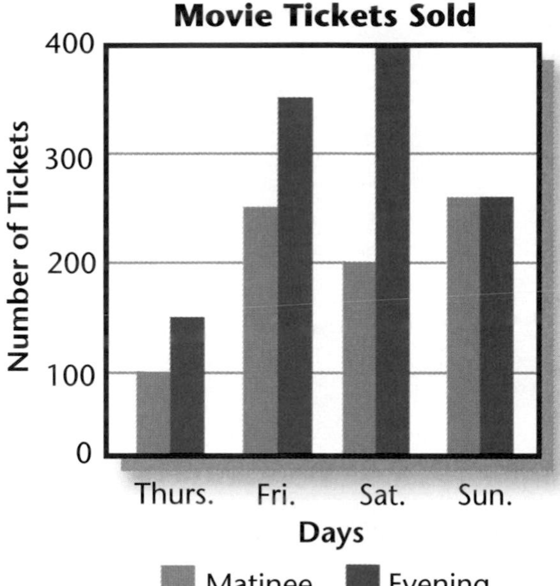

9. On what day were the same number of tickets sold for the matinee and evening shows?

A. Thursday **C.** Saturday
B. Friday **D.** Sunday

10. How many more tickets were sold for the Friday evening show than the matinee?

F. 100 **H.** 250
G. 200 **J.** 600

11. How many tickets were sold in all for Friday and Saturday matinee shows?

A. 1,200 **C.** 250
B. 450 **D.** 200

12. On which day were the most tickets sold for the evening shows?

F. Thursday **H.** Saturday
G. Friday **J.** Sunday

Algebra and Functions

13. What number completes the table?

8	9	10	11	12
96	108	120	■	144

A. 121 **C.** 130
B. 128 **D.** 132

14. What is the next dividend in the pattern?

$8 \div 4 = 2$
$12 \div 4 = 3$
$16 \div 4 = 4$
$20 \div 4 = 5$

F. 24 **H.** 6
G. 7 **J.** 4

15. Complete the number sentence.

$(3 \times 4) \times 8$ ● $288 \div 3$

A. $<$ **C.** $=$
B. $>$ **D.** Not Here

16. How much do 6 CDs cost?

1 CD costs $8.95
2 CDs cost $17.90
3 CDs cost $26.85

F. $35.80 **H.** $53.70
G. $44.75 **J.** $62.65

CHAPTER

10 Geometry

Theme: Shaping the World

Use the Data

- As you can see in the photograph, buildings often show many different shapes. What 2-dimensional shapes can you find? What 3-dimensional geometric figures do you see?

What You Will Learn

In this chapter you will learn how to

- classify 2- and 3-dimensional figures and their parts.
- classify triangles and quadrilaterals.
- identify congruent, similar, or symmetrical figures.
- use formulas to find the perimeter, area, and volume.
- use strategies to solve problems.

Objective: Identify, describe, and classify 3-dimensional objects.

10·1 3-Dimensional Figures

Learn

I. M. Pei designed the Grand Louvre, the main entrance to the Louvre Museum in Paris, France. How would you describe the shape?

Math Words

3-dimensional figure a figure in space

cone

cube

cylinder

rectangular prism

sphere

square pyramid

triangular prism

triangular pyramid

face a flat side of a 3-dimensional figure

base a face of a 3-dimensional figure, usually the one on which it stands

edge a line segment where two faces of a 3-dimensional figure meet

vertex the common point of the two sides of a polygon

net a 2-dimensional figure that can be folded to make a 3-dimensional figure

Example 1

You can describe a **3-dimensional figure** by its parts.

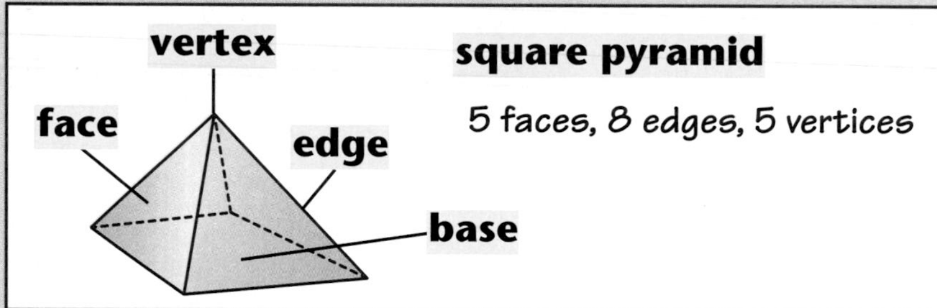

The Grand Louvre is a square pyramid with 5 faces, 8 edges, and 5 vertices.

More Examples

cube
6 faces, 12 edges, 8 vertices

triangular pyramid
4 faces, 6 edges, 4 vertices

rectangular prism
6 faces, 12 edges, 8 vertices

sphere

cone
1 circular base

triangular prism
5 faces, 9 edges, 6 vertices

cylinder
2 circular bases

You want to make a **net** for a square pyramid. What will it look like?

Example 2

Think about what a square pyramid would look like if it is "folded out."

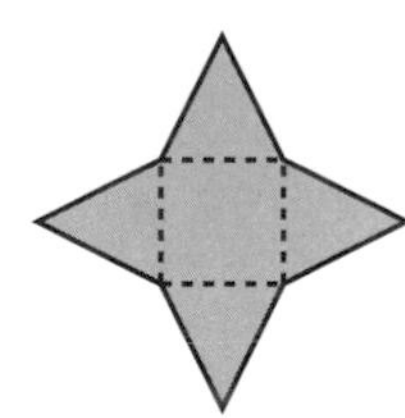

Net of square pyramid

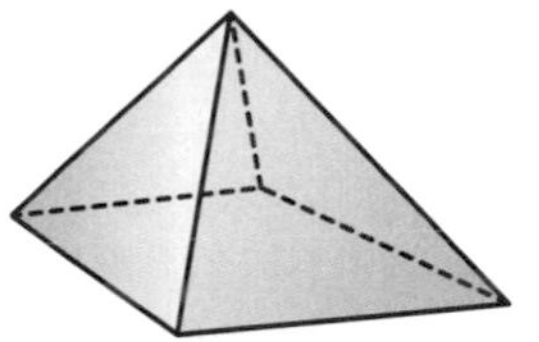

More Examples

Here are examples of nets for some other 3-dimensional figures.

cube	**rectangular prism**	**triangular prism**	**triangular pyramid**
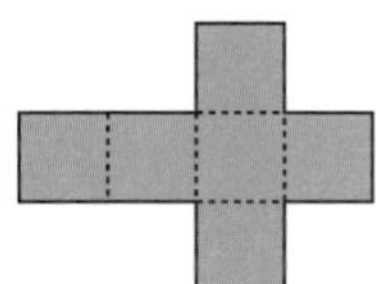	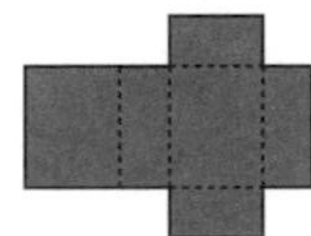	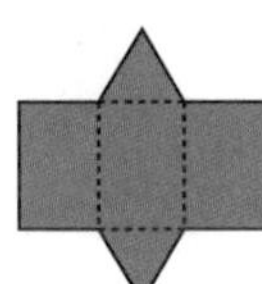	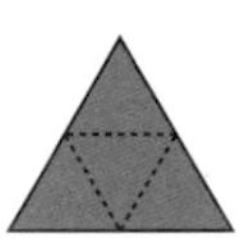

Try It **Identify the 3-dimensional figure the object looks like. Tell how many faces, edges, and vertices it has.**

1. 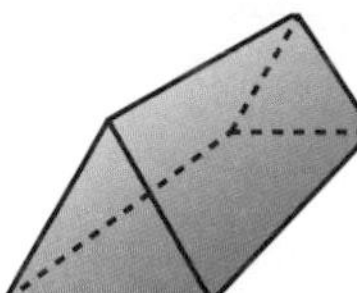

2. 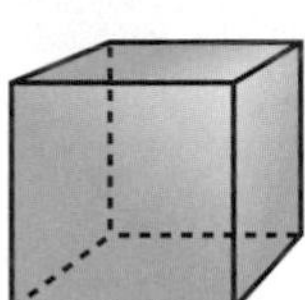

3. 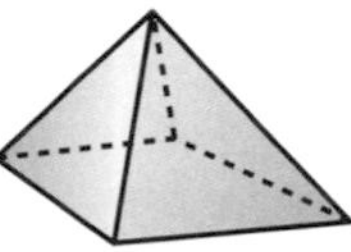

Copy and fold. Identify the 3-dimensional shape.

4. 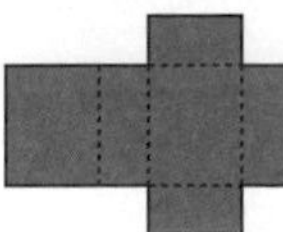

5. 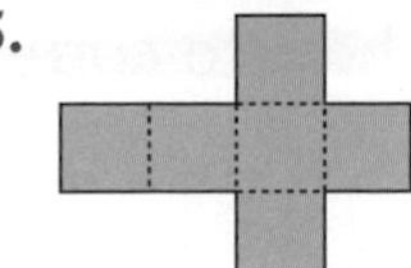

6. 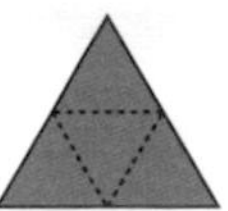

Choose one 3-dimensional figure and describe it. Ask another student to name the figure you have described.

Practice **Identify the 3-dimensional figure each object looks like. Tell how many faces or bases, edges, and vertices it has.**

7. 

8. 

9. 

Identify the figures used to construct this office building.

10. 

Copy and fold. Identify the 3-dimensional shape.

11. 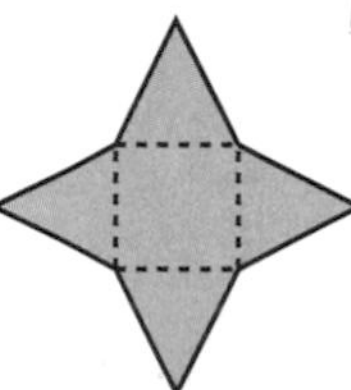

12. 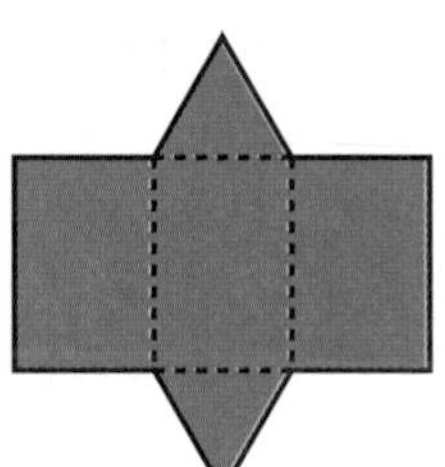

13. 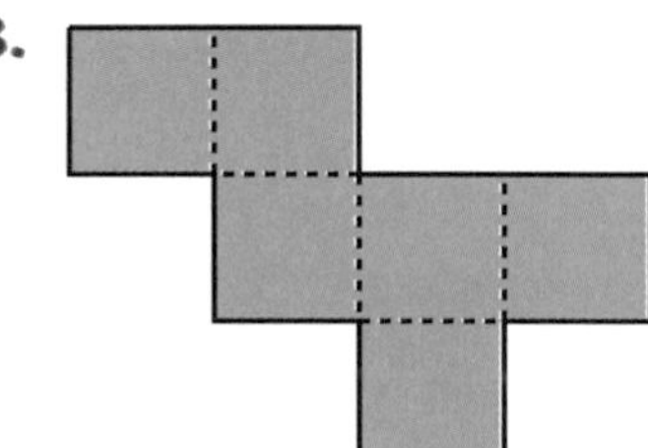

Algebra & functions **What could the next shape be?**

14. 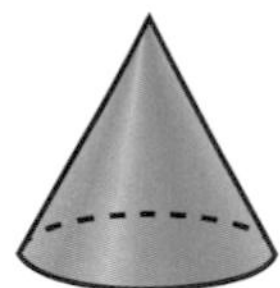  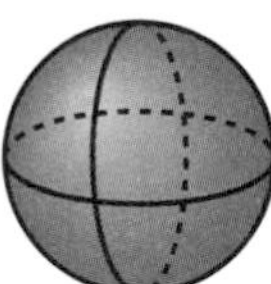 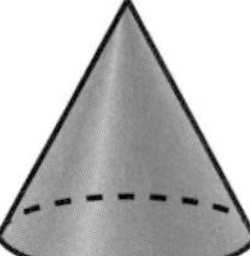  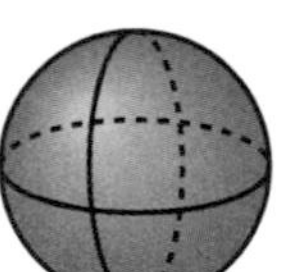 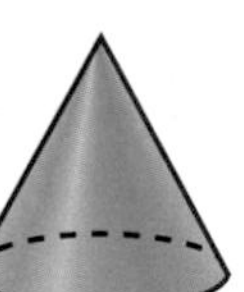

15. 

Here's how Amy drew a net for a cube. Tell what mistake she made. Explain how to correct it.

Problem Solving

16. Spatial Reasoning: Matthew made a 3-dimensional figure out of construction paper. His figure has 2 bases, but nothing else that is flat or straight. What could his figure be?

17. Summarize: What characteristics are used to classify 3-dimensional figures?

Average House in the 1930s

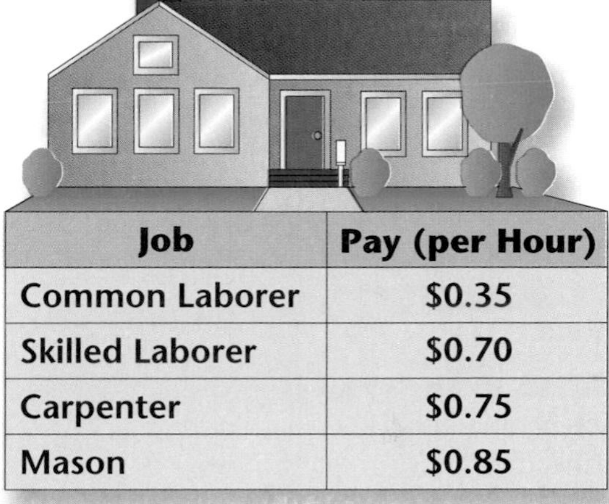

Job	Pay (per Hour)
Common Laborer	$0.35
Skilled Laborer	$0.70
Carpenter	$0.75
Mason	$0.85

Use data from the chart for problems 18–20.

18. How much did a carpenter get paid if he worked 40 hours each week for 4 weeks?

19. How much more was a mason paid than a skilled laborer for 40 hours of work?

20. A skilled laborer was paid $28 for 40 hours of work. How much would a common laborer have gotten for that same amount of work?

21. Compare and contrast a prism and a pyramid.

22. Social Studies: An architect plans to design a building based on the Egyptian monument to King Cheops. The monument stands 450 feet high and has a base with square corners and 4 sides that measure 755 feet each. It has 4 triangular faces that meet at a point. What kind of figure is this?

23. Collect Data: Look around the school and in your neighborhood. What kinds of 3-dimensional figures do you see the most. Discuss with other students why these figures are the most common. Display your results in a graph.

★24. What shape could you get if a cube is split in half?

★25. What shape shadow does a square pyramid cast?

Spiral Review and Test Prep

26. 37×46 **27.** $87 \div 6$ **28.** $346 \div 14$ **29.** $3{,}467 + 6{,}179$ **30.** $3{,}832 - 568$

Choose the correct answer.

31. How many pints are in 2 quarts?

A. 2 **C.** 6
B. 4 **D.** 8

32. Jamie wants to share 36 cookies among 12 people. What number sentence describes the number of cookies each person will get?

F. $36 - 12 = ■$ **H.** $36 \div 12 = ■$
G. $36 + 12 = ■$ **J.** $36 \times 12 = ■$

Objective: Identify, describe, and classify 2-dimensional figures and polygons.

10•2

2-Dimensional Figures and Polygons

Learn

Math Words

2-dimensional figure a figure on a plane

open a figure that does not start and end at the same point

closed a figure that starts and ends at the same point

polygon a closed 2-dimensional figure that has straight sides

side

square

rectangle

triangle

pentagon

hexagon

octagon

Pablo Picasso was a famous artist who was born in Malaga, Spain. In 1909 he painted this painting. Are there any open figures in this painting?

Brick Factory in Tortosa by Pablo Picasso

Example 1

A **2-dimensional figure** can be open or closed.

The painting has no open figures.

Picasso's painting shows examples of several different **polygons**. Identify the polygons.

Example 2

Polygons are closed 2-dimensional figures that have straight **sides**. A circle is a closed figure, but it does not have straight sides. A circle is not a polygon.

You can group polygons by the number of sides that they have.

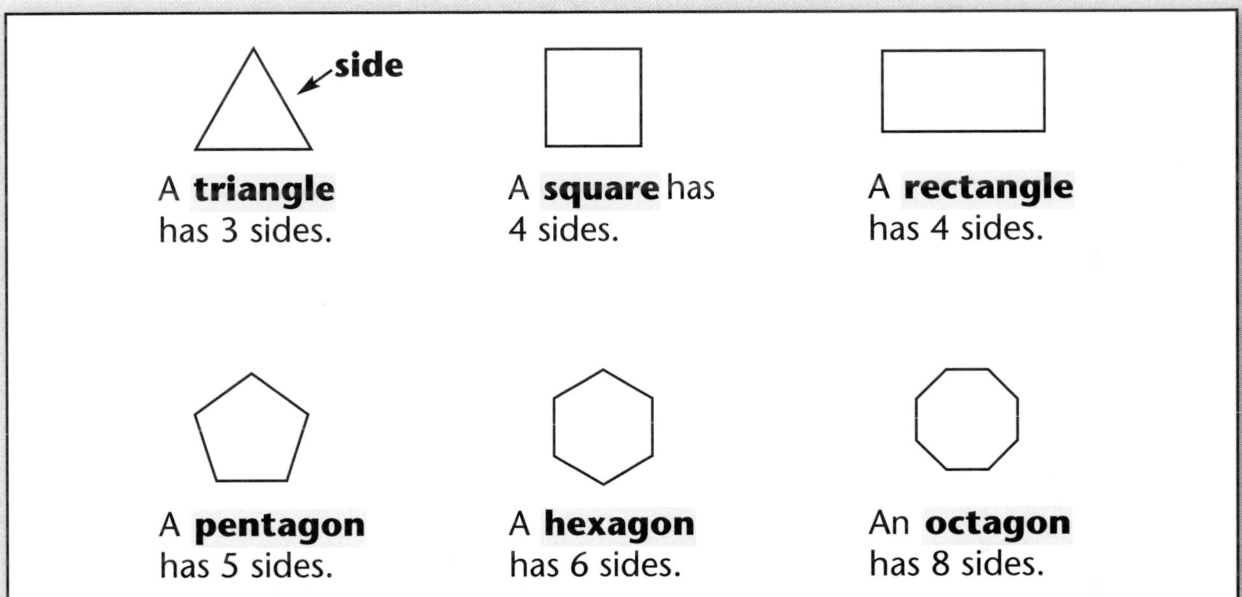

In Picasso's painting, there are triangles, rectangles, and pentagons.

Try It **Tell whether each figure is open or closed. Is it a polygon? If so, classify the figure.**

1. 

2. 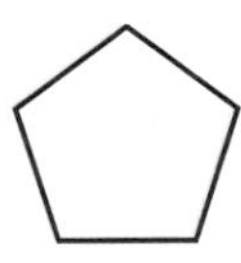

3. 

4. 

Sum it Up! Is this figure a polygon? Explain why or why not.

Practice **Tell whether each figure is open or closed. Is it a polygon? If so, classify the figure.**

5\.

6\.

7\.

8\. 

9\. 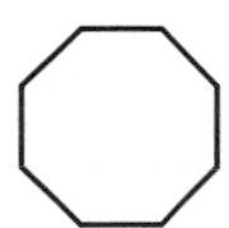

10\. 

★11. 

★12. 

Draw the figure and identify it.

13\. a 3-sided polygon

14\. a closed figure that is not a polygon

15\. a 4-sided polygon

16\. a 5-sided polygon

Algebra & functions **Locate each set of points. Then connect the points to make a geometric figure. Identify the figure.**

17\. (2, 5) (2, 7) (5, 5) (5, 7)

18\. (2, 5) (4, 5) (2, 7) (4, 7)

19\. (1, 1) (3, 1) (1, 3) (3, 3) (5, 2)

20\. (3, 1) (5, 3) (6, 1)

21\.

For homework, Ramona had to describe and name a polygon. Here is what she did. Tell what mistake she made. Explain how to correct it.

Problem Solving

22\. **Spatial Reasoning:** When you look at only one side of a 3-dimensional object, you see a triangle. What figure could you be looking at?

23\. An art exhibit has 3 rooms of paintings on display. There are 27 paintings in each room. How many paintings are on display altogether?

Use data from the picture for problems 24–25.

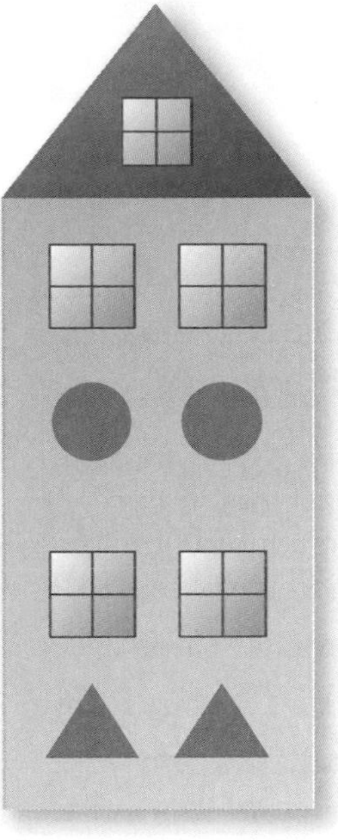

24. How many triangles are in the building? rectangles? squares? circles?

★**25.** How many polygons are in the building? Which figure is not a polygon?

26. Name a polygon you could make by putting two triangles together. Draw and label the figure.

27. Name a polygon you could make by putting two squares together. Draw and label the figure.

★**28.** Make a drawing that includes many different 2-dimensional figures. Describe the figures in as many ways as you can.

29. **Explain** whether or not all closed figures are polygons.

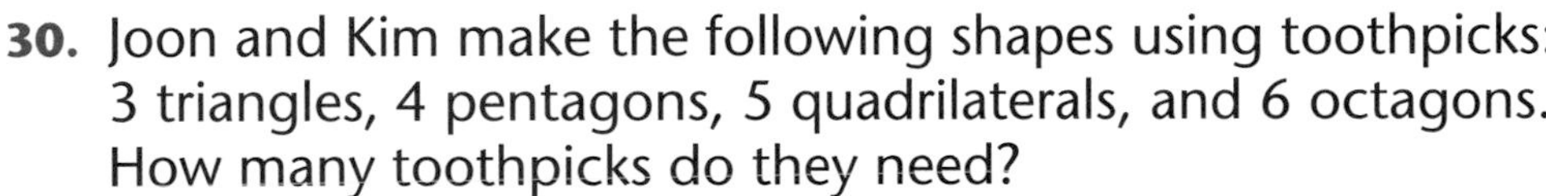

30. Joon and Kim make the following shapes using toothpicks: 3 triangles, 4 pentagons, 5 quadrilaterals, and 6 octagons. How many toothpicks do they need?

31. **Spatial Reasoning:** When you look at the bottom of a 3-dimensional figure, you see a square. What figure could you be looking at?

Spiral Review and Test Prep

Write the number that makes each sentence true.

32. 300 mm = ■ cm　**33.** 4 qt = ■ c　**34.** 5 mi = ■ yd

35. 1 T = ■ lb　**36.** 2 L = ■ mL　**37.** 96 in. = ■ ft

Choose the correct answer.

38. If the air temperature is 17°C, what should you wear?

A. Bathing suit　**C.** Shorts
B. Sweater　**D.** Heavy coat

39. Anya studies between 45 and 54 minutes each night. About how many minutes will she study in 5 nights?

F. 200 minutes　**H.** 250 minutes
G. 300 minutes　**J.** Not Here

Extra Practice, page 457

10•3

Objective: Identify, describe, and classify lines, line segments, and rays.

Lines, Line Segments, and Rays

Learn

Math Words

line a straight path that goes in two directions without ending

parallel lines ||

intersecting lines

perpendicular lines ⊥

Parts of a line
- **endpoint**
- **line segment**
- **ray**

Parts of a circle
- **chord**
- **diameter**
- **radius**

Biltmore Estate in Asheville, North Carolina, was designed by architect Richard Morris Hunt. The Entrance Hall shows examples of how an architect uses geometry.

Example 1

Architects use many different figures in their work.

A **line** goes on forever in both directions.	A **ray** has one endpoint and goes on forever in only one direction.	A **line segment** has two **endpoints**.
A $\overleftrightarrow{AB}$ B	C $\overrightarrow{CD}$ D	E $\overline{EF}$ F
Read: line AB	Read: ray CD	Read: line segment EF

You can describe the line segments in the photo of the Entrance Hall by the way they meet or cross each other.

If they stay the same distance apart from each other, they are **parallel**.
Note: You can use the || symbol to show that two lines are parallel.

$\overline{JK} \parallel \overline{LM}$

If they meet or cross each other, they are **intersecting**.

$\overline{AB}$ intersects $\overline{CD}$

If they meet or cross each other to form square corners, they are **perpendicular** to each other.

Note:
You can use the ⊥ symbol to show that two lines are perpendicular.

$\overline{EF} \perp \overline{GH}$

Architects also use circles and parts of circles.

Example 2

A circle is a closed, 2-dimensional figure. All of the points on the circle are the same distance from the center of the circle.

The center of this circle is point *C*.

A **chord** is a line segment that connects two points on a circle.

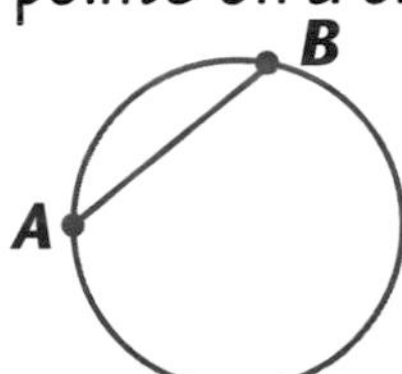

$\overline{AB}$ is a chord.

The **diameter** of a circle is a chord that goes through the center of a circle.

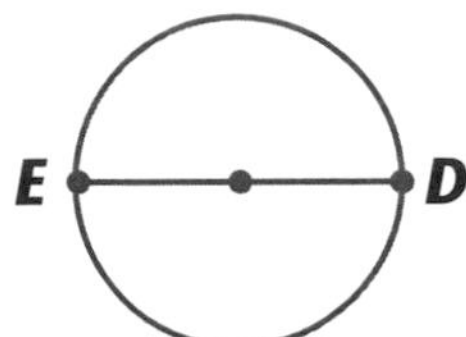

$\overline{ED}$ is a diameter.

The **radius** of a circle is the line segment from the center of a circle to every point on a circle.

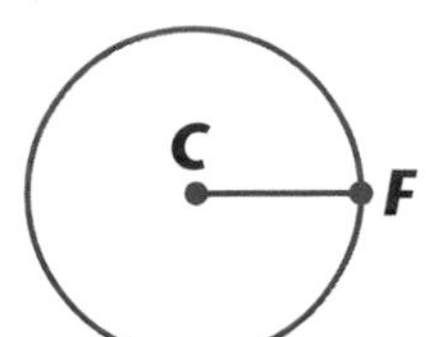

$\overline{CF}$ is a radius.

Try It **Identify each figure.**

1.

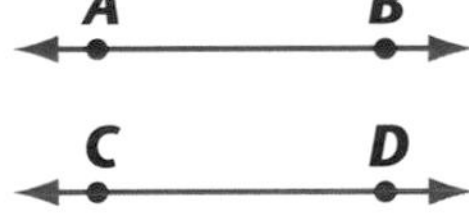

2.

3.

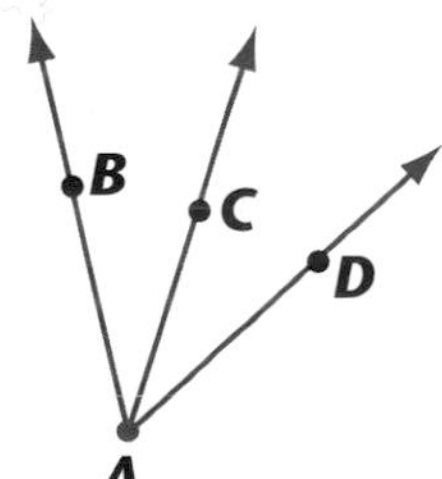

Identify the parts of a circle.

4.

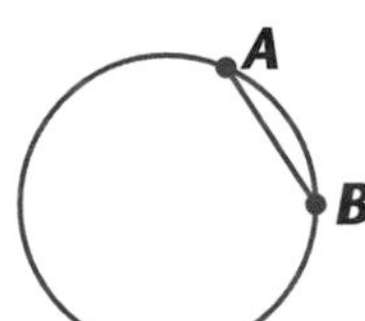

5.

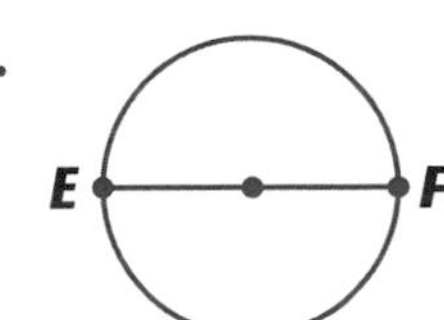

6.

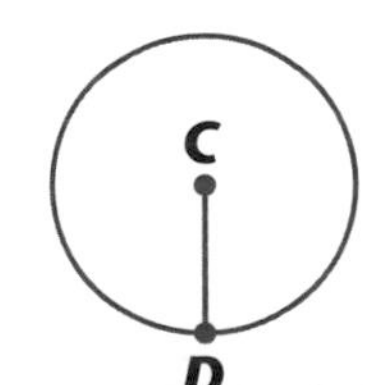

Sum it Up Draw and label a design using straight figures and circles.

Practice Identify each figure.

7. A———B
C———D

8.

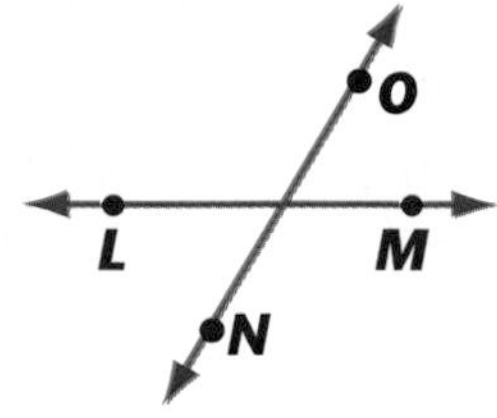

9.

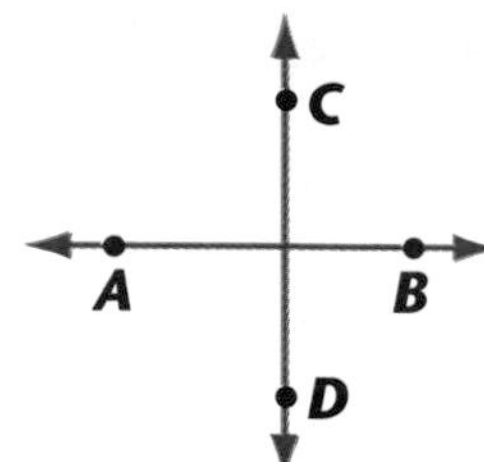

10.

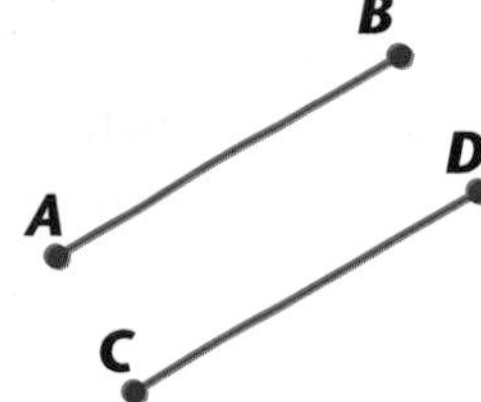

11. E———F

12.

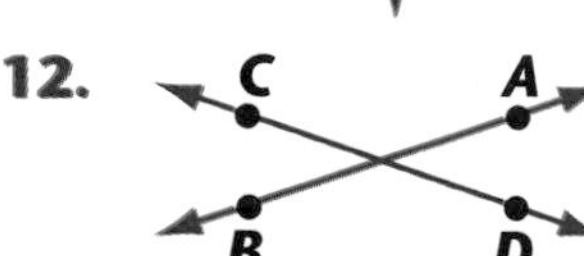

Identify the parts of a circle.

13.

14.

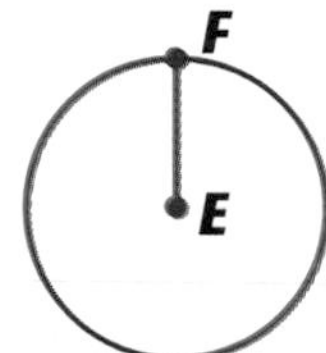

15.

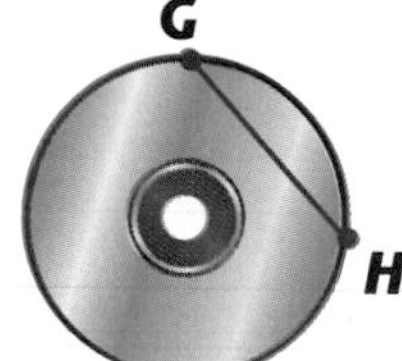

16.

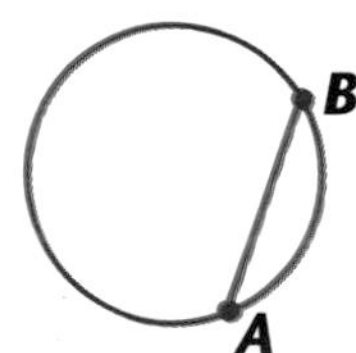

17.

★18.

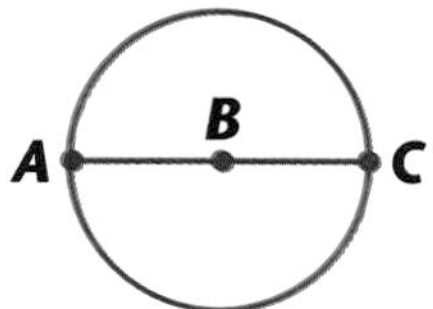

Algebra & functions **Locate each set of points. Then connect the points to draw line segments. Classify the lines as perpendicular or parallel.**

19. Line segment *AB*: (1, 1), (2, 2), (3, 3), (4, 4)
Line segment *CD*: (1, 3), (2, 4), (3, 5), (4, 6)

20. Line segment *EF*: (2, 2) (2, 3) (2, 4) (2, 5), (2, 6)
Line segment *GH*: (4, 2), (4, 3), (4, 4), (4, 5)

21.

Here's how Melvin drew and described these lines. Tell what mistake he made. Explain how to correct it.

Problem Solving

22. **Art:** Artists use a variety of sizes of circles and straight figures to make interesting, colorful designs. Use circles and straight figures to make your own design. Describe your design using the math words in this lesson.

★23. Make a point on a sheet of paper. Use either a compass or 2 pencils and a paper clip to draw a circle. Then draw line segments and label parts of the circle.

Use data from the cube for problems 24–26.

24. **Spatial Reasoning:** Which line segments are parallel to line segment CD?

25. Name all of the line segments in the cube.

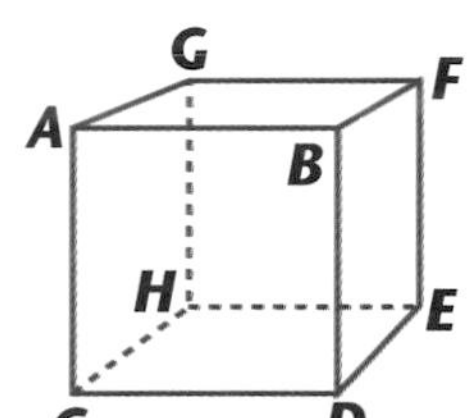

26. **Create a problem** about the cube. Solve it. Ask others to solve it.

27. Give a real-world example of how an architect might use parallel line segments.

28. **Career:** If an architect earns $6,250 each month, how much would the architect earn in one year?

29. **Compare** the number of line segments in a hexagon and a triangle. Write a comparison statement.

30. Stephen built a 3-dimensional figure out of straws. His figure has 8 vertices, 12 edges, and 6 faces. What could his figure be?

31. Draw some polygons. Describe them using the terms *line segment, parallel lines,* and *intersecting lines.*

32. The horizon is a real-world example of a line. List a real-world example of a *line segment, parallel lines,* and *intersecting lines.*

Spiral Review and Test Prep

33. 5,739 + 438 + 97
34. 688 × 49
35. $4.75 ÷ 25
36. 493 ÷ 8
37. 8,424 − 5,365
38. $62.48 ÷ 35

Choose the correct answer.

39. What is the median of the data?

4, 6, 2, 1, 4, 5, 2, 3, 4, 2, 3

A. 2
B. 3
C. 4
D. 5

40. 50,000 milliliters is the same as ▮

F. 500 liters
G. 50 liters
H. 500 quarts
J. 50 quarts

Extra Practice, page 457

Angles

Learn

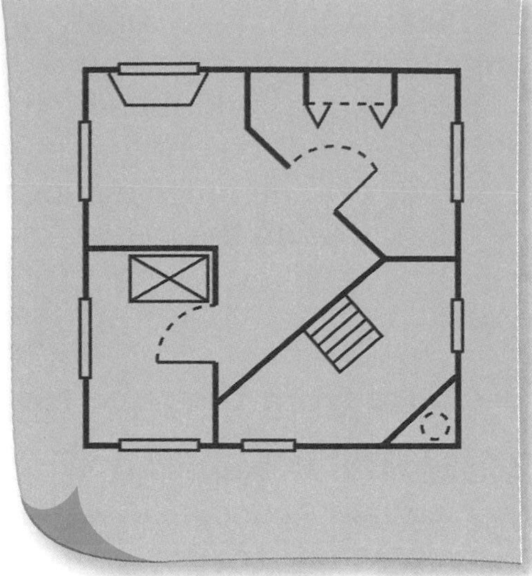

Math Words

angle a figure formed by two rays with the same endpoint

right angle

acute angle

obtuse angle

Sam's dad is an architect. He works with angles in his drawings. What do you notice about the sizes of the different angles in the drawing?

Example

A **right angle** is formed by perpendicular lines. A right angle forms a square corner and measures 90°.

An **acute angle** has a measure less than a right angle.

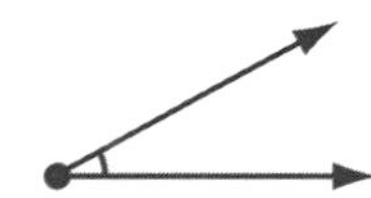

An **obtuse angle** has a measure greater than a right angle (90°) but less than 180°.

Angles are measured in degrees. Think of a circle to understand this.

An angle that is 90° is $\frac{1}{4}$ turn on a circle. It is also a right angle.

90° $\frac{1}{4}$ turn

An angle that is 180° is $\frac{1}{2}$ turn on a circle.

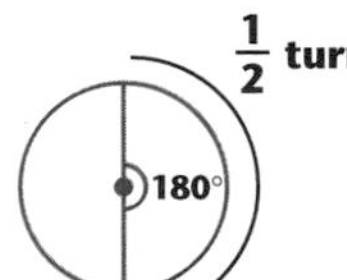

An angle that is 270° is $\frac{3}{4}$ turn on a circle.

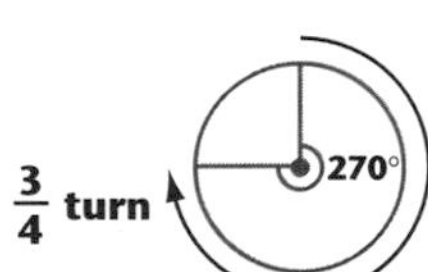

An angle that is 360° is a full turn on a circle.

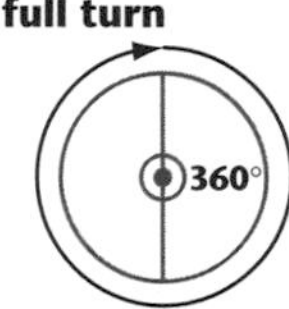

The drawing includes right, acute, and obtuse angles.

Try It

Write *acute, obtuse,* or *right* for each angle.

1. 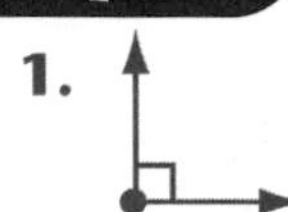

2.

3. 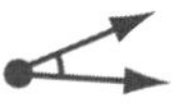

Explain the difference between a right angle, an acute angle, and an obtuse angle.

Practice **Write *acute, obtuse,* or *right* for each angle.**

4. 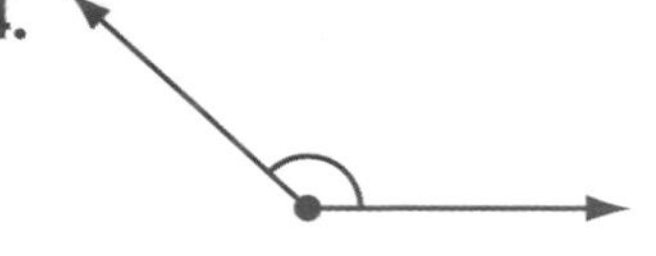

5. 

6. 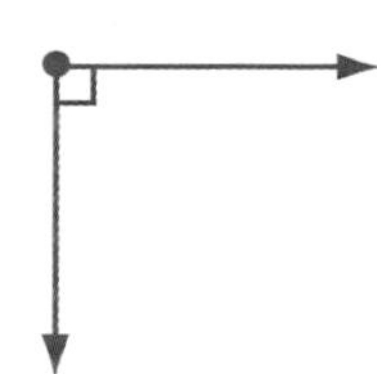

Write the degree measure and fraction of a turn for each angle.

7. 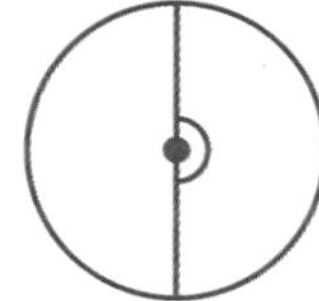

8. 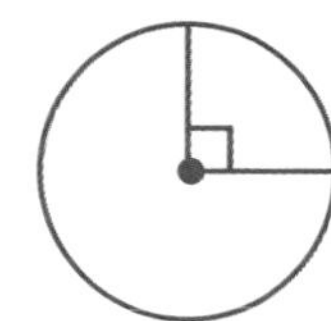

9. 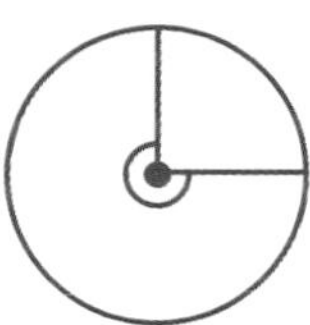

Draw each figure.

★**10.** a 3-sided figure with 1 right angle

★**11.** a 5-sided figure with 1 obtuse angle and at least 1 acute angle

Problem Solving

12. An architect is drawing plans for a building that has hexagons, rectangles, squares, and triangles. Draw each figure and write the number and kind of angles it has.

13. Make a table with the headings 3, 4, 5, 6, and 8. Draw a polygon under each heading that has the same number of sides as the heading. How many angles are in each? What do you notice about the number of sides and angles?

★**14.** **Music:** This picture shows a whole note. Describe this figure in as many ways as possible.

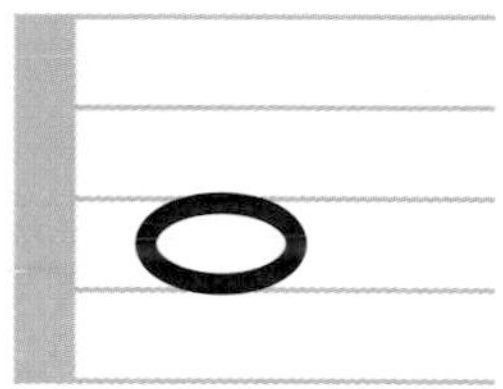

15. **Analyze:** Using a sheet of paper, how could you tell if an angle is obtuse or acute?

16. **Create a problem** using a bar graph of the following information. A survey of architects shows that 400 like contemporary houses; 1,000 prefer colonial; 200 favor English cottage; and 400 like Tudor. Solve it. Ask others to solve it.

Spiral Review and Test Prep

17. 839 − 76 **18.** \$66.75 × 28 **19.** 7,609 ÷ 18 **20.** 1,329 + 697

Choose the correct answer.

21. Which would you use to measure the capacity of a garbage can?

A. Cup **C.** Quart
B. Pint **D.** Gallon

22. What is the mean of the data?
10, 12, 8, 10, 11, 9

F. 4 **H.** 10
G. 9 **J.** 12

Objective: Identify, describe, and classify triangles and quadrilaterals.

10•5 Triangles and Quadrilaterals

Learn

Math Words

Triangles
- **acute triangle**
- **equilateral triangle**
- **isosceles triangle**
- **obtuse triangle**
- **right triangle**
- **scalene triangle**

Quadrilaterals
- **parallelogram**
- **rhombus**
- **trapezoid**

The original building of the National Gallery of Art in Washington, D.C., was designed by the architect John Russell Pope. What kinds of triangles do you see in this building?

Example 1

There are many ways to identify triangles.

An **isosceles triangle** has at least two sides or angles that are equal.

An **equilateral triangle** has three sides and angles that are equal.

A **scalene triangle** has no sides or angles that are equal.

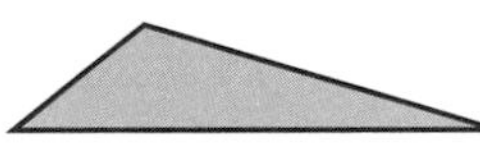

An **obtuse triangle** has one obtuse angle.

An **acute triangle** has three acute angles.

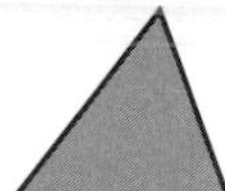

A **right triangle** has one right angle.

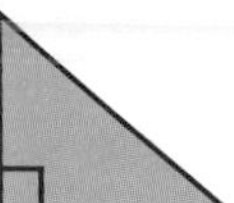

The triangle shown on the National Gallery of Art building is both an isosceles triangle and an obtuse triangle.

An architect is using pictures of houses to design a logo. Here are two sample drawings he did. Which quadrilaterals are used?

Drawing A

Drawing B

Example 2

All **quadrilaterals** have 4 sides and 4 angles.

A square has 4 equal sides and 4 right angles. Opposite sides of a square are parallel.

A rectangle has 4 sides and 4 right angles. Opposite sides of a rectangle are equal and parallel.

A **parallelogram** has 2 pairs of parallel sides. Opposite sides of a parallelogram are equal and parallel.

A **rhombus** has 4 equal sides and 2 pairs of parallel sides. Opposite sides of a rhombus are parallel.

A **trapezoid** has 1 pair of parallel sides.

Drawing A has a square and a trapezoid. Drawing B has a rectangle and a trapezoid.

Try It **Classify each in as many ways as possible.**

1. 2cm, 2cm

2. 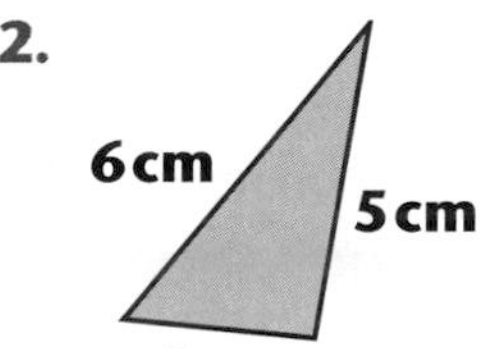

3. 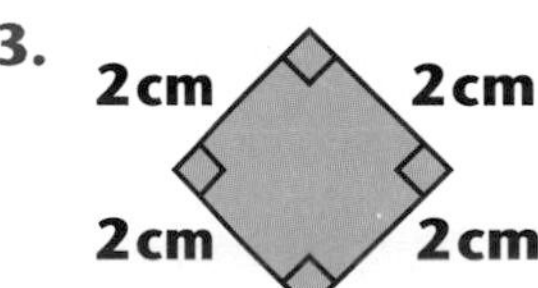

4. 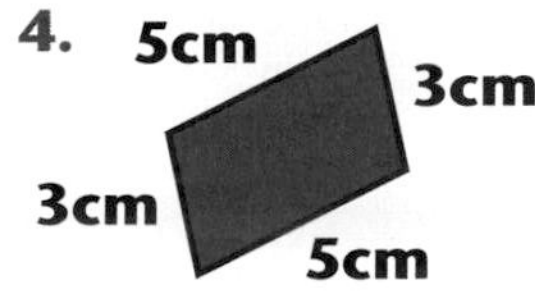

What are the different ways used to identify triangles and quadrilaterals?

Practice

Classify each triangle as *equilateral, isosceles,* or *scalene.* Then classify each triangle as *right, acute,* or *obtuse.*

5. 3 cm, 3 cm, 3 cm

6. 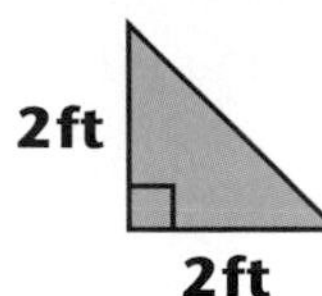

7. 10 in., 20 in., 15 in.

Identify each quadrilateral.

8. 

9. 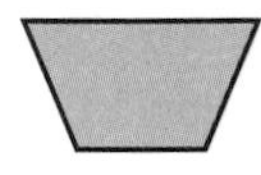

10. 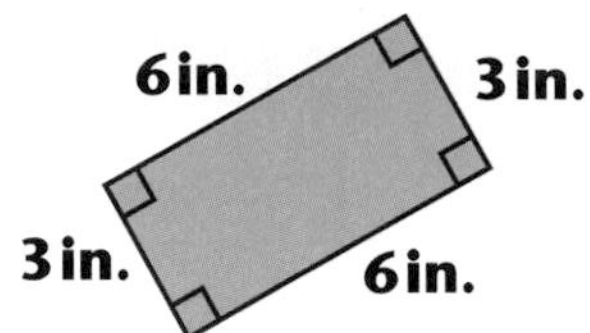

Tell if each statement is *true* or *false.* Explain why.

11. Some right triangles are also isosceles triangles.

12. All rhombuses are also squares.

13. A rhombus is also a parallelogram.

14. No acute triangles are equilateral.

15. No obtuse triangle is also a scalene triangle.

16. Some isosceles triangles are also obtuse.

17. Some rectangles are also squares.

★18. An equilateral triangle can never be a right triangle.

★19. Some parallelograms are squares.

20. 

Here is how Julia drew an isosceles triangle. Tell what mistake she made. Explain how to correct it.

Algebra & functions **21.** Copy and complete. Describe a pattern you see.

Polygon	Number of Triangles Used to Make the Polygon	Number of Sides in the Polygon
Triangle	1	3
Square	2	4
Pentagon	3	5
Hexagon	■	6
Heptagon	5	■
Octagon	■	8

Problem Solving

22. A building is shaped like a triangle with 3 equal sides and 3 equal angles. Beatrice said the building is an equilateral triangle. Todd said the building is an isosceles triangle. Who is correct? Explain.

23. Generalize: You know that an obtuse triangle has one obtuse angle. Can an obtuse triangle have 2 obtuse angles? If not, what type of angle do the other 2 angles have to be?

24. Draw a design that uses many kinds of triangles and quadrilaterals. Name the types of each you used.

25. Compare: A rectangle is a type of parallelogram. Tell how they are alike and different.

★**26. Analyze:** Draw and cut out a picture of a triangle. Then cut off the corners and place them side-by-side to form a straight line. Do the same with other triangles. What do you notice? What is the sum of the measures of all three angles of a triangle?

★**27. Language Arts:** An analogy is a comparison of words or ideas, for example, hot is to cold as warm is to cool. How would you complete this analogy? Rectangle is to parallelogram as square is to ____.

Spiral Review and Test Prep

28. $17\overline{)\$36.89}$ **29.** 419×8 **30.** $6,085 + 3,784$ **31.** $5,456 - 2,643$ **32.** 548×7

Choose the correct answer.

33. A museum tour started at 2:10 and ended at 3:05. How long was the tour?

A. 45 minutes **C.** 1 h 5 minutes
B. 55 minutes **D.** 1 h 10 minutes

34. About how much does a calculator weigh?

F. 13 grams **H.** 130 ounces
G. 130 grams **J.** Not Here

Extra Practice, page 458

Objective: Use illustrations and diagrams to solve problems.

Problem Solving: Reading for Math

Use a Diagram

Budding Picassos Found at Library

Read Ruby used a rectangle and an equilateral triangle in her painting. How long is side A?

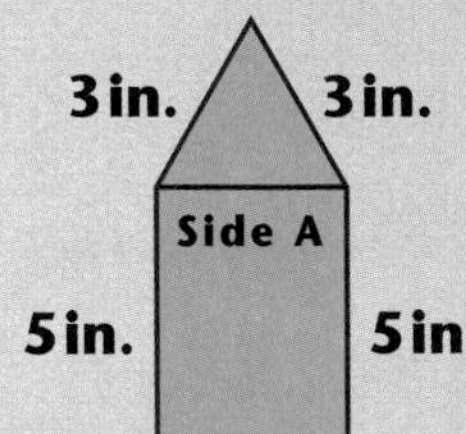

READING SKILL ▶

Use an Illustration

An illustration is a picture that represents information. It shows relationships among the parts of a whole.

- **What do you know?** **The rectangle is 5 in. long and 3 in. wide; two sides of the equilateral triangle are each 3 in. long.**
- **What do you need to find?** **Length of side A**

MATH SKILL ▶

Use a Diagram

- A diagram can show how different items can be combined to form a whole.

Plan You must identify the length of side A. You can use your knowledge of rectangles and triangles.

Solve The opposite sides of a rectangle are parallel and equal.

The three sides of an equilateral triangle are equal.

So side A must have the same measure as the width of the rectangle and one side of the triangle. Side A is 3 in.

Look Back

- Could you have solved this problem without knowing the length of one side of the triangle?

How did using a diagram help you solve this problem?

Practice **Use the diagram to solve each problem.**

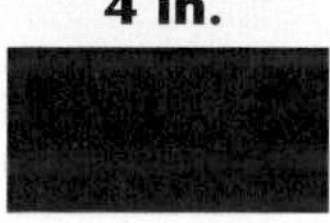

1. On another painting, Ruby drew this figure. Describe Ruby's figure in more than one way.

2. Can Ruby draw a triangle with sides measuring 2 cm, 3 cm, and 8 cm? a triangle with sides 2 cm, 3 cm, 5 cm?

Use data from the diagram for problems 3–6.

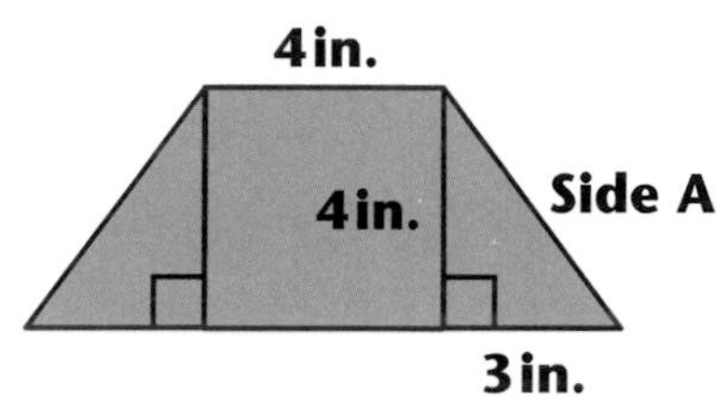

3. Ali drew this figure on her painting. Describe the polygons she used to form the figure.
4. What is the length of the line segment common to these polygons?
5. Can side A be 7 in. long? Explain why or why not.
6. Can side A be 5 in. long? Explain why or why not.
7. Paul made a frame for his painting. He connected two 4-inch pieces of frame, a 5-inch piece, and a 6-inch piece. How would you describe his frame?
8. Sue painted this figure on her painting. What is the length of side A?

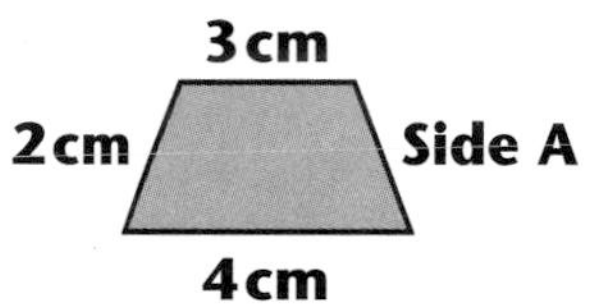

Spiral Review and Test Prep

Choose the correct answer.

Henri uses a square, two isosceles right triangles and a equilateral triangle in his drawing. How long is side A?

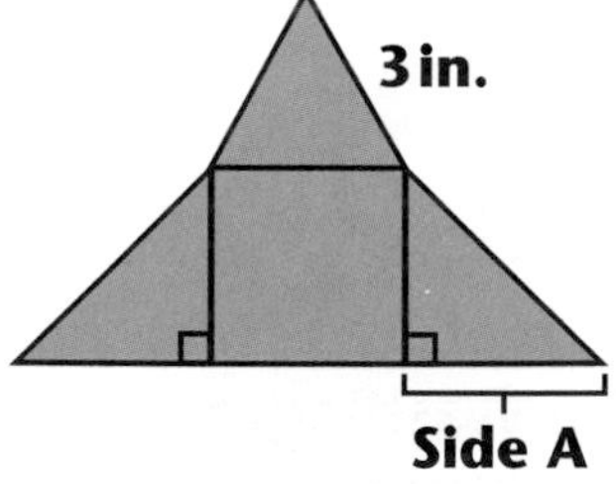

9. Which statement is true?
   - **A.** Side A has the same length as one side of the square.
   - **B.** The length of side A must be greater than 3 inches.
   - **C.** All sides of the figure are the same length.

10. You can find the length of side A because ____
    - **F.** it is part of a right triangle.
    - **G.** two sides of an isosceles triangle are equal.
    - **H.** all sides of all of the triangles shown are equal.

Check Your Progress A

Classify each figure. Tell how many faces, bases, edges, and vertices it has. (pages 408–411)

1. 

2. 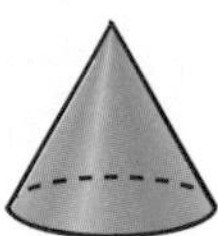

3. 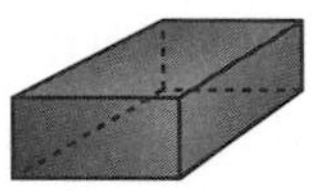

Tell whether each figure is open or closed. Is it a polygon? If so, classify the figure. (pages 412–415)

4. 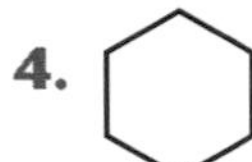

5. 

6. 

Identify each figure. (pages 416–419)

7. 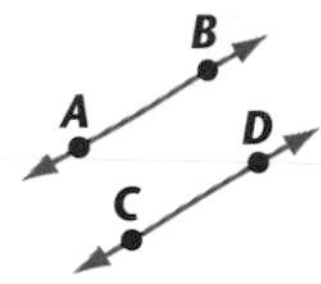

8. 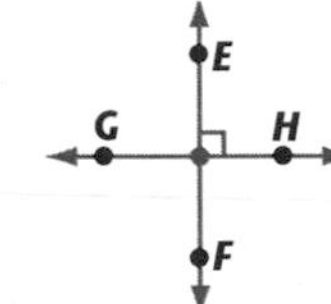

9. C D

Classify each angle as acute, obtuse, or right. (pages 420–421)

10. 

11. 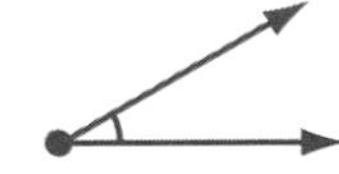

12. 

Classify each triangle as equilateral, isosceles, or scalene. Then classify each triangle as right, acute, or obtuse. (pages 422–425)

13. 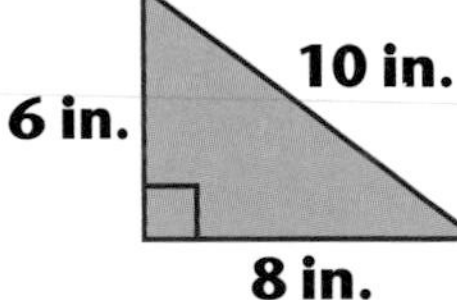

14. 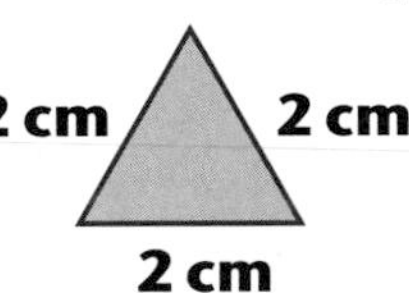

15. 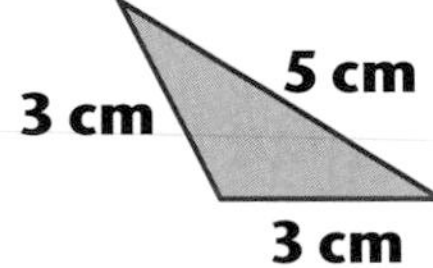

Identify each quadrilateral. (pages 422–425)

16. 

17. 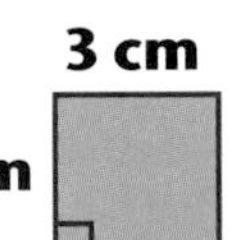

18. 

Solve. (pages 408–427)

19. **Social Studies:** The top of the Washington Monument in Washington, D.C., is a square pyramid and the bottom is a rectangular prism. Draw it.

20. **Generalize:** Tell how you would classify 2-dimensional figures.

Additional activities at www.mhschool.com/math

Draw Congruent Figures

Petra is designing a quilt. She wants to draw congruent pentagons to use in her design. Draw any pentagon. Then draw a congruent pentagon.

You can use a drawing program with geometry tools to draw congruent geometric figures.

- Click on the geometry tools.
- Choose the freeform polygon tool. Draw a pentagon.
- Use the duplicate tool to draw a congruent pentagon.
- Use the measurement tool to find the length of each side and the measure of each angle.

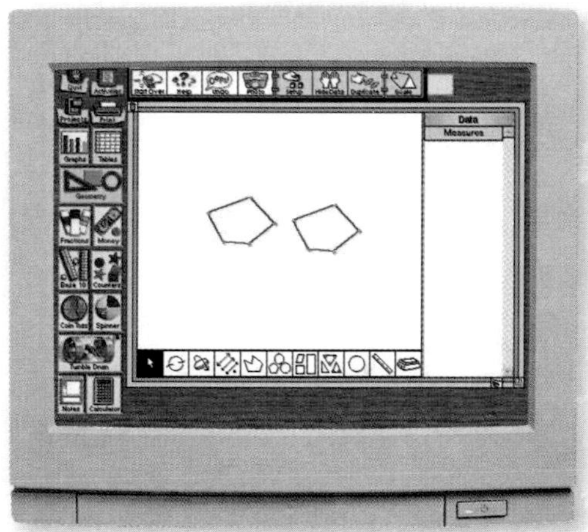

How do you know the figures are congruent?

Use the computer to draw each figure. Then draw a figure congruent to it. Show that they are congruent.

1. triangle **2.** quadrilateral **3.** hexagon

Solve.

4. Kurt wants to create a design for a book cover. He wants to draw congruent regular octagons to use in his design. Draw a regular octagon. Then draw a congruent octagon.

5. Two pictures in a magazine are to be outlined with congruent rectangles. Draw two rectangles that could be used to outline the pictures. Explain how you know that your figures are correct.

6. Analyze: How do the geometry and measurement tools help you draw congruent figures?

For more practice, use Math Traveler™.

Objective: Identify congruent and similar 2-dimensional figures.

10•7 Congruent and Similar

Learn

Math Words

congruent figures that have the same shape and same size

similar figures that are the same shape, may be different sizes

Priscilla Warren is a Navajo rug weaver from Shiprock, New Mexico. She uses congruent and similar shapes in her rug designs.

Priscilla Warren

Example 1

Find **congruent** and **similar** figures.

Look at the two pentagons on the dot paper. The sides have the same number of dots and are in the same position.

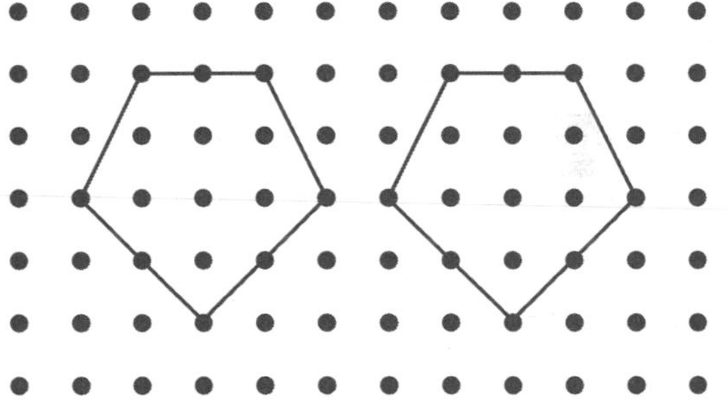

The pentagons are congruent and similar.

The following figures are not congruent, and not similar.

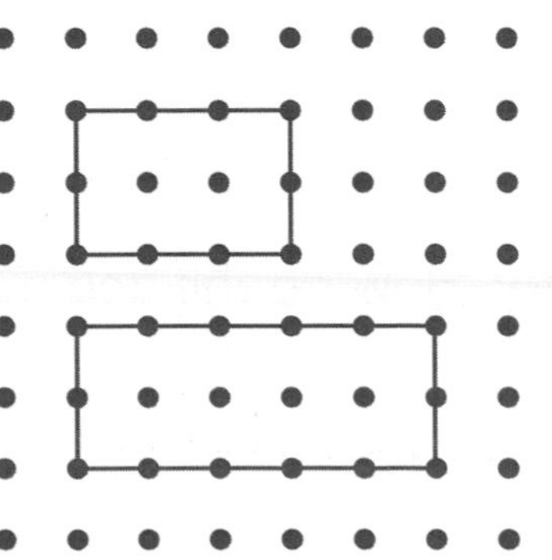

What if you want to draw a figure that has the same shape but is larger than the original figure?

Example 2

Find similar figures.

Count the number of dots on the sides of the figures.
The sides of the second figure are two times the size of the first figure and are in the same position.

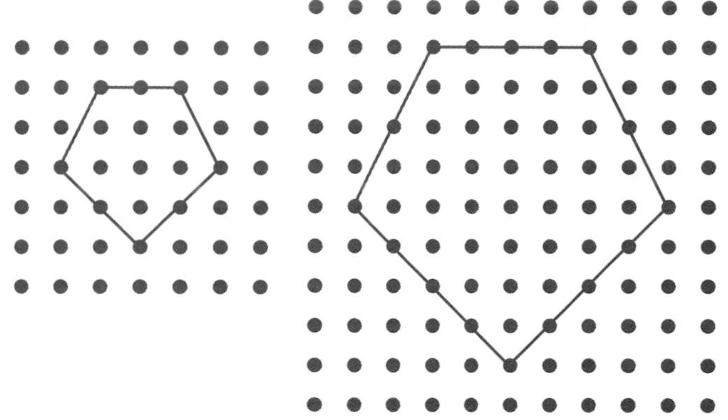

The following figures are not similar.

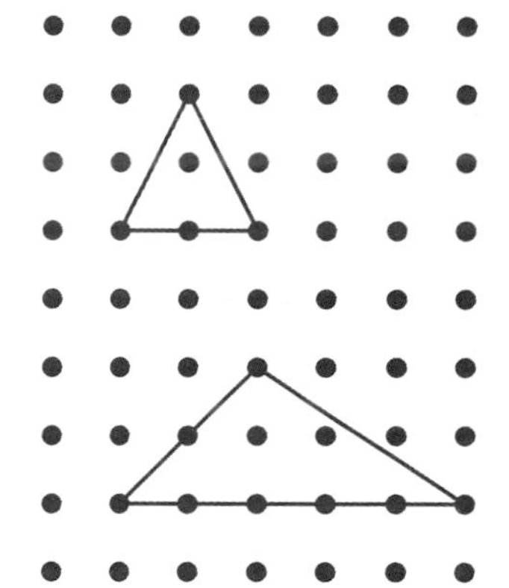

The figures are similar, but not congruent.

Try It **Write whether the figures are similar. Then write whether the figures are congruent.**

1\.

2\.

3\.

Copy the figure on dot paper. Then draw one congruent figure and one similar figure.

4\. 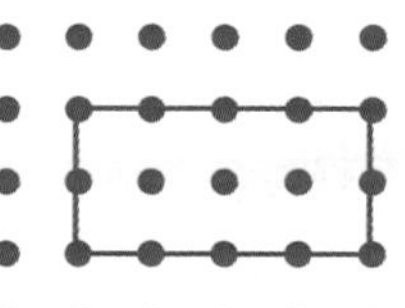

5\. 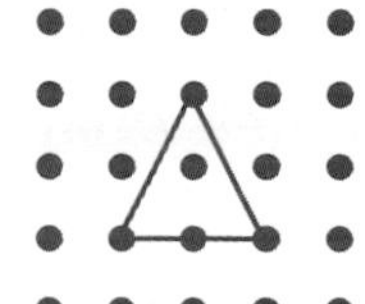

6\. 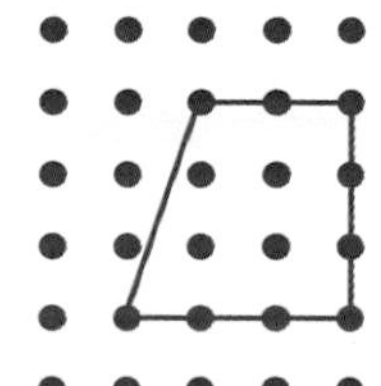

Sum it Up How can you show that two figures are congruent? similar?

Practice **Write whether the figures are similar. Then write whether the figures are congruent.**

7.

8. 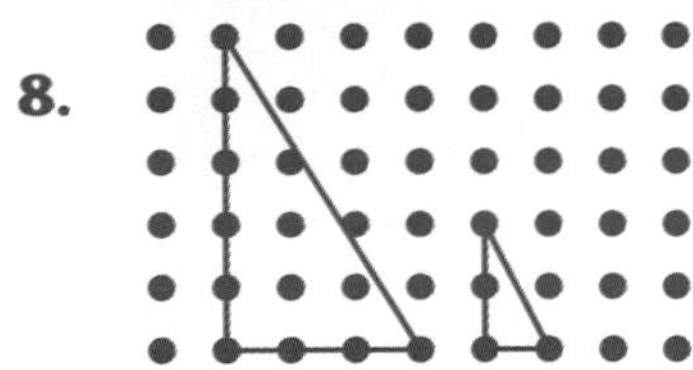

9. 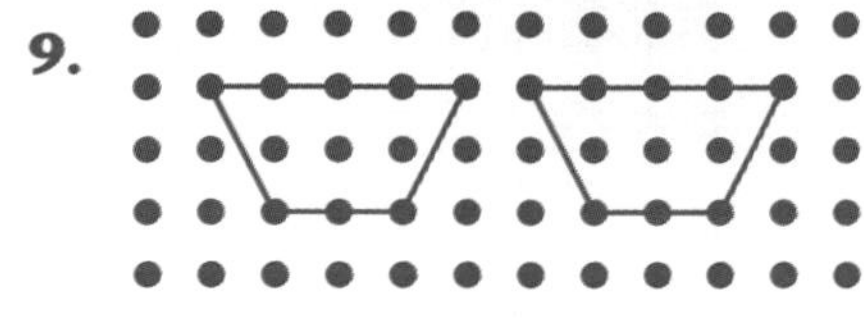

Copy the figure on paper. Then draw one congruent figure and one similar figure.

10. 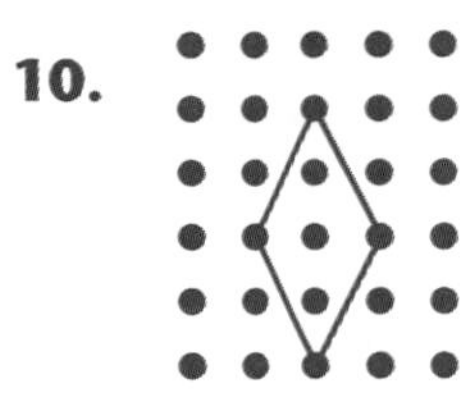

11. 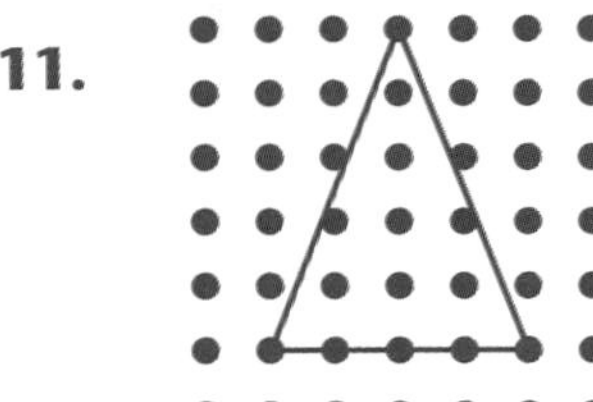

12. 

13. 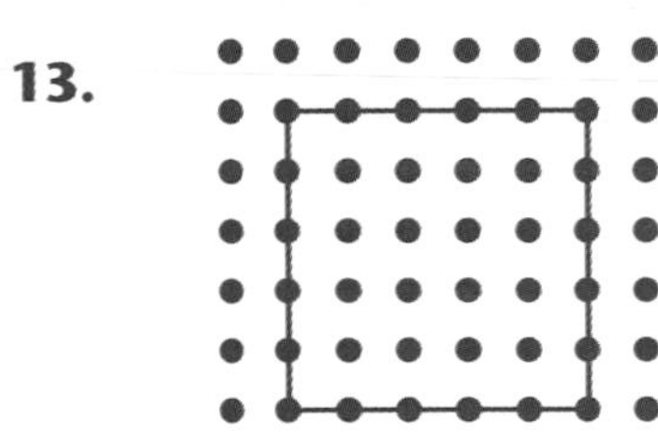

14. 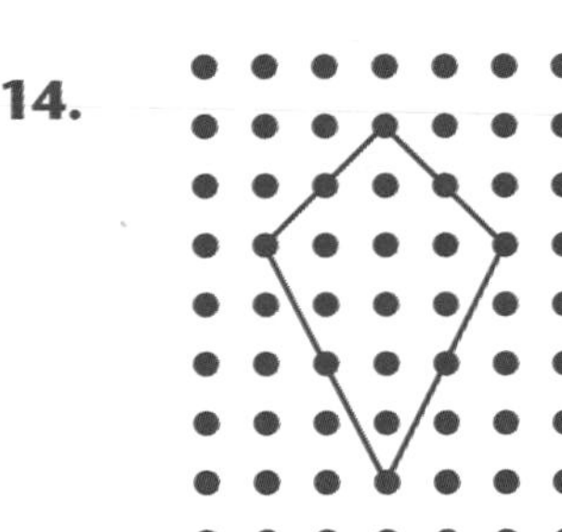

15. 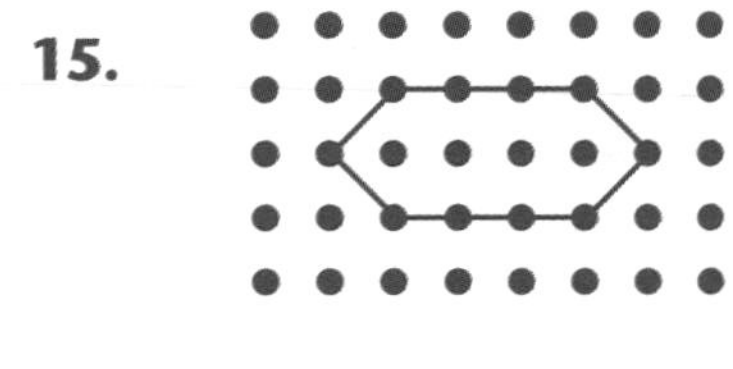

Algebra & functions **Draw the figures and write ordered pairs.**

16. Draw a figure on a coordinate grid. Then draw a similar figure that is half the size of the original. Write the ordered pairs for all vertices.

17. Draw a figure on a coordinate grid. Then draw a similar figure that is 3 times the size of the original. Write the ordered pairs for all vertices.

18. 

Here's how Kerstin drew a figure and a figure similar to it. Tell what mistake she made. Explain how to correct it.

Problem Solving

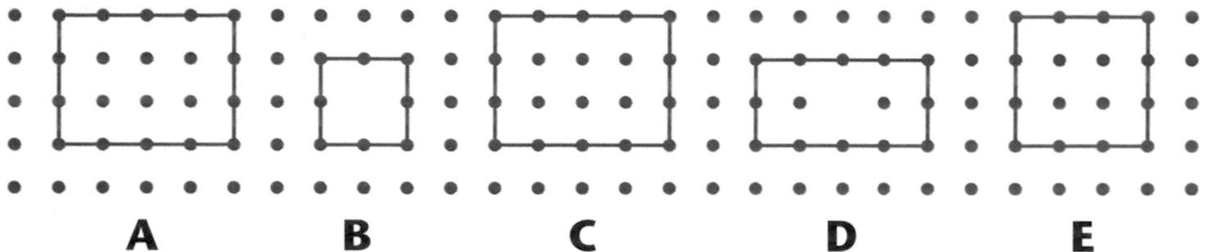

19. Which two figures are similar? Which two figures are congruent?

20. **Analyze:** What happens to a rectangle when you multiply or divide the length and width by the same number and draw a new rectangle?

Congruent or Similar?

	Original Figure	Other Figures
A		
B		
C		

Use data from the chart for problems 21–23.

21. Which row shows other figures that are congruent to the original figure?

22. Which row shows other figures that are similar to the original figure?

23. Which row shows other figures that are neither congruent nor similar to the original figure?

24. Draw a figure on dot paper. Give the paper to a partner. Have your partner draw a congruent and similar figure.

25. An interior designer buys a rectangular poster to be framed. The perimeter of the poster is 92 inches. If the width is 10 inches, what is the length? If the frame is $0.55 per inch, how much would it cost to have the poster framed?

26. **Science:** Examples of congruent and similar figures can be seen in nature. Look at this picture of a honeycomb. How would you describe the figures that make up the honeycomb?

Spiral Review and Test Prep

27. 509,004 − 77,899

28. $7,611.52 + $79.88

29. 3,486 ÷ 29

Choose the correct answer.

30. A figure has 8 sides. What figure is it?
    - **A.** Triangle
    - **B.** Pentagon
    - **C.** Octagon
    - **D.** Decagon

31. What unit of measure would you use to describe the distance between San Francisco and Seattle?
    - **F.** Kilometers
    - **G.** Meters
    - **H.** Decimeters
    - **J.** Centimeters

Extra Practice, page 458

Objective: Investigate and predict the results of motion.

10•8 Explore Translations, Reflections, and Rotations

Learn

Math Words

reflection (flip) a movement of a figure across a line, producing a mirror image

rotation (turn) a figure that is rotated around a point

translation (slide) a figure that is moved along a straight line.

You can use dot paper to explore motion.

Work Together

You Will Need
- dot paper

► Draw a figure. Use dot paper to show a translation, a reflection, and a rotation of that figure.

- You can slide a figure across a line to show a **translation**.
- You can flip a figure over a line to show a **reflection**.
- You can turn a figure around a point on a line to show a **rotation**.

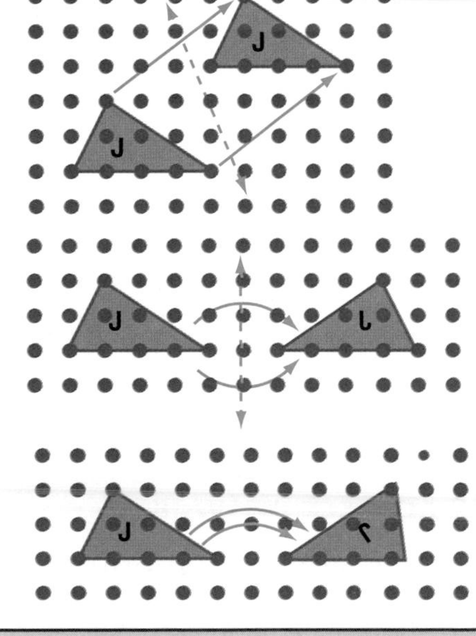

The original figure and the translation, reflection or rotation are congruent figures.

► Draw a figure that shows a translation, reflection, or rotation. Have your partner tell which one you used.

Make Connections

Here is how to make and identify translations, reflections, and rotations.

Using Shapes	Writing a Description
Translation: 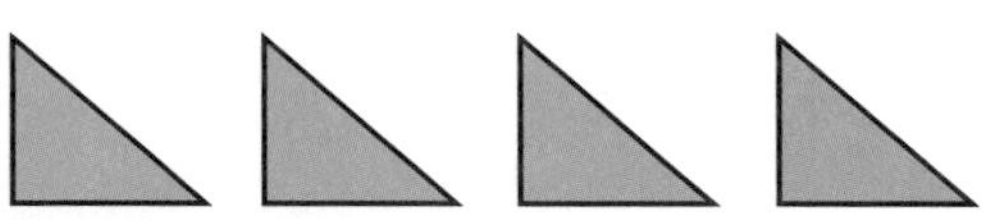	In this translation, the shape was slid 3 times.
Reflection: 	In this reflection, the shape was flipped 3 times.
Rotation:    	In this rotation, the shape was turned 3 times.

Try It **Write *translation, reflection,* or *rotation* to describe how the figure was moved.**

1. 

2.

3.

Sum it Up How can you tell when a figure is a translation, rotation, or reflection of the original?

Practice **Write *translation, reflection,* or *rotation* to describe how the figure was moved.**

4.

5. 

6.

7. **Compare:** It can be difficult to tell how some figures were moved. Look at this design with equilateral triangles. How could you describe the movement?

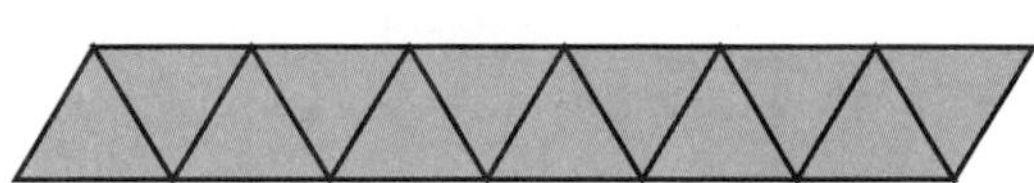

Objective: Identify, describe, and draw symmetrical objects with bilateral or rotational symmetry.

Symmetry

Learn

Math Words

line of symmetry a line on which a figure can be folded so that its two halves match exactly

bilateral symmetry a figure with a line of symmetry

rotational symmetry a figure that matches itself after being turned 180° or less

The Taj Mahal in India is one of the most famous buildings in the world. Does this building have a line of symmetry? Explain your answer.

Example 1

You can fold a figure to find out if it is symmetrical. The fold line is a **line of symmetry**. The figure has **bilateral symmetry** if, when you fold it, one side fits exactly over the other side.

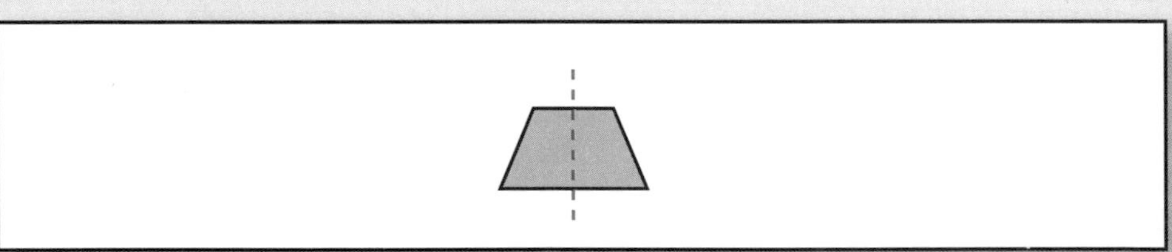

Figures can have more than one line of symmetry.

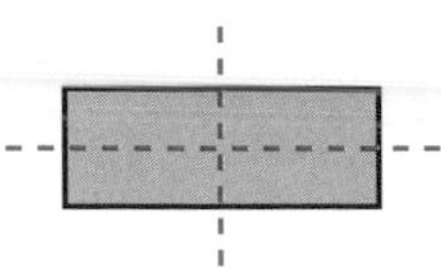

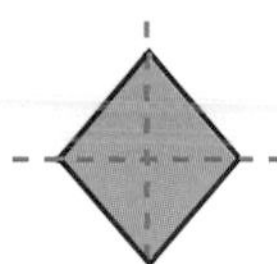

The Taj Mahal does have bilateral symmetry. If you draw a line down the center of the building, it is the same on both sides.

What does a figure with **rotational symmetry** look like?

Example 2

If a figure will fit exactly over itself after being rotated clockwise or counterclockwise 180° or less, then the figure has rotational symmetry.

An equilateral triangle has rotational symmetry.

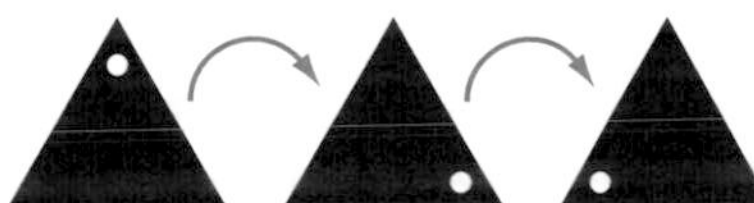

The following figure does not have rotational symmetry.

Try It **Is the dotted line a line of symmetry?**

1.

2.

3.

Does the figure have rotational symmetry?

4.

5.

6.

Can a figure with bilateral symmetry also have rotational symmetry? Draw an example.

Practice Is the dotted line a line of symmetry?

7. 

8. 

9. 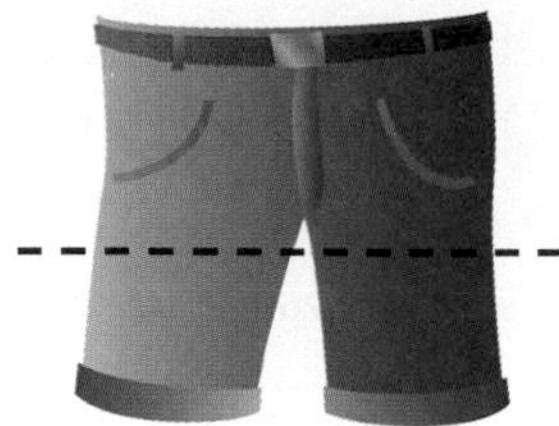

Is the figure symmetrical? If yes, draw its line of symmetry.

10. 4

11. L

12. 

Draw each figure.

13. Draw a figure with bilateral symmetry and show the lines of symmetry.

14. Draw a figure with rotational symmetry.

Complete the drawing to make it symmetrical.

★15. 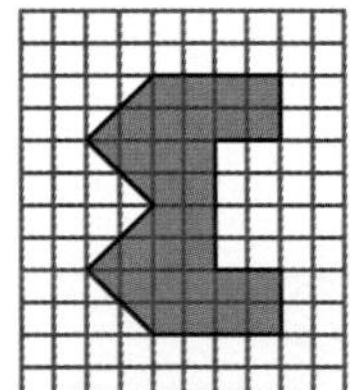

★16. 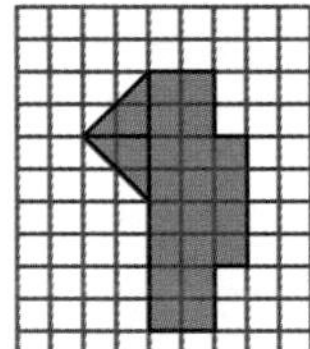

★17. 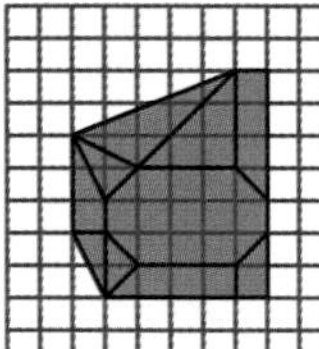

18. 

Here's how Marc drew a line of symmetry for this figure. Tell what mistake he made. Explain how to correct it.

Problem Solving

19. A 9-foot by 12-foot oriental rug costs $3,775.49 at Far East Carpets. A similar rug at Quality Carpets costs $3,550.99. Which is more expensive? What is the difference in price?

20. **Collect Data:** Make a list of four objects that have symmetry. Tell whether the symmetry is bilateral or rotational.

Use data from *Did You Know?* for problems 21–23.

21. Find a part of the map that has bilateral symmetry. Draw a sketch of this part and then draw a line of symmetry through it.
22. Name some different figures you see on the map.
23. Look at the red lines on the map. Sketch a pair of intersecting lines like this. Does this figure have rotational symmetry? Explain.

★ 24. **Analyze:** Sal says the parts of a figure with bilateral symmetry are congruent. Do you agree or disagree? Explain.

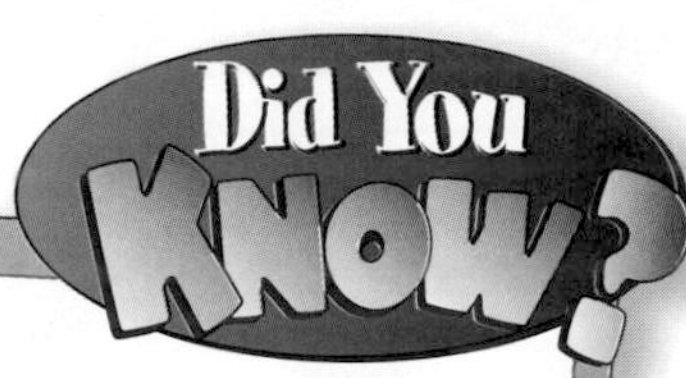

The Taj Mahal is part of a larger structure. There is a main gateway, a garden, a mosque, and other walls. The layout of the structure can be seen on this map.

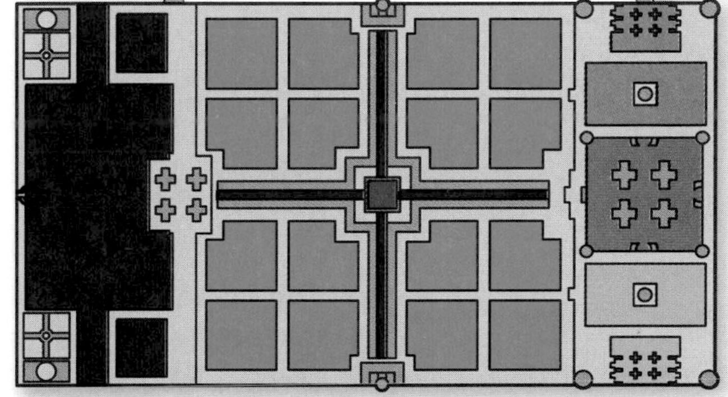

Use data from the picture for problems 25–26.

25. Oriental rugs such as this might be seen in the Taj Mahal. How many lines of symmetry does the rug have?
26. Does the rug have bilateral symmetry or rotational symmetry? Explain your answer.
27. An artist was painting a scene of the Taj Mahal. The painting has two pairs of equal sides and four right angles. Tell what polygon this is and tell if it has a line of symmetry.
28. **History:** The Taj Mahal was completed in 1649. About how many years ago was it built?

Spiral Review and Test Prep

29. $927 \div 43$ 30. $(12 \times 3) + (8 \times 4)$ 31. $180{,}000 \div 20$ 32. 649×28

Choose the correct answer.

33. Which is longest?
    A. 70 centimeters **C.** 7 feet
    B. 7 meters **D.** 7 decimeters

34. What number is missing?
    42, 36, 30, ____, 18, 12
    F. 28 **H.** 25
    G. 24 **J.** 20

Objective: Find a pattern to solve a problem.

Problem Solving: Strategy
Find a Pattern

Math Word

tessellation an arrangement of shapes that covers an area without any gaps or overlaps

Read

Read the problem carefully.

A **tessellation** is made when shapes are fitted together without overlapping and with no spaces between them. Tessellations are thousands of years old. They can be found all over the world in many forms and in many cultures. The tessellation shown here is an old mosaic pattern from Italy.

You need to make a copy of this tessellation for a wall panel. What pattern was used to make the tessellation?

- **What do you know?** parallelograms are used in the tessellation
- **What do you need to find?** what pattern was used to make the tessellation

Plan

One way to solve the problem is to find a pattern.

Solve

Find any shapes that look familiar, such as a parallelogram. Look for translations, reflections, and how the colors are used in the patterns.

Think: A parallelogram has been slid down vertically and flipped horizontally.

One way to create this tessellation is to use translations and reflections of parallelograms. The color changes as it moves.

Look Back

Has the question been answered?
Is your answer reasonable?

How did you find a pattern to solve the problem?

Practice **Use data from the tessellations for problems 1–4.**

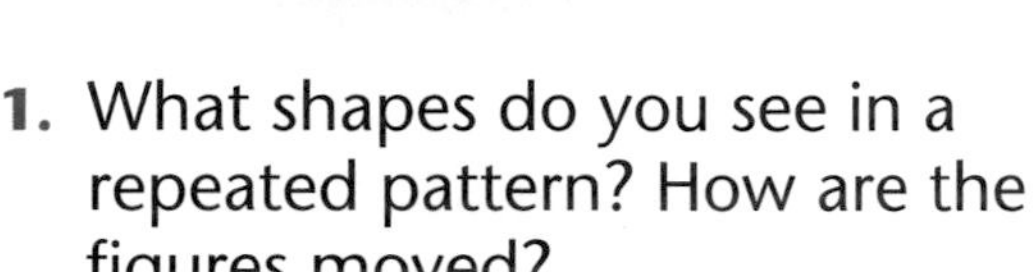

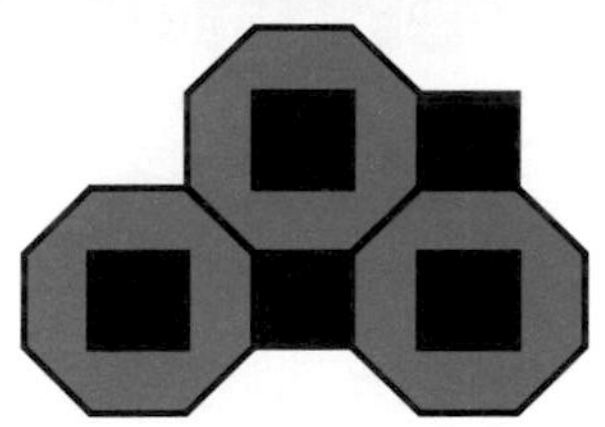

1. What shapes do you see in a repeated pattern? How are the figures moved?

2. Copy the pattern and complete the missing pieces.

3. Describe the pattern using shapes.

4. Copy the pattern and add two pieces.

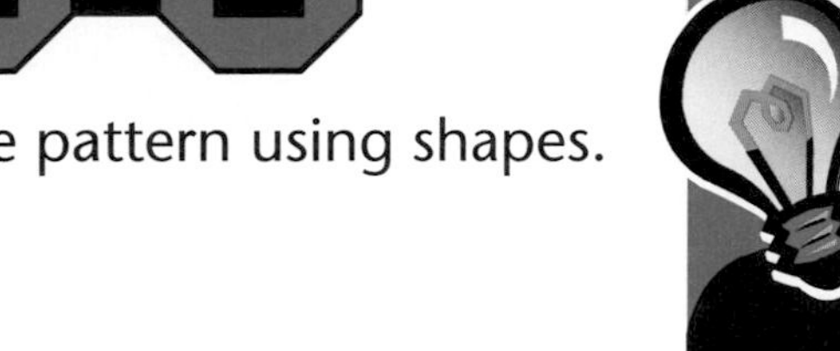

Mixed Strategy Review

5. An art teacher has a budget of $200 to buy art supplies. She buys 40 colored pencils for $0.49 each, 40 markers for $1.39 each, and 20 sketch pads for $4.95 each. Does she go over her budget? If not, how much is left over?

6. An architect designs a deck with dimensions of 12 feet by 24 feet. What are the dimensions in yards?

7. Sam buys 8 hand-blown glass bowls for a total price of $4,200. How much does each bowl cost?

8. An architect is designing a skyscraper that is 27 stories high. The plans call for 1,080 windows. If each story has the same number of windows, how many windows are there on each story?

9. **Create a problem** using a tessellation. Solve it. Ask others to solve it.

★10. Several artists' work is on display at Sunset Art Gallery. Each painting done by the same artist is the same price. Johnson has 3 paintings at $425 each, Cooper has 6 paintings at $545 each, Henderson has 11 paintings at $315 each, and Walker has 5 paintings at $595 each. What is the total value of the paintings in the gallery?

CHOOSE A STRATEGY

- Logical Reasoning
- Draw a Picture
- Make a Graph
- Act It Out
- Make a Table or List
- Find a Pattern
- Guess and Check
- Write a Number Sentence
- Work Backward
- Solve a Simpler Problem

Extra Practice, page 459

Objective: Estimate or determine the perimeter of a polygon.

10•11 Perimeter

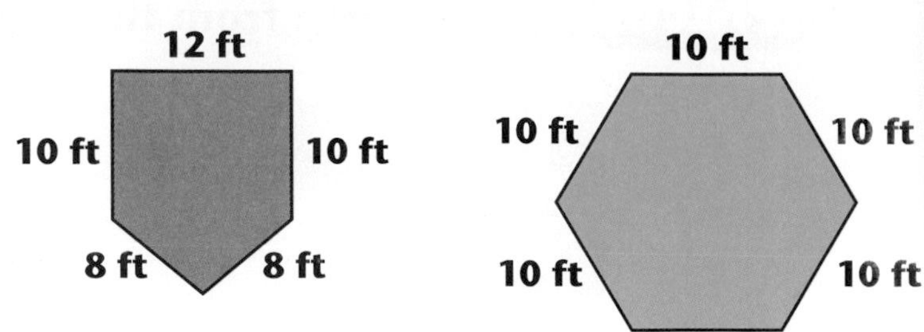

Learn

Math Word

perimeter the distance around a closed figure

Rene is making plans for his house that include a courtyard. He is considering the three different shapes shown. He wants to find the perimeter of each figure.

8 ft
8 ft 8 ft
8 ft 8 ft
8 ft 8 ft
8 ft

There's more than one way!

Method A

*You can find the **perimeter** of any polygon by adding the lengths of its sides.*

Pentagon $12 + 10 + 10 + 8 + 8 = 48$

The perimeter of the pentagon is 48 feet.

Hexagon $10 + 10 + 10 + 10 + 10 + 10 = 60$

The perimeter of the hexagon is 60 feet.

Octagon $8 + 8 + 8 + 8 + 8 + 8 + 8 + 8 = 64$

The perimeter of the octagon is 64 feet.

Method B

You can use formulas for finding the perimeter of a rectangle and a square.

Rectangle

4 cm

8 cm

Since opposite sides of a rectangle are equal, the perimeter equals two times length plus two times width.

$P = 2l + 2w$

$P = (2 \times 8) + (2 \times 4)$

$P = 24$ centimeters

Square

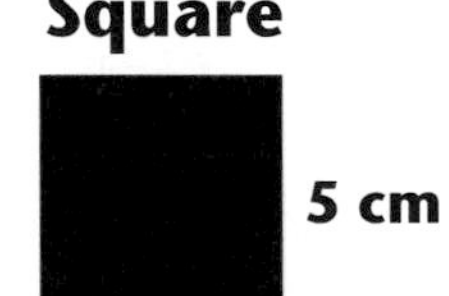

5 cm

Since all four sides of a square are equal, the perimeter equals 4 times the length of a side.

$P = 4s$

$P = 4 \times 5$

$P = 20$ centimeters

You can also find the perimeter of figures in a coordinate plane. Find the perimeter of this rectangle.

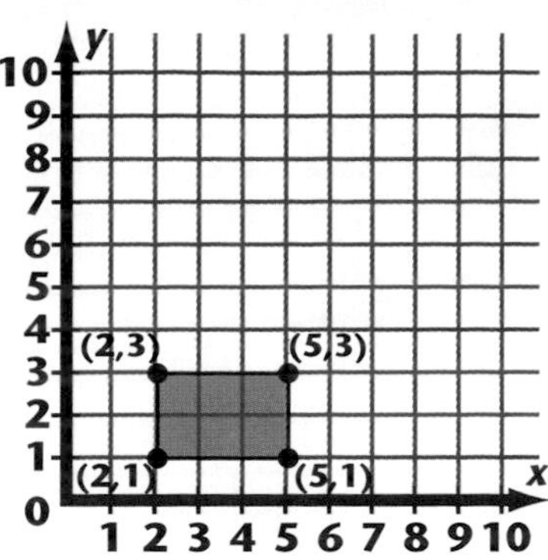

Example

1

Find the length of the horizontal line segment by finding the difference between the x-coordinates.

The x-coordinate is the first number in each ordered pair. $x = 5$ and $x = 2$

Find: $5 - 2 = 3$

The lengths of the horizontal lines are 3 units each.

2

Find the length of the vertical line segment by finding the difference between the y-coordinates.

The y-coordinate is the second number in each ordered pair. $y = 3$ and $y = 1$

Find: $3 - 1 = 2$

The lengths of the vertical lines are 2 units each.

3

Add the lengths of the sides to find the perimeter.

$$\begin{array}{r} 3 \\ 3 \\ 2 \\ +2 \\ \hline 10 \end{array}$$

The perimeter of the rectangle is 10 units.

Try It **Find the perimeter of each figure.**

1. 6 cm 6 cm 6 cm

2. 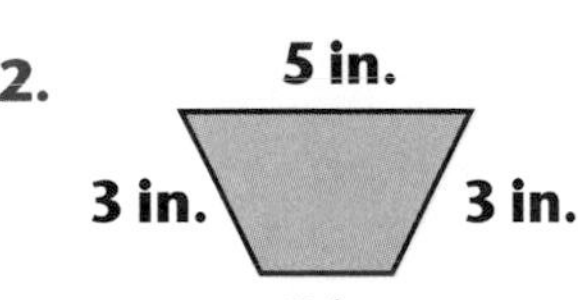

3. 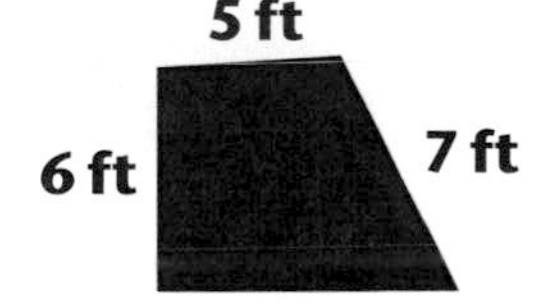

4. 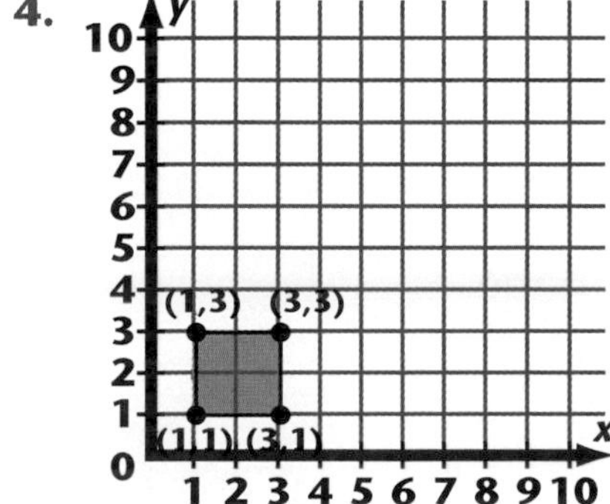

5. 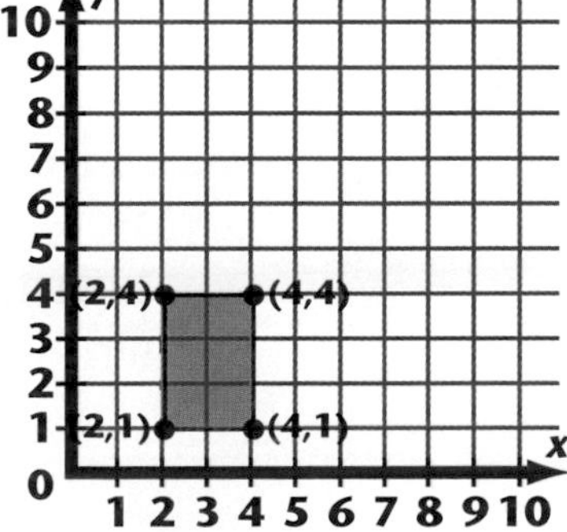

6. 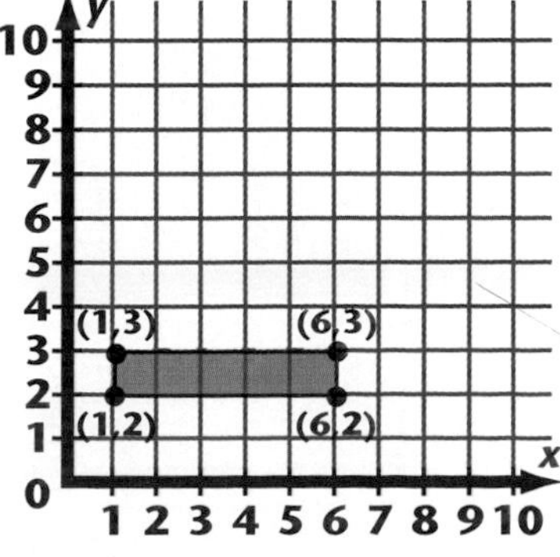

What are two ways to find the perimeter of a figure that has all equal sides?

Practice Find the perimeter of each figure.

7. 3 in. 7 in. 9 in.

8. 

9. 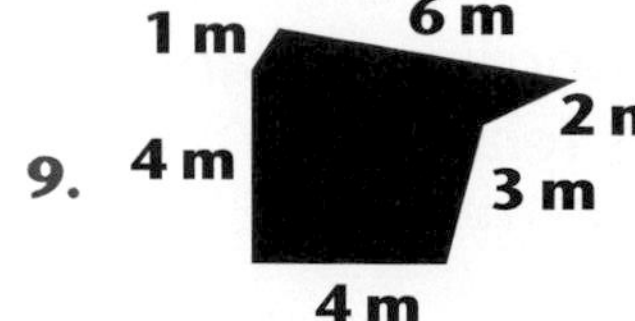

10. (3,5) (4,5) (3,1) (4,1)

11. 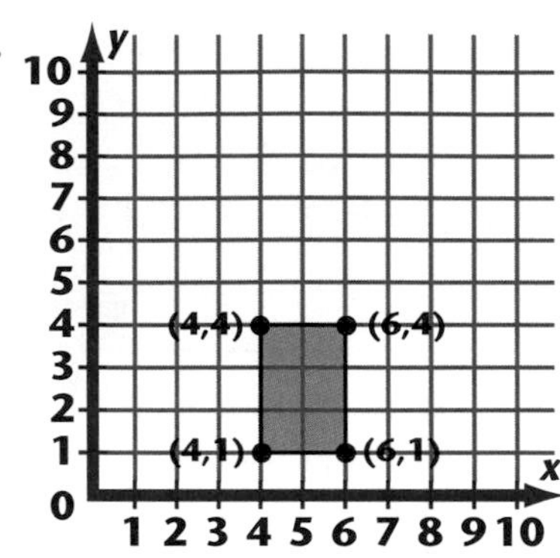

12. 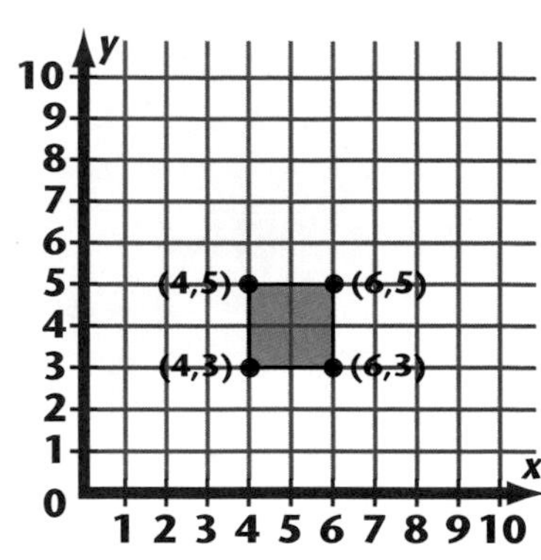

13. 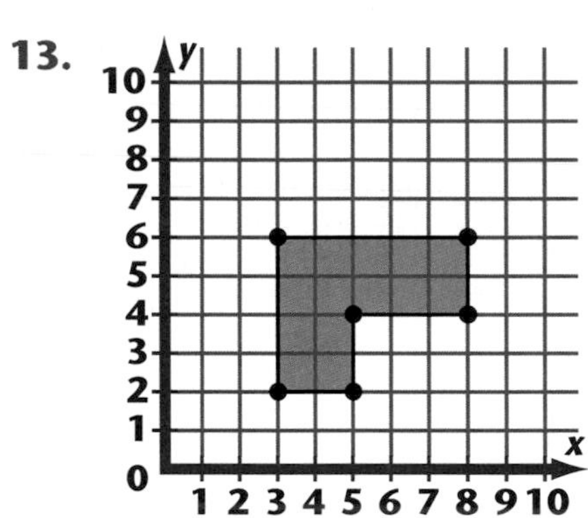

14. 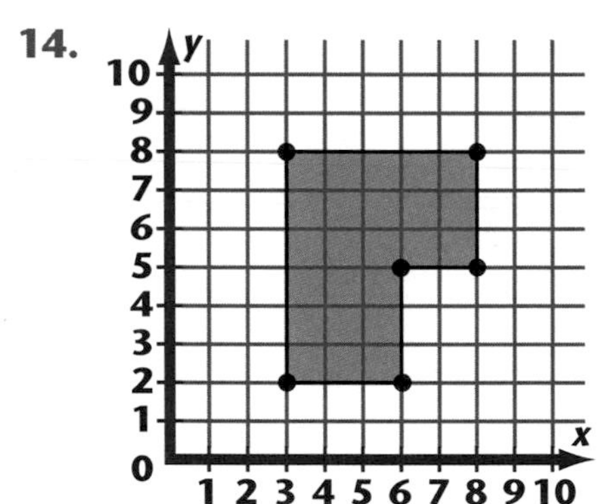

Algebra & functions Find the length of each missing side.

★ 15. 

P = 18 cm

★ 16. 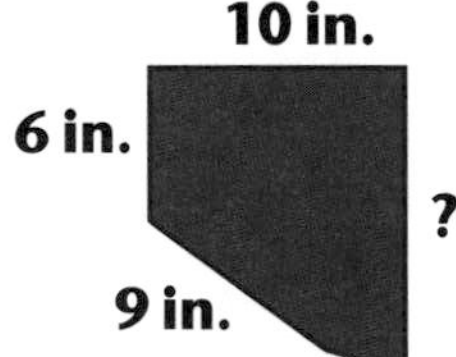

P = 40 in.

★ 17. 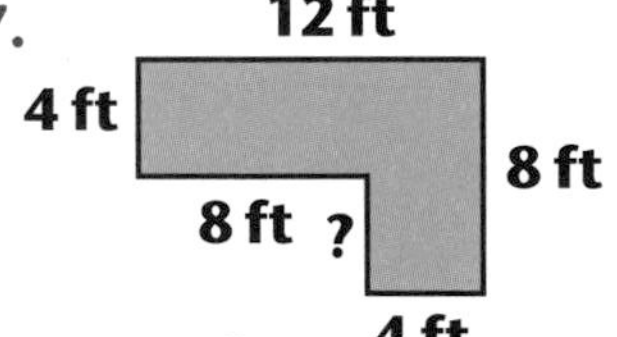

P = 40 ft

18. 

Here's how Ming found the perimeter of a figure. Tell what mistake he made. Explain how to correct it.

Problem Solving

Use data from the plans for problems 19–22.

Master Bedroom 13 ft x 17 ft

Bedroom 2 13 ft x 10 ft

Bedroom 3 13 ft x 10 ft

Bedroom 4 11 ft x 10 ft

19. What is the perimeter of bedroom 2?

20. Convert your answer in problem 19 to yards and inches.

★**21.** Write the names of 2 polygons you see on the plans.

22. What is the total perimeter of the master bedroom and bedroom 2 together? Hint: Do not count the wall that the rooms share.

23. A set of floor plans shows a rectangular house. It measures 56 feet by 30 feet. What is the perimeter of the house?

24. An architect designed a museum that cost $2,637,550 to build. Write the word name for this number.

25. **Analyze:** How many addends will you have if you find the perimeter of:
a. a figure with 6 sides?
b. a figure with 18 sides?

26. An interior decorator uses 8 rolls of wallpaper to cover the walls of a room. Each roll of wallpaper costs $4.50. How much does it cost?

27. If you doubled the length of each side of a square, is the perimeter always doubled? Give an example to explain.

28. If you doubled the length and width of each side of a rectangle, is the perimeter always doubled? Give an example to explain.

★**29.** Circumference is the distance around a circle. You can measure it by putting a piece of string around the circle and measuring the string with a ruler. Measure the circumference of the circle shown.

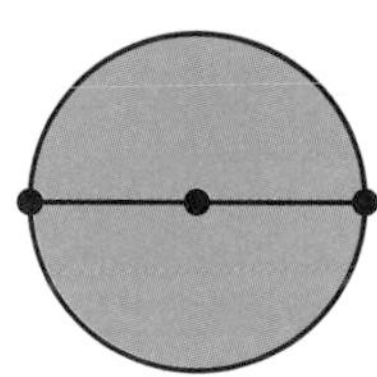

C=20 cm

Spiral Review and Test Prep

30. 4,628 + 3,903 **31.** 8,405 − 2,788 **32.** 526 × 9 **33.** 409 ÷ 7

Choose the correct answer.

34. In order of operations, which is performed first?
A. Multiply and divide
B. Add and subtract
C. Inside parentheses
D. Not Here

35. If the temperature is 50°F, what would you do outside?
F. Swim
G. Hike
H. Snowboard
J. Ice skate

Extra Practice, page 459

Objective: Estimate or determine the area of a shape using a formula.

10•12

Area

Algebra & functions

Learn

Math Words

area the number of square units needed to cover a region or figure

Martin and his father design a flower garden for a dollhouse. What is the area of the garden?

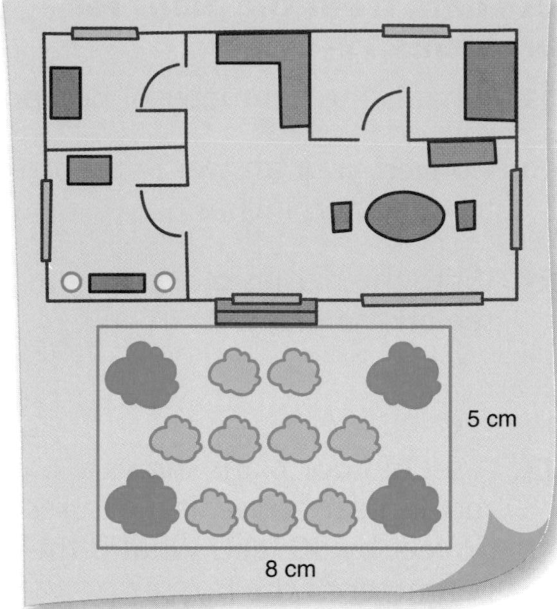

There's more than one way!

Method 

You can count the square units on graph paper to find the **area** of a rectangle.

Count the number of centimeter squares in the rectangle.

There are 40 square centimeters.

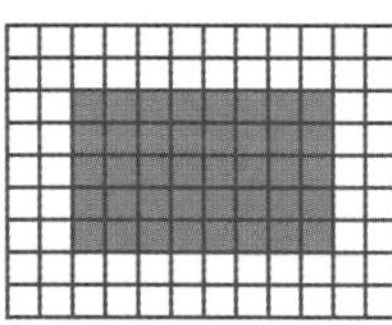

Method 

You can use a formula to find the area.

Area = length × width

$A = l \times w$

$= 8 \text{ cm} \times 5 \text{ cm}$

$= 40$ square centimeters (cm^2)

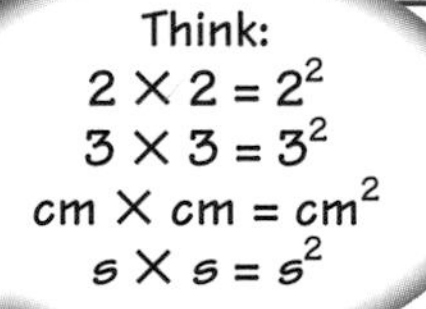

The area of the garden is 40 cm^2.

Another Example

Find the area of a square with 3 centimeter sides.

$A = \text{side} \times \text{side}$ $\quad A = 3 \text{ cm} \times 3 \text{ cm}$

$A = s^2$ $\quad A = 9 \text{ cm}^2$

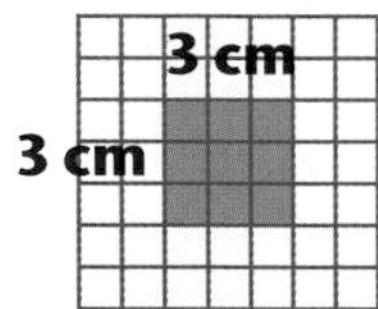

Martin and his father are now designing an herb garden. This diagram shows the outline of the garden. What is the area?

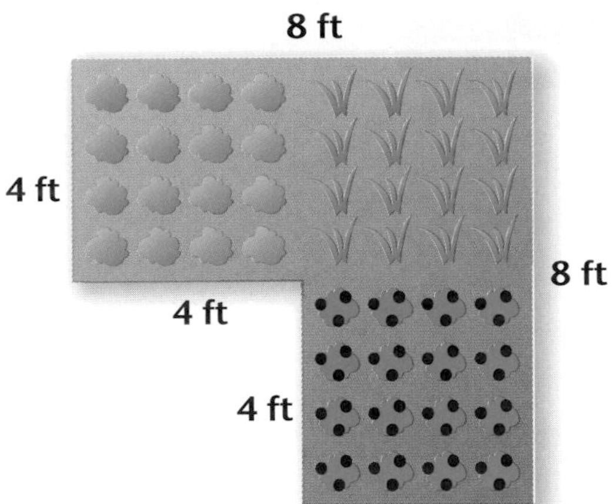

Example

To find the area of a complex figure, break it into smaller parts.

1

Try to divide the figure into rectangles and/or squares.

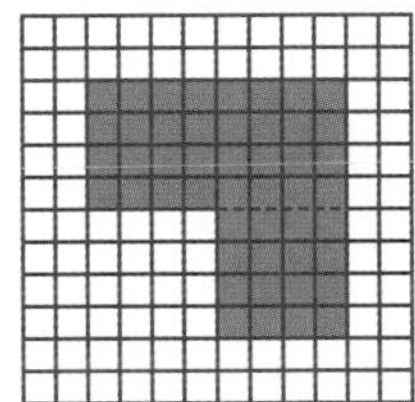

The dotted line shows how to make a rectangle and a square.

2

Find the area of each smaller figure.

Area of rectangle:

$A = l \times w$

$8 \times 4 = 32 \text{ ft}^2$

Area of square:

$A = s \times s$, or s^2

$4 \times 4 = 16 \text{ ft}^2$

3

Add the area of both smaller figures.

$32 \text{ ft}^2 + 16 \text{ ft}^2 = 48 \text{ ft}^2$

The area of the herb garden is 48 square feet.

Try It **Find the area of each figure.**

1. 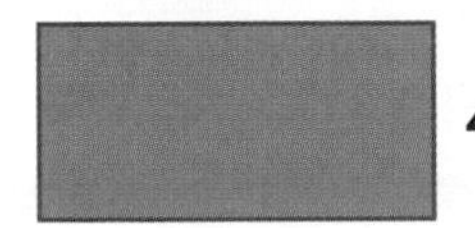

2. 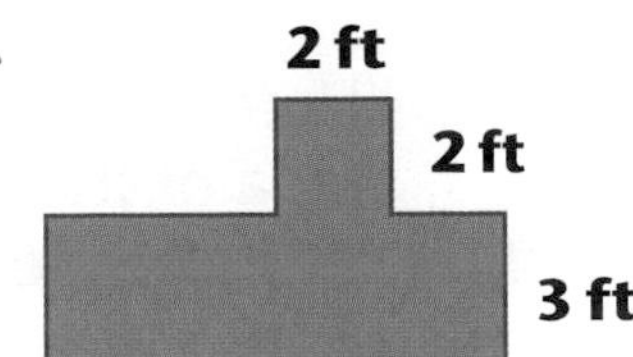

3. 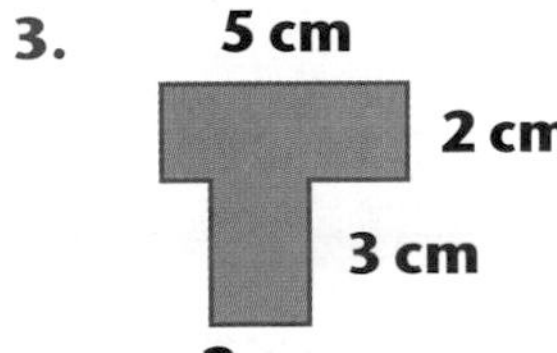

Write a rule for finding the area of complex figures.

Practice **Find the area of each figure.**

4.
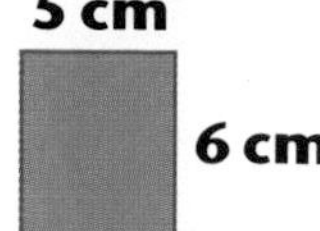

5.
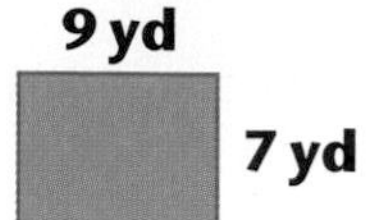

6.
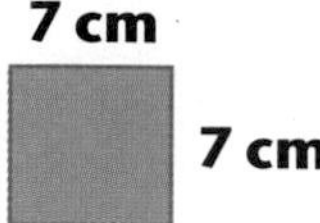

7.
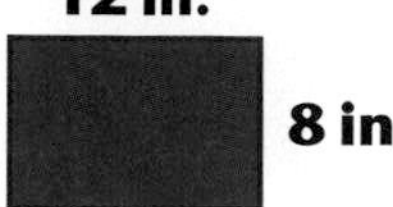

★8.
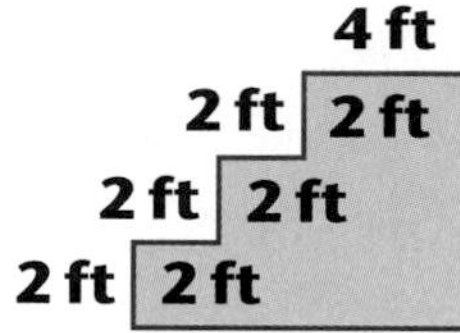

★9.
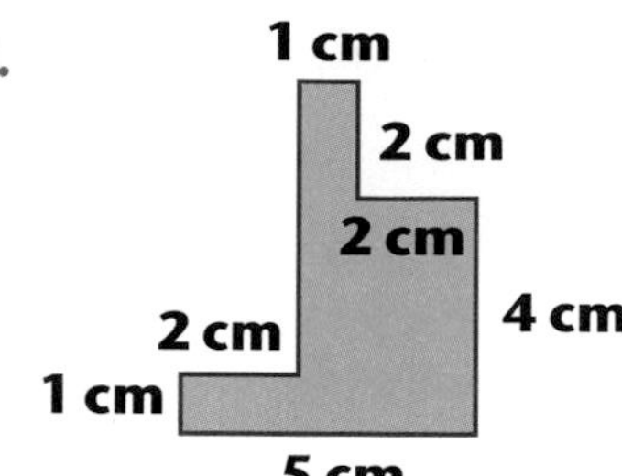

Use graph paper to draw each figure. Tell what the figure is and find the area.

10. Length: 6 cm
Width: 7 cm

11. Length: 8 cm
Width: 8 cm

12. Length: 6 cm
Width: 3 cm

Find the area and perimeter of each figure.

13.

14.
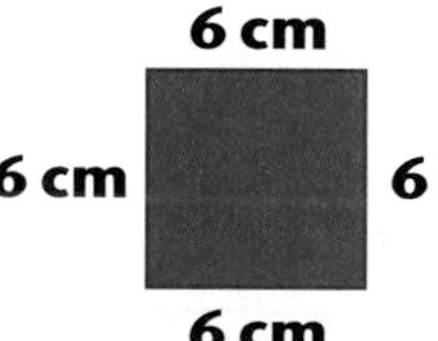

15.
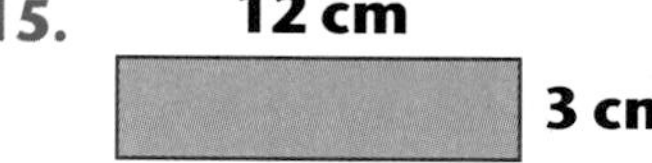

16. Compare the area and perimeter of each figure in problems 13–15. What do you find?

17. **Analyze:** Given an area of 30 square units, how many rectangles with whole number lengths are there? How can you tell without drawing them?

18.

Here's how Katya found the area of the square. Tell what mistake she made. Explain how to correct it.

Problem Solving

Use data from *Did You Know?* for problem 19.

19. In the beginning of March, Janet planted 9 rows of seeds with 35 seeds in each row. How many seeds did she plant? When should they germinate?

Did You Know?

Licorice mint is an herb that can be used in tea and in salads. The seed usually germinates in 1 to 3 months. The young shoots should be harvested when they are about 10-15 centimeters tall.

20. Language Arts: The Dewey Decimal System is a cataloging method that libraries use to classify nonfiction. Books related to the arts are classified between 700.0 and 760.0. Books on architecture are classified between 710.0 and 720.0. Vince is looking in 735.0 for a book on landscape architecture. Is he likely to find it? Explain why or why not.

21. Explain what happens to the area when the length and width of a rectangle are doubled. What happens when the length and width are tripled?

★**22.** How can you use what you have learned about finding the area of rectangles and squares to find the area of right triangles? Draw examples to show your reasoning. Can you write a formula?

★**23.** A large rectangular garden measuring 240 meters by 100 meters needs to be fertilized. Each bag of fertilized covers 2,000 square meters and costs $10. Find the cost of the fertilizer needed.

24. Michael exercises by jogging in his neighborhood park. He jogs 37 miles each week for 7 weeks. He then jogs 49 miles each week for 20 weeks. How many miles did he run altogether?

Spiral Review and Test Prep

25. $4{,}506 + 569$

26. $81{,}089 - 113$

27. 738×6

28. $8\overline{)1{,}032}$

29. 481×8

Choose the correct answer.

30. What is the missing number in this number sentence?
$(4 \times 3) \times 6 = ■ \times (3 \times 6)$

A. 2 **C.** 4
B. 3 **D.** 72

31. Which is the same as 60 decimeters?

F. 60 millimeters **H.** 600 centimeters
G. 60 centimeters **J.** 600 millimeters

Explore Volume

Algebra & functions

Learn

Math Words

volume the amount of space that a 3-dimensional figure encloses

cubic unit the volume of a cube, one of whose sides is the given unit of length

You can use connecting cubes to explore volume. What different rectangular prisms can you make using 30 cubes?

Work Together

You Will Need
- connecting cubes

▶ Use 30 connecting cubes to build rectangular prisms.

- First, build a prism that has only one layer of blocks. Next, build a prism that has two layers, three layers, and so on.

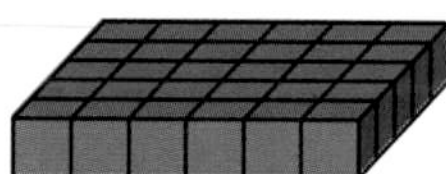 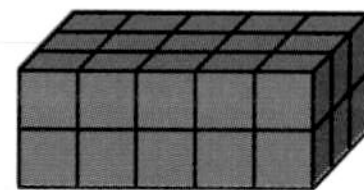 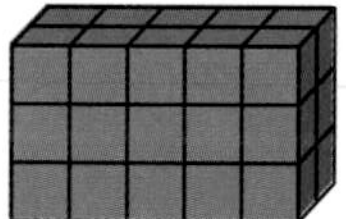

- Each prism includes 30 cubes. The **volume** of each prism is 30 **cubic units**.
- Record the length, width, height, and volume of the rectangular prisms in a table.

Length	Width	Height	Volume
6 cm	5 cm	1 cm	30 cubic cm

▶ Use different numbers of connecting cubes to build rectangular prisms. Find the volume of each rectangular prism. Record the length, width, height, and volume in a table.

Make Connections

What if you exactly fill a box with centimeter cubes? The volume of the box is measured by the exact number of cubes it holds.

Using Models	Using Paper and Pencil
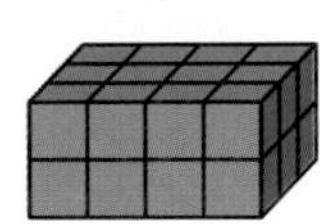 You can count the number of cubes in the box. The top layer has 12 cubes and the bottom layer has 12 cubes. $12 + 12 = 24$	You can use multiplication to find the volume of the box. There are 4 cubes in the length of the box and 3 cubes in the width of the box. So $4 \times 3 = 12$ cubes in one layer. Since there are 2 layers, multiply 12×2 to find the volume.

The volume of the box is 24 cubic centimeters (cm^3).

Try It **Find the volume of each rectangular prism.**

1. 
2. 
3. 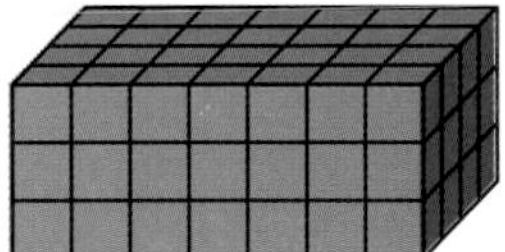

Explain why you multiply the length by the width by the height to find the volume of a rectangular prism.

Practice **Find the volume of each rectangular prism.**

4. 
5. 
6. 

7. Length: 3 in.
   Width: 8 in.
   Height: 5 in.
8. Length: 4 ft
   Width: 12 ft
   Height: 3 ft
9. Length: 7 in.
   Width: 5 in.
   Height: 6 in.
10. Length: 7 cm
    Width: 3 cm
    Height: 4 cm

11. **Measurement:** Name as many units as you can that could be used to measure the volume of a container.

Extra Practice, page 459

Objective: Analyze data and make decisions.

Problem Solving: Application
Decision Making

What dimensions should he choose for the garden?

Mr. Harris is making a flower garden next to his house. The garden will be 64 square feet in area. Mr. Harris wants to place a decorative fence around the garden. He has $150.00 to spend.

PICKET FENCING
$3.50 each foot
$8.50 each foot for fencing and installation

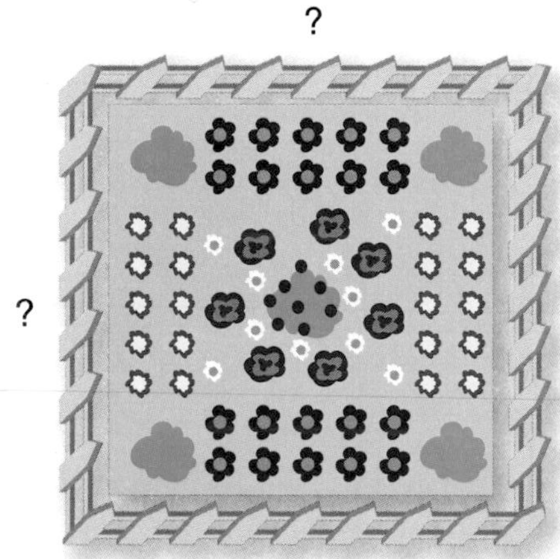

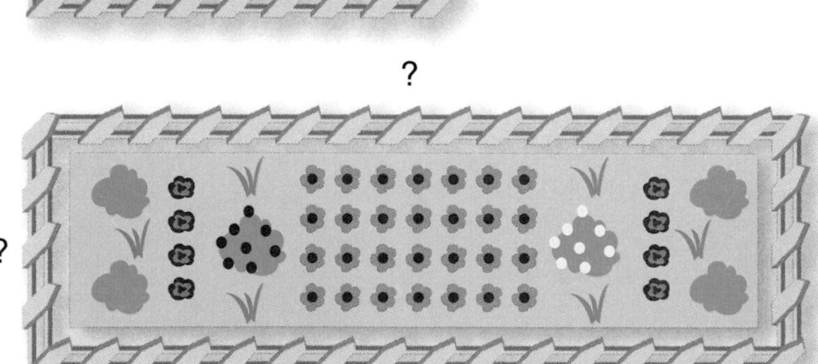
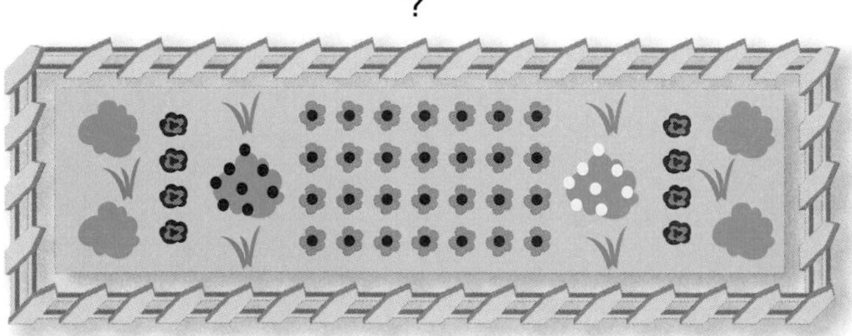

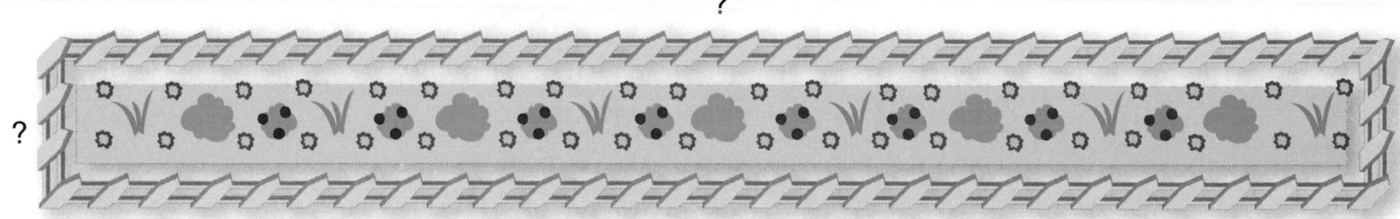

Read for Understanding

1. How large of an area does Mr. Harris want to fence off?
2. How much does he have to spend?
3. What are some possible shapes that Mr. Harris might use for the garden?
4. How much does the fencing cost alone? How much does it cost for the fence with installation?

Make Decisions

5. How many possible rectangles with whole number lengths are there with an area of 64 square units? What are the dimensions?
6. Can you make a square with an area of 64 square units? What would the dimensions be?
7. What other complex figures could Mr. Harris use that have an area of 64 square units? Draw and label 2 examples.
8. Would you use area or perimeter of the figure to find out how much fencing is needed?
9. What is the cost of fencing for each of the rectangles?
10. Find the cost of fencing for the square.
11. Does it make sense for Mr. Harris to consider all of the possible rectangles as being suitable for a garden? Explain your reasoning.
12. What is the cost of fencing in one of the complex figures you drew in problem 7?
13. Compare the cost for fencing in the rectangles with the cost for fencing in the square. What do you find?
14. Suppose Mr. Harris wants to consider having the fence installed. How much would it cost to fence in the least expensive rectangle?
15. Does Mr. Harris have enough money to have the fence installed for any of the figures? Explain.
16. Does Mr. Harris have enough money to fence in all the complex figures you drew? Why or why not?

What is your recommendation for Mr. Harris? Explain your reasoning.

Problem Solving

Objective: *Apply perimeter and area to investigate science concepts.*

Problem Solving: Math and Science

How well do you make patterns?

Have you ever tried to give a friend directions to your home? It's not as easy as it seems.

You Will Need
- **pattern blocks and other mixed objects**
- **textbook**

In this activity, you will use shapes to create patterns. Then you will use geometry words to give and take directions.

Hypothesize

On a scale of 1 (best) to 5 (worst), rate how well you think you will follow directions to make patterns.

Procedure

1. Work with a partner. Take turns. Make the textbook a wall between you and your partner.
2. Build a geometric pattern using some or all of the shapes. Describe that pattern to your partner. Give other information such as the size, number of sides, angles, position and height. See the *Hint* for more words.
3. The other partner should follow the directions and recreate the pattern. Don't peek!
4. Compare the two patterns. Rate how well you followed directions.
5. Switch jobs and try again.

Data

Make a sketch of your structure. Copy and complete the chart to record the rating.

Drawing of Structure	Rating

Hint:
Use words like...
triangle, pentagon, sphere, cube, angle, obtuse, symmetry, over, under, behind, next to, line

Conclude and Apply

- How well did you follow directions? Do you have enough data to decide?
- Talk about what was hard or easy about giving and following the directions.
- Make a list of words that helped you give directions.
- Describe how a camouflage pattern gives some animals a survival advantage.

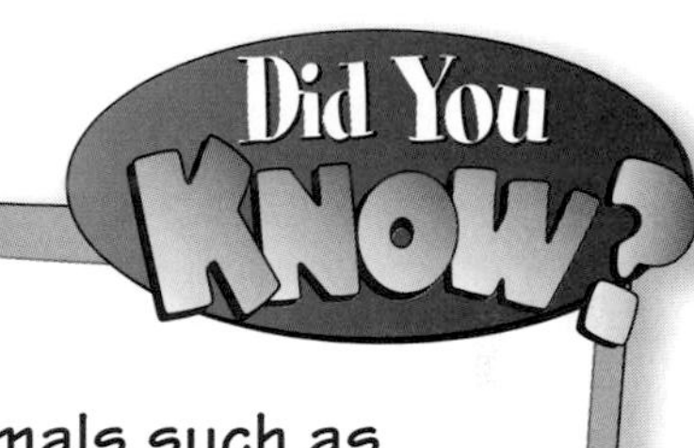

Animals such as leopards, chameleons, and zebras use patterns to camouflage themselves.

Going Further

1. Design and complete an activity to find how many shapes you can use in a structure and still follow directions easily. How many shapes make following directions hard?

2. Make a structure with any or all of the shapes. What did you make? Write a story about that structure.

3. Design and complete an activity to find how many numbers you can repeat given a set of numbers. Did you use a pattern to help you remember the numbers?

Check Your Progress B

Write whether the figures are similar. Then write whether the figures are congruent. (pages 430–433)

1. 

2. 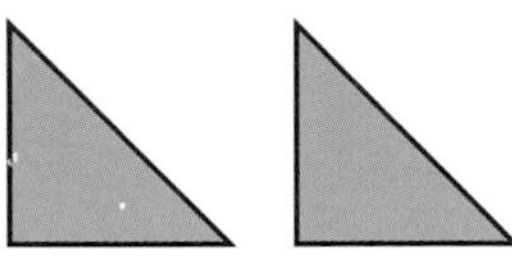

Write *translation, reflection,* or *rotation* to tell how the figure was moved. (pages 434–435)

3. 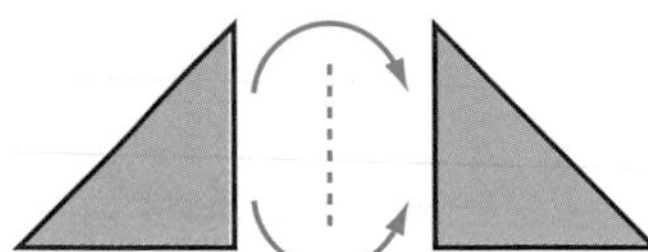

4. 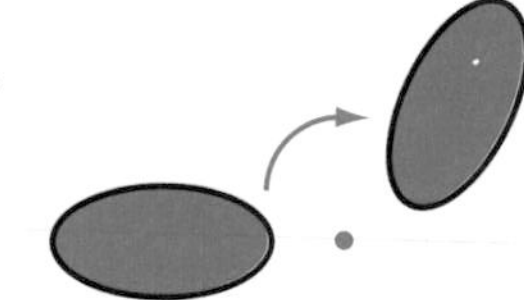

Is the dotted line a line of symmetry? (pages 436–439)

5. 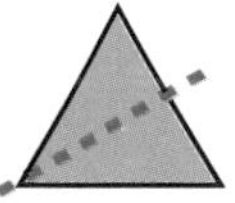

6. 

Find the perimeter and area. (pages 446–445)

7. 

Find the volume. (pages 450–451)

8. 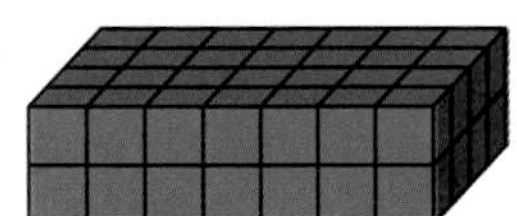

Solve. (pages 430–451)

9. Draw a tessellation using squares and triangles. Describe the pattern you used.

10. **Explain** how you can find the area of the floor in your classroom.

Additional activities at www.mhschool.com/math

Extra Practice

3-Dimensional Figures (pages 408–411)

Describe the figure. Tell how many faces, edges, and vertices it has.

1. 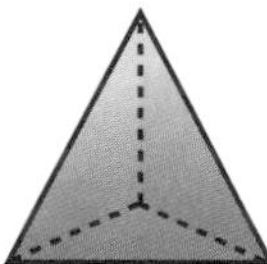

2. 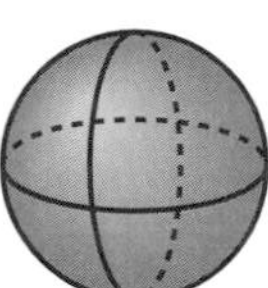

3. 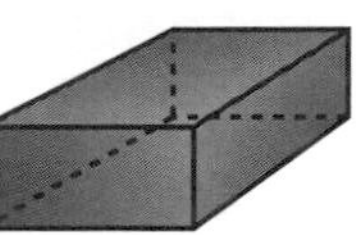

2-Dimensional Figures and Polygons (pages 412–415)

Identify each figure as open or closed.
Is it a polygon? If so, classify the figure.

1. 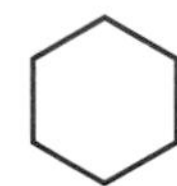

2. 

3. 

Lines, Line Segments, and Rays (pages 416–419)

Identify each figure.

1. 

2. 

3. 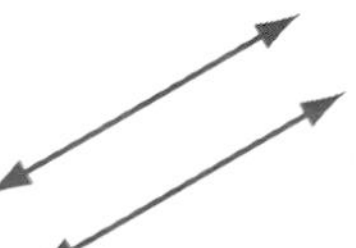

Angles (pages 420–421)

Write *acute, obtuse,* or *right* for each angle.

1. 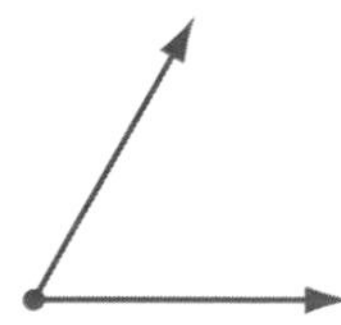

2. 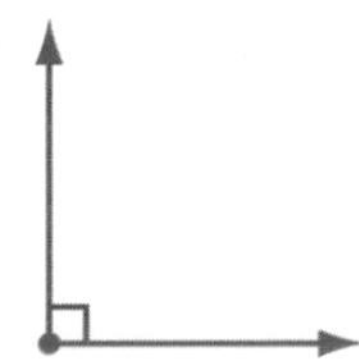

3. 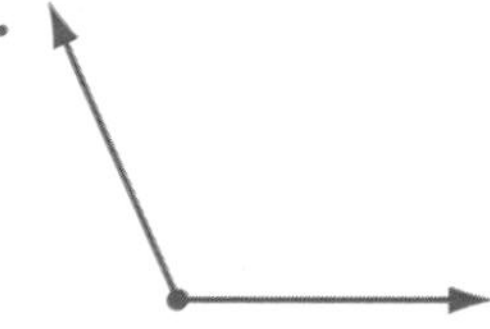

Solve.

4. An artist named her painting 180 Degrees. She explained that the two right angles in her painting equal 180°. That's where she came up with the name. Do you agree or disagree? Explain your reasoning.

Extra Practice

Triangles and Quadrilaterals (pages 422–425)

Classify each triangle as equilateral, isosceles, or scalene. Then classify each triangle as right, acute, or obtuse.

1. 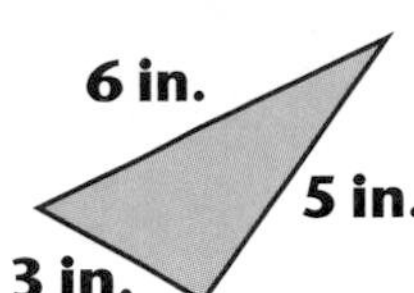

2. 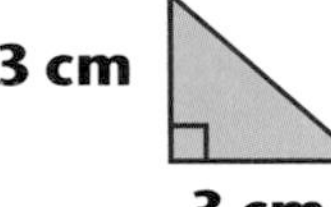

3. 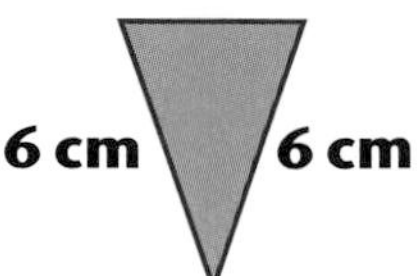

Identify the quadrilateral in as many ways as you can.

1. 

2. 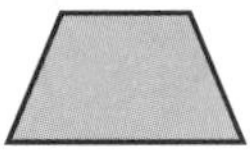

3. 

Problem Solving: Reading for Math Use a Diagram (pages 426–427)

Solve.

1. Mike, Bob, Melanie, and Susan are taking a painting class. Frank, Lois, Melanie, Sam, and Bob are taking a drawing class. Make a diagram that shows this.

Congruent and Similar (pages 430–433)

Draw the figure on dot paper. Then draw one figure that is similar to the original and one that is congruent and similar.

1. 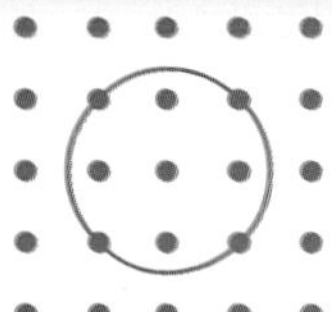

2. 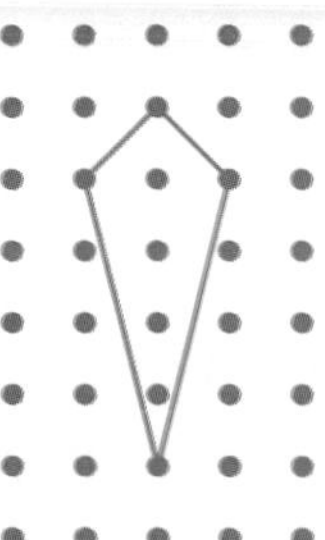

3. 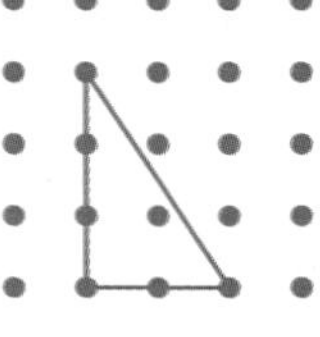

Extra Practice

Symmetry (pages 436–439)

Is the dotted line a line of symmetry?

1. 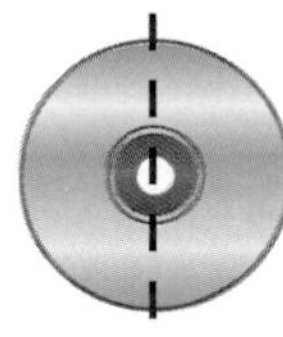

2. 

3. 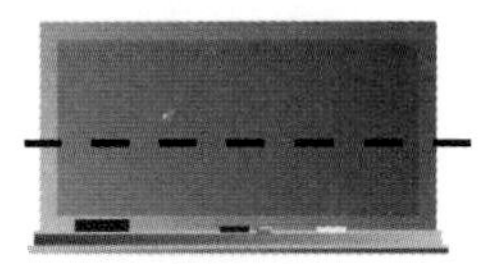

Problem Solving: Strategy Find a Pattern (pages 440–441)

Solve.

1. In the summer Misha draws for 25 minutes every day. She increases her time by 5 minutes every week. In the sixth week, how many minutes does she draw each day?

2. Mr. Dobson put 3 papers in the first row, 6 in the second, and 12 in the fourth. The numbers continue to increase in the same way. How many papers are in the third row?

Perimeter (pages 442–445)

Find the perimeter of each figure.

1. 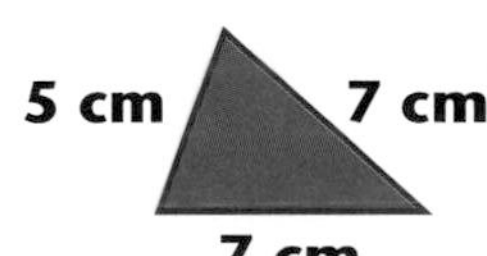

2. 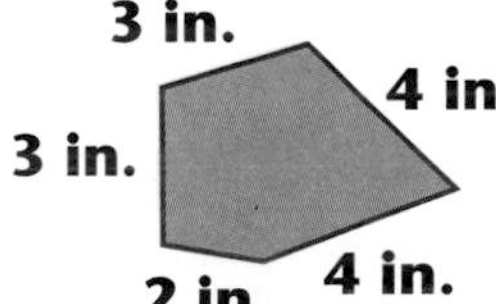

3. 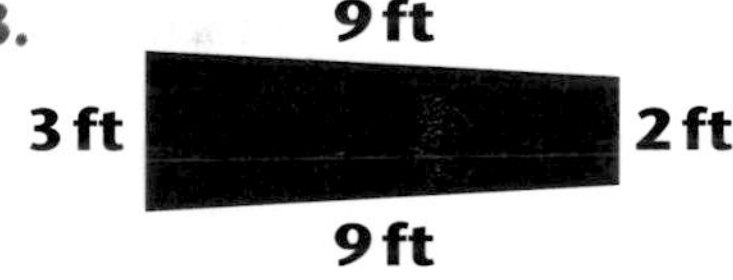

Area (pages 446–449)

Find the area of each figure.

1. 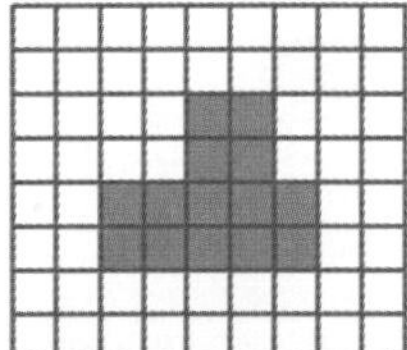

2. 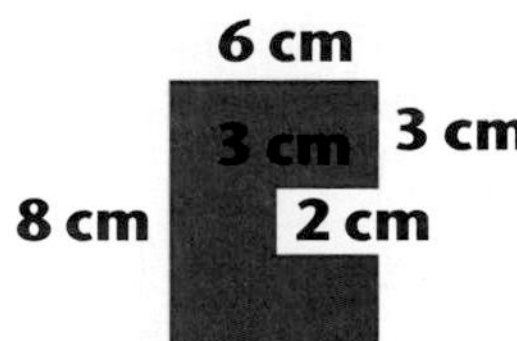

3. 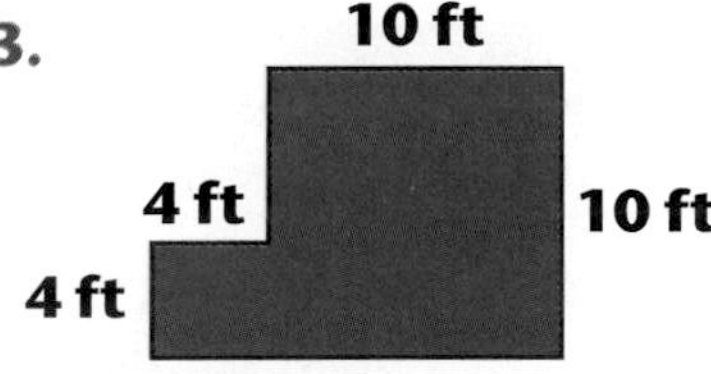

Explore Volume (pages 450–451)

Find the volume for each rectangular prism.

1. 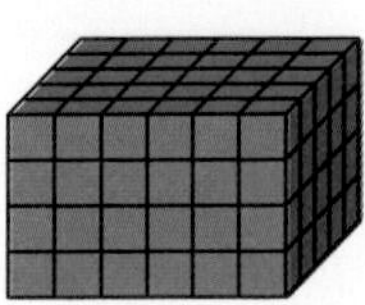

2. 

Chapter Study Guide

Language and Math

Complete. Use a word from the list.

1. A parallelogram with 4 equal sides and 4 right angles is a ____.
2. If two lines never meet, they are ____.
3. If a figure has two pairs of opposite sides that are parallel, it is a ____.
4. An angle that measures 90° is a ____.

Math Words

obtuse
parallel
parallelogram
perpendicular
right angle
square

Skills and Applications

Classify 2- and 3-dimensional figures and their parts. (pages 408–421)

Example

Describe and name the figure and its parts.

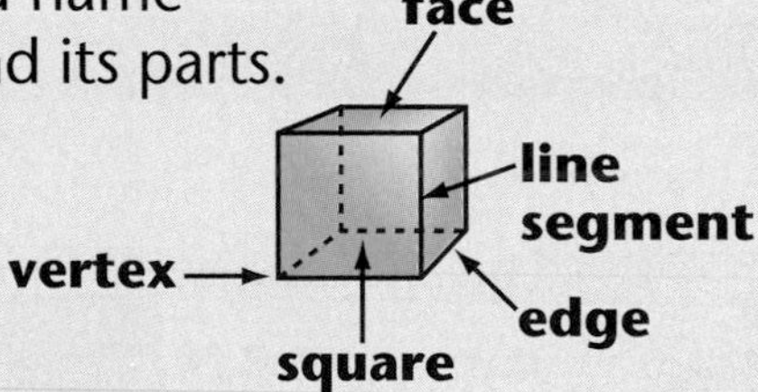

Solution

You can describe a figure by naming its parts. It has 6 square faces, 12 edges, and 8 vertices. The figure is a cube.

Name each figure.

5. 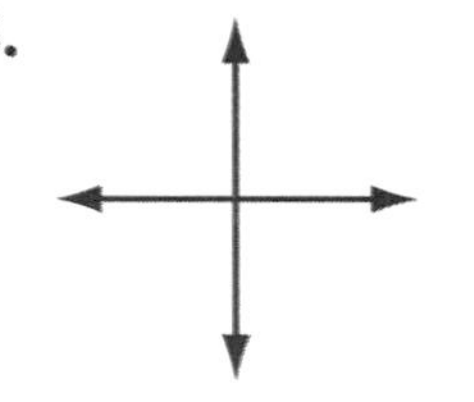

6. 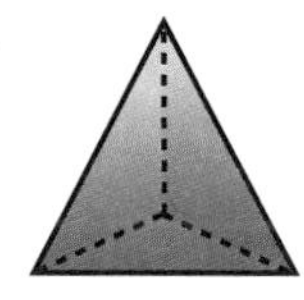

7. 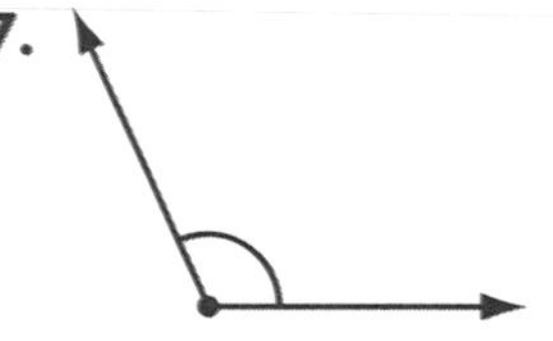

Classify triangles and quadrilaterals. (pages 422–425)

Example

Describe and name the figure.

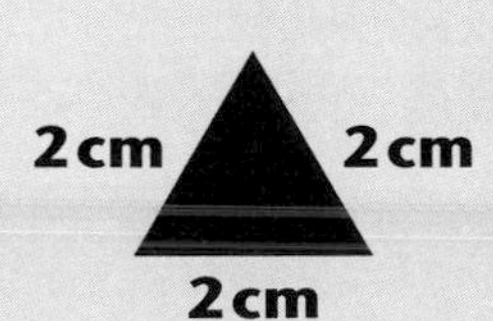

Solution

You can name a polygon by looking at its sides and angles. This figure has 3 equal sides. It has 3 equal, acute angles. It is an equilateral triangle.

Name each figure.

8. 

9. 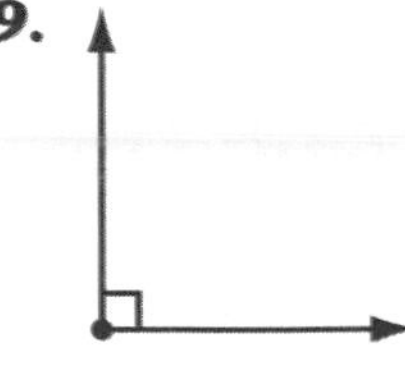

10 

Identify congruent, similar, and symmetrical figures. (pages 430–433, 436–439)

Example

Tell which figures are similar and congruent.

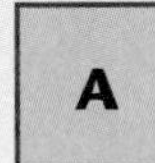

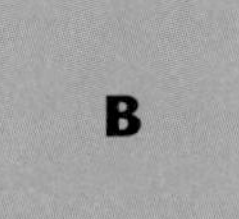

C

Solution

Figure B is similar to the others, but it is a different size. Figures A and C are similar and congruent.

Tell which figures are similar and congruent.

11.

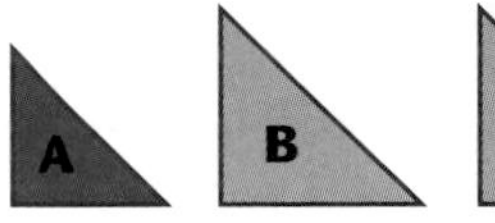

12.

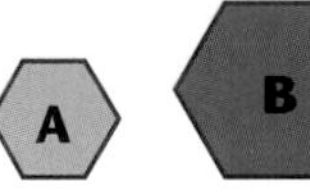

Does each figure have bilateral symmetry or rotational symmetry?

13.

14.

Find the perimeter, area, and volume. (pages 442-451)

Example

Find the perimeter and area of this figure.

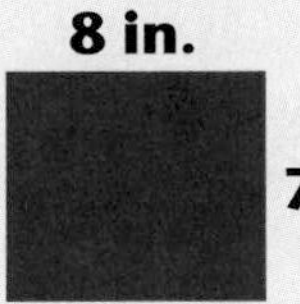

Solution

$P = 2l + 2w$

$(2 \times 8) + (2 \times 7) = 30$

Perimeter = 30 in.

$A = l \times w$

$8 \times 7 = 56$

Area = 56 in.^{2}

Find the perimeter and area of each rectangle.

15. length: 8 inches; width = 4 inches

16. length: 10 inches; width = 6 inches

17. length: 3 feet; width = 14 feet

Find the volume.

18.

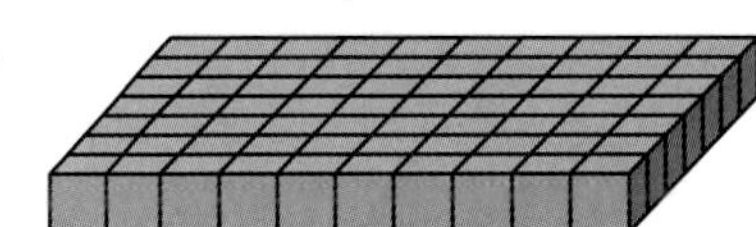

Use strategies to solve problems. (pages 426–427, 440–441)

Example

What figures are used in the design? How are these figures moved to make the design?

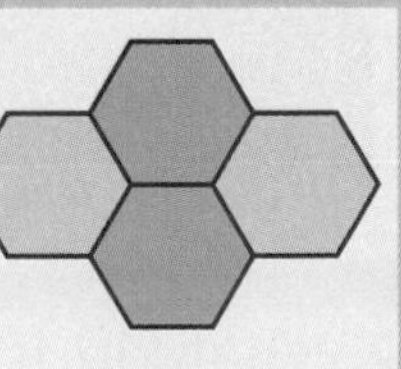

Solution

The design is made up of hexagons. The pattern is formed by translations to the left, up and down, or diagonally.

Solve.

19. Copy the design in the example on grid paper. Then add 4 more pieces to the design.

20. A figure has 4 sides. The opposite sides are the same length. There are two obtuse angles and two acute angles. What figure is it?

Chapter Test

Identify each figure.

1. 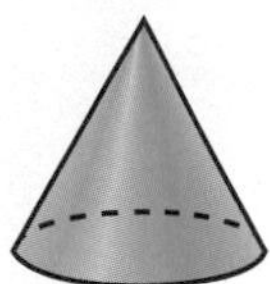

2. 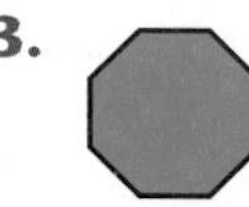

3. 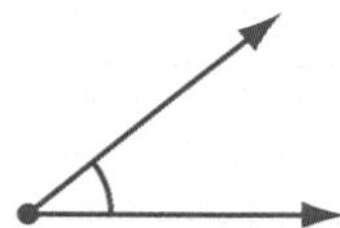

4. 

5. 

6. 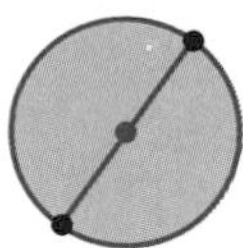

7. 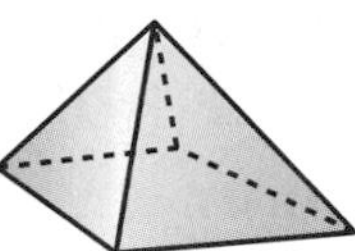

8. 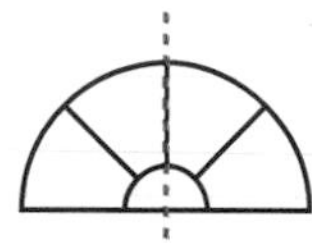

Write *bilateral symmetry* or *rotational symmetry* for each item.

9. 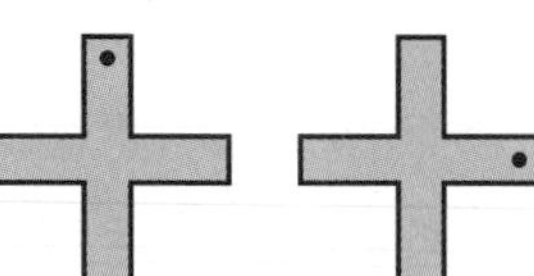

10. 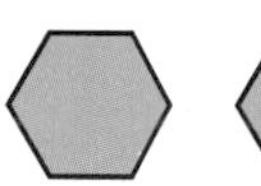

Write whether the figures are similar. Then write whether the figures are congruent.

11. 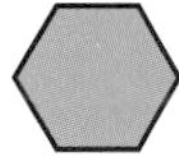

12. 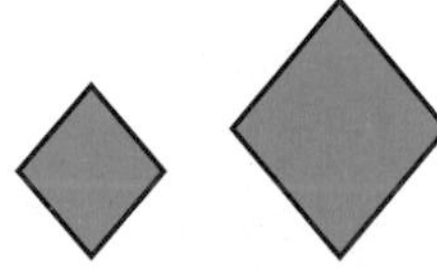

Find the area and perimeter of each figure.

13. 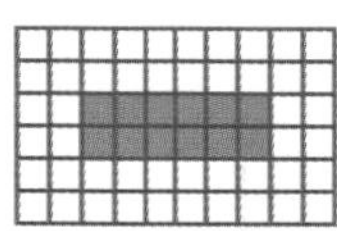

14. 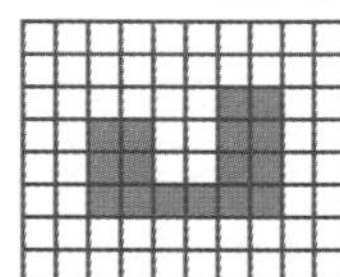

Find the volume.

15. 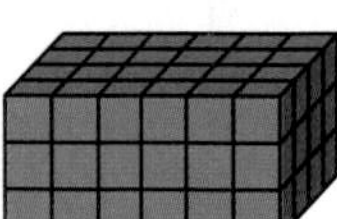

16. 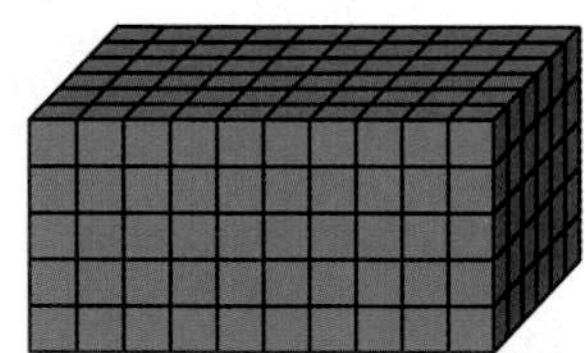

Solve.

17. The floor of a house has 6 sides. What kind of figure is this?

18. What kinds of line segments are two segments on a square that touch?

19. House plans show that a rectangular shaped garage has a length of 28 feet and a width of 24 feet. What is the area?

20. Use an equilateral triangle to make a tessellation. Tell how you made the pattern.

Performance Assessment

Building designers use geometric shapes all the time when they create plans for new buildings.

You are designing a new office building. Make a sketch of what your building will look like.

Use as many different geometric shapes as you can.

Remember that you can also change the position of a shape to make it look different.

Find the perimeter and area of the building's base. Then find the volume of the entire building.

A Good Answer

- shows that you used a variety of geometric shapes.
- includes a list of the shapes you used.
- shows a sketched-out plan for a building that includes many different geometric shapes.
- gives the perimeter, area, and volume and how you found them.

You may want to save this work for your portfolio.

Enrichment

Area of Irregular Shapes

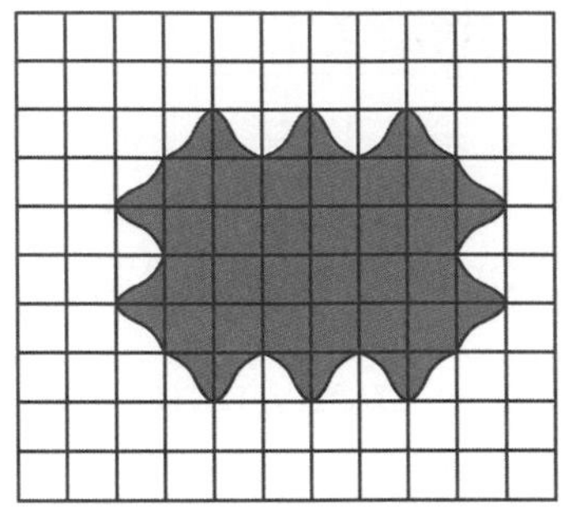

Some shapes are not shaped like squares or triangles. They are irregular shapes.

There are no formulas to help you find areas of irregular shapes, but you can estimate the area.

Look at the shape shown on the grid. What is the area in square units?

- Count the whole squares first. There are 24 whole squares in the shape.
- Now count the partial squares. There are 20 squares where the shape covers $\frac{1}{2}$ of a square. You can think of them as 10 wholes.
- So the area of the shape is about 24 + 10 or 34 square units.

1. **Analyze:** How could you have used the formula for area of a rectangle to help you estimate the area of the shape shown above?

Estimate the area of each shape.

2. 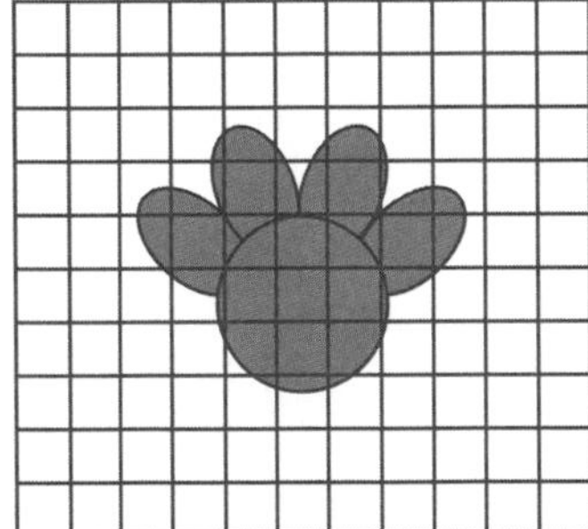

3. 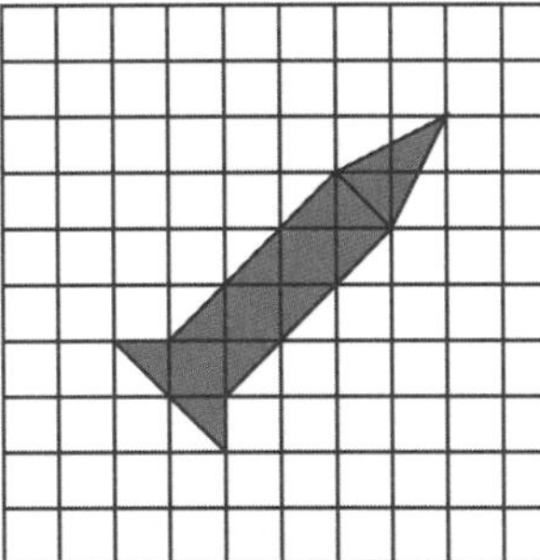

4. 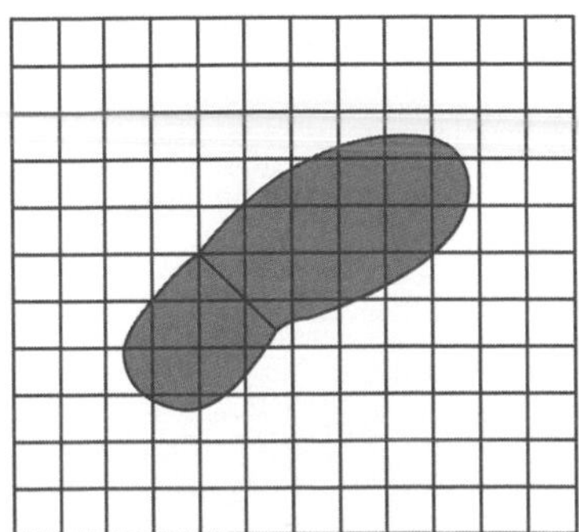

5. 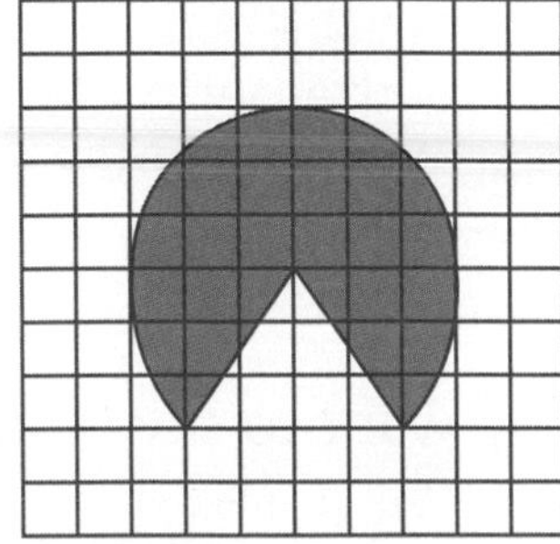

Test-Taking Tips

For some types of test questions, you need to use information from a picture to find the answer.

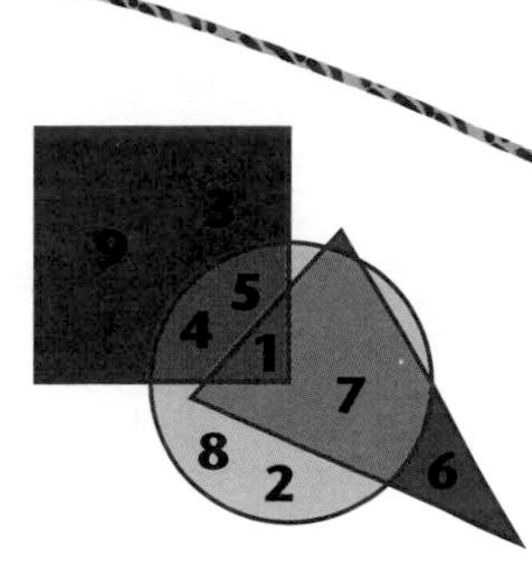

Which numbers are only in the circle and the square?

A. 1 **C.** 4, 5, and 1
B. 4 and 5 **D.** 4, 5, 8, and 2

Find the part of the picture that is in the square and the circle. Do not include the part with 1 in it. That part is also in the triangle.

The part that is only in the circle and the square has 4 and 5 in it. The correct answer is B.

Check for Success

Before turning in a test, go back one last time to check.

☑ I understood and answered the questions asked.
☑ I checked my work for errors.
☑ My answers make sense.

Choose the correct answer. Use the information in the picture.

1. Which figures have 4 right angles?

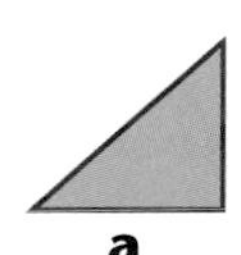
a

b

c

d

A. a, d **C.** a, b, c
B. a, b, d **D.** b, d

2. Find two shapes in which one shape has a perimeter that is twice that of the other?

a
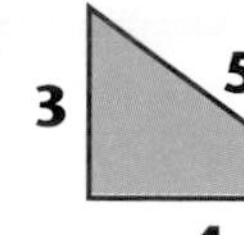

b
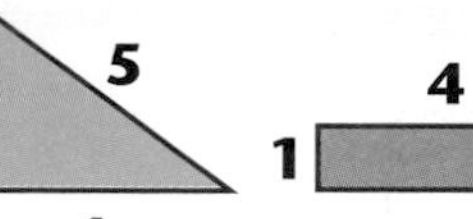
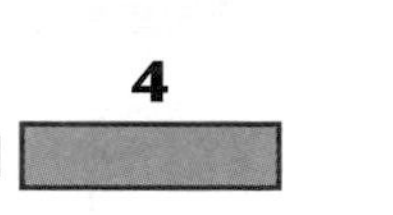

c
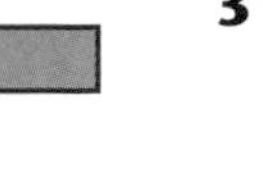

d

F. a and b **H.** a and d
G. c and d **J.** b and c

3. Which is the best estimate of the shaded part?

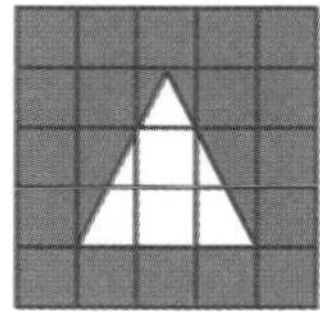

A. 5 sq. units **C.** 25 sq. units
B. 20 sq. units **D.** 30 sq. units

4. Which two shapes have the same shape and size?

a

b

c

d

F. c and d **H.** a and b
G. a and c **J.** a and d

Spiral Review and Test Prep

Chapters 1–10

Choose the correct answer.

Number Sense

1. Write the number in standard form.
   30,000 + 5,000 + 40 + 2
   A. 30,542 C. 35,420
   B. 35,042 D. 354,200

2. A colored pencil set has 3 rows with 12 pencils in each row. How many pencils are there in the set?
   F. 15 H. 36
   G. 24 J. 48

3. An office building has 4 wings. There are 5 floors in each wing and 12 offices on each floor. How many offices are there in the building?
   A. 240 C. 32
   B. 21 D. Not Here

4. A house sold for less than the price the owners wanted. If they wanted $124,900, what could the selling price be?
   F. $124,950 H. $124,999
   G. $125,000 J. $124,000

Measurement and Geometry

5. Which name could not be given to a square?
   A. Quadrilateral C. Open figure
   B. Polygon D. Parallelogram

6. A window is 120 centimeters long. What is its length in millimeters?
   F. 12 millimeters
   G. 1,200 millimeters
   H. 12,000 millimeters
   J. 120,000 millimeters

7. Which figure shows a congruent rhombus?

A. C. 

B. D. 

8. How many faces and edges does this shape have?

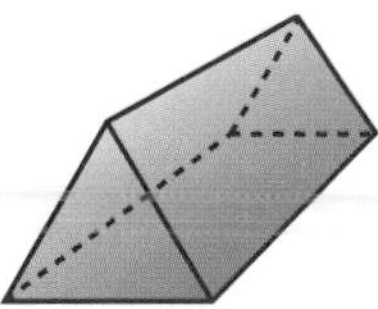

   F. 5 faces, 9 edges
   G. 4 faces, 9 edges
   H. 5 faces, 8 edges
   J. 9 faces, 5 edges

Statistics, Data Analysis, and Probability

Use data from the graph for problems 9–12.

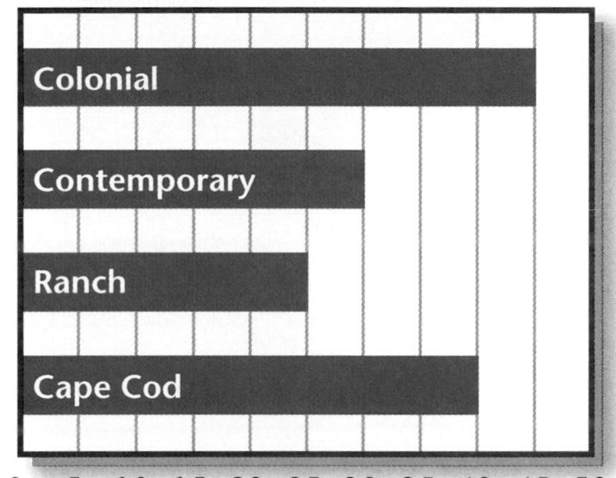

9. Which kind of house did the company design most of?
   - A. Ranch
   - B. Cape Cod
   - C. Colonial
   - D. Contemporary

10. How many more contemporaries did they design than ranches?
    - F. 5
    - G. 15
    - H. 20
    - J. Not Here

11. How many houses did the company design in all?
    - A. 100
    - B. 130
    - C. 140
    - D. 150

12. Write a conclusion you can make from the information in the graph.

Algebra and Functions

13. What is the missing number in the pattern?
    $6 \times 7 = 42$
    $60 \times 7 = 420$
    $60 \times \blacksquare = 4,200$
    - A. 7
    - B. 70
    - C. 60
    - D. 700

14. Which is an example of the Distributive Property?
    - F. $4 \times 6 = 6 \times 4$
    - G. $6 \times 19 = (6 \times 10) + (6 \times 9)$
    - H. $7 \times 1 = 7$
    - J. $3 \times (5 \times 6) = (3 \times 5) \times 6$

15. What are the coordinates for the star?

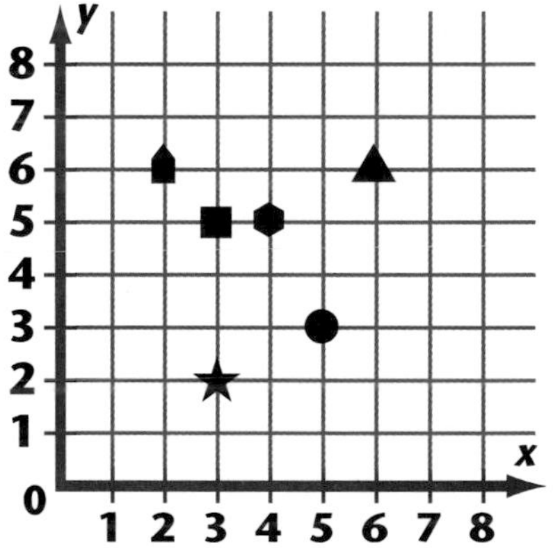

   - A. (3, 3)
   - B. (4, 3)
   - C. (2, 3)
   - D. (3, 2)

16. What object is located at (5, 3) in the grid above?
    - F. Square
    - G. Hexagon
    - H. Circle
    - J. Star

Spiral Review and Test Prep

Fractions and Probability

Theme: Amusement Parks

Waiting Time for Rides

Ride	Waiting Time
Roller Coaster	$1\frac{1}{4}$ hours
Water Slide	$1\frac{1}{2}$ hours
Haunted House	$\frac{3}{4}$ hour
Bumper Cars	$\frac{1}{2}$ hour
Ferris Wheel	$\frac{1}{4}$ hour

- **What if** you and your family are spending a day at an amusement park? You want to plan how you will spend your day. How could you use fractions to tell how many minutes are in $\frac{1}{4}$, $\frac{1}{2}$, or $\frac{3}{4}$ of an hour?

What You Will Learn

In this chapter you will learn how to
- identify, read, and write fractions and mixed numbers.
- compare, order, and find equivalent and simpler fractions.
- find probability.
- use strategies to solve problems.

Objective: Review identifying, reading, and writing fractions for parts of a whole.

11·1

Parts of a Whole

Learn

Alex plays a ball toss game at the amusement park. There are 2 parts of the target that are red. Write a **fraction** to show what part of the target is red.

Math Words

fraction the number that names part of a whole or part of a group

numerator the number above the bar in a fraction

denominator the number below the bar in a fraction

Example

You can say that 2 of the 6 parts are red.

Write: red parts → 2 ← **numerator**
parts in all → 6 ← **denominator**

Read: Two sixths of the target is red.

So $\frac{2}{6}$ of the target is red.

More Examples

A

What fraction of the target is yellow?

$\frac{1}{6}$ 1 ← yellow parts
6 ← parts in all

One sixth of the wheel is yellow.

B

How long is the paperclip?

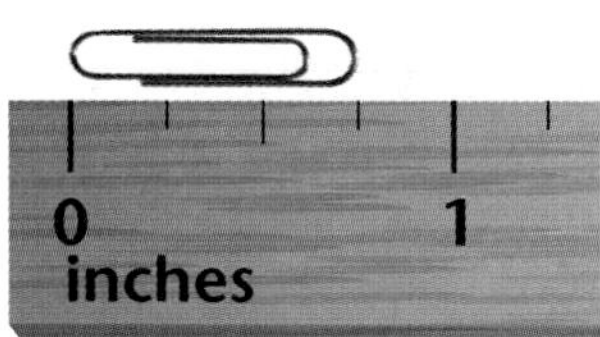

The paper clip is $\frac{3}{4}$ of an inch long.

Try It

Write a fraction for the part that is shaded.

1. 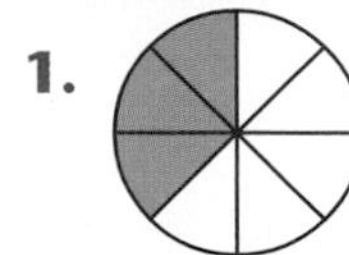

2. 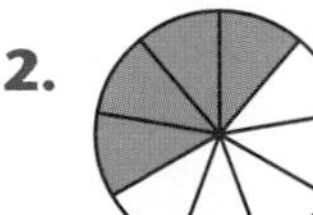

3. 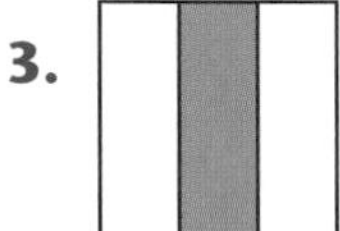

4. 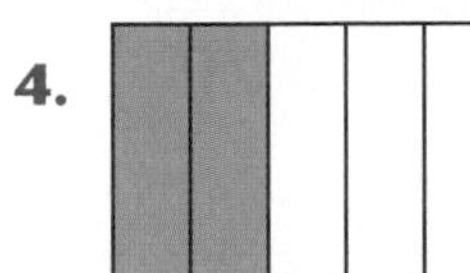

Sum it Up! What part of the target is either blue or red? How do you know?

Practice Write a fraction for the part indicated.

5.

6. 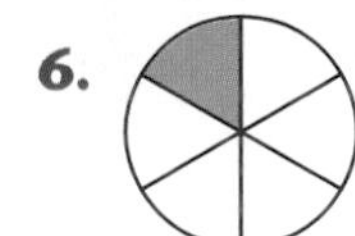

7. 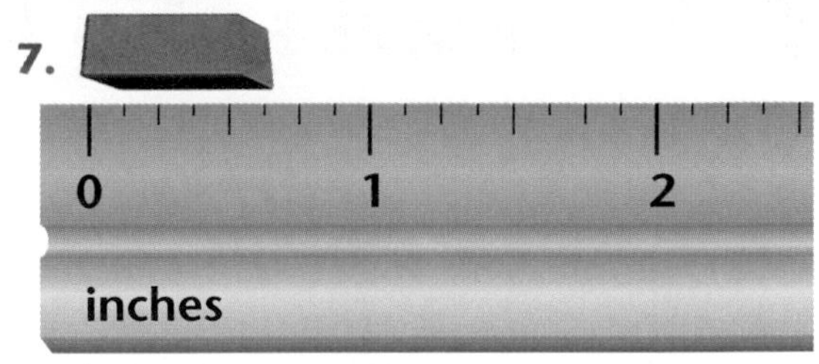

Draw a rectangle with the fraction shaded.

8. $\frac{2}{3}$ 9. $\frac{1}{4}$ 10. $\frac{5}{8}$ 11. $\frac{1}{2}$ 12. $\frac{5}{9}$ 13. $\frac{3}{4}$ 14. $\frac{1}{3}$ 15. $\frac{7}{8}$

Problem Solving

Use data from *Did You Know?* for problems 16–19.

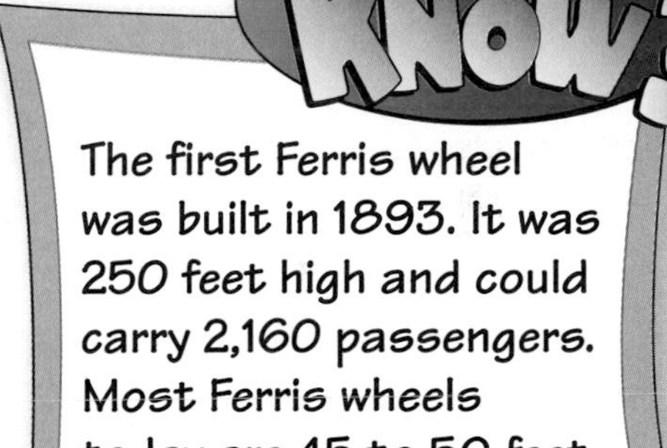

16. The height of today's Ferris wheel is what fraction of the height of the first Ferris wheel?

17. The first Ferris wheel ran 23 times a day, and each time it was filled with passengers. How many passengers could ride in one day? in one week?

18. **Social Studies:** A London Ferris wheel built in 1894 was 328 feet high. How many feet higher was the London wheel than the first Ferris wheel?

19. **Create a problem** using the data. Solve it. Ask others to solve it.

20. If a Ferris wheel carries 48 riders for each ride, how many riders could the wheel carry in 35 rides?

21. Estimate the fraction shown by the shaded part.

22. **Analyze:** A Ferris wheel has 9 cars. There are 4 red cars. What fraction shows how many of the cars are not red?

Spiral Review and Test Prep

23. $56 + 104$ 24. $319 - 99$ 25. 410×20 26. $525 \div 25$

Choose the correct answer.

27. Estimate the product. 475×57
   - A. about 30,000
   - B. about 20,000
   - C. about 3,000
   - D. about 2,000

28. Compare. 300 mm ● 32 cm
   - F. $<$
   - G. $>$
   - H. $=$
   - J. Not Here

Extra Practice, page 503

Objective: Review identifying, reading, and writing fractions for parts of a group.

11•2

Parts of a Group

Tracy and her brother win a stuffed animal at an amusement park. What fraction shows how many of the stuffed animals are pigs?

Example

Use a fraction to describe a part of the group.

There are 5 pigs out of a total of 9 animals.

Write: numerator → 5 ← number of pigs denominator → 9 ← total animals	**Read:**	Five ninths of the stuffed animals are pigs.

Of the stuffed animals, $\frac{5}{9}$ are pigs.

More Examples

A

What fraction shows how many animals are either ducks or frogs?

$\frac{2}{9}$ ← 2 = number of ducks or frogs; 9 = total animals

B

What fraction shows how many animals are not dogs or elephants?

$\frac{7}{9}$ ← 7 = number not dogs or elephants; 9 = total animals

Write a fraction that names a part.

1. Red
2. Gray
3. Blue or black
4. Not black

If you know that 5 of 9 stuffed animals are ducks and pigs, how many are not ducks and pigs? Explain.

Practice **Write a fraction that names what part is blue.**

5. 

6. 

7. 

Draw a picture, and then write a fraction.

8. Five of seven people are wearing hats.
9. Three of eleven people are smiling.
10. One of five stuffed animals is a cat.
11. All of 6 balls are red.

Problem Solving

★12. **Time:** Fifteen seconds is what fraction of a minute? Ten minutes is what fraction of an hour? Three days is what fraction of a week?

13. **Social Studies:** The first amusement park was built in 1846 in Bristol, Connecticut. How many years ago was that?

14. **Spatial Reasoning:** You have 2 squares of the same size. You cut each square to get 2 equal triangles. What different shapes can you create with the 4 triangles?

15. An arcade has a row of 12 boats in water. Sam knocks down 5 of the boats. What fraction shows how many of the boats were not knocked down?

16. **Language Arts:** Look at the words in the sign. What fraction shows how many of the letters are consonants? What fraction shows how many of the letters are vowels?

Spiral Review and Test Prep

17. $\begin{array}{r} 514 \\ \times\ 23 \\ \hline \end{array}$

18. $56\overline{)12{,}936}$

19. $19\overline{)13{,}205}$

20. $\begin{array}{r} \$45.89 \\ \times\ \ \ \ 56 \\ \hline \end{array}$

Choose the correct answer.

21. What is the rule for this table?

Input	3	4	5	6
Output	9	12	15	18

A. Multiply by 2.
B. Multiply by 3.
C. Multiply by 4.
D. Add 6.

22. Find the remainder for 5,603 ÷ 17.

F. 3
G. 10
H. 15
J. 17

Extra Practice, page 503

Objective: Review finding equivalent fractions and writing fractions in simplest form.

Find Equivalent Fractions and Fractions in Simplest Form

Math Words

equivalent fractions two or more fractions that name the same number

simplest form a fraction in which the numerator and the denominator have no common factor greater than 1

Learn

May and her friends buy T-shirts at Funland Amusement Park. Six shirts are blue and 6 are red, so May says that $\frac{6}{12}$ of the shirts are blue. What other fractions could May use to tell how many of the shirts are blue?

There's more than one way!

You can use fraction strips to show other fractions that name the same number.

Method A

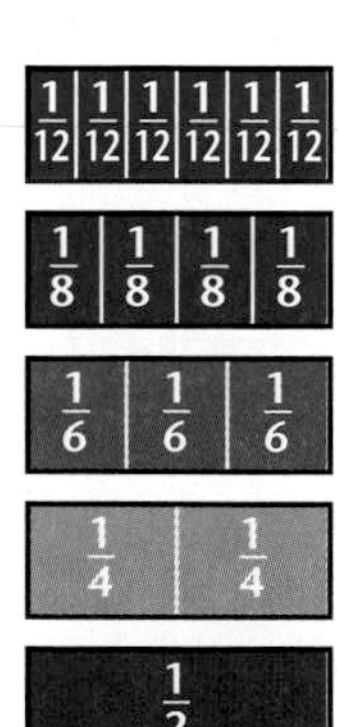

Equivalent Fractions for $\frac{6}{12}$

Fraction Strip Used	Number of Sections	Equivalent Fraction
$\frac{1}{8}$	4	$\frac{4}{8}$
$\frac{1}{6}$	3	$\frac{3}{6}$
$\frac{1}{4}$	2	$\frac{2}{4}$

These are called **equivalent fractions**.

Method B

You can multiply to find equivalent fractions. Multiply the numerator and the denominator by the same number.

Think: equals multiplied by equals are equal

$\frac{1}{2} = \frac{1 \times 2}{2 \times 2} = \frac{2}{4}$ $\frac{2 \times 2}{4 \times 2} = \frac{4}{8}$ $\frac{1}{2} = \frac{1 \times 3}{2 \times 3} = \frac{3}{6}$

May could use $\frac{1}{2}$, $\frac{2}{4}$, $\frac{3}{6}$, or $\frac{4}{8}$ to tell what fraction of the shirts are blue.

May and her friends ride a roller coaster. The roller coaster has 12 cars. Four of the cars are blue. How can you write a fraction for the blue cars in **simplest form**?

Example

Find the simplest form of $\frac{4}{12}$.

1

Find the common factors.

Factors of 4: 1, 2, 4

Factors of 12: 1, 2, 3, 4, 6, 12

Common factors: 2 and 4

2

Divide the numerator and the denominator by the greatest common factor.

$$\frac{4 \div 4}{12 \div 4} = \frac{1}{3}$$

The simplest form of $\frac{4}{12}$ is $\frac{1}{3}$.

Try It

Complete to name each equivalent fraction.

1. 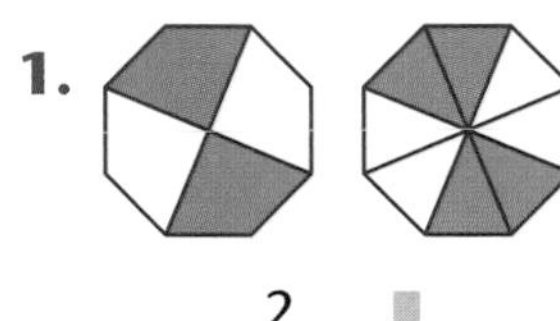

$\frac{2}{4} = \frac{\blacksquare}{8}$

2. 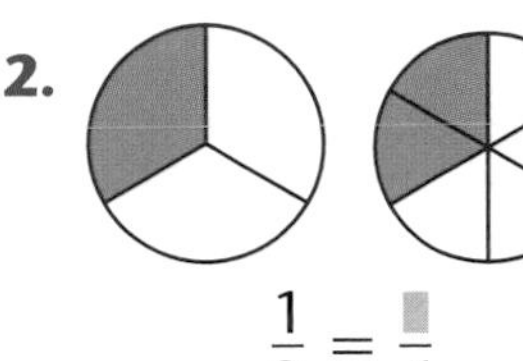

$\frac{1}{3} = \frac{\blacksquare}{6}$

3. 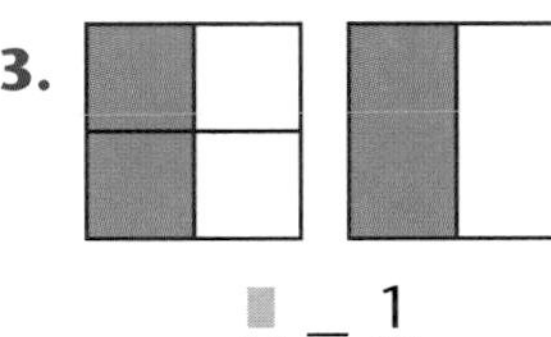

$\frac{\blacksquare}{4} = \frac{1}{2}$

Copy and complete.

4. $\frac{\blacksquare \times 2}{4 \times 2} = \frac{2}{8}$

5. $\frac{4 \times \blacksquare}{6 \div 2} = \frac{\blacksquare}{3}$

6. $\frac{3 \times 3}{5 \times \blacksquare} = \frac{9}{15}$

7. $\frac{4 \div \blacksquare}{8 \div 4} = \frac{\blacksquare}{2}$

8. $\frac{1}{2} = \frac{\blacksquare}{16}$

9. $\frac{8}{24} = \frac{\blacksquare}{3}$

10. $\frac{3}{8} = \frac{6}{\blacksquare}$

11. $\frac{9}{27} = \frac{\blacksquare}{3}$

Name an equivalent fraction for each.

12. $\frac{2}{3}$

13. $\frac{1}{4}$

14. $\frac{1}{5}$

15. $\frac{4}{5}$

16. $\frac{1}{3}$

17. $\frac{1}{8}$

Write each fraction in simplest form. Show your method.

18. $\frac{4}{16}$

19. $\frac{6}{8}$

20. $\frac{7}{21}$

21. $\frac{18}{30}$

22. $\frac{10}{35}$

23. $\frac{6}{36}$

Sum it Up! Explain why $\frac{3}{4}$, $\frac{6}{8}$, and $\frac{9}{12}$ are equivalent fractions. Which fraction is in simplest form?

Practice

Draw an equivalent fraction for each.

24. 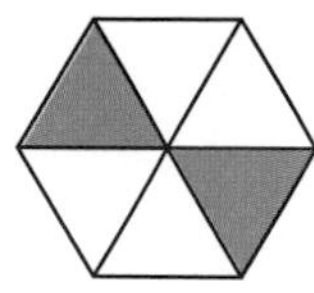

25. 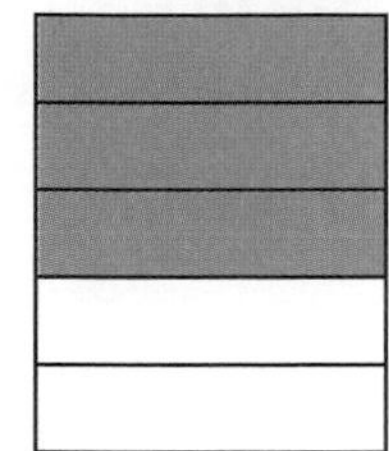

26. 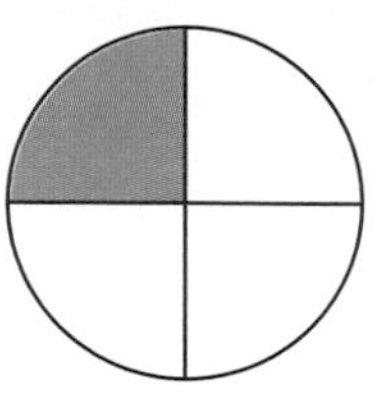

Copy and complete to find equivalent fractions.

27. $\frac{2 \times 2}{4 \times \blacksquare} = \frac{4}{\blacksquare}$

28. $\frac{7 \div \blacksquare}{14 \div 7} = \frac{\blacksquare}{2}$

29. $\frac{3 \times 4}{4 \times \blacksquare} = \frac{12}{\blacksquare}$

30. $\frac{8 \div \blacksquare}{12 \div 4} = \frac{\blacksquare}{3}$

31. $\frac{9}{15} = \frac{\blacksquare}{5}$

32. $\frac{2}{3} = \frac{\blacksquare}{12}$

33. $\frac{10}{45} = \frac{2}{\blacksquare}$

34. $\frac{8}{64} = \frac{1}{\blacksquare}$

Name an equivalent fraction for each.

35. $\frac{2}{7}$

36. $\frac{2}{5}$

37. $\frac{3}{5}$

38. $\frac{2}{12}$

39. $\frac{8}{12}$

40. $\frac{2}{3}$

Write each fraction in simplest form.

41. $\frac{7}{21}$

42. $\frac{2}{10}$

43. $\frac{6}{8}$

44. $\frac{4}{16}$

45. $\frac{9}{18}$

46. $\frac{3}{27}$

47. $\frac{14}{16}$

48. $\frac{15}{18}$

49. $\frac{10}{35}$

50. $\frac{24}{28}$

51. $\frac{15}{24}$

52. $\frac{12}{40}$

★53. $\frac{63}{98}$

★54. $\frac{81}{117}$

★55. $\frac{121}{154}$

Algebra & functions **Complete the pattern of equivalent fractions.**

56. $\frac{1}{2} = \frac{\blacksquare}{4} = \frac{\blacksquare}{6} = \frac{4}{\blacksquare} = \frac{5}{\blacksquare} = \frac{\blacksquare}{12}$

57. $\frac{1}{5} = \frac{\blacksquare}{10} = \frac{\blacksquare}{15} = \frac{4}{\blacksquare} = \frac{5}{\blacksquare} = \frac{\blacksquare}{30}$

58. $\frac{3}{4} = \frac{\blacksquare}{8} = \frac{\blacksquare}{12} = \frac{12}{\blacksquare} = \frac{15}{\blacksquare} = \frac{\blacksquare}{24}$

59. $\frac{2}{3} = \frac{\blacksquare}{6} = \frac{\blacksquare}{9} = \frac{8}{\blacksquare} = \frac{10}{\blacksquare} = \frac{\blacksquare}{18}$

60. 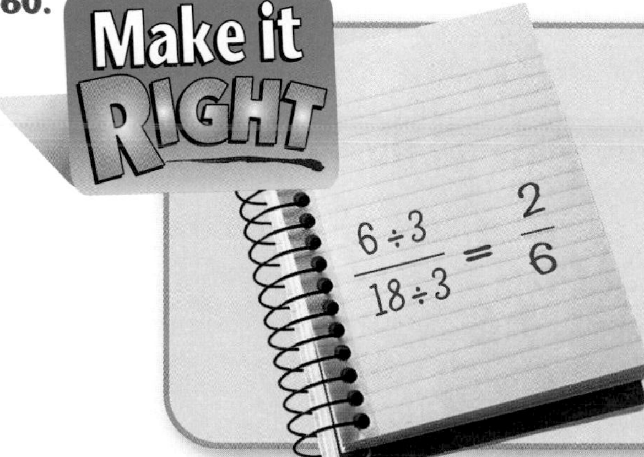

Here is how Rachel wrote $\frac{6}{18}$ in simplest form. Explain what mistake she made. Tell how to correct it.

Problem Solving

Use data from the bar graph for problems 61–63.

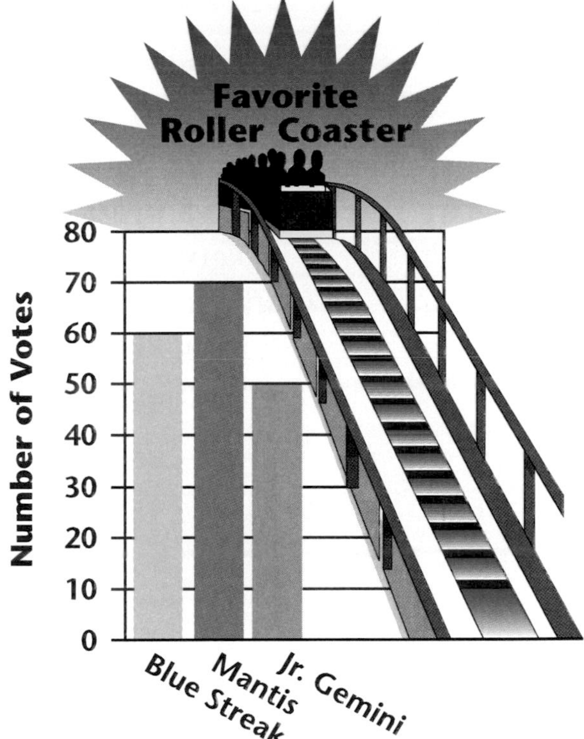

61. What fraction shows how many people liked Blue Streak the most? Write your answer in simplest form.

62. How many more people voted for Mantis than for Blue Streak?

63. **Logical Reasoning:** What fraction shows how many people did not like Blue Streak the most? Write your answer in simplest form.

64. **Art:** A painter mixes paint for a roller coaster. The paint calls for one part red, one part blue, and two parts yellow. Write a fraction for each of the parts.

65. **Measurement:** One of the highest roller coasters in the world is Superman The Escape. It is 415 feet tall. How many inches tall is the roller coaster?

66. **Collect Data:** Take a survey of the favorite amusement park rides of each member of your class. Write statements using fractions to describe the data.

67. **Summarize:** Describe how you would find an equivalent fraction for $\frac{6}{15}$. Can you always find an equivalent fraction for a fraction? Explain.

Spiral Review and Test Prep

Write the number that makes each sentence true.

68. 4 ft = ▮ in **69.** 4 T = ▮ lb **70.** 7 pt = ▮ c **71.** 320 oz = ▮ lb

Choose the correct answer.

72. A rectangle is 28 millimeters long and 16 millimeters wide. What is its area?

A. 448 square millimeters
B. 440 square millimeters
C. 144 square millimeters
D. 48 square millimeters

73. Renee has a tablecloth that is 3 meters long. How many centimeters is that?

F. 30,000 centimeters
G. 3,000 centimeters
H. 300 centimeters
J. 30 centimeters

Extra Practice, page 503

Objective: Review comparing and ordering fractions.

11•4 Compare and Order Fractions

Algebra & functions

Learn

Miko and Ruben each buy a book of tickets for the attractions at the amusement park. Miko uses $\frac{3}{4}$ of her tickets. Ruben uses $\frac{5}{8}$ of his tickets. Who uses more tickets?

There's more than one way!

Compare $\frac{3}{4}$ and $\frac{5}{8}$ to solve.

Method 

You can use fraction strips to compare fractions.

$\frac{1}{4}$	$\frac{1}{4}$	$\frac{1}{4}$	$\frac{3}{4}$

$\frac{1}{8}$	$\frac{1}{8}$	$\frac{1}{8}$	$\frac{1}{8}$	$\frac{1}{8}$	$\frac{5}{8}$

$\frac{3}{4} > \frac{5}{8}$

Method 

You can use a number line to compare fractions.

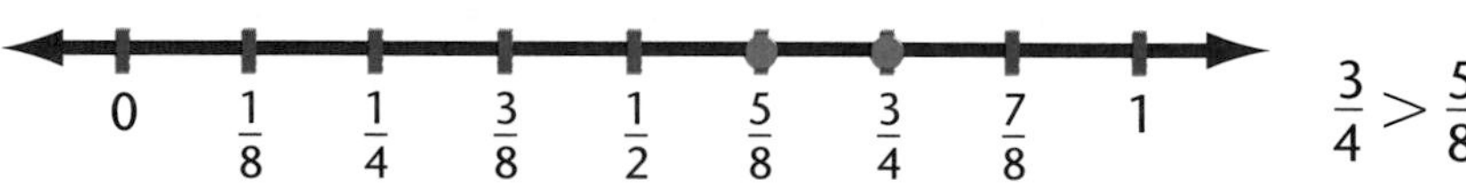

$\frac{3}{4} > \frac{5}{8}$

Method C

You can write equivalent fractions with the same denominator.

$\frac{3}{4} = \frac{3 \times 2}{4 \times 2} = \frac{6}{8}$

Since $\frac{6}{8} > \frac{5}{8}$, then $\frac{3}{4} > \frac{5}{8}$.

Miko uses more of her tickets.

Jill has a book of tickets that is $\frac{1}{2}$ full. Maya's ticket book is $\frac{1}{4}$ full, and Josh's book is $\frac{3}{8}$ full. Order the ticket books from least to full.

Example

Order $\frac{1}{2}$, $\frac{1}{4}$, and $\frac{3}{8}$ from least to greatest.

1 Write equivalent fractions with the same denominator.

$$\frac{1}{2} = \frac{1 \times 4}{2 \times 4} = \frac{4}{8}$$

$$\frac{1}{4} = \frac{1 \times 2}{4 \times 2} = \frac{2}{8}$$

$$\frac{3}{8}$$

2 Compare the numerators.

$\frac{4}{8}$ **Think:** 4 is the greatest.

$\frac{2}{8}$ **Think:** 2 is the least.

$\frac{3}{8}$

The order from least to greatest is $\frac{1}{4}$, $\frac{3}{8}$, and $\frac{1}{2}$.

Try It **Compare. Write >, <, or =.**

1. 

$\frac{1}{8}$ ● $\frac{3}{8}$

2. 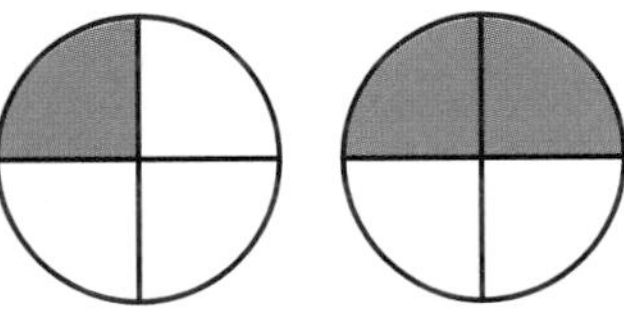

$\frac{1}{4}$ ● $\frac{1}{2}$

3. 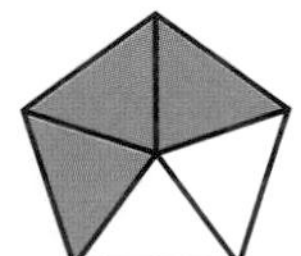 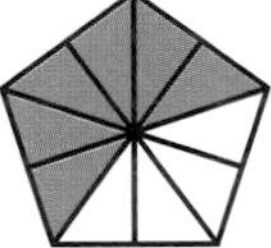

$\frac{3}{5}$ ● $\frac{6}{10}$

4. $\frac{1}{4}$ ● $\frac{3}{4}$
5. $\frac{7}{8}$ ● $\frac{3}{4}$
6. $\frac{2}{3}$ ● $\frac{5}{6}$
7. $\frac{1}{2}$ ● $\frac{3}{8}$
8. $\frac{2}{5}$ ● $\frac{4}{10}$
9. $\frac{3}{5}$ ● $\frac{1}{3}$
10. $\frac{2}{7}$ ● $\frac{4}{14}$
11. $\frac{1}{10}$ ● $\frac{1}{11}$
12. $\frac{5}{12}$ ● $\frac{1}{2}$
13. $\frac{4}{5}$ ● $\frac{5}{8}$

Order from least to greatest.

14. $\frac{3}{8}, \frac{7}{8}, \frac{1}{8}$
15. $\frac{4}{5}, \frac{1}{5}, \frac{3}{5}$
16. $\frac{1}{4}, \frac{1}{8}, \frac{1}{2}$
17. $\frac{1}{16}, \frac{1}{8}, \frac{1}{4}$
18. $\frac{5}{9}, \frac{2}{3}, \frac{3}{6}$
19. $\frac{5}{6}, \frac{4}{6}, \frac{2}{6}$
20. $\frac{2}{9}, \frac{2}{5}, \frac{2}{4}$
21. $\frac{4}{5}, \frac{3}{10}, \frac{1}{2}$

How would you compare $\frac{2}{3}$ and $\frac{3}{5}$? Explain.

Practice

Compare. Write >, <, or =.

22. $\frac{1}{4}$ ● $\frac{2}{3}$ **23.** $\frac{3}{5}$ ● $\frac{5}{6}$ **24.** $\frac{6}{9}$ ● $\frac{2}{3}$ **25.** $\frac{3}{10}$ ● $\frac{2}{5}$ **26.** $\frac{6}{7}$ ● $\frac{5}{8}$

Order from least to greatest.

27. $\frac{5}{8}, \frac{3}{8}, \frac{3}{4}$ **28.** $\frac{1}{3}, \frac{5}{6}, \frac{1}{6}$ **29.** $\frac{4}{5}, \frac{3}{10}, \frac{1}{2}$ **30.** $\frac{1}{3}, \frac{5}{7}, \frac{4}{21}$

31. $\frac{3}{4}, \frac{7}{8}, \frac{5}{8}$ **32.** $\frac{5}{10}, \frac{3}{10}, \frac{3}{5}$ **33.** $\frac{3}{15}, \frac{2}{5}, \frac{4}{5}$ **34.** $\frac{7}{9}, \frac{2}{3}, \frac{3}{18}$

Order from greatest to least.

35. $\frac{4}{7}, \frac{2}{7}, \frac{6}{7}$ **36.** $\frac{1}{3}, \frac{1}{2}, \frac{1}{6}$ **37.** $\frac{3}{4}, \frac{1}{3}, \frac{5}{6}$ **38.** $\frac{3}{8}, \frac{1}{2}, \frac{1}{4}$

39. $\frac{5}{7}, \frac{3}{7}, \frac{12}{21}$ **40.** $\frac{1}{10}, \frac{2}{5}, \frac{1}{2}$ **41.** $\frac{7}{8}, \frac{13}{16}, \frac{1}{4}$ **★42.** $\frac{5}{8}, \frac{35}{40}, \frac{45}{64}$

43.

Here is how Jessica compared $\frac{5}{6}$ and $\frac{11}{12}$. Tell what mistake she made. Explain how to correct it.

Problem Solving

44. Three friends visit an amusement park and each brings \$30. Jen spends $\frac{1}{5}$ of her amount, Felicia spends $\frac{3}{10}$ of her amount, and Miguel spends $\frac{4}{10}$ of his amount. Who spends the most? the least?

45. Time: The Cooper family spends $\frac{1}{3}$ hour waiting in line to go on the Giant Water Slide. The Wells family waits in line for 30 minutes. The Green family waits for $\frac{1}{4}$ hour. Which family waits the longest amount of time? the least amount of time?

★46. Use the numerals 2, 3, and 5 to write three sentences that compare fractions. Use >, <, or =, using different fractions each time.

47. Three sisters each want to save \$30. Judy has $\frac{1}{4}$ of the amount. Julia has $\frac{3}{8}$ of the amount and Jill has $\frac{5}{8}$. Who has the most? least?

Use data from the graph for problems 48–51.

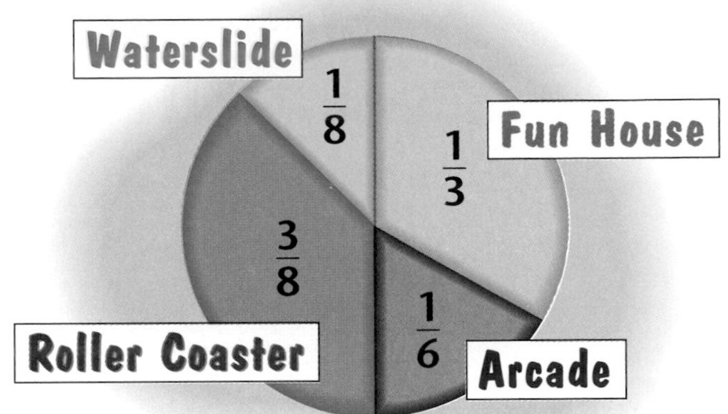

48. Which attraction made the most money?

49. Which attractions made less money than the Fun House?

50. **Logical Reasoning:** If the Fun House makes $\frac{1}{3}$ of the money at the amusement park, how much do the other attractions make?

51. **Create a problem** using the information in the graph. Solve it. Ask others to solve it.

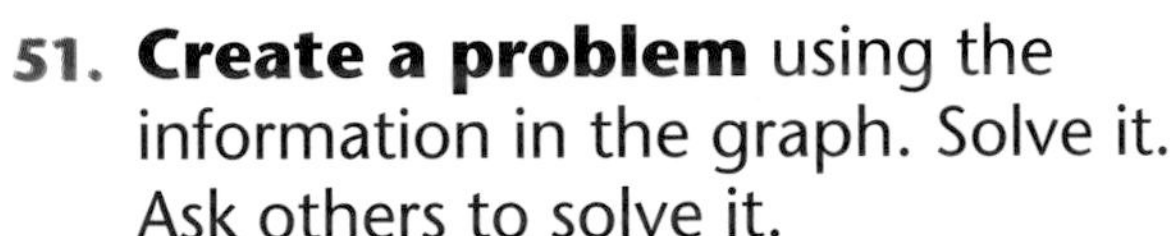

★**52.** A roller coaster travels 1 mile in 10 minutes. How many miles would the roller coaster travel in $1\frac{1}{2}$ hours?

53. A vertical-drop ride drops 180 feet into a tunnel. Estimate how many inches the ride drops.

54. A giant Ferris wheel holds a total of 292 people. If each car holds 4 people, how many cars are on the Ferris wheel?

55. **Generalize:** If the numerator of two fractions is the same, tell how you can compare the fractions.

Spiral Review and Test Prep

Write *obtuse, acute,* or *right* for each angle in the figure.

56. 

57. 

58. 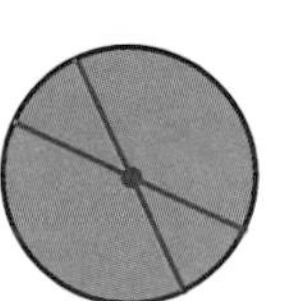

59. 

60. 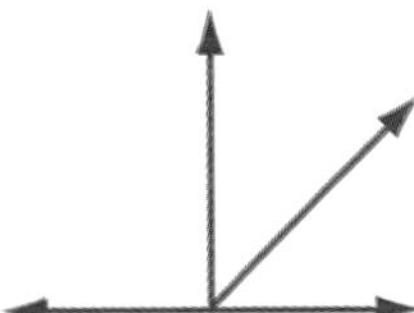

61. 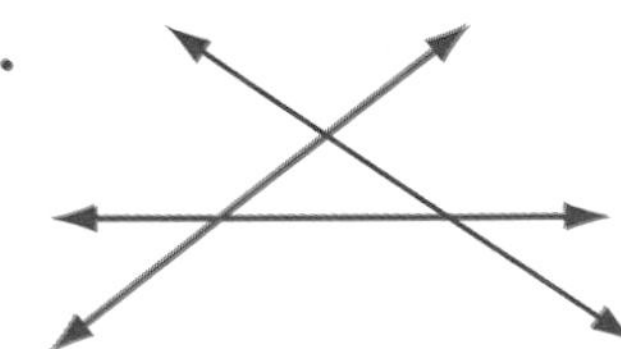

Choose the correct answer.

62. A rectangle has a length of 42 inches and a width of 24 inches. What is the perimeter?

A. 66 inches **C.** 108 inches
B. 132 inches **D.** 1,008 inches

63. A shape has 4 sides, 2 obtuse angles, 2 acute angles, and 1 set of parallel lines. What shape is it?

F. Square **H.** Rectangle
G. Trapezoid **J.** Rhombus

Extra Practice, page 504

11•5

Objective: Use prior knowledge to check for reasonableness of a solution.

Problem Solving: Reading for Math

Check for Reasonableness

What a Ride!

Read

Of the dozen students who went to the amusement park, $\frac{3}{4}$ of them rode the carousel. Cindy guesses that 9 students went on the carousel.

Is this reasonable?

READING SKILL ▶ **Use Prior Knowledge**

Prior knowledge is everything that you already know. Sometimes, you must use prior knowledge to solve a problem.

- What do you know? — **A dozen students; $\frac{3}{4}$ of them rode the carousel.**
- What prior knowledge will help solve this problem? — **12 students = 1 dozen**
- What do you need to find? — **Is it a reasonable guess.**

MATH SKILL ▶ **Check for Reasonableness**

When checking the reasonableness of an answer, think about the facts given in the problem and what you know.

Plan

You need to find $\frac{3}{4}$ of 12.

Solve

12 = 4 groups of 3; 3 of the groups rode on the carousel.
3 groups of 3 students = 9 students
So 9 students on the carousel is a reasonable guess.

Look Back

How could you check your answer?

Explain how you would find the number of students who did not ride the carousel.

Practice Answer each question. Check for reasonableness.

1. A group of 16 students rode a Ferris wheel. Of the group, $\frac{1}{2}$ rode in red chairs. Is it reasonable to say 8 students rode in red chairs?

2. A group of 8 students went on the Sky Train together. Of the group, 5 students rode in the first car, the others rode in the last car. Did $\frac{3}{5}$ of the group ride in the first car?

Use data from the chart for problems 3–8.

Ride Log	
Student	Ride
Clay	8 rides
Emma	1 dozen rides
Flora	10 rides
Nari	9 rides

3. Of all of Clay's rides, $\frac{1}{2}$ of them were on the Alpine Slide. How many times did he ride the Alpine Slide?

4. Nari spent $\frac{2}{3}$ of her rides on the Water Bash. How many times did she ride the Water Bash?

5. Flora chose to ride on the Flying Swings $\frac{3}{5}$ of the time. How many times did she ride the Flying Swings?

6. Emma rode the Alpine Slide $\frac{1}{4}$ of the time. How many times did she ride the Alpine Slide?

7. Flora rode on the Rocky Roasters $\frac{2}{5}$ of the time. How many times did she ride other rides?

8. What fraction of all of the rides taken by the group were taken by Emma?

Spiral Review and Test Prep

Choose the correct answer.

A total of 20 students rode the Ferris wheel. Of these students, $\frac{2}{5}$ also had ridden on the bumper cars. How many students also had ridden on the bumper cars?

9. Which statement is true?
   - **A.** 20 students rode bumper cars.
   - **B.** Of the students, $\frac{3}{5}$ had not ridden on the bumper cars.
   - **C.** $\frac{2}{5}$ of the students rode the Ferris wheel.

10. A reasonable answer for this problem would be
    - **F.** greater than 20.
    - **G.** less than 4.
    - **H.** greater than 4 but less than 10.

Problem Solving

Extra Practice, page 504

Objective: Review finding parts of a group.

11·6 Explore Finding Parts of a Group

Learn

You can use connecting cubes to explore parts of a group.

What is $\frac{3}{4}$ of 20?

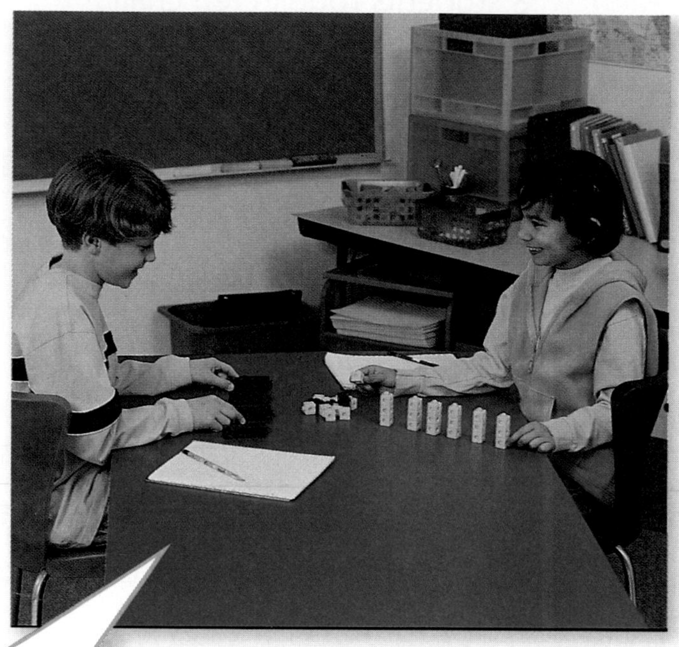

Work Together

You Will Need
- **connecting cubes**

- Use connecting cubes to show $\frac{3}{4}$ of 20.
- The denominator tells how many equal groups to make.
- The numerator tells how many of the groups to count.

> • Put 20 cubes into 4 equal groups.
> • Count one of the groups.

- Record your answer.
- Multiply that answer by the number of groups in the numerator of the fraction $\frac{3}{4}$. Answer the question above.
- Use connecting cubes to help you find a fraction of each group. Think about how you arrange the cubes to make equal groups. Record your work.

$\frac{1}{3}$ of 24 $\frac{3}{4}$ of 16 $\frac{5}{6}$ of 18 $\frac{7}{8}$ of 24

Make Connections

At lunchtime $\frac{2}{5}$ of the 20 students have sandwiches.

How many students eat sandwiches?

Here are two ways you can find $\frac{2}{5}$ of 20.

Using Models	Using Paper and Pencil
Make equal stacks of cubes to show the denominator.  *Count the total in two groups to show the numerator.*	*You can use division and multiplication to find a fraction of a group.* Find $\frac{1}{5}$ of 20. Use the denominator. Divide the total into that many groups. **Think:** The denominator is 5. $20 \div 5 = 4$ Multiply by the numerator. **Think:** The numerator is 2. $2 \times 4 = 8$ So $\frac{2}{5}$ of 20 is 8.

Eight of the students have sandwiches.

Try It **Find the fraction of each number. You may use connecting cubes.**

1. $\frac{1}{3}$ of 15
2. $\frac{3}{4}$ of 24
3. $\frac{3}{5}$ of 10
4. $\frac{5}{8}$ of 24
5. $\frac{5}{6}$ of 12
6. $\frac{2}{7}$ of 14
7. $\frac{1}{9}$ of 18
8. $\frac{3}{10}$ of 30
9. $\frac{1}{6}$ of 36
10. $\frac{1}{12}$ of 24

How would you find $\frac{2}{3}$ of 18? Explain.

Practice **Find the fraction of each number.**

11. $\frac{1}{8}$ of 24
12. $\frac{2}{3}$ of 21
13. $\frac{1}{6}$ of 36
14. $\frac{3}{4}$ of 12
15. $\frac{2}{5}$ of 25
16. $\frac{1}{3}$ of 21
17. $\frac{1}{10}$ of 50
18. $\frac{1}{4}$ of 28
19. $\frac{3}{5}$ of 35
20. $\frac{1}{7}$ of 21
21. **Analyze:** When you are finding $\frac{2}{3}$ of 15, what does the numerator tell you?

Extra Practice, page 504

Objective: Review reading and writing mixed numbers.

11•7 Mixed Numbers

Learn

The Kent family rides a water log ride. They need $1\frac{1}{4}$ logs for their family. How many fourths is that?

Math Words

mixed number
a number named by a whole number and a fraction

improper fraction
a fraction with a numerator that is greater than or equal to the denominator

Example 1

Rename the **mixed number** $1\frac{1}{4}$ as an **improper fraction**.

1 Rename the whole number as a fraction.

$$1 = \frac{4}{4}$$

2 Add the fractions.

$$\frac{4}{4} + \frac{1}{4} = \frac{5}{4}$$

They need $\frac{5}{4}$ logs for their family.

You can rename a fraction as a mixed number.
What is $\frac{7}{4}$ as a mixed number?

Example 2

1 Divide the numerator by the denominator.

$$\frac{7}{4} \rightarrow 7 \div 4 = 1 \text{ R}3$$

2 Write the quotient as the whole number part. Write the remainder over the divisor.

$$1\frac{3}{4}$$

Try It

Rename each as a mixed number or fraction in simplest form.

1. $\frac{8}{7}$ **2.** $1\frac{1}{3}$ **3.** $\frac{15}{2}$ **4.** $\frac{11}{4}$ **5.** $2\frac{1}{6}$ **6.** $\frac{11}{3}$

Explain how to rename $\frac{9}{8}$ as a mixed number.

Practice

Rename each as a mixed number or fraction in simplest form.

7. $\frac{13}{4}$ **8.** $1\frac{2}{5}$ **9.** $2\frac{1}{4}$ **10.** $\frac{16}{6}$ **11.** $\frac{14}{10}$ **12.** $\frac{68}{8}$

13. $\frac{11}{7}$ **14.** $\frac{29}{3}$ **15.** $\frac{48}{9}$ **16.** $\frac{21}{14}$ **★17.** $\frac{369}{72}$ **★18.** $\frac{448}{63}$

Use the number line to compare. Write >, <, or =.

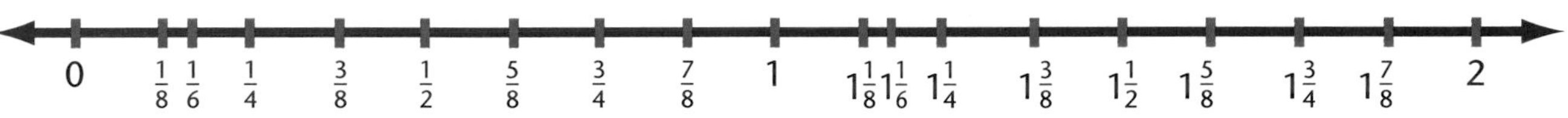

19. $1\frac{1}{4}$ ● $1\frac{3}{4}$ **20.** $1\frac{3}{8}$ ● $1\frac{5}{8}$ **21.** $1\frac{1}{4}$ ● $\frac{3}{4}$ **22.** 1 ● $\frac{3}{4}$

23. $1\frac{1}{8}$ ● $1\frac{5}{8}$ **24.** 1 ● $\frac{4}{4}$ **★25.** $\frac{5}{8}$ ● $\frac{1}{2}$ **★26.** $1\frac{5}{8}$ ● $1\frac{1}{6}$

Problem Solving

Use data from the chart for problems 27–29.

27. Logical Reasoning: A measure of music has 4 beats. If 6 notes of a measure are ♪, how many could be ♩?

28. Music: Write a mixed number to show how many beats are represented by the top row of notes at the right, and another mixed number to show how many beats are represented by the bottom row of notes.

★29. Compare: Which row of notes has more beats?

30. Explain how you change a mixed number into an improper fraction.

Note	Beats
♩	**1**
♪	$\frac{1}{2}$
𝅘𝅥𝅯	$\frac{1}{4}$

𝅘𝅥𝅯 𝅘𝅥𝅯 ♩ ♪ ♩ ♪

♩ ♪ 𝅘𝅥𝅯 ♩ ♩

Spiral Review and Test Prep

Name the figure.

31. **32.** **33.**  **34.** 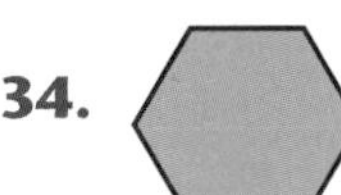

Choose the correct answer.

35. I am a 4-sided polygon. All my sides are equal in length. I have 2 acute angles and 2 obtuse angles. What am I?

A. Rectangle **C.** Rhombus
B. Square **D.** Hexagon

36. A tea cup ride has 18 cups. Each cup seats 6 people. Which number sentence shows how many people can go on the ride?

F. $18 - 6$ **H.** $18 \div 6$
G. $18 + 6$ **J.** 18×6

Extra Practice, page 504

Check Your Progress A

Write a fraction for the part that is shaded. **(pages 470–471)**

1. 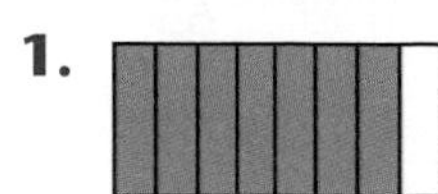
2. 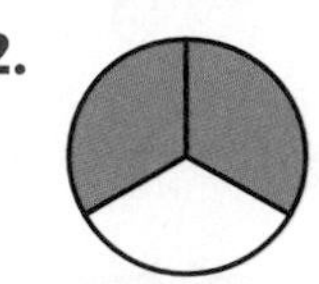
3.

Write a fraction that names which part is red. **(pages 472–473)**

4.
5.
6.

Name an equivalent fraction for each. **(pages 474–477)**

7. $\frac{1}{6}$ 8. $\frac{2}{3}$ 9. $\frac{4}{5}$ 10. $\frac{2}{4}$ 11. $\frac{1}{2}$ 12. $\frac{6}{10}$

Write each fraction in simplest form. **(pages 474–477)**

13. $\frac{3}{9}$ 14. $\frac{14}{21}$ 15. $\frac{10}{16}$ 16. $\frac{9}{12}$ 17. $\frac{8}{48}$ 18. $\frac{14}{35}$

Compare. Write >, <, or =. **(pages 478–481)**

19. $\frac{1}{8}$ ● $\frac{2}{4}$ 20. $\frac{1}{2}$ ● $\frac{5}{12}$ 21. $\frac{2}{5}$ ● $\frac{7}{15}$ 22. $\frac{1}{2}$ ● $\frac{8}{16}$

Find the fraction of each number. **(pages 484–485)**

23. $\frac{2}{5}$ of 15 24. $\frac{2}{3}$ of 9 25. $\frac{1}{2}$ of 18 26. $\frac{1}{3}$ of 24

Rename as a whole number or a mixed number in simplest form. **(pages 486–487)**

27. $\frac{4}{3}$ 28. $\frac{15}{5}$ 29. $\frac{12}{8}$ 30. $\frac{26}{6}$ 31. $\frac{19}{4}$

Solve.

32. Three students have an equal number of tickets. Adam uses $\frac{3}{4}$ of his tickets, Ming uses $\frac{1}{2}$ of hers, and Kahlil uses $\frac{7}{8}$ of his. Did Kahlil use the most tickets? Explain.

33. **Explain** how you compare two mixed numbers.

Additional activities at www.mhschool.com/math

Find Probability

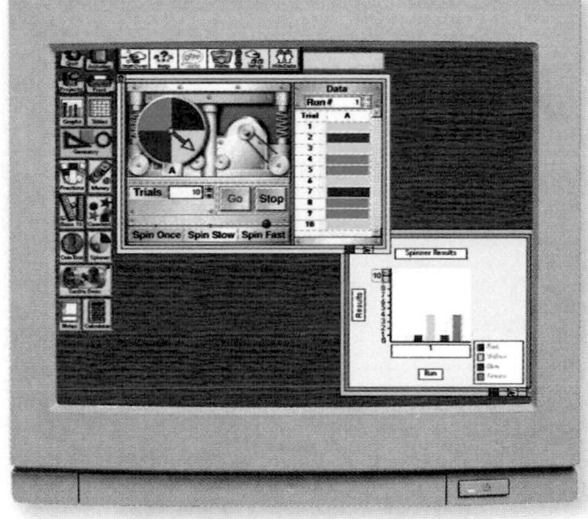

Briana is using a spinner to conduct an experiment. She uses a spinner with four sections; one green, one red, one yellow, and one blue. She spins the spinner 10 times and draws a bar graph of the results. Conduct the experiment and draw a bar graph of the results. On which color did the spinner land the most? the least?

You can use a spinner to conduct the experiment.

- Set Trials to 10.
- Click on Spin Slow or Spin Fast.
- Click on the link at the bottom of the Data table.
- Choose Bar Graph. The graph that shows the data is drawn.
- On which color did the spinner land the most?
- The least?

Use the computer to spin a four-color spinner the number of times given. Draw a bar graph of the results. State the color the spinner landed on the most and the least.

1. 15 **2.** 20 **3.** 30 **4.** 50

Solve.

5. Toss a coin 25 times and draw a bar graph of the results. Did the coin land on heads or tails more often?

6. Spin a six-colored spinner 30 times. Draw a bar graph of the results. On which color did the spinner land the most? the least?

7. **Analyze:** How do the probability tools help you conduct an experiment and draw a bar graph of the results?

For more practice, use Math Traveler™.

Objective: Identify the likeliness of events.

11-8 Likely and Unlikely

Learn

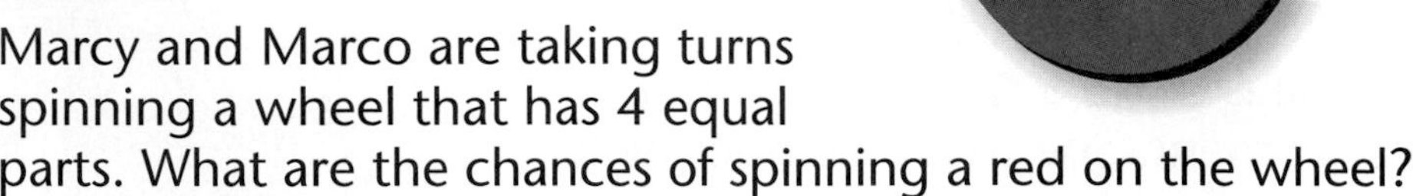

Marcy and Marco are taking turns spinning a wheel that has 4 equal parts. What are the chances of spinning a red on the wheel?

Math Words

probability the chance that an event will happen

likely an event will probably happen

equally likely an event that is just as likely to happen as not to happen

unlikely an event is not likely to happen

impossible an event that cannot happen

certain an event will definitely happen

Example 1

The chance, or likelihood that something happens, is called its **probability**. *You can describe probability in terms of how* **likely** *it is for an event to occur.*

The spinner above has 1 blue and 3 red sections. It is more likely that you would spin red than any other color.

Example 2

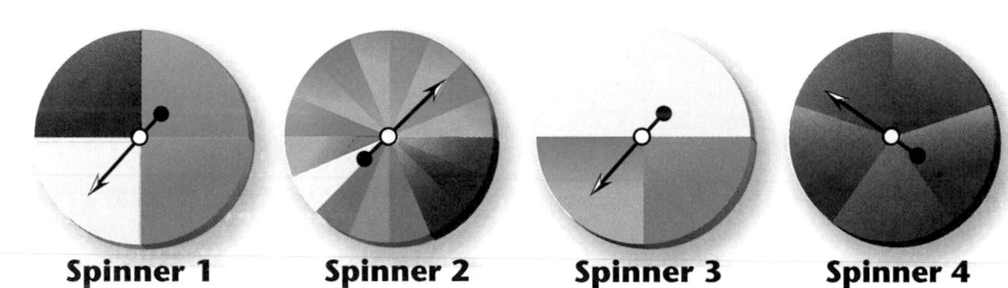

Spinner 1 | Spinner 2 | Spinner 3 | Spinner 4

In Spinner 1, there is an **equally likely** chance of spinning red, blue, green, and yellow.

Spinner 2 is more likely to spin blue than any other color. It is **unlikely** to spin yellow.

In Spinner 3, it is **impossible** to spin red.

Spinner 4 is **certain** to spin red.

Try It

Use the words *likely, equally likely, certain, unlikely,* or *impossible* to describe the probability.

1. Red **2.** Yellow **3.** White

Sum it Up

Describe the probability of spinning a 4 on a spinner that has sections that are all labeled with a 4. Explain.

Practice

Use the words *likely, equally likely, certain, unlikely,* or *impossible* to describe the probability.

4. Red or blue
5. Green
6. White

Describe the probability of picking a certain color cube from a bag.

7. Red
8. Blue
9. Black
10. Green or yellow
11. Blue or red
12. Red, green, yellow, or blue

Describe the probability.

13. The day after Sunday will be Tuesday.
14. The sun will rise in the morning.

Problem Solving

Use data from *Did You Know?* for problems 15–16.

15. An amusement park takes up 12 acres. How many square feet is that?
16. If $\frac{1}{5}$ of Disney World is taken up by the Magic Kingdom, how many acres is that?

★17. A spinner has 4 sections. It is impossible to spin red. It is most likely to spin green. It is less likely to spin yellow. Draw the spinner.

18. **Generalize:** Tell how you can use this statement to make a decision: It will most likely rain today.

Spiral Review and Test Prep

Write each fraction in simplest form.

19. $\frac{5}{25}$
20. $\frac{21}{27}$
21. $\frac{6}{12}$
22. $\frac{3}{30}$
23. $\frac{20}{45}$
24. $\frac{8}{32}$

Choose the correct answer.

25. An equivalent fraction for $\frac{3}{5}$ is:
   A. $\frac{6}{10}$ **B.** $\frac{2}{5}$ **C.** $\frac{4}{6}$ **D.** $\frac{1}{3}$

26. $\frac{8}{20}$ in simplest form is:
   F. $\frac{4}{20}$ **G.** $\frac{2}{5}$ **H.** $\frac{4}{10}$ **J.** $\frac{2}{10}$

Extra Practice, page 505

Objective: Organize, display, and analyze the results of probability experiments.

Explore Probability

Learn

Math Words

favorable outcomes desired results in a probability experiment

possible outcomes any of the results that could occur in a probability experiment

You can use a number cube to explore probability. What is the probability of tossing a 6 on a number cube? How many times will you toss it in 50 tries?

Work Together

You Will Need
- number cube

▶ Use a number cube to find how many times you toss a 6 in 50 tries.

- Make a line plot to show your results. Put an X above each number to show how many times that number was rolled.

1 2 3 4 5 6

▶ How many times did you toss a 6? Compare your results with those of others.

Make Connections

What is the chance, or the probability, of tossing 3 or 4?

Using Models	Using Paper and Pencil
The **favorable outcomes** are 3 and 4. There are 6 **possible outcomes**: 1, 2, 3, 4, 5, and 6.	Use a fraction to show the probability. **Think:** Favorable outcomes → 2 Possible outcomes → 6 The probability of winning is $\frac{2}{6}$. You can also say that the probability of a favorable outcome is 2 out of 6 or 1 out of 3.

Try It

Find the probability of spinning the color.

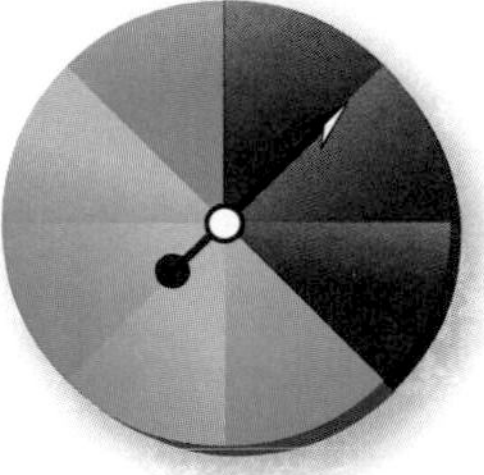

1. Red
2. Blue
3. Green
4. Red or blue
5. Blue or green
6. Yellow

What is the probability of tossing a 6 on the number cube used on page 492?

Practice

Find the probability of picking the color.

7. Yellow
8. Blue
9. Green
10. Yellow or blue
11. Blue or green
12. Red

Find the probability of picking the shape.

13. Star
14. Triangle
15. Circle
16. Square
17. Star or triangle
18. Circle or triangle

19. **Analyze:** Which type of card are you least likely to pick; Why?

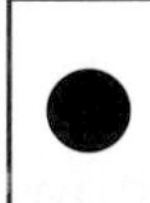

Objective: Solve problems by drawing and using a tree diagram.

Problem Solving: Strategy
Draw a Tree Diagram

Read

Read the problem carefully.

Ben plays a target game at a boardwalk amusement arcade. What are all the possible outcomes if Ben tosses one ball at each of the two targets below?

Math Word
tree diagram a diagram of all the possible outcomes of an event

- **What do you know?**
  how many sections are on each target

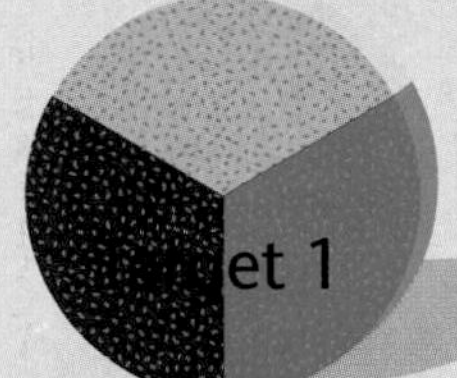

- **What do you need to find?**
  all the possible outcomes of tossing a ball at each of the two targets

Plan

One way to solve the problem is to make a **tree diagram** that shows all of the possible outcomes.

Solve

Start with the first target. Make branches to show all of the possible outcomes for the first toss. Then make branches to show all of the possible outcomes for the second toss.

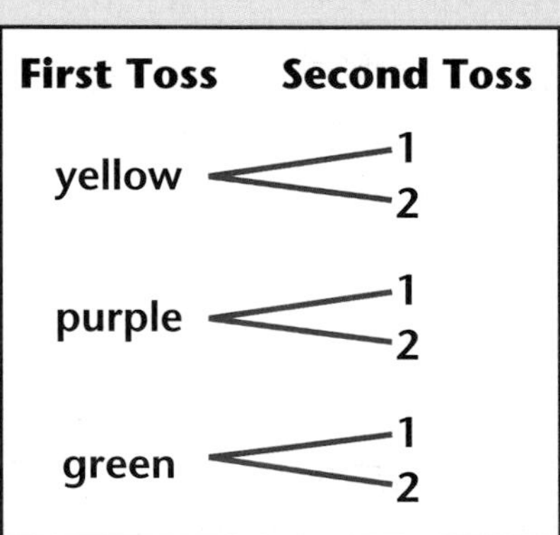

There are 6 possible combinations for the game: yellow, 1; yellow, 2; purple, 1; purple, 2; green, 1; green, 2.

Look Back

How could you use a table to solve the problem?

Tell how a tree diagram helps you find the possible outcomes.

Practice **Make a tree diagram to solve.**

1. What are all the possible outcomes of tossing a number cube and flipping a coin?

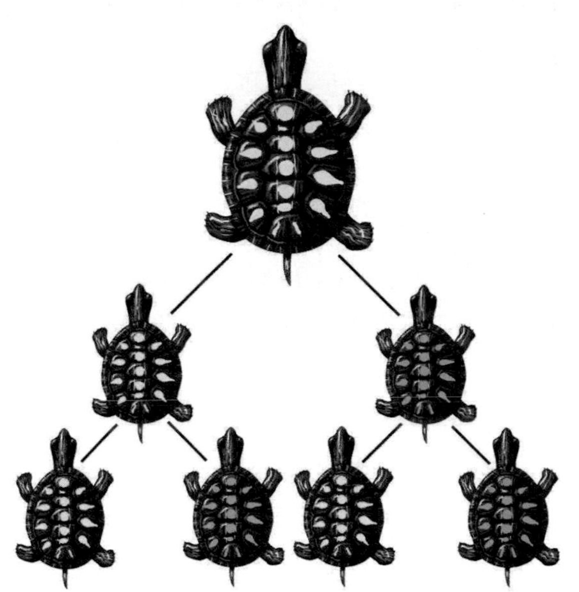

2. **Science:** The boardwalk aquarium has a turtle house. The tree diagram shows the number of spotted yellow and spotted green offspring for 3 generations. If this pattern continues for 2 more generations, how many turtles will have green spots? yellow spots?

3. Ben gets a yogurt cone at the arcade. He can choose vanilla, chocolate, or strawberry yogurt. He can choose a cup, wafer cone, or sugar cone. What are all the possible combinations?

Mixed Strategy Review

4. **What if** you toss 2 number cubes? What are the possible sums? What is the probability of tossing an 8?

5. The gift store owner is making a bottle of sand art. The bottle holds 12 inches of sand. He wants to put 1 more inch of blue sand than yellow sand and 4 more inches of pink sand than blue sand. How many inches of each color sand will he fill in the bottle?

6. **Collect Data:** Take a survey of the favorite board games of your classmates. Find out if the board game uses spinners, number cubes, or cards. Make a graph to show your results. Draw a conclusion based on the data.

7. **Logical Reasoning:** You multiply a number by 5 and get an even number. Is the number you multiplied by odd or even? Explain.

8. **Create a problem** that could be solved by conducting an experiment. Solve it. Ask others to solve it.

CHOOSE A STRATEGY

- Logical Reasoning
- Draw a Picture
- Make a Graph
- Act It Out
- Make a Table or List
- Find a Pattern
- Guess and Check
- Write a Number Sentence
- Work Backward
- Solve a Simpler Problem

Extra Practice, page 505

Objective: Predict the outcome in an experiment.

11-11 Explore Making Predictions

Learn

You can use a spinner to explore making predictions. Predict how many times you would spin a 1 in 50 spins.

Work Together

► *Use a spinner to conduct an experiment.*

You Will Need
- **spinner**

- List the possible outcomes for the spinner.
- Predict the number of times you will spin a 1 in 50 spins.
- Record your prediction.
- Experiment by spinning the spinner 50 times.
- Record the number you spin for each try in a table.

Number Spun									
0	1	2	3	4	5	6	7	8	9

- Compare your results with your prediction. Compare your results with those of others.

► *Spin the spinner 30 more times. How many times do you predict you will spin a 3 in 30 spins? in 80 spins?*

Make Connections

How many times would you spin a 6 in 50 spins?

Using Models	Using Paper and Pencil
The possible outcomes are 0, 1, 2, 3, 4, 5, 6, 7, 8, 9.	Use probability to predict the outcome.

Think:

Probability $= \frac{\text{Favorable outcomes}}{\text{Possible outcomes}} = \frac{1}{10}$

The probability of spinning 6 is 1 out of 10.

1 out of 10 is $\frac{1}{10}$.

$\frac{1}{10}$ of 50 is 5.

It is reasonable to predict that you would spin 6 five times out of 50.

Try It **Use the spinner for problems 1–2.**

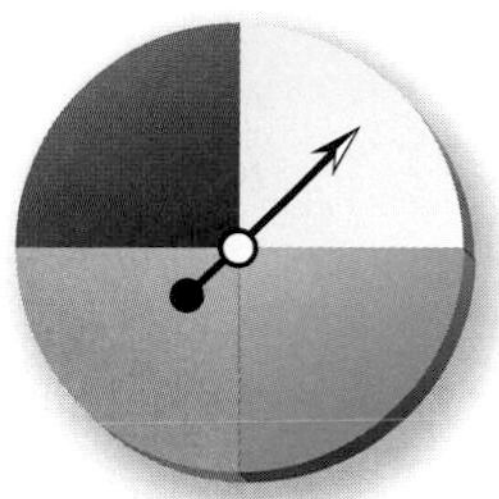

1. If you spin the spinner 100 times, how many times will you land on blue?
2. If you spin the spinner 50 times, how many times will you land on pink or purple?

You spin the above spinner 40 times. Is it reasonable to predict that you will land on purple 30 times? Explain.

Practice **Use the cubes for problems 3–4.**

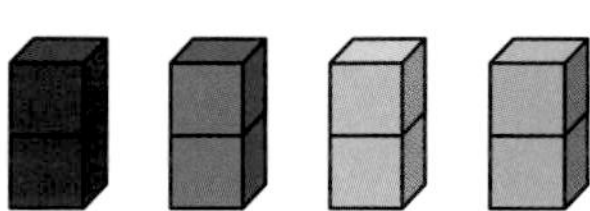

3. If you pick a cube out of a bag 80 times, what is the probability that you will pick a green cube?
4. Is it reasonable to predict that you will pick a yellow cube 6 out of 24 tries?
5. **Analyze:** A paper bag contains 30 cubes of one color, 15 cubes of another color, and 5 cubes of a third color. Red is picked from the bag 57 times. Blue is picked from the bag 28 times, and white is picked from the bag 12 times. How many cubes of each color do you think are in the bag?

Extra Practice, page 505

Objective: Analyze data and make decisions.

Problem Solving: Application
Decision Making

How can you create 3 games that are fair?

Monty and Anne are setting up some backyard amusement games. They want to create 3 games that are fair using spinners, cards, and checkerboards. A game is fair if each outcome is equally likely. Which games are fair? Which games are unfair?

Monty and Anne Stambler invented a game players can use fractions to play.

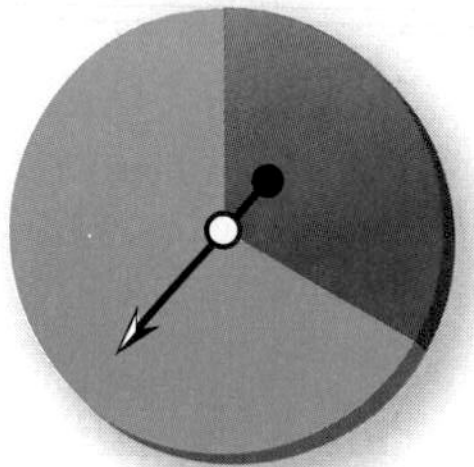

Spinner A

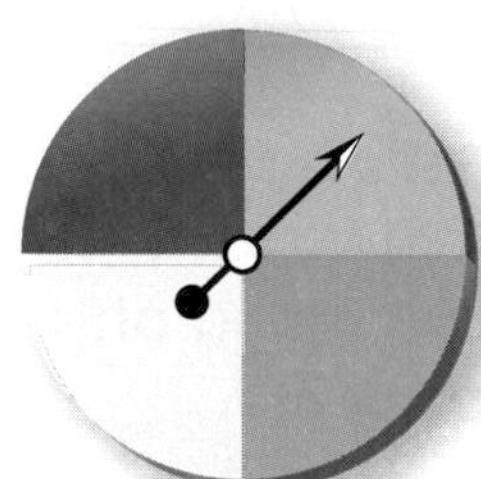

Spinner B

Spinner C

Spinner D

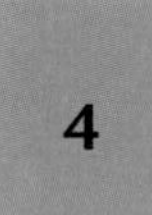

Cards A

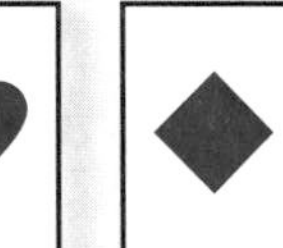

Cards B

Checkerboard A

Checkerboard B

Read for Understanding

1. What are the possible outcomes for Spinner A? Do you have an equally likely chance of landing on red and green?
2. What is the probability of landing on blue in Spinner B? Are you more likely to land on red or blue?
3. Is it likely, unlikely, or impossible to pick the card with the square on it in Cards B?
4. What if you toss a coin on Checkerboard B? What is the probability of landing on black?
5. Do you have an equally likely chance of spinning yellow in Spinner B as in Spinner D? Explain.
6. **What if** you need to pick a card with a six on it to win? What is the probability of winning in Cards A?

Make Decisions

7. Two students play a game with Spinner A. If one student spins a green, she wins the game. If the other student spins a red, he wins. Is this a fair or unfair game? Explain.
8. A spinner game is played in which you can score a point by landing on red. Would you be more likely to land on red in Spinner C or Spinner D? Explain. Which spinner would be a fair game?
9. You set up a coin toss game where you win a prize by landing on white. Which checkerboard should you use to set up a fair game? Explain.
10. Students set up a game in which two spinners are used. Which two spinners should they use to create a fair game? Explain.
11. You want to change Spinner C to make a fair game. How can you do this?
12. You want to change the cards in Cards B to make it a fair game. How can you do this?
13. A student wants to set up a game in which Cards A and a spinner are used. If she uses Spinner D, what is the probability that the player will draw a 1-RED? Explain.
14. How can you change Checkerboard B so that the probability of tossing a coin on all three colors is $\frac{1}{3}$?

Describe the three fair games you would recommend.

Objective: Apply fractions and probability to investigate science concepts.

Problem Solving: Math and Science

How does size affect how fast a solid dissolves?

You Will Need

- 3 seltzer tablets
- 3 clear plastic 8-ounce cups
- water
- timer or clock

You open a lemonade stand. To make the lemonade, you must dissolve a large amount of sugar in the water. Will it be easier if you use big sugar cubes or crushed (granulated) sugar?

In this activity, you will explore whether solids (such as salt, sugar, or seltzer tablets) dissolve faster when they are whole or broken into pieces.

Hypothesize

Will a seltzer tablet dissolve faster whole or broken into pieces?

Procedure

1. Work in a group of three people. Take turns.
2. Fill each cup $\frac{3}{4}$ full with water.
3. Add one **whole**, unbroken seltzer tablet to the first cup.
4. Time how long it takes until the water stops fizzing.
5. Break a seltzer tablet in **half**. Add the pieces to the second cup.
6. Time how long it takes to dissolve.
7. Repeat the experiment again with the seltzer tablet broken into **quarters**.

Data

Make your own chart to record the dissolving time for each seltzer tablet.

Tablet	Time to Dissolve
Whole	
Half	
Quarter	

Conclude and Apply

- Rank the seltzer tablets in order from fastest to slowest.
- What would happen if you broke the seltzer into eighths? Why?
- Describe a plan to make the seltzer dissolve as fast as possible.
- Did you collect enough data in this activity to make any strong conclusions? Explain your answer.
- Explain the results of the activity in terms of **surface area.**

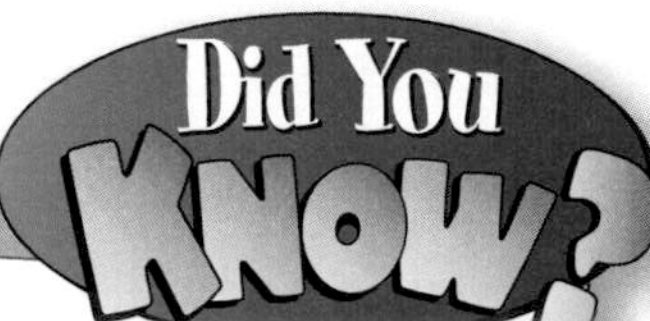

Surface area is the amount of area on the outside of a 3-dimensional object. Your surface area would be equal to the area of your skin.

Going Further

1. Design and do an activity to determine whether salt dissolves faster in cold or hot water.
2. Design and complete an activity to determine how stirring affects how fast salt will dissolve.

Check Your Progress B

Use the words *likely, equally likely, certain, unlikely,* or *impossible* to describe the probability. **(pages 490–491)**

1. Yellow
2. Green
3. Black
4. Blue
5. Yellow, green, or blue

Find the probability of picking the cube from a bag. **(pages 492–493)**

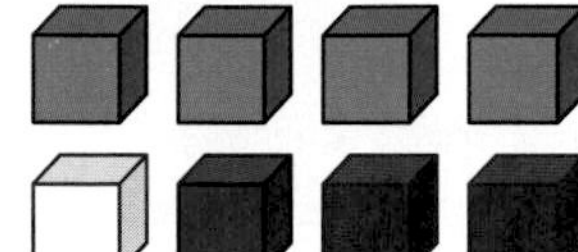

6. Blue
7. White
8. Green
9. Black or red
10. Blue or white
11. Black or blue

Find the probability of picking the card from a bag. **(pages 492–493)**

1 1 2 2

2 2 3 3

3 4 5 6

12. 

13. 

14. 

15. 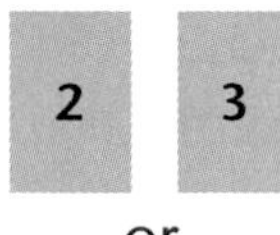

16. 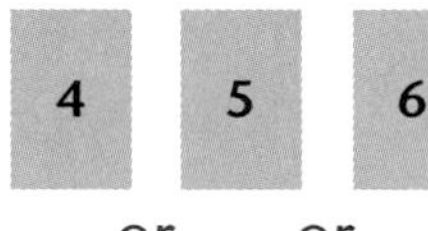

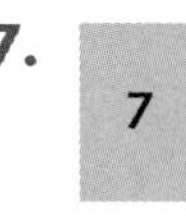

17. 7

Use the spinners for problems 18–19. **(pages 496–497)**

18. How many possible outcomes are there if you spin only Spinner 1? What are they?
19. How many possible combinations are there if you spin both spinners once each? What are they?

Spinner 1

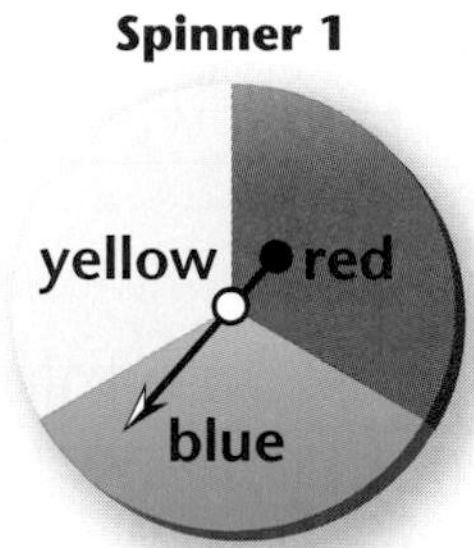

Spinner 2

20. **Summarize:** You are conducting an experiment to see how many times you would choose a blue cube from a bag of 5 white cubes and 1 blue cube. Tell how you predict how many times you will pick blue in 60 tries.

Additional activities at
www.mhschool.com/math

Extra Practice

Parts of a Whole (pages 470–471)

Write a fraction for the part that is orange.

1. 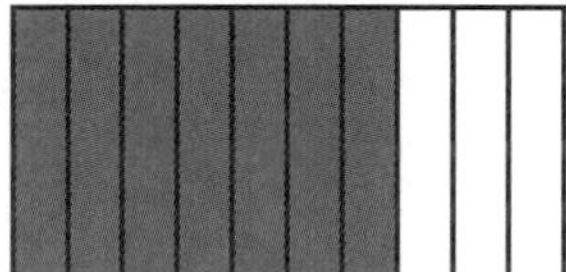
2. 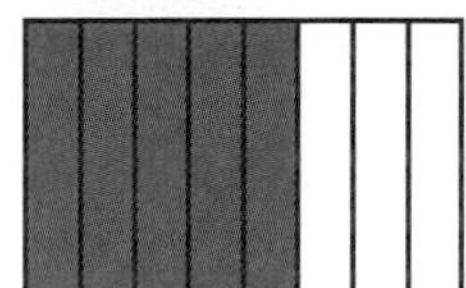
3. 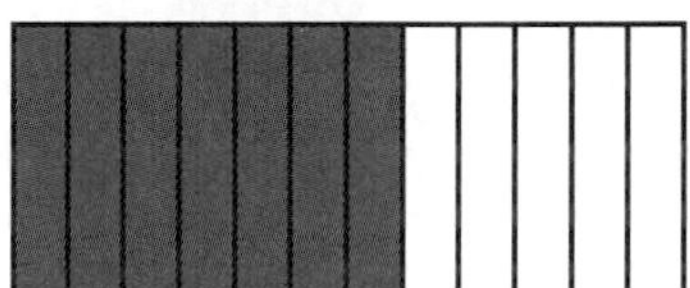

Solve.

4. A spinning game has a wheel that is divided into 15 equal parts. Nine of the parts are blue. What fraction of the wheel is blue? What fraction of the wheel is not blue?

Parts of a Group (pages 472–473)

Write a fraction that names what part is green.

1. 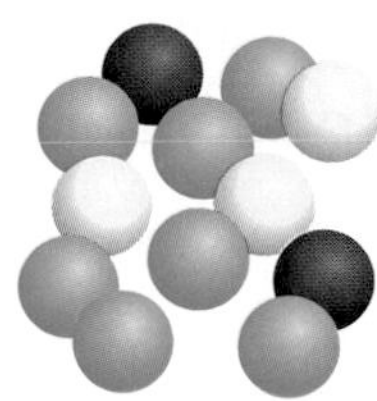
2. 
3. 

Solve.

4. Four of five pins in a ball toss are white. What fraction shows how many of the pins are white? What fraction shows how many of the pins are not white?
5. There are 12 cars on a train ride. Five of the cars are full. What fraction shows how many of the cars are not full?

Find Equivalent Fractions and Fractions in Simplest Form (pages 474–477)

Name an equivalent fraction for each.

1. $\frac{4}{7}$
2. $\frac{2}{4}$
3. $\frac{3}{5}$
4. $\frac{1}{8}$
5. $\frac{2}{9}$

Write each fraction in simplest form.

6. $\frac{4}{18}$
7. $\frac{4}{44}$
8. $\frac{5}{50}$
9. $\frac{8}{64}$
10. $\frac{4}{48}$
11. $\frac{14}{21}$
12. $\frac{12}{54}$
13. $\frac{18}{21}$
14. $\frac{15}{55}$
15. $\frac{21}{63}$
16. $\frac{25}{45}$
17. $\frac{24}{32}$

Extra Practice

Compare and Order Fractions (pages 478–481)

Compare. Write >, <, or =.

1. $\frac{7}{14} \bullet \frac{2}{3}$
2. $\frac{12}{15} \bullet \frac{4}{5}$
3. $\frac{3}{8} \bullet \frac{1}{4}$
4. $\frac{7}{8} \bullet \frac{12}{16}$
5. $\frac{9}{15} \bullet \frac{2}{3}$

Order from least to greatest.

6. $\frac{3}{4}, \frac{5}{6}, \frac{5}{12}$
7. $\frac{3}{4}, \frac{3}{8}, \frac{1}{2}$
8. $\frac{5}{10}, \frac{1}{3}, \frac{4}{5}$
9. $\frac{5}{6}, \frac{1}{2}, \frac{2}{3}$

Problem Solving: Reading for Math Check for Reasonableness (pages 482–483)

Solve.

1. There are 14 cars on a ride. Four of the cars are green. Is it reasonable to say that fewer than half of the cars are green? Explain.
2. There are 64 squares on a checkerboard. Half of the squares are black. Is it reasonable to say that $\frac{36}{64}$ are black? Explain.

Explore Finding Parts of a Group (pages 484–485)

Find the fraction of each number.

1. $\frac{1}{2}$ of 18
2. $\frac{4}{5}$ of 45
3. $\frac{2}{3}$ of 33
4. $\frac{5}{7}$ of 21
5. $\frac{4}{10}$ of 80

Mixed Numbers (pages 486–487)

Rename each as a mixed number or fraction in simplest form.

1. $2\frac{1}{3}$
2. $\frac{25}{6}$
3. $\frac{52}{8}$
4. $1\frac{3}{4}$
5. $\frac{41}{5}$
6. $3\frac{3}{5}$
7. $\frac{11}{5}$
8. $\frac{33}{9}$
9. $\frac{40}{6}$
10. $3\frac{1}{4}$
11. $\frac{20}{8}$
12. $6\frac{3}{8}$

Solve.

13. Roger fills a water cooler with 13 cups of water. Write a mixed number to show how many quarts are in the cooler.
14. A sign is 25 feet high. Write a mixed number to show how many yards high the sign is.

Extra Practice

Likely and Unlikely (pages 490–491)

Use the words *likely, equally likely, certain, unlikely,* or *impossible* to describe the probability.

1. Picking a green ball
2. Picking a yellow ball
3. Picking a pink ball
4. A bag is filled with red and green apples. What is the probability that you will pick either a red or a green apple?

Explore Probability (pages 492–493)

Find the probability of spinning each color.

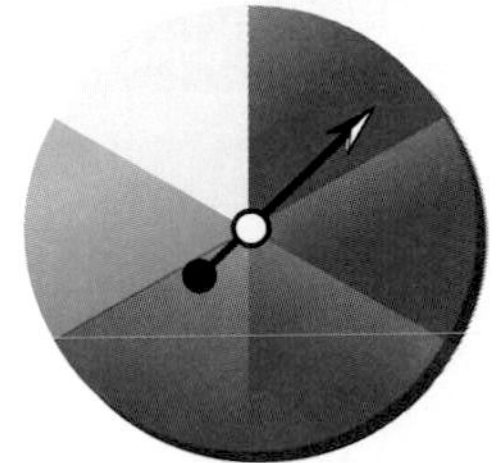

1. Blue
2. Red or blue
3. Yellow or blue
4. Green

Problem Solving: Strategy Draw a Tree Diagram (pages 494–495)

Make a tree diagram to solve.

1. What if you spin each spinner once. What are all of the possible outcomes?

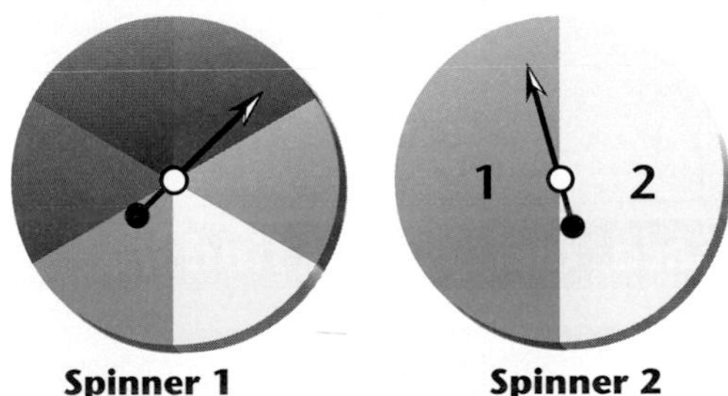

Spinner 1 Spinner 2

Explore Making Predictions (pages 496–497)

Find the probability of picking the color.

1. If you pick a cube from a bag 60 times, what is the probability that you will pick a green cube?
2. Is it reasonable to predict that you will pick either a yellow or red cube 12 out of 18 times?

Chapter Study Guide

Language and Math

Complete. Use a word from the list.

1. Eight-thirds is an example of a (an) ____.
2. In the fraction $\frac{4}{5}$, the 4 is the ____.
3. A spinner with 3 equal sections of red, blue, and yellow has 3 ____.
4. Two or more fractions that name the same number are called ____.

Math Words

- denominator
- improper fraction
- numerator
- possible outcomes
- probability
- equivalent fractions

Skills and Applications

Identify, read, and write fractions and mixed numbers. (pages 470–473, 486–487)

Example

Write a fraction for the part that is shaded.

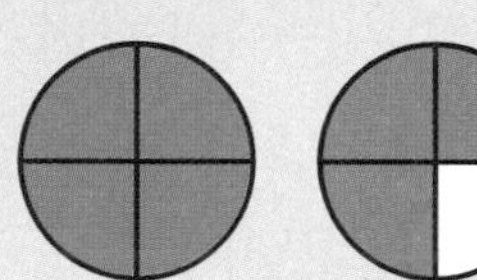

Solution

7 quarters is $\frac{7}{4}$.

Change to a mixed number.

$4\overline{)7}$ = 1 R3 → $1\frac{3}{4}$

Write a fraction for the part that is shaded.

5. 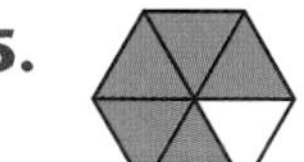
6. 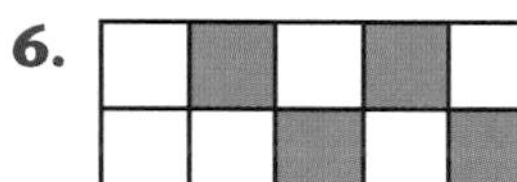

Rename as a whole number or a mixed number in simplest form.

7. $\frac{9}{9}$
8. $\frac{13}{3}$
9. $\frac{8}{5}$
10. $\frac{22}{4}$
11. $\frac{25}{10}$
12. $\frac{6}{3}$
13. $\frac{14}{6}$
14. $\frac{9}{2}$

Compare, order, and find equivalent fractions. (pages 474–481)

Example

Compare $\frac{2}{5}$ and $\frac{3}{10}$.

Solution

Find equivalent fractions with the same denominator.

Multiply the numerator and the denominator by the same number.

$\frac{2 \times 2}{5 \times 2} = \frac{4}{10}$

$\frac{4}{10} > \frac{3}{10}$ so $\frac{2}{5} > \frac{3}{10}$.

Name an equivalent fraction for each.

15. $\frac{1}{5}$
16. $\frac{6}{16}$
17. $\frac{4}{6}$
18. $\frac{6}{9}$
19. $\frac{3}{8}$

Compare. Write >, <, or =.

20. $\frac{2}{3}$ ● $\frac{4}{6}$
21. $\frac{5}{8}$ ● $\frac{3}{4}$
22. $\frac{3}{8}$ ● $\frac{3}{12}$

Write in order from least to greatest.

23. $\frac{3}{4}, \frac{7}{12}, \frac{1}{2}$
24. $\frac{3}{8}, \frac{7}{8}, \frac{8}{16}$

Find the number of outcomes and the probability for given situations. (pages 490–493, 496–497)

Example

What is the probability of spinning green?

Solution

Number of favorable outcomes: 1

Number of possible outcomes: 5

There is a 1 out of 5, or $\frac{1}{5}$, probability.

Find the probability of picking the marble from a bag.

25. Red
26. Blue
27. Purple
28. Red or yellow
29. List all the possible outcomes.
30. Predict how many times you would pick yellow if you picked 36 times.

Use strategies to solve problems. (pages 482–483, 494–495)

Example

What if you flip a coin and spin a spinner with red, blue, and yellow sections? What are all the possible combinations?

Solution

Make a tree diagram.

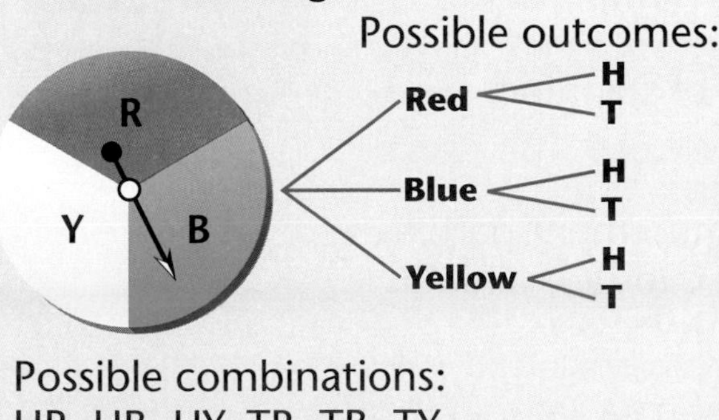

Possible combinations:
HR, HB, HY, TR, TB, TY

Solve.

31. What are the possible outcomes of tossing a number cube with numbers 1 to 6 and spinning a spinner with 1 red and 1 blue section?
32. Sally has used up $\frac{1}{3}$ of 24 tickets. Is it reasonable to say that she has used up 20 tickets? Explain.
33. There are 6 blocks in a bag. Two blocks are white, 3 are black, and 1 is red. What is the probability of choosing a black or red block?

Chapter Test

Write a fraction for the part that is shaded blue.

1. 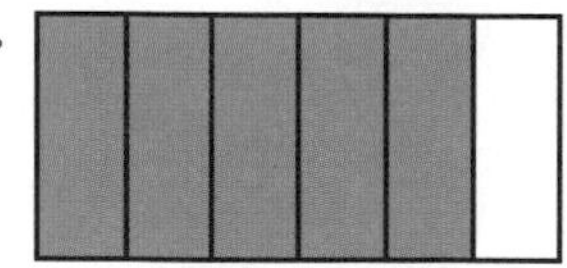

2. 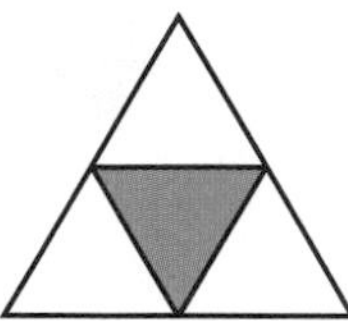

3. 

Write each fraction in simplest form.

4. $\frac{9}{24}$
5. $\frac{4}{12}$
6. $\frac{28}{35}$
7. $\frac{18}{27}$
8. $\frac{20}{55}$
9. $\frac{18}{42}$

Compare. Write >, <, or =.

10. $\frac{5}{8}$ ● $\frac{3}{4}$
11. $\frac{10}{12}$ ● $\frac{2}{3}$
12. $\frac{8}{18}$ ● $\frac{5}{9}$
13. $\frac{8}{10}$ ● $\frac{4}{5}$

Order from least to greatest.

14. $\frac{7}{9}, \frac{2}{3}, \frac{3}{9}$
15. $\frac{2}{4}, \frac{5}{6}, \frac{5}{12}$
16. $\frac{3}{8}, \frac{5}{16}, \frac{3}{4}$

Rename each as an improper fraction, a mixed number, or fraction in simplest form.

17. $6\frac{3}{4}$
18. $\frac{19}{3}$
19. $\frac{29}{6}$
20. $4\frac{2}{5}$
21. $\frac{15}{2}$

Solve.

22. Describe the probability of spinning red on the spinner. Use the words *likely, unlikely, impossible,* or *certain.*

23. Write a fraction that shows the probability of spinning black on the spinner.

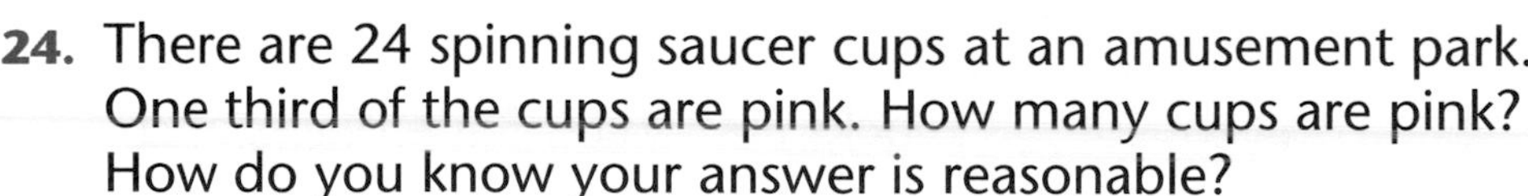

24. There are 24 spinning saucer cups at an amusement park. One third of the cups are pink. How many cups are pink? How do you know your answer is reasonable?

25. Liza plays a game with a spinner and a coin. The spinner has 4 equal sections of red, blue, yellow, and green. She flips the coin and spins the spinner once each. Draw a tree diagram to show all the possible combinations.

Performance Assessment

You serve a mixture of snacks at your movie party. Put different-color cubes in a bag to represent different snacks. You can use six colors: yellow = popcorn, red = dried fruit, blue = raisins, green = peanuts, orange = carrot sticks, purple = baked corn chips.

Decide how many of each color will go into the bag. Then determine the probability of picking each snack. Write the numbers as fractions. Predict how many times you would pick each snack in 10 turns.

Now take 10 turns picking snacks from the bag. Return the snack picked each time. Write the results of the experiment as fractions.

Graph the results, using a different color pencil for each snack.

Compare the probabilities to the results. What conclusions can you draw?

A Good Answer
- shows the probability of each color as a fraction.
- shows the results as fractions.
- displays the results on a graph.
- describes the conclusions that can be made.

You may want to save this work for your portfolio.

Assessment

Enrichment

Combinations

Nancy is playing a game in which you must toss a coin to see if you move up (heads) or down (tails).

Then you spin the spinner shown at the right to see how many spaces you should move.

What is the total number of possible outcomes when you flip the coin and spin the spinner?

Coin toss:	There are two possible outcomes that are equally likely: heads and tails (H and T).
Spinner:	There are six possible outcomes that are equally likely: 1, 2, 3, 4, 5, 6.

The possible outcomes when you toss the coin and spin the spinner are: H1, H2, H3, H4, H5, H6, T1, T2, T3, T4, T5, T6.

The total number of possible outcomes is 12.

Another way to find the total number of outcomes is to multiply the number of outcomes for the coin toss by the number of outcomes for the spinner.

2 coin toss outcomes $\times$ 6 spinner outcomes $=$ 12 possible outcomes.

Use the spinner and cards for 1 and 2.

1. You pick a card and spin the spinner. How many outcomes are possible? List them.
2. **What if** you add another card, D? How would that change the number of outcomes?

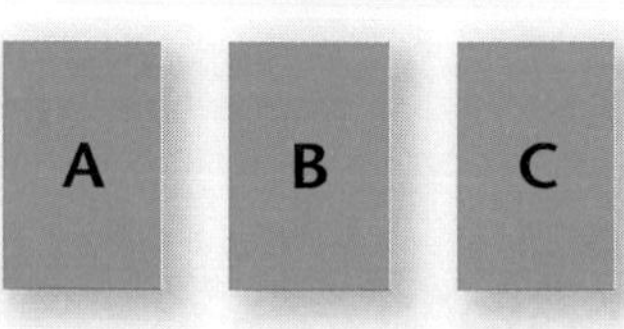

Test-Taking Tips

A long-answer type of test does not give you any answer choices. You have to write out your answer and show your work. These questions are often worth more than multiple-choice questions. Plan your time accordingly.

You want the spinner to land on blue. Which spinner should you use?

Explain below which spinner you chose and why you chose it.

If I use the four-part spinner, I have a 1 out of 4 chance of spinning blue. If I use the eight-part spinner, I have a 1 out of 8 chance of spinning blue. I have a better chance of spinning blue with the four-part spinner.

Check for Success

Before turning in a test, go back one last time to check.

- ☑ I understood and answered the questions asked.
- ☑ I checked my work for errors.
- ☑ My answers make sense.

For this type of question, always be sure that your explanation really describes the thinking you used to get your answer.

Read the problem carefully. Then write your answer.

1. Make 2 sets of cards, each containing 5 numbers. Form the greatest number possible from each set of cards. Then subtract to find the difference between the numbers. Explain the steps you followed.
2. Write a problem that uses multiplication where the answer is "528 miles."
3. Write a problem that uses division where the answer is "12 cupcakes."
4. Draw an object, using inches to describe its length, width, and height. Then write these measurements in centimeters.

Spiral Review and Test Prep

Chapters 1–11

Choose the correct answer.

Number Sense

1. A roller coaster holds a total of 272 people. If each car holds 8 people, how many cars are there? Choose the number sentence that solves the problem.

   A. $272 \div 8$ **C.** 8×272
   B. $272 - 8$ **D.** $272 + 8$

2. A theme park has special 3-day passes. The pass costs $79.95. If a 1-day entrance to the park costs $32.29, how much would you save if you went for 3 days and bought the special pass?

   F. $47.66 **H.** $16.92
   G. $37.66 **J.** $16.72

3. Which statement describes the numbers on the number line below?

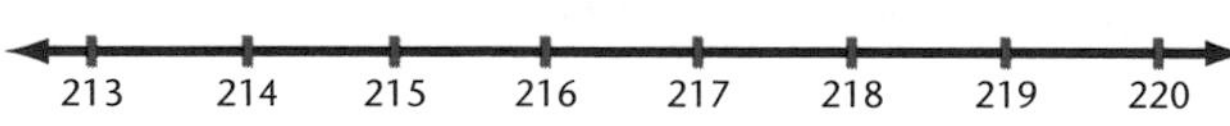

   A. All whole numbers greater than 213
   B. All whole numbers less than 220
   C. All whole numbers greater than 212 and less than 221
   D. All whole numbers between 213 and 220

4. Which shows $\frac{5}{8}$?

   F. $\frac{1}{3}$ **H.** $\frac{1}{4}$ | $\frac{1}{4}$ | $\frac{1}{4}$
   G. $\frac{1}{8}$ | $\frac{1}{8}$ | $\frac{1}{8}$ | $\frac{1}{8}$ | $\frac{1}{8}$ **J.** $\frac{1}{6}$ | $\frac{1}{6}$

Measurement and Geometry

5. A parking lot has a length of 42 feet and a width of 27 feet. What is the area of the parking lot?

   A. 69 square feet
   B. 138 square feet
   C. 1,134 square feet
   D. Not Here

6. A roller coaster has a track that is $\frac{1}{4}$ of a kilometer long. How many meters is that?

   F. 1000 meters **H.** 250 meters
   G. 500 meters **J.** 250 kilometers

7. Which is the most reasonable measurement? A bathtub holds about 100 ■ of water.

   A. liters **C.** grams
   B. milliliters **D.** ounces

8. What is not shown in the diagram?

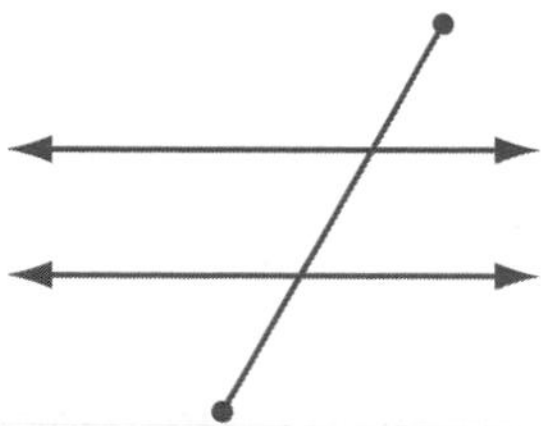

   F. Parallel lines **H.** Line segment
   G. Intersecting lines **J.** Perpendicular lines

Statistics, Data Analysis, and Probability

Use the picture of the spinner for problems 9–11.

9. What is the probability of spinning blue?

   A. $\frac{1}{8}$ C. $\frac{3}{8}$

   B. $\frac{2}{8}$ D. $\frac{1}{4}$

10. What fraction of the spinner is red or yellow?

   F. $\frac{1}{2}$ H. $\frac{3}{8}$

   G. $\frac{3}{4}$ J. $\frac{2}{6}$

11. If you spin the spinner once and flip a coin, how many possible outcomes are there?

   A. 2 C. 16

   B. 8 D. 32

12. If each ✪ stands for 2 persons, how can you show 10 people?

   F. ✪ ✪ H. ✪ ✪ ✪ ✪ ✪

   G. ✪ ✪ ✪ ✪ ✪ ✪ ✪ ✪ ✪ ✪ J. Not Here

Mathematical Reasoning

13. If one number is removed from each number sentence below and placed in the other, the products would be equal. Which numbers should be moved?

   10×80 5×40

   A. 10, 40 C. 5, 80

   B. 5, 10 D. 40, 80

14. Harry has $18 at the end of the week. During the week, he took out $6 and put back $4. Which method could you use to find out how much money he had at the beginning of the week?

   F. Add $4 to $18, then subtract $6. H. Subtract $4 from $18, then add $6.

   G. Subtract $6 from $15, then add $3. J. Add $6 and $4 to $18.

15. What two numbers are likely to be next?

   1, 3, 7, 13, _, _

   A. 17, 31 C. 21, 31

   B. 23, 33 D. 17, 23

16. You have 6 coins in your pocket that equal $1.00. What could the coins be? Explain.

CHAPTER 12 Fraction Operations

Theme: Food for Thought

Use the Data

One Serving of Fruit	One Serving of Vegetables
$\frac{1}{2}$ cup fruit salad	$\frac{1}{2}$ cup cooked or canned vegetables
$\frac{1}{4}$ cup dried fruit, such as raisins	1 cup raw, leafy greens
$\frac{3}{4}$ cup fruit juice	$\frac{3}{4}$ cup vegetable juice

Fruit and vegetables are an important part of our daily diet. In fact, we should eat 3 to 5 servings each of fruits and vegetables every day.

- How many cups of dried fruit should you eat to get the minimum number of servings you need each day? How could you use addition with fractions to solve the problem?

What You Will Learn

In this chapter you will learn how to
- add fractions with like and unlike denominators.
- subtract fractions with like and unlike denominators.
- use properties to add and subtract fractions.
- use strategies to solve problems.

Objective: Add fractions with like denominators.

12·1 Add Fractions with Like Denominators

Math Words

numerator the part of a whole

denominator the total number of parts in a whole

simplest form a fraction in which the numerator and denominator have no common factor greater than 1

greatest common factor greatest number that is a common factor of two or more numbers

Learn

The 8 fourth-grade classes at Memorial School are having a food festival. Each class brings in dishes from a different country. One class brought in food from Canada, one brought in food from the United States, and one from Mexico. What fraction of the classes brought in food from North America?

There's more than one way!

There are 8 classes in all. Each class is $\frac{1}{8}$ of the total number of classes. To solve the problem, add $\frac{1}{8} + \frac{1}{8} + \frac{1}{8}$.

Method A

You can use fraction strips to add.

$\frac{1}{8} + \frac{1}{8} + \frac{1}{8} = \frac{3}{8}$

Method B

1. Add the **numerators**.

$\frac{1}{8} + \frac{1}{8} + \frac{1}{8} = \frac{3}{8}$

2. Use the common **denominator**.

$\frac{1}{8} + \frac{1}{8} + \frac{1}{8} = \frac{3}{8}$

3. Write the sum in **simplest form**.

Think: Divide the numerator and denominator by the **greatest common factor.**

$\frac{3}{8}$ of the class brought in food from North America.

Try It

Add. Write each sum in simplest form.

1. $\frac{1}{10} + \frac{5}{10}$ **2.** $\frac{3}{12} + \frac{5}{12}$ **3.** $\frac{7}{8} + \frac{5}{8}$ **4.** $\frac{2}{11} + \frac{9}{11}$ **5.** $\frac{1}{6} + \frac{1}{6}$

Why do you not add the denominators when you add fractions?

Practice Add. Write each sum in simplest form.

6. $\begin{array}{r} \frac{3}{8} \\ +\frac{1}{8} \\ \hline \end{array}$

7. $\begin{array}{r} \frac{6}{10} \\ +\frac{3}{10} \\ \hline \end{array}$

8. $\begin{array}{r} \frac{1}{6} \\ +\frac{5}{6} \\ \hline \end{array}$

9. $\begin{array}{r} \frac{3}{12} \\ +\frac{7}{12} \\ \hline \end{array}$

10. $\begin{array}{r} \frac{5}{6} \\ +\frac{5}{6} \\ \hline \end{array}$

11. $\begin{array}{r} \frac{1}{4} \\ +\frac{1}{4} \\ \hline \end{array}$

12. $\begin{array}{r} \frac{9}{10} \\ +\frac{7}{10} \\ \hline \end{array}$

13. $\begin{array}{r} \frac{1}{2} \\ +\frac{1}{2} \\ \hline \end{array}$

★14. $\begin{array}{r} \frac{5}{12} \\ \frac{1}{12} \\ +\frac{7}{12} \\ \hline \end{array}$

★15. $\begin{array}{r} \frac{3}{8} \\ \frac{1}{8} \\ +\frac{3}{8} \\ \hline \end{array}$

16. $\frac{3}{9} + \frac{2}{9}$
17. $\frac{5}{8} + \frac{1}{8}$
18. $\frac{4}{5} + \frac{1}{5}$
19. $\frac{3}{10} + \frac{5}{10}$
20. $\frac{1}{12} + \frac{4}{12}$

21. $\frac{1}{4} + \frac{2}{4}$
22. $\frac{2}{9} + \frac{5}{9}$
23. $\frac{3}{11} + \frac{5}{11}$
24. $\frac{2}{10} + \frac{2}{10}$
25. $\frac{1}{3} + \frac{2}{3}$

Algebra & functions **Compare. Write >, <, or =.**

26. $\frac{1}{3} + \frac{2}{3}$ ● 1
27. $\frac{2}{5} + \frac{1}{5}$ ● 1
28. $\frac{3}{11} + \frac{9}{11}$ ● 1
29. $\frac{3}{8} + \frac{7}{8}$ ● 1

Problem Solving

30. **Music:** Written music is divided into parts that are called measures. Notes in these measures are fractions of a beat. How many beats are in this measure?

31. **Analyze:** How can you tell if a sum will be closest to 0, $\frac{1}{2}$, or 1?

★32. At a Thai restaurant, $\frac{1}{3}$ of the meals are very spicy and $\frac{1}{3}$ are somewhat spicy. The rest of the meals are mild. What fraction of the meals are mild?

Spiral Review and Test Prep

33. 1,325 + 9,467
34. 3,108 ÷ 32
35. \$459 × 12
36. 8,631 − 479

Choose the correct answer.

37. What is $\frac{3}{4}$ of 36?
A. 27
B. 12
C. 9
D. 4

38. Tani uses $1\frac{1}{2}$ lb of beef to make hamburger. How many ounces of beef is this?
F. 16 ounces
G. 20 ounces
H. 24 ounces
J. Not Here

Extra Practice, page 545

Objective: Subtract fractions with like denominators.

12-2 Subtract Fractions with Like Denominators

At *nabemono* restaurants stews are cooked in a pot right at the table.

Learn

One *nabemono* recipe has $\frac{3}{4}$ cup of mushrooms and $\frac{1}{4}$ cup of celery. How much less celery is in the stew than mushrooms?

There's more than one way!

Find $\frac{3}{4} - \frac{1}{4}$ to solve.

Method A

You can use fraction strips to subtract.

$$\frac{3}{4} - \frac{1}{4} = \frac{2}{4} = \frac{1}{2}$$

Method B

1. Subtract the numerators. $\frac{3}{4} - \frac{1}{4} = 2$
2. Use the common denominator. $\frac{3}{4} - \frac{1}{4} = \frac{2}{4}$
3. Write the difference in simplest form. $\frac{2 \div 2}{4 \div 2} = \frac{1}{2}$

Think: Divide the numerator and denominator by the greatest common factor.

There is $\frac{1}{2}$ cup less celery than mushrooms in the stew.

Try It

Subtract. Write each difference in simplest form.

1. $\frac{7}{10} - \frac{5}{10}$
2. $\frac{5}{8} - \frac{4}{8}$
3. $\frac{8}{9} - \frac{4}{9}$
4. $\frac{3}{5} - \frac{2}{5}$
5. $\frac{7}{12} - \frac{6}{12}$

Sum it Up Why is it important that the fractions have a common denominator before subtracting?

Practice **Subtract. Write each difference in simplest form.**

6. $\frac{7}{8} - \frac{5}{8}$
7. $\frac{6}{11} - \frac{2}{11}$
8. $\frac{5}{7} - \frac{2}{7}$
9. $\frac{7}{12} - \frac{5}{12}$
10. $\frac{4}{5} - \frac{1}{5}$
11. $\frac{7}{8} - \frac{1}{8}$

12. $\frac{8}{9} - \frac{5}{9}$
13. $\frac{2}{10} - \frac{1}{10}$
14. $\frac{3}{5} - \frac{3}{5}$
15. $\frac{4}{6} - \frac{1}{6}$
16. $\frac{5}{6} - \frac{1}{6}$
17. $\frac{9}{12} - \frac{7}{12}$

18. $\frac{5}{6} - \frac{1}{6}$
19. $\frac{7}{9} - \frac{4}{9}$
20. $\frac{11}{12} - \frac{9}{12}$
21. $\frac{8}{8} - \frac{3}{8}$
22. $\frac{7}{9} - \frac{6}{9}$

23. $\frac{9}{10} - \frac{3}{10}$
24. $\frac{8}{11} - \frac{7}{11}$
25. $\frac{7}{10} - \frac{2}{10}$
26. $\frac{5}{12} - \frac{4}{12}$
27. $\frac{5}{8} - \frac{1}{8}$

28. $\frac{2}{3} - \frac{1}{3}$
29. $\frac{9}{9} - \frac{2}{9}$
30. $\frac{3}{4} - \frac{3}{4}$
★31. $\frac{12}{5} - \frac{8}{5}$
★32. $\frac{13}{8} - \frac{7}{8}$

Algebra & functions **Compare. Write >, <, or =.**

33. $\frac{8}{11} - \frac{5}{11}$ ● $\frac{6}{11} - \frac{3}{11}$
34. $\frac{5}{12} - \frac{1}{12}$ ● $\frac{11}{12} - \frac{10}{12}$
35. $\frac{5}{6} - \frac{2}{6}$ ● $\frac{4}{6} - \frac{1}{6}$

Problem Solving

36. **Generalize:** How could you use addition to check the difference when subtracting fractions? Use an example to explain.

★37. A stew has 1 cup of chopped chicken, $\frac{1}{4}$ cup of onions, and $\frac{1}{4}$ cup of celery. How much more meat is in the stew than vegetables?

38. **Language Arts:** The Japanese word *nabemono* means a quickly-cooked stew. How many vowels are in this word? Write a fraction comparing the number of vowels to the number of letters in the word.

Spiral Review and Test Prep

Find the fraction of the number.

39. $\frac{1}{3}$ of 15
40. $\frac{3}{4}$ of 16
41. $\frac{3}{10}$ of 100
42. $\frac{1}{5}$ of 30

Choose the correct answer.

43. Gina makes 4 cups of a seafood stew. How many ounces of stew does she make?
   - **A.** 64 ounces
   - **B.** 32 ounces
   - **C.** 16 ounces
   - **D.** 8 ounces

44. Which fraction is equivalent to $\frac{3}{12}$?
   - **F.** $\frac{1}{3}$
   - **G.** $\frac{1}{2}$
   - **H.** $\frac{3}{8}$
   - **J.** $\frac{1}{4}$

Objective: Make a judgment to decide the best operation to use.

12•3

Problem Solving: Reading for Math

Choose an Operation

A Taste of Korea

Read

Jin made *pahjun*, a Korean vegetable pancake, for his family. He cut the *pahjun* into 8 slices. His family ate 3 slices. What fraction of the *pahjun* is left?

READING SKILL ▶

Make a Judgment

When you make a judgment, you decide something. Your decision is based on what you know and the information given in the problem.

- **What do you know?** 8 slices in all; 3 slices eaten
- **What do you need to find?** Fraction of *pahjun* left
- **What judgment is called for?** Decide which operation to use

MATH SKILL ▶

Choose the Operation

- Understanding what you need to find in a problem can help you decide the operation to use.

Plan

Subtract to find what fraction of the *pahjun* is left.

Solve

$\frac{8}{8}$ represents Jin's whole *pahjun*.

$\frac{3}{8}$ represents the eaten slices. $\frac{8}{8} - \frac{3}{8} = \frac{5}{8}$

There is $\frac{5}{8}$ of the *pahjun* left.

Look Back

Is your answer reasonable?

How do you decide to subtract fractions to solve a problem?

Practice **Solve. Tell how you chose the operation.**

1. Jin also baked a dozen cookies. He gave 5 cookies to friends. What part of the dozen cookies is left?

2. Jin used $\frac{1}{8}$ stick of butter for one recipe and $\frac{3}{8}$ stick of butter in another recipe. How much butter did he use altogether?

Use data from the recipe for problems 3–9.

3. What is the total amount of pine nuts and raisins?

4. Are there more peanuts or sunflower seeds in the recipe? How much more?

5. How many more raisins than pine nuts are needed?

6. What is the total amount of peanuts and sunflower seeds in the recipe?

7. Miko uses $\frac{5}{8}$ cup of sunflower seeds in her recipe. How much more does she use than Yoshi?

8. What is the total amount of all the ingredients in the recipe?

YOSHI'S YUMMY SNACKS
$\frac{3}{8}$ cup sunflower seeds
$\frac{6}{8}$ cup raisins
$\frac{5}{8}$ cup peanuts
$\frac{1}{8}$ cup pine nuts

★9. Liah decides to add $\frac{2}{8}$ cup of almonds to the recipe and to reduce the amount of peanuts by $\frac{2}{8}$. What is the total amount of nuts used?

Spiral Review and Test Prep

Choose the correct answer.

Kim uses $\frac{1}{4}$ cup of milk and $\frac{3}{4}$ cup of broth in her sauce. How much liquid does she use in all?

10. Which of these statements is true?
    - **A.** Kim uses $\frac{3}{4}$ cup of milk.
    - **B.** Kim uses more milk than broth.
    - **C.** Kim uses $\frac{1}{4}$ cup of milk.

11. Which operation can you use to solve the problem?
    - **F.** Addition
    - **G.** Subtraction
    - **H.** Multiplication

Extra Practice, page 546

Check Your Progress A

Add. Write each sum in simplest form. **(pages 516–517)**

1. $\frac{1}{3} + \frac{1}{3}$
2. $\frac{4}{11} + \frac{2}{11}$
3. $\frac{2}{9} + \frac{7}{9}$
4. $\frac{1}{6} + \frac{5}{6}$
5. $\frac{3}{8} + \frac{4}{8}$
6. $\frac{5}{6} + \frac{2}{6}$
7. $\frac{3}{5} + \frac{2}{5}$
8. $\frac{7}{10} + \frac{5}{10}$
9. $\frac{3}{12} + \frac{8}{12}$
10. $\frac{5}{8} + \frac{7}{8} + \frac{1}{8}$

Subtract. Write each difference in simplest form. **(pages 518–519)**

11. $\frac{6}{7} - \frac{4}{7}$
12. $\frac{7}{8} - \frac{3}{8}$
13. $\frac{5}{12} - \frac{4}{12}$
14. $\frac{3}{4} - \frac{2}{4}$
15. $\frac{11}{12} - \frac{6}{12}$
16. $\frac{9}{10} - \frac{4}{10}$
17. $\frac{9}{12} - \frac{7}{12}$
18. $\frac{7}{10} - \frac{2}{10}$
19. $\frac{6}{6} - \frac{5}{6}$
20. $\frac{7}{9} - \frac{5}{9}$
21. $\frac{2}{3} - \frac{1}{3}$

Solve. **(pages 516–521)**

22. One bunch of grapes weighs 1 pound. Another bunch of grapes weighs $\frac{3}{4}$ pound. How much more does one bunch weigh than the other? Tell why you chose the operation you used to solve the problem.

23. Katrina cuts a loaf of banana bread into 12 equal pieces. She shares the bread with her friends. When they are done eating, $\frac{7}{12}$ of the loaf is left. How many pieces did they eat?

24. Marco makes a pound of bread dough. He freezes $\frac{1}{3}$ of the dough and bakes the rest. How much dough does he bake?

25. **Explain** how subtraction with fractions and subtraction with whole numbers are alike. How are they different?

Additional activities at www.mhschool.com/math

Use Fraction Strips to Add

Marian gave $\frac{1}{2}$ of the cookies she made to her friend. She then gave $\frac{1}{3}$ of the cookies to her brother. What fraction of her cookies did she give away?

You can model the number of cookies Marian gave away using fraction strips.

- Choose addition for the mat type.
- Stamp out a $\frac{1}{2}$ fraction strip in one section.
- Stamp out a $\frac{1}{3}$ fraction strip in the other section.

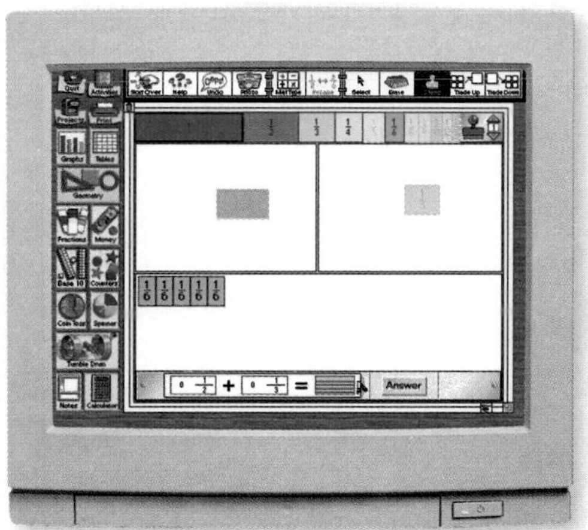

The number boxes show that you are finding $\frac{1}{2} + \frac{1}{3}$.

What fraction of her cookies did she give away?

Use the computer to model each addition. Then find each sum.

1. $\frac{1}{3} + \frac{1}{4}$ **2.** $\frac{1}{2} + \frac{1}{4}$ **3.** $\frac{1}{4} + \frac{1}{6}$ **4.** $\frac{2}{3} + \frac{1}{4}$

Solve.

5. Geoff put $\frac{1}{2}$ of his books on one shelf and $\frac{1}{6}$ on another shelf. What fraction of his book did he put on these two shelves?

6. Mr. Harmon mowed $\frac{2}{6}$ of his lawn before dinner and $\frac{1}{2}$ of his lawn after dinner. What fraction of his lawn did he mow?

7. Analyze: How do fraction strips help you add fractions?

For more practice, use Math Traveler™.

Objective: Explore adding fractions with unlike denominators.

12·4 Explore Adding Fractions with Unlike Denominators

Learn

Math Word

common denominator the same denominator shared by two or more fractions

You can use fraction strips to explore adding fractions with unlike denominators.

What is $\frac{3}{4} + \frac{1}{2}$?

Work Together

► Add $\frac{3}{4} + \frac{1}{2}$ by using fraction strips.

You Will Need
- **fraction strips**

- Get the $\frac{1}{4}$ strips and $\frac{1}{2}$ strips that you need.
- Use the fraction strips to find a **common denominator**.
- Find the total number of strips you have.

$\frac{1}{2}$

$\frac{1}{4}$ $\frac{1}{4}$ $\leftarrow \frac{1}{2} = \frac{2}{4}$

$$\frac{3}{4} + \frac{2}{4} = \frac{5}{4} = 1\frac{1}{4}$$

- Record your work.

► Use fraction strips to add. Record your work.

$\frac{1}{3} + \frac{5}{6}$ $\frac{1}{6} + \frac{1}{4}$ $\frac{1}{2} + \frac{5}{6}$ $\frac{2}{10} + \frac{1}{5}$

Make Connections

Here is how to find and write a sum in simplest form.

Using Models

Find the simplest form.

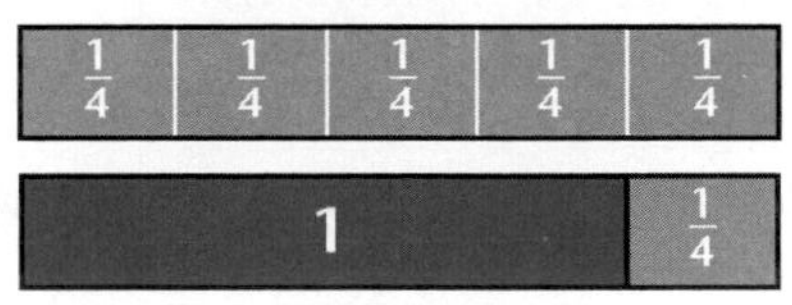

$\frac{5}{4} = 1\frac{1}{4}$

Using Paper and Pencil

Find an equivalent fraction with a common denominator.

$$\frac{3}{4} + \frac{1}{2} = \frac{3}{4} + \frac{2}{4}$$

Add the numerator. Use the common denominator. Write the fraction in simplest form.

$$\frac{3}{4} + \frac{2}{4} = \frac{5}{4} = 1\frac{1}{4}$$

Try It **Add. Write the answer in simplest form. You may want to use models.**

1. $\frac{1}{4} + \frac{3}{8}$
2. $\frac{5}{6} + \frac{2}{3}$
3. $\frac{5}{12} + \frac{1}{4}$
4. $\frac{3}{5} + \frac{7}{10} + \frac{1}{5}$
5. $\frac{1}{2} + \frac{4}{6}$
6. $\frac{4}{5} + \frac{1}{10}$
7. $\frac{3}{12} + \frac{3}{6}$
8. $\frac{3}{4} + \frac{1}{2} + \frac{1}{8}$
9. $\frac{2}{4} + \frac{1}{6}$
10. $\frac{2}{3} + \frac{1}{6}$
11. $\frac{1}{12} + \frac{2}{3}$
12. $\frac{1}{6} + \frac{1}{4} + \frac{1}{3}$

How can you use fraction strips to add fractions with denominators that are different?

Practice **Add. Write the answer in simplest form.**

13. $\frac{1}{6} + \frac{7}{12}$
14. $\frac{3}{8} + \frac{3}{4}$
15. $\frac{2}{3} + \frac{5}{9}$
16. $\frac{1}{12} + \frac{3}{4} + \frac{5}{12}$
17. $\frac{9}{10} + \frac{2}{5}$
18. $\frac{1}{2} + \frac{7}{8}$
19. $\frac{1}{3} + \frac{1}{4}$
20. $\frac{1}{2} + \frac{1}{4} + \frac{3}{8}$
21. $\frac{2}{10} + \frac{3}{5}$
22. $\frac{2}{9} + \frac{2}{3}$
23. $\frac{3}{4} + \frac{1}{16}$
24. $\frac{2}{12} + \frac{5}{6} + \frac{1}{3}$
25. $\frac{5}{18} + \frac{5}{6}$
26. $\frac{3}{4} + \frac{4}{5}$
27. $\frac{3}{16} + \frac{1}{2}$
28. $\frac{1}{3} + \frac{7}{18} + \frac{2}{3}$
29. **Analyze:** How did you solve $\frac{1}{12} + \frac{3}{4} + \frac{5}{12}$?

Objective: Add fractions with unlike denominators.

12•5 Add Fractions with Unlike Denominators

Learn

You can eat different foods to get the calcium you need for strong bones and teeth.

You eat $\frac{1}{4}$ cup of mozzarella cheese and 1 large tomato. What fraction of the daily amount of calcium do you eat?

Fraction of Amount of Calcium Needed Daily

6 ounces yogurt	$\frac{1}{5}$
8 ounces milk	$\frac{1}{4}$
$\frac{1}{4}$ cup mozzarella cheese	$\frac{1}{5}$
large tomato	$\frac{1}{10}$

sunshine yogurt

Nutrition Facts
Serving Size: $\frac{1}{2}$ cup (144g)
Servings per Container: 2

Amount per Serving	
Calories 90	Calories from Fat 30
	% Daily Value
Calcium	**33%**

Example 1

Find: $\frac{1}{5} + \frac{1}{10}$

1

Find equivalent fractions with a common denominator.

$$\frac{1}{5} + \frac{1}{10}$$

Think: Multiples of 5: 5, 10
Multiples of 10: 10
So, 10 is the common denominator.

$$\frac{1}{5} = \frac{1 \times 2}{5 \times 2} = \frac{2}{10}$$
$$+\frac{1}{10} \qquad +\frac{1}{10}$$

2

Add the numerators. Use the common denominator. Write the sum in simplest form, if needed.

$$\frac{2}{10} + \frac{1}{10} = \frac{3}{10}$$

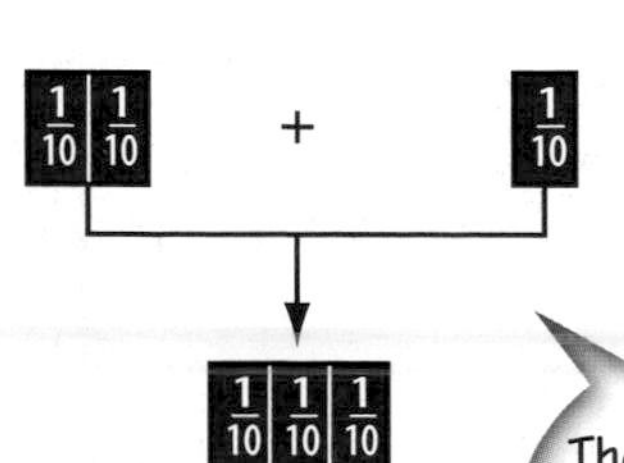

Think:
The greatest common factor of 3 and 10 is 1, so $\frac{3}{10}$ is in simplest form.

You eat $\frac{3}{10}$ of the daily amount of calcium.

You eat 6 ounces of yogurt and drink 8 ounces of milk. What fraction of the daily amount of calcium do you eat?

Example 2

Find: $\frac{1}{5} + \frac{1}{4}$

1 Find equivalent fractions with a common denominator.

$\frac{1}{5} = \frac{1 \times 4}{5 \times 4} = \frac{4}{20}$

$\frac{1}{4} = \frac{1 \times 5}{4 \times 5} = \frac{5}{20}$

Think: Multiples of 5: 5, 10, 15, 20 Multiples of 4: 4, 8, 12, 16, 20

The common denominator is 20.

2 Add the numerators. Use the common denominator. Write the sum in simplest form, if needed.

$\frac{4}{20} + \frac{5}{20} = \frac{9}{20}$

Think: The greatest common factor of 9 and 20 is 1, so $\frac{9}{20}$ is in simplest form.

You eat $\frac{9}{20}$ of the daily amount of calcium.

More Examples

A

$\frac{2}{3} = \frac{2 \times 6}{3 \times 6} = \frac{12}{18}$

$+\frac{5}{6} = \frac{5}{6} \times \frac{3}{3} \quad +\frac{15}{18}$

$\frac{27}{18} = 1\frac{9}{18} = 1\frac{1}{2}$

Think: You can always find a common denominator by multiplying the denominators.

B

$\frac{2}{5} = \frac{2 \times 2}{5 \times 2} = \frac{4}{10}$

$\frac{1}{2} = \frac{1 \times 5}{2 \times 5} = \frac{5}{10}$

$+\frac{7}{10} \quad\quad +\frac{7}{10}$

$\frac{16}{10} = 1\frac{6}{10} = 1\frac{3}{5}$

Try It **Add. Write each sum in simplest form.**

1. $\frac{7}{8} + \frac{1}{8}$
2. $\frac{9}{10} + \frac{1}{5}$
3. $\frac{7}{8} + \frac{2}{3}$
4. $\frac{1}{9} + \frac{5}{12}$
5. $\frac{1}{4} + \frac{3}{4}$
6. $\frac{1}{3} + \frac{5}{12}$
7. $\frac{1}{2} + \frac{1}{6}$
8. $\frac{4}{5} + \frac{3}{10}$
9. $\frac{5}{12} + \frac{2}{3}$
10. $\frac{1}{12} + \frac{1}{2} + \frac{1}{6}$

Explain how you would add $\frac{3}{4} + \frac{5}{6}$.

Practice **Add. Write each sum in the simplest form.**

11. $\frac{2}{10} + \frac{3}{5}$

12. $\frac{1}{8} + \frac{1}{2}$

13. $\frac{1}{15} + \frac{2}{5}$

14. $\frac{1}{4} + \frac{7}{12}$

15. $\frac{2}{3} + \frac{2}{6}$

16. $\frac{1}{3} + \frac{1}{3} + \frac{2}{3}$

17. $\frac{2}{5} + \frac{1}{3}$

18. $\frac{4}{5} + \frac{7}{10}$

19. $\frac{3}{4} + \frac{2}{8}$

20. $\frac{5}{12} + \frac{1}{6}$

21. $\frac{1}{12} + \frac{1}{4}$

22. $\frac{5}{9} + \frac{1}{3} + \frac{7}{9}$

23. $\frac{5}{6} + \frac{5}{12} + \frac{11}{12}$

24. $\frac{1}{10} + \frac{1}{5} + \frac{7}{10}$

★25. $\frac{11}{12} + \frac{3}{4} + \frac{1}{6} + \frac{5}{12}$

★26. $\frac{2}{3} + \frac{3}{5} + \frac{2}{15} + \frac{3}{5}$

★27. $\frac{1}{12} + \frac{2}{3} + \frac{5}{6} + \frac{7}{12}$

Algebra & functions **Compare. Write >, <, or =.**

28. $\frac{1}{3} + \frac{7}{12}$ ● $\frac{1}{4} + \frac{1}{3}$

29. $\frac{3}{8} + \frac{1}{8}$ ● $\frac{1}{2} + \frac{3}{4}$

30. $\frac{1}{9} + \frac{2}{3}$ ● $\frac{1}{2} + \frac{1}{8}$

31. $\frac{2}{12} + \frac{1}{4}$ ● $\frac{3}{12} + \frac{1}{6}$

32. $\frac{2}{5} + \frac{3}{10}$ ● $\frac{1}{2} + \frac{2}{3}$

33. $\frac{3}{8} + \frac{5}{16}$ ● $\frac{3}{4} + \frac{1}{2}$

34.

This is how Taran solved the addition problem $\frac{2}{3} + \frac{2}{6}$. Tell what mistake he made and how to correct it.

Problem Solving

35. **Art:** Mark makes centerpieces out of vegetables and other foods. In one centerpiece he uses 3 celery stalks, 7 radishes, and 5 carrots. What fraction of the vegetables are celery stalks? carrots?

36. Cara tries to drink more than 2 cups of milk every day. In the morning, she drinks $\frac{7}{8}$ cup. In the afternoon, she drinks $\frac{3}{4}$ cup. In the evening, she drinks $\frac{1}{2}$ cup. Does she drink more than 2 cups of milk? How much does she drink?

Use data from *Did You Know?* for problems 37–39.

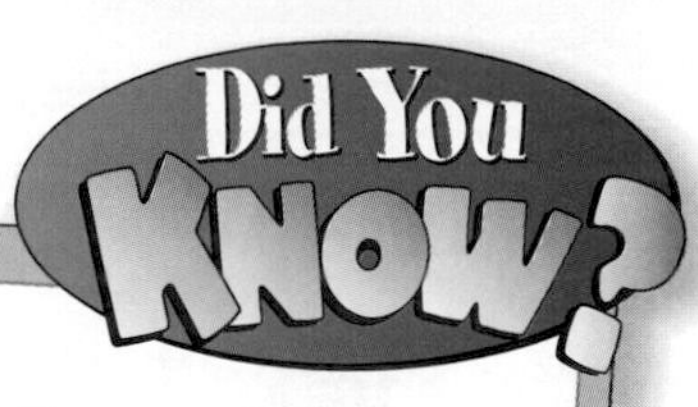

The Kpelle people of Liberia, Africa, measure rice by using a samoko (sah-MOH-koh), or "salmon cup." Larger measurements are also used. 12 samokos = 1 boke (BAH-kee)
2 bokes = 1 tin
4 bokes = 1 boro (BAH-ro)

37. What fraction of a *boke* is a *samoko*?

38. What fraction of a *boro* is a *boke*?

39. You have $\frac{1}{2}$ *boke* of rice. How many *samokos* is this?

40. A recipe uses $\frac{1}{4}$ cup of carrots. A second recipe uses $\frac{1}{8}$ cup more carrots. What fraction of a cup of carrots do you need for the second recipe?

41. Clarissa buys a dozen apples. She gives $\frac{1}{6}$ of them to Jin. How many apples did Jin get?

Use data from the graph for problems 42–45.

42. **Health:** This circle graph shows what Fran usually eats each day. The fractions show what part each food group is of her total diet. What fraction of her diet is fruits and vegetables?

43. What fraction of her diet is meat and vegetables?

44. What fraction of her diet is bread and fruits?

★45. **Analyze:** Add all the fractions in the circle graph. What do you find? Why do you think this is so?

46. **Create a problem** using the data in the circle graph. Solve it. Ask others to solve it.

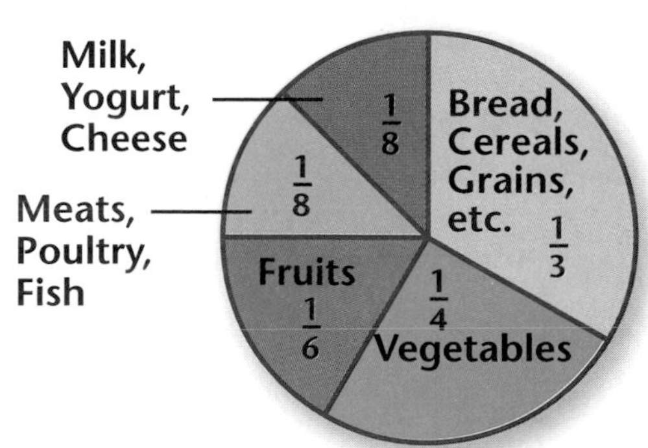

Spiral Review and Test Prep

47. 252 ÷ 15
48. 268 × 15
49. 32,109 + 3,249
50. 6,852 − 1,579

Choose the correct answer.

51. What number is shown by this model?

   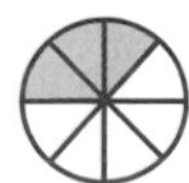

A. $\frac{3}{8}$
B. $2\frac{3}{8}$
C. $3\frac{1}{8}$
D. $3\frac{3}{8}$

52. Which color are you the least likely to spin?

F. Blue
G. Red
H. Green
J. Yellow

Extra Practice, page 546

Objective: Solve a simpler problem to determine how to solve a problem.

Problem Solving: Strategy

Solve a Simpler Problem

Read

Read the problem carefully.

Martina is making a deli platter for a party. She wants to have the same amount of meat and cheese on the platter. Look at her list. Does she have the same amount of meat and cheese?

Meat & Cheese

$\frac{1}{4}$ pound roast beef

$\frac{1}{2}$ pound turkey breast

$\frac{1}{4}$ pound ham

$\frac{1}{4}$ pound salami

$\frac{1}{3}$ pound American Cheese

$\frac{1}{3}$ pound Swiss cheese

$\frac{1}{3}$ pound provolone cheese

- **What do you know?** The amount of meat and cheese she has
- **What do you need to find?** Whether they are the same amounts

Plan

You can sometimes see how to solve a problem by first solving a simpler problem. Use easy whole numbers to see how to solve the problem.

Solve

Add to find how much meat. ⟶ $1 + 2 + 1 + 1 = 5$ pounds

Add to find how much cheese. ⟶ $1 + 1 + 1 = 3$ pounds

Compare the amounts. ⟶ $5 > 3$, so there is more meat.

Now solve the problem the same way, using the fractions.

Add to find how much meat. ⟶ $\frac{1}{4} + \frac{1}{2} + \frac{1}{4} + \frac{1}{4} = 1\frac{1}{4}$ pounds

Add to find how much cheese. ⟶ $\frac{1}{3} + \frac{1}{3} + \frac{1}{3} = 1$ pound

Compare the amounts. ⟶ $1\frac{1}{4} > 1$ so there is more meat than cheese.

Look Back

Is your answer reasonable? Explain.

How does using simpler numbers help you solve the problem?

Practice Solve.

1. Josh buys a 5-pound watermelon for \$0.49 per pound and 2 pounds of grapes for \$1.29 per pound. Sabrina buys an 8-pound watermelon for \$0.29 per pound and 3 pounds of grapes for \$0.99 per pound. Who spends more money? how much more?

2. On Monday Roger drinks $\frac{7}{8}$ cup of milk at breakfast, $\frac{3}{4}$ cup at lunch, and $\frac{1}{2}$ cup at dinner. On Tuesday he drinks $\frac{3}{4}$ cup of milk at each meal. On which day does he drink more milk? how much more?

3. A customer pays \$2.45 for 5 pounds of bananas. What is the price for 1 pound of bananas?

4. Recipe A uses $\frac{3}{4}$ cup of beef broth and $\frac{3}{8}$ cup of water. Recipe B uses $\frac{1}{3}$ cup of beef broth, $\frac{3}{8}$ cup of water, and $\frac{1}{4}$ cup of soy sauce. Which recipe makes more sauce?

Problem Solving

Mixed Strategy Review

5. Mario buys 2 pounds of peppers for \$0.98 per pound and 3 pounds of tomatoes for \$1.19 per pound. He gets \$4.47 back in change. How much money did Mario give the clerk?

6. **Logical Reasoning:** There are 39 plants in a garden. There are twice as many tomato plants as pepper plants and 3 more cucumber plants than pepper plants. How many of each kind of plant is in the garden?

★7. **Career:** Jay is training to be a chef at a restaurant. Each week he works 5 more hours than the week before. If Jay starts out at 10 hours, how many weeks will it take until he works a 40-hour week?

8. A recipe calls for $\frac{1}{4}$ cup of tomato sauce. You want to double the recipe. How much sauce will you use? how much to triple the recipe?

9. Jenna and Max bought some cherries. Jenna bought $\frac{7}{10}$ lb and Max bought $\frac{3}{5}$ lb of cherries. Did they buy the same amount? Explain.

10. **Create a problem** that involves adding fractions. Show how to solve a simpler problem. Then solve the original problem. Ask others to solve it.

CHOOSE A STRATEGY

- Logical Reasoning
- Draw a Picture
- Make a Graph
- Act It Out
- Make a Table or List
- Find a Pattern
- Guess and Check
- Write a Number Sentence
- Work Backward
- Solve a Simpler Problem

Extra Practice, page 546

Objective: Explore subtracting fractions with unlike denominators.

12•7 Explore Subtracting Fractions with Unlike Denominators

Learn

You can use fraction strips to explore subtracting fractions with unlike denominators.

What is $\frac{9}{10} - \frac{1}{2}$?

Work Together

You Will Need
- **fraction strips**

► Find $\frac{9}{10} - \frac{1}{2}$ using fraction strips.

- Get the $\frac{1}{10}$ strips and $\frac{1}{2}$ strips that you need.

- Use the strips to find a common denominator.
- Find the difference.

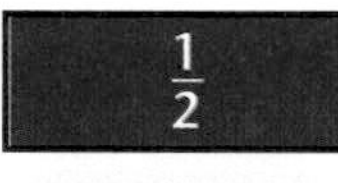

$\frac{1}{2} = \frac{5}{10}$

1/10 1/10 1/10 1/10 1/10 1/10 1/10 1/10 1/10

- Record your work and answer the question.

► Use fraction strips to subtract. Record your work.

$\frac{7}{12} - \frac{1}{6}$ $\frac{3}{4} - \frac{3}{8}$ $\frac{2}{3} - \frac{1}{4}$ $\frac{5}{6} - \frac{1}{3}$ $\frac{2}{3} - \frac{1}{2}$

Make Connections

Here is how to find and write a difference in simplest form.

Using Models	Using Paper and Pencil
$\frac{1}{10}$ $\frac{1}{10}$ $\frac{1}{10}$ $\frac{1}{10}$ $\frac{1}{5}$ $\frac{1}{5}$ $\frac{9}{10} - \frac{1}{2} = \frac{4}{10} = \frac{2}{5}$	Find an equivalent fraction with a common denominator. $\frac{9}{10} - \frac{1}{2} = \frac{9}{10} - \frac{5}{10}$ Subtract the numerator. Use the common denominator. Write the fraction in simplest form. $\frac{9}{10} - \frac{1}{2} = \frac{9}{10} - \frac{5}{10} = \frac{4}{10} = \frac{2}{5}$

Try It **Subtract. Write each answer in simplest form. You may wish to use models.**

1. $\frac{3}{4} - \frac{1}{8}$
2. $\frac{5}{6} - \frac{1}{3}$
3. $\frac{7}{12} - \frac{1}{4}$
4. $\frac{4}{5} - \frac{7}{10}$
5. $\frac{7}{12} - \frac{1}{4}$
6. $\frac{2}{8} - \frac{1}{12}$
7. $\frac{6}{10} - \frac{1}{3}$
8. $\frac{5}{6} - \frac{2}{3}$

How can you use fraction strips to subtract fractions with denominators that are different?

Practice **Subtract. Write each answer in simplest form.**

9. $\frac{1}{2} - \frac{1}{6}$
10. $\frac{5}{8} - \frac{1}{2}$
11. $\frac{3}{4} - \frac{2}{8}$
12. $\frac{1}{8} - \frac{2}{16}$
13. $\frac{2}{3} - \frac{1}{9}$
14. $\frac{5}{6} - \frac{5}{12}$
15. $\frac{7}{8} - \frac{3}{4}$
16. $\frac{2}{3} - \frac{1}{9}$
17. $\frac{3}{4} - \frac{5}{12}$
18. $\frac{1}{2} - \frac{1}{8}$
19. $\frac{9}{10} - \frac{3}{5}$
20. $\frac{1}{2} - \frac{3}{8}$
21. $\frac{2}{3} - \frac{1}{4}$
22. **Analyze:** Sam estimates that the difference between $\frac{11}{22}$ and $\frac{4}{6}$ is about $\frac{1}{2}$. Is this reasonable? Explain.

Objective: Subtract fractions with unlike denominators.

12•8 Subtract Fractions with Unlike Denominators

Learn

You are buying limes.
You put 2 limes on the scale.
The scale shows $\frac{1}{2}$ pound.
You add another lime.
The weight is shown on the scale in the picture.
How much does the third lime weigh?

Example 1

Find: $\frac{3}{4} - \frac{1}{2}$

1 Find equivalent fractions with a common denominator.

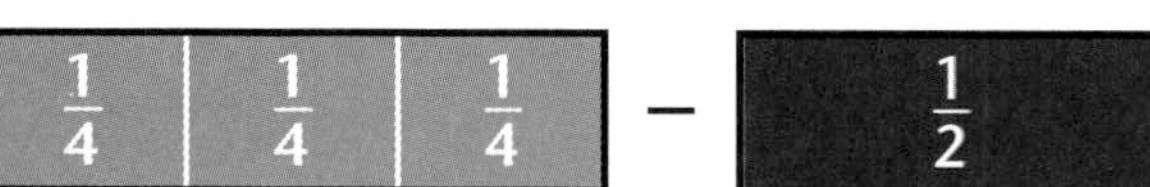

$\frac{3}{4} = \frac{3}{4}$ $\qquad$ $\frac{1}{2} = \frac{1 \times 2}{2 \times 2} = \frac{2}{4}$

Think:
Multiples of 4: 4
Multiples of 2: 2, 4
4 is the common denominator.

2 Subtract the numerators. Use the common denominator. Write the difference in simplest form, if needed.

$$\begin{array}{r} \frac{3}{4} \\ -\frac{2}{4} \\ \hline \frac{1}{4} \end{array}$$

Think:
Since 1 is the greatest common factor of 1 and 4, $\frac{1}{4}$ is in simplest form.

One pepper weighs $\frac{2}{3}$ pound. A smaller pepper weighs $\frac{1}{4}$ pound. How much more does the heavier pepper weigh than the lighter pepper?

Example 2

Find: $\frac{2}{3} - \frac{1}{4}$

Find equivalent fractions with a common denominator.

$$\frac{2}{3} = \frac{2 \times 4}{3 \times 4} = \frac{8}{12}$$

$$\frac{1}{4} = \frac{1 \times 3}{4 \times 3} = \frac{3}{12}$$

Think:
Multiples of 3: 3, 6, 9, 12
Multiples of 4: 4, 8, 12

12 is the common denominator.

2

Subtract the numerators. Use the common denominator. Write the answer in simplest form, if needed.

$$\frac{8}{12} - \frac{3}{12} = \frac{5}{12}$$

Think:
The greatest common factor of 5 and 12 is 1, so $\frac{5}{12}$ is in simplest form.

The heavier pepper weighs $\frac{5}{12}$ pound more than the lighter one.

More Examples

$$\frac{7}{8} - \frac{1}{4} \qquad \frac{1}{4} = \frac{1 \times 2}{4 \times 2} = \frac{2}{8} \qquad \frac{7}{8} - \frac{2}{8} = \frac{5}{8}$$

B

$$\frac{2}{3} - \frac{1}{6} \qquad \frac{2}{3} = \frac{2 \times 2}{3 \times 2} = \frac{4}{6} \qquad \frac{4}{6} - \frac{1}{6} = \frac{3}{6} = \frac{3 \div 3}{6 \div 3} = \frac{1}{2}$$

Try It **Subtract. Write each difference in simplest form.**

1. $\frac{7}{8} - \frac{3}{8}$
2. $\frac{9}{10} - \frac{1}{5}$
3. $\frac{7}{8} - \frac{1}{2}$
4. $\frac{8}{9} - \frac{2}{3}$
5. $\frac{5}{8} - \frac{1}{6}$
6. $\frac{5}{6} - \frac{2}{3}$
7. $\frac{1}{2} - \frac{1}{6}$
8. $\frac{4}{5} - \frac{3}{10}$
9. $\frac{11}{12} - \frac{2}{3}$
10. $\frac{7}{8} - \frac{5}{6}$
11. $\frac{11}{15} - \frac{2}{5}$

How can you find the difference of $\frac{5}{6} - \frac{1}{2}$ in simplest form?

Practice **Subtract. Write each difference in simplest form.**

12. $\frac{9}{10} - \frac{3}{5}$

13. $\frac{5}{8} - \frac{1}{2}$

14. $\frac{11}{12} - \frac{3}{8}$

15. $\frac{2}{3} - \frac{3}{10}$

16. $\frac{7}{9} - \frac{1}{3}$

17. $\frac{7}{10} - \frac{1}{4}$

18. $\frac{4}{5} - \frac{1}{3}$

19. $\frac{3}{5} - \frac{1}{10}$

20. $\frac{3}{4} - \frac{1}{8}$

21. $\frac{5}{12} - \frac{1}{6}$

22. $\frac{5}{9} - \frac{1}{3}$

23. $\frac{10}{12} - \frac{2}{3}$

24. $\frac{7}{9} - \frac{1}{3}$

25. $\frac{2}{6} - \frac{2}{12}$

★ **26.** $\frac{3}{4} - \frac{3}{25}$

★ **27.** $\frac{4}{5} - \frac{5}{12}$

★ **28.** $\frac{8}{15} - \frac{1}{2}$

★ **29.** $\frac{7}{12} - \frac{9}{30}$

Algebra & functions **Find each missing number.**

30. $\frac{2}{3} - \frac{1}{12} = \frac{■}{12}$

31. $\frac{7}{8} - \frac{1}{■} = \frac{3}{8}$

32. $\frac{10}{12} - \frac{1}{■} = \frac{7}{12}$

★ **33.** $\frac{3}{5} - \frac{1}{3} = \frac{■}{15}$

★ **34.** $\frac{5}{6} - \frac{7}{12} = \frac{1}{■}$

★ **35.** $\frac{3}{4} - \frac{1}{■} = \frac{7}{12}$

36. **Make it RIGHT**

This is how Tami solved the subtraction problem $\frac{5}{6} - \frac{1}{3}$. Tell what mistake she made. Tell how to correct it.

Problem Solving

37. **Social Studies:** One year India sold 891,000 metric tons of rice to other countries. In the same year Pakistan sold 984,000 metric tons to other countries. How much more rice did Pakistan sell that year than India?

★ **38.** **Time:** Roberto spends $\frac{1}{3}$ hour making breakfast. He spends $\frac{3}{4}$ hour making dinner. How much more time does it take him to make dinner than breakfast? Write your answer as a fraction of an hour and in minutes.

Use data from *Did You Know?* for problems 39–40.

39. About how much would $\frac{1}{2}$ pound of saffron powder cost? About how much would 3 pounds cost?

40. Nala bought a pound of saffron for her restaurant. So far she has used $\frac{1}{4}$ pound. How much does she have left?

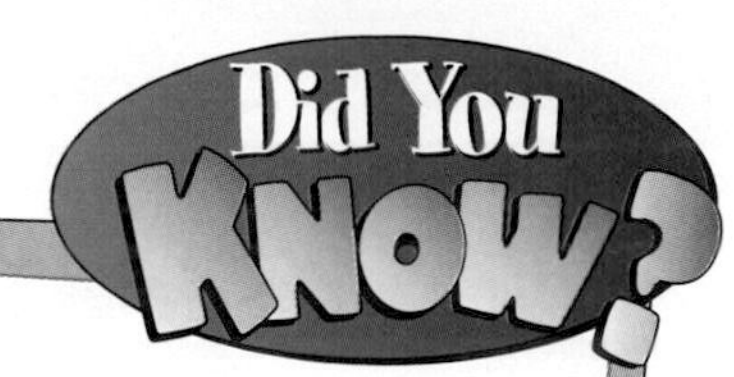

Saffron powder is used to color cakes, breads, and dressings. It is also known as the world's most expensive food. A single pound of saffron powder sells for over $2,600.

Use data from the list for problems 41–45.

41. How many more pounds of grapes than melon are in the fruit salad?

42. How many more pounds of bananas are there than raspberries?

43. How many more pounds of melon are there than blueberries?

★44. **Estimate** the cost to buy the ingredients for the fruit salad.

45. **Create a problem** using the information in the recipe or sign. Solve it. Ask others to solve it.

FRUIT SALAD RECIPE

- $\frac{3}{4}$ pound grapes
- $\frac{1}{3}$ pound blueberries
- $\frac{3}{8}$ pound raspberries
- $\frac{1}{2}$ pound bananas
- $\frac{2}{3}$ pound melon

Grapes: $1.00/lb
Blueberries: $1.80/lb
Raspberries: $3.00/lb
Bananas: $0.50/lb
Melon: $0.90/lb

Journal 46. **Explain** how to find the difference of $\frac{7}{8} - \frac{1}{4}$ using different common denominators. What do you notice about both answers?

Spiral Review and Test Prep

47. $456 \div 22$

48. 238×34

49. $62,960 - 1,845$

Choose the correct answer.

50. Which is not a possible outcome of spinning the spinner?
   - A. Yellow
   - B. Green
   - C. Red
   - D. Blue

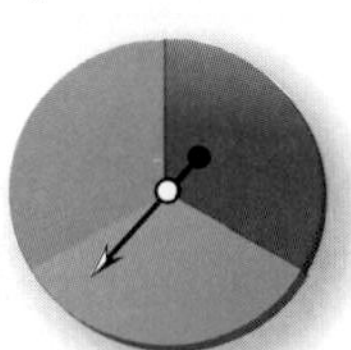

51. A chef uses 12 peppers to make a recipe. One third of the peppers are green. How many green peppers does the chef use?
   - F. 3
   - G. 4
   - H. 6
   - J. 8

Objective: Use properties to find sums and differences of fractions.

Properties of Fractions

Algebra & functions

Madhur Jaffrey, chef and cookbook author, New York, NY

Learn

Math Words

Commutative Property of Addition

$4 + 6 = 6 + 4 = 10$

Associative Property of Addition

$(5 + 3) + 7 =$
$5 + (3 + 7) = 15$

Identity Property of Addition

$8 + 0 = 8$

What if Madhur creates a strawberry drink? She puts $\frac{7}{8}$ cup of frozen yogurt in the blender. Then she uses $\frac{3}{4}$ cup of skim milk along with $\frac{1}{8}$ cup of strawberry syrup. She mixes all the ingredients. How many cups does this recipe make?

Example

You can use the **Commutative** and **Associative Properties** to make it easier to add.

Find: $\frac{7}{8} + \frac{3}{4} + \frac{1}{8}$

1 Change the order of the addends.

$\frac{7}{8} + \frac{1}{8} + \frac{3}{4}$

2 Group the addends to make it easier to add.

$\left(\frac{7}{8} + \frac{1}{8}\right) + \frac{3}{4}$

3 Add.

$\frac{7}{8} + \frac{1}{8} = 1$

$1 + \frac{3}{4} = 1\frac{3}{4}$

The recipe makes $1\frac{3}{4}$ cups.

More Examples

You can use the **Identity Property** to help add.

A $\frac{3}{4} + n = \frac{3}{4}$; $\frac{3}{4} + 0 = \frac{3}{4}$; $n = 0$

B $\frac{7}{8} - m = 0$; $\frac{7}{8} - \frac{7}{8} = 0$; $m = 0$

Try It

Find the missing number. Tell which property you used.

1. $\frac{1}{4} + \frac{3}{8} = a + \frac{1}{4}$
2. $\frac{7}{10} + \left(\frac{3}{10} + \frac{1}{5}\right) = \left(\frac{7}{10} + \frac{3}{10}\right) + b$

Tell how you would use properties to help you solve $\frac{7}{8} + n + \frac{1}{8} = 1$

Practice Use properties to find each missing number.

3. $\frac{1}{2} + \frac{1}{6} = \frac{1}{6} + c$

4. $\frac{3}{8} + \left(\frac{5}{8} + \frac{1}{2}\right) = \left(\frac{3}{8} + d\right) + \frac{1}{2}$

5. $\frac{3}{9} + e = \frac{3}{9}$

6. $\frac{3}{5} + \frac{3}{10} = f + \frac{3}{5}$

7. $\left(\frac{3}{4} + \frac{1}{12}\right) + \frac{11}{12} = \frac{3}{4} + \left(\frac{1}{12} + g\right)$

8. $\frac{1}{8} - h = \frac{1}{8}$

9. $i - 0 = \frac{9}{10}$

10. $\frac{1}{6} + \frac{2}{3} = \frac{2}{3} + j$

11. $\frac{1}{3} + \left(\frac{2}{3} + \frac{1}{4}\right) = \left(\frac{1}{3} + k\right) + \frac{1}{4}$

★12. $\frac{3}{5} + \left(m + \frac{2}{5}\right) = \left(\frac{3}{5} + n\right) + \frac{3}{10} = 1\frac{3}{10}$

★13. $\left(\frac{1}{12} + p\right) + \frac{5}{12} = \left(\frac{1}{12} + r\right) + \frac{3}{8} = \frac{7}{8}$

Add. Then use the property to write a different number sentence.

14. $\frac{2}{5} + \frac{7}{10}$
Commutative

15. $\frac{2}{3} + \frac{5}{6}$
Identity

16. $\left(\frac{1}{4} + \frac{1}{4}\right) + \frac{5}{8}$
Associative

Problem Solving

Use data from the pictograph for problems 17–19.

17. Which kind of food do the people surveyed prefer?

18. How many people prefer Italian food? This is what fraction of those who prefer Mexican food?

★19. How many people like Thai food?

Kind of Food Preferred

Key: = 2 people

20. Diane mixes together $\frac{3}{4}$ cup of orange juice, $\frac{1}{2}$ cup of grapefruit juice, and $\frac{1}{4}$ cup of pineapple juice. How many cups is this in all? Write a number sentence.

Spiral Review and Test Prep

21. 135×25

22. $3{,}587 + 5{,}942$

23. $21\overline{)592}$

24. $6{,}703 - 4{,}984$

Choose the correct answer.

25. For lunch, students can choose from pizza, chicken, or a sandwich. They can have milk or juice to drink. How many combinations of food and drink are there?

A. 6 **C.** 9
B. 5 **D.** 3

26. Which outcome is impossible?

F. Spin 0 **H.** Spin 4
G. Spin 2 **J.** Spin 3

Extra Practice, page 547

Objective: Analyze data and make decisions.

Problem Solving: Application
Decision Making

What combinations of juices can they use to make exactly 1 quart of fruit punch?

Joseph and his sister are making fruit punch. They are using a 1-quart container to hold the punch. Joseph's mom puts several containers of juice on the table. She tells them to use any combination of juices that they want to.

All of the juice in the containers they choose, must be used.

Read for Understanding

1. How much mixed citrus juice is there?
2. There is $\frac{1}{2}$ quart of what kind of juice?
3. How much grape juice is there?
4. There is $\frac{5}{8}$ quart of what kind of juice?
5. There is $\frac{1}{4}$ quart of which kinds of juice?
6. How much fresh berry juice is there?

Problem Solving

Make Decisions

7. There is the most of which kind of juice?
8. There is the least of which kind of juice?
9. How much juice would there be if you combined the cranberry and apple juice?
10. How much juice would there be if you combined the pineapple and cranberry juice?
11. If you mixed the orange juice and mixed citrus juice, would you have more or less than 1 quart?
12. What juices could not be combined with mixed citrus juice to make 1 quart or less?
13. If you combined the pineapple and grapefruit juice, how much juice would you have?
14. If you combined the mixed berry and cranberry juice, how much less than a quart would you have?
15. If you combined the orange and pineapple juice, how much less than 1 quart would you have?
16. What juices could you combine with the mixed citrus juice to make exactly 1 quart?
17. What else do you need to think about before making fruit punch?
18. If you combined pineapple and grapefruit juice, what is the only other juice you could use?

What is your recommendation for Joseph and his sister? Explain.

Objective: Apply fraction operations to investigate science concepts.

Problem Solving: Application

Which objects can hold a static charge?

Have you ever rubbed a balloon in your hair and made it stick?

An object that can hold a static charge can attract other objects. In this activity, you will explore which objects can hold a static charge.

You Will Need

- **string**
- **scissors**
- **ruler**
- **pencil**
- **balloon (blown up)**
- **five connecting cubes (attached)**
- **crayon**

Hypothesize

Which of these objects will hold a static charge—connecting cubes, balloon, crayon, your hand, sock?

Procedure

1. Work with a partner.
2. Cut 30 cm of string and tie it around the center of the pencil.
3. Hold the pencil by the ends, so the string hangs freely.
4. Rub the balloon in your hair. Hold the balloon near the end of the string.
5. Repeat with the connecting cubes, crayon, sock, and your hand.

Safety

Be careful when working with scissors. Wear goggles in case the balloon bursts.

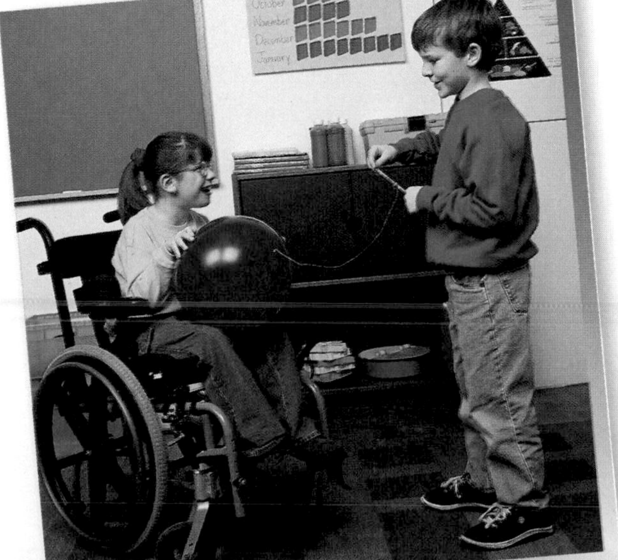

Data

Copy and complete the chart to record your observations of the string.

Material Observations	
Balloon	
Cubes	
Crayon	
Sock	
Hand	

Did You Know?

Static electricity is created when an object holds an uneven amount of positive and negative charges on its surface. This imbalance lets objects attract each other with an electric force.

Conclude and Apply

- What happened to the string when a charged object came near it?
- Which objects held a static charge? How do you know?
- What fraction of the objects held a static charge? Construct a circle graph to display your results.
- What fraction of all objects in the world do you think hold a static charge? Think about how the objects you used represent all things in the world.
- Explain the results of the activity in terms of **static electricity.**

Going Further

1. Design and complete an activity that determines how long an object can hold a static charge.
2. Write a story about a person who always has a static charge. Include the words "static electricity," "positive charge," "negative charge," and "electric force."

Check Your Progress B

Add. Write each sum in simplest form. (pages 526–529)

1. $\frac{2}{3} + \frac{1}{6}$
2. $\frac{3}{11} + \frac{5}{11}$
3. $\frac{2}{9} + \frac{1}{3}$
4. $\frac{5}{6} + \frac{1}{4}$
5. $\frac{7}{10} + \frac{2}{5}$
6. $\frac{1}{12} + \frac{5}{6}$
7. $\frac{5}{12} + \frac{1}{4}$
8. $\frac{1}{8} + \frac{3}{4} + \frac{1}{8}$

Subtract. Write each difference in simplest form. (pages 534–537)

9. $\frac{5}{8} - \frac{1}{4}$
10. $\frac{3}{4} - \frac{1}{8}$
11. $\frac{2}{3} - \frac{2}{9}$
12. $\frac{3}{5} - \frac{1}{3}$
13. $\frac{7}{12} - \frac{1}{6}$
14. $\frac{7}{10} - \frac{1}{5}$
15. $\frac{5}{6} - \frac{2}{3}$
16. $\frac{8}{9} - \frac{4}{9}$

Use properties to find each missing number. (pages 538–539)

17. $\frac{3}{4} + \frac{2}{3} = \blacksquare + \frac{3}{4}$
18. $\left(\frac{3}{5} + \frac{7}{10}\right) + \frac{3}{10} = \frac{3}{5} + \left(\blacksquare + \frac{3}{10}\right)$
19. $\frac{3}{4} + \frac{7}{8} = \frac{7}{8} + \blacksquare$
20. $\frac{1}{3} + \left(\frac{1}{4} + \frac{2}{3}\right) = \frac{1}{4} + \left(\blacksquare + \frac{2}{3}\right)$

Use data from the recipe to solve problems 21–24.

21. How much more sugar than flour is in the recipe?
22. The first step in making the filling is to combine the flour and sugar. How many cups is this in all?
23. The next step is to add the cinnamon, nutmeg, lemon peel, and salt. How many teaspoons is this?
24. How much more cinnamon is in the recipe than nutmeg?

Blackberry Pie

$\frac{2}{3}$ cup sugar	$\frac{1}{4}$ teaspoon nutmeg
$\frac{1}{4}$ cup flour	5 cups blackberries
$\frac{1}{2}$ teaspoon grated lemon peel	1 tablespoon butter
$\frac{1}{8}$ teaspoon salt	pie pastry
$\frac{1}{2}$ teaspoon cinnamon	

25. **Summarize:** List the steps you would follow to add fractions with unlike denominators.

Additional activities at www.mhschool.com/math

Extra Practice

Add Fractions with Like Denominators (pages 516–517)

Add. Write each sum in simplest form.

1. $\frac{1}{9} + \frac{4}{9}$ **2.** $\frac{3}{5} + \frac{1}{5}$ **3.** $\frac{5}{10} + \frac{1}{10}$ **4.** $\frac{2}{8} + \frac{7}{8}$ **5.** $\frac{5}{12} + \frac{1}{12}$ **6.** $\frac{1}{5} + \frac{1}{5}$

7. $\frac{2}{12} + \frac{3}{12}$ **8.** $\frac{2}{5} + \frac{2}{5}$ **9.** $\frac{1}{8} + \frac{5}{8}$ **10.** $\frac{2}{11} + \frac{6}{11}$ **11.** $\frac{7}{9} + \frac{3}{9}$ **12.** $\frac{2}{3} + \frac{1}{6}$

13. $\frac{2}{6} + \frac{1}{6}$ **14.** $\frac{1}{10} + \frac{3}{10}$ **15.** $\frac{5}{11} + \frac{5}{11}$ **16.** $\frac{3}{4} + \frac{2}{4}$ **17.** $\frac{2}{3} + \frac{2}{3}$

18. $\frac{1}{5} + \frac{4}{5}$ **19.** $\frac{2}{9} + \frac{4}{9}$ **20.** $\frac{1}{8} + \frac{3}{8}$ **21.** $\frac{1}{3} + \frac{1}{3}$ **22.** $\frac{3}{10} + \frac{3}{10}$

Solve.

23. A recipe calls for $\frac{1}{4}$ teaspoon each of salt and pepper. How much is this in all?

Subtract Fractions with Like Denominators (pages 518–519)

Subtract. Write each difference in simplest form.

1. $\frac{3}{4} - \frac{2}{4}$ **2.** $\frac{11}{12} - \frac{9}{12}$ **3.** $\frac{2}{3} - \frac{1}{3}$ **4.** $\frac{6}{8} - \frac{3}{8}$ **5.** $\frac{4}{12} - \frac{3}{12}$ **6.** $\frac{7}{15} - \frac{2}{15}$

7. $\frac{7}{8} - \frac{3}{8}$ **8.** $\frac{5}{12} - \frac{1}{12}$ **9.** $\frac{3}{10} - \frac{1}{10}$ **10.** $\frac{3}{12} - \frac{1}{12}$ **11.** $\frac{2}{5} - \frac{1}{5}$ **12.** $\frac{3}{6} - \frac{1}{6}$

13. $\frac{7}{10} - \frac{2}{10}$ **14.** $\frac{5}{6} - \frac{3}{6}$ **15.** $\frac{7}{8} - \frac{3}{8}$ **16.** $\frac{5}{12} - \frac{1}{12}$ **17.** $\frac{5}{9} - \frac{4}{9}$

18. $\frac{7}{9} - \frac{5}{9}$ **19.** $\frac{8}{11} - \frac{5}{11}$ **20.** $\frac{9}{10} - \frac{3}{10}$ **21.** $\frac{2}{3} - \frac{2}{3}$ **22.** $\frac{5}{5} - \frac{4}{5}$

Solve.

23. Alyssa has $\frac{3}{4}$ cup of broth in a measuring cup. She pours $\frac{1}{4}$ cup into the pan. How much broth is left in the measuring cup?

Extra Practice

Problem Solving: Reading for Math
Choose an Operation (pages 520–521)

Solve. Tell how you chose the operation.

1. Lu used $\frac{1}{3}$ cup of sugar and $\frac{2}{3}$ cup of flour in a recipe. How much sugar and flour did Lu use altogether?

2. Kaya used $\frac{7}{8}$ cup of flour and $\frac{3}{8}$ cup of sugar in a recipe. How much more flour did she use than sugar?

3. Maria used $\frac{2}{5}$ cup of brown sugar in a recipe. Kay used $\frac{4}{5}$ cup of brown sugar. How much more did Kay use than Maria?

Add Fractions with Unlike Denominators (pages 526–529)

Add. Write each sum in simplest form.

1. $\frac{2}{3} + \frac{1}{12}$
2. $\frac{3}{5} + \frac{7}{10}$
3. $\frac{1}{4} + \frac{5}{6}$
4. $\frac{3}{8} + \frac{1}{2}$
5. $\frac{2}{15} + \frac{3}{5}$
6. $\frac{3}{8} + \frac{1}{6}$
7. $\frac{3}{8} + \frac{3}{4}$
8. $\frac{2}{3} + \frac{1}{4}$
9. $\frac{1}{3} + \frac{3}{5}$
10. $\frac{7}{10} + \frac{2}{5}$
11. $\frac{1}{12} + \frac{1}{8}$
12. $\frac{1}{8} + \frac{1}{2}$
13. $\frac{1}{3} + \frac{5}{6}$
14. $\frac{1}{6} + \frac{7}{12}$
15. $\frac{3}{4} + \frac{1}{8}$
16. $\frac{1}{6} + \frac{1}{8}$

Problem Solving: Strategy
Solve a Simpler Problem (pages 530–531)

Use data from the advertisement to solve problems 1–3.

1. How much would it cost to buy 2 pounds of ground beef and 2 pounds of chicken wings?

2. Which would cost more, 3 pounds of pork chops or 2 pounds of boneless chicken breasts? how much more?

3. Which would cost more, 7 pounds of chicken wings or 2 pounds of sirloin steak tips? how much more?

4. Alana bought $\frac{7}{8}$ pound of chicken and $\frac{1}{2}$ pound of steak. Aki bought $\frac{3}{4}$ pound of pork and $\frac{5}{8}$ pound of chicken. Who bought more meat? how much more?

Extra Practice

Subtract Fractions with Unlike Denominators (page 534–537)

Subtract. Write each difference in simplest form.

1. $\begin{array}{r} \frac{9}{10} \\ -\frac{3}{5} \\ \hline \end{array}$ **2.** $\begin{array}{r} \frac{8}{9} \\ -\frac{1}{3} \\ \hline \end{array}$ **3.** $\begin{array}{r} \frac{7}{12} \\ -\frac{1}{4} \\ \hline \end{array}$ **4.** $\begin{array}{r} \frac{1}{3} \\ -\frac{1}{4} \\ \hline \end{array}$ **5.** $\begin{array}{r} \frac{4}{5} \\ -\frac{1}{15} \\ \hline \end{array}$ **6.** $\begin{array}{r} \frac{5}{12} \\ -\frac{1}{8} \\ \hline \end{array}$

7. $\frac{4}{5} - \frac{1}{10}$ **8.** $\frac{4}{4} - \frac{1}{8}$ **9.** $\frac{11}{12} - \frac{5}{6}$ **10.** $\frac{7}{9} - \frac{2}{3}$ **11.** $\frac{3}{3} - 0$

12. $\frac{10}{12} - \frac{1}{3}$ **13.** $\frac{7}{8} - \frac{3}{8}$ **14.** $\frac{4}{5} - \frac{1}{3}$ **15.** $\frac{3}{4} - \frac{2}{8}$ **16.** $\frac{8}{8} - \frac{1}{3}$

Solve.

17. Michael spends $\frac{3}{4}$ hour making his dinner. Kyle takes $\frac{2}{3}$ hour to make his dinner. Who spends more time? how much more?

18. Explain how you could use equivalent fractions and mental math to solve problem 15.

Properties of Fractions (pages 538–539)

Use properties to find each missing number.

1. $\frac{1}{3} + \frac{3}{4} = \blacksquare + \frac{1}{3}$

2. $\frac{2}{3} + \blacksquare = \frac{2}{3}$

3. $\left(\frac{1}{4} + \frac{2}{3}\right) + \frac{1}{3} = \frac{1}{4} + \left(\blacksquare + \frac{1}{3}\right)$

4. $0 + \blacksquare = \frac{1}{10}$

5. $\frac{5}{6} + \frac{1}{3} = \frac{1}{3} + \blacksquare$

6. $\left(\frac{3}{8} + \blacksquare\right) + \frac{1}{4} = \frac{3}{8} + \left(\frac{3}{4} + \frac{1}{4}\right)$

7. $\frac{3}{5} - \blacksquare = 0$

8. $\blacksquare - \frac{1}{4} = 0$

9. $\frac{1}{5} - \frac{1}{5} = \blacksquare$

10. $\frac{1}{8} - \blacksquare = \frac{1}{8}$

11. $\frac{1}{10} - \frac{1}{10} = \blacksquare$

12. $\blacksquare - \frac{2}{3} = 0$

Solve.

13. How can you use the properties of addition to add $\frac{1}{5} + \frac{2}{3} + \frac{4}{5}$ without finding a common denominator?

Chapter Study Guide

Language and Math

Math Words
- Commutative
- denominator
- Identity
- numerator
- simplest form

Complete. Use a word from the list.

1. The ____ Property of Addition states that when 0 is an addend, the sum is the other addend.
2. The ____ in the fraction $\frac{2}{3}$ is 2.
3. The fraction $\frac{10}{12}$ is written as $\frac{5}{6}$ in ____.
4. The ____ in the fraction $\frac{3}{10}$ is 10.

Add fractions with like and unlike denominators.

(pages 516–517, 524–529)

Example

$\frac{1}{10} + \frac{2}{5}$

Solution

Find a common denominator.

$$\begin{array}{r} \frac{1}{10} \\ +\frac{2}{5} \\ \hline \end{array} \quad \begin{array}{l} \\ =2\times2 \\ =5\times2 \end{array} \quad \begin{array}{r} \frac{1}{10} \\ +\frac{4}{10} \\ \hline \end{array}$$

$$\frac{1}{10} + \frac{4}{10} = \frac{5}{10} = \frac{1}{2}$$

Add. Write each sum in simplest form.

5. $\frac{2}{12} + \frac{5}{12}$
6. $\frac{3}{4} + \frac{1}{4}$
7. $\frac{5}{6} + \frac{1}{3}$
8. $\frac{7}{8} + \frac{3}{8}$
9. $\frac{1}{3} + \frac{3}{6}$
10. $\frac{3}{12} + \frac{5}{12}$
11. $\frac{1}{4} + \frac{1}{8}$
12. $\frac{3}{10} + \frac{2}{5}$
13. $\frac{2}{3} + \frac{2}{5}$
14. $\frac{1}{9} + \frac{2}{9}$

Subtract fractions with like and unlike denominators.

(pages 518–519, 532–537)

Example

$\frac{4}{5} - \frac{1}{10}$

Solution

Find a common denominator.

$$\begin{array}{r} \frac{4}{5} \\ -\frac{2}{10} \\ \hline \end{array} \quad \begin{array}{l} =4\times2 \\ =5\times2 \end{array} = \quad \begin{array}{r} \frac{8}{10} \\ -\frac{2}{10} \\ \hline \end{array}$$

$$\frac{8}{10} - \frac{2}{10} = \frac{6}{10} = \frac{3}{5}$$

15. $\begin{array}{r} \frac{4}{5} \\ -\frac{3}{5} \\ \hline \end{array}$
16. $\begin{array}{r} \frac{7}{8} \\ -\frac{3}{8} \\ \hline \end{array}$
17. $\frac{9}{10} - \frac{2}{5}$
18. $\frac{7}{9} - \frac{1}{3}$
19. $\frac{10}{12} - \frac{1}{6}$
20. $\frac{5}{6} - \frac{3}{6}$
21. $\frac{2}{3} - \frac{2}{6}$
22. $\frac{8}{9} - \frac{2}{3}$
23. $\frac{7}{10} - \frac{1}{10}$
24. $\frac{3}{4} - \frac{1}{2}$

Use properties to solve. (pages 538–539)

Example

$\frac{3}{4} + \frac{1}{12} + \frac{1}{4}$

Solution

Use Commutative and Associative Properties to reorder addends and make it easier to add.

$\frac{3}{4} + \left(\frac{1}{12} + \frac{1}{4}\right) = \left(\frac{3}{4} + \frac{1}{4}\right) + \frac{1}{12} = 1\frac{1}{12}$

Use properties to find each missing number.

25. $\frac{1}{3} + \left(\frac{2}{3} + \frac{1}{4}\right) = \left(\frac{1}{3} + ■\right) + \frac{1}{4}$

26. $\frac{1}{6} + \frac{1}{3} = ■ + \frac{1}{6}$

27. $\left(\frac{3}{8} + \frac{1}{4}\right) + \frac{1}{4} = \frac{3}{8} + \left(\frac{1}{4} + ■\right)$

28. $\frac{1}{5} + ■ = \frac{1}{5}$

29. $\frac{1}{2} + \frac{2}{6} = \frac{2}{6} + ■$

Use strategies to solve problems. (pages 520–521, 530–531)

Example

One recipe for dressing uses $\frac{3}{8}$ cup vinegar and $\frac{3}{4}$ cup oil. Another recipe uses $\frac{1}{3}$ cup vinegar and $\frac{2}{3}$ cup oil. Which recipe makes more dressing?

Solution

Use simpler numbers.

Recipe 1: $\frac{3}{8} + \frac{3}{4} = \frac{3}{8} + \frac{6}{8} = \frac{9}{8} = 1\frac{1}{8}$

Recipe 2: $\frac{1}{3} + \frac{2}{3} = \frac{3}{3} = 1$

Compare $1\frac{1}{8} > 1$, so recipe 1 makes more.

Now use actual numbers.

Recipe 1: $\frac{3}{8} + \frac{3}{4} = 1\frac{1}{8}$

Recipe 2: $\frac{1}{3} + \frac{2}{3} = 1$

Compare $1\frac{1}{8} > 1$, so recipe 1 makes more.

30. Janet has $\frac{3}{4}$ bottle of water and drinks $\frac{1}{2}$ of the bottle. Pete has $\frac{1}{2}$ bottle and drinks $\frac{1}{8}$ of it. Who has more left? How much more?

31. One sauce uses $\frac{2}{3}$ cup of broth. Another sauce uses $\frac{1}{2}$ cup of broth. How much more broth is in the first sauce than the second?

32. Which costs more, 3 pounds of grapes at $0.99 per pound or 2 pounds of grapes at $1.49 per pound? How much more?

33. Explain how you chose the operation you used to solve problem 32.

Chapter Test

Add. Write each sum in simplest form.

1. $\frac{2}{9} + \frac{3}{9}$

2. $\frac{1}{3} + \frac{1}{5}$

3. $\frac{3}{12} + \frac{1}{12}$

4. $\frac{4}{9} + \frac{1}{3}$

5. $\frac{3}{10} + \frac{4}{10}$

6. $\frac{1}{3} + \frac{5}{6}$

7. $\frac{5}{6} + \frac{5}{12}$

8. $\frac{7}{8} + \frac{1}{4}$

Subtract. Write each difference in simplest form.

9. $\frac{4}{5} - \frac{2}{10}$

10. $\frac{2}{3} - \frac{1}{5}$

11. $\frac{5}{6} - \frac{1}{6}$

12. $\frac{8}{9} - \frac{2}{9}$

13. $\frac{9}{11} - \frac{5}{11}$

14. $\frac{7}{10} - \frac{2}{5}$

15. $\frac{7}{8} - \frac{1}{4}$

16. $\frac{11}{12} - \frac{3}{4}$

Use properties to find each missing number.

17. $\frac{3}{10} + \frac{1}{5} = s + \frac{3}{10}$

18. $\frac{5}{9} - t = \frac{5}{9}$

19. $\frac{1}{8} + \left(\frac{3}{8} + \frac{1}{4}\right) = \left(\frac{1}{8} + u\right) + \frac{1}{4}$

20. $\frac{4}{5} + v = \frac{3}{5} + \frac{4}{5}$

21. $\frac{3}{8} - \frac{3}{8} = w$

22. $\frac{1}{3} + \left(\frac{5}{12} + y\right) = \left(\frac{1}{3} + \frac{5}{12}\right) + \frac{1}{12}$

Solve.

23. A recipe says to combine $\frac{3}{4}$ cup of sugar and $\frac{1}{3}$ cup of butter. How many cups are in this mixture? Explain how you chose the operation you used.

24. Frieda makes a gallon of tomato sauce. She uses $\frac{1}{2}$ of the gallon to make meatballs. Then she uses $\frac{1}{2}$ of what was left of the sauce to make pizza. After that, how much is left of the original gallon of sauce?

25. Some expensive cheeses are sold in small packages. Antonio buys $\frac{1}{3}$ pound and $\frac{1}{4}$ pound of cheese. Brandon buys a $\frac{3}{8}$-pound package and a $\frac{1}{4}$-pound package of cheese. Who buys more cheese? how much more?

Performance Assessment

You love to cook! One of your favorite things is creating new recipes.

Create a recipe that uses fractions. (Not all your ingredients need to have fractional parts.) List each of the ingredients on a chart like the one below. Then double your recipe. Show your work. Write two questions comparing the amounts in both recipes.

Ingredient Amount	Recipe Name	Double Recipe

A Good Answer

- shows a clearly completed chart.
- includes a recipe that uses fractions.
- shows the steps you followed to double your recipe.
- compares the amounts in both recipes.

You may want to save this work for your portfolio.

Assessment

Enrichment

Add and Subtract Mixed Numbers

When you add or subtract mixed numbers, add or subtract the fractions first. The add or subtract the whole numbers.

Subtract: $3\frac{5}{8} - 1\frac{3}{8}$

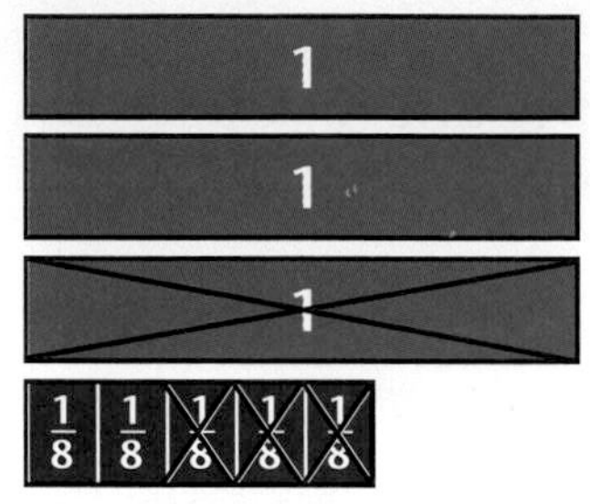

$$\begin{array}{r} 3\frac{5}{8} \\ -1\frac{3}{8} \\ \hline 2\frac{2}{8} \end{array}$$

Subtract the fractions. Then subtract the whole numbers.

Simplify: $2\frac{2}{8} = 2\frac{1}{4}$

Sometimes you need to rename when the denominators are not the same.

Add: $1\frac{2}{3} + 1\frac{5}{6}$.

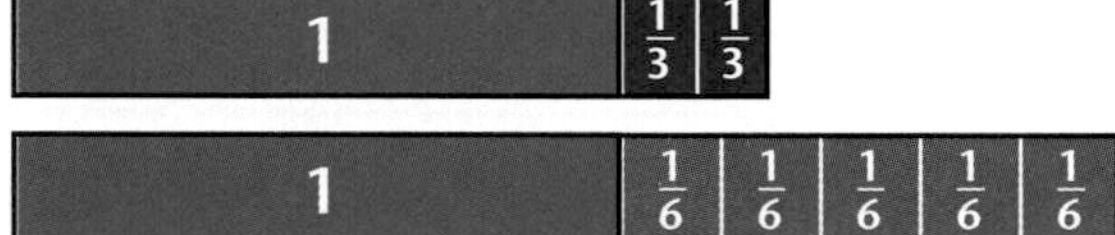

$$\begin{array}{rcr} 1\frac{2}{3} & = & 1\frac{4}{6} \\ +1\frac{5}{6} & = & +1\frac{5}{6} \\ \hline & & 2\frac{9}{6} \end{array}$$

Rename $\frac{2}{3}$ as $\frac{4}{6}$. Add the fractions. Add the whole numbers.

Simplify: $2\frac{9}{6} = 2 + 1\frac{3}{6} = 3\frac{3}{6} = 3\frac{1}{2}$

Add or subtract. Write each answer in simplest form.

1. $\begin{array}{r} 6\frac{7}{8} \\ -2\frac{3}{8} \\ \hline \end{array}$

2. $\begin{array}{r} 12\frac{1}{3} \\ -3\frac{1}{3} \\ \hline \end{array}$

3. $\begin{array}{r} 6\frac{1}{2} \\ +4\frac{1}{2} \\ \hline \end{array}$

4. $\begin{array}{r} 2\frac{3}{4} \\ +3\frac{5}{8} \\ \hline \end{array}$

5. $\begin{array}{r} 5\frac{3}{8} \\ -2\frac{5}{8} \\ \hline \end{array}$

6. $\begin{array}{r} 7\frac{3}{6} \\ +2\frac{1}{3} \\ \hline \end{array}$

7. $\begin{array}{r} 4\frac{5}{6} \\ +5\frac{9}{12} \\ \hline \end{array}$

8. $\begin{array}{r} 6\frac{3}{5} \\ +4\frac{4}{10} \\ \hline \end{array}$

Test-Taking Tips

Sometimes you need to use information in a chart to answer questions on a test.

The chart shows the amounts of pie eaten at a country fair.

Type of Pie	Amount Eaten
Apple	$\frac{5}{12}$
Blackberry	$\frac{9}{12}$
Lemon	$\frac{3}{12}$
Peach	$\frac{6}{12}$

Be sure to choose the correct information to solve the problem.

Which kind of pie is the most popular?

A. Apple **B.** Blackberry **C.** Lemon **D.** Peach

Look at the column in the chart called "Amount Eaten." Each pie was cut into 12 slices. The greater number tells you which pie was most popular.

The correct choice is B.

Check for Success

Before turning in a test, go back one last time to check.

☑ I understood and answered the questions asked.

☑ I checked my work for errors.

☑ My answers make sense.

Student	Amount of Hot Dogs Eaten (in pounds)
Sasha	$\frac{3}{4}$
Tim	$\frac{4}{8}$
Brenda	$\frac{2}{16}$
Raymond	$\frac{1}{2}$

Use data from the chart on the right to choose the correct answer.

1. Who ate the most hot dogs?

A. Sasha **B.** Tim **C.** Brenda **D.** Raymond

2. Who ate exactly the same amount of hot dogs?

F. Sasha and Raymond **G.** Brenda and Tim **H.** Sasha and Brenda **J.** Tim and Raymond

3. Who ate the fewest hot dogs?

A. Sasha **B.** Tim **C.** Brenda **D.** Raymond

4. Which is another way to write how many hot dogs Brenda ate?

F. $\frac{2}{3}$ **G.** $\frac{5}{6}$ **H.** $\frac{1}{8}$ **J.** $\frac{3}{8}$

Spiral Review and Test Prep

Chapters 1–12

Choose the correct answer.

Number Sense

1. 12×45
   - **A.** $12 + (40 \times 5)$
   - **B.** $12 \times 40 \times 5$
   - **C.** $(12 \times 40) + (5 \times 40)$
   - **D.** $(12 \times 40) + (12 \times 5)$

2. Erin buys two 2-pound packages and two $\frac{1}{2}$-pound packages of ground beef. How many total pounds is this?
   - **F.** 4 pounds
   - **G.** 5 pounds
   - **H.** 6 pounds
   - **J.** 7 pounds

3. A store manager orders 3 cases of juice boxes. There are 3 boxes in each package and 12 packages in a case. How many juice boxes is this altogether?
   - **A.** 36
   - **B.** 108
   - **C.** 18
   - **D.** Not Here

4. A restaurant serves between 60,000 and 65,000 customers each year. Which could not be the actual number of customers served?
   - **F.** 65,011
   - **G.** 61,055
   - **H.** 60,030
   - **J.** 64,950

Measurement and Geometry

5. Sammy's Sandwiches is famous for its 2-foot sandwich. Three friends share one of these sandwiches equally. What length will they cut each piece?
   - **A.** 8 feet
   - **B.** 6 inches
   - **C.** 8 inches
   - **D.** 3 feet

6. The inside of a can of soup is 14 ounces. Which best describes this capacity?
   - **F.** Almost 2 cups
   - **G.** More than 1 quart
   - **H.** Less than 1 cup
   - **J.** Almost 1 gallon

7. A can of tomatoes weighs 28 ounces. Which item weighs less than a can of tomatoes?
   - **A.** 6-pound watermelon
   - **B.** Kernel of popcorn
   - **C.** 5-pound bag of potatoes
   - **D.** 3-pound bunch of bananas

8. Which figure best describes the shape of an orange?
   - **F.** Prism
   - **G.** Sphere
   - **H.** Pyramid
   - **J.** Cone

Statistics, Data Analysis, and Probability

Use data from the table for problems 9–12.

Pizza		$1.25 slice
Salad		$2.75
Tuna Sandwich		$2.25
Hot Dog		$1.50
Beverages		
Juice	Small	$0.75
	Large	$1.25
Milk		$0.75
Bottled Water		$1.00

9. How much does it cost for 2 slices of pizza and a large juice?
   A. $2.50 **C.** $3.75
   B. $3.25 **D.** $4.25

10. How much more would you pay for a salad and water than a tuna sandwich and milk?
   F. $0.50 **H.** $1.00
   G. $0.75 **J.** $1.25

11. How many combinations of food and beverage are possible, including both sizes of juice, if you buy one food and one beverage?
   A. 16 **C.** 12
   B. 8 **D.** 20

12. Create a problem based on the information in the table. Explain how to solve your problem.

Mathematical Reasoning

13. What is the next quotient in this pattern?
   $320 \div 40 = 8$
   $3{,}200 \div 40 = 80$
   $32{,}000 \div 40 = 800$
   A. 8,000 **C.** 80
   B. 800 **D.** 8

14. A recipe uses $\frac{3}{4}$ pound of meat and serves 4 people. How many pounds of meat do you need to make the recipe for 8 people?
   F. $2\frac{1}{4}$ pounds **H.** $\frac{3}{8}$ pound
   G. 3 pounds **J.** $1\frac{1}{2}$ pounds

15. Look at the pattern. What is the price for 1 person?
   Group Prices for Buffet Meals
   10 people = $120
   15 people = $180
   20 people = $240
   A. $10 **C.** $15
   B. $12 **D.** $120

16. Which number sentence is not a part of the same fact family as the others?
   F. $3 \times 4 = 12$ **H.** $12 \div 3 = 4$
   G. $4 + 3 = 7$ **J.** $4 \times 3 = 12$

CHAPTER 13 Relate Fractions and Decimals

Theme: Bright Lights, Big Cities

Use the Data

Total Precipitation for One Year

Name	Amount in Inches
San Diego, California	9.30
Jackson,Mississippi	58.94
Tampa, Florida	67.71
New Orleans, Louisiana	51.68

- Which city gets the most amount of precipitation? How can you use the data to put the cities in order from least to greatest according to how much precipitation they get?

What You Will Learn

In this chapter you will learn how to
- identify fraction and decimal equivalents.
- read and write decimals to thousandths.
- compare, order, and round decimals.
- use strategies to solve problems.

Objective: Use models to relate fractions and decimals.

13·1 Explore Fractions and Decimals

Learn

You can use models to explore fractions and decimals.

How can you show twenty-five hundredths as a decimal?

Math Words

decimal a number that uses place value and a decimal point to show tenths, hundredths, and thousandths

decimal point a period separating the ones and the tenths in a decimal

equivalent decimals decimals that name the same number

Work Together

You Will Need

- centimeter graph paper

▶ Use graph paper to model fractions and decimals.

- Count 10 rows of 10 squares each for a total of 100 squares.
- Color 25 squares in your 100-square grid.

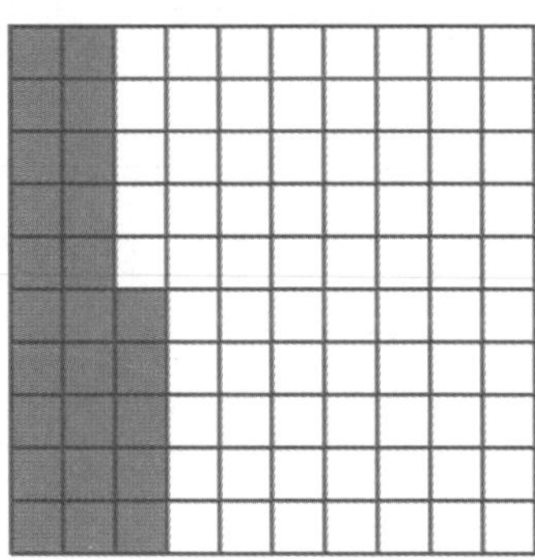

- Write what fraction of the grid has been shaded.
- Write a **decimal** number to show what part of the grid has been shaded.
- Record your work in a chart like the one shown.

Fraction	Decimal
$\frac{25}{100}$	0.25

▶ Model these fractions using graph paper. Write them as decimals. Record your work.

$\frac{4}{10}$ $\frac{5}{10}$ $\frac{10}{100}$ $\frac{75}{100}$ $\frac{38}{100}$

Make Connections

You can use a model and a place-value chart to read and write decimals. The **decimal point** separates the ones from the tenths.

Using Models

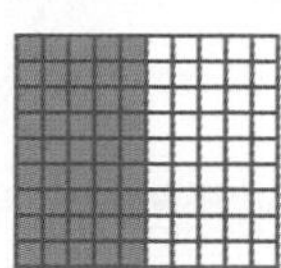

Think: $\frac{50}{100}$ of the grid is shaded.

Simplify: $\frac{50}{100} = \frac{5}{10} = \frac{1}{2}$

Using Paper and Pencil

Ones		Tenths	Hundredths
0	.	5	0

0.50 and 0.5 are **equivalent decimals** because they represent the same amount. $\frac{1}{2}$ is equivalent to 0.50.

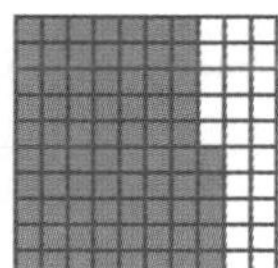

Think: $\frac{75}{100}$ of the grid is shaded.

Simplify: $\frac{75}{100} = \frac{3}{4}$

Ones		Tenths	Hundredths
0	.	7	5

$\frac{3}{4}$ is equivalent to 0.75.

Try It **Write a fraction and a decimal for each shaded part. Then write the fraction in simplest form.**

1. 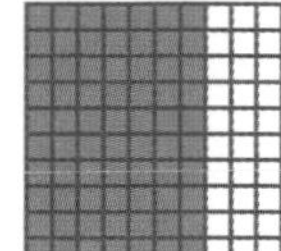
2. 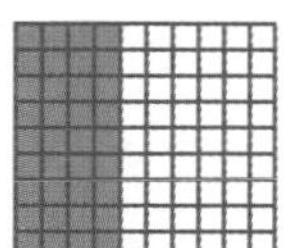
3. 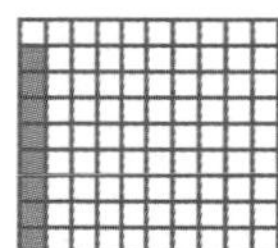
4. 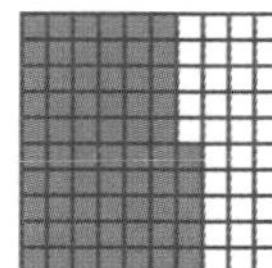

How are 0.2 and 0.20 equivalent? 0.2 and $\frac{2}{10}$?

Practice **Write a fraction and a decimal for each shaded part. Then write the fraction in simplest form.**

5. 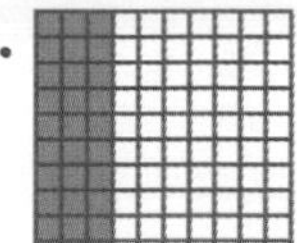
6. 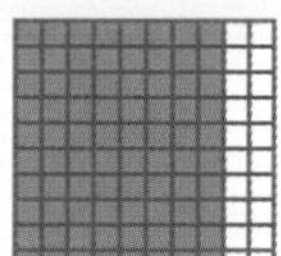
7. 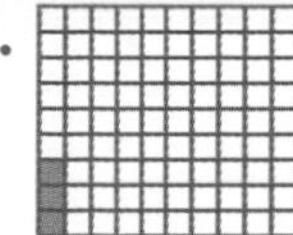
8. 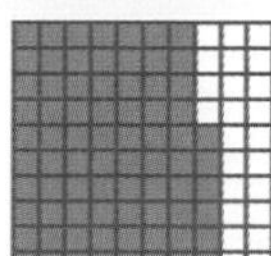

Write each as a decimal.

9. $\frac{1}{10}$ 10. $\frac{1}{4}$ 11. $\frac{30}{100}$ 12. $\frac{3}{5}$ 13. $\frac{5}{100}$ 14. $\frac{65}{100}$

Objective: Read and write tenths and hundredths as decimals and fractions.

13·2

Tenths and Hundredths

Learn

What if Chief Harvard said the crime rate in Atlanta, Georgia decreased by $\frac{2}{10}$ last month. How can she write this amount as a decimal?

Atlanta Chief of Police Beverly Harvard

Example

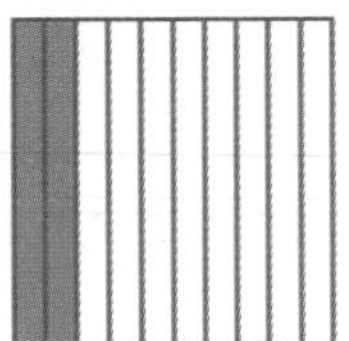

Ones		Tenths	Hundredths
0	.	2	

Read: two tenths **Write:** 0.2

Read a decimal by reading the number and the place value of the last digit at the right.

She can write it as 0.2.

More Examples

A

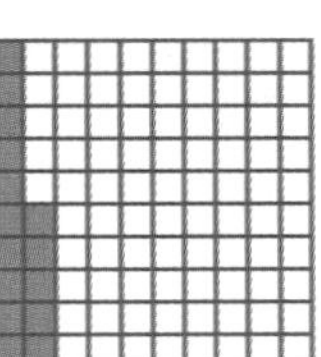

Read: fifteen hundredths
Write: 0.15

B

Show $\frac{3}{5}$ as a decimal.

$$\frac{3 \times 2}{5 \times 2} = \frac{6}{10} = 0.6$$

Read: six tenths
Write: 0.6

Try It

Write a fraction and a decimal for each part that is shaded.

1. 
2. 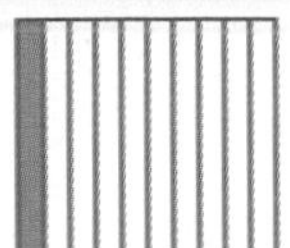
3. 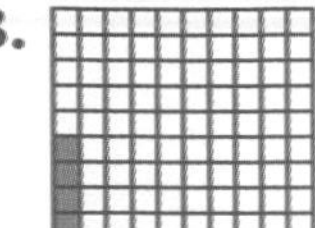
4. 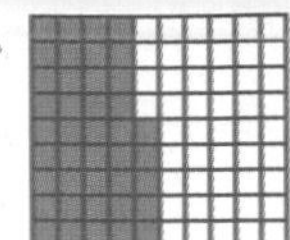

Sum it Up How is the 5 in 0.5 different from the 5 in 0.05?

Practice Write a fraction and a decimal for each part that is shaded.

5. 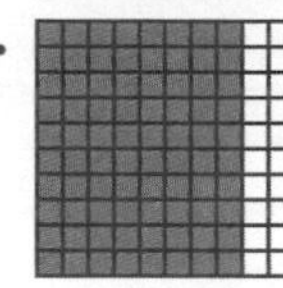

6. 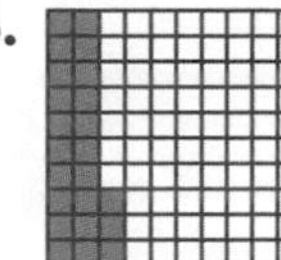

7. 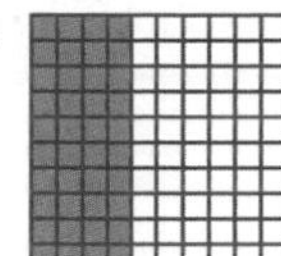

8. 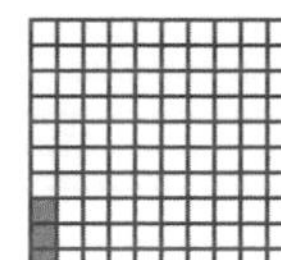

Write each as a decimal.

9. $\frac{1}{5}$
10. $\frac{17}{100}$
11. $\frac{3}{4}$
12. $\frac{89}{100}$
13. $\frac{44}{100}$
14. $\frac{6}{100}$
15. eight tenths
16. thirteen hundredths
17. nine hundredths

Write a fraction and decimal for each point. Tell if it is close to 0, $\frac{1}{2}$, or 1.

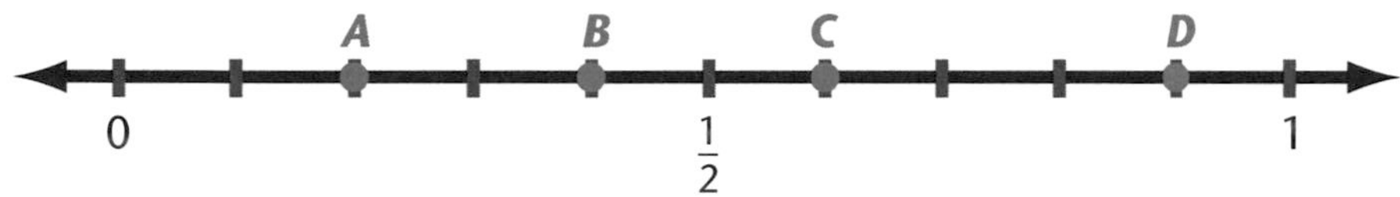

18. A
19. B
20. C
21. D

What number is being added each time? What numbers are missing?

22. $1.00, $1.10, $1.20, ■, ■, ■
23. 0.01, 0.06, 0.11, ■, ■, ■

Problem Solving

24. **Spatial Reasoning:** Derek shades all the squares on the edge of a 10-by-10 grid. Write a fraction and a decimal to show the shaded part.

★25. Walter has 0.1 of a dollar in coins. He gets another 0.23 of a dollar in coins. How much money does Walter have?

Spiral Review and Test Prep

26. $425 + 625$
27. $5{,}000 - 2{,}999$
28. 450×9
29. $800 \div 40$

Choose the correct answer.

30. Three tickets to the ballet cost $104.85. How much does each ticket cost?
    - A. $34.95
    - B. $44.95
    - C. $52.43
    - D. $314.55

31. The Arts Center has 3 tiers of seats. If each row seats 83 people and each tier has 14 rows, how many seats are in the Arts Center?
    - F. 249
    - G. 1,162
    - H. 3,486
    - J. Not Here

Extra Practice, page 583

Objective: Understand the meaning of thousandths.

13·3

Thousandths

Learn

Wow! Could he hit a ball! Ted Williams of the Boston Red Sox had a lifetime batting average of 0.344. How can you write the word name for this decimal?

Example

Ones		Tenths	Hundredths	Thousandths
0	.	3	4	4

Read: three hundred forty-four thousandths

Fraction: $\frac{344}{1{,}000}$ **Decimal:** 0.344

Read a decimal by reading the number and the place value of the last digit at the right.

More Examples

A

Ones		Tenths	Hundredths	Thousandths
0	.	0	2	7

Read: twenty-seven thousandths

Fraction: $\frac{27}{1{,}000}$ **Decimal:** 0.027

B

Ones		Tenths	Hundredths	Thousandths
0	.	0	0	5

Read: five thousandths

Fraction: $\frac{5}{1{,}000}$ **Decimal:** 0.005

Try It

Write each as a decimal.

1. $\frac{7}{1{,}000}$
2. $\frac{78}{1{,}000}$
3. $\frac{502}{1{,}000}$

What does the 5 in 0.539 mean? What does the 3 mean? What does the 9 mean?

Practice Write each as a decimal.

4. $\frac{4}{1,000}$ 5. $\frac{13}{1,000}$ 6. $\frac{411}{1,000}$ 7. $\frac{50}{1,000}$ ★8. $\frac{4,234}{10,000}$ ★9. $\frac{1,295}{10,000}$

10. eighty-nine thousandths
11. six hundred sixty-four thousandths
12. five hundred thousandths
13. four hundred six thousandths

Algebra & functions **Copy and complete.**

14.

Millimeters	Centimeters	Decimeters	Meters
▮	0.5	0.05	0.005
7	▮	▮	▮
▮	▮	▮	0.012

Use data from *Did You Know?* for problem 15.

15. **Social Studies:** All of the games the Cincinnati Red Stockings won in the 1869–1870 season lasted nine innings. How many innings did they play in those games?

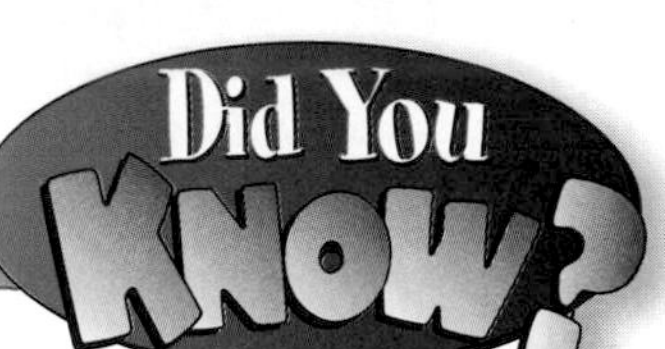

The first professional baseball team was the Cincinnati Red Stockings in Cincinnati, Ohio. They won 91 and tied 1 of their first 92 games in the 1869–1870 season.

Problem Solving

16. **Social Studies:** Ty Cobb of the Detroit Tigers and the Philadelphia Athletics holds the record batting average of 0.366. Write the word name for this decimal.

17. **Collect data:** Find out the highest batting average on your favorite baseball team.

Spiral Review and Test Prep

Add. Write each sum in simplest form.

18. $\frac{1}{4} + \frac{2}{4}$ 19. $\frac{2}{10} + \frac{3}{10}$ 20. $\frac{2}{5} + \frac{2}{5}$

Choose the correct answer.

21. What fraction of the spinner is not red?

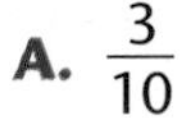

A. $\frac{3}{10}$ B. $\frac{4}{10}$ C. $\frac{5}{10}$ D. $\frac{6}{10}$

22. What is the probability of spinning green?

F. $\frac{1}{5}$ G. $\frac{2}{5}$ H. $\frac{3}{5}$ J. $\frac{4}{5}$

13•4

Objective: Compare and contrast information to choose a representation.

Problem Solving: Reading for Math

Choose a Representation

Straphangers Surveyed

Read Out of 100 subway riders surveyed, 0.25 of the riders stated they ride Train A the most and $\frac{3}{4}$ of the riders stated they ride Train B the most. Do more riders take Train A or Train B?

READING SKILL ▶ **Compare and Contrast**

When you compare and contrast, you look at two or more items. You note how the items are alike and different.

- **What do you know?** **0.25 take Train A; $\frac{3}{4}$ take Train B**
- **What do you need to find?** **Which train more riders take**

MATH SKILL ▶ **Choose a Representation**

You can represent part of a whole as either a fraction or a decimal. You should use the same form when comparing.

Plan You need to change the way one amount is represented so you can compare.

Solve You can either change a decimal to a fraction or you can change a fraction to a decimal. Then compare.

$0.25 = \frac{1}{4}$ $\quad 0.25 < 0.75$ $\qquad \frac{3}{4} = 0.75$ $\quad \frac{1}{4} < \frac{3}{4}$

A greater number of riders take Train B.

Look Back How could you check your answer?

Why do you need to make sure the numbers you use are in the same form to solve a problem?

Practice Choose a representation and solve.

1. Another question asked riders how often they take the subway. Of the people who answered, 0.3 said they ride less than 4 times a week and $\frac{7}{10}$ said more than 5 times a week. How did the greater number of people respond to this question?

2. A third survey question asked riders how long they have been taking the subway. Of the people surveyed, $\frac{1}{2}$ said they ride less than 2 years and 0.5 said more than 2 years. Which answer got the greater number of responses?

Use data from the table for problems 3–8.

Survey of 100 Riders	
Question: How much money do you spend each week on transportation?	
Less than \$5	25
Between \$5 and \$10	50
More than \$10	25

3. What fraction represents the number of people who spend more than \$10 a week on transportation?

4. What decimal represents the number of people who spend between \$5 and \$10 on transportation each week?

5. What fraction represents the amount of people who spend less than \$5 a week on transportation?

6. Paul says half of the people asked spend either less than \$5 or more than \$10. Is his statement reasonable?

7. Celia says $\frac{3}{4}$ of those asked spend \$10 or less. Is her statement reasonable?

8. What fraction of those surveyed ride for free?

Spiral Review and Test Prep

Choose the correct answer.

Anne rode the subway 3 days out of 4 last week. Is it reasonable to say she rode 0.75 of the days?

9. Which statement is true?
   - **A.** Anne rode the subway for 4 straight days.
   - **B.** Anne rode for $\frac{1}{4}$ the days.
   - **C.** Anne rode for 3 out of the 4 days.

10. The statement is reasonable because
   - **F.** $3 > 4$.
   - **G.** $0.75 = \frac{3}{4}$.
   - **H.** $4 - 3 = 1$.

Extra Practice, page 583

Check Your Progress A

Write a fraction and a decimal for each shaded part. Then write the fraction in simplest form. (pages 558–561)

1. 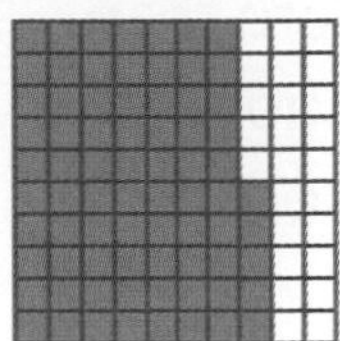

2. 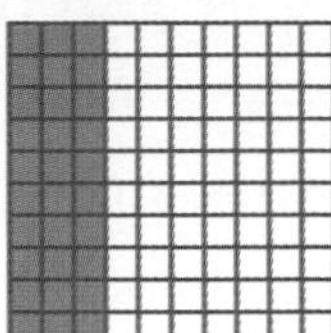

3. 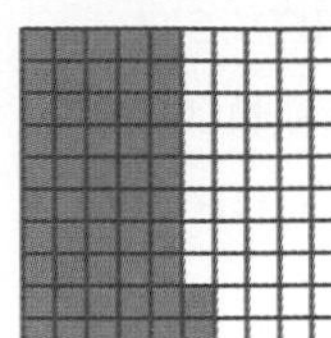

4. 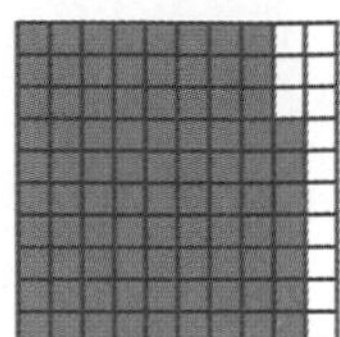

Write each as a decimal. (pages 558–561)

5. $\frac{1}{10}$ **6.** $\frac{14}{100}$ **7.** $\frac{70}{100}$ **8.** $\frac{45}{100}$ **9.** $\frac{75}{100}$

10. $\frac{37}{100}$ **11.** one tenth **12.** twenty-three hundredths **13.** ninety hundredths

Write each as a decimal. (pages 562–563)

14. $\frac{6}{1,000}$ **15.** $\frac{20}{1,000}$ **16.** $\frac{450}{1,000}$ **17.** $\frac{37}{1,000}$

18. $\frac{800}{1,000}$ **19.** $\frac{674}{1,000}$ **20.** seventy thousandths **21.** five hundred three thousandths

Solve. (pages 558–565)

22. In Tibet there are suspension bridges that are over $\frac{7}{100}$ kilometer long. Write this fraction as a decimal.

23. Mark measures a distance of 0.2 centimeter. Rita measures a distance of 0.2 meter. Who measures the greater distance?

24. Of the people surveyed, $\frac{1}{5}$ say they prefer to use tunnels rather than bridges. More than 0.75 of those surveyed preferred bridges over tunnels. Which choice did more people prefer to use?

25. **Analyze:** Write three different decimals using the numbers 4, 0, and 3. You may use all or some of the numbers. Write at least one decimal each for tenths, hundredths, and thousandths.

Additional activities at www.mhschool.com/math

Use Place-Value Models to Show Decimals

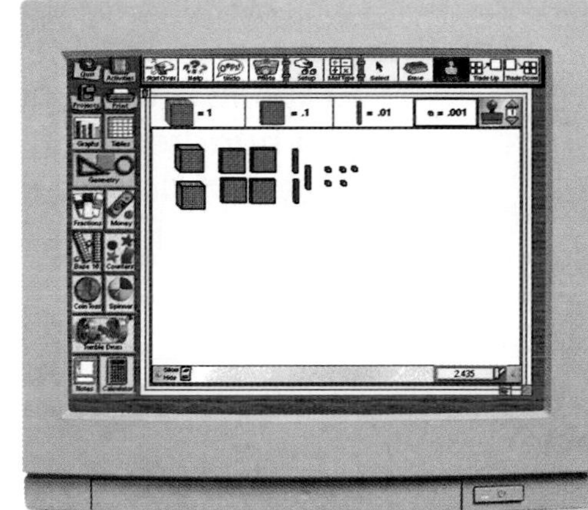

Brent found that the height of the fence around his backyard is 2.435 meters. How many ones are in this measure? How many tenths? How many hundredths? How many thousandths?

You can build a model of the measure using place-value or base-ten models.

- Choose Setup. Select the block on the left to represent 1.
- Start with the 2. Stamp out that many ones.
- Move to the 4 and stamp out that many tenths.
- Move to the 3 and stamp out that many hundredths.
- Move to the 5 and stamp out that many thousandths.

The number box keeps count as you stamp.

- How many ones are in his measure?
- How many tenths?
- How many hundredths?
- How many thousandths?

Use the computer to model each number. Then name the value of each digit.

1. 6.24 **2.** 8.253 **3.** 9.082 **4.** 4.607

Solve.

5. Adrian ran 2.45 miles on Tuesday. How many ones are in this measure? How many tenths? How many hundredths?

6. Michael filled his gas tank with 9.345 gallons of gas. How many ones are in this measure? How many tenths? hundredths? thousandths?

7. Analyze: How does using the model help you name the value of each digit in the number?

For more practice, use Math Traveler™.

Objective: Understand decimals greater than 1.

13•5 Decimals Greater Than 1

Learn

Santa Fe is one and thirty-two hundredths miles above sea level. How can you write this number as a decimal?

Santa Fe, New Mexico, is the city with the highest elevation in the United States.

Example

Write $1\frac{32}{100}$ as a decimal.

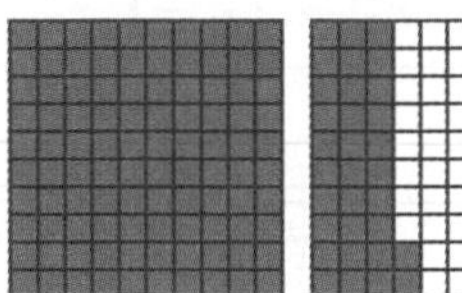

Mixed number: $1\frac{32}{100}$

Ones		Tenths	Hundredths
1	.	3	2

Read: one and thirty-two hundredths
Write: 1.32

More Examples

A

Ones		Tenths	Hundredths
4	.	9	

Read: four and nine tenths
Mixed number: $4\frac{9}{10}$
Decimal: 4.9

B

Tens	Ones		Tenths	Hundredths
3	8	.	0	5

Read: thirty-eight and five hundredths
Mixed number: $38\frac{5}{100}$
Decimal: 38.05

Try It

Write a mixed number and a decimal to tell how much is shaded.

1. 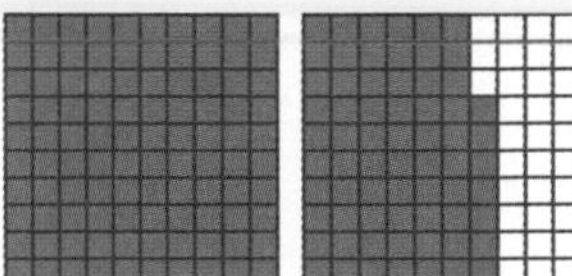

2.  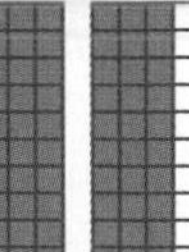

Do the decimals 4.5 and 4.50 name the same number? Draw decimal models to help you.

Practice **Write a mixed number and a decimal to tell how much is shaded.**

3. 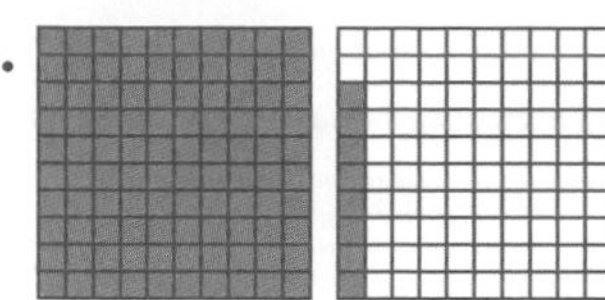

4. 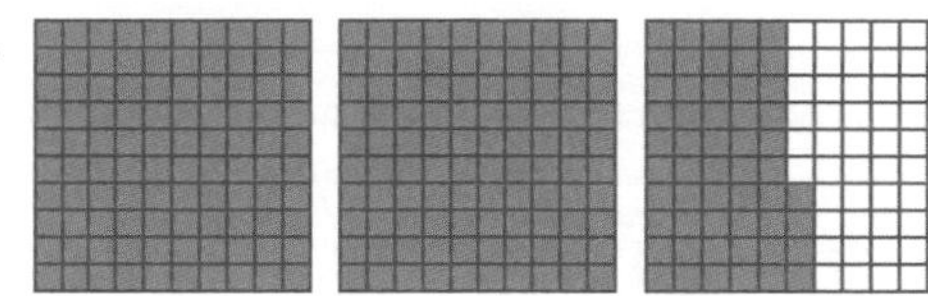

Write the decimal.

5. $8\frac{5}{10}$
6. $4\frac{28}{100}$
7. $7\frac{6}{10}$
8. $4\frac{56}{1{,}000}$
9. $12\frac{9}{100}$
10. $100\frac{4}{10}$
11. $6\frac{6}{1{,}000}$
12. $52\frac{6}{10}$

★13. $2\frac{3}{10{,}000}$

★14. $45\frac{255}{10{,}000}$

15. sixty-seven and three thousandths
16. three hundred and fifty-six hundredths
17. nine and one hundred thirteen thousandths

Problem Solving

18. Sal pours $1\frac{3}{4}$ liters of water in a pool. Write a decimal to show how much water he pours.

★19. **Science:** Sea levels rise an average of 1.2 mm each year. How many centimeters will the average sea levels rise in 100 years?

Use data from the chart for problems 20–22.

20. About how many times higher is the elevation of Atlanta than Gulfport?
21. Which city is about 50 times higher than San Diego?
22. **Create a problem** using the data in the chart. Solve it. Ask others to solve it.

Elevation Above Sea Level

City	Feet
Asheville, North Carolina	2,134
Atlanta, Georgia	1,050
Gulfport, Mississippi	25
San Diego, California	40

Spiral Review and Test Prep

Copy and complete.

23. 50 mm = ▮ cm
24. 8,000 mL = ▮ L
25. 7 kg = ▮ g

Choose the correct answer.

26. Beth has three 500 mL cans of juice. How many more milliliters does she need to fill a 3 L punch bowl?

A. 2 L C. 1,500 mL
B. 1 L D. 1,000 mL

27. Matt and Jill are reading the same book. Matt has read $\frac{4}{8}$ of the book. Which fraction is equivalent to $\frac{4}{8}$?

F. $\frac{1}{2}$ G. $\frac{5}{6}$ H. $\frac{3}{4}$ J. Not Here

Objective: Compare and order decimals.

13•6 Compare and Order Decimals

San Francisco, 1906	8.3
Mexico City, 1985	8.1

Algebra & functions

Learn

Readings from the Richter scale measure the power of these earthquakes. Was the San Francisco earthquake more or less powerful than the earthquake in Mexico City?

There's more than one way!

You can compare decimals to solve this problem.

Method 

Use a number line to compare 8.3 and 8.1.

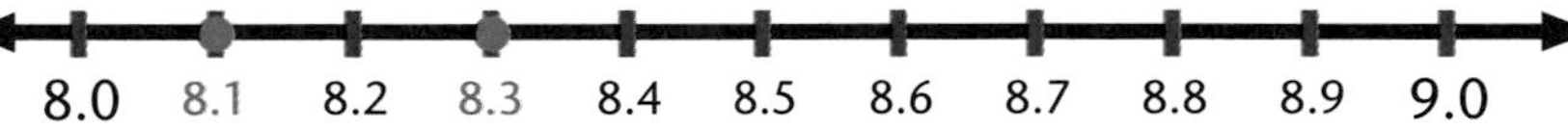

8.1 is to the left of 8.3, $8.1 < 8.3$

Method B

Use place-value to compare 8.3 and 8.1.

1 *Compare the ones.*

8.1 **Think:** $8 = 8$
8.3

2 *Compare the tenths.*

8.1 **Think:** $1 < 3$
8.3 $8.1 < 8.3$

The earthquake in San Francisco was more powerful than the one in Mexico City.

Example 1

Compare 1.29 and 1.26.

Compare the ones.
1.29 **Think:** $1 = 1$
1.26

Compare the tenths.
1.**2**9 **Think:** $2 = 2$
1.**2**6

Compare the hundredths.
1.2**9** **Think:** $9 > 6$
1.2**6**

$1.29 > 1.26$

Example 2

Order 6.49, 6.41, 6.57, and 7.03 from greatest to least.

1 Line up the decimal points.

6.49
6.41
6.57
7.03

Think: 7 > 6
So 7.03 is the greatest decimal.

2 Compare the tenths.

6.49
6.41
6.57

Think: 6.57 > 6.49
6.57 > 6.41

3 Compare the hundredths.

6.49
6.41

Think: 6.49 > 6.41

The order from greatest to least is 7.03, 6.57, 6.49, 6.41.

More Examples

A

Order from least to greatest: 0.433, 0.471, and 0.474.

0.433	
0.474	0.474
0.471	0.471

0.433 < 0.471 and 0.474
0.471 < 0.474

From least to greatest:
0.433, 0.471, 0.474

B

Order from greatest to least: 0.112, 0.102, 0.121.

0.112	0.112
0.102	0.102
0.121	

0.121 > 0.112 and 0.102
0.112 > 0.102

From greatest to least:
0.121, 0.112, 0.102

Try It **Compare. Write >, <, or =.**

1. 0.5 ● 0.50
2. 4.2 ● 4.5
3. 0.23 ● 0.27
4. 4.72 ● 4.71

Order from greatest to least.

5. 3.2, 4.5, 3.9, 4.1
6. 5.33, 4.91, 5.19, 5.52
7. 0.764, 0.684, 0.746

Tell how you would compare 5.8 and 5.3. Which number is greater?

Practice

Compare. Write >, <, or =.

8. 4.7 ● 0.47 **9.** 16.03 ● 16.30 **10.** 0.56 ● 0.58 **11.** 0.6 ● 0.60

12. 7.46 ● 7.49 **13.** 0.5 ● 0.05 **14.** 5.670 ● 5.6 **15.** 18.1 ● 18.10

Write in order from greatest to least.

16. 0.54, 0.45, 0.50 **17.** 0.08, 0.88, 0.80 **18.** 14.9, 14.7, 17.4

19. 0.35, 0.34, 0.39 **20.** 1.27, 1.19, 1.25 **21.** 0.617, 0.613, 0.620

Use each digit once to form decimals with the least and greatest value.

★**22.** 9, 7, 6, 0 ★**23.** 5, 4, 0, 0 ★**24.** 8, 7, 3, 1

Write in order from least to greatest.

25. 7.11, 7.01, 7.12 **26.** 13.9, 13.91, 13.09 **27.** 0.07, 0.70, 0.77

28. 2.07, 2.70, 2.67 **29.** 4.59, 4.95, 5.94 **30.** 0.045, 0.405, 0.005

31.

Here is how Jasmine ordered these decimals from greatest to least. Tell what mistake she made. Explain how to correct it.

Problem Solving

32. Yoshi is training for a race. He ran 24.45 kilometers on Friday, 25.08 kilometers on Saturday, and 24.61 kilometers on Sunday. Order the distances he ran from least to greatest.

33. **Science:** A tsunami is a large wave that is produced by underwater earthquakes. It may reach a height of 37 meters. How many centimeters is that?

34. **Spatial Reasoning:** The blocks in the picture are the only remaining blocks left out of a group of 100 blocks. Write a decimal to show the amount of blocks left in the group.

Use data from the chart for problems 35–38.

35. Which earthquake had a reading that was less than 6.0?

36. Which earthquakes were weaker than the one in Northridge, California?

37. Write the locations of the three strongest earthquakes in order from greatest to least.

38. **Create a problem** using the information in the chart. Solve it. Ask others to solve it.

20th Century Earthquakes

Place	Date	Richter-Scale
Azores, Portugal	1998	5.8
W. Pakistan	1997	7.3
Kobe, Japan	1995	7.2
Northridge, CA	1994	6.8
Southwest India	1993	6.4

Source: World Almanac, 1999

★ 39. Josh's research tells him that there were 60 earthquakes in the past 5 years. Out of the 60, $\frac{1}{4}$ of them had readings of 7.0 or greater. How many earthquakes had readings less than 7.0?

40. Name a decimal that is greater than 1.1 but less than 1.2.

41. **Time:** On May 3, 1998, there was an earthquake on Ryukyu Island near Taiwan. On June 1, 1998 there was an earthquake in Kamchatka, Russia. How many days passed between the two earthquakes?

Spiral Review and Test Prep

Write the answer in simplest form.

42. $\frac{7}{8} + \frac{5}{8}$

43. $\frac{9}{10} - \frac{5}{10}$

44. $\frac{11}{12} - \frac{7}{12}$

45. $\frac{5}{6} + \frac{1}{6}$

46. $\frac{5}{8} - \frac{1}{2}$

47. $\frac{8}{10} + \frac{1}{5}$

48. $\frac{13}{16} - \frac{3}{4}$

49. $\frac{3}{4} + \frac{3}{8}$

Choose the correct answer.

50. What fraction of the cubes are not shaded blue?

A. $\frac{2}{9}$

C. $\frac{4}{9}$

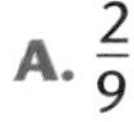

B. $\frac{3}{9}$

D. $\frac{5}{9}$

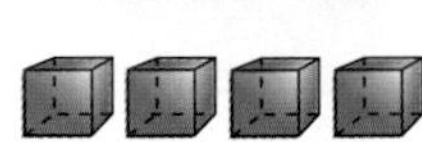

51. What is the probability of picking a green marble?

F. Likely

G. Certain

H. Unlikely

J. Impossible

Objective: Draw diagrams to solve problems.

Problem Solving: Strategy
Draw a Diagram

Read

Read the problem carefully.

Marshall and his father are taking a tour of his state. He lives in Boontown. The list shows the distances to Greentree, Rockford, and Park City. He wants to travel to the cities in order from east to west. Going from east to west, put the cities in order.

Greentree is 4.5 km east of Boontown
Rockford is 3.5 km east of Greentree
Park City is 3.1 km east of Greentree

- **What do you know?** the distance between the cities
- **What do you need to find?** the order of the cities

Plan

One way to solve the problem is to draw a diagram.

Solve

- Use a centimeter ruler to draw a diagram.
- Draw a diagram of the distance from Boontown to Greentree using 1 cm for each km.
- Draw the distances of Park City and Rockford from Greentree.
- You know that 3.5 km is equivalent to 3.5 cm.
- The cities in order from west to east are Boontown, Greentree, Park City, and Rockford.
- The cities in order from east to west are Rockford, Park City, Greentree, and Boontown.

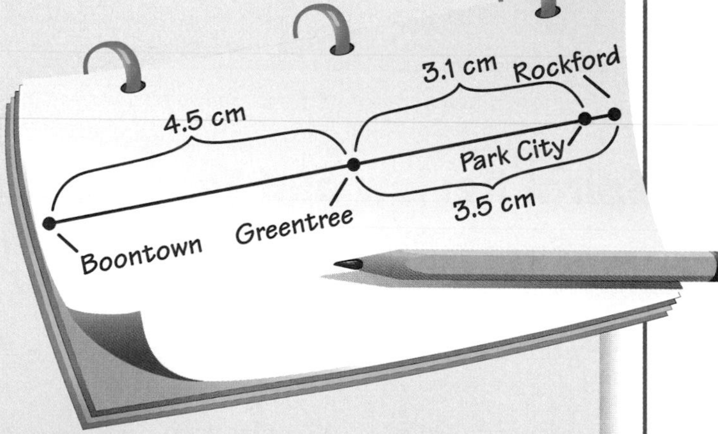

Look Back

How can you check your answer?

How did the diagram help you solve the problem?

Practice Draw a diagram to solve.

1. Kendra wants to go to a mall. The Loews Mall is 3.9 miles east of her town. The Bergen Mall is 1.8 miles west of the Loews Mall. King's Mall is 2.9 miles east of Bergen Mall. Which mall is the closest to Kendra's town? the farthest from her town?

2. The park is 1 kilometer south of the beach. Jamaal lives 2.72 kilometers north of the beach. Ron lives 3.27 kilometers south of the park. Kara lives 2 kilometers south of Ron. Who lives the closest to the beach? the farthest?

3. Max rides the elevator 4 floors up from his office. He then goes down 6 floors, where he meets Jenna. Jenna rides up 5 floors to her office. How many floors away is Jenna's office from Max's?

4. Hightstown is 3.5 miles directly east of Allentown. Warren City is 3.5 miles directly south of Allentown. Harbor City is 3.5 miles directly west of Hightstown. Is this possible? Why or why not?

Mixed Strategy Review

5. Laura owes Alan $2.65. She has only quarters. How many quarters should she give him to pay him back? How much change should he give her?

6. **Logical Reasoning:** Four children are standing in line for a movie. Haley is ahead of Mark; Audrey is behind Mark. Haley is behind Rodney. What is the order of the children in line?

★ 7. The Center City Sports Arena has an audience of 6,069 people. There are 17 rows of seats in the arena, and 595 people are seated in chairs around the court. The rest are seated in the rows. How many people can sit in each row?

8. Cameron runs a city vegetable stand that sells tomatoes for $0.35 each and corn for $0.22 an ear. Mary buys 12 tomatoes and 8 ears of corn. How much does she spend?

9. **Create a problem** that you can solve by drawing a diagram. Solve it. Ask others to solve it.

CHOOSE A STRATEGY

- Logical Reasoning
- Draw a Picture
- Make a Graph
- Act It Out
- Make a Table or List
- Find a Pattern
- Guess and Check
- Write a Number Sentence
- Work Backward
- Solve a Simpler Problem

Extra Practice, page 585

Objective: Use rounding to estimate decimals.

13•8 Round Decimals

Learn

Florence Griffith-Joyner ran incredibly fast in the 100-meter race in the 1988 Olympic Games in Seoul, Korea. How can you round her speed to the nearest whole number? to the nearest tenth?

Example

Round 24.58 to the nearest whole number.

Use a number line.

24.58

24 24.1 24.2 24.3 24.4 24.5 24.6 24.7 24.8 24.9 25

Round up to 25.

Think: 24.58 is closer to 25 than it is to 24.

Round 24.58 to the nearest tenth.

1

Use place-value.
Look at the digit in the place to the right of where you want to round.
24.58

2

Compare the digit to 5.
If it is less than 5, round down. If it is greater than 5, round up.
Round up to 24.6

More Examples

A

Round 23.42 to the nearest whole number.

23.42 **Think:** $4 < 5$

Round down to 23.

B

Round 34.78 to the nearest tenth.

34.78 **Think:** $8 > 5$

Round up to 34.8.

C

Round 4.562 to the nearest hundredth.

4.562 **Think:** $2 < 5$

Round down to 4.56.

Try It

Round to the nearest whole number.

1. 5.54 **2.** 6.17 **3.** 4.59 **4.** 67.21 **5.** 82.09 **6.** 28.84

Sum it Up Explain how rounding decimals is like rounding whole numbers. How is it different?

Practice

Round to the nearest whole number.

7. 8.23   8. 4.97   9. 3.52   10. 74.81   11. 35.11   12. 16.73

Round to the nearest tenth.

13. 17.45   14. 32.86   15. 68.32   16. 7.34   17. 9.97   18. 47.21

19. 82.09   20. 15.44   21. 2.74   22. 78.47   ★23. 5.3678   ★24. 2.0954

Round to the nearest hundredth.

25. 6.197   26. 4.781   27. 3.390   28. 5.821   29. 7.901   30. 4.555

31. 15.345   32. 61.942   33. 41.358   34. 27.067   ★35. 8.0323   ★36. 6.70667

Problem Solving

37. In 1988 Carl Lewis reached a speed of 26.95 miles an hour. What is his speed rounded to the nearest whole number?

38. **Compare:** Which is greater when rounded to the nearest hundredth, 1.765 or 1.799?

Use data from *Did You Know?* for problems 39–40.

39. How many years ago were the first Olympic games?

40. About how many years passed from the first Olympics until they were revived?

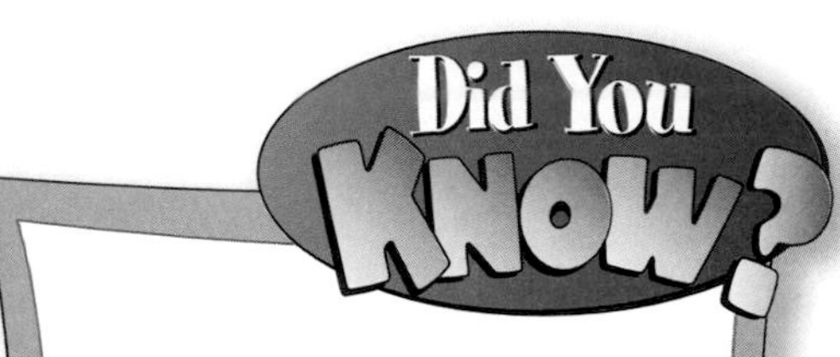

The first Olympic games are believed to have been held in Athens, Greece, in 776 B.C. The games were revived in Athens in 1896.

Spiral Review and Test Prep

Write each as a decimal.

41. $\frac{3}{10}$ 42. $\frac{9}{10}$ 43. $\frac{70}{100}$ 44. $\frac{95}{100}$ 45. $\frac{8}{100}$ 46. $\frac{56}{100}$

47. $\frac{5}{1,000}$ 48. $\frac{67}{1,000}$ 49. $\frac{999}{1,000}$ 50. $6\frac{4}{10}$ 51. $8\frac{9}{100}$ 52. $27\frac{5}{100}$

Choose the correct answer.

53. Uma buys a map for $4.95 and 2 pitas for $2.69 each. She pays with a ten-dollar bill and a five-dollar bill. What is her change?

A. $0.47   C. $5.67
B. $4.67   D. $10.33

54. Dmitri saves a penny on Sunday. Each day after that he saves twice as much as the day before. How much will he save in one week?

F. $1.27   H. $0.32
G. $0.64   J. $0.70

Objective: Analyze data and make decisions.

Problem Solving: Application

Decision Making

What models should they put in the area where people live?

What models should they put in the business area?

For a social studies project, Kit and Rammel are building a model of a city they create. They will build their model on a 1-meter by 1-meter piece of plywood. They have $25 to spend on the model.

$2.95 for an apartment building, 9 cm by 8 cm by 22 cm tall

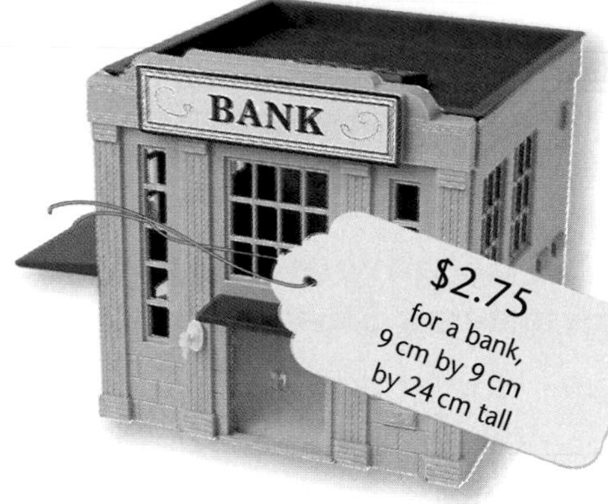

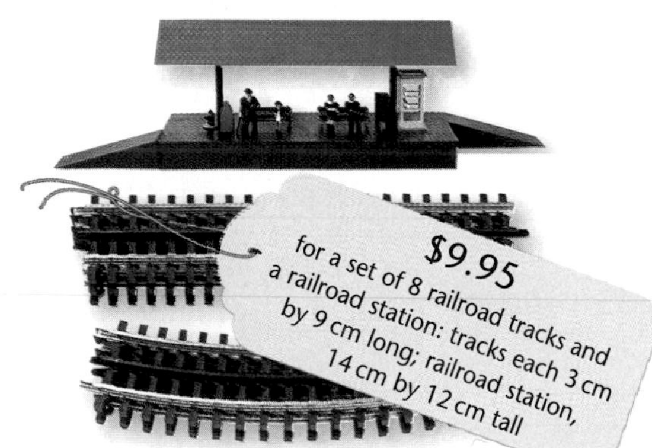

Read for Understanding

1. Which is taller, the apartment building or the railroad station? How can you tell?
2. Which has a larger base, the bank or the apartment building? How can you tell?
3. Which costs more, the homes or the stores? How can you tell?
4. When you buy the railroad tracks, railroad station, and school, how much will you have left to spend on other models?
5. How much would you spend if you bought a box of trees and a box of stores?
6. If you lay the 8 railroad tracks end to end will they fit on the plywood? How can you tell?

Making Decisions

7. Which models would Kit and Rammel use if they decide to build only places where people live? Why?
8. Which models would be best for a business district? Why?
9. Is $25 enough to buy models for people's homes? for a business district? Why or why not?
10. Draw the plywood base. Let each unit on a sheet of graph paper stand for 10 centimeters. What is the area of the base?
11. When Kit and Rammel decide to use homes, apartment buildings, and trees to build an area where people live, how many boxes of each should they buy? How much will it cost?
12. When Kit and Rammel decide to use stores, railroad tracks, a railroad station, and a school in a business area, how many boxes of each should they buy? How much will it cost?
13. You decide to buy the homes. How will you arrange them on the plywood? How much space will you leave between each home?
14. Make a list of information you need to think about before deciding which models to buy and how many of each you will need.

What is your recommendation for Kit and Rammel? Explain.

Objective: Apply fractions and decimals to investigate science concepts.

Problem Solving: Math and Science

How does distance affect how many strikes you throw?

You Will Need

- **paper ball**
- **sheet of paper**
- **tape**
- **ruler or meterstick**

Major League pitchers must throw a ball sixty feet, six inches into the catcher's glove. Would it be easier if the pitcher were standing closer to the catcher? In this activity, you will discover whether it is harder or easier to throw a strike as you move away from the target.

Hypothesize

Of ten tries, how many strikes will you throw from 1.5 meters away? from 6 meters away?

Procedure

1. Work with a partner. Take turns.
2. Tape a sheet of paper to the board or wall 1 meter from the floor. (This paper is the catcher's mitt—if you hit it, you make a strike.)
3. Try 10 pitches from 1.5 meters (m) away. Record how many strikes you make.
4. Repeat from 3, 4.5, and 6 meters away.

Data

Record the number of strikes you made.
Write each answer as a decimal.

Distance	Attempts	Strikes	Answer as a Decimal
1.5 m	10		
3.0 m	10		
4.5 m	10		
6.0 m	10		

Conclude and Apply

1. At which distance was it easiest to make strikes? Explain your answer.

2. Put the decimals in order from least to greatest. If you made a lot of strikes, was the decimal greater or less than the other numbers?

3. What fraction of all the throws are strikes? Write the fraction as a decimal.

4. Use your answer in number 3 to compare your ability to throw strikes with that of major league baseball pitchers.

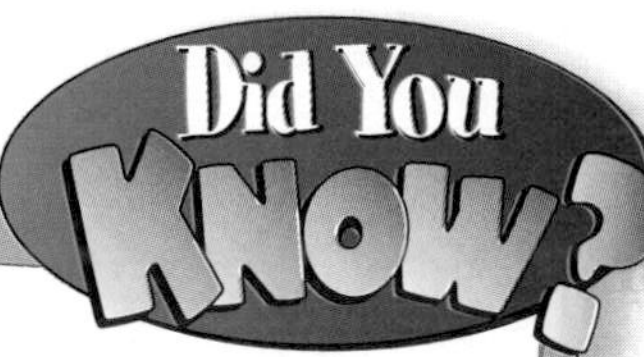

A major league baseball pitcher throws a strike about 0.7 of the time.

Going Further

1. Design and complete an activity to find the farthest distance you can be from the target and still make at least 1 strike in 10 throws.

2. Design and complete an activity to explore whether practice makes it easier to throw strikes.

Check Your Progress B

Write each as a mixed number in simplest form and as a decimal to tell how much is shaded. (pages 568–569)

1. 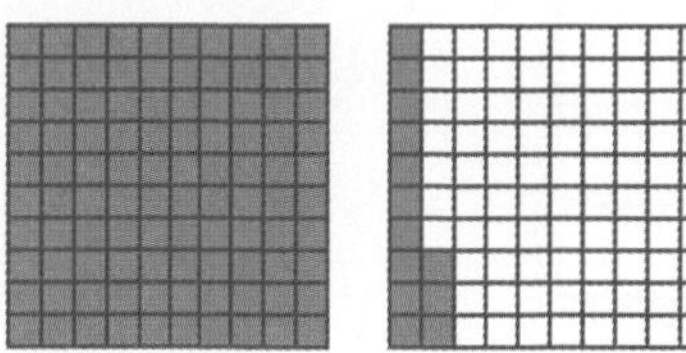

2. 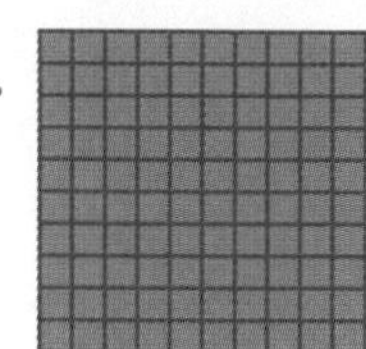

Write each as a decimal. (pages 568–569)

3. $6\frac{3}{10}$ 4. $1\frac{57}{100}$ 5. $14\frac{5}{100}$ 6. $9\frac{77}{1,000}$ 7. $8\frac{452}{1,000}$ 8. $6\frac{9}{1,000}$

Compare. Write >, <, or =. (pages 570–573)

9. 4.50 ● 0.45 10. 0.37 ● 0.370 11. 5.12 ● 5.1 12. 1.73 ● 1.63

Write in order from greatest to least. (pages 570–573)

13. 0.47, 4.70, 0.48 14. 16.03, 16.30, 16.06 15. 62.8, 62.4, 63.0

Round to the nearest tenth. (pages 576–577)

16. 13.90 17. 6.17 18. 45.89 19. 6.45 20. 19.19 21. 8.27

Solve. (pages 568–577)

22. The weather bureau in Jackson, Mississippi, records the amount of snowfall each year. These numbers are the inches of snowfall for the last five years: 4.8, 3.9, 3.7, 4.2, 5.1. List the amounts of snowfall from greatest to least.

23. Jamie lives 5.2 kilometers north of the city center. Chen lives 6.7 kilometers south of Jamie. Kara lives 4.4 kilometers north of Chen. Who lives the closest to the city center?

24. Samantha lives 15.74 miles from the city fairgrounds. What is this distance rounded to the nearest whole number?

25. **Explain** how you would put these decimals in order from least to greatest: 5.72, 5.73, 6.75, 6.62.

Additional activities at
www.mhschool.com/math

Extra Practice

Tenths and Hundredths (pages 560–561)

Write a fraction in its simplest form and a decimal for each shaded part.

1. 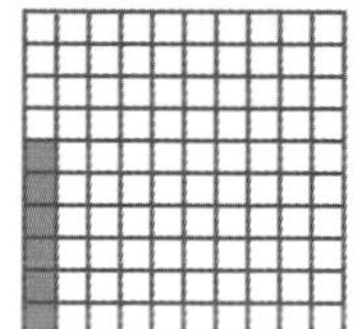

2. 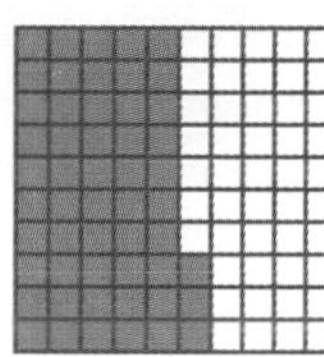

3. 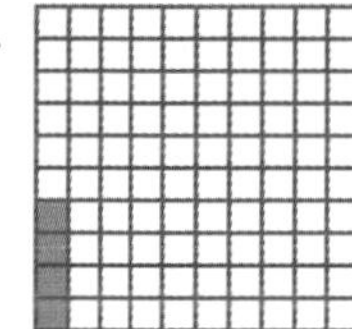

4. 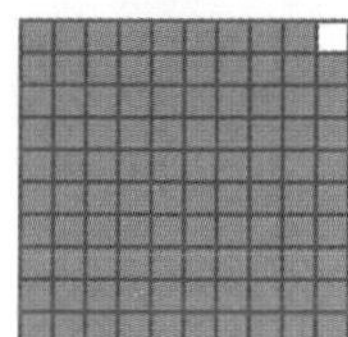

Write each as a decimal.

5. $\frac{4}{5}$
6. $\frac{19}{100}$
7. $\frac{75}{100}$
8. one tenth
9. eight hundredths

Solve.

10. Nineteen out of 100 cities surveyed have art centers. Write a decimal to show how many cities have art centers.
11. If twenty-three students spend $201.25 on ballet tickets, how much does one ticket cost?

Thousandths (pages 562–563)

Write each as a decimal.

1. $\frac{5}{1,000}$
2. $\frac{24}{1,000}$
3. $\frac{50}{1,000}$
4. $\frac{3}{1,000}$
5. four-hundred one thousandths

Solve.

6. In a one thousand person baseball survey, one hundred twenty people chose the Angels as their favorite team. Write a decimal to show how many chose the Angels.

Problem Solving: Reading for Math Choose a Representation (pages 564–565)

Solve.

1. Out of 100 subway riders, $\frac{3}{10}$ were under the age of 18. And 0.25 were over 65. Which age group had more people?
2. In a group of 48 subway riders, 0.75 of them wore sneakers. Is it correct to say over $\frac{7}{8}$ of the people wore sneakers? Explain.

Extra Practice

Decimals Greater Than 1 (pages 568–569)

Write a mixed number and a decimal to tell how much is shaded.

1. 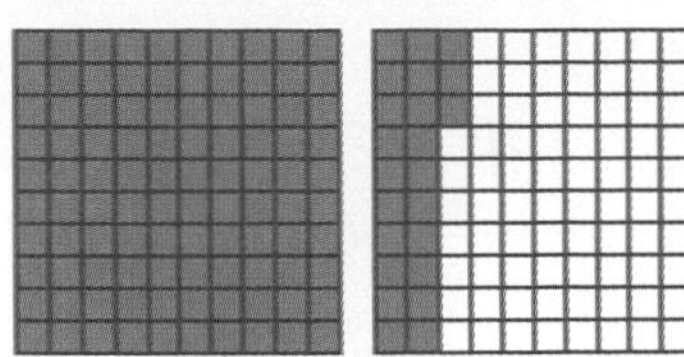

2. 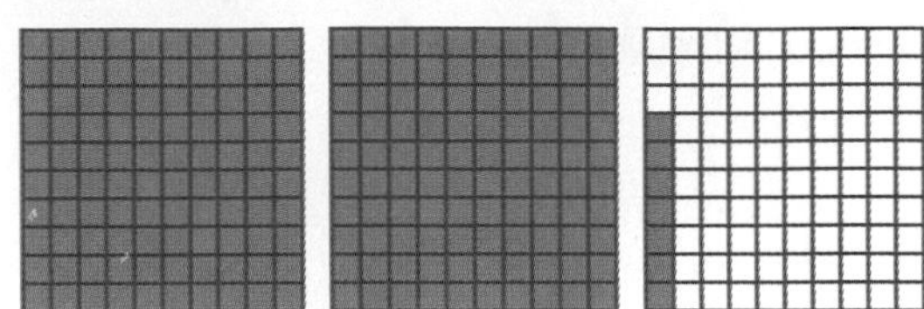

Write each as a decimal.

3. $9\frac{3}{4}$
4. $6\frac{34}{100}$
5. $5\frac{7}{10}$
6. $9\frac{472}{1,000}$
7. $16\frac{3}{100}$
8. $3\frac{89}{1,000}$
9. $4\frac{28}{100}$
10. $78\frac{2}{5}$
11. $3\frac{97}{1,000}$
12. $50\frac{123}{1,000}$
13. eighty-five and four thousandths
14. fifty-two and fifty-two hundredths

Solve.

15. Stamps come in sheets of 100. A post office worker has 8 sheets and $\frac{45}{100}$ of another sheet. Write a decimal to show how many sheets of stamps there are.

16. Roy is second at bat. Jane is after Roy, but before Bob. Paula is after Bob and Jose is before Roy. What is the batting order?

Compare and Order Decimals (pages 570–573)

Compare. Write >, <, or =.

1. 0.06 ● 0.60
2. 14.56 ● 14.55
3. 0.30 ● 0.3
4. 5.34 ● 5.55
5. 13.09 ● 13.03
6. 6.090 ● 6.90
7. 3.37 ● 3.73
8. 45.38 ● 45.35

Write in order from greatest to least.

9. 6.71, 6.07, 6.61
10. 0.40, 0.04, 0.44
11. 15.5, 15.55, 15.05

Write in order from least to greatest.

12. 3.48, 3.50, 3.08
13. 14.3, 14.4, 13.4
14. 3.5, 3.05, 3.59

Solve.

15. Normal annual precipitation for Charleston, South Carolina, is 53.51 inches each year. Write a decimal that is greater than and a decimal that is less than 53.51.

Extra Practice

Problem Solving Strategy: Draw a Diagram (pages 574–575)

Solve.

1. **Logical Reasoning:** In a city, a fruit stand is between a hot dog stand and a vegetable stand. A newspaper stand is the farthest to the left. The vegetable stand is next to the newspaper stand. Tell how the four stands are lined up from left to right.

2. A construction worker works from 6:15 A.M. until 2:15 P.M. She gets 45 minutes for lunch and two 10-minute breaks. She then works an additional $2\frac{1}{2}$ hours. How long does she work altogether?

3. Lyn lives 4.5 city blocks north of the subway station. Ming lives 4.2 city blocks east of the subway station. Jackson lives 2 city blocks east of Barry who lives 3 city blocks east of the subway station. Who lives the closest to the subway station? the farthest?

4. A rectangular city park is 1,400 square feet. If the longer sides each measure 40 feet, then what is the length of each of the shorter sides?

5. On Sunday 278 newspapers were sold for $1.75 each. On Monday a newsstand sold 418 papers for $0.50 each. How much more money did the newsstand get for papers sold on Sunday than Monday?

Round decimals (pages 576–577)

Round to the nearest whole number.

1. 6.38 2. 14.09 3. 27.47 4. 9.69 5. 55.61 6. 4.78

Round to the nearest tenth.

7. 69.56 8. 13.05 9. 29.99 10. 7.44 11. 11.36 12. 10.53

Round to the nearest hundredth.

13. 7.097 14. 5.478 15. 2.905 16. 6.588 17. 47.006 18. 82.045

Solve.

19. Brett has 17 quarters. How much money does he have rounded to the nearest dollar? to the nearest ten cents?

Chapter Study Guide

Language and Math

Math Words

decimal point
decimal
equivalent decimals

Complete. Use a word from the list.

1. The . in the number 3.45 is called a ______.
2. The number 85.006 is called a ______.

Identify fraction and decimal equivalents. (pages 558–559)

Example

Write a fraction and a decimal for each shaded part. Then write the fraction in simplest form.

Solution

Think: $\frac{50}{100}$

Decimal: 0.50

Simplify: $\frac{50}{100} = \frac{1}{2}$

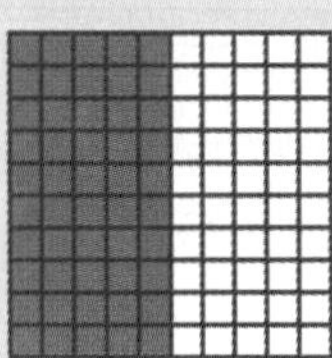

Write each as a decimal.

3. $\frac{3}{4}$
4. $\frac{1}{4}$
5. $\frac{2}{8}$
6. $\frac{5}{10}$
7. $\frac{6}{8}$
8. $\frac{2}{4}$
9. Felicia measures $1\frac{3}{4}$ cups of melon and $2\frac{5}{10}$ cups of strawberries for a fruit salad. Write two decimals to show how much fruit she put into the salad.

Read and write decimals to thousandths. (pages 560–563)

Example

Write the shaded part as a decimal.

Solution

Count the number of shaded squares out of 100.

Think: $\frac{42}{100}$

Write: 0.42

Write each as a decimal.

10. $\frac{2}{10}$
11. $\frac{10}{100}$
12. $\frac{53}{100}$
13. $\frac{6}{1,000}$
14. $\frac{72}{1,000}$
15. $4\frac{15}{1,000}$
16. $6\frac{7}{10}$
17. $5\frac{78}{1,000}$
18. $100\frac{60}{1,000}$

Compare, order, and round decimals. (pages 570–573, 576–577)

Example

Put 3.65, 3.67, and 4.68 in order from greatest to least.

Solution

Step 1 Line up the decimal points. Compare each place.

3.65

3.67

4.68

4.68 is the greatest

Step 2

3.65

3.67

3.67 > 3.65

So the order from greatest to least is 4.68, 3.67, 3.65.

Compare. Write >, <, or =.

19. 1.25 ● 1.29 **20.** 2.80 ● 2.8

21. 0.077 ● 0.007 **22.** 0.33 ● 0.03

Write in order from least to greatest.

23. 1.17, 1.07, 1.27 **24.** 5.4, 5.9, 4.8

Round to the nearest tenth.

25. 4.57 **26.** 5.08 **27.** 12.62

Round to the nearest hundredth.

28. 4.038 **29.** 10.989 **30.** 8.005

31. The average annual rainfall in City A is 13.79 inches, in City B it is 13.92 inches, and in City C it is 13.97 inches. Which city has the most rainfall? the least?

Use strategies to solve problems. (pages 564–565, 574–575)

Example

Nikki lives 3.5 miles to the west of the city museum. Juan lives 2.7 miles to the east of the museum. Jessie lives 1 mile north of the train station which is 2 miles north of the museum. Who lives the farthest away?

Solution

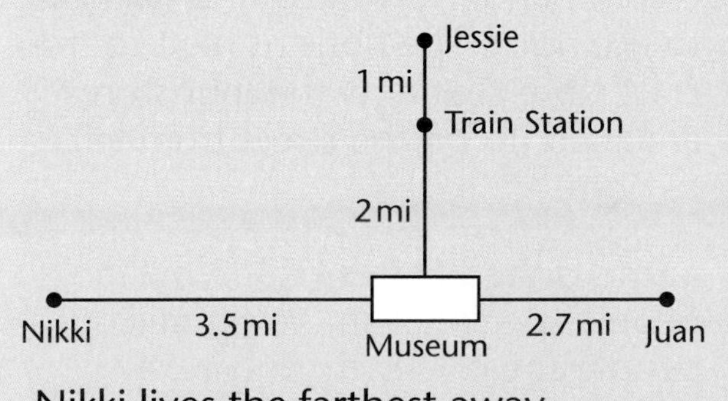

Nikki lives the farthest away.

Solve.

32. A playground covers $\frac{3}{10}$ of a park. A garden covers 0.40 of the park. Which is larger, the playground or the garden?

33. A train station is 2.5 city blocks north of the subway station. The bus station is 2.9 city blocks south of the subway station. Molly lives 1 block south of the subway station. Is she closer to the train station or the bus station?

Chapter Test

Write a fraction and a decimal for each shaded part.

1. 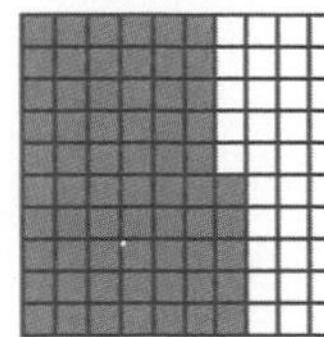

2. 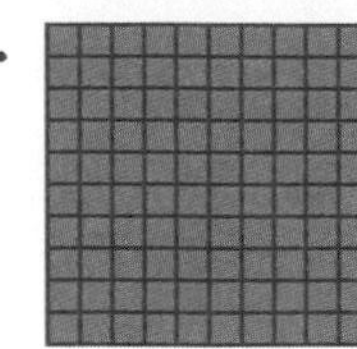 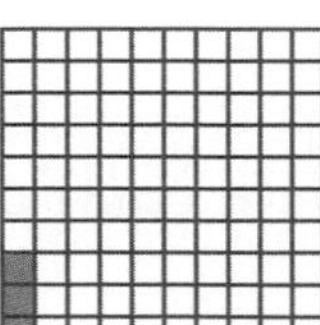

Write each as a decimal.

3. $\frac{5}{10}$

4. $\frac{7}{100}$

5. $\frac{48}{100}$

6. $\frac{80}{100}$

7. $\frac{567}{1,000}$

8. $9\frac{82}{100}$

9. $7\frac{6}{10}$

Compare. Write >, < or =.

10. 0.75 ● 1.7

11. 1.67 ● 1.09

12. 4.1 ● 3.979

Write in order from greatest to least.

13. 9.97, 0.97, 9.79

14. 0.12, 0.21, 2.01

Round to the nearest tenth.

15. 5.77

16. 0.32

17. 66.09

18. 4.12

Round to the nearest hundredth.

19. 0.678

20. 5.008

21. 7.092

Solve.

22. Nico traveled 32.8 kilometers from Portsmith to Truro. From Truro he traveled 33.1 kilometers to Pearl River. From Pearl River he traveled 33.9 kilometers to Bennington. Between which two cities did he travel the greatest distance?

23. A city business district has four stores in a row on one block. The stationery store is between a florist and an ice cream parlor. A craft store is farthest to the right. The florist is next to the craft store. Tell how the four stores are lined up on the street from left to right.

24. A concert stand takes up 0.5 of the Arts Center. Cheryl says that the concert stand takes up one half of the Arts Center. Is this reasonable?

25. In the United States, 1.309 million people speak Italian, 1.709 million people speak French, and 1.547 million people speak German. Which language is spoken the most? the least?

Performance Assessment

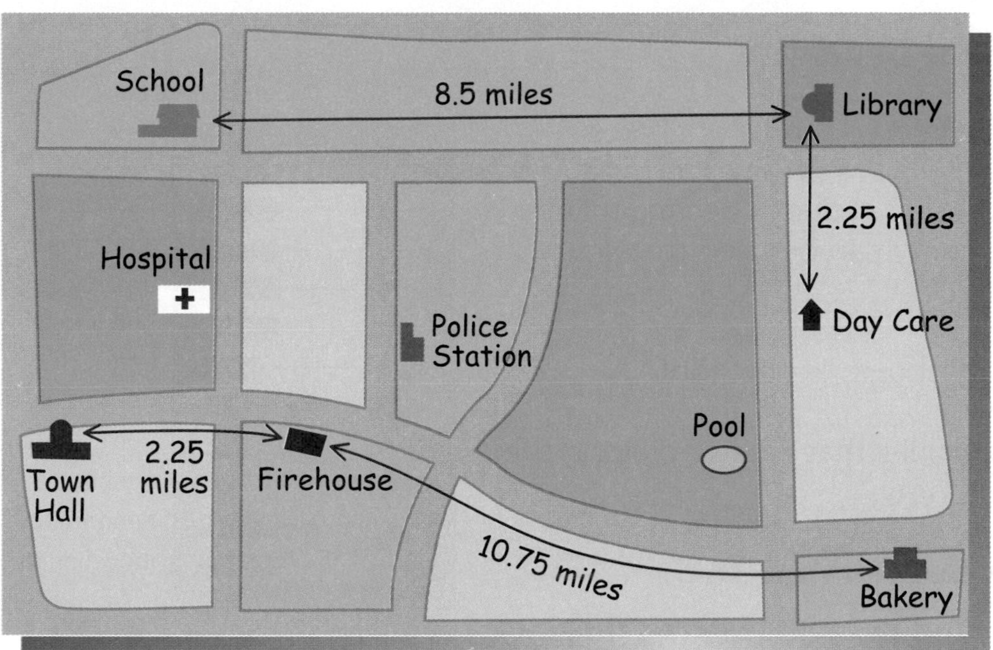

You have the chance to design a whole new city! You will need to sketch a map of the city that includes at least 10 locations.

- Mark the distances between locations with decimal numbers.
- After your map is complete, write 5 different sentences that compare the distances between sets of 2 locations on the map. Use "less than" (<) or "greater than" (>) wording.

A Good Answer

- shows a clearly marked map with at least 10 different locations labeled.
- shows that you used decimals to describe the distances between locations on your map.
- shows the correct use of "<" and ">" signs when comparing decimal numbers.

You may want to save this work in your portfolio.

Enrichment

Russian Abacus

Russian people have used a type of abacus called a *schoty* (SHOH-tee). A salesperson can use one because it includes decimal places. This means the schoty can be used to calculate money amounts.

Look at the schoty shown at the right.

Notice the place values that are listed along the right side of the schoty.

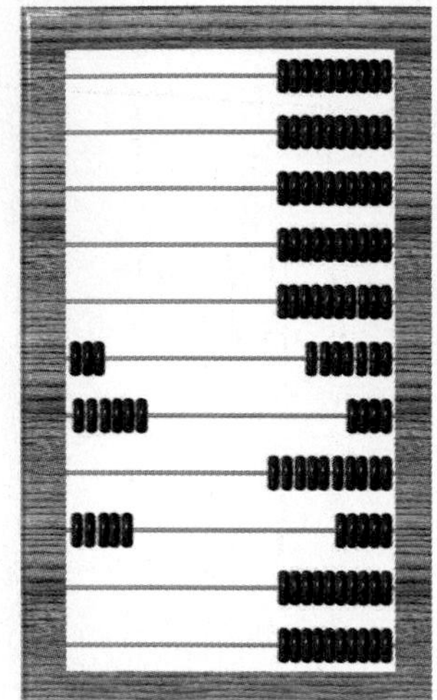

This schoty shows the number 36.5.

1. Explain how the positions of the beads show this number.

Write the number shown by each abacus.

2. 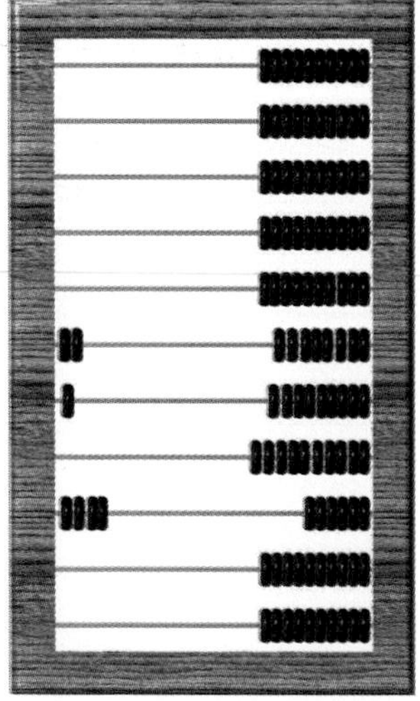

3. 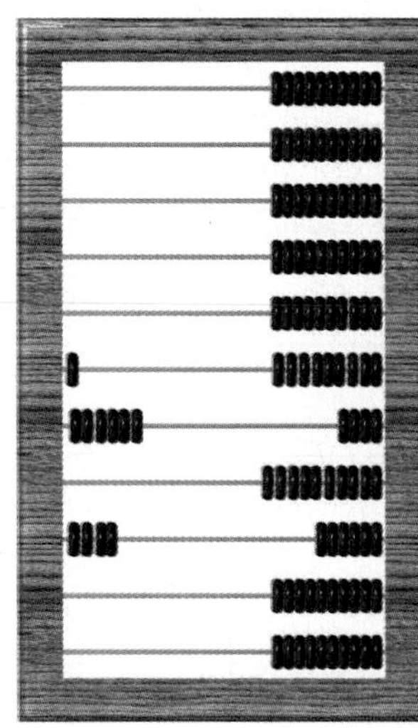

4. 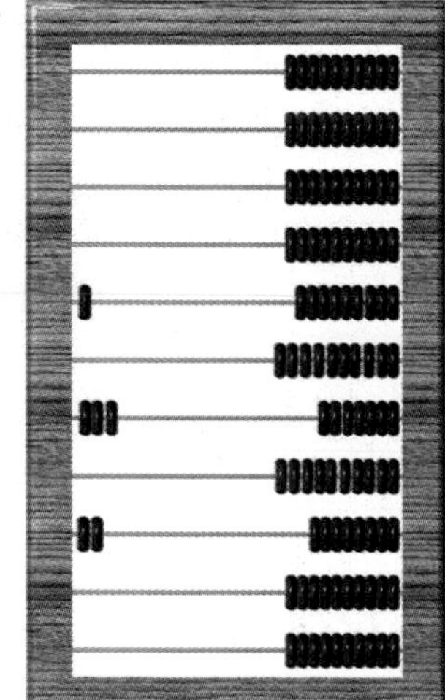

Draw a schoty to show each number.

5. 22.2
6. 46.1
7. 50
8. 123
9. 1,325

Test-Taking Tips

With a multistep problem you need to use several steps to solve the problem.

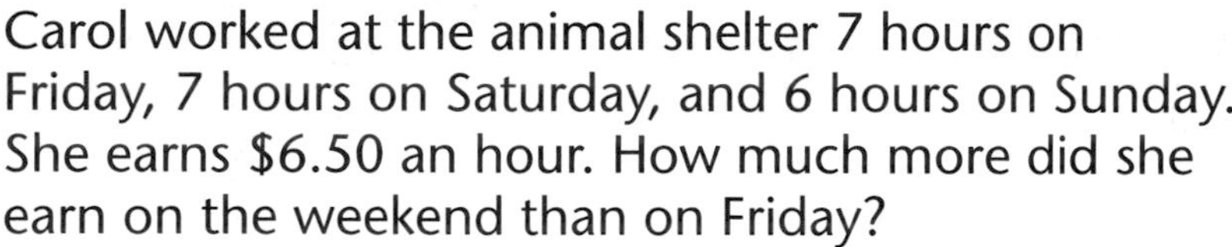

Carol worked at the animal shelter 7 hours on Friday, 7 hours on Saturday, and 6 hours on Sunday. She earns \$6.50 an hour. How much more did she earn on the weekend than on Friday?

A. \$45.50 **C.** \$26.00
B. \$39.00 **D.** \$6.50

First, find the total number of hours that Carol worked on the weekend.
$7 + 6 = 13$ hours

Then subtract to find how many more hours she worked on the weekend.
$13 - 7 = 6$

Finally, multiply to find how much more he earned.
$\$6.50 \times 6 = \$39.00$

The correct choice is B.

Check for Success

- ☑ I understood and answered the questions asked.
- ☑ I checked my work for errors.
- ☑ My answers make sense.

Read each problem carefully. Then choose the correct answer.

1. Carl can buy sports socks in packages of 4 pairs for \$8.60 or 2 pairs for \$4.48. How much can he save if he buys 8 pairs of the better buy?
   A. \$17.20 **C.** \$2.15
   B. \$2.24 **D.** \$0.72

2. Ann and Allison order french fries for \$1.97, onion rings for \$2.19, and two glasses of juice for \$0.90 each. The tax and tip is \$2.20. How much change should they get from a twenty-dollar bill?
   F. \$7.26 **H.** \$11.84
   G. \$8.16 **J.** \$12.84

3. Marcie, Cathy, and Dot each pay \$5.25 for a movie ticket, \$2.45 for popcorn, and \$1.29 for soda. How much do they pay altogether?
   A. \$26.97 **C.** \$12.60
   B. \$15.75 **D.** \$8.99

4. Of the 48 students in a class, $\frac{1}{6}$ of them have brown eyes, $\frac{1}{3}$ blue eyes, and the rest have green eyes. How many students have green eyes?
   F. 8 **H.** 20
   G. 12 **J.** 24

Spiral Review and Test Prep

Chapters 1–13

Choose the correct answer.

Number Sense

1. The population of Greentree City was 289,815 in 1990. Ten years later, the population was 295,041. What is the difference in population over the 10-year period?

   A. 4,226 **C.** 5,226
   B. 4,326 **D.** 5,336

2. Write six hundred thirty-seven thousandths as a decimal.

   F. 6.37 **H.** 0.637
   G. 637 **J.** Not Here

3. Which decimal is greater than the one shown?

   A. 0.045 **C.** 1.42
   B. 0.089 **D.** 1.57

4. Becka is making a birdhouse. She cuts a piece of wood that is $7\frac{3}{8}$ inches long and another piece of wood that is $4\frac{1}{2}$ inches long. How much wood does she cut?

   F. $11\frac{7}{8}$ inches **H.** $11\frac{4}{10}$ inches
   G. $11\frac{3}{8}$ inches **J.** $3\frac{1}{4}$ inches

Measurement and Geometry

5. A city parking lot is shaped like a square. One side is 36 feet long. What is the perimeter of the parking lot?

   A. 72 feet **C.** 1,296 sq. feet
   B. 144 feet **D.** Not Here

6. Which is the greatest measurement?

   F. 0.5 kilometer **H.** 0.5 decimeter
   G. 0.5 meter **J.** 0.5 centimeter

7. Find the area of the shaded part of the figure.

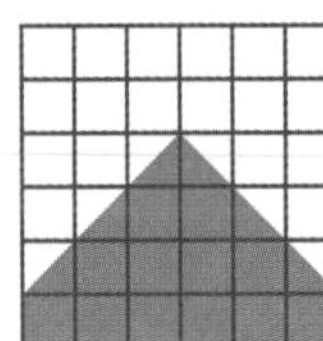

   A. 5 square units **C.** 15 square units
   B. 13 square units **D.** 36 square units

8. Name the figure.

   F. Parallelogram **H.** Trapezoid
   G. Rhombus **J.** Rectangle

Statistics, Data Analysis, and Probability

Use data from the chart for problems 9–10.

Average Daily Temperature in June	
Sea Bright	76.9°
Inlet Beach	76.2°
Belle Harbor	74.8°
Rock Point	77.1°

9. Which city has the lowest daily temperature for June?
   A. Sea Bright C. Inlet Beach
   B. Belle Harbor D. Rock Point

10. What is the order of the towns from greatest to least temperature?
    F. Rock Point, Sea Bright, Inlet Beach, Belle Harbor
    G. Sea Bright, Inlet Beach, Rock Point, Belle Harbor
    H. Rock Point, Sea Bright, Belle Harbor, Inlet Beach
    J. Belle Harbor, Inlet Beach, Sea Bright, Rock Point

Use data from the picture for problems 11–12.

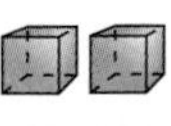

11. What is the likelihood of picking a blue cube from the bag?
    A. Certain C. Unlikely
    B. Likely D. Impossible

12. Explain how you can find the probability of picking a green cube from the bag.

Mathematical Reasoning

13. Adam bought a bag of apples. He gave 5 to his grandmother, ate 1, and lost 1. He has 6 apples left. How many were in the bag to start with?
    A. 7 C. 11
    B. 8 D. 13

14. Ms. Daley wants to catch the 12:20 P.M. train to the city. It takes her 20 minutes to walk to the train station. On the way, she wants to stop for 35 minutes to have lunch with a friend. What time should she leave in order to ride the train?
    F. 11:25 A.M. H. 12:00 P.M.
    G. 11:25 P.M. J. 11:15 A.M.

15. The city zoo has 936 visitors in one day. There are twice as many children as there are adults. How many children go to the zoo that day?
    A. 936 C. 468
    B. 624 D. 312

16. Keiko's house is 6.3 miles north of the city monument. Lisa's house is 7.6 miles south of Keiko's house. Billy's house is 3.8 miles north of Lisa's house. Chad's house is 7.3 miles south of Billy's house. Who lives closest to the city monument?
    F. Keiko H. Lisa
    G. Chad J. Billy

CHAPTER 14 Decimal Operations

Theme: Planes, Trains, and Automobiles

Use the Data

Fastest Trains

Train	Miles per Hour
Nozomi/MLX01, Japan	345.6
TGV, France	311.9
ICE, Germany	255.3
X2000, Sweden	172.8

- Each of the numbers in the chart shows a decimal. How can you use the information in the chart to tell how much faster one train travels than another?

What You Will Learn

In this chapter you will learn how to
- add and subtract decimals to thousandths.
- use properties to find sums and differences.
- estimate decimal sums and differences.
- use strategies to solve problems.

Objective: Use models to add decimals.

14·1 Explore Adding Decimals

Learn

You can use 10-by-10 grids to explore adding decimals. What is 1.5 + 0.35?

You Will Need
- **centimeter graph paper**
- **red crayons, markers, or pencils**
- **blue crayons, markers, or pencils**

Work Together

▶ *Use 10-by-10 grids to find the exact decimal sum.*

- Draw 10-by-10 grids on graph paper.
- Show 1.5 by coloring grids in red.
- Show 0.35 by coloring the remaining part in blue.

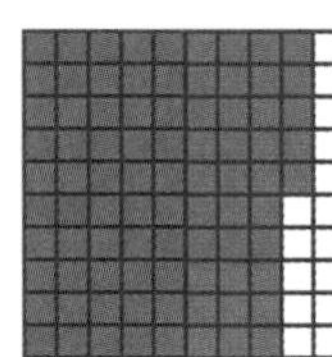

- Count how many grids are completely shaded.
- Count how many rows in the second grid are completely shaded.
- Then count how many squares in the incompletely shaded row are shaded.
- Write a decimal to show the total number of shaded squares. Record your work.
- Answer the question above.

▶ *Use grids to find each sum.*

0.72 + 0.14   2.3 + 1.47   1.42 + 0.3   0.87 + 0.34   1.6 + 0.7

Make Connections

Here is how you can add 1.17 + 1.38.

Using Models

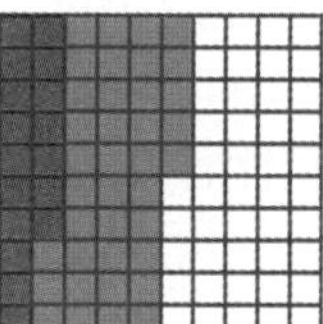

Using Paper and Pencil

Add each place. Regroup if needed.

$$\begin{array}{r} 1.17 \\ +1.38 \\ \hline 2.55 \end{array}$$

Try It

Find each sum. You may wish to use models.

1. $\begin{array}{r} 0.3 \\ +0.6 \\ \hline \end{array}$
2. $\begin{array}{r} 3.38 \\ +0.34 \\ \hline \end{array}$
3. $\begin{array}{r} 2.07 \\ +1.45 \\ \hline \end{array}$
4. $\begin{array}{r} 1.83 \\ +1.52 \\ \hline \end{array}$
5. $\begin{array}{r} 0.4 \\ +0.9 \\ \hline \end{array}$
6. $\begin{array}{r} 4.29 \\ +0.85 \\ \hline \end{array}$
7. $\begin{array}{r} 3.18 \\ +2.56 \\ \hline \end{array}$
8. $\begin{array}{r} 7.06 \\ +4.96 \\ \hline \end{array}$
9. 0.41 + 0.45
10. 1.25 + 0.5
11. 1.3 + 1.49
12. 0.8 + 1.63

How could you use models to add 1.56 + 0.6?

Practice

Find each sum.

13. $\begin{array}{r} 1.8 \\ +2.6 \\ \hline \end{array}$
14. $\begin{array}{r} 7.3 \\ +1.4 \\ \hline \end{array}$
15. $\begin{array}{r} 6.45 \\ +0.82 \\ \hline \end{array}$
16. $\begin{array}{r} 2.49 \\ +5.30 \\ \hline \end{array}$
17. $\begin{array}{r} 0.48 \\ +0.67 \\ \hline \end{array}$
18. $\begin{array}{r} 3.47 \\ +0.96 \\ \hline \end{array}$
19. $\begin{array}{r} 8.68 \\ +1.52 \\ \hline \end{array}$
20. $\begin{array}{r} 5.67 \\ +2.23 \\ \hline \end{array}$
21. 1.3 + 1.8
22. 0.4 + 0.9
23. 2.15 + 1.04
24. 2.5 + 0.42
25. 0.9 + 0.06
26. 0.75 + 0.15
27. 1.13 + 0.58
28. 1.4 + 1.45
29. 1.6 + 1.25
30. 1.42 + 0.37
31. 0.5 + 1.96
32. 2.12 + 0.96
33. **Generalize:** When do you need to regroup when adding tenths? hundredths?

Objective: Add decimals.

14-2 Add Decimals

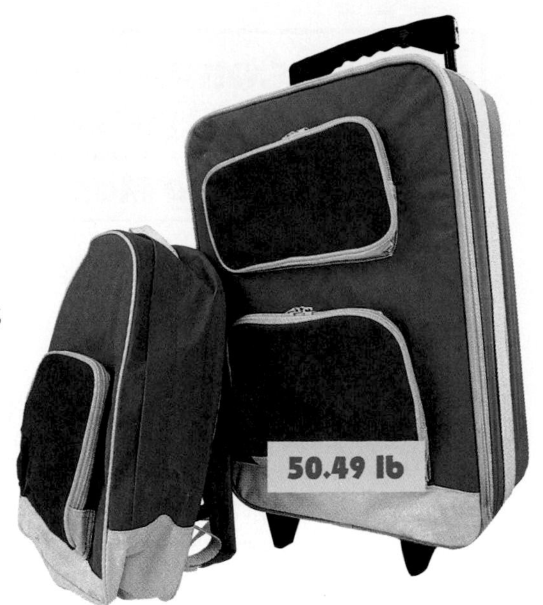

Learn

Luis is traveling by plane to visit his grandmother. He has two bags to check in at the airport counter. One bag weighs 24.67 pounds. Another bag sits on the scale to be weighed. How much do the bags weigh in all?

Example 1

Find 24.67 + 50.49 to solve.

Adding decimals is like adding whole numbers.

Whole Numbers

$$\begin{array}{r} {}^{1\,1} \\ 2467 \\ +5049 \\ \hline 7516 \end{array}$$

Decimals

$$\begin{array}{r} {}^{1\,\,\,1} \\ 24.67 \\ +50.49 \\ \hline 75.16 \end{array}$$

Write the decimal point in the sum.

1 *Line up the decimal points.*

$$\begin{array}{r} 24.67 \\ +50.49 \\ \hline \end{array}$$

2 *Add each place. Regroup if needed. Write the decimal point.*

$$\begin{array}{r} {}^{1\,\,\,1} \\ 24.67 \\ +50.49 \\ \hline 75.16 \end{array}$$

The bags weigh 75.16 pounds in all.

More Examples

A

$$\begin{array}{r} 15.9 \\ +\ 1.3 \\ \hline 17.2 \end{array}$$

B

$$\begin{array}{r} 12.782 \\ +73.038 \\ \hline 85.820 \end{array}$$

Luis sends three packages home. One package weighs 0.9 pound. The second package weighs 2.57 pounds. The third package weighs 3.52 pounds. How many pounds do the packages weigh in all?

Example 2

Find 0.9 + 2.57 + 3.52 to solve.

1 Line up the decimal points. Add zeros if necessary.

```
  2.57
  0.90
 +3.52
```

2 Add as you would with whole numbers. Write the decimal point in the sum.

```
  1
  2.57
  0.90
 +3.52
 -----
  6.99
```

Think: Look for doubles or make a ten to make it easier to add.

The packages weigh 6.99 pounds.

More Examples

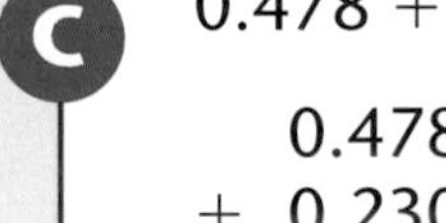

C 0.478 + 0.23

```
    0.478
 +  0.230
 --------
    0.708
```

D 52.6 + 0.832

```
   52.600
 +  0.832
 --------
   53.432
```

Try It

Add.

1. 0.36 + 0.46
2. 6.33 + 0.40
3. 7.09 + 1.62
4. 51.40 + 5.89
5. 8.891 + 2.572 + 3.210
6. 30.63 + 4.60
7. 73.08 + 20.34
8. 32.078 + 1.453
9. 100.15 + 7.92
10. 516.833 + 41.920
11. 7.2 + 8.4 + 0.09
12. 4.510 + 5.6
13. 30.16 + 5.71

Why is it important to line up the decimal points before you add?

Practice Add.

14. $\begin{array}{r} 0.47 \\ +0.79 \\ \hline \end{array}$

15. $\begin{array}{r} 2.07 \\ +4.91 \\ \hline \end{array}$

16. $\begin{array}{r} 5.79 \\ +3.60 \\ \hline \end{array}$

17. $\begin{array}{r} 18.44 \\ +\ 8.59 \\ \hline \end{array}$

18. $\begin{array}{r} 45.909 \\ +\ 3.622 \\ \hline \end{array}$

19. $\begin{array}{r} 6.7 \\ +3.4 \\ \hline \end{array}$

20. $\begin{array}{r} 4.052 \\ +0.560 \\ \hline \end{array}$

21. $\begin{array}{r} 13.990 \\ +\ 0.067 \\ \hline \end{array}$

22. $\begin{array}{r} 0.79 \\ +0.80 \\ \hline \end{array}$

23. $\begin{array}{r} 0.078 \\ +0.600 \\ \hline \end{array}$

24. $\begin{array}{r} 26.27 \\ 0.47 \\ +\ 2.89 \\ \hline \end{array}$

25. $\begin{array}{r} 4.718 \\ 5.200 \\ +3.989 \\ \hline \end{array}$

26. $\begin{array}{r} 4.5 \\ 23.6 \\ +56.9 \\ \hline \end{array}$

27. $\begin{array}{r} 3.086 \\ 9.007 \\ +0.567 \\ \hline \end{array}$

28. $\begin{array}{r} 0.780 \\ 0.451 \\ +4.225 \\ \hline \end{array}$

29. 4.3 + 9.7
30. 5.78 + 9.672
31. 7.3 + 0.745
32. 3.82 + 0.041

33. 0.67 + 0.583 + 2.3
★34. 13.5739 + 5.6
★35. 0.0076 + 6.9784

Algebra & functions Find the number you need to add to complete the pattern.

36. 1.5, 2.0, 2.5, ■, ■, ■
37. 0.25, 0.55, ■, ■, ■, 1.75
38. 0.09, 1.19, ■, ■, 4.49, ■
39. 3.95, 3.955, ■, 3.965, ■, ■

40.

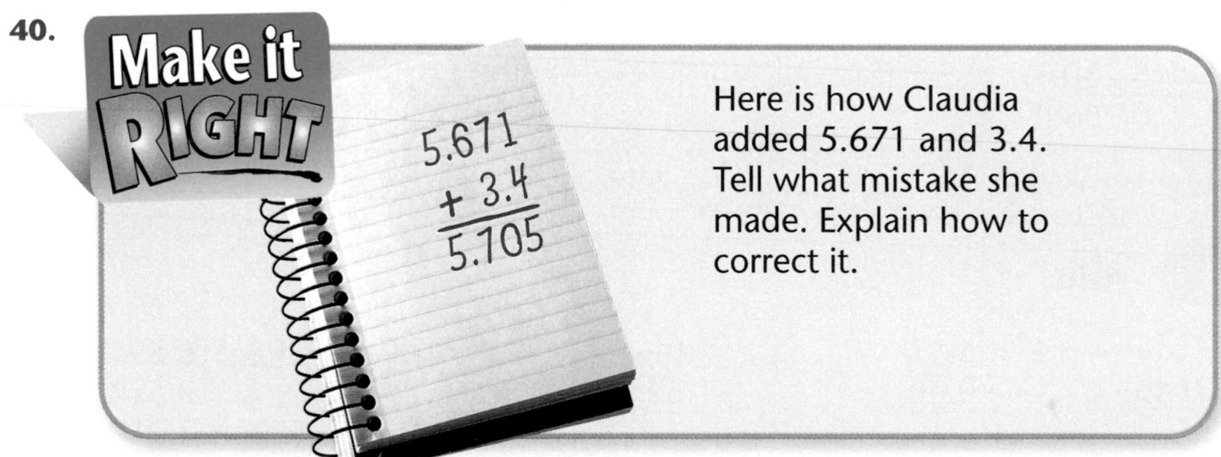

Here is how Claudia added 5.671 and 3.4. Tell what mistake she made. Explain how to correct it.

Problem Solving

41. An airline charges $2.35 for each pound of overweight baggage. Mac's luggage is 13 pounds overweight. How much does he pay in overweight charges?

42. **Measurement:** An airport is shaped like a pentagon that measures 2,075 yards around. All of the sides of the airport measure 375 yards except one. How long is the unequal side?

Use data from *Did You Know?* for problem 43.

43. **Science:** Sound travels through air at a speed of about 335.38 meters per second. How fast does the Concorde fly?

44. **Time:** Melissa is catching a 3:05 P.M. plane to Chicago. The flight is 2 hours 15 minutes long. At Chicago she will need 35 minutes to change planes. The second half of the trip is 3 hours 55 minutes. What time will she arrive at her destination?

45. Suppose you traveled the 24,902 miles around Earth's equator. About how many miles would you need to travel in one day if you made the trip in 80 days?

Use data from the chart for problems 46–47.

46. How much would it cost to send a 6-pound package and a 1-pound package?

★47. Marcel sends two 4-pound packages and one 2-pound package by Air Freight. How much change should she get if she gives the clerk two twenty-dollar bills?

Air Freight Overnight Delivery	
1 lb - 2 lb	$9.95
3 lb - 5 lb	$10.75
6 lb - 10 lb	$13.50
11 lb - 50 lb	$25.95

48. **Explain** how you can use compensation to add 3.9 and 1.2 mentally.

49. **Create a problem** adding decimals. Solve it. Ask others to solve it.

Spiral Review and Test Prep

Round to the nearest tenth.

50. 15.07 51. 41.63 52. 42.51 53. 8.46 54. 9.09 55. 57.75

Choose the correct answer.

56. Matt has $75.63 in his bank account. How much does he have rounded to the nearest dollar?
A. $75 C. $75.60
B. $76 D. $76.50

57. Len has $45.17, Mark has $45.29, Jill has $43.95, and Gina has $43.35. Who has the most money?
F. Len H. Mark
G. Jill J. Gina

Objective: Estimate sums.

14-3 Estimate Sums

An odometer measures distance to the nearest tenth of a mile.

Learn

An odometer is an instrument in a car that measures the number of miles a car has traveled. Kyle traveled 17.7 miles to go to the store, then another 13.4 miles to visit a friend. About how many miles did he travel?

Example

Estimate 17.7 + 13.4 to solve.

To estimate, round each addend to the nearest whole number.

17.7	+	13.4		
↓		↓		
18	+	13	=	31

Think: $7 > 5$ Round up.

Think: $4 < 5$ Round down.

Kyle traveled about 31 miles.

More Examples

A

6.59 + 4.01
↓ ↓
7 + 4 = 11

B

27.3 + 4.61
↓ ↓
27 + 5 = 32

C

\$5.67 + \$8.24
↓ ↓
\$6 + \$8 = \$14

Try It

Estimate. Round to the nearest whole number.

1. 5.7 + 4.1 **2.** 8.9 + 3.5 **3.** 6.2 + 5.1

4. 7.81 + 4.94 + 6.25 **5.** 1.24 + 0.98 + 1.78

How is estimating sums with decimals similar to estimating sums with money? How is it different?

Practice

Estimate. Round to the nearest whole number.

6. 7.3 + 8.3
7. 9.76 + 4.25
8. 8.5 + 13.7
9. 14.84 + 13.94
10. 24.5 + 18.4
11. $16.07 + $11.25
12. 9.97 + 10.55
13. 42.8 + 7.5

Add. Check your answers.

14. $7.45 + $3.97
15. 15.40 + 9.89
16. $9.95 + $9.22
17. 65.8 + 34.4
18. 4.5 + 3.7 + 2.8
19. 5.67 + 8.44 + 2.99
20. $1.55 + $4.66 + $2.88
21. 4.1 + 4.7 + 0.8

★22. 3.718 + 4.552 + 3.077

★23. 5.008 + 6.537 + 8.199

Algebra & functions **Compare. Use > or <.**

24. 3.6 + 3.7 ● 7.1 + 2.2
25. 6.1 + 2.1 ● 3.6 + 7.7
26. 5.2 + 5.1 ● 5.1 + 4.2

Problem Solving

Use data from the mileage chart for problems 26–28.

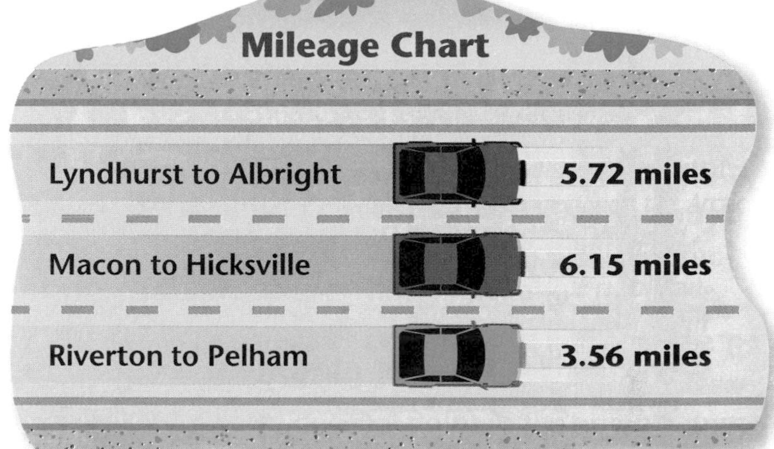

27. Marta travels from Lyndhurst to Albright, then she drives another 5.13 miles to Macon. About how many miles does she drive in all?
28. Between which two towns is the greatest distance?
29. **Create a problem** using the data from the mileage chart. Solve it. Ask others to solve it.
30. **Analyze:** Is 0.368 + 0.421 greater than 0.7? How can you tell?

Spiral Review and Test Prep

Write the number that makes each sentence true.

31. 40 dm = ▮ cm
32. 5,000 mL = ▮ L
33. 6 m = ▮ dm
34. 72 kg = ▮ g
35. 70 cm = ▮ mm
36. 1.5 kg = ▮ g

Choose the correct answer.

37. Which is $\frac{24}{80}$ in simplest form?
    A. $\frac{2}{5}$
    B. $\frac{3}{10}$
    C. $\frac{6}{20}$
    D. $\frac{12}{40}$
38. It is $^{-}2$°C outside. What activity are you most likely to do?
    F. Ice skate
    G. Rake leaves
    H. Hike
    J. Swim

Extra Practice, page 625

Objective: Make a judgment to decide the best operation to use.

14•4

Problem Solving: Reading for Math

Choose an Operation

Wheeling to Work!

Read Jeb rides his bicycle to work and back home again each work day. The distance from home to work is 3.25 miles. How long is the round trip?

READING SKILL ▶

Make a Judgment

When you make a judgment, you decide something. You use what you know and the information given in the problem.

- **What do you know?** Distance from home to work is 3.25 miles
- **What do you need to find?** Total distance from home to work and back again
- **What judgment is called for?** Which operation to use

MATH SKILL ▶

Choose the Operation

Understanding what the problem is asking you to find can help you decide which operation to use.

Plan You need to find the total distance Jeb travels. You can add.

Solve The distance from Jeb's home to work is 3.25 miles.

$3.25 + 3.25 = 6.5$ The round trip is 6.5 miles.

Look Back
- Is your answer reasonable?

How do you decide to add decimals to solve problems?

Practice **Solve. Tell how you chose the operation.**

1. Tia rides her bicycle to deliver newspapers. Last week, she rode a total of 8.2 miles. This week, she rode 2.15 miles more than last week. How far did Tia ride this week?

2. Bud is preparing for a cycling competition. Each day, he increases his distance by 1.15 mile. Yesterday, Bud rode for 5.25 miles. How far will Bud ride today?

Use data from the chart for problems 3–8.

3. How far will Clyde travel if he goes from the Post Office to the Medical Center and then to the Bank?

4. How would you order the distances from least to greatest?

5. Yesterday, Clyde rode from the Hospital to the Wilson Building to the Post Office. How far did he travel?

6. On a very busy day, Clyde rode his bicycle between each set of locations listed. How far did he travel?

7. As a messenger, Clyde rides his bicycle all over the city. Today he rode from the Medical Center to the Bank and then to the Hospital. How far did Clyde ride?

8. From Clyde's home to the Bank is 1.7 miles. Tomorrow he will ride from home to the Bank and then to the Medical Center. How far will he travel?

Delivery Distances	
Bank to Hospital	1.45 miles
Hospital to Wilson Building	2.7 miles
Medical Center to Post Office	4.35 miles
Medical Center to Bank	3.1 miles
Wilson Building to Post Office	1.8 miles

Spiral Review and Test Prep

Choose the correct answer.

Bo rode 3.45 miles from home to the mall. Then he rode 1.6 miles to a friend's house. How far did Bo ride?

9. Which statement is true?
   - **A.** Bo got a ride to the mall.
   - **B.** The distance from home to the mall is greater than the distance from the mall to Bo's friend's house.
   - **C.** Bo rode 1.6 miles to the mall.

10. Which number sentence can you use to solve the problem?
   - **F.** $3.45 - 1.6 = 1.85$
   - **G.** $1.45 + 3.0 = 4.45$
   - **H.** $3.45 + 1.6 = 5.05$

Check Your Progress A

Add. Check for reasonableness. **(pages 598–599)**

1. $\begin{array}{r} 0.27 \\ +0.53 \\ \hline \end{array}$

2. $\begin{array}{r} 4.22 \\ +0.90 \\ \hline \end{array}$

3. $\begin{array}{r} 5.03 \\ +1.58 \\ \hline \end{array}$

4. $\begin{array}{r} 26.405 \\ +\ 4.896 \\ \hline \end{array}$

5. $\begin{array}{r} 9.67 \\ +10.10 \\ \hline \end{array}$

6. $\begin{array}{r} 27.94 \\ 47.30 \\ +70.10 \\ \hline \end{array}$

7. $\begin{array}{r} \$2.85 \\ 6.09 \\ +\ 0.25 \\ \hline \end{array}$

8. $\begin{array}{r} 8.900 \\ 0.456 \\ +13.210 \\ \hline \end{array}$

9. 5.8 + 10.4

10. 8.193 + 6.9

11. 18.918 + 6.4

Estimate. Round to the nearest whole number. **(pages 600–603)**

12. 6.2 + 4.3

13. 7.5 + 6.7

14. 3.4 + 8.6

15. 6.45 + 3.81

16. 6.03 + 1.22

17. \$9.50 + \$2.41

18. 3.5 + 8.7 + 1.2

19. 5.24 + 7.05 + 2.69

20. 1.82 + 2.56 + 10.54

21. 1.9 + 3.5 + 7.2 + 6.3

Solve. **(pages 604–605)**

22. A train travels 4.5 miles to the first stop, 3.7 miles to the second stop, and 7.2 miles to the third stop. About how many miles does the train travel?

23. The distance from New York City to Los Angeles is 2,451 miles. The distance from New York City to Mexico City is 2,090 miles. The distance from New York City to Montreal is 331 miles. Which two cities are the closest together?

24. Jean rode 22.58 kilometers on her bike. After she rested she rode another 10.7 kilometers. How many kilometers did she ride altogether?

25. How would you add 0.734 and 23.2?

Additional activities at
www.mhschool.com/math

Use Place Value Models to Add

Suzie bought two packages of fish. One package weighed 4.56 pounds and the other 3.66 pounds. What is the total weight of both packages?

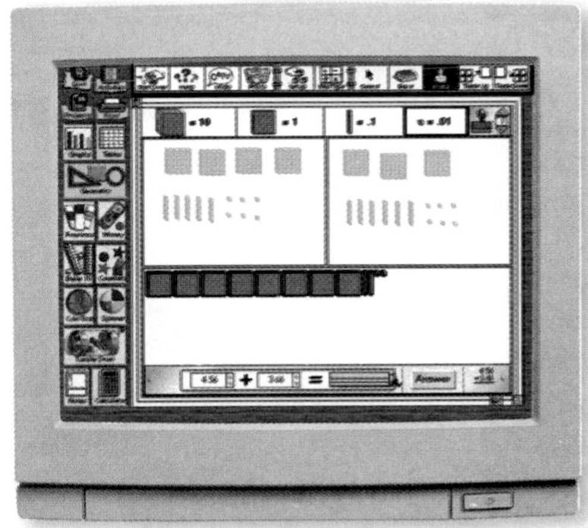

You can build a model of the total weight of both packages using place value or base-ten models.

- Choose addition as the type of mat.
- Choose Setup. Select the second block from the left.
- Stamp out 4.56 in one section.
- Stamp out 3.66 in the other section.

The number boxes show that you are finding 4.56 + 3.66.

- What is the total weight of both packages?

Use the computer to model each addition. Then write the sum.

1. 5.29 + 3.18 **2.** 10.46 + 7.35 **3.** 18.5 + 3.76 **4.** 25.93 + 6.7

Solve.

5. Yvette bought 1.86 pounds of apples and 3.68 pounds of oranges. How many pounds of fruit did she buy?

6. Gregg took 10.35 pounds of newspaper to the recycling center on Monday. He took 8.9 pounds on Tuesday. How many pounds of newspapers did he recycle?

7. Analyze: How does modeling the problem help you add?

For more practice, use Math Traveler™.

Objective: Use models to subtract decimals.

14•5 Explore Subtracting Decimals

Learn

You can use 10-by-10 grids to explore subtracting decimals. What is 2.5 − 1.9?

You Will Need
- **centimeter graph paper**
- **red color pencils, markers, or crayons**
- **red and blue colored pencils, markers, or crayons**

Work Together

► *Use 10-by-10 grids to find the exact difference.*
- Draw 10-by-10 graph on graph paper.
- Show 2.5 by coloring grids in red.
- Cross out 1.9 to show subtraction.

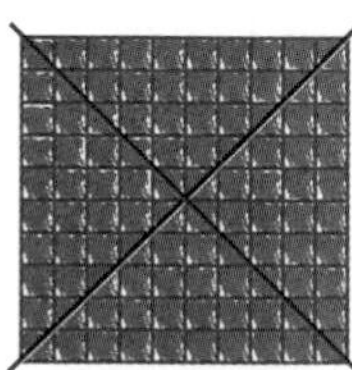 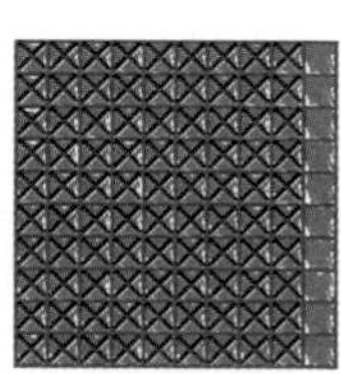 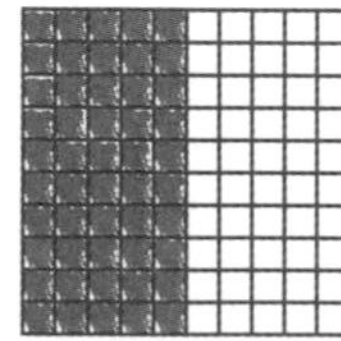

- Count how many squares are not crossed out.
- Write a decimal to show the total number of squares that are left. Record your work.
- Answer the question above.

► *Use grids to find each difference.*

0.75 − 0.23 2.4 − 1.6 1.34 − 0.7 4.0 − 1.3 2.8 − 1.16

Make Connections

Here is how you can find 1.65 − 1.28.

Using Models	Using Paper and Pencil
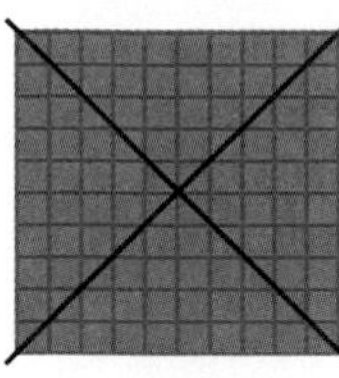 	Subtract each place. Regroup if needed. $\begin{array}{r} 1.65 \\ -1.28 \\ \hline 0.37 \end{array}$

Try It **Find each difference. You may wish to use models.**

1. $\begin{array}{r} 0.9 \\ -0.2 \\ \hline \end{array}$
2. $\begin{array}{r} 4.38 \\ -0.34 \\ \hline \end{array}$
3. $\begin{array}{r} 7.03 \\ -2.45 \\ \hline \end{array}$
4. $\begin{array}{r} 6.83 \\ -1.52 \\ \hline \end{array}$
5. 0.98 − 0.43
6. 1.45 − 0.7
7. 1.2 − 1.08
8. 1.8 − 1.34

How would you use models to subtract 1.06 – 0.55?

Practice **Find each difference.**

9. $\begin{array}{r} 8.5 \\ -2.6 \\ \hline \end{array}$
10. $\begin{array}{r} 4.3 \\ -2.8 \\ \hline \end{array}$
11. $\begin{array}{r} 6.45 \\ -0.82 \\ \hline \end{array}$
12. $\begin{array}{r} 7.49 \\ -5.30 \\ \hline \end{array}$
13. $\begin{array}{r} 2.12 \\ -0.99 \\ \hline \end{array}$
14. $\begin{array}{r} 6.73 \\ -2.81 \\ \hline \end{array}$
15. $\begin{array}{r} 8.11 \\ -0.21 \\ \hline \end{array}$
16. $\begin{array}{r} 6.53 \\ -4.14 \\ \hline \end{array}$
17. $\begin{array}{r} 8.11 \\ -2.22 \\ \hline \end{array}$
18. $\begin{array}{r} 3.38 \\ -2.91 \\ \hline \end{array}$
19. $\begin{array}{r} 6.87 \\ -1.99 \\ \hline \end{array}$
20. $\begin{array}{r} 4.21 \\ -1.83 \\ \hline \end{array}$
21. 1.9 − 1.2
22. 0.7 − 0.3
23. 2.22 − 1.55
24 1.95 − 0.34
25. 1.99 − 1.66
26. 0.90 − 0.15
27. 1.25 − 1.09
28. 1.6 − 0.56
29. 0.9 − 0.06
30. 1.75 − 1.37
31. 1.04 − 0.38
32. 1.8 − 0.65
33. **Generalize:** How does crossing out decimal squares show subtraction?

Objective: Subtract decimals.

14•6 Subtract Decimals

Learn

Each year, the International Balloon Fiesta is held in Albuquerque, New Mexico. This year the shortest balloon is 14.25 meters high. The tallest balloon is 25.8 meters high. What is the difference in height between the two balloons?

Example 1

Find: 25.8 − 14.25

Subtracting decimals is like subtracting whole numbers.	**Whole Numbers**	**Decimals**
	7 10 25~~8~~~~0~~ −1425 1155	7 10 25.~~8~~~~0~~ −14.25 11.55

Write the decimal point in the difference.

1 Line up the decimal points. Add zeros if needed.

$$\begin{array}{r} 25.80 \\ -14.25 \\ \hline \end{array}$$

2 Subtract each place. Regroup if needed. Write the decimal point.

7 10
25.~~8~~~~0~~
−14.25
11.55

3 You can use the inverse relationship between addition and subtraction to check.

$11.55 + 14.25 = 25.80$

The difference in height between the two balloons is 11.55 meters.

A red balloon travels 2.6 miles an hour and a blue balloon travels 1.45 miles an hour. How much faster is the red balloon?

Example 2

Find: 2.6 − 1.45

1 Line up the decimal points. Add zeros if necessary.

$$\begin{array}{r} 2.60 \\ -1.45 \\ \hline \end{array}$$

2 Subtract as you would with whole numbers. Write the decimal point in the sum.

$$\begin{array}{r} \scriptstyle 5\ 10 \\ 2.\not{6}\not{0} \\ -1.4\ 5 \\ \hline 1.15 \end{array}$$

3 You can use the inverse relationship between addition and subtraction to check.

1.15 + 1.45 = 2.60

The red balloon travels 1.15 miles an hour faster.

More Examples

A 3.5 − 0.583

$$\begin{array}{r} \scriptstyle 2\ 14\ \overset{9}{10}\ 10 \\ \not{3}.\not{5}\not{0}\not{0} \\ -0.5\ 8\ 3 \\ \hline 2.9\ 1\ 7 \end{array}$$

B 47.02 − 5.4

$$\begin{array}{r} \scriptstyle 6\ 10 \\ 4\not{7}.\not{0}2 \\ -\ 5.40 \\ \hline 41.62 \end{array}$$

C 0.9 − 0.327

$$\begin{array}{r} \scriptstyle 8\ \overset{9}{10}\ 10 \\ 0.\not{9}\not{0}\not{0} \\ -0.3\ 2\ 7 \\ \hline 0.5\ 7\ 3 \end{array}$$

Try It **Subtract. Check each answer.**

1. $\begin{array}{r} 0.96 \\ -0.29 \\ \hline \end{array}$ **2.** $\begin{array}{r} 1.54 \\ -0.39 \\ \hline \end{array}$ **3.** $\begin{array}{r} 8.20 \\ -0.99 \\ \hline \end{array}$ **4.** $\begin{array}{r} 3.452 \\ -0.670 \\ \hline \end{array}$ **5.** $\begin{array}{r} 5.006 \\ -1.358 \\ \hline \end{array}$

6. 8.4 − 3.5 **7.** 9.772 − 0.56 **8.** 41.06 − 5.831

9. 0.8 − 0.17 **10.** 1.04 − 0.97 **11.** 6.072 − 1.46

How is subtracting decimals similar to subtracting money? How is it different?

Practice Subtract. Check each answer.

12. $1.77 - 0.50$ **13.** $0.45 - 0.03$ **14.** $8.92 - 1.44$ **15.** $9.321 - 0.789$ **16.** $15.03 - 4.50$

17. $0.703 - 0.118$ **18.** $11.562 - 4.900$ **19.** $6.300 - 0.496$ **20.** $13.205 - 6.476$ **21.** $6.90 - 4.55$

22. $3.56 - 1.27$ **23.** $4.509 - 2.909$ **24.** $6.78 - 0.90$ **25.** $4.510 - 0.732$ **26.** $4.11 - 3.05$

27. $11.2 - 4.5$ **28.** $8.412 - 3.3$ **29.** $6.7 - 1.9$

30. $14.67 - 3.9$ ★**31.** $19.4067 - 3.7$ ★**32.** $14.0074 - 5.822$

Algebra & functions Find each missing number.

33. $6.53 - n = 0.52$ **34.** $8.2 + t = 10.07$ **35.** $7.2 - a = 2.6$

36. $r - 5.62 = 1.12$ **37.** $m + 0.75 = 0.91$ **38.** $x + 3.09 = 11.34$

39.

Here is how Edward found 8.152 − 2.7. Tell what mistake he made. Explain how to correct it.

Problem Solving

40. A total of 875 balloons were at this year's Balloon Fiesta. Of those, $\frac{1}{5}$ were from the United States. How many balloons were not from the United States?

41. A new balloon costs about $20,000. Five people decide to share the cost of a new balloon equally. About how much will each person pay?

★**42.** Fiesta T-shirts are $14.79. Ms. Plath buys four T-shirts to bring home to her family. Tax on each T-shirt is $0.75. How much does she spend?

Use data from *Did You Know?* for problems 43–44.

43. In 1981 the Double Eagle V balloon crossed the Pacific Ocean, traveling 9,282.7 kilometers. How much farther did the Orbiter 3 travel than the Double Eagle V?

★44. **Time:** How many hours did the balloon trip take? Write your answer as a decimal.

45. **Collect data** about balloon races. Use your data to write a problem. Solve it. Ask others to solve it.

46. **Measurement:** A hot-air balloon carries 4 people with a total weight of 585 pounds. A helium balloon carries four people with a total weight of 597 pounds. How many more ounces are carried in the helium balloon?

47. **Logical Reasoning:** Jeff, Anne, and Corey share a pizza for lunch. The pizza is cut into 6 equal slices. Jeff had more slices than Anne or Corey. Corey had more slices than Anne. Write a fraction to show how many pieces of pizza each person had.

48. **Analyze:** Sara writes 30 + 2 + 0.6 + 0.09. What decimal is this? How do you know?

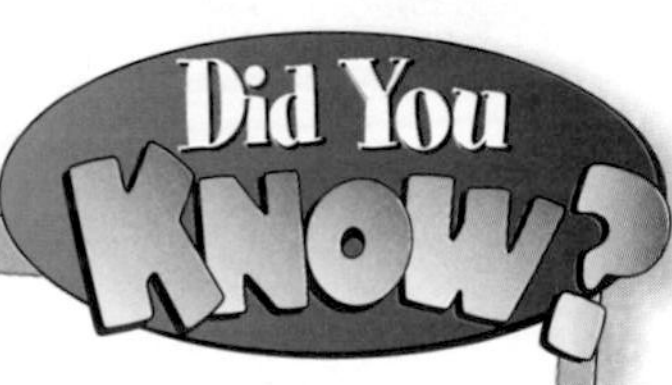

On March 20, 1999, Bertrand Piccard and Brian Jones became the first aviators to circle Earth nonstop in a hot-air balloon—the Breitling Orbiter 3. It took them 19 days, 1 hour, and 49 minutes to travel the 42,810 kilometers.

Spiral Review and Test Prep

49. 5,690 + 43,095
50. 55,032 − 1,927
51. 35 × 542
52. 46,725 ÷ 25
53. $390.78 + $45.77
54. $854.22 − $78.99
55. $67.35 × 18
56. $6,531.84 ÷ 16
57. 35 × 15 × 8

Choose the correct answer.

58. Niles buys 3 round-trip train tickets to go to the Balloon Fiesta. Each ticket costs $12.85 one way. How much does Niles spend?
   - A. $38.55
   - B. $67.10
   - C. $77.10
   - D. Not Here

59. T-shirts for the Balloon Fiesta are 3 for $36. How much do 9 T-shirts cost?
   - F. $72
   - G. $96
   - H. $108
   - J. $324

Objective: Estimate differences.

Estimate Differences

Bill Becoat, Alton, Illinois, inventor of a two-wheel drive system for bicycles.

Learn

What if Bill tested a bike by riding it a total of 29.72 miles in two days? He biked 13.21 miles the first day. About how many miles does he bike the second day?

Example

Estimate 29.72 − 13.21 to solve.

To estimate, round decimals to the nearest whole number.

29.72	−	13.21		
↓		↓		
30	−	13	=	17
Think: $7 > 5$ Round up.		**Think:** $2 < 5$ Round down.		

Bill bikes about 17 miles on the second day.

More Examples

A	B	C
7.32 − 5.15	15.69 − 9.47	\$8.34 − \$2.68
↓ ↓	↓ ↓	↓ ↓
7 − 5 = 2	16 − 9 = 7	\$8 − \$3 = \$5

Try It

Estimate. Round to the nearest whole number.

1. 28.7 − 13.4 **2.** 11.2 − 1.6 **3.** 18.2 − 9.9

4. 15.71 − 4.63 **5.** 13.52 − 4.71 **6.** 34.28 − 11.93

How is estimating differences with decimals similar to estimating differences with whole numbers? How is it different?

Practice

Estimate. Round to the nearest whole number.

7. 9.7 − 4.3 **8.** 18.5 − 6.1 **9.** 7.24 − 1.89 **10.** 19.44 − 8.72

11. 7.75 − 5.9 **12.** \$23.65 − \$5.60 **13.** 15.4 − 6.7 **14.** 35.18 − 5.56

Subtract. Check your answer.

15. 27.07 − 6.87 **16.** \$19.95 − \$4.15 **17.** 23.8 − 7.90 **18.** 99.99 − 30.13

19. 40.75 − 4.57 ★**20.** 10.629 − 5.067 ★**21.** 14.337 − 6.678

Algebra & functions **Compare. Use > or <.**

22. 8.9 − 4.5 ● 12.2 − 6.1 **23.** 10.6 − 2.2 ● 8.3 − 4.7 **24.** 5.5 − 1.9 ● 7.6 − 3.4

Problem Solving

Use data from the diagram for problems 25–26.

25. About how much faster was the fastest speed for the bicycle than the unicycle?

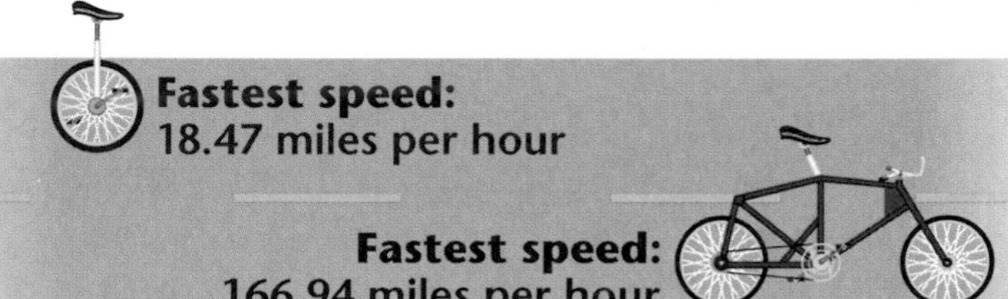

26. **What if** a person walks at a speed of 3.45 miles an hour? About how much faster is the speed for a unicycle?

27. **Science:** The large gear on a bicycle makes 36 revolutions a minute. The small gear makes twice as many revolutions a minute. How many revolutions does the large gear make in 5 minutes? the small gear?

28. **Analyze:** Look at your estimate for problem 11. Do you think the actual answer is greater than or less than your estimate? Explain.

29. **Generalize:** Why should you estimate to check the reasonableness of your answer?

Spiral Review and Test Prep

Add or subtract. Write each answer in simplest form.

30. $\frac{2}{3} + \frac{1}{6}$ **31.** $\frac{11}{15} - \frac{1}{3}$ **32.** $\frac{3}{7} + \frac{4}{7}$ **33.** $\frac{7}{12} - \frac{1}{4}$

Choose the correct answer.

34. Rename $\frac{23}{4}$ as a mixed number.

A. $2\frac{3}{4}$ **C.** $23\frac{1}{4}$

B. $5\frac{3}{4}$ **D.** Not Here

35. The side of a square is 6 centimeters. What is the area of the square?

F. 36 sq cm **H.** 36 cm

G. 24 sq cm **J.** 24 cm

Objective: Solve a complex problem by solving a simpler problem.

14·8 Problem Solving: Strategy
Solve Simpler Problems

Adult $8.29 Each
Youth $5.49 Each

Read **Read the problem carefully.**

The Vaughn family takes a train trip. They buy 3 adult tickets and 3 youth tickets. How much does the Vaughn family spend for tickets?

- **What do you know?** **The price of an adult ticket and the price of a youth ticket**
- **What are you asked to find out?** **How much 3 adult tickets and 3 youth tickets cost**

Plan One way to solve the problem is to first solve a simpler problem.

Solve Try using smaller and easier numbers than the numbers in the original problem.

Think:

Adult Ticket costs $8. Youth Ticket costs $5.

Try the simpler problem.

Adult Ticket: $3 \times \$8 = \$24$ Youth Ticket: $3 \times \$5 = \$15$

Total ticket cost: $\$24 + \$15 = \$39$

Now, solve the problem the same way.

$3 \times \$8.29 = \$24.87$ $3 \times \$5.49 = \$16.47$

Total ticket cost: $41.34

The Vaughn family spends $41.34 on train tickets.

Look Back How could you solve the problem another way?

Sum it Up! How does using the solution to the simpler problem help you in finding the solution to the original problem?

Practice Solve using a simpler problem.

1. Railroad tracks come in lengths of 1 yard. Each yard costs $29.95. How much will it cost to build a track that is 45 yards long?
2. A train conductor earns $18.45 an hour. A ticket checker earns $12.95 an hour. How much do both workers earn in an 8-hour day?
3. A newsstand sells 85 copies of a magazine for $4.95 each. It also sells 28 copies of a newspaper for $0.50 each. How much does the newsstand make selling the magazines and the newspapers?
4. A train travels at a speed of 37 miles an hour. An express train travels at a speed of 46 miles an hour. How much farther does the express train travel if both trains travel for 28 hours?

Mixed Strategy Review

CHOOSE A STRATEGY
- Logical Reasoning
- Draw a Picture
- Make a Graph
- Act It Out
- Make a Table or List
- Find a Pattern
- Guess and Check
- Write a Number Sentence
- Work Backward
- Solve a Simpler Problem

5. **Art:** An artist is going to tile the ceiling of the train station with panels that are 4 feet by 3 feet. Each panel has a design of squares that measures 12 inches by 12 inches. The design is made up of smaller square tiles that are 1 inch by 1 inch. How many of the smaller tiles are needed to make one large panel?
6. Each car on a train holds 95 passengers. There are 2 seats along the right side of the car and 3 seats along the left side of the car. How many rows of seats are there in the car?

Use data from the table for problems 7–8.

Fastest Train Trips in the World

Cities	Speed (miles per hour)
Hiroshima to Kokura, Japan	162.7
Madrid to Seville, Spain	129.9
Baltimore to Wilmington, U.S.	97.7

7. How much faster is the train in Japan than the train in the United States? than the train in Spain?
8. **Create a problem** using the information in the table. Solve it. Ask others to solve it.
9. Latisha spends $3.40 on lunch, $5.50 on a train ticket, and $0.60 on a newspaper. How much does she spend in all?

Extra Practice, page 627

Objective: Use properties to find decimal sums and differences mentally.

Use Properties to Add and Subtract

Learn

NASA astronauts are conducting an experiment inside the Space Shuttle. How many grams of samples are the astronauts using?

The samples have masses of 1.2 g, 3.4 g, and 0.8 g

Math Words

Associative Property when adding, the grouping of the numbers does not affect the result

Commutative Property when adding, the order of the numbers does not affect the result

Identity Property in addition, the sum of 0 and a number is the number

Example

Use properties of addition to find the sum mentally.

Find 1.2 + 3.4 + 0.8 to solve.

(1.2 + 3.4) + 0.8	Look for compatible numbers to add.
(3.4 + 1.2) + 0.8	Use the **Commutative Property**.
3.4 + (1.2 + 0.8)	Use the **Associative Property**.
3.4 + 2.0 = 5.4	Add the compatible numbers.

The astronauts are using 5.4 grams of samples.

More Examples

A

Use the **Identity Property** to find sums.

Add: 5.5 + 0

5.5 + 0 = 5.5

Think: Zero added to a number is the number

B

Use the Identity Property to find differences.

Subtract: 0.4 − 0.4

0.4 − 0.4 = 0

Think: A number subtracted from itself is zero.

Try It

Add or subtract mentally.

1. 4.2 + 1.8 **2.** 6.7 + 0 **3.** 5.7 − 0.7 **4.** 9.9 − 0

How does the Associative Property help you add?

Practice Add or subtract mentally.

5. 1.45 + 0.05
6. 3.07 + 0.6
7. 7.92 + 0.9
8. 8.93 − 8
9. 11.03 + 1.97
10. 14.16 − 0.17
11. 20.11 − 10.01
12. 16.88 − 8.44
13. 4.7 + 2.9 + 0.3
14. 8.3 + 0.8 + 1.2
15. 1.2 + 3.6 − 0.2

★16. 2 × (7.2 + 0.8)
★17. 5 × (4.7 − 0.7)
★18. (9.1 + 0.9) × 10

Algebra & functions Find each missing number.

19. $3.7 + k = 3.7$
20. $8.4 - m = 0$
21. $0.56 + p = 1.9 + 0.56$
22. $g - 0 = 7.081$
23. $1.2 - n = 1.2$
24. $(f + 12.5) + 7.5 = 20$

Problem Solving

Use data from the chart for problems 25–27.

25. How much larger was the Apollo capsule than the Mercury capsule?
26. If you were to line up all three capsules end to end, how long would they be?
27. **Create a problem** using the data in the chart. Solve it. Ask others to solve it.

Capsule Sizes for NASA Space Programs

Capsule	Size
Mercury Capsule	2.9 m
Gemini Capsule	5.8 m
Apollo Capsule	10.4 m

28. **Social Studies:** One of the longest space shuttle flights lasted 423 hours 53 minutes 18 seconds. What is the total number of minutes and seconds spent in space?
29. **Explain** how you can use properties to add 7.4 + 9.2 + 0.6.

Spiral Review and Test Prep

30. 17.3 + 14.7
31. 29.1 − 14.9
32. 50.45 + 8.93
33. 100.42 − 49.57

Choose the correct answer.

34. An astronaut drinks $\frac{3}{4}$ cup of juice for a snack. Which decimal shows how much the astronaut drank?
    - A. 0.25
    - B. 0.34
    - C. 0.50
    - D. 0.75

35. On the moon, astronauts weigh $\frac{1}{6}$ of their weight on Earth. How much does a 216-pound person weigh on the moon?
    - F. 216 pounds
    - G. 108 pounds
    - H. 36 pounds
    - J. Not Here

Objective: Analyze data and make decisions.

Problem Solving: Application

Decision Making

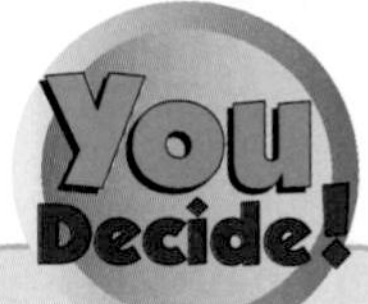

Should they take Route 35, the Parkway, or the Old Turnpike to the lake?

Carlos and Jennifer Lopez and their son Ricky are going on a trip to Lake Matawan for one week. They will travel by car, leaving from Marion on Saturday and returning the following Friday.

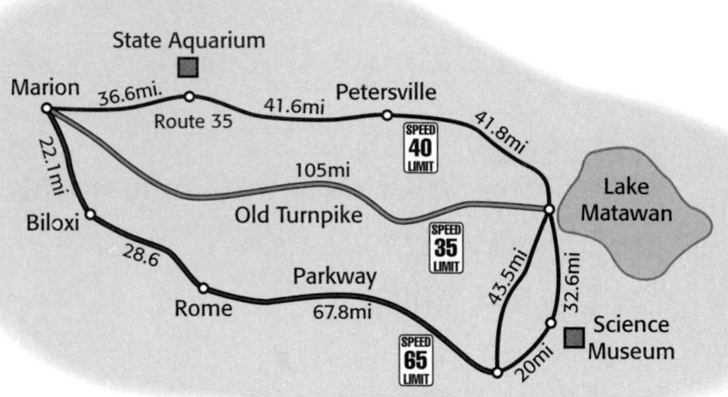

Science Museum

Adults	$5.75
Youth	$2.95

Hours: Tuesday-Saturday
9:00 AM to 4:30 PM

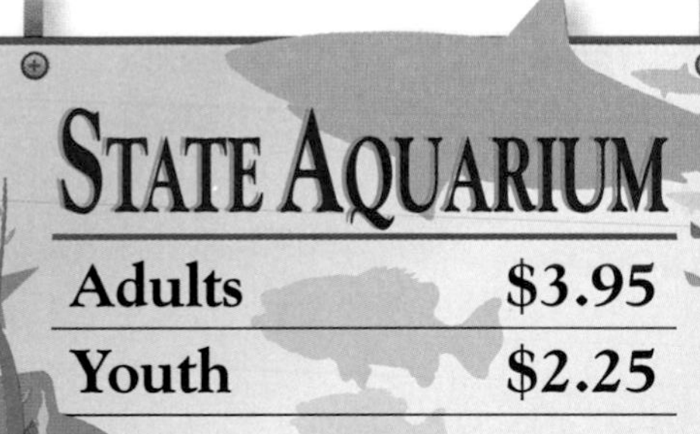

GASOLINE
(EACH GALLON)

Regular	$1.07
High-test	$1.17
Super	$1.27

Read for Understanding

1. If the Lopezes take Route 35 directly to Lake Matawan, how many miles will they drive?
2. If the Lopezes take the Parkway to Lake Matawan, how many miles will they drive?
3. The Lopez's car has a 13-gallon gas tank. If they fill the tank with Super, how much will it cost?
4. Ricky wants to visit the Science Museum. How much will it cost the Lopez family?
5. How many more miles is it to take the Parkway to the lake than the Old Turnpike?
6. How much less will it cost the Lopez family to visit the State Aquarium than the Science Museum?

Make Decisions

7. If the Lopez family drives at the speed limit directly from Marion to the lake along the Parkway, about how long will it take them?
8. If the Lopezes travel along Route 35 at the speed limit and make a $\frac{1}{2}$-hour stop for lunch, about how long will it take them to get to the lake?
9. Mrs. Lopez wants to stop at the State Aquarium on the way to the lake. It takes about 1 hour to drive from Marion to the Aquarium. If the Lopez family stops for 45 minutes for breakfast, what time must they leave to get to the Aquarium when it opens?
10. There are 20 traffic lights along the Old Turnpike. Each red light lasts for $1\frac{1}{2}$ minutes. Suppose the Lopezes take the turnpike and drive the speed limit. If they hit every other red light, how long will it take to drive to the lake?
11. Ricky wants to stop at the Science Museum on the way to the lake. How many miles will the trip be from Marion to the lake if the Lopezes make this stop along the Parkway?
12. Mrs. Lopez suggests they take the Old Turnpike to the lake and then go to the Science Museum. What are the advantages of taking this route instead of the Parkway? What are the disadvantages?
13. Mr. Lopez's car gets 27 miles to the gallon. He decides to take the Parkway to the lake. How much will he spend for gas if he uses super? How much will he save if he uses regular?
14. What else should they think about before deciding on a route?

Problem Solving

What is your recommendation for the Lopez family? Explain.

Objective: Apply adding and subtracting decimals to investigate science concepts.

Problem Solving: Math and Science

How would you conserve electricity?

You can save money and help the environment by using less electricity. You want to reduce your electricity use so that you can save at least $0.50 each day.

In this activity, you find different ways to save $0.50 each day and decide which conservation plan you would choose.

The appliances in your home require electricity to work.

Hypothesize

Think about the ways you use electricity. Estimate how much less time you would need to spend doing those things to save $0.50 each day.

Procedure

1. Work with a partner.
2. The information in this chart shows how many cents it costs to use the electricity for one hour.
3. List three different ways you could save $0.50 each day.

Appliance	Cents/ Hour	Appliance	Cents/ Hour
Air Conditioner (small)	9	Light bulb (40W)	0.5
Air Conditioner (large)	17	Light bulb (100W)	1
Computer	3	Microwave	14
Clothes Dryer (small)	28	Radiator (small)	12
Clothes Dryer (large)	46	Radiator (large)	28
Coffee Machine	7	Range	50
Dishwasher	28	Refrigerator	1.5
Fan	0.6	Small Appliance (radio, etc.)	3
Freezer (small)	1.5	Television	3
Freezer (large)	3	Toaster	7

Data

Copy and complete the chart. Use data from the table to make your three plans.

Plan 1		
Activity	Time Saved	Money Saved
Total:		
Plan 2		
Activity	Time Saved	Money Saved
Total:		
Plan 3		
Activity	Time Saved	Money Saved
Total:		

Conclude and Apply

- Which of your three plans would you prefer to use? Explain your answer.
- Which of your three plans might you actually use? Explain your answer.
- Look at the plan you like best. How much money would you save in a month? in a year?
- Compare the advantages and disadvantages of the different ways to produce electricity. Think about costs, energy efficiency, and stress to the environment.

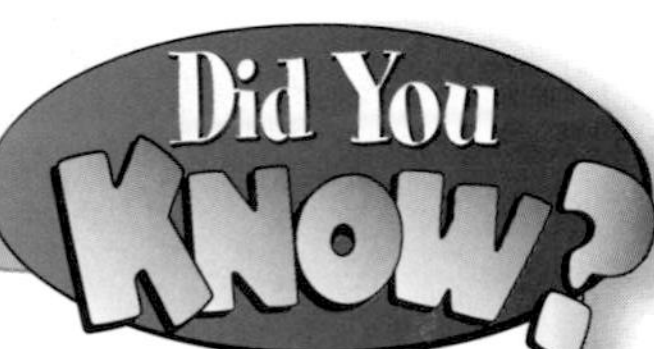

Electricity is usually produced by burning coal, oil, or natural gas; building a dam; or running a nuclear power plant. It can also be generated from wind and solar energy.

Going Further

Talk to friends, family, and teachers about ways you can conserve electricity at home and at school.

Problem Solving

Check Your Progress B

Subtract. (pages 610–611)

1. $\begin{array}{r} 0.8 \\ -\ 0.3 \\ \hline \end{array}$
2. $\begin{array}{r} 6.24 \\ -\ 0.57 \\ \hline \end{array}$
3. $\begin{array}{r} 7.04 \\ -\ 0.99 \\ \hline \end{array}$
4. $\begin{array}{r} 8.600 \\ -\ 2.476 \\ \hline \end{array}$
5. 15.603 − 13.4
6. 8.067 − 0.51
7. 7.32 − 0.529

Estimate. Round to the nearest whole number. (pages 612–615)

8. 6.5 − 2.3
9. 10.8 − 4.5
10. 15.65 − 5.9
11. \$18.95 − \$7.29

Find each missing number. (pages 618–619)

12. $9.2 + n = 9.2$
13. $5.24 - t = 0$
14. $0.8 + p = 6.82 + 0.8$

Add or subtract mentally. (pages 618–619)

15. 0.50 + 1.25
16. 4.08 + 0.7
17. 3.7 + 3.7 − 0.7
18. 8.9 + 0.1 − 9
19. 7.8 + 4.9 + 0.2
20. 7.4 + 1.5 + 0.6
21. 2.7 + 3.6 + 0.3

Solve. (pages 610–619)

22. A gas tank in a car holds 16 gallons of gasoline. How much does it cost to fill the tank if gas costs \$1.19 a gallon?
23. Carmen travels 1.5 miles each day for 3 days and 1.25 miles each day after that for 2 days. How many miles does she travel?
24. Round-trip fare to London is \$289.57 for students. The fare is \$389.29 for adults. How much would it cost for a group of 9 students and 2 teachers to go to London?

25. **Explain** how you would add mentally 8.2 + 7.1 + 0.8.

Additional activities at www.mhschool.com/math

Extra Practice

Add Decimals (pages 598–601)

Add.

1. $\begin{array}{r} 2.6 \\ +4.9 \\ \hline \end{array}$
2. $\begin{array}{r} 3.71 \\ +0.86 \\ \hline \end{array}$
3. $\begin{array}{r} 14.2 \\ +\ 7.6 \\ \hline \end{array}$
4. $\begin{array}{r} 0.86 \\ +0.37 \\ \hline \end{array}$
5. $\begin{array}{r} 4.78 \\ +1.99 \\ \hline \end{array}$

6. 6.1 + 5.9 + 8.7
7. 4.51 + 2.03 + 5.66
8. 53.9 + 4.7 + 0.6

Solve.

9. A mountain bike weighs 25.5 pounds. A racing bike weighs 17.9 pounds. How much more does the mountain bike weigh than the racing bike?

Estimate Sums (pages 602–603)

Estimate.

1. 4.5 + 3.9
2. 6.7 + 9.9
3. 3.2 + 11.6
4. 5.67 + 5.33
5. 8.21 + 3.4
6. 6.82 + 5.09
7. 7.1 + 14.5
8. 15.33 + 9.08

Add. Check for reasonableness.

9. 19.5 + 23.7
10. 27.6 + 13.04
11. \$2.34 + \$4.52
12. \$56.09 + \$3.14
13. 4.4 + 5.5 + 1.7
14. 6.4 + 3.2 + 11.1
15. 7.1 + 8.4 + 9.6
16. 8.7 + 6.5 + 0.7

Solve.

17. Barbara spends \$4.25 for a sandwich, \$1.79 for juice, and \$0.59 for an apple. About how much does she spend?

Problem Solving: Reading for Math Choose an Operation (pages 604–605)

Solve. Tell which operation you used.

1. Martina traveled a total of 98.5 miles one weekend. If she traveled 46.7 miles on Saturday, how many miles did she travel on Sunday?

2. Mr. Young drives a bus. He drove 38.7 miles before stopping at a rest area. Then he drove 49.67 miles more to reach his destination. How far did he drive altogether?

Extra Practice

Subtract Decimals (pages 610–613)

Subtract. Check your answers.

1. $\begin{array}{r} 2.8 \\ -0.9 \\ \hline \end{array}$ 2. $\begin{array}{r} 0.67 \\ -0.30 \\ \hline \end{array}$ 3. $\begin{array}{r} 3.66 \\ -1.44 \\ \hline \end{array}$ 4. $\begin{array}{r} 7.09 \\ -5.32 \\ \hline \end{array}$

5. $\begin{array}{r} 0.45 \\ -0.38 \\ \hline \end{array}$ 6. $\begin{array}{r} 0.589 \\ -0.078 \\ \hline \end{array}$ 7. $\begin{array}{r} 8.890 \\ -3.447 \\ \hline \end{array}$ 8. $\begin{array}{r} 7.54 \\ -1.93 \\ \hline \end{array}$

9. $\begin{array}{r} 14.009 \\ -\ \ 7.437 \\ \hline \end{array}$ 10. $\begin{array}{r} 5.890 \\ -0.667 \\ \hline \end{array}$ 11. 16.4 − 9.3 12. 23.7 − 0.57

13. 4.12 − 1.367 14. 10.909 − 3.556 15. 7.045 − 0.007 16. 32.6 − 1.845

Solve.

17. Make this problem and its answer reasonable by replacing each ■ with one of these numbers: 1.3, 3.9, 5.2. Write a number sentence to represent the data.
    - Pete's balloon flew for ■ miles.
    - Brittany's balloon flew for ■ miles.
    - Pete's balloon flew for ■ miles more than Brittany's balloon.

Estimate differences (pages 614–615)

Estimate.

1. 9.7 − 3.4 2. 5.9 − 5.1 3. 8.21 − 3.73 4. 12.5 − 5.8

5. 5.78 − 4.67 6. 10.97 − 4.66 7. 18.5 − 9.4 8. 13.99 − 4.33

Subtract. Check for reasonableness.

9. 23.4 − 8.2 10. 16.7 − 10.3 11. 25.25 − 10.90 12. 32.62 − 11.67

13. \$4.25 − \$1.35 14. \$15.59 − \$8.64 15. \$75.09 − \$5.88 16. \$47.06 − \$29.50

Solve.

17. Walter buys two new wheels for his bike. Each wheel costs \$23.59. He also buys a new bike helmet for \$27.95. About how much more do two new wheels cost than the bike helmet?

18. **Logical Reasoning:** Sheila divides a number by 7. Then she subtracts 3 from the quotient to get 6. What number did she start with?

Extra Practice

Problem Solving: Strategy Solve a Simpler Problem (pages 616–617)

Solve. Use any method.

1. Ben spends an average of 48.32 hours commuting by train each month. Ronna spends an average of 39.45 hours commuting each month. Who spends more time on the train? How much more?

2. **Social Studies:** Plans for the first U.S. Continental Railroad were made in 1845. The railroad was completed in 1869. How many years elapsed from the planning stage to the completion of the railroad?

3. Suzanna can travel in first class or coach. She can take a 5:00 P.M., a 6:30 P.M., or a 7:15 P.M. train. How many choices does she have? List the choices.

4. **Time:** A train takes 1 hour 35 minutes to get to Garnerville, 55 minutes to get to Pelham, and 1 hour 12 minutes to get to Pomona. How long does the trip from Garnerville to Pelham take?

5. Fifteen members of a fourth-grade scout troop took a train trip with two scout leaders. Youth tickets are \$2.29 each. Adult tickets are \$3.95 each. How much did it cost the scout troop to take the train trip?

6. Penn Station had 2,194 passengers board trains on Monday; 1,975 passengers on Tuesday; and 2,504 passengers on Wednesday. How many passengers boarded the trains on all three days?

Use Properties to Add or Subtract (pages 618–619)

Add or subtract mentally.

1. $2.09 + 0.91$	2. $0.55 + 1.55$	3. $6.34 - 0.3$	4. $9.45 - 9.45$
5. $14.57 + 6.03$	6. $8.99 - 1.98$	7. $6.27 + 1.13$	8. $30.55 - 15.05$

Solve.

9. Shaun has \$35.96 in his bank account. If he saves \$5 each week for 20 weeks, how much will he have?

10. Five astronauts have spent the following number of hours in space: 96, 73, 35, 28, and 53. What is their average number of hours spent in space?

Chapter Study Guide

Language and Math

Complete. Use a word from the list.

1. 5.6 + 0 = 5.6 is an example of the ____.
2. 1.3 + 4.5 = 4.5 + 1.3 is an example of the ____.

Math Words

Associative Property
Commutative Property
Identity Property

Skills and Applications

Add decimals to thousandths. (pages 596–601)

Example

Find: 5.66 + 0.36

Solution

Line up the decimal points.
Add zeros if necessary.
Add each place. Regroup if needed.

$$\begin{array}{r} 5.66 \\ +\ 0.36 \\ \hline 6.02 \end{array}$$

Write the decimal point.

Add.

3. $\begin{array}{r} 0.36 \\ +0.47 \\ \hline \end{array}$
4. $\begin{array}{r} 6.33 \\ +2.68 \\ \hline \end{array}$
5. $\begin{array}{r} 0.561 \\ +0.032 \\ \hline \end{array}$
6. $\begin{array}{r} 7.036 \\ +3.471 \\ \hline \end{array}$
7. 0.4 + 0.57
8. 3.603 + 1.9
9. 4.5 + 3.078 + 6.09 + 0.451

Subtract decimals to thousandths. (pages 608–611)

Example

Find: 9.452 − 1.7

Solution

Line up the decimal points.
Add zeros if necessary.
Subtract each place. Regroup if needed.

$$\begin{array}{r} 9.452 \\ -\ 1.700 \\ \hline 7.752 \end{array}$$

Write the decimal point.

Subtract.

10. $\begin{array}{r} 2.4 \\ -0.9 \\ \hline \end{array}$
11. $\begin{array}{r} 7.84 \\ -2.87 \\ \hline \end{array}$
12. $\begin{array}{r} 0.905 \\ -0.178 \\ \hline \end{array}$
13. $\begin{array}{r} 13.890 \\ -\ 6.006 \\ \hline \end{array}$
14. 18.4 − 4.32
15. 9.709 − 5.4
16. 4.567 − 0.82
17. 7.3 − 1.06

Estimate decimal sums and differences. (pages 602–603, 614–615)

Example

Estimate 5.31 + 7.62

Solution

Round to the nearest whole number.

5.31 + 7.62

↓ ↓

5 + 8 = 13

Estimate.

18. 5.1 + 7.3
19. 2.7 + 0.9
20. 8.45 + 0.89
21. 5.13 + 8.67
22. 7.3 − 3.5
23. 12.6 − 6.3
24. 4.85 − 1.27
25. 13.66 − 5.89

Use properties to find sums and differences. (pages 618–619)

Example

Use properties and mental math to add.

5.7 + 4.8 + 0.3

Solution

Use the Commutative Property.

5.7 + (0.3 + 4.8)

Use the Associative Property to add compatible numbers first.

(5.7 + 0.3) + 4.8

6 + 4.8 = 10.8

Add or subtract.

26. 3.04 + 4.06
27. 9.77 − 0.07
28. 3.1 + 4.7 + 1.9
29. 8.1 + 8.9 − 5.9
30. 6.4 + 4.7 − 1.4
31. 4.5 + 0.6 + 2.5

Use strategies to solve problems. (pages 604–605, 616–617)

Example

Jonathan buys two new car seat covers for $39.95 each. Then he buys four new tires for $46.27 each. How much does he spend?

Solution

Solve a simpler problem.

2 × $40 = $80   4 × $50 = $200

$80 + $200 = $280

2 × $39.95 = $79.90

4 × $46.27 = $185.08

$79.90 + $185.08 = $264.98

Jonathan spends $264.98.

Solve.

32. Monika takes a bus and a train each day to work. The bus costs $0.75 and the train costs $1.95 to ride. If she works 5 days a week, how much does she spend for transportation each week?
33. Nester travels 35.7 kilometers each way to work. Sally travels 23.8 kilometers each way to work. She also travels another 14.7 kilometers round trip to the day care center. How many kilometers do they travel altogether? What operation did you use? Why?

Chapter Test

Add.

1. $\begin{array}{r} 0.73 \\ +0.81 \\ \hline \end{array}$
2. $\begin{array}{r} 56.9 \\ +\ 4.8 \\ \hline \end{array}$
3. $\begin{array}{r} 13.843 \\ +\ 9.406 \\ \hline \end{array}$
4. $6.785 + 0.09$
5. $52.946 + 3.04$

Subtract.

6. $\begin{array}{r} 3.7 \\ -0.9 \\ \hline \end{array}$
7. $\begin{array}{r} 6.52 \\ -1.95 \\ \hline \end{array}$
8. $\begin{array}{r} 14.804 \\ -\ 2.965 \\ \hline \end{array}$
9. $8.045 - 4.7$
10. $16.8 - 6.436$
11. \$13.78 − \$5.46

Estimate.

12. $6.3 + 2.9$
13. $0.8 + 11.5$
14. $7.34 + 5.19$
15. $3.77 + 8.62$
16. $7.8 - 3.9$
17. $15.2 - 6.4$
18. $9.29 - 2.57$
19. $17.38 - 7.52$

Find each missing number.

20. $7.03 + p = 8.20$
21. $9.55 - q = 9.55$
22. $1.2 + r + 0.8 = 6.6$
23. $8.4 + 0.4 - 0.4 = s$

Solve.

24. Sharona travels 95.67 kilometers to Boston, then 67.32 kilometers to Redding, then 78.55 kilometers to Burlington. How many kilometers does she travel in all?
25. Mr. Sandusky spent \$23.95 on gas the first week of May. He spent \$17.67 the second week and \$28.58 the third week. How much more did he spend in the third week than in the second week? Tell how you chose the operation.

Performance Assessment

You have just bought a new car and want to take two long trips. For the first trip, you travel to the beach. The round trip is 27 miles. You spend $11.75 in gas and $3.45 in tolls.

For the second trip, you visit your uncle. The trip there is 42 miles. You spend $16.98 in gas. The trip back, taking the scenic route, is 53 miles. You spend $7.54 in gas and $1.65 in tolls.

Figure out the costs and mileage for each trip. Compare both trips. Which trip costs more in gas? Which costs more in tolls? How much more for each? How many total miles did you drive for both trips? How much did you spend on gas and tolls altogether? Show all your work.

A Good Answer

- shows the costs and mileage for each trip.
- shows that you have compared the distances and costs of both trips.
- shows all work done to calculate and compare the total distances and costs.

You may want to save this work for your portfolio.

Enrichment

Relating Fractions, Decimals, and Percents

You have seen how fractions and decimals name parts of a whole. **Percent** is another way of naming part of a whole.

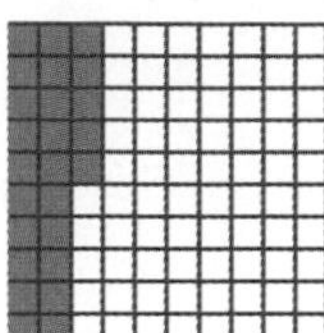

Percent means per hundred. The grid shows that 25 out of 100 squares are shaded. You can write this as a percent: 25% of the grid is shaded.

You can also write the amount as a fraction:
25 out of 100 $= \frac{25}{100} = \frac{1}{4}$

You can write the amount as a decimal:
25 out of 100 = 25 hundredths = 0.25
$25\% = \frac{25}{100} = 0.25$

Write the percent for the shaded part. Then write the percent as a fraction in simplest form, and as a decimal in simplest form.

1. 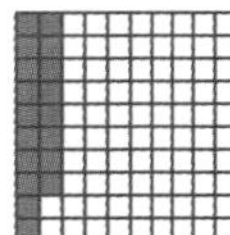

2. 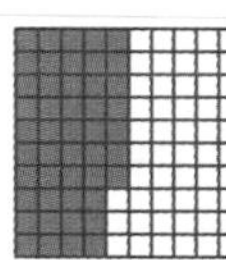

3. 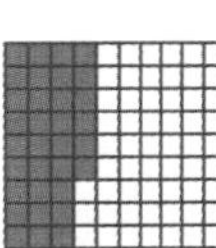

4. 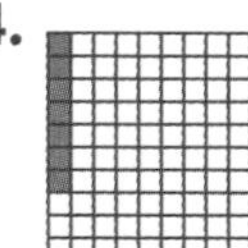

5. 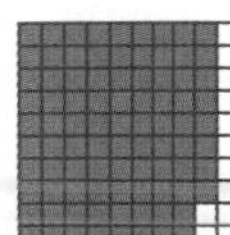

6. 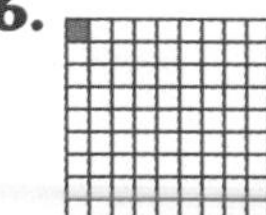

Write the percent as both a fraction and a decimal.

7. 50%

8. 10%

9. 44%

10. 77%

11. What is 100% as a fraction? as a decimal?

Test-Taking Tips

Sometimes the numbers in the problem make it seem more difficult than it actually is. It may help to **use simpler numbers** for decimals and fractions.

Rose used $7\frac{1}{2}$ yards of material to make her play costume. Nancy used $6\frac{1}{4}$ yards. How much more fabric did Rose use than Nancy?

A. $\frac{1}{4}$ yard **C.** $1\frac{3}{4}$ yards
B. $1\frac{1}{4}$ yards **D.** $13\frac{3}{4}$ yards

Substitute whole numbers for the fraction numbers:
Rose used 7 yards of material.
Nancy used 6 yards.

Then decide how to solve the problem. You need to find the difference, so subtract. Go back to the original problem and subtract.

$7\frac{1}{2} - 6\frac{1}{4} = 7\frac{2}{4} - 6\frac{1}{4} = 1\frac{1}{4}$

Rose used $1\frac{1}{4}$ yards more. The correct choice is B.

Check for Success

Before turning in a test, go back one last time to check.

- ☑ I understood and answered the questions asked.
- ☑ I checked my work for errors.
- ☑ My answers make sense.

Chose the correct answer. Use simpler numbers to help you.

1. Tia worked 3.25 hours on Friday and 9.75 hours on Saturday. Ty worked 4.5 hours on Friday and 9.25 hours on Saturday. How many more hours did Ty work than Tia?
   A. 0.05 hours **C.** 0.80 hours
   B. 0.75 hours **D.** 1.75 hours

2. The width of Ana's room is $11\frac{1}{2}$ ft. How much more or less is this than the length of 3 yard sticks?
   F. $\frac{1}{2}$ foot less **H.** $2\frac{1}{2}$ feet less
   G. $\frac{1}{2}$ foot more **J.** $2\frac{1}{2}$ feet more

3. It is exactly 14.25 miles between Tim's house and Dan's house. Tina's house is 4 times as far as that from Dan's house. How far is Tina's house from Dan's?
   A. 18 miles **C.** 56 miles
   B. 18.25 miles **D.** 57 miles

4. Bertha walked 3.75 miles to the mall. The next day she walked 6.25 miles on a hiking trail. Bob walked 9.5 miles in a marathon. Later he walked 2.75 miles to the zoo. How many more miles did Bob walk than Bertha?
   F. 1.5 miles **H.** 2.25 miles
   G. 2 miles **J.** 3.755 miles

Spiral Review and Test Prep

Chapters 1–14

Choose the correct answer.

Number Sense

1. What is 45,783 rounded to the nearest thousand?
   A. 45,000 C. 46,000
   B. 45,700 D. 50,000

2. Melly bought a sandwich for \$4.59 and juice for \$1.77. She paid with a ten-dollar bill. What is her change?
   F. 4 one-dollar bills, 2 quarters, 1 dime, 4 pennies
   G. 3 one-dollar bills, 3 quarters, 1 dime, 4 pennies
   H. 3 one-dollar bills, 2 quarters, 1 dime, 4 pennies
   J. 3 one-dollar bills, 3 quarters, 4 pennies

3. An airplane travels 39,753 miles in one week. What is the average number of miles the airplane travels in one day?
   A. 4,979 miles C. 5,679 miles
   B. 5,579 miles D. 6,047 miles

4. An airplane travels at a speed of 329.47 miles an hour. A train travels at a speed of 59.63 miles an hour. How much faster does the airplane travel?
   F. 269.84 miles an hour
   G. 26.984 miles an hour
   H. 26,984 miles an hour
   J. 2,698.4 miles an hour

Measurement and Geometry

5. What is the perimeter of this rectangle?

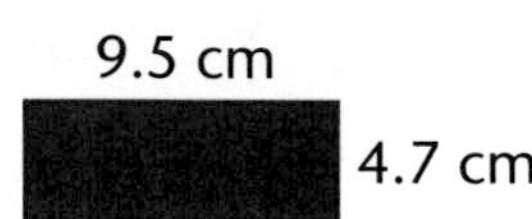

   A. 14.2 centimeters
   B. 28.4 centimeters
   C. 45.65 centimeters
   D. Not Here

6. Ned uses $1\frac{3}{4}$ cups of orange juice and $2\frac{1}{2}$ cups of cranberry juice to make a punch. How many cups are in the punch?
   F. $3\frac{1}{4}$ cups H. $4\frac{3}{4}$ cups
   G. $4\frac{1}{4}$ cups J. $5\frac{3}{4}$ cups

7. Jackie runs a mile in exactly 5 minutes. How many feet does she run each minute?
   A. 1,056 feet C. 586 feet
   B. 1,760 feet D. Not Here

8. Which is a true statement?
   F. All quadrilaterals have four sides and 4 angles.
   G. A right angle is greater than an obtuse angle.
   H. Perpendicular lines are lines that never intersect.
   J. A pyramid is a 3-dimensional figure that has parallelograms for faces.

Statistics, Data Analysis, and Probability

Use data from the bar graph for problems 9–10.

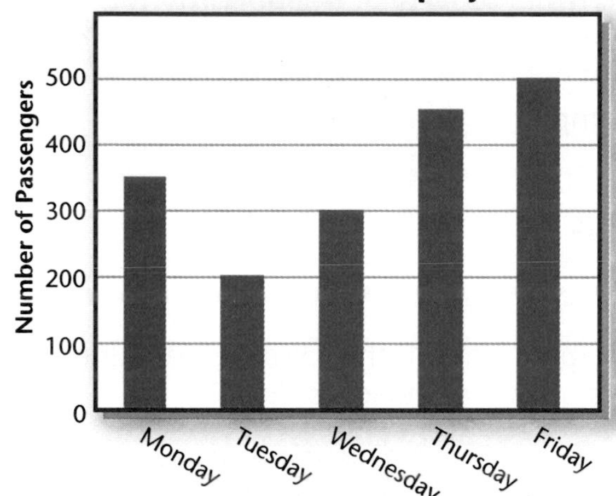

9. How many fewer passengers traveled on Monday and Tuesday than the rest of the week?

A. 150 **C.** 700
B. 600 **D.** 1,250

10. One-sixth of the total number of passengers traveled on what day?

F. Monday **H.** Wednesday
G. Tuesday **J.** Thursday

Use the spinner for problem 11.

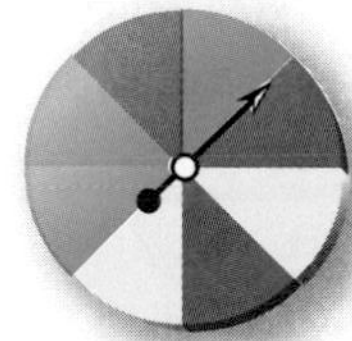

11. What is the likelihood of spinning red or blue?

A. $\frac{2}{8}$ **C.** $\frac{5}{8}$
B. $\frac{3}{8}$ **D.** Impossible

12. What is the median of the following set of data?

3.2 3.8 3.8 3.6 4.0 4.0
3.9 3.2 3.4 4.0 4.0

F. 3.2 **H.** 3.6
G. 3.4 **J.** 3.8

Mathematical Reasoning

13. Becka is thinking of a decimal number that is an even number. It has a 5 in the tenths and tens place. The digit in the ones place is half of the digit in the hundredths place. The digit in the ones place is less than 3. What is the number?

A. 56.53 **C.** 54.58
B. 55.50 **D.** 52.54

14. A train travels from the station for 1 hour 35 minutes and stops in Duluth. It travels for another 35 minutes and stops in Portsmouth at 1:05 P.M. What time did the train leave the station?

F. 10:05 A.M. **H.** 11:05 P.M.
G. 10:55 A.M. **J.** 11:30 A.M.

15. How many triangles are in the figure?

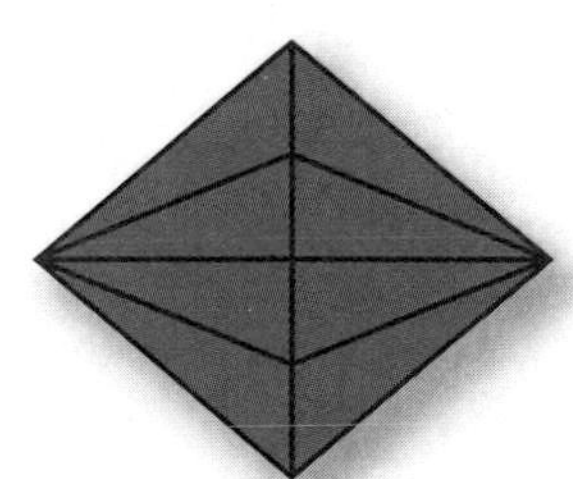

A. 24 **C.** 12
B. 16 **D.** 8

16. There are 357 people going on a bus trip. Each bus holds 48 passengers. How many buses are needed for the trip? Explain your reasoning.

Glossary

(*Italicized* terms are defined elsewhere in this glossary.)

acute angle An *angle* that has a measure less than a *right angle* (90°). (p. 420)

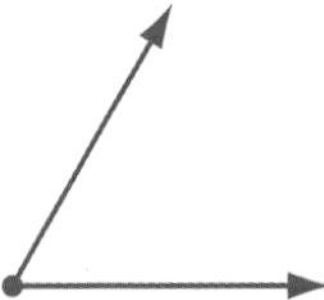

acute triangle A *triangle* with three *acute angles.* (p. 422)

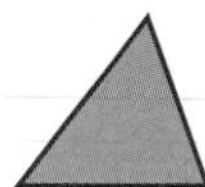

addend A number to be added. (p. 52)

A.M. A name for time between 12:00 midnight and 12:00 noon. (p. 92)

angle A figure formed by two rays with the same endpoint. (p. 420)

area The number of square units needed to cover a region or figure. (p. 446)

array Objects or symbols displayed in rows and columns. (p. 138)

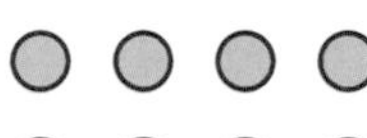

Associative Property of Addition When adding, the grouping of *addends* does not affect the result. (p. 48)
Example: $(3 + 5) + 4 = 12$
$3 + (5 + 4) = 12$

Associative Property of Multiplication When multiplying, the grouping of *factors* does not change the result. (p. 140)
Example: $2 \times (4 \times 3) = 24$
$(2 \times 4) \times 3 = 24$

average another word for *mean.* (p. 302)

bar graph A graph that displays data using bars of different heights. (p. 114)

base A *face* of a *3-dimensional figure,* usually the one on which it stands. (p. 408)

bilateral symmetry A figure with a line of symmetry. (p. 436)

C

capacity A measure of dry or liquid volume of a container. (p. 366)

centimeter (cm) A metric unit for measuring *length.* (p. 378) (See Table of Measures.)

certain An event will definitely happen. (p. 490)

chord A *line* that connects two points on a *circle.* (p. 417)

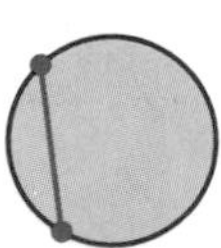

circle A closed, *2-dimensional figure* having all points the same distance from a given point. (p. 417)

closed figure A figure that starts and ends at the same point. (p. 412)

common denominator The same *denominator* shared by two or more *fractions.* (p. 524)

Commutative Property of Addition When adding, the order of the numbers does not affect the *sum.* (p. 44)

Example: 23 + 45 = 68
45 + 23 = 68

Commutative Property of Multiplication When multiplying, the order of *factors* does not change the result. (p. 140)

Example: $9 \times 3 = 27$
$3 \times 9 = 27$

compatible numbers Numbers that are close to the numbers in a problem and easy to divide mentally. (p. 288)

compensation When adding, add a number to one *addend* and subtract the same number from the other addend to find the *sum.* (p. 52)

cone A pointed *3-dimensional figure* with a circular *base.* (p. 408)

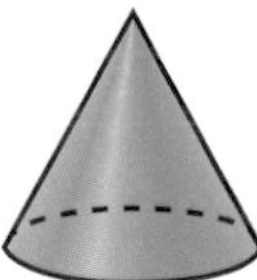

congruent figures Figures that have the same shape and same size. (p. 430)

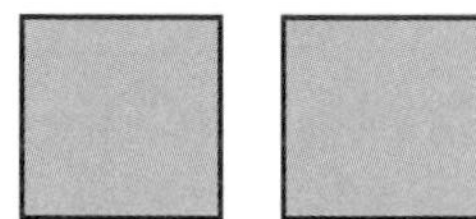

coordinates The numbers in an *ordered pair.* (p. 212)

cube A *3-dimensional figure* with six square *faces.* (p. 408)

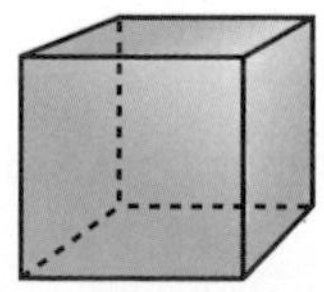

cubic unit The volume of a cube, one of whose sides is the given unit of length. (p. 450)

cup (c) A customary unit for measuring *capacity.* (p. 366) (See Table of Measures.)

cylinder A *3-dimensional figure* with two congruent, circular *faces.* (p. 408)

D

decimal A number that uses place value and a *decimal point* to show tenths, hundredths, and thousandths. (p. 558)

decimal point A period separating the ones and the tenths in a *decimal.* (p. 559)

Examples: 0.6, 2.3, 87.24
↑ ↑ ↑
decimal point

decimeter (dm) A metric unit for measuring *length.* (p. 378) (See Table of Measures.)

degrees Celsius A unit for measuring *temperature.* (p. 388)

degrees Fahrenheit A unit for measuring *temperature.* (p. 388)

denominator The number below the bar in a *fraction.* (p. 470)

Example: $\frac{2}{3}$ ← denominator

diameter A *chord* that goes through the center of a *circle.* (p. 417)

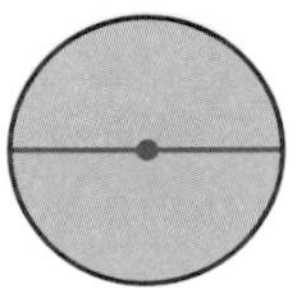

difference An answer to a subtraction problem. (p. 60)

digit Any of the symbols used to write numbers (0, 1, 2, 3, 4, 5, 6, 7, 8, 9). (p. 4)

dividend A number to be divided. (p. 160)

division An operation on two numbers that tells how many groups or how many in each group. (p. 160)

divisor The number by which the *dividend* is divided. (p. 160)

edge A *line segment* where two *faces* of a *3-dimensional figure* meet. (p. 408)

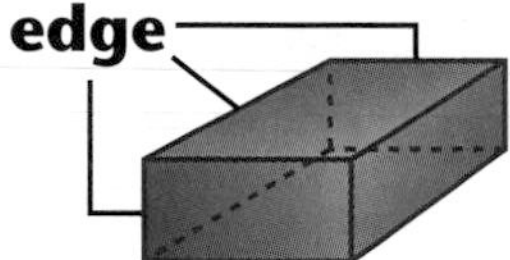

elapsed time The amount of time that passes from the start to the end of an activity. (p. 96)

endpoint A point at the end of a *ray* or *line segment.* (p. 416)

equally likely An event that is just as *likely* to happen as not to happen. (p. 490)

equation A mathematical statement with an equal sign. (p. 212)

equilateral triangle A *triangle* with three sides and *angles* that are equal. (p. 422)

equivalent decimals *Decimals* that name the same number. (p. 559)

equivalent fractions Two or more *fractions* that name the same number. (p. 474)

estimate An answer that is close to the exact answer. (p. 54)

expanded form A way of writing a number as the *sum* of the values of its *digits.* (p. 4)

expression A group of numbers and symbols that shows a mathematical quantity. (p. 344)

face A flat side of a *3-dimensional figure.* (p. 408)

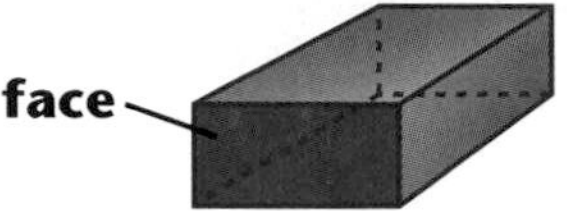

fact family A group of related facts using the same numbers. (p. 44)

factors Numbers that are multiplied to give a *product.* (p. 138)

favorable outcomes Desired results in a *probability* experiment. (p. 493)

fluid ounce (fl oz) A customary unit for measuring *capacity.* (p. 366) (See Table of Measures.)

foot (ft) A customary unit for measuring *length.* (p. 364) (See Table of Measures.)

fraction The number that names part of a whole or part of a group. (p. 470)

function A relationship in which one quantity depends upon another quantity. (p. 212)

gallon (gal) A customary unit for measuring *capacity.* (p. 366) (See Table of Measures.)

gram (g) A metric unit for measuring *mass.* (p. 381) (See Table of Measures.)

greatest common factor Greatest number that is a *common factor* of two or more numbers. (p. 516)

hexagon A *polygon* with 6 sides. (p. 413)

I

Identity Property of Addition When 0 is added to a number, the *sum* is the number. (p. 44)

Identity Property of Multiplication When a number is multiplied by 1, the *product* is the number. (p. 140)

impossible An event that cannot happen. (p. 490)

improper fraction A *fraction* with a *numerator* that is greater than or equal to the *denominator.* (p. 486)

inch (in.) A customary unit for measuring *length.* (p. 364) (See Table of Measures.)

intersecting lines *Lines* that meet or cross each other. (p. 416)

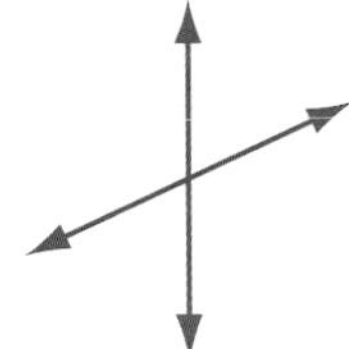

is greater than (>) Symbol to show that the first number is greater than the second. (p. 8)
Example: $12 > 8$

is less than (<) Symbol to show that the first number is less than the second. (p. 8)
Example: $13 < 25$

isosceles triangle A triangle with at least two sides or angles that are equal. (p. 422)

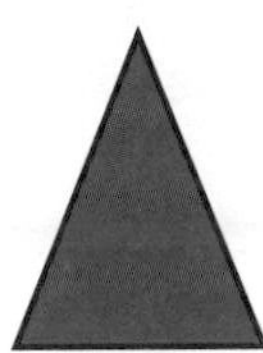

key A key tells how many items each symbol stands for. (p. 110)

kilogram (kg) A metric unit for measuring *mass.* (p. 381) (See Table of Measures.)

kilometer (km) A metric unit for measuring *length.* (p. 378) (See Table of Measures.)

length The measurement of distance between two *endpoints.* (p. 364)

likely An event will probably happen. (p. 490)

line A straight path that goes in two directions without ending. (p. 416)

line graph A graph that uses a line to show the relationship between two sets of data. (p. 118)

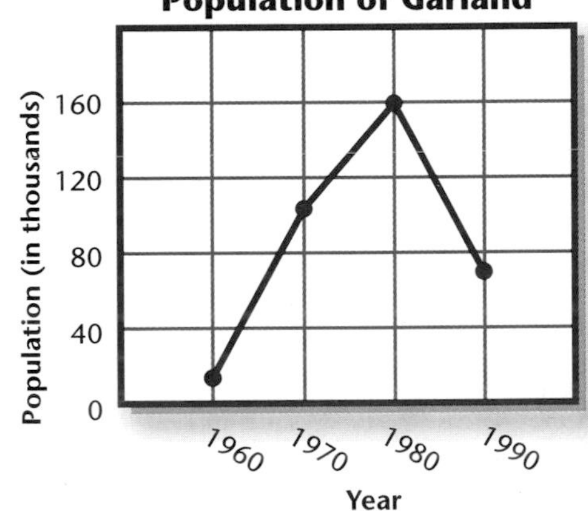

line of symmetry A line on which a figure can be folded so that its two halves match exactly. (p. 436)

line plot A vertical graph that uses Xs above a number line to show data. (p. 100)

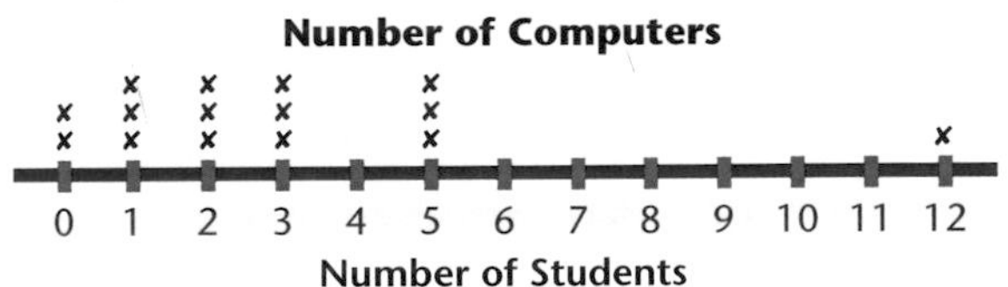

line segment A *line* with two *endpoints.* (p. 416)

liter (L) A metric unit for measuring *capacity.* (p. 380) (See Table of Measures.)

mass Amount of matter an object has. (p. 381)

mean The quotient when the *sum* of two or more numbers is divided by the number of *addends.* (p. 102)

median The middle number in a group of numbers arranged in numerical order. (p. 102)

Example: The median of 3, 6, and 8 is 6.

meter (m) A metric unit for measuring *length.* (p. 378) (See Table of Measures.)

mile (mi) A customary unit for measuring *length.* (p. 364) (See Table of Measures.)

milliliter (mL) A metric unit for measuring *capacity.* (p. 380) (See Table of Measures.)

millimeter (mm) A metric unit for measuring *length.* (p. 378) (See Table of Measures.)

mixed number A number named by a whole number and a *fraction.* (p. 486)

Example: $1\frac{3}{4}$

mode The number or numbers that occur most often in a collection of data. (p. 102)

Example: 3, 5, 4, 6, 7, 4, 2, 3, 4
The mode is 4.

multiple The *product* of a number and any whole number. (p. 142)

multiplication An operation using at least two numbers to find a number, called a *product.* (p. 138)

negative number A number less than zero. (p. 24)

net A *2-dimensional figure* that can be folded to make a *3-dimensional figure.* (p. 409)

numerator The number above the bar in a *fraction.* (p. 470)

Example: $\frac{2}{3}$ ← numerator

obtuse angle An *angle* that has a measure greater than a *right angle* (90°) but less than 180°. (p. 420)

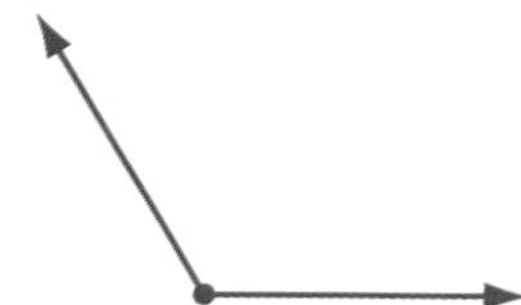

obtuse triangle A *triangle* with one *obtuse angle.* (p. 422)

octagon A *polygon* with 8 sides. (p. 413)

open figure A figure that does not start and end at the same point. (p. 412)

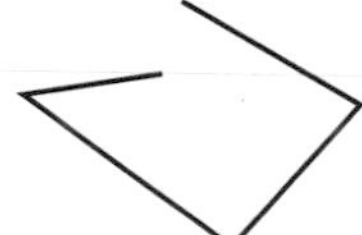

ordered pair A pair of numbers that gives the location of a point on a graph, map, or grid. (p. 116)

ordinal number A number used to tell order or position. (p. 98)

ounce (oz) A customary unit for measuring *weight.* (p. 367) (See Table of Measures.)

parallel lines ∥ *Lines* that stay the same distance apart from each other. (p. 416)

parallelogram A *quadrilateral* with two pairs of *parallel sides.* (p. 423)

pattern A series of numbers or figures that follows a rule. (p. 46)

Examples: 2, 4, 6, 8, 10

pentagon A *polygon* with 5 sides and 5 *angles.* (p. 413)

perimeter The distance around a closed figure. (p. 442)

per For each. (p. 298)

period Each group of three *digits* in a *place-value chart.* (p. 4)

Thousands Period			Ones Period		
Hundred Thousands	Ten Thousands	Thousands	Hundreds	Tens	Ones
2	7	0	2	7	1

perpendicular lines (⊥) Lines that meet or cross each other to form *right angles.* (p. 416)

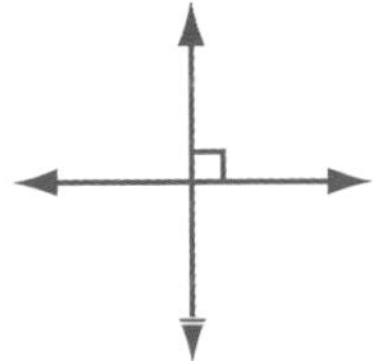

pictograph A graph that shows data by using symbols. (p. 110)

pint (pt) A customary unit for measuring *capacity.* (p. 366) (See Table of Measures.)

place value The value given to a *digit* by its place in a number. (p. 4)

P.M. A name for time between 12:00 noon and 12:00 midnight. (p. 92)

polygon A closed *2-dimensional figure* that has straight sides. (p. 413)

positive number A number greater than zero. (p. 24)

possible outcomes Any of the results that could occur in a probability experiment. (p. 493)

pound (lb) A customary unit for measuring *weight.* (p. 367) (See Table of Measures.)

prime number A whole number greater than 1 with only itself and 1 as *factors.* (p. 152)

prism A *3-dimensional figure* with two *parallel, congruent* bases and *rectangles* or *parallelograms* for faces. (p. 408)

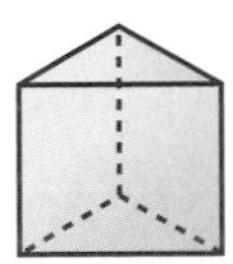

probability The chance that an event will happen. (p. 490)

product The answer in multiplication. (p. 138)

Example: $8 \times 3 = 24 \leftarrow$ product

pyramid A *3-dimensional figure* that is shaped by *triangles* on a *base.* (p. 408)

quadrilateral A polygon with 4 sides. (p. 423)

quart (qt) A customary unit for measuring *capacity.* (p. 366) (See Table of Measures.)

quotient The result of division. (p. 160)

Example: $20 \div 5 = 4 \leftarrow$ quotient

R

radius The distance from the center of a *circle* to every point on a circle. (p. 417)

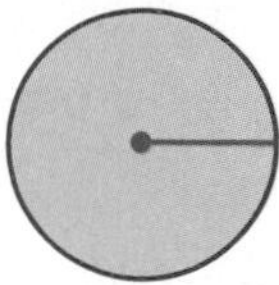

range The difference between the greatest and the least numbers in a group of numbers. (p. 102)

ray A *line* that has one *endpoint* and goes on forever in only one direction. (p. 416)

rectangle A polygon with 4 *right angles;* opposite sides are equal and *parallel.* (p. 423)

rectangular prism A *3-dimensional figure* with six rectangular sides. (p. 408)

reflection (flip) A movement of a figure across a line, producing a mirror image. (p. 434)

remainder The number less than the *divisor* that remains after the division is completed. (p. 279)

Example: $31 \div 5 = 6$ R1 ← remainder

rhombus A *quadrilateral* with 4 equal sides and 2 pairs of *parallel sides;* opposite sides are *parallel.* (p. 423)

right angle An *angle* formed by *perpendicular lines* that measure 90°. (p. 420)

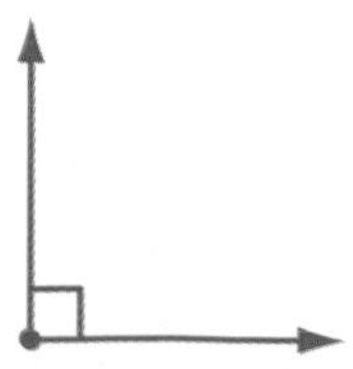

right triangle A *triangle* with one *right angle.* (p. 422)

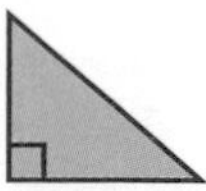

rotation (turn) A figure that is rotated around a point. (p. 434)

rotational symmetry A figure that matches itself after a 180° turn or less. (p. 437)

round To find the nearest value of a number based on a given *place value.* (p. 200)

S

scale Equally spaced marks along a graph. (p. 114)

scalene triangle A *triangle* with no sides and *angles* that are equal. (p. 422)

side One of the *line segments* in a polygon. (p. 413)

similar Same shape, may be different size. (p. 430)

simplest form A *fraction* in which the *numerator* and the *denominator* have no *common factor* greater than 1. (p. 475)

skip-count To count by twos, fives, tens, and so on. (p. 142)

sphere A *3-dimensional figure* that has the shape of a round ball. (p. 408)

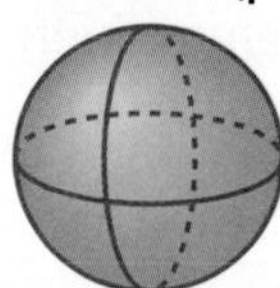

square A polygon with 4 equal sides and 4 *right angles;* opposite sides of a square are *parallel.* (p. 423)

square number The *product* of a number multiplied by itself. (p. 152)

square pyramid A pyramid whose *base* is a *square.* (p. 408)

square units The area of a square, one of whose sides is the given unit of length. (p. 446)

standard form A way to write a number that shows only its *digits.* (p. 4)

sum The answer for an addition problem. (p. 46)

survey A collection of data that answers a question or questions. (p. 100)

tally A way of counting by making a mark for each item counted. (p. 100)

temperature A measurement that tells how hot or cold something is. (p. 388)

tessellation An arrangement of shapes that covers an area without any gaps or overlaps. (p. 440)

3-dimensional figure A figure in space. (p. 408)

ton (T) A customary unit for measuring *weight.* (p. 367) (See Table of Measures.)

translation (slide) A figure that is moved along a straight line. (p. 434)

trapezoid A *quadrilateral* with exactly 1 pair of *parallel* sides. (p. 423)

tree diagram A diagram of all the possible outcomes of an event. (p. 495)

triangle A *polygon* with 3 sides. (p. 413)

triangular prism A *prism* whose opposite sides are *triangles.* (p. 408)

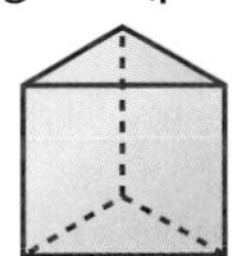

triangular pyramid A pyramid whose *base* is a *triangle.* (p. 408)

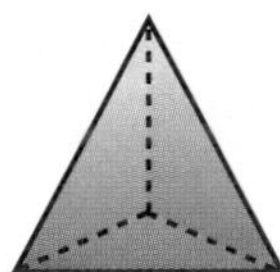

2-dimensional figure A figure on a plane. (p. 412)

unit price A price given as the cost for a single unit. (p. 298)

unlikely An event that is not *likely* to happen. (p. 490)

variable A symbol used to represent a number or group of numbers. (p. 44)

vertex The common point of the two sides of a *polygon.* (p. 408)

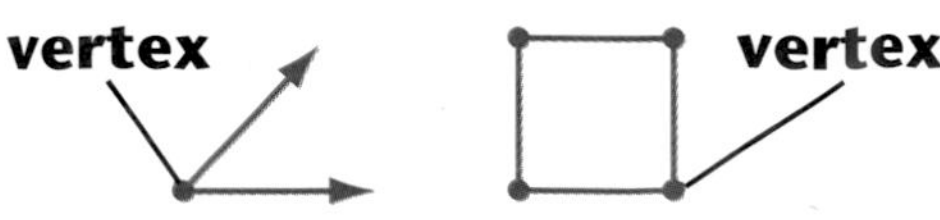

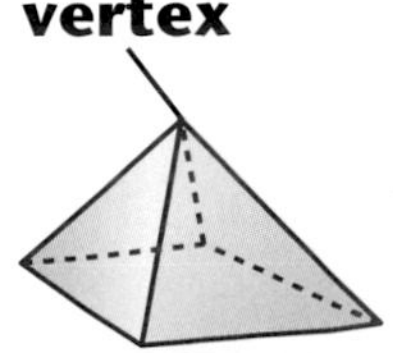

volume The amount of space that a *3-dimensional figure* encloses. (p. 450)

W

weight A measurement that tells how heavy an object is. (p. 366)

Y

yard (yd) A customary unit for measuring *length.* (p. 364) (See Table of Measures.)

Z

Zero Property of Multiplication Any number multiplied by zero is zero. (p. 140)
Example: $57 \times 0 = 0$

Table of Measures

Customary

Length	Weight	Capacity
1 foot (ft) = 12 inches (in.)	1 pound (lb) = 16 ounces (oz)	1 cup (c) = 8 fluid ounces
1 yard (yd) = 3 feet, or 36 inches	1 ton (t) = 2,000 pounds	1 pint (pt) = 2 cups (c)
1 mile (mi) = 5,280 feet or 1,760 yards		1 quart (qt) = 2 pints
		1 gallon (gal) = 4 quarts

Metric

Length

1 meter (m) = 1,000 millimeters (mm)
1 meter = 100 centimeters (cm)
1 decimeters (dm) = 10 centimeters
1 meter = 10 decimeters
1,000 meters = 1 kilometer

Mass

1 kilogram (kg) = 1,000 grams

Capacity

1 liter (L) = 1,000 milliliters (mL)

Symbols

$<$	is less than
$>$	is greater than
$=$	is equal to
\$	dollar
¢	cent
°	degree
$\leftrightarrow$	line
—	line segment
$\rightarrow$	ray
$\angle$	angle
(5, 3)	ordered pair 5, 3
$\perp$	perpendicular
$\parallel$	parallel

Formulas

Formula	Meaning
$P = 2\ell + 2w$	Perimeter of a rectangle
$A = \ell \times w$	Area of a rectangle
$V = \ell \times w \times h$	Volume of a rectangular prism

Table of Measures

Index

C

D

E

F

P

Index

Credits

COVER PHOTOGRAPHY David Muir for MHSD

PHOTOGRAHY CREDITS

All photographs are by McGraw-Hill School Division (MHSD) and Ken Karp, Peter Brandt and Doug David for MHSD except as noted below.

Table of Contents xiii: tr, 6-RAGA-@India/Stock Market • xvii: tr, Benjamin Rondel/Stock Market • vi: tr, Bob Daemmrich /Stock Boston • xii: tr, Ed Bock/Stock Market • ix: tr, Louie Bunde/Visuals Unlimited • viii: tr, Peter Walton /International Stock • xv: tr, Richard Dranitzke/Photo Researchers • xi: tr, Rudi Bon Briel/Photo Edit • xvi: tr, SuperStock • iv: tr, Tim Davis/Stone • xiv: tr, Tom & Dee Ann McCarthy/Stock Market • **Chapter 1** 1: all,Tim Davis/Stone • 14: tr, Chuck Place/Place Stock Photo • 17: cr, Robert Maier/Animals, Animals/Earth Scenes • 22: tr, Richard Hutchings for MHSD • 28: tr, Richard Hutchings for MHSD; **Chapter 2** 44: tl, Richard Hutchings for MHSD • 52: tr, Richard Hutchings for MHSD • 62: tr, Stephen Ogilvy for MHSD • 66: tr, Helping Hearts • 68: tr, Richard Hutchings for MHSD • 73: cr, Tribune Media Services • 74: cr, Ian O'leary /Stone • 74: cr, SuperStock/Superstock • 76: tr, Richard Hutchings for MHSD • 76: cr, Stephen Oligvy for MHSD; **Chapter 3** 90: all, Jeffrey Rich Nature Photography • 93: bl, Myra Miller/Liaison International • 93: br, Bob Daemmrich/Stock Boston • 94: tl, Tom Mccarthy/Unicorn Stock • 94: tr, Melanie Carr/Zephyr Images • 100: tr, Stephen Ogilvy for MHSD • 104: tr, Michele & Tom Grimm/International Stock • 106: tc, Haushahn/Stock Market • 106: tr, Mary Kate Denny/Stone • 118: tr, Stephen Ogilvy for MHSD • 120: tl, Bill Bachmann/Photo Edit • 120: tr, Edward F. Wolff/Animals,Animals • 120: cl, Peter Campbell /Zephyr Pictures • 120: cr, Ian O'leary /Stone • 120: bl, Arthur Tilley/FPG • 120: br, Bob Daemmrich /Stock Boston • 122: tr, Amy Etra/Photo Edit • 122: bc, Stephen Ogilvy for MHSD • 123: br, Chris Hamilton 1994 • 125: tc, Super Stock • 125: tr, Ian Shaw/Stone; **Chapter 4** 136: all, Lynton Gardiner Photography • 138: tr, Stephen Ogilvy for MHSD • 148: tr, Stephen Ogilvy for MHSD • 156: tr, Stuart Crump/Creative Communications • 160: tr, Richard Hutchings for MHSD • 165: t, Ken Cavanaugh for MHSD • 165: tc, Ken Cavanaugh for MHSD • 165: tc, Ken Cavanaugh for MHSD • 168: tr, Richard Hutchings for MHSD • 173: br, Stephen Ogilvy for MHSD • 174: tr, International Stock • 174: cr, Photodisc • 176: tr, Bill Horsman/Stock Boston • 176: br, Stephen Ogilvy for MHSD; **Chapter 5** 190: all, Mark Segal/Index Stock • 194: tr, Stephen Ogilvy for MHSD • 196: tr, Ken Cavanaugh for MHSD • 196: cr, Ken Cavanaugh for MHSD • 196: br: Ken Cavanaugh for MHSD • 200: tr, Alan Kearney/FPG International • 200: tr, Ken Cavanaugh for MHSD • 202: tr, D. Young-Wolff/Photo Edit • 206: tr, U. S. Dept. Interior • 209: cr, Peter Walton /Int'l Stock • 210: tr, Ken Cavanaugh for MHSD • 212: tr, Ron Thomas/FPG International • 218: tr, Aaron Haupt/Stock Boston; **Chapter 6** 232: all, James P. Rowan/DRK Photo • 234: tr, David Young-Wolff /Photo Edit • 236: tr, Stephen Ogilvy for MHSD • 238: tl, Ira Block/Image Bank • 242: tc, Chuck Place/Place Photography • 246: tc, Tony Arruza/Bruce Coleman • 250: tr, Index Stock • 254: tr, Cindy Charles/Photo Edit • 256: tr, Index Stock • 258: c, Louie Bunde/Visuals Unlimited • 258: b, Frederick Mckinney/FPG International • 258: b, Mark Gibson/Visuals Unlimited • 258: bc, Ariel Skelley/Stock Market • 260: tr, John Serafin for MHSD • 260: br, John Serafin for MHSD • 261: br, Nancy Sheehan/Photo Edit • 272: cr, Davies & Starr/Stone; **Chapter 7** 274: all, Lori Adamski Peek/Stone • 284: tr, David S. Hwang • 286: tr, Lori Adamski Peek/Stone • 288: tc, Bryan F. Peterson/Stock Market • 288: tr, Ken Cavanaugh for MHSD • 289: cr, Jack Holtel/Photographik • 290: tr, Ken Cavanaugh for MHSD • 294: tr, Hugh Rooney/Corbis • 302: tr, Jack Holtel/Photographik; **Chapter 8** 322: all, Paul Barton/Stock Market • 324: tr, Bob Daemmrich /Stock Boston • 328: tr, Superstock • 329: cr, John Livzey/Stone • 334: tr, Mike Coy/The Health Club • 338: tr, Rudi Bon Briel/Photo Edit • 348: tr, W. Myers/Uniphoto • 348: bc, Stephen Ogilvy for MHSD; **Chapter 9** 362: c, Rob Tringali Jr./SportsChrome USA • 364: bl, Michael Newman/Photo Edit • 365: tl, Ken Cavanaugh for MHSD • 365: tl, Ken Cavanaugh for MHSD • 365: cl, Yellow Dog Prods./Image Bank • 366: bl, Ken Cavanaugh for MHSD • 367: tl, Inga Spence/Visuals Unlimited • 367: tc, Michael Newman/Stock Market • 367: tr, Ford Motor Co./FPG International • 367: bc, Ken Cavanaugh for MHSD • 368: cl, Charles Winters/Photo Researchers • 368: cr, Tom Brakefield/Stock Market • 368: bl, Leonard Lessin/Peter Arnold • 368: bc, Delair Grouping LLC. • 370: tr, Gary R. Zahm/DRK Photo • 374: tr, Juan Carlos Ferrufino/Mark Palmer • 376: tl, Photodisc • 376: tc, Renee Comet/Uniphoto • 379: cl, Kenneth Jarecke/Stock Market • 379: bl, David Young-Wolff/Photo Edit • 380: cr, Ron W. Perry/TransImage • 380: bc, E.R. Degginger /Animals Animals/Earth Scenes • 381: tc, Ken Cavanaugh for MHSD • 381: bl, Roy Schneider/Stock Market • 382: tl, David Arky/Stone • 382: tl, Index Stock • 382: tc, Ken Cavanaugh for MHSD • 382: tr, Doug Adams/Unicorn Stock • 382: tr, Photodisc • 384: tr, SuperStock • 386: tr, Ken Cavanaugh for MHSD • 388: tr, Ed Bock/Stock Market • 392: tr, Andrew Itkoff for MHSD • 392: bc, Stephen Ogilvy for MHSD • 394: tl, David Young-Wolff/Photo Edit • 394: tc, Tom Mareschal/Image Bank • 394: tr, Michael Newman/Photo Edit • 395: tl, Photodisc • 395: tc, David Young-Wolff/Photo Edit • 395: tc, Vollrath • 395: tr, Richard Thom/Visuals Unlimited • 395: tr, SuperStock • 395: c, Manuel Denner/International Stock • 395: c, Michael Newman/Photo Edit • 395: cl, Ron W. Perry/TransImage • 395: cl, Superstock • 395: cr, Ken Cavanagh for MHSD • 395: cr, Leonard Lessin/Peter Arnold • 398: cl, William Whitehurst/Stock Market • 398: bl, Leonard Lessin/Peter Arnold; 401: br, Dave Mager for MHSD **Chapter 10** 406: all, SuperStock • 407: tc, Joe Cornish/Stone • 408: tr, H.P. Merten/Stock Market • 410: tl, SuperStock/Superstock • 410: tc, Deborah Denker/Liaison International • 410: tr, Index Stock • 412: tr, Hermitage Museum/SuperStock • 414: tl, A. Zalon/ FPG International • 414: tc, SuperStock/SuperStock • 416: tr, Paul Johnson/Liaison International • 416: tr, Used with permission from Biltmore Estate, Asheville, North Carolina • 422: tr, K.H. Photo/International Stock • 433: cr, J.C. Carton/Bruce Coleman • 436: tr, 6-RAGA-@India /Stock Market • 437: c, Berenholtz/Stock Market • 437: cl, John Lawrence/Stone • 437: cr, Stewart Cohen/Stone • 438: tc, Mark Newman/Bruce Coleman • 439: cr, Will & Deni Mcintrye/Photo Researchers • 450: tr, Stephen Ogilvy for MHSD • 454: tr, Bruno Maso/Photo Researchers • 461: c, Alan Schein/Stock Market; **Chapter 11** 468: all, Tom & Dee Ann McCarthy/Stock Market • 470: cr, Davies & Starr/Stone • 472: tr, Ken Cavanaugh for MHSD • 482: tr, Photodisc • 484: tr, Stephen Ogilvy for MHSD • 500: tr, Craig Hammall/Stock Market; **Chapter 12** 514: all, Tom McCarthy /Photo Edit • 518: tr, Earl & Nazima Kowall/Corbis • 520: tr, Mary Kate Denny/Photo Edit • 524: tr, Stephen Ogilvy for MHSD • 529: tr, Richard Dranitzke/Photo Researchers • 538: tr, Tom Pilston/Liaison Agency • 542: tr, Davis Barber/Photo Edit; **Chapter 13** 556: all, SuperStock • 558: tr, Stephen Ogilvy for MHSD • 560: tr, Eric Jordan/ADP Photo Lab for MHSD • 568: tr, Travelpix /FPG International • 576: tr, Mike Powell/Allsport • 578: tl, Ken Cavanaugh for MHSD • 578: tr, Ken Cavanaugh for MHSD • 578: cl, Ken Cavanaugh for MHSD • 578: cr, Ken Cavanaugh for MHSD • 578: cr, Ken Cavanaugh for MHSD • 578: bl, Ken Cavanaugh for MHSD • 578: br, Ken Cavanaugh for MHSD • 580: tr, Chris Hamilton • 581: br, Jim Cummins/FPG International; **Chapter 14** 594: all, Dallas & John Heaton/Stock Boston • 598: tr, Myrleen Ferguson/Photo Edit • 601: tr, Benjamin Rondel/Stock Market • 602: tr, Aneal Vohra/Unicorn Stock • 604: cr, Lawrence Migdale • 610: tr, Randy Wells /Stone • 613: cr, Nicolas le Corre/Liaison Agency • 614: tr, Bill Becoat for MHSD • 618: tr, NASA/Science Photo Library • 622: tr, Richard Hutchings for MHSD • 623: br, Richard Hutchings for MHSD.

ILLUSTRATION CREDITS

Kenneth Batelman: 48, 60, 72, 147, 344, 364, 402, 410, 415, 420, 438, 445, 446, 447, 452, 459, 461, 472, 473, 474, 487, 503, 505, 534, 589 • Annie Bissett: 144 • Paul DiMare: 573 • Stephen Durke: 95, 116, 117, 120, 124, 130, 139, 140, 141, 158, 158, 161, 164, 342, 486, 495, 507, 590, 616, 620 • Colin Hayes: 143, 144, 145, 166, 402, 439, 470, 491, 494, 615 • Patricia Rasch: 85 • Marty Smith: 91, 92, 96, 98, 99, 103, 105, 106, 109, 110, 111, 112, 114, 115, 119, 120, 124, 125, 127, 135, 233, 241, 242, 245, 246, 247, 253, 254, 255, 258, 260, 273, 411

Credits

Contents

Calculator Handbook

ACTIVITY 1

Objective: Increase and decrease a number by a given amount.

More or Less

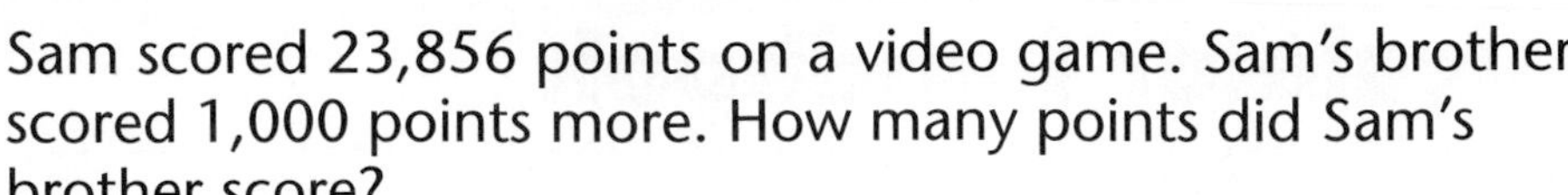

Sam scored 23,856 points on a video game. Sam's brother scored 1,000 points more. How many points did Sam's brother score?

To answer the question, you can solve the problem below:

23,856 + 1,000 = ■

Using the TI-15

To find the sum, enter the following:

2 3 8 5 6 + 1 0 0 0 Enter =

23856+1000=
24856

So, 23,856 + 1,000 = 24,856. Sam's brother scored 24,856 points.

Sam scored 10,000 points less than his brother. If his brother scored 49,930, how many points did Sam score?

To answer the question, you can solve the problem below:

49,930 − 10,000 = ■

To find the difference, enter the following:

4 9 9 3 0 − 1 0 0 0 0 Enter =

49930-10000
= 39930

So, 49,930 − 10,000 = 39,930. Sam scored 39,930 points.

Practice **Find 100 more and 100 less than the number given.**

1. 38,930
2. 458,731
3. 907,325
4. 632,018

Solve.

5. Sharon scored 237,005 on her video game. Her sister scored a 100,000 less. What did her sister score?

ACTIVITY 2

Objective: Use the place-value key on the calculator.

Place Value

Diane searched the Internet for art and found 218,573 sites. What is the place value of the 2?

Using the TI-15

You can use the problem-solving mode to identify place value. Enter the following:

218573
2 _ _ _ _ _

218573
2 -> 100000

218573

To get out of the problem-solving mode, press  again

So, 2 is in the hundred thousands place.

What digit is in the thousands place?

Enter the following:

1000.

So, 8 is in the thousands place.

Practice

Name the place of the 5 in each number.

1. 5,296,134
2. 4,096,352
3. 258,903,147

Name the digit in the place named.

4. 104,286,753; ten millions
5. 73,892,546; ten thousands
6. 47,309,876; millions

Solve.

7. Diane searched the Internet for sites on cars. She found 56,834 sites. How many thousands did she find?

Calculator Activities

ACTIVITY 3

Objective: Use the addition and parenthesis keys to investigate the Commutative Property, Associative Property, and Identity Property.

Addition Properties

Gina has 56 stickers and she bought 48 more. Mary has 48 stickers and she bought 56 more. Who has more stickers?

To find the answer, solve this problem.

56 + 48 ● 48 + 56

Using the TI-15

To find the answer, enter the following:

5 6 + 4 8 Enter =   56+48= 104

4 8 + 5 6 Enter =   48+56= 104

So, 56 + 48 = 48 + 56. This is an example of the Commutative Property of Addition. Gina and Mary have the same number of stickers.

Find each pair of sums: 72 + (37 + 43) ● (72 + 37) + 43.

To find the answer, enter the following:

7 2 + (3 7 + 4 3) Enter =

72+(37+43)=
152

(7 2 + 3 7) + 4 3 Enter =

(72+37)+43=
152

So, 72 + (37 + 43) = (72 + 37) + 43. This is an example of the Associative Property of Addition.

Practice **Find each pair of sums. If two sums are equal, state which property of addition they show.**

1. 68 + 57 ● 57 + 68
2. 25 + (49 + 58) ● (49 + 25) + 57
3. 124 + 0 ● 124
4. (138 + 412) + 78 ● 138 + (412 + 78)
5. 0 + 506 ● 5,060
6. 634 + 421 ● 421 + 634

ACTIVITY 4

Objective: Use the Problem Solving Mode to find missing factors.

Missing Factors

Kirk is setting up 108 chairs. If he puts 9 chairs in each row, how many rows will he make?

Find the missing factor in the problem below.

9 × ▮ = 108

Using the TI-15

You can use the problem-solving mode to find the missing factor. Enter the following:

9 × ? = 108
1 SOL

9 × ? = 108

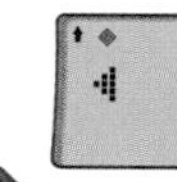

To get out of the problem-solving mode, press ◈ again

Kirk will make 12 rows of chairs.

Practice **Use you calculator to find the missing factors. What is your score?**

1. 8 × ▮ = 72 **2.** 6 × ▮ = 48 **3.** 5 × ▮ = 60 **4.** 7 × ▮ = 49

5. ▮ × 9 = 63 **6.** ▮ × 4 = 32 **7.** ▮ × 3 = 24 **8.** ▮ × 6 = 54

Solve.

9. Kirk has 345 chairs to set up in 15 rows. If each row has the same number of chairs, how many chairs are in each row?

10. Janet wants to make photo albums with 6 pictures on each page. Each album can hold 32 pages. If she has 576 pictures, how many photo albums will she need?

Calculator Activities

ACTIVITY 5

Objective: Use the backspace key to correct a wrong numerical entry.

Error Corrections

Lonnie added 3,852 + 375 on her calculator. She wanted to add 3,852 + 475. How can she fix the mistake without starting over? What is the sum?

Using the TI-15

To correct a mistake, enter the following:

3 8 5 2 + 3 7 5 → 3852+375

◁ ◁ ← 4 → 3852+445

Enter = → 3852+475= 4327

Lonnie fixed the mistake by using the ◁ key to move the cursor back and the ← key to delete the 3.

The sum is 4,327.

Practice **Enter the problem into your calculator, then correct the problem by entering the number in brackets. Find the sum.**

1. 927 + 832 [842]
2. 2,518 [2,578] + 642
3. 863 + 1,257 [1,557]
4. 3,516 [3,816] + 762
5. 3,413 [3,453] + 1,212
6. 2,257 + 4,740 [4,748]
7. 2,345 [2,748] + 4,358
8. 7,035 + 2,358 [2,468]
9. 7,395 [7,495] + 1,136
10. 2,345 [2,748] + 4,358
11. 7,035 + 2,358 [2,468]
12. 3,247 [4,342] + 1,400

Solve.

13. Gregg entered 3,876 + 5,431 into his calculator. He wanted to enter 3,965 + 5,431. What is the sum he should have?

14. Jenny was using her calculator to add 5,973 + 2,347. She made a mistake and entered 5,873 + 2,347. How many times must she press the left arrow key to change the 9 to an 8?

Objective: Use the backspace key to correct a wrong numerical entry after pressing the Enter key.

Error Corrections

A department store had 2,784 customers in one day. If they had that many customers for the next 55 days, how many customers total would they have served for the 56 days?

To solve this problem, Denise entered 56 × 2,884 in her calculator and got 161,504 for an answer. How can she fix the mistake without starting over? What is the product?

Using the TI-15

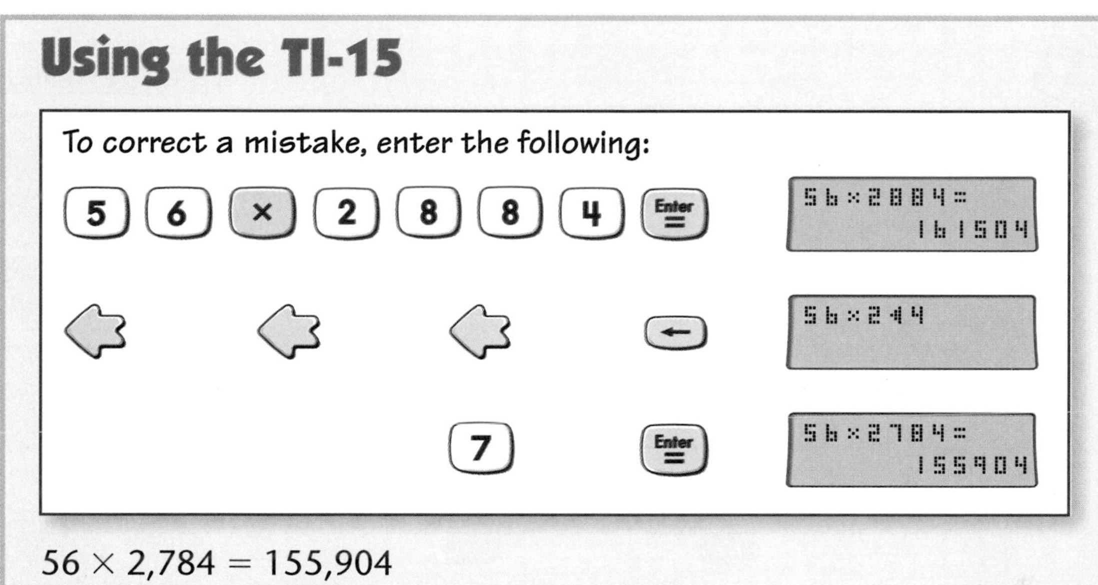

56 × 2,784 = 155,904

So, the store would serve 155,904 customers.

Practice **Enter the problem into your calculator, then correct the problem by entering the number in brackets. Find the product.**

1. 42 × 2,132 [2,332]
2. 48 × 3,407 [4,407]
3. 4,785 × 73 [43]
4. 6,230 × 94 [74]
5. 2,358 × 82 [93]
6. 61 × 3,508 [6,518]
7. 1,738 [1,938] × 62
8. 4,351 [5,251] × 83

Solve.

9. Kate entered 52 × 6,049 into her calculator. She wanted to enter 82 × 6,049. How much larger is the right answer than the answer Kate got?

ACTIVITY 7

Objective: Use the Fix *key for rounding whole numbers.*

Rounding

Brian read that there are 13,875,942 trees in a national park near his city. Round this number to the nearest ten, hundred, and thousand.

Using the TI-15

To round to the nearest ten, enter the following:

Fix
13875942=
13875940.

13,875,942 rounded to the nearest ten is 13,875,940.

To round to the nearest hundred, enter the following:

Fix 100.

Fix
13875942=
13875900.

13,875,942 rounded to the nearest hundred is 13,875,900.

To round to the nearest thousand, enter the following:

Fix 1000.

Fix
13875942=
13876000.

To remove a setting for rounding, press Fix (.).

13,875,942 rounded to the nearest thousand is 13,876,000.

Practice **Round each number to the nearest ten, hundred, and thousand.**

1. 38,479

2. 59,945

3. 78,754

4. 64,208

5. 19,721

6. 35,436

7. 83,743

8. 95,159

9. 53,688

10. 129,548

11. 238,967

12. 415,738

Solve.

13. In the national park there are an estimated 476,932 plants. Round the number of plants to the nearest thousand.

ACTIVITY 8

Objective: Use the Int÷ key to find a quotient with a remainder.

Unit Conversion

Bob is 58 inches tall. How tall is he in feet and inches? (Remember: 12 inches = 1 foot)

Solve 58 ÷ 12 to answer this question.

Using the TI-15

Enter the following:

5 8 Int÷ 1 2 Enter =

58÷12= 4r10

So, 58 ÷ 12 = 4 R 10. Bob is 4 feet 10 inches tall.

Bob's dad is 83 inches tall. How tall is his dad in feet and inches?

Solve 83 ÷ 12 to answer this question.

Enter the following:

8 3 Int÷ 1 2 Enter =

83÷12= 6r11

So, 83 ÷ 12 = 6 R 11. Bob's dad is 6 feet 11 inches tall.

Practice **Change each measurement to feet and inches.**

1. 78 inches	**2.** 93 inches	**3.** 134 inches	**4.** 215 inches
5. 345 inches	**6.** 487 inches	**7.** 564 inches	**8.** 685 inches
9. 773 inches	**10.** 836 inches	**11.** 941 inches	**12.** 2,853 inches
13. 1,456 inches	**14.** 2,133 inches	**15.** 3,952 inches	**16.** 4,691 inches

Solve.

17. Lacy bought 147 inches of rope on sale. How many feet and inches of rope did she buy?

ACTIVITY 9

Objective: Use the Op1 key to perform multiplication by the same factor.

Repeated Constants

Carla created a multiplication chart. How can she use the calculator to check her entries for 9 × 7, 9 × 8, 9 × 9, and 9 × 10?

Using the TI-15

To multiply several numbers by 9, enter the following:

Keys	Display
Op1 × 9 Op1	×9
7 Op1	7×9 / 1 63
8 Op1	8×9 / 1 72
9 Op1	9×9 / 1 81
1 0 Op1	10×9 / 1 90

To clear the contents of Op1, enter the following:

Mode ▽ ▽ Enter/= Mode — Display: 4

To multiply several numbers by 6, enter:

Op1 × 6 Op1 — Display: ×6

Practice **Complete the multiplication table and check using the Op1 key.**

X	6	7	8	9	10	11	12
6	36	42					
7							
8							
9							
10							
11							
12							

ACTIVITY 10

Objective: Use the Op1 and Op2 keys to perform repeated operations.

Repeated Operations

A local club sold tickets to their winter picnic. They also gave away 52 tickets. They set up 86 tables with 8 seats at each to seat all of the people. How many tickets did they sell?

To answer this question guess and check your answer to the problem: $(\blacksquare + 52) \div 8 = 86$.

Using the TI-15

To set up the problem, enter the following:

To try 900 as your first guess, enter the following:

Since 900 gave an answer of 119, the next guess should be less than 900. Try 636.

So, $(636 + 52) \div 8 = 86$. They sold 636 tickets.
To clear the contents of Op1 or Op2, enter the following:

Select Op1 or Op2 by pressing ⇨. Then press Mode.

Practice

Find the missing number using your calculator.

1. $(\blacksquare + 13) \div 4 = 9$

2. $(\blacksquare + 28) \div 6 = 12$

3. $(\blacksquare - 20) \times 4 = 60$

4. $(\blacksquare - 18) \div 7 = 15$

5. Jason gave away 22 baseball cards to his friends and then divided the rest evenly among his 3 brothers. If each brother got 10 cards, how many cards did he have to start with?

ACTIVITY 11

Objective: Use the F↔D key.

Fractions to Decimals and Decimals to Fractions

Gregg estimated that he jumped $\frac{4}{5}$ of a meter. What is $\frac{4}{5}$ written as a decimal?

Using the TI-15

To change a fraction to a decimal, enter the following:

4 n 5 d Enter = F↔D → 0.8

So, Gregg jumped 0.8 of a meter.

Gregg measured a relay baton to be 0.25 of a meter. What fraction of a meter is the baton?

To change the decimal to a fraction, enter the following:

0 . 2 5 Enter = F↔D → $\frac{25}{100}$

So, the baton is $\frac{25}{100}$ of a meter.

Practice **Change each fraction to a decimal.**

1. $\frac{3}{4}$ **2.** $\frac{1}{4}$ **3.** $\frac{3}{5}$ **4.** $\frac{5}{10}$ **5.** $\frac{3}{10}$

6. $\frac{13}{100}$ **7.** $\frac{27}{100}$ **8.** $\frac{1}{5}$ **9.** $\frac{9}{10}$ **10.** $\frac{37}{100}$

Change each decimal to a fraction.

11. 0.36 **12.** 0.45 **13.** 0.29 **14.** 0.7 **15.** 0.53

16. 0.81 **17.** 0.67 **18.** 0.90 **19.** 0.95 **20.** 0.75

Solve.

21. Martin needs $\frac{1}{2}$ of a board that is 1 meter long. What decimal portion of the board does he need?

ACTIVITY 12

Objective: Use the memory keys.

Memory

Adam took a 4-hour flight. Every hour Adam calculated how many minutes he had flown. How many minutes was Adam's airplane in the air after 1 hour? 2 hours? 3 hours? 4 hours?

(Remember: 60 minutes = 1 hour)

Using the TI-15

To find the answer, enter the following:

    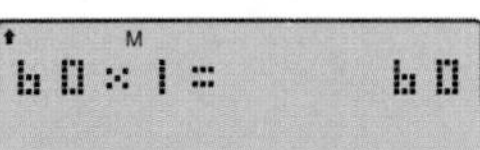

    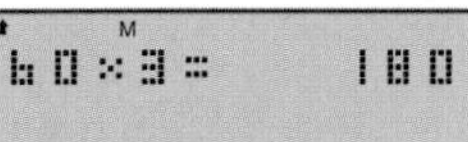

So, Adam was in the air for 60 minutes after 1 hour, 120 minutes after 2 hours, 180 minutes after 3 hours, and 240 minutes after 4 hours.

To clear the memory, enter MR/MC MR/MC.

Practice **Find the number of minutes for each number of hours given.**

1. 7 hours
2. 15 hours
3. 48 hours
4. 93 hours
5. 108 hours
6. 235 hours
7. 285 hours
8. 320 hours
9. 456 hours
10. 681 hours

Solve.

11. Rhonda makes $7 an hour. How much would she make for working 10 hours, 15 hours, 20 hours, and 25 hours?

ACTIVITY 13

Objective: Use the Simp *key to simplify fractions.*

Simplifying Fractions

In a survey, $\frac{24}{60}$ of the people chose the Internet as their number one source for shopping. What is this fraction in simplest form?

To simplify the fraction, you must divide the numerator and denominator by the same number.

Using the TI-15

Enter the following:

       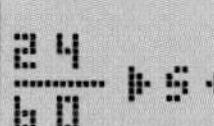

To divide the numerator and denominator by 4, enter the following:

The $\frac{N}{D} \rightarrow \frac{n}{d}$ in the calculator display indicates that the fraction can be simplified further.

To continue simplifying the fraction, enter the following:

   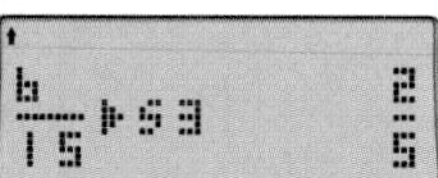

So, $\frac{6}{15}$ is $\frac{2}{5}$ in simplest form.

Practice **Write each fraction in simplest form.**

1. $\frac{6}{8}$
2. $\frac{5}{10}$
3. $\frac{3}{12}$
4. $\frac{4}{6}$
5. $\frac{8}{10}$
6. $\frac{4}{16}$
7. $\frac{14}{21}$
8. $\frac{6}{24}$
9. $\frac{2}{12}$
10. $\frac{9}{36}$

Solve.

11. In a survey, $\frac{32}{60}$ of the people chose shopping malls as their number one source for shopping. Write the fraction in simplest form.

Objective: Use the Fac key to see what factor was used to simplify a fraction.

Simplifying Fractions II

Nancy bought sodas for a party. Of the sodas, $\frac{10}{20}$ were cherry. She wrote the fraction as $\frac{1}{2}$. What did she divide the numerator and denominator by to simplify the fraction?

Using the TI-15

To find the answer, enter the following:

To see what number the calculator divided both numerator and denominator by, enter the following: Fac → 2

To get back to the fraction, enter: Fac → $\frac{5}{10}$

Simp Enter → $\frac{5}{10}$ ▸S $\frac{1}{2}$

Fac → 5

Fac → $\frac{1}{2}$

$$\frac{10 \div 2}{20 \div 2} = \frac{5}{10} = \frac{5 \div 5}{10 \div 5} = \frac{1}{2}$$

So, Nancy divided the numerator and denominator by 2 and by 5. She also could have divided the numerator and denominator by 10.

Practice **Identify what number was used to simplify each fraction.**

1. $\frac{6}{12} = \frac{1}{2}$
2. $\frac{12}{16} = \frac{3}{4}$
3. $\frac{8}{20} = \frac{2}{5}$
4. $\frac{10}{15} = \frac{2}{3}$
5. $\frac{12}{15} = \frac{4}{5}$
6. $\frac{12}{28} = \frac{3}{7}$
7. $\frac{18}{27} = \frac{2}{3}$
8. $\frac{8}{32} = \frac{1}{4}$
9. $\frac{12}{66} = \frac{2}{11}$
10. $\frac{120}{130} = \frac{12}{13}$

ACTIVITY 15

Objective: Add fractions using the  *and*  *keys.*

Adding Fractions

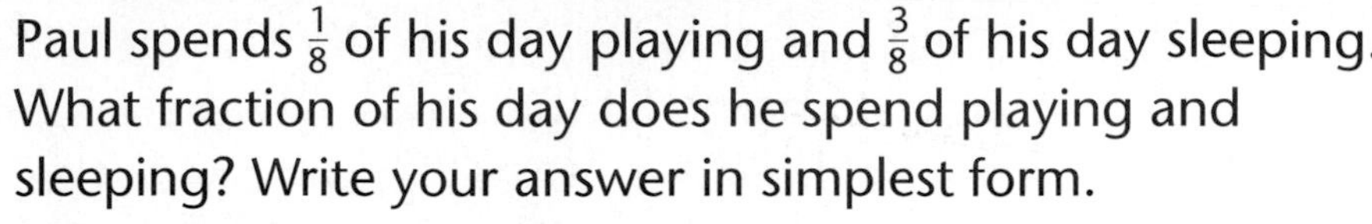

Paul spends $\frac{1}{8}$ of his day playing and $\frac{3}{8}$ of his day sleeping. What fraction of his day does he spend playing and sleeping? Write your answer in simplest form.

You can answer the question by solving the following problem:

$\frac{1}{8} + \frac{3}{8} = \blacksquare$

Using the TI-15

To add fractions, enter the following:

$\frac{1}{8} + \frac{3}{8} = \frac{4}{8} = \frac{1}{2}$

So, Paul spends $\frac{1}{2}$ of his day sleeping and playing.

Practice **Add. Write each answer in simplest form.**

1. $\frac{1}{3} + \frac{1}{3}$	**2.** $\frac{2}{5} + \frac{1}{5}$	**3.** $\frac{1}{6} + \frac{4}{6}$	**4.** $\frac{1}{8} + \frac{1}{8}$
5. $\frac{1}{6} + \frac{1}{6}$	**6.** $\frac{1}{4} + \frac{1}{4}$	**7.** $\frac{1}{6} + \frac{2}{6}$	**8.** $\frac{2}{8} + \frac{2}{8}$
9. $\frac{1}{4} + \frac{2}{4}$	**10.** $\frac{2}{5} + \frac{2}{5}$	**11.** $\frac{3}{6} + \frac{1}{6}$	**12.** $\frac{3}{8} + \frac{4}{8}$

Solve.

13. Lori finished $\frac{3}{12}$ of her homework on Friday after school and $\frac{7}{12}$ on Saturday. How much of her homework has she finished?

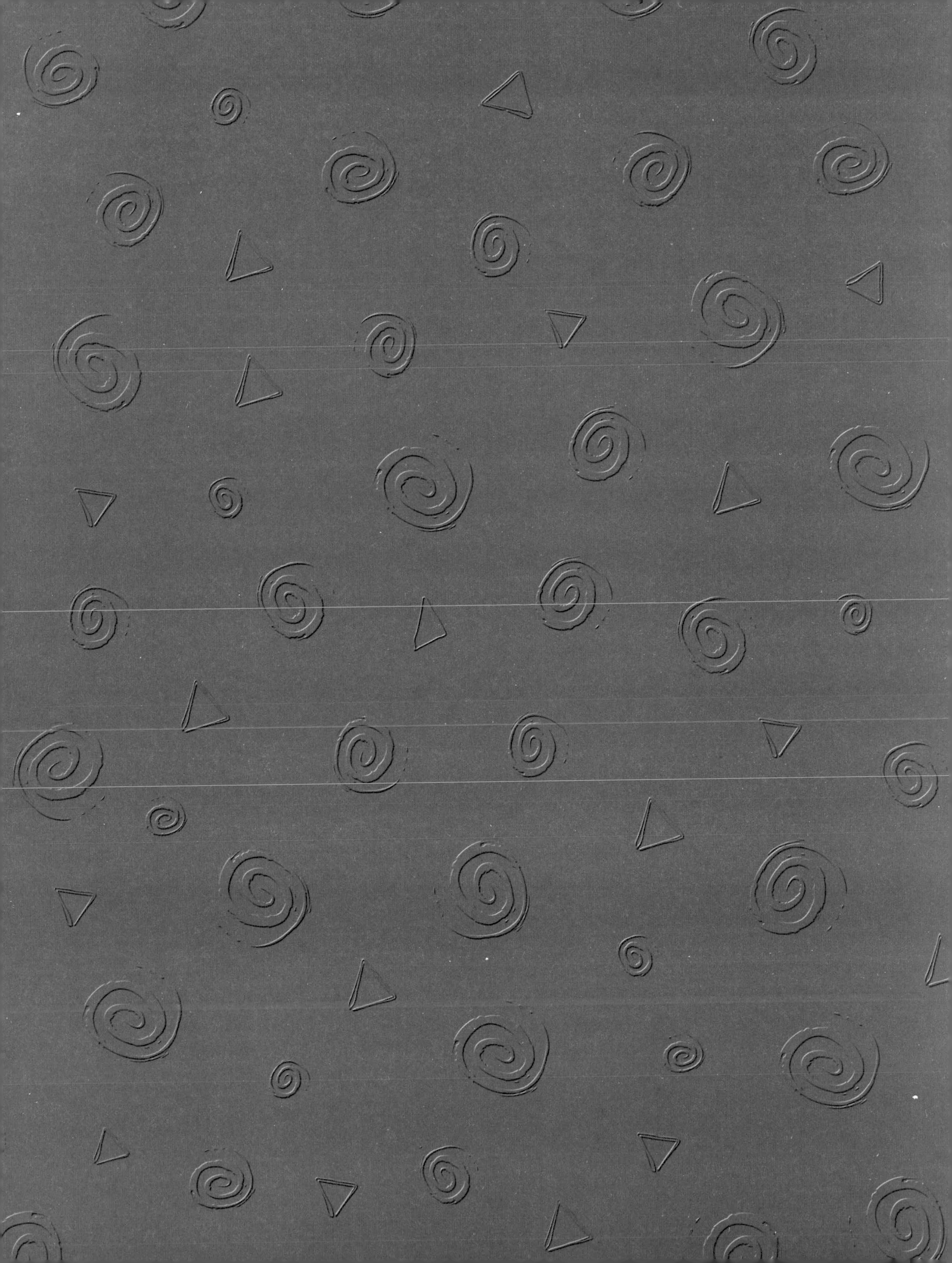